The Good Society

The Good Society

An Introduction to Comparative Politics

Third Edition

Alan Draper
St. Lawrence University

Ansil Ramsay
St. Lawrence University

PEARSON

Boston   Columbus   Indianapolis   New York   San Francisco   Amsterdam
Cape Town   Dubai   London   Madrid   Milan   Munich   Paris   Montréal   Toronto
Delhi   Mexico City   São Paulo   Sydney   Hong Kong   Seoul   Singapore   Taipei   Tokyo

Editorial Director: Dickson Musslewhite
Publisher: Charlyce Jones-Owen
Editorial Assistant: Maureen Diana
Program Manager: Rob DeGeorge
Project Manager: Gail Cocker
Procurement Manager: MaryAnn Gloriande
Art Director: Maria Lange
Cover Art: Zhu Difeng/Shutterstock
Director, Digital Studio: Sacha Laustein
Media Project Manager: Tina Gagliostro
Full-Service Project Management and Composition: Sneha Pant/Lumina Datamatics, Inc.
Printer/Binder and Cover Printer: Courier/Kendallville
Text Font: Palatino LT Pro

Acknowledgements of third party content appear here; page 353, which constitutes an extension of this copyright page.

Copyright © 2016, 2012, 2008 Pearson Education, Inc., 330 Hudson Avenue, Hoboken, NJ. All rights reserved. Manufactured in the United States of America. This publication is protected by Copyright, and permission should be obtained from the publisher prior to any prohibited reproduction, storage in a retrieval system, or transmission in any form or by any means, electronic, mechanical, photocopying, recording, or likewise. To obtain permission(s) to use material from this work, please submit a written request to Pearson Education, Inc., Permissions Department, 330 Hudson Ave., Hoboken, NJ.

Library of Congress Cataloging-in-Publication Data
Draper, Alan.
　The good society: an introduction to comparative politics / Alan Draper, St. Lawrence University, Ansil Ramsay, St. Lawrence University. — 3rd ed.
　　　pages cm
　Includes index.
　ISBN 978-0-13-397485-0 — ISBN 0-13-397485-5
　1. Comparative government—Textbooks.　I. Ramsay, Ansil.　II. Title.
JF51.D73 2014
320.3—dc23

2014036622

V011
10 9 8 7 6 5 4 3 2

Student Edition
ISBN-10: 0-133-97485-5
ISBN-13: 978-0-133-97485-0

Instructor's Review Copy:
ISBN 10: 0-133-97503-7
ISBN 13: 978-0-133-97503-1

Books á la carte:
ISBN-10: 0-133-97495-2
ISBN-13: 978-0-133-97495-9

PEARSON

Brief Contents

1 Comparative Politics and the Good Society — 1
2 The State — 26
3 State and Society — 55
4 Political Culture and Identity — 74
5 Political Economy — 98
6 Authoritarianism — 126
7 Democracy — 152
8 Economic and Human Development — 175
9 Developed Countries and the Good Society — 203
10 Less-Developed Countries and the Good Society — 250
11 Communism, Postcommunism, and the Good Society — 290

Contents

Preface   xiii

1   Comparative Politics and the Good Society   1

Learning Objectives   1
Introduction   2
The Logic and Practice of Comparative Politics   4
Figure 1.1 Wealthier Is Healthier   8
Visions of the Good Society: Gross National Product and Gross National Happiness   10
Figure 1.2 Gross Domestic Product Per Capita (PPP), 2011   11
Figure 1.3 Countries Ranked by Happiness   15
In Brief: Criticisms of GDP and GDH as Measures of the Good Society   16
Capabilities and the Quality of Life   17
    Physical Well-being   17
In-Depth: Costa Rica—Doing More with Less   18
    Informed Decision Making   18
    Safety   19
    Democracy   20
    Some Caveats   21
In Brief: Operationalizing Capabilities   21
Responding to Criticisms of the Capabilities Approach   21
Conclusion   23
    Suggested Readings   24
    Critical Thinking Questions   25

2   The State   26

Learning Objectives   26
Introduction   27
Institutions and Power   28
The State   30
In-Depth: Somalia—The Weightlessness of Statelessness   32
The Origins of States   32
Political Institutions   34
    Federal and Unitary Systems   36
    The Legislature   37
In Brief: Federal and Unitary Systems   37
    The Executive   40
    The Bureaucracy   41
In Brief: Bureaucracy   42
    The Military   43
    The Judiciary   44
Comparative Political Analysis: Does the Design of Political Institutions Make a Difference in People's Lives?   46
Weak States, Strong States, and the Good Society   47
    Physical Well-being   49
    Informed Decision Making   49
Figure 2.1 State Quality and Infant Mortality Rates   49
Figure 2.2 State Quality and Literacy Rates   50
    Safety   50
Figure 2.3 State Quality and Homicide Rates   51
    Democracy   51
Figure 2.4 State Quality and Democracy   52
Conclusion   52
    Suggested Readings   53
    Critical Thinking Questions   54

3   State and Society   55

Learning Objectives   55
Introduction   56
Political Participation   58
Political Parties   60
In Brief: Strong and Weak Political Parties   62

In-Depth: Iraq—From Bullets to Ballots (and Perhaps Back Again)	63	Political Culture, Identity, and the Good Society	91
Interest Groups	64	Physical Well-being	91
Table 3.1 Interest Group Systems	67	Figure 4.2 Social Trust and Infant Mortality Rates	92
In Brief: Pluralist and Corporatist Interest Groups	67	Informed Decision Making	92
Social Movements	68	Figure 4.3 Social Trust and Literacy Rates	93
Comparative Political Analysis: Does Civic Engagement Contribute to Good Government?	70	Safety	93
		Figure 4.4 Social Trust and Homicide Rates	94
		Democracy	94
Patron–Client Relations	71	Figure 4.5 Social Trust and Democracy	95
Conclusion	72	Conclusion	95
Suggested Readings	72	Suggested Readings	96
Critical Thinking Questions	73	Critical Thinking Questions	97

4 Political Culture and Identity — 74

5 Political Economy — 98

Learning Objectives	74	Learning Objectives	98
Introduction	75	Introduction	99
Political Culture	76	In Brief: Market Systems	101
Two Approaches to Political Culture	77	States and Markets	101
The Civic Culture Approach	77	The Advantages of Market Systems	103
The Self-Expression Approach	78	The Dark Side of Markets	105
Figure 4.1 Two Dimensions of Value Change	79	In Brief: The Advantages and Disadvantages of Market Systems	107
In Brief: The Civic Culture and Self-Expression Approaches	80	The Shifting Balance Between States and Markets	107
Social Capital	81	In-Depth: India—From States to Markets	110
In-Depth: The Good Society—Getting to Denmark	83	Globalization	110
Politics of Identity	84	Comparative Political Analysis: Does Globalization Help or Hurt Workers in the Developing World?	115
Identity	84		
Ethnicity	84		
In Brief: Distinguishing between Race and Ethnicity	85	Forms of State Intervention	115
		Fiscal Policy	115
Nationalism	85	Table 5.1 Government Expenditures and Revenues as a Percentage of GDP, 2011	116
Religion	86		
Table 4.1 Importance of Religion in People's Lives, 2006–2008	87	Monetary Policy	117
		Regulations	117
Contentious Identity Politics	87	Nationalization	118
Explaining Why Identity Leads to Violence	88	States, Markets, and the Good Society	119
Comparative Political Analysis: Is Ethnic Diversity the Root Cause of Civil Wars?	89	Figure 5.1 Capitalism and Infant Mortality Rates	120

Physical Well-being	120	Conclusion	149
Informed Decision Making	120	Suggested Readings	151
Figure 5.2 Capitalism and Literacy Rates	**121**	Critical Thinking Questions	151
Safety	121		
Figure 5.3 Capitalism and Homicide Rates	**121**	**7 Democracy**	**152**
Democracy	122	Learning Objectives	152
Figure 5.4 Capitalism and Democracy	**122**	Introduction	153
Conclusion	123	Transitions to Democracy	154
Suggested Readings	124	**In-Depth: Mauritius—A Democratic Enigma**	**156**
Critical Thinking Questions	125		

6 Authoritarianism 126

		Figure 7.1 Global Trends in Governance, 1946–2012	**157**
Learning Objectives	126	**Comparative Political Analysis: Does Diversity Undermine Democracy?**	**159**
Introduction	127		
Authoritarian Politics	129	Presidential and Parliamentary Democracy	159
Types of Authoritarian Regimes	130	**In Brief: Presidential Systems**	**160**
Monarchy	130	**In Brief: Parliamentary Systems**	**161**
Military Regimes	131	Electoral Rules and Party Systems	162
One-Party Regimes	133	Democracy, Authoritarianism, and Economic Development	167
In-Depth: Zimbabwe—How to Wreck and Economy and Weaken Capabilities	**135**	Democracy, Authoritarianism, and the Good Society	169
Personalist Regimes	135	Physical Well-being	169
In Brief: Types of Authoritarian Rule	**136**	**Figure 7.2 Democracy and Infant Mortality Rates**	**170**
Comparative Political Analysis: Why Do Elections Lead to Democratization in Some Authoritarian Regimes but Not Others?	**137**	Informed Decision Making	170
		Safety	170
Explaining Authoritarian Persistence	138	**Figure 7.3 Democracy and Literacy Rates**	**171**
In Brief: Domestic Explanations for Authoritarian Persistence	**142**	**Figure 7.4 Democracy and Homicide Rates**	**172**
Authoritarianism and the Good Society	142	Conclusion	172
Physical Well-being	144	Suggested Readings	173
Figure 6.1 Authoritarian Regime Type and Infant Mortality Rate per 1,000 (2011)	**144**	Critical Thinking Questions	174

8 Economic and Human Development 175

Informed Decision Making	145	
Figure 6.2 Regime Type and Adult Literacy (2009–2011)	**146**	Learning Objectives	175
		Introduction	176
Safety	146	Economic Development and Human Development	177
Figure 6.3 Regime Type and Homicide Rates (2011)	**147**		
Democracy	148	**In-Depth: South Korea—From Least Likely to Succeed to Most Successful in Its Class**	**179**
Figure 6.4 Regime Type and Democracy (2012)	**148**		

In Brief: Economic Development and Human Development	180
Differing Levels of Development Among Countries	181
Table 8.1 Countries Compared by Level of Economic and Human Development	181
Comparing Incomes Between Countries with High and Low Levels of Development	182
Comparing Capabilities Between Countries with High and Low Levels of Development	183
Table 8.2 Capabilities in the Top 20 Countries and Bottom 20 Countries Ranked by HDI (2010)	184
Comparing Economic Growth Rates Between Countries with High and Low Levels of Development	184
States and Development	185
Table 8.3 Corruption Perceptions Index 2012	187
Why Did Some Countries Become More Economically Developed Than Others?	188
Geography	188
Culture	190
Colonialism	191
Institutions	192
Comparative Political Analysis: Institutions as the Main Cause of Development and Underdevelopment	195
Leadership	196
In Brief: Five Explanations for Different Levels of Development Among Countries	196
Development, Underdevelopment, and the Good Society	197
Physical Well-Being	197
Figure 8.1 Income per Capita and Infant Mortality Rates	197
Informed Decision Making	198
Figure 8.2 Income Per Capita and Literacy Rates	198
Safety	199
Figure 8.3 Income per Capita and Homicide Rates	199
Figure 8.4 Income per Capita and Democracy Index	200
Democracy	200

Conclusion	200
Suggested Readings	201
Critical Thinking Questions	202

9 Developed Countries and the Good Society 203

Learning Objectives	203
Introduction	204
Social Democracy	206
Sweden	208
Historical Background	208
The State	209
State and Society	211
Table 9.1 Sweden Votes	214
Political Culture	214
Political Economy	216
Extreme Market Democracy	219
The United Kingdom of Great Britain and Northern Ireland	220
Historical Background	220
The State	222
State and Society	228
Table 9.2 British Election Results	230
Political Culture	230
Political Economy	231
Christian Democracy	233
Germany	234
Historical Background	234
The State	237
State and Society	239
Political Culture	240
Table 9.3 Germany Votes	241
Political Economy	242
Comparing Capabilities Among Sweden, the United Kingdom, and Germany	245
Physical Well-Being	246
Table 9.4 Poverty Rates	246
Informed Decision Making	246
Table 9.5 Literacy Skills	246
Safety	247
Table 9.6 Safety	247
Democracy	247
Table 9.7 Quality of Democracy	247

Conclusion	248
Suggested Readings	248
Critical Thinking Questions	249

10 Less-Developed Countries and the Good Society — 250

Learning Objectives	250
Introduction	251
Flawed Democracy	252
Brazil	253
Historical Background	254
The State	256
State and Society	257
Table 10.1 Brazil's Income Distribution in Comparative Perspective	257
Political Culture	260
Political Economy	261
Semi-Democracy	263
Nigeria	264
Historical Background	264
The State	265
State and Society	268
Political Culture	270
Political Economy	271
Electoral Authoritarianism	272
Iran	273
Historical Background	273
The State	276
Figure 10.1 Iranian Political Institutions	277
State and Society	280
Political Culture	282
Political Economy	283
Comparing Capabilities Among Brazil, Nigeria, and Iran	285
Physical Well-Being	285
Informed Decision Making	285
Table 10.2 Infant Mortality Rates per 1,000 Live Births	285
Table 10.3 Literacy Rates, 15 Years Old and Older, Selected Years	286
Safety	286
Democracy	286
Table 10.4 Homicide Rates in Brazil, Iran, and Nigeria, per 100,000 People, 2011	286
Table 10.5 Democracy Ratings for Brazil, Nigeria, and Iran	287
Conclusion	287
Suggested Readings	288
Critical Thinking Questions	289

11 Communism, Postcommunism, and the Good Society — 290

Learning Objectives	290
Introduction	291
The Institutional Basis of Communist Regimes	291
Communist Party Rule	292
In-Depth: Socialism and Communism	292
State-Owned, Centrally Planned Economies	293
Russia	293
Historical Background	295
The State	297
Figure 11.1 Russian Political Institutions	299
State and Society	301
Political Culture	304
Political Economy	306
China	309
Historical Background	309
The State	314
Figure 11.2 Chinese Political Institutions	315
State and Society	317
Political Culture	320
Political Economy	321
Table 11.1 Differing Chinese and Russian Political Values	321
Comparing Capabilities Between Russia And China	325
Table 11.2 Infant Mortality Rates in Russia and China per 1,000 Live Births	**326**
Physical Well-Being	326
Informed Decision Making	326
Table 11.3 Youth and Adult Literacy Rates in Russia and China, 2010	326
Table 11.4 Homicide Rates in Russia and China per 100,000 People (2011)	327

Safety	327	Table 1.2 Adult Literacy Rates	333
Democracy	327	Table 1.3 Homicide Rates per 100,000	335
Table 11.5 Rule of Law in Russia and China, 2012	327	Table 1.4 Democracy Index	338
		Table 2.1 Failed States Index	341
Table 11.6 Democracy Index, 2013	328	Table 5.2 Economic Freedom Index	344
Table 11.7 Voice and Accountability in Russia and China, 2012	328		
Suggested Readings	328	Glossary	346
Critical Thinking Questions	329	Credits	353
		Index	358

APPENDIX 330

Table 1.1 Infant Mortality Rates 330

Preface

The *Lonely Planet* guidebook describes Siena, Italy, as a charming city whose medieval center is a UNESCO World Heritage Site. The travel guide recommends simply wandering the narrow streets of the city and visiting its ornate churches and small museums. In the very center of the city is its famous town square—the Piazza del Campo—where tourists eat and drink at outdoor cafes that line its perimeter. Twice a year, the square is packed with spectators who come to watch horses representing the city's different neighborhoods race around its circumference. Crowds of up to 20,000 line the infield, shops, restaurants, and upstairs apartments to watch the horses compete. The event is so famous and picturesque that it served as the backdrop for the opening action sequence in the 2008 James Bond movie, *Quantum of Solace*.

The most imposing and beautiful building on the town square is City Hall, the Palazzo Pubblico. It dates back to the 13th century, when the Republic of Siena was formed. The Sienese were remarkably progressive for their time, first freeing themselves from control by the Church and then from the aristocracy to form a self-governing city-state. Today, the Palazzo Pubblico is no longer the local seat of government but an art museum. Almost every room in the museum contains frescoes, paintings that are drawn on walls as opposed to canvas, from the epic period of the Republic of Siena (1287 to 1355). The most famous of the frescoes is a set of three, collectively known as "Allegory and Effects of Good and Bad Government" by Ambrogio Lorenzetti. These are located on the second floor of the museum, in the room where the Nine Governors and Defenders of the Republic of Siena, the city's governing council, would meet. On the room's left wall is Lorenzetti's painting of bad government. It portrays a society in ruins. Farms in the distance are abandoned or burning. The fields lie fallow. The city, which is portrayed on the right-hand side of the painting, is desolate. Buildings are rundown, and violence is pervasive. In one scene, a woman is being robbed; in another, a building is being destroyed; and in still another scene, someone lies unattended, bleeding from a wound. In the center of the painting, a devil figure representing Tyranny sits on the throne, surrounded by Cruelty, Treason, Fraud, Furor, Conflict and War. Justice lies bound and defeated at its feet.

On the opposite wall, Lorenzetti depicts the effects of good government, which are a counterpoint to the awful scenes on the other side of the room. Here, the Common Good, not tyranny, rules.[1] The effects of good government are evident in the scenes of wealth and serenity represented in the picture. Crops are bountiful, markets are lively, houses are well maintained, and people are portrayed dancing in the streets, practicing their crafts, and harvesting their fields. Peace and prosperity prevail.[2]

Unfortunately, the sharp contrast between good and bad government displayed so vividly in the Lorenzetti frescoes are still with us.

---

[1] Nicolai Rubenstein, "Political Ideas in Sienese Art: The Frescoes by Ambrogio Lorenzetti and Taddeo di Bartolo in the Palazzo Pubblico," *Journal of the Warburg and Courtauld Institutes* (July–December, 1958), vol. 21, no. 3/4, , pp. 179–207.

[2] Randolph Starn and Loren Partridge, *Arts of Power: Three Halls of State in Italy, 1300–1600* (Berkeley: University of California Press, 1992).

Some countries today display all the symptoms of bad government—carnage, poverty, and misery—shown in one of the frescoes, whereas others exhibit all the signs of good government—affluence, security, and happiness—that are depicted in Lorenzetti's other painting. For example, consider the case of Juarez in Mexico and El Paso, Texas, in the United States, which are separated by the narrow band of the Rio Grande River. The Mayor of El Paso can actually see downtown Juarez from his office, but the quality of life for residents of the two cities could not be more different. In 2012, El Paso was ranked as the safest city in the United States with a population over 500,000,[3] with only 16 homicides recorded in 2011; more than 1,000 people were murdered in Juarez that same year. The infant mortality rate—the number of newborns per 1,000 who die before their first birthday—in El Paso was 3.9 in 2010. In comparison, the infant mortality rate was five times higher across the river in Juarez, and although 78 percent of El Paso residents completed high school in 2010, only 63 percent did so in Juarez.

This tale of two cities is at the heart of our book *The Good Society*, whose central theme is why some countries are more successful than others at creating conditions that promote their citizens' well-being. Why do people in the United States live so much better than those who live just across the border in Mexico? How can a river loom as wide as an ocean in terms of the quality of life for those who live on opposite shores? Why, in other words, do some countries reflect the symptoms of bad government found on the left wall in the room where the leaders of Sienna would meet, whereas others display the signs of good government found on the opposite wall in Sienna's governing chambers?

These questions give unity to a wide range of topics in comparative politics by asking how political institutions in different countries affect citizens' quality of life. Students are interested in comparative politics—and appropriately so—because of what it might teach them about how different political institutions affect people's lives. It is our experience that few students who enroll in "Introduction to Comparative Politics" are intrinsically curious about the details of other countries' political institutions or about the conceptual repertoire of comparative politics. However, they are curious about why some countries do a better job than others of providing for their citizens. Students want to know how political systems work because they are interested in how they can work better. The wonderful, exciting quality of comparative politics is that it is in a privileged position to pose and answer such large and meaningful questions. Comparison permits students to make normative judgments about the merits of different political systems. These are the kinds of issues that first attracted us as students to comparative politics. We believe today's students will find the fresh, normative approach to comparative politics in *The Good Society* equally compelling.

We believe the approach to comparative politics that *The Good Society* offers is a bold departure from existing comparative politics textbooks. Most textbooks in the field use the case study approach, in which students study a series of individual countries in depth. We find such textbooks to be richly descriptive but oddly uninformative. The case studies provide evocative detail but are not related to one another, nor is their collective meaning and significance clear. Textbooks using a thematic approach are also unsatisfying. They familiarize readers with core concepts in comparative politics but often fail to explain how those concepts could be applied or would be useful to explain the politics of any particular country. In short—and to be blunt—existing comparative politics textbooks generally offer either too little comparison or too little politics. They leave students asking "so what?" and wondering in what

---

[3] El Paso Ranks Safest City in US. (June 25, 2012) www.kvia.com/news/El-Paso-Ranks-Safest-City-In-US/.

ways the fine detail and conceptual clarity these textbooks offer matter.

We have not dispensed with case study and thematic approaches to comparative politics. We believe each is valuable, and we use them here by situating them within a larger argument about the *purpose* of government. We use case studies to typify different political models, and we illustrate how concepts can be applied to the study of individual countries. We offer case studies of individual countries to assess their performance against the standard of the good society. We review the conceptual nuts and bolts of the field because such terms as *state*, *market*, and *democracy* represent ways people have organized their lives. However, they are means to an end, not the end itself, which is to maximize people's ability to live well. *The Good Society* introduces students to a variety of countries and the conceptual apparatus of comparative politics in ways that we hope they will find relevant and meaningful.

New to This Edition

This is the third edition of the Good Society. While we continue to introduce concepts, describe political institutions, and assess government performance in different countries against the standards of the good society, there is also much that is new here. Revisions to the thematic chapters for the Third Edition include the following:

- **The introductory chapter** (Chapter 1) presents more vividly, with new updated examples, how higher economic growth does not necessarily result in better living conditions for people.
- **The chapter on political participation** (Chapter 3) devotes more attention to the political impact of social media. It also discusses the emergence of the Arab Spring that challenged dictators throughout the Middle East, and the rise of the Occupy Movement that protested rising inequality in Europe and the United States.
- **The chapter on political culture** now includes new sections on value change, describing changes from traditional to secular values, and survival to self-expression values. There is also an expanded section on social capital, and a new section on contentious identity politics.
- **The authoritarianism** chapter uses a new approach that focuses on how authoritarian regimes solve problems of power sharing and control. It also has new material on why most authoritarian Arab regimes survived the Arab Spring.
- **The chapter on democracy** includes more on the current period when democracies are neither growing in number nor receding. It argues that the third wave of democratic growth has crested, but democracy has neither consolidated nor collapsed.
- **The chapter on economic and human development** incorporates new scholarship by Daron Acemoglu and James A. Robinson on extractive and inclusive institutions.

The chapters covering individual countries have been revised and updated for the Third Edition as follows:

- **New case study of the United Kingdom.** In this edition, the United Kingdom replaces the United States as the model of extreme market democracies. We believe the British case study will be more useful for faculty teaching American students about comparative politics.
- **Germany**—analyzes the 2013 election results, how Germany fared in the Great Recession, and Germany's emergence as the "indispensable nation" within Europe.
- **Sweden**—includes more coverage of foreign policy and more analysis of the cultural and political challenges that immigration and diversity pose in Sweden.
- **Brazil**—examines the massive popular protests in Brazil in 2013, the effect of slowing

economic growth on politics, and the rise of racially based politics.

- **Nigeria**—delves further into the problems posed by Nigeria's weak state and includes new material on the growing threat of the Islamic fundamentalist group, Boko Haram.
- **Iran**—describes the 2013 presidential election and the surprising victory of Hassan Rouhani. It also considers whether President Rouhani will be able to carry out his reform program.
- **Russia**—includes more on the personalist regime led by President Vladimir Putin and his efforts to maintain authoritarian control by using nationalism, anti-Westernism, and the conservative social values of the Russian Orthodox Church.
- **China**—describes the transition of Chinese Communist Party leadership to Xi Jinping and the challenges he faces as economic and environmental protests increase, income and regional inequality worsen, and economic growth slows.

We also continued to provide more pedagogical assistance to users of the book. Several pedagogical features were retained from previous editions. These include emphasis on the practice of comparative politics, application of concepts to countries in "In-Depth" boxes that show how topics discussed in conceptual chapters may be applied to countries, "In Brief" text boxes to highlight key concepts in the chapter; key terms in boldface type, figures and tables, maps with accompanying economic and demographic data, and selected readings at the end of each chapter, to guide students to some of the best and most recent scholarship.

For the Third Edition, the pedagogy has been improved in the following ways:

- **Learning Objectives:** Learning objectives now appear at the beginning of each chapter and subheading. These aids signal students what to expect and indicate what they should take away from each section.
- **Improved presentation of data:** Scatter diagrams have been improved by adding countries' names to their locations in the scatter diagrams. This makes it easier for students to see relationships among countries and stimulates questions about why some countries are outliers.

REVEL™

Educational technology designed for the way today's students read, think, and learn

When students are engaged deeply, they learn more effectively and perform better in their courses. This simple fact inspired the creation of REVEL: an immersive learning experience designed for the way today's students read, think, and learn. Built in collaboration with educators and students nationwide, REVEL is the newest, fully digital way to deliver respected Pearson content.

REVEL enlivens course content with media interactives and assessments—integrated directly within the author's narrative—that provide opportunities for students to read about and practice course material in tandem. This immersive educational technology boosts student engagement, which leads to better understanding of concepts and improved performance throughout the course.

Learn more about REVEL <http://www.pearsonhighered.com/revel/>

Features

CHAPTER 1. COMPARATIVE POLITICS AND THE GOOD SOCIETY. The opening chapter introduces students to the field of Comparative Politics and the comparative method. It then proceeds to ask: What does the good society look like? The answer to this question becomes the measure, the standard, by which we compare and evaluate how well different countries perform. We consider alternative visions of the good society, including gross national product and gross national happiness rankings, before presenting our own view that is based on "the capabilities approach," developed by Amartya Sen and Martha Nussbaum. According to this approach, the good society is one in which certain minimal conditions are met that permit people to flourish or thrive. These include physical well-being, safety from violence, the ability to make informed choices about one's life, and the freedom to participate in meaningful political activity. After proposing ways to apply these concepts to compare how countries perform, we respond to different criticisms of this approach.

CHAPTER 2. THE STATE. Chapter 2 introduces students to the concept of the state. States are sovereign, meaning they are the ultimate authorities within a territory, creating and enforcing rules within it. As a result, groups struggle to gain control over the state and try to influence its procedures and decisions. The chapter then proceeds to describe the origins of the modern state and examines its components or parts, such as legislatures, judiciaries, executives, bureaucracies, militaries, and more local or regional authorities. It concludes by examining whether the quality of the state, correlates with our measures of the good society.

CHAPTER 3. STATE AND SOCIETY. Chapter 3 examines the ways in which states and societies are linked together through political parties, interest groups, social movements, and patron–client relations. The chapter also explores ways in which states try to use these linkages to gain more influence over society, at the same time groups in society try to exploit these connections to increase their influence over the state.

CHAPTER 4. POLITICAL CULTURE AND IDENTITY. This chapter first describes the civic culture and self-expression approaches to the study of political culture. It then turns to an analysis of social capital and collective action. The next section examines how political identities are formed, how groups based on national, ethnic, and religious identities engage in political struggles, and why these struggles sometimes become violent. Finally, the chapter asks whether the level of generalized trust within countries affects the degree to which they approach the good society.

CHAPTER 5. POLITICAL ECONOMY. Chapter 5 looks at different economic systems and how each strikes a different balance between states and markets. It begins by arguing that markets are not antagonistic to states but presume them. Markets require states to set the rules so that production and exchange can take place. We then discuss the market's virtues and vices, and the different means through which states intervene in the operation of market economies. The chapter then proceeds to discuss globalization. Finally, we examine whether more market-oriented economies do a better job than statist systems in promoting the capabilities of citizens.

CHAPTER 6. AUTHORITARIANISM. Chapter 6 defines authoritarianism as well as describing its different forms: monarchy, military rule, one-party rule, and personal rule. Each type of regime is discussed in terms of how it solves the problem of power sharing among members of the leadership group and the problem of authoritarian control over the population. It also examines the surprising persistence of authoritarianism in many countries, despite the trend toward democracy in recent decades. This section focuses on authoritarian rule in the Middle East, and why most Arab authoritarian regimes survived the Arab Spring. The chapter ends with an analysis of how well different types of authoritarian rule do in meeting the criteria of the good society.

CHAPTER 7. DEMOCRACY. Chapter 7 parallels the previous chapter by defining democracy and describes its two dominant forms, parliamentary and presidential systems. It also considers the successive waves of democratization and how electoral rules shape party competition and party systems. The chapter ends by assessing whether democracies perform better than authoritarian states in contributing to economic development and in meeting the standards of the good society.

CHAPTER 8. ECONOMIC AND HUMAN DEVELOPMENT. This chapter begins by distinguishing between economic development and human development. It next examines how rich and poor countries differ in levels of poverty, capabilities, economic growth, and state strength. The chapter then examines five different explanations for why development gaps have emerged among countries: imperialism, geography, culture, colonialism, institutions, and leadership. It concludes with an examination of the relationship between economic development and meeting the standards of the good society.

CHAPTER 9. DEVELOPED COUNTRIES AND THE GOOD SOCIETY. Chapter 9 begins our analysis of the developed countries, which include the rich democracies of North America and Western Europe, as well as those of Japan, New Zealand, and Australia. It examines three "families of nation," or distinct models of politics and policy found within them: social democracies, extreme market democracies, and Christian democracies. We then offer case studies for each of the three types: Sweden represents the social democratic model; the United Kingdom typifies extreme market democracies; and Germany exemplifies the Christian democracies. Finally, the chapter compares these countries' performance to see which of them—and the political models they represent—comes closest to meeting the standards of the good society.

CHAPTER 10. LESS DEVELOPED COUNTRIES AND THE GOOD SOCIETY. This chapter begins with a description of the main features of less-developed countries, while noting that they are a more numerous and diverse lot than their developed counterparts. Many of them are not democracies—and the quality of democracy varies considerably among those that are—and they differ greatly in terms of economic performance. The chapter examines three common types of regimes with different degrees of democracy: flawed democracies that share some of the same features as democracies in high-income countries but fall short on others; semi-democracies that exist in a gray area between democracy and authoritarianism; and regimes that use the trappings of democracy to maintain authoritarian control. Brazil is presented as an example of a flawed democracy, Nigeria is offered as a model of semi-democracy, and Iran is submitted as a case study of how authoritarian regimes use elections as a means of authoritarian control. The chapter concludes with a comparison of how well these countries—and the types of regimes they represent—perform in promoting their citizens' well-being and meeting the criteria of the good society.

CHAPTER 11. COMMUNISM, POST-COMMUNISM, AND THE GOOD SOCIETY. Chapter 11 begins with a discussion of the institutional features of communist regimes prior to their demise. It examines why the Soviet Union collapsed, why Russia was not able to sustain democratic politics and came under personal rule, and explores how the Chinese Communist Party has managed to avoid the fate of the Soviet Union. In both countries the chapter explains how authoritarian rulers solve problems of power sharing within the leadership group and control over the population. The chapter concludes by comparing the two countries' degree of success in promoting their citizens' well-being and approximating the good society.

Supplements

Pearson is pleased to offer several resources to qualified adopters of The Good Society and their students that will make teaching and learning from this book even more effective and enjoyable. Several of the supplements for this book are available at the Instructor Resource Center (IRC), an online hub that allows in- structors to quickly download book-specific supplements. Please visit the IRC welcome page at www.pearsonhighered.com/irc to register for access.

INSTRUCTOR'S MANUAL/TEST BANK. This resource includes chapter overviews, learning objectives, lecture outlines, key terms, and numerous multiple-choice, short answer, and essay questions for each chapter. Available exclusively at the IRC.

PEARSON MYTEST. This powerful assessment generation program includes all of the items in the test bank. Questions and tests can be easily created, customized, saved online, and then printed, allowing flexibility to manage assessments anytime and anywhere. To learn more, please visit www.mypearsontest.com or contact your Pearson representative.

POWERPOINT PRESENTATIONS. Organized around a lecture outline, these multimedia presentations include photos, figures, and tables from each chapter. Available exclusively on the IRC.

LONGMAN ATLAS OF WORLD ISSUES (0-205-78020-2). From population and political systems to energy use and women's rights, the Longman Atlas of World Issues features full-color thematic maps that examine the forces shaping the world. Featuring maps from the latest edition of The Penguin State of the World Atlas, this excerpt includes critical thinking exercises to promote a deeper understanding of how geography affects many global issues. Available at no additional charge when packaged with this book.

GOODE'S WORLD ATLAS (0-321-65200-2). First published by Rand McNally in 1923, *Goode's World Atlas* has set the standard for college reference atlases. It features hundreds of physical, political, and thematic maps as well as graphs, tables, and a pronouncing index. Available at a discount when packaged with this book.

Acknowledgments

As authors, the first edition had all the excitement of a debutante's coming out party to us. We were the new kids on the block with a fresh approach for introducing students to Comparative Politics. The second edition was a chance to fix missteps and include new insights that only became apparent months after the debutante's ball had ended. Now that the book actually existed we could see more clearly ways to improve it. The third edition, we hope, is when we finally get things right—or, at least, more right. We have put the exuberance and mistakes of youth behind us and can offer a more mature text; one that still retains its unique normative thrust—the vision of our youth--but is now more seasoned and tested.

Writing is a solitary occupation, but publishing a book is not. It requires the help and cooperation of many people. We appreciate the confidence of our editor at Pearson, Charlyce Jones-Owen, who recognized and valued our distinctive approach to Comparative Politics. Only we know how much she has delivered for us. We are truly grateful. We also appreciate the outstanding work of the production team at nSight in charge of the production process. Their professionalism and skill made it a significantly better book. We owe special thanks to Mary Stone who guided us through the details of book production. She was meticulous and thorough, compensating for qualities that were too often in short supply on our end. She also showed extraordinary patience in responding to our requests for last minute changes to chapters. Gail Cocker and Sneha Pant then took over and midwifed the book while it was in the last, most crucial, stage of labor. They coordinated multiple passes of the text, keeping track of the track changes we submitted The devil, they say, is in the details. We did not fear the devil because they took care of him for us.

We also owe thanks to several scholars who shared with us unpublished manuscripts and data, and provided answers to political questions that sometimes eluded us. They include Barbara Geddes (UCLA), Jonathan Hanson (Syracuse University), Patrick Heller (Brown University), Jie Lu (American University), Steve Saideman (Carleton University), and Christian Welzel (Leuphana University, Lueneburg Germany).

Paul Doty, a librarian at our home institution, St. Lawrence University, was like a forensic investigator, hunting down requests for sources and information, and sending journal articles to us when we were not on campus. But we owe the greatest debt to our former colleague Sandy Hinchman who, once again, patiently edited almost every chapter of the book. She turned our prose from analog to HD. She added pixels to the page by sharpening our sentences and clarifying their meaning.

We would also like to thank the reviewers Pearson commissioned who offered suggestions in response to our revision proposal. J.D. Bowen, St. Louis University; Robert Dayley, The College of Idaho; Maria Fornella-Oehninger, Old Dominion University; Peggy Kahn, The University of Michigan—Flint; Steven L. Taylor, Troy University; and Jiangnan Zhu, University of Nevada—Reno.

Finally, we dedicate this book to those who mean the most to us—our parents and our families—Robert and Clarice Draper; Pat Ellis; Sam and Rachel Draper; Bryan and Trevor Ellis; Estelle K. Ramsay; Eva Turknett-Ramsay; Douglas and David Ramsay; Brian and Alan Mobley; and Jeni Flint.

Alan Draper
Ansil Ramsay

Chapter 1
Comparative Politics and the Good Society

Learning Objectives

1.1 Define comparative politics and illustrate the value and usefulness of studying it.

1.2 Outline the steps involved in doing comparative political analysis.

1.3 Analyze wealth and happiness as measures of the good society.

1.4 Define and apply the capabilities approach.

Introduction

1.1 Define comparative politics and illustrate the value and usefulness of studying it.

All of us want to enjoy richer, fuller lives. We may disagree about exactly what richer and fuller means—it may involve becoming the next Nobel Prize winner in medicine or an Olympic gold medalist in track and field—but we all want to realize our dreams, whatever they may be. Our ability to make our dreams come true depends in part on raw talent. As much as we would like to find a cure for a deadly disease or be an athletic star, most of us are not smart or athletic enough, no matter how hard we try or how much we study or practice. But our potential is constrained not only by the limits of our innate talents but by the kind of society we live in. As President Lyndon Baines Johnson explained in a famous address he gave in the 1960s, ability is not simply "the product of birth"; it is "stretched or stunted by the family that you live with, and the neighborhood you live in—by the school you go to and the poverty or richness of your surroundings. It is the product of a hundred unseen forces playing upon the little infant, the child, and finally the man."[1]

According to Johnson, our ability to realize our potential is conditioned by the circumstances in which we live. For example, it would be difficult at best to be a great scientist or outstanding athlete if we had to work six days a week making bricks, as some children do in Pakistan; if we had to subsist on one dollar a day, as millions do in India; or if we could not read or write, as is true for a majority of adults in the African country of Niger. People in such dire circumstances—deprived of a childhood, destitute, and denied an education—would find it exceedingly difficult to fulfill their potential, regardless of their natural gifts. On the other hand, some people are more fortunate and live in countries that help them realize their potential. People who are lucky enough to live in countries that require children to attend schools that actually teach them to read and write; who have access to health care, nourishment, and shelter; who are safe from physical assault and the ravages of war; and where there are large reserves of mutual trust in which governments and citizens play by the rules are in a much better place to succeed, to realize their potentials, than those who don't. The famed investor Warren Buffet attributed his economic success to the fact that, "When I was a kid, I got all kinds of good things. I had the advantage of a home where people talked about interesting things, and I had intelligent parents and I went to decent schools. . . . I was born at the right time and place."[2] Of course, not everyone who went to good schools and grew up in a good home with loving parents is as economically successful as Warren Buffet, but Buffet is wise and humble enough to know that his success would not have been possible without them. In short, the quality of our lives is improved or impoverished, depending on the type of society we live in.

This book argues that some countries are better than others are at creating conditions that permit citizens to realize their potential. This issue is our entrance into the field of comparative politics. **Comparative politics** identifies similarities and differences between countries, explains why they occur, and probes their consequences. For example, some countries are organized in ways that permit their citizens to flourish and thrive, whereas in others, people's lives are blighted and stunted. Consider the case of Nicaragua and Costa Rica, two former Spanish colonies that border each other in Central America. Both possess sun-drenched beaches on their Caribbean and Pacific coasts, beautiful mountain ranges with verdant rainforests in their interiors, and arable farmland to produce goods and seaworthy ports from which to export them. Yet, with so much in common, the life chances of those who live in Costa Rica are much greater than those who live just across the border in Nicaragua. In Nicaragua, 22 out of every 1,000 babies died before their first birthday in 2012; infant mortality rates were half that in Costa Rica. Nicaraguans could expect to live six years less, on average, than citizens in neighboring Costa Rica, and Nicaragua's per capita income was less than one-third that of Costa Rica's in 2012. Why is the quality of life so much better in Costa Rica than in Nicaragua?

On the other hand, take the case of how natural disasters result in death and destruction in some cases and not in others. In 2008, a category 4 cyclone, Nargis, created a sea surge that went 7 miles upstream the densely populated Irrawaddy River in Myanmar. More than 100,000 people died as floods inundated homes and villages along the river. Sometimes whole villages were wiped out. Damage was estimated to be over $10 billion. Just a year before, an even stronger, category 5, cyclone hit neighboring Bangladesh, but the government of Bangladesh had invested in warning systems, shelters, and coastal housing standards designed to withstand storm surges. Only 4,000 died when the storm struck because of precautions Bangladesh had taken. There is little governments can do to avoid the wrath of Mother Nature in the form of earthquakes, tornados, tsunamis, and cyclones, but there is much governments can do to mitigate their effects.[3]

Comparative politics enables us not only to compare different countries but to appreciate what is special or distinctive about our own. It provides a standard or point of reference that permits us to recognize unique features of our country by comparing it to another. We may find that what we take for granted and assume is common elsewhere in fact may be quite distinctive and unusual. For example, few countries have anything resembling the American two-party system. Indeed, few democracies model themselves on American political institutions and its system of checks and balances. The institutions that Americans take pride in, assume to be prevalent, and embody the essence of democracy are actually quite rare. Few democracies have adopted them. Comparative politics provides a sense of perspective with which to view—and check—ourselves. It helps us see ourselves better and with more insight.

Comparative Politics
A subfield of political science that studies similarities and differences among countries' politics, why they exist, and the consequences they have.

Finally, comparison is valuable because it helps us discover which policies work best in improving people's lives. Many countries face similar challenges, such as making sure that water is safe to drink, that garbage is collected, and that traffic moves safely. Comparative politics helps us discover what policies work best and reveals those that are ineffective. We can learn from other countries' successes and failures as they try to solve similar problems.

Comparative politics is a subfield of political science and is distinct from international relations, another subfield of the discipline with which it is sometimes confused. The former studies politics *within* countries; the latter studies politics *among* them. But the border separating these subfields is quite porous because what happens among countries can and often does affect what happens within them and vice versa. For example, international agreements among European countries to share a common currency, the Euro—which is within the domain of international relations—have led states to change the way they budget for taxes and spending and affected election results among the parties within them—all of which is the stuff of comparative politics. Comparative politics is not walled off from the other branches of political science but bleeds into them, just as it accepts transfusions from them as well.

The Logic and Practice of Comparative Politics

1.2 Outline the steps involved in doing comparative political analysis.

Hypothesis
Proposed relationship among variables. An educated guess about how one thing affects another.

Dependent Variable
What the analyst is trying to explain; what the independent variable acts on.

Independent Variable
The agent of change in a hypothesis. What the analyst believes explains the change to the dependent variable.

Just like the man who was pleased and surprised to learn he always had been speaking prose, readers might similarly be surprised to learn they have been doing comparative analysis all their lives. We compare all the time. Students compare the merits of different colleges when they decide where to enroll, and men and women compare the merits of potential partners when they decide whom to date. Instead of comparing colleges or potential dates, comparative politics analyzes how and why the politics of countries differ and what consequences those differences may have. However, comparative political analysis differs from the comparisons we normally make in its use of systematic procedures. Comparative political analysis requires practitioners to form hypotheses about how different variables or concepts are related to one another. **Hypotheses** simply present relationships that we expect to find among these variables. They often take the form of "if, then" statements, such as if a country's wealth increases, then its citizens will be healthier. The two variables in this hypothesis are a country's wealth and health. Differences in health among countries are the **dependent variable**, or what we are trying to explain, whereas differences in wealth among countries are the **independent variable**, or what we believe explains them.

How do we know which countries are wealthier or healthier? Wealth and health are only concepts. They are abstract and do not provide specific criteria with which to make comparisons among countries. For example, we might safely assume that Germany is wealthier than Bangladesh, but is it wealthier than Austria, its neighbor to the south? We might reasonably believe that Canadians are healthier than Haitians, but are they healthier than Americans? To make comparisons like these, we need to find measurable, real-world approximations for wealth and health to see whether Germans are wealthier than Austrians or Canadians are healthier than Americans. We need to **operationalize** our variables. This means finding specific, concrete alternatives to use in place of such abstract terms as *wealth* and *health*. For example, we can operationally define health, our dependent variable, in terms of life expectancy and compare it across countries. We can do the same for our independent variable, wealth, by using per capita gross domestic product (GDP) in place of it. Per capita GDP refers to the total value of a country's goods and services sold each year divided by the number of people in it. Both life expectancy and per capita GDP are measurable; they actually exist in the real world and capture the concepts of health and wealth they are meant to represent. Once we operationally define our variables, we can now determine whether and to what degree wealth influences health.

Operationalize Variables
When we substitute specific, real-life, measurable alternatives in place of concepts that are too abstract and general for use in testing hypotheses.

We might find that as per capita GDP increases, so does life expectancy, as our hypothesis anticipated, but this only reveals a correlation or pattern between our variables; it does not prove that our independent variable, wealth, actually caused life expectancy to increase. The positive result confirming our hypothesis might be due to other factors that we did not take into account. For example, before the polio vaccine was discovered, public health experts noted that polio outbreaks increased with the consumption of ice cream, leading to speculation that ice cream contributed to the crippling disease. It turned out that polio outbreaks were more common in the summer when people ate more ice cream, and that the summer treat was only associated with the disease but did not cause it.[4] Ice cream was innocent of the vicious charge leveled against it once researchers included **controls** in their tests. Controls hold other factors constant to see whether we still obtain the same results or whether they were spurious due to intervening factors. For example, parenting studies found that teenagers who ate dinner regularly with their parents were healthier, happier, got in less trouble, and did better in school. However, when researchers controlled for income and other factors, they found that as long as parents found other ways to connect with their kids, they needn't worry that their teenager would end up a drug addict if they didn't have dinner regularly as a family.[5]

Control Variables
When researchers hold other factors constant so they can determine whether their independent variable, as opposed to some extraneous factor, was indeed responsible for a change to their dependent variable.

An excellent example of comparative research using controls was one recently conducted by Dan Zuberi. Zuberi was interested in whether Canadian workers lived better than their American counterparts. He conducted research in cities that were otherwise quite similar on either side of the border, Vancouver and Seattle, on workers who did the same job for the same employer and belonged to the same union in each city.[6] By doing so, Zuberi could have confidence that any difference in Canadian and American workers' life chances was not due to differences in occupation, employer, union status, or urban environment but, as he concluded, could be attributed to the political power Canadian workers enjoyed in comparison to their American counterparts. When we control for variables, we are more confident that any correlations we find are not accidental but are the result of causation. We are more confident that it is safe to eat ice cream without the fear that it increases our chances of contracting polio.

Comparative political analysis uses three methods to test hypotheses. One approach is to do a case study that examines a topic in depth within a single country. Case studies examine a particular case to develop or test hypotheses. For instance, political scientist Kellee Tsai's case study of China tested the hypothesis that the emergence of large numbers of capitalists (independent variable) would result in democratization within China (dependent variable). Supporters of the hypothesis believe private entrepreneurs will increasingly resent the restrictions imposed by the Communist Party and demand democratic reforms. However, contrary to these expectations, Tsai found that as the number of entrepreneurs in China increased, democratic reforms did not occur. Entrepreneurs have not been in the vanguard of democratic reform because Tsai found that they have been able to advance their interests through other means. Chinese entrepreneurs succeeded so well in promoting their interests through the one-party dictatorship of the Chinese Communist Party that they had little need, or appetite, for democratic reform.[7]

The case study approach offers detail and depth, but it does so at the expense of breadth. Like a camera that zooms in for a close-up, the high definition that the case study of a single country provides comes at the expense of how much is included in the picture. Using the case study method, researchers may be confident about their results for the country they studied but cannot generalize beyond it with any assurance. Case studies are also susceptible to charges of selection bias in which researchers inappropriately select cases that confirm what they want to prove.

Another approach, the comparative cases method, attempts to make broad generalizations by examining a few countries in depth instead of just one, as case studies do. Political scientist Bo Rothstein uses the comparative cases method to explain why the Asian country of Singapore has been so much more successful than the Caribbean country of Jamaica in promoting economic development and the well-being of its citizens. Both were former British colonies, had similar per capita incomes, and were comparable in terms of population when they each achieved independence in the 1960s. If anything, Jamaica seemed better poised for success. It had large deposits of valuable raw materials, was less ethnically divided than Singapore, and followed a democratic path after independence, whereas Singapore did not. Yet by 2011, Singapore's gross national income per capita was over $50,000 a year; Jamaica's was only $6,500.[8] Singaporeans live longer and enjoy much lower infant mortality and homicide rates. Rothstein believes the contrasts are explained by differences in the quality of government in the two countries. Jamaica's political leaders packed the civil service with political appointees who used their positions to trade favors for votes instead of implementing policies impartially. Political parties recruited police and criminal gangs to intimidate political opponents and coerce voters. Corruption and violence flourished at the expense of economic development and citizens' well-being. Singapore's leaders, by contrast, appointed and promoted civil servants according to merit. Rothstein believes that Singapore's professional and competent civil service is a key variable explaining its relative success in promoting economic development and improving its citizens' health and safety.[9]

But Jamaica and Singapore have many other differences between them that might account for why Singapore outperformed Jamaica since they became independent. It is hard to control for all the variables that might influence results when researchers use the comparative cases method. In addition, it is hard to distinguish the effects of a particular institution, such as a professional and competent civil service, from the conditions under which it functions. Perhaps other aspects about Jamaica and Singapore made the presence or absence of a professional civil service loom so large between them. It is difficult to isolate the effects of institutions, such as a professional civil service, from the circumstances in which they exist.[10]

Finally, researchers can compare many countries instead of just a few or just one. Such studies often use quantitative data. An example of this approach is provided in the following scatter diagram, testing the hypothesis that wealthier countries are healthier, which we mentioned previously. The independent variable, wealth—operationally defined as per capita GDP in terms of purchasing power parity (PPP), which adjusts for differences in living costs among countries—is located along the horizontal x axis on the bottom of the scatter diagram. The dependent variable, health—operationalized as life expectancy—is located along the vertical y axis. To avoid charges that we cherry-picked our countries to reach certain results, we selected countries in a neutral and impartial fashion to include in Figure 1.1. Starting from the country reporting the lowest average per capita GDP, the Democratic Republic of the Congo in Africa at $400, we went up the chart and included every tenth country from the list of 226 we used to obtain our data, all the way to tiny Liechtenstein nudged between Austria and Switzerland in Europe, which topped the charts at a $141,100. We let the chips fall where they may, which fortunately captured some familiar countries, such as Bangladesh, Indonesia, and France, but also included more obscure ones such as Djibouti and the Federated States of Micronesia. In addition to these countries, the figure includes the developed and less developed countries we profile in Chapter 9 (Britain, Germany, and Sweden) and Chapter 10 (Brazil, Iran, and Nigeria), as well as Russia and China highlighted in Chapter 11. Finally, the figure also includes the United States, which we thought might interest some readers.

Figure 1.1 Wealthier Is Healthier

SOURCES: For GDP per capita (PPP) see: www.indexmundi.com/g/r.aspx?v=67. For "Life Expectancy for Countries, 2013" see: www.infoplease.com/world statistics/life expectancy-country.html

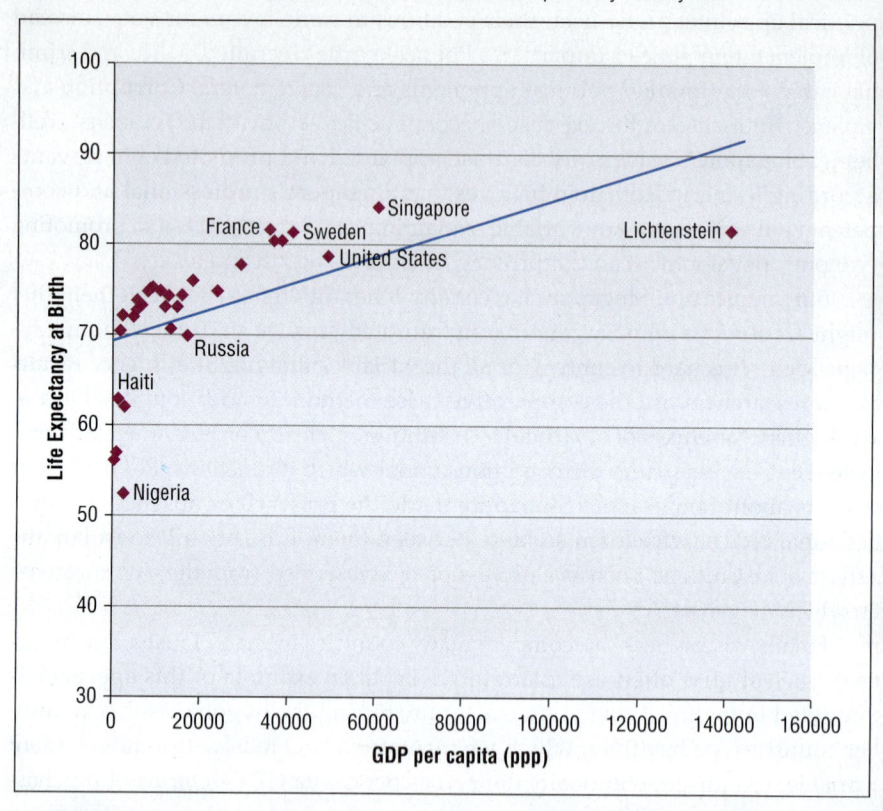

As can be seen in Figure 1.1, the relationship between wealth and health generally follows the pattern we expected to find: As per capita GDP increases, so does life expectancy. What is called the regression line running through the results represents the line closest to all the points in Figure 1.1. All the countries above the line performed better than predicted given their average per capita GDPs. They are getting more health for their wealth. Countries closest to the line are getting the average life expectancy you would expect given their average per capita GDP. All those below the line are getting less health than their wealth would have predicted. France is getting more health for its level of wealth than any other country, whereas Nigeria is getting the least.

The advantage of comparing many countries in this way is that it gives researchers confidence that their results apply broadly because of the number of countries included. Nevertheless, although this approach may reveal statistical relationships among variables, it does not provide as much insight as the other approaches about why those relationships exist. Depth is sacrificed for breadth. In addition, it is more difficult to find reliable and comparable data as the number of countries included in the data set increases. Countries may differ in how they define activities and in their accuracy and efficiency in recording them.

In summary, proceeding systematically with comparative political analysis requires a lot more effort than proceeding intuitively, as we do when we make everyday comparisons. Nevertheless, it is worth the effort because forming hypotheses, operationally defining variables, and choosing a method to test them leads to more accurate results than relying on intuition and common sense. Proceeding systematically gives us a procedure to validate whose intuition is correct when people disagree. What is more, judgments relying on common sense are sometimes flat-out wrong because they do not incorporate controls. Relying on common sense to wean people from ice cream would not have done much to prevent polio. Furthermore, sometimes what we think we see plainly with our own eyes deceives us. The absence of conflict in societies marked by inequality may falsely lead us to believe that those at the bottom accept their fate as fair and legitimate. In fact, they may consider their conditions unjust but are reluctant to complain because they lack the power to change their circumstances and fear what may happen to them if they tried to do so.

Finally, doing systematic comparative political analysis can be very satisfying because it poses puzzles to solve. For instance, in 1948 Costa Rica erupted in civil war following a close election for president that was tainted by charges of fraud. The Congress in Costa Rica proceeded to select the winner who officially received fewer votes. A half-century later in another country, a similar scenario unfolded but people accepted the result without much fuss. In the 2000 U.S. presidential election, Republican and Democratic candidates finished in a dead heat amidst allegations of fraud, and the Supreme Court declared the candidate who received fewer votes the winner. Why did Costa Rica erupt in violence that claimed the lives of 300 people, but Americans calmly accepted the results? Why did losers protest violently in one case and go home peacefully in the other?[11] How can we explain this?

Solving puzzles like this can be interesting, but these are not just ordinary puzzles. They pertain to the quality of people's lives. It is important to solve them to find the right answer because people's well-being depends on it.

We have argued that the value of comparison is that it offers insight into how countries' political conditions differ and the consequences those differences have. It permits us to check our intuitions about a country's politics by examining whether they apply in other circumstances. But comparison is also useful because it permits us to evaluate and form judgments that help us make sense of the world around us. Those judgments may be empirical and objective, such as when we say that Sweden spends more on its welfare state (28 percent of GDP in 2012) than the United States (19 percent of GDP)[12] or that Germany has higher turnout in parliamentary elections (85.4 percent of registered voters) than Switzerland (56.5 percent of registered voters).[13] Our judgments may be normative and moral, such as when we say that something is better or worse than something else, or that Sweden is kinder and gentler than the United States because it makes a greater welfare effort, or that Germany's democracy is superior to Switzerland's because it has higher voter turnout. Comparison permits us to make objective and normative judgments that help us make sense of the world.

This book tries to combine both forms of comparison, the empirical and the normative, to probe more deeply into the political life around us. We are interested in how countries govern themselves not only because it gives us insight into our own circumstances but because it helps us make moral judgments about them. The question at the heart of our text is: What constitutes a good society, and why are some countries better than others at creating one?

In this chapter, we develop some general criteria by which to examine and evaluate government performance in creating a good society. Our argument begins by suggesting that some kinds of behavior, widely condemned throughout the world, would not meet most people's criteria of a good society. We then evaluate two common standards—wealth and happiness—that are frequently used to compare government performance. Because we find comparisons of both wealth and happiness inadequate, we then offer a different standard, called the capabilities approach, to compare the performance of countries. Finally, the chapter anticipates and responds to criticism that it is inappropriate to evaluate countries according to *any* common standard. To do so is a form of cultural imperialism in which we are imposing our values on others. We address this argument at the end of the chapter.

Visions of the Good Society: Gross National Product and Gross National Happiness

1.3 Analyze wealth and happiness as measures of the good society.

Few people anywhere in the world would argue that a society based on slavery, where people can be bought and sold like cattle, is a good society, especially if one happened to be a slave. Few would agree that a society in which one group of people slaughters fellow citizens from another ethnic or religious group exemplifies good governance, especially if one happened to be part of the persecuted minority. And few would say that a society in which thousands of children die each year from preventable diseases is exemplary, especially if one of those children happened to be yours.

These are not hypothetical examples. Slavery still exists. Slaves include girls as young as fifteen who are involuntarily held in brothels in Thailand and children as young as six who make bricks all day in Pakistan. Today, the proportion of the world's population condemned to do forced labor is smaller than it has ever been. At the same time, however, the *absolute* number of people who are held in slavery is greater than ever before. "According to historians," Gary A. Haugan and Victor Boutros write, "about 11 million people were extracted from Africa *during four hundred years* of the Atlantic slave trade.—which is as little as half of the number of people held in slavery in our world *this year*."[14]

Just as slavery remains prevalent and extensive, ethnic and religious mass murder persists and is widespread. Shiite and Sunni Muslims slaughter each other in Iraq, and rival Tutsi and Hutu ethnic groups murdered each other in Africa in 1994. Finally, millions of infants suffer and die from preventable diseases each year. In the African country of Sierra Leone, more than one out of every ten babies who are born dies before his or her first birthday.

It would be relatively easy to get widespread agreement that these are undesirable outcomes in any country or culture. Our sense of moral outrage might be particularly acute if they were to happen to us. But is it possible to move beyond these specific examples to develop general criteria that can be used to decide what constitutes a good society? In the following paragraphs, we discuss the merits of using wealth and happiness to judge societies.

It is generally and appropriately assumed that the higher a country's level of economic development, the better off its citizens will tend to be. In wealthier countries, few people are held as slaves, large-scale ethnic and religious violence is rare, and few people die from preventable diseases. Economic development is often measured by a country's per capita gross domestic product, which we defined earlier, in which purchasing power is held constant.[15]

Figure 1.2 gives the GDP per capita (with purchasing power held constant) for those countries plotted in Figure 1.1. By this criterion, Liechtenstein was the

Figure 1.2 Gross Domestic Product per Capita (PPP), 2011

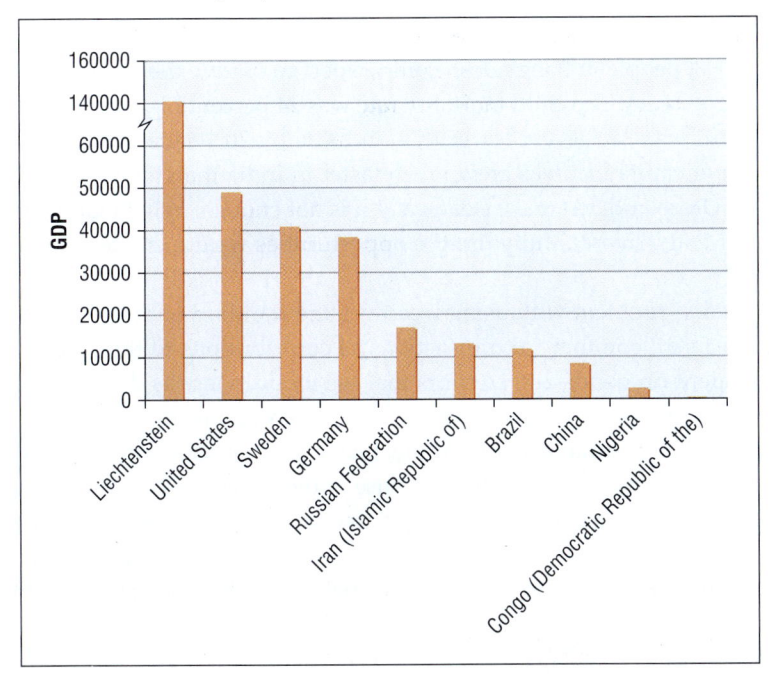

SOURCE: www.indexmundi.com/g/r.aspx?v=67

most successful with a per capita GDP of $141,100 in 2011, whereas the Democratic Republic of the Congo was the least successful with a per capita GDP of only $400.[16] Countries with high levels of per capita income to purchase an array of goods and services can afford to send their children to school instead of to work, can satisfy the competing claims of different ethnic and religious groups instead of inciting one group to slaughter another, and can provide health care services to people instead of presiding over people dying needlessly

Yet, political leaders and social scientists are increasingly dissatisfied with this measure of a good society and of good governance. In fact, in February 2008, the president of France, Nicholas Sarkozy, was so disgruntled that he commissioned a group of the world's leading economists, including two Nobel Prize winners, to propose a better alternative.[17] One problem with using wealth or per capita income as the measure of a good society, Sarkozy's commission noted, was that it assumes more wealth contributes to improved living conditions. But a country may or may not use its wealth to improve living conditions for its citizens. For example, Jean Dreze and Amartya Sen show that economic success and social failure have gone hand in hand in India. Per capita income in India grew at a remarkable compound rate of close to five percent from 1999 through 2009, but even as India leaped ahead of other South Asian countries in terms of economic development, it fell behind many of them in terms of citizens' well-being. Compare India and Bangladesh. India's GDP per capita was 60 percent higher than neighboring Bangladesh in 1990 and grew to almost double Bangladesh's GDP by 2010. Nevertheless, during that same period of outstanding economic performance by India, as the wealth gap between Bangladesh and India widened, Bangladesh overtook India on a wide range of social indicators, including greater life expectancy, higher immunization rates, and lower infant mortality rates. Life expectancy was four years longer in India than in Bangladesh in 1990, but by 2008, people in Bangladesh could expect to outlive their neighbors in India by three years. The child mortality rate was 24 percent higher in Bangladesh in 1990 but was 24 percent lower than in India by 2009—despite the fact that average per capita incomes grew much faster in India than they did in Bangladesh. As Dreze and Sen make clear, wealth is not enough. What matters more is "whether countries skillfully use the opportunities wealth creates to make life better."[18]

A second problem with using wealth as the standard of the good society is that it treats all commercial transactions as contributions to the greater good. Money spent on goods and services that we would view as detestable are regarded as morally equivalent to money spent on goods and services that we would consider desirable. For example, major oil spills from ocean-going tankers contribute to economic growth because of the expense to clean them up, but few of us would regard a coastline ravaged with oil slicks as something that improves people's lives. GDP treats money spent on prisons as equivalent to money spent on education, but few of us believe that money spent on prisons is as productive for society as that devoted to education. A standard that simply measures how much money is spent and is indifferent to what it is spent on is morally blind.

Moreover, a focus on GDP alone may ignore its hidden costs and thus misrepresent the benefits society derives from it. For example, China has achieved remarkable rates of economic growth recently, but this has been achieved at the expense of increasing inequality, environmental degradation, and ruinous corruption. Alistair Thornton, an economist who studies China, recently commented, "Digging a hole and filling it in again gives you GDP growth. It doesn't give you economic value. A lot of the economic activity in China over the last few years has been digging holes and filling them back in again"—anything from bailing out solar companies to building thousands of apartments in which no one lives.[19] High-quality economic growth that imposes minimal costs on society needs to be distinguished from low-quality growth that inflicts costly damage. The kind of growth that occurs is as important to social well-being as the rate of growth.

Finally, using GDP per capita as a measure of good governance may hide considerable differences in how it is distributed. According to this standard, it does not matter whether a higher average per capita income is achieved by increasing the incomes of the few at the top, permitting them to purchase private yachts and jets, or whether it is realized by increasing the incomes of the many at the bottom, permitting them to purchase food and medicine they need. Between 1995 and 2008, Nigeria's economy grew to an extent that it was poised to surpass South Africa as the largest economy in Africa (and eventually did pass South Africa in 2014). Over those same thirteen years (1995-2008) in which Nigeria's economy closed the gap with South Africa, "real incomes for the bottom two-thirds of Nigerians declined."[20] In his novel *Hard Times*, Charles Dickens composed a clever scene to convey the idea that higher national incomes contribute to well-being only when their benefits are distributed widely. The teacher in Dickens's novel tries to convince students that wealth equaled well-being by telling them to imagine that their classroom is a nation endowed with "fifty millions of money." The teacher then asks whether this didn't make them all prosperous and lucky to live in such a thriving country, to which one of the students replies: "I couldn't know whether it was a prosperous nation or not and whether I was in a thriving state or not unless I knew who got the money and whether any of it was mine."[21]

We do not mean to suggest that economic development and the accumulation of wealth is unimportant. According to economist Paul Collier, "Growth is not a cure all, but lack of growth is a kill-all."[22] Dani Rodrik concurs and writes, "Historically nothing has worked better than economic growth in enabling societies to improve the life chances of their members, including those at the very bottom."[23] Countries that fail to grow economically lack the financial resources to improve citizens' health care, increase their educational opportunities, and insure their safety. Poor countries are also more prone to debilitating corruption and destructive civil wars that threaten people's well-being. However, higher GDP growth and per capita incomes, by themselves, are no assurance that people's needs are met. It depends on how the money is spent and how widely it is distributed. According to the economists Jean Dreze and Amartya Sen, "While economic growth is an important tool for enhancing living conditions, its reach and impact depend greatly upon what is done with the fruits of growth. . . . Economic growth is indeed important, not for itself, but for what it allows a country to do with the resources that are generated."[24] In other words, what matters for development is not how much countries have—albeit, it is better to have more than less—but how wisely they invest it to improve people's lives.

As much as economic growth and higher per capita incomes are desirable, they are only a means to an end; they are not ends in themselves. Consequently, some social scientists have proposed happiness as the goal of a good society that wealth can help us achieve. They argue that a country's gross domestic product is only important in as much as it contributes to a country's gross domestic happiness (GDH), which is the true measure of the good society. More is better only if it makes us happier. Derek Bok, the former president of Harvard University, argues that, "A nation's total production of goods and services is at best a means to other ends, and often a dubious one at that. In contrast, happiness or satisfaction with life, can lay claim to being . . . the end that most people consider more important than any other."[25]

One country that took happiness seriously as the measure of the good society was the Kingdom of Bhutan, located high in the Himalayan mountains, between China and India. Under a new constitution that Bhutan adopted in 2008, government programs were judged according to the happiness they produced, not the economic benefits they created.[26] The government then proceeded to classify happiness in terms of four pillars (economy, culture, environment, and good governance), with nine domains under them, which could, in turn, be measured by seventy-two indicators. The domain of psychological well-being, for example, came under the pillar of culture and was indicated by the frequencies of prayer and meditation, fewer feelings of selfishness and jealousy, and more feelings of calm and compassion.[27]

Bhutan developed complex mathematical formulas for measuring happiness, but it is hard to apply these formulas comparatively to other countries. Fortunately, the World Values Survey asked how happy people were in different countries, making such comparisons possible. Surveys conducted in 97 countries between 1995 and 2005 found that Denmark had the highest average life satisfaction score while Zimbabwe's negative result indicated that a majority of people there were unhappy with their lives. Figure 1.3 provides a sample of how different countries scored when it came to happiness.[28] Although skeptics of using polls to assess happiness criticize their subjectivity, advocates defend them as "the most democratic of well-being measures, since they reflect not what

Figure 1.3 Countries Ranked by Happiness

SOURCE: "Despite Frustrations Americans Are Pretty Darned Happy." National Science Foundation Press Release, June 30, 2008. nsf.gov.www.nsf.gov/news/newsmedia/pr111725/pr111725.pdf

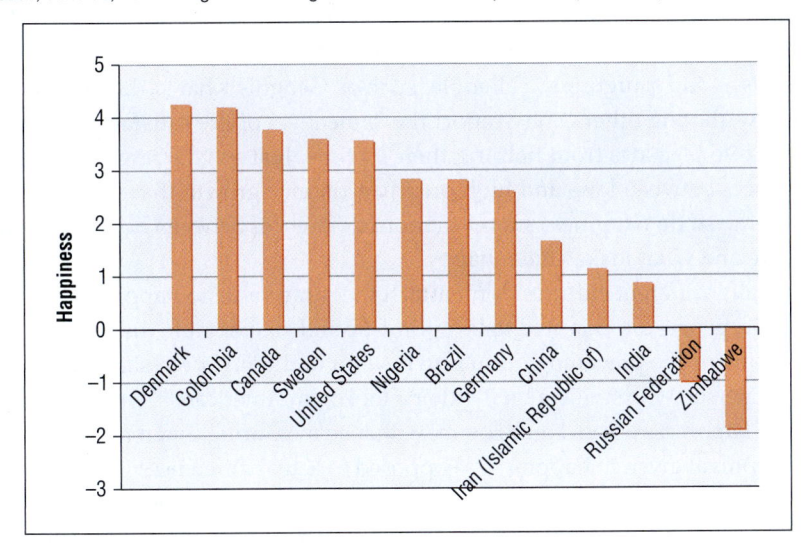

experts or governments think should define a good life, but instead represent a direct personal judgment about . . . how happy YOU feel."[29]

However, just as there were good reasons to be skeptical of average per capita income as an indicator of the good society, so are there good reasons to be suspicious of happiness as the measure of government performance. First, when life is hard, people adapt to adversity and find happiness with less. That is, people who are deprived "come to want only what they can have" and be content with this. Consequently, poor people tend to apply lower standards to evaluate their happiness than wealthier citizens.[30] Amartya Sen writes that "hopelessly deprived people adjust their desires and expectations to what little they see as feasible . . . [and] train themselves to take pleasure in small mercies."[31] Although reports of happiness by poor people may be genuine, they are also expressions of acceptance of conditions they would probably change if they had the power to do so.[32] It appears that happiness depends heavily upon one's reference group and expectations.

Second, although happiness may be a good thing, it is not the only thing. Indeed, people may desire other worthy goals that require sacrifice and hardship to attain them. People's yearning for purpose and meaning in life may require them to forgo pleasures that would bring them happiness. In addition, although maximizing satisfaction may make sense for individuals, it may not be an optimal strategy for society.[33] As Elizabeth Kolbert argues, making sure the environment is sustainable may be more important than trashing it, even if we derive more pleasure from the latter than the former.[34]

Third, just as GDP measures ignore the purpose for which goods and services are produced, so do happiness measures overlook the different ways in which people find satisfaction. Genghis Khan is alleged to have said, "The greatest happiness is to vanquish your enemies, to chase them before you, to rob them of their wealth, to see those dear to them bathed in tears, to clasp to your bosom their wives and daughters."[35] People, such as Genghis Khan, who get pleasure from humiliating others, may report the same level of life satisfaction as those who derive pleasure from helping their victims. Just as GDP measures ignore differences between low- and high-quality economic growth that we mentioned previously, so do happiness surveys ignore differences between how people find pleasure and what makes them happy.

Finally, different cultures don't attach the same value to happiness. In some countries, people are expected to be optimistic and exuberant in the face of adversity; in others, the prevailing norm is to be dour and grim. A Russian adage holds that, "A person who smiles a lot is either a fool or an American."[36] Survey comparisons of happiness across countries may thus be measuring differences in the cultural approval given to happiness as opposed to actual differences in happiness.[37]

Neither gross domestic product nor gross domestic happiness is satisfactory as a standard to evaluate government performance and compare quality of life across countries. The question remains: What standard is appropriate by which to measure the good society? We propose to use **the capabilities approach** developed by Nobel Prize–winning economist Amartya Sen and the philosopher Martha Nussbaum to answer this question. According to the capabilities approach, a good society "ensures all individuals a set of basic resources that will equalize their chances to reach their full potential." Governments cannot equalize abilities to become a brilliant and creative scientist like Albert Einstein or a basketball player with the grace and power of LeBron James. Some of this is genetic, but "it is possible for those who happen to have ambitions in those fields

The Capabilities Approach
This approach argues that societies should be evaluated according to the freedoms their members enjoy to develop their potential in ways they value.

In Brief: Criticisms of GDP and GDH as Measures of the Good Society

GDP
- More wealth may not translate into better social conditions.
- GDP is not sensitive to issues of distribution.
- GDP devalues activity that is not bought and sold.

GDH
- GDH discounts that people's sense of satisfaction may depend more on their reference group or expectations than on their actual circumstances.
- GDH is indifferent to the ways people might find happiness.
- GDH ignores cultural differences in the approval or sanction given to happiness.

to realize their talents ... by giving them access to certain goods and services that are likely to enhance their capabilities of reaching their full potential."[38] Empowering people, giving them access to certain goods and services so they can pursue values of importance to them—to be a scientist, athlete, or whatever—is the best way of assessing individuals' quality of life and the measure of the good society.

Capabilities and the Quality of Life

1.4   Define and apply the capabilities approach.

Nussbaum describes the capabilities approach as one that defines "achievement in terms of the opportunities available to each person."[39] The key issue, she argues, is "what each person is able to do and to be."[40] However, if the concept of "capabilities" is to be useful in comparative analysis, we need to make it more precise and measurable. We propose to make it less abstract by suggesting there are four dimensions to capabilities that make people free to live the life they choose, which apply in all countries. Instead of one dial, such as GDP or GDH, to measure the quality of life in different countries, we propose a dashboard containing different gauges. Just as one dial won't tell you how well a car is running, so do you need to check various gauges on the dashboard—electricity, gas, temperature, and pressure—to assess how well a car is performing.[41] In a good society, people are able to:

- Meet their physical needs.
- Make informed decisions.
- Live in safety.
- Exercise democratic rights.

Physical Well-being

Physical well-being includes nourishment, health care, and housing sufficient to support a long life. People cannot lead rich, full lives if they are malnourished, chronically sick, or exposed to the elements because they lack shelter. One way of assessing physical needs is to compare poverty rates across countries, but doing so is problematic. Many countries do not draw a poverty line, an income threshold below which people are considered poor, as the United States does, and a 2014 poverty line of $23,850 for a family of four in the United States would look like riches to millions of poor people in the rest of the world whose annual incomes are much less. Alternatively, poverty can be defined as including those whose income is 50 percent below the median income in a country. However, this measure really compares inequality among countries, not poverty, because the median income differs from one country to the next. People who are below 50 percent where the median income is high would live much better than those who are below that threshold where the median income is low.

In-Depth: Costa Rica—Doing More with Less

The general pattern is that wealthier countries are healthier, as we saw in Figure 1.1, and that the wealthiest countries have the lowest infant mortality rates. Costa Rica is an exception. This small democratic country of four and a half million people in Central America has one of the best infant mortality records in the world for a country at its income level.

Dramatically reducing infant mortality rates does not require expensive, sophisticated medical technology. It does, however, require safe drinking water, adequate nutrition, and basic health care for pregnant mothers and newborns. Costa Rica has done an excellent job of providing these necessities to poor mothers and infants who need them most. Safe drinking water is readily available to over 90 percent of the population, poor families receive assistance to alleviate malnutrition, and basic medical care is available to mothers in all parts of the country, especially in rural areas that traditionally lacked access to health care workers.

Costa Rica's success in reducing infant mortality is due, first, to the traditions and vibrancy of its democracy. The country is one of the oldest, most established democracies in the Americas, boasting competitive political parties and high voter turnout by peasants and workers. Second, for most of the latter part of the last century, the government was controlled by a political party whose leaders were determined to help the rural poor. Finally, groups opposed to its policies were politically weak. Doctors, hospitals, and insurance companies were publicly controlled and funded, which weakened their ability to oppose the government's policies.

For Further Discussion

1. Given Costa Rica's success in reducing infant mortality, why haven't other developing countries rushed to copy its formula?
2. Costa Rica is fairly wealthy compared to its Central American neighbors, which have much higher infant mortality rates. Why not just explain its success by saying it has more money to spend on health care?

To avoid these problems, we will steer clear of poverty rates entirely. We propose to examine physical well-being across countries by comparing infant mortality rates, the number of children who die during their first year of life. Infant mortality rates (see Table 1.1 in the appendix) provide a revealing window into social conditions because new babies are particularly susceptible to poor diets, deadly diseases, and extreme weather. Some countries do an excellent job of keeping infants alive and healthy, whereas others do not. In developed countries, such as Sweden and Japan, fewer than three newborn babies die per 1,000 births. In contrast, in Sierra Leone, there were 119 deaths for every 1,000 babies born in 2011.[42]

Informed Decision Making

Knowledge is power. In the modern world, the ability to make choices that improve one's quality of life depends on access to information and the skills to understand its meaning. In India, a new right-to-information law permits poor people to hold the bureaucracy accountable and find out what happened to the money that was budgeted for them. Whereas previously an unresponsive bureaucracy had to be bribed, activists now say that "simply filing an inquiry about a missing ration card, a wayward pension application, or a birth certificate is nowadays enough to force the once stodgy bureaucracy to deliver."[43] Nevertheless, access to information is insufficient without the skills to make sense of it. People need to be literate and numerate so they can negotiate their lives more effectively. People who are illiterate are said to be blind; they cannot decipher street signs or understand medical prescriptions and are handicapped in providing for their families.[44] Their awareness of the ways in which their lives could be improved is limited, and they are vulnerable to others who can take advantage of these shortcomings. One study found that Americans who lacked basic knowledge about finances and could not do simple calculations were more likely to lose their home to foreclosure in the recent recession than those who were more financially literate. "The less people know," James Surowieki writes, "the more they run into trouble."[45] Citizens' ability to promote their interests and make thoughtful choices about their lives can be dramatically improved by access to education. For example, in the award-winning Hollywood movie, "Precious," (2009) an obese, illiterate, teenager who is abused by her mother and pregnant with a second child by her father, develops self-confidence after attending an alternative school and learning how to read. Literacy gives her the capacity to protect her children and find work, to escape her dysfunctional family and surroundings, and to take advantage of opportunities that were previously closed to her.[46]

The more people know, the more they have a sense of possibility. The knowledge that the civil rights movement imparted and the profound changes it gave to blacks in the South is captured in a story told by an aged southern black farmer: "A little boy was selling puppies last week for two dollars. He came around again this week, selling the same puppies for six dollars. I asked him why the price had gone up and he said because their eyes were open now. That's the way it is with us colored folk. . . . Our eyes are open now."[47]

To assess informed decision making, we compare literacy rates across countries (see Table 1.2 in the appendix).

Safety

People cannot lead a good life if they are victims of, or live in constant fear of being beaten, imprisoned, robbed, shot, enslaved, raped, or tortured. If you are not safe, nothing else matters. The biggest fear of the poorest people in the world, according to a United Nations report, was not going hungry, losing your home, or getting sick, but being hurt by violence.[48] The problem is not the law, but lawlessness, in which people are subject to predators and outside the protection of basic law enforcement. Security is a precondition to improving people's lives because the best efforts to meet people's physical needs and educate them will fail if they are subject to predatory violence. Lawless violence reduces economic growth, redistributes income from the poor to the rich, undermines valuable public goods such as trust, and lowers productivity. Amartya Sen writes, "Freedom from fear is as important as freedom from want. It is impossible to truly enjoy one of those rights without the other." Or as one African villager eloquently explained in the World Bank's *Voices of the Poor* study: "Where there is no security, there is no life."[49] Just as there are substantial differences in the degree to which countries meet their citizens' physical needs, there are also profound differences in the extent to which they meet their citizens' need for safety and security. We measure physical safety by comparing homicide rates across countries (see Table 1.3 in the appendix). Homicide rates avoid different definitions of criminal offenses that might exist in different countries and minimize the different rates at which crimes are reported and recorded by police. Being dead is the same everywhere, and people are more likely to report a murder, and the police are more likely to record it than other crimes.

According to this measure, countries differ greatly in their ability to provide a safe environment for their citizens. Canadians are much less likely to murder each other than Americans, who live just across the border. Where appropriate, we supplement the use of homicide rates to capture our standard of safety by looking also at the incidence of war. People's safety is not only threatened by isolated murderers but by organized soldiers and the collateral damage that accompanies warfare. Millions of people have died in violent political conflicts between states, and especially in civil wars within them, in places ranging from Syria in the Middle East to the Democratic Republic of the Congo in Africa.

Democracy

The ability "to participate effectively in political choices that govern one's life; . . . the right of political participation; protections of free speech and association" underpin the other three conditions for a good society.[50] Without influence over the laws that govern them, people cannot press for improvements in their physical well-being, safety, and education, nor can they defend gains they have already made, as former slaves discovered in the American South in the aftermath of the Civil War. By the end of Reconstruction, many southern blacks lost access to their farms, lived in fear of being lynched, and had to send their children to segregated and inferior schools once they had lost the right to vote.

Democracy, which entails political equality, the rule of law, and choosing leaders in free and fair elections, is more common today than in the past, but just because citizens gain formal, legal rights does not mean people can actually use them. Citizens in the former Soviet Union would often joke that Americans were unsophisticated about democratic rights. "What's important is not freedom of speech," they would lecture naïve Americans, "but rather freedom *after* speech." A constitution that enumerates rights does not mean that those are enforced or that people are free to enjoy them. In many countries, people are unable to exercise their civil and political rights because they are subject to the vindictive power of employers, husbands, landlords, urban bosses, or even their relatives. In these circumstances, people are reluctant to exercise their legal rights because it might cost them their jobs, access to land, or even their lives.[51]

Unlike our other standards, there is no shortage of indexes measuring democracy. Efforts by governments and international agencies to promote democracy led to more efforts to monitor and assess it. The problem with democracy indexes is not their frequency but their quality. Some indexes define democracy in such a way that it includes too much, whereas others include too little. We will use the Economist Intelligence Unit's Index of Democracy, which uses five categories, from a supportive political culture to sufficient political participation, to measure democratic robustness across countries on a scale of 1 to 10.[52]

Some Caveats

The four categories we have described represent the minimum that people need to fulfill their potentials and enhance their quality of life. Several points must be stressed here before we respond to criticisms of these criteria to define the good society. First, it may be that all "good things do not necessarily go together," and trade-offs among physical well-being, safety, education, and democracy may be necessary.[53] Progress on one dimension of capabilities may require concessions on others. Second, the goal of a good society is to make it possible for each individual in a country to enjoy a high quality of life, not just for the average quality of life to be high. Third, our approach does not specify a particular set of economic, political, or social institutions that are necessary for a good society. Some argue that good societies can be created only by relying on free markets, private property rights, and a minimal role for states. Others argue that a good society requires institutions that do just the opposite. Finally, our approach does not assert that it is the state's responsibility to ensure that all individuals develop their potential. It is, however, the role of the state to create conditions in which persons can *choose* to develop their potential. One way of thinking about this difference, Nussbaum suggests, is to distinguish between dieting and starving. People may choose to go on a diet that restricts their intake of food. By contrast, starvation is not a choice. People can choose not to eat but it is the job of the government to ensure that food is available for those who want to.[54] If people who are sick choose not to take advantage of health care resources, that is their business; but it is quite another matter if sick people cannot access health care because it is unavailable or unaffordable.[55]

In Brief: Operationalizing Capabilities

- Meeting physical needs: infant mortality rates
- Informed decision-making: literacy rates
- Safety: homicide rates
- Democracy: Index of Democracy

Responding to Criticisms of the Capabilities Approach

1.5 Analyze criticisms of the capabilities approach.

The capabilities approach has won widespread support in recent years from eminent scholars and important international organizations. Recently, Peter A. Hall of Harvard and former president of the Comparative Politics section of the

American Political Science Association encouraged his colleagues to move beyond their concern with how societies distribute income to think more broadly "about the distribution of life chances and about the ways in which institutional and cultural frameworks . . . contribute to individual and collective well-being."[56] He and a number of colleagues have collaborated on a project that investigates the sources of successful societies.[57] A number of organizations, such as the United Nations, have also adopted the capabilities approach. The 2002 Human Development Report issued by the UN stated: "Fundamental to enlarging human choices is building capability: the range of things that people can do or be."[58] American states have also begun to develop an alternative to GDP inspired by the capabilities approach to measure the well-being of their citizens. Maryland and Vermont have officially adopted Genuine Progress Indicator (GPI), which assesses 26 economic, environmental, and social indicators, such as inequality, the costs of climate change, and the value of volunteering to measure performance, with more states considering doing so.[59] There is even a scholarly journal, *The Journal of Human Development and Capabilities*, devoted to work using the capabilities approach.

Despite support from prominent scholars and influential organizations, the capabilities approach still has its critics.[60] A skeptic might dismiss this approach as too idealistic, asserting with some justification that no country can meet these conditions for every single citizen. Not even the wealthiest countries in the world have met these standards, no less poorer countries in Africa, Asia, and Latin America. Although it may be idealistic to assume that every citizen in every country can enjoy a high quality of life, it is not idealistic to believe that many countries can perform better than they currently do. Performance on these standards varies widely among countries that are quite similar to one another in other respects, indicating that there probably is room for improvement. Furthermore, many of the poorest countries in the world have made improvements in their citizens' capabilities in recent decades, demonstrating that progress is possible even in unlikely circumstances.[61]

Other readers will argue that our approach is contrary to human nature. Some critics may be sympathetic to the goals of the capabilites approach but believe that people are too competitive, greedy, and selfish to create the kind of good society it envisions. Nevertheless, people are capable of a wide range of behavior, from the most greedy and selfish to the most altruistic and cooperative. It is not any more natural to be greedy and selfish than to be caring and cooperative. As Amartya Sen reminds us, we do not have to be a Gandhi, a Mandela, or a Mother Theresa "to recognize that we can have aims or priorities that differ from the single-minded pursuit of our own well-being only."[62] In addition, insisting that there is a universal human nature makes it hard to explain why there are dramatic differences in citizens' capabilities from one country to another. Those who insist that flaws in human nature prevent substantial improvements in people's lives cannot explain why Americans kill each other more frequently than do Canadians; why Denmark has remarkably little government corruption, but it is routine in Nigeria; or why South Korea has achieved extraordinary economic growth since 1960, but North Korea has plunged into poverty and famine.

Finally, **cultural relativists** believe that it is inappropriate to try to establish criteria for a good society that apply to all of the world's countries. They claim that each society should be evaluated only by using criteria from that society.[63] If some countries choose not to practice democratic politics, that is up to them. If some countries do not want female children to be educated, that is their prerogative. These are not necessarily practices that we would approve of, but other countries and cultures have the right to decide on their own rules, just as we do. Cultural relativism is attractive because it appeals to our desire to be tolerant and open-minded toward people who have different beliefs from our own.[64]

However, cultural relativism is not as innocent and impartial as it appears. Cultural relativists simply legitimize the power of those who have triumphed over others in the conflict over prevailing social values. Cultures are seldom, if ever, monolithic in which everyone agrees but are often filled with different and sometimes conflicting interpretations. Where many interpretations of a culture's values exist, cultural relativism sides with those who are able to enforce their values on others. The Taliban's oppression of women, for example, only represented Afghani culture because it was able to defeat other Afghani groups who had a more progressive view of women.

In addition, cultural relativists assume wrongly that the liberal values at the heart of the capabilities approach are distinctively western. To the contrary, many ideas about each individual's intrinsic worth developed elsewhere before they appeared in the West. Ideas were imported from other cultures and became part of the Western tradition, just as spices imported from the East became part of the West's culinary tradition. Elements that are uniquely Western "should not be dismissed because cultures borrow and learn from each other all the time."[65] All cultures are blended. Relativists assume a cultural purity and isolation that simply does not exist.

Cultural Relativism: The premise that countries should be evaluated according to their own cultural values as opposed to judging them according to values outsiders impose on them.

Conclusion

Comparative politics examines why countries are organized in different ways and what consequences those differences may have. It examines differences within countries as opposed to relations between them, which is the domain of international relations, a subfield within political science. Comparative politics is a valuable field of study not only because it makes us familiar with other countries but because it gives us perspective about our own. It also reveals best and worst practices as countries try to meet similar challenges. Comparative political analysis provides a reference point or standard by which we can make judgments about government performance.

Comparative political analysis proceeds systematically, which entails forming hypotheses, operationally defining variables, and selecting a method to test them. We then assessed different standards of the good society by which to compare countries. One standard defines the good society according to wealth, whereas another does so according to happiness. Both are inadequate because they are insensitive to distributional issues. A society may be wealthy, but the people within it are not because its wealth is unevenly distributed, and the poor may use lower standards than the rich to define happiness because that is all they think they can obtain or deserve.

We then introduced the capabilities approach, which defines the good society in terms of "the progress of human freedom and capability to lead the kind of life that people have reason to value."[66] That is, the good society is one in which certain minimal conditions exist that permit people to flourish. These conditions include physical well-being, safety from violence, the ability to make thoughtful choices about one's life, and the possession of civil and political rights.

Finally, the chapter responded to critics of the capabilities approach who condemn it for foolish idealism or cultural imperialism. However, it is not idealistic to suggest that some countries can do better at promoting their citizens' capabilities because other countries with similar levels of resources are outperforming them. Nor is the capabilities approach guilty of imposing values on another culture. Rather, it provides consistent standards to apply in making judgments about how well governments perform in promoting their citizens' well-being.

Suggested Readings

Alexander Kaufman, (ed.), *Capabilities Equality: Basic Issues and Problems* (NewYork: Routledge, 2006). An edited volume that includes chapters sympathetic to the capabilities approach and criticisms of it.

Todd Landman, *Issues and Methods of Comparative Politics: An Introduction* (New York: Routledge, 2000). Makes the case for why we compare countries and how to make comparisons using a single country, a few countries, or many countries.

Derek Bok, *The Politics of Happiness: What Government Can Learn from the New Research on Well-Being* (Princeton: Princeton University Press, 2010). A good brief on behalf of happiness research and its use to steer policy.

Martha Nussbaum, *Creating Capabilities: The Human Development Approach* (Cambridge: Harvard University Press, 2011). An introduction to the capabilities approach. It suggests the success of a society should be evaluated primarily by the freedoms its members enjoy.

Critical Thinking Questions

1. What principles does your vision of the good society reflect? What prerequisites do you think the good society should include?
2. We use concepts, such as democracy or freedom, all the time, or we often say that workers in some country are more class conscious than those in another, or that ethnic tensions are greater here than there. Nevertheless, operationally defining these concepts so they can be used in comparative political analysis is tricky and takes a great deal of imagination. How would you operationally define these concepts (democracy, freedom, class consciousness, ethnic tension) so they can be compared across countries?
3. What are the advantages and disadvantages of the different comparative methods we reviewed: the case study approach that examines one country intensively; a paired country approach that tries to find countries that are similar to each other while other variables are held constant; or comparisons that involve many countries so analysts can test their hypothesis against many cases? Which method do you think is best and why?
4. Even if we accept that wealth (GDP per capita) is not sufficient for the good society, do you think it is, at least, necessary?
5. What criteria do you believe should be used to evaluate how states perform?

Chapter 2
The State

Learning Objectives

2.1 Analyze the relationship between states and societies.

2.2 Define power and distinguish the different cultural, economic, and political forms it takes.

2.3 Define the state.

2.4 Evaluate different perspectives that explain the rise of states.

2.5 Compare the different ways states are organized.

2.6 Evaluate the performance of strong and weak states according to the standards of the good society.

Introduction

2.1 Analyze the relationship between states and societies.

States viewed forests initially as sources of revenue for the timber that could be extracted and sold from them. To increase their yields, states turned to scientific forestry, which involved replacing the diverse, chaotic, old-growth forest with one that was easier to manipulate, measure, and assess. The underbrush needed to be cleared, the number of species needed to be reduced, and the trees needed to be planted at the same time and in straight rows for easy harvesting. The forest had been replaced by tree farming. Scientific forestry promised to deliver maximum production of a uniform commodity that could be managed, extracted, and sold easily.[1]

In the short run, the simplification of the forest to a single commodity was a success. Timber yields increased, but after the second rotation of saplings had been planted, the quality of the timber began to decline. Scientific forestry destroyed the complex ecology that the forest had once provided to nourish and protect the trees. The absence of biomass on the forest floor due to the clearing of underbrush led to thinner and less nutritious soil. Trees that were all of the same kind attracted pests that specialized in that species, and James C. Scott writes, "same age, same-species forests . . . were more susceptible to massive storm-felling."[2] Efforts to bring order and control to the forest in pursuit of higher yields were incompatible with the complex ecosystems on which healthy trees depended.

Nevertheless, scientific forestry matured. The regimentation of nature as a way to manage forests and increase their yield was abandoned. New ways of cultivating forests were developed that did not destroy the biodiversity that trees required. Scientific forestry, which initially imposed an order on nature that harmed it, now permitted the state to extract more revenue from it in ways that also maintained this vital resource. The kind of planning and order that states imposed became the basis for realizing higher timber yields that would not have been possible without it. This parable of the forest tells us a lot about states. They have certain interests—in this instance, raising revenue—and they try to bring order to chaos in pursuit of them. Like the forest, society is diverse and complex, with a complicated ecology, and the state's efforts to impose order on such a complex social organism can make things worse. In these cases, as Scott quips, the state can't see "the forest for the trees."[3] At other times, the state's effort to plan, coordinate, and administer permits societies to achieve things they could not have done otherwise. The state can both frustrate society's ambitions and help realize them.

This chapter argues that the good society depends on a society's institutional arrangements, and the most powerful institution of all is the state. The good society, as we established earlier, is based on a set of defensible universal values. First, people should be able to meet their physical needs: People should be able to obtain the food, shelter, and health care they need to work, play, and procreate. It is hard to achieve your life's goals if you are hungry from lack of food, cold from lack of shelter, or sick from lack of medical care. Second, people should be safe from harm: They should be secure enough that others, including agents of the government, will not harm them physically or take their personal property. Third, people should have the ability to make educated choices about how they live: They must have the opportunity to obtain the knowledge they need to make informed decisions. Finally, people should have civil and political rights to protect the conditions in which they might freely develop their capabilities. People should be allowed to participate in open public debate about the policies and leaders most likely to produce conditions in which they can thrive.

States can promote conditions that develop people's capabilities or impede them. They can manage forests in ways that reduce their yield or increase it. Since states loom so large in thwarting or enhancing people's lives, this chapter examines the origins of the state and its different parts or components. These include its legislative, executive, and judicial branches, its bureaucratic and military arms, and its subnational or federal levels. Since states matter so much, it is important to look inside them.

Finally, the chapter examines whether strong states contribute more to the good society than do weak states. According to Samuel P. Huntington, "the most important distinction between countries concerns not their form, but their degree of government." Some countries have "strong, adaptable, coherent political institutions" in which the probability is high that policies will be implemented as the government intended.[4] In countries with strong states, you can be fairly sure that water is safe to drink because regulators have inspected it, police will arrive when you dial 911, and children will be educated when you send them to school. In countries with weak states, the opposite is true. These countries suffer from a crisis of governability. Laws are not enforced, basic public services are not delivered, and officials are corrupt. The government rules but does not govern. The chapter concludes by asking whether people are better off with strong rather than weak states.

Institutions and Power

2.2 Define power and illustrate the different cultural, economic, and political forms it takes.

Institutions
Institutions refer not only to rules but to the organizations that make them. Institutions create patterns of behavior that give order to society.

The degree to which countries meet the standards of the good society depends on their institutional arrangements. **Institutions** create and embody written and unwritten rules that constrain individuals' behavior into patterned actions. These rules make a social life together possible by giving it order and predictability. Without these rules, our lives together would be chaotic and fraught with anxiety. Just as individual words in a paragraph would sound like gibberish if we did not use them within the context of established rules, so do institutions give meaning and structure to our relations with each other. Institutions provide the grammar of our lives.

To appreciate the importance of institutions, just imagine how dangerous the simple act of driving a car would be if there were no traffic laws. We could not be sure that incoming traffic would stop at red lights, that cars on our side of the road would go in the same direction, or that drivers would operate at safe speeds. The result would be chaos and danger. This is precisely what happened in Baghdad, Iraq, "when the rules vanished in the chaos of the American invasion, when there was no electricity for stoplights, and no police officers to enforce the law." According to *New York Times* reporter John Tierney, "Every intersection became a perpetual game of chicken among cars, trucks, buses and carts drawn by horses and donkeys. Every lane became potentially two-way, even on expressways, where there quickly became no distinction between entrance and exit ramps."[5] To make traffic flow smoothly, to create the order and predictability that makes daily life tolerable, institutions must constrain people's conduct. They must exert power. Some people make and enforce the traffic rules that drivers follow so that there can be a safe and predictable flow of traffic. Investing institutions with power over our behavior is the price we pay to enjoy the benefits of a social life together, of keeping traffic moving safely and smoothly. Institutions, one might say, are "the ground of both our freedoms and unfreedoms."[6] They make it possible for drivers to get from place to place safely, but only by exerting power, and imposing and enforcing rules on them.

All kinds of institutions impose rules, such as families and schools. Parents tell their children when they should be home, and teachers tell students how they should behave in class. They exert **power**, which is the ability to make people do things that they would not have chosen to do on their own or to prevail in getting what you want in the presence of opposing claims and competing interests.[7] To paraphrase Dr. Martin Luther King, power is the ability to get people to say "Yes" when they really want to say "No."[8] Or as someone once said, power is about who gets it and who gets it put to them.

Power is one of the most contested and elusive terms in political science. After lyrically characterizing power as "the pinch of necessity, the coercion of consent, the extraction of obedience," the historian Daniel Rodgers conceded that it is "easy to feel and hard to describe."[9] Sometimes the exercise of power is overt, such as when force or coercion is used. At other times, power is concealed, such as when people are manipulated without realizing it. Sometimes power is used to make people do something, to elicit change; at other times, it is used to ensure that people do nothing, to preserve the status quo. Power is distinct from authority in which those who comply think it is legitimate or morally appropriate to do so. **Authority** is a form of power that has been accepted as right and proper by those who submit to it.

Power takes three forms: cultural, economic, and political. Cultural power exists when some people can convince others to adopt their values, ideas, and

Power
The ability to influence people's ideas and behavior; to influence others to comply with your wishes.

Authority
When power is exercised in a way that people recognize as legitimate or appropriate. Authority is power that is rightfully employed. People may have power but lack authority, but people cannot have authority without also having power.

premises as their own. People comply with what others want because they think it is the right thing to do. For example, students sit quietly through a painfully boring lecture because they are socialized to think that is the proper way to behave in school. This form of power can be insidious because people may not even be aware they are subject to it. The values and ideas they thought were their own are actually those they have been socialized to adopt and accept. They obey because they have been led to believe the rules to which they submit are fair and legitimate.

The second form of power is material or economic power. People who control critical scarce resources, such as land or capital, obtain compliance from those who need them. For example, to return to our previous example, students may sit quietly through a boring lecture because they don't want to risk offending professors who grade them. Professors dispense rewards that students are willing to feign interest to obtain. Economic power occurs when rewards are offered or denied to obtain compliance.

Finally, there is political power. Political power is grounded in coercion and control over the means of violence. Returning to the classroom example, students sit quietly because professors can tell disruptive students to leave class or have the campus police evict them. Not all forms of political power involve the use of violence, but they do involve the threat of violence; that is, if people do not obey commands, those who wield political power have ways of making them do so.[10]

The power institutions exert is based on control over the content of social beliefs, essential material resources, and the means of violence. Institutions wield cultural, economic, and political power to create rules that channel people's behavior into regular patterns. They create incentives for people to act in certain ways. Rules grounded in power make civilization possible. Of course, the quality of that civilization—whether it resembles the scenes of desolation and war portrayed in the fresco of bad government or the picture of abundance and peace representing good government that are on the walls of the former City Hall in Sienna, Italy—depends on the institutions in place, what the rules are, and how they are enforced.

The State

2.3 Define the state.

Although power may take many forms, political power trumps its cultural and economic acquaintances. Political power is necessary for cultural and economic power to be exercised in an orderly manner. For example, all economic systems presuppose political power to enforce rules of exchange and trade. Political power, thus, takes functional priority over other forms.[11] In addition, political power is necessary to protect cultural and economic power from outside threats.

Political power is paramount because it keeps rivals who are not subject to ideological indoctrination or material incentives in check. Political power not only comes first but is foremost.

The institution that embodies political power is **the state**. The state refers to a set of organizations imbued with sovereignty over a given area through its control of the means of violence. There are four distinct parts to this definition. First is the notion of the state as an organization, a distinct administrative entity. People who are vested with political power are granted it by virtue of their place within this organization. Power belongs to the office, not to the person. This is as true of presidents who are elected as it is of kings who ascend to the throne by accident of birth.

Second is the concept of sovereignty, which refers to absolute power. The state has ultimate power over the population. The only limits to its power are those it creates and accepts itself. It sets the rules by which others must play.

Third is the idea of territoriality. The state's power extends over a specific area with clear boundaries. It exercises sovereign rule over this territory, whose integrity it protects against encroachment.[12] The concept of territoriality is codified in customs officials who check passports and visas, deciding whom to let in and whom to keep out; in fences, walls, and electronic monitoring devices to prevent and detect movement across borders; and in armed checkpoints and guards to dissuade and catch trespassers.

Finally, there is the issue of coercion and violence. The state enjoys a monopoly over the means of violence within its territory. That is, the only legitimate or legal use of violence is by those the state mandates or authorizes to use it. Control over the means of coercion permits the state to make its rules effective against internal challengers and foreign rivals. This does not mean that the state exercises power primarily through coercion and violence, but that these are available as a last resort in enforcing its laws.

These dimensions of the state—an organization that is sovereign within a bounded territory through its control of the means of coercion—are captured in the pithy phrase, "one government, one land, one law, one gun."

The powers of states can be truly awesome. States can dictate what people wear, what language they speak, and what job they do. Consequently, groups struggle for control of the state and its power to make rules that others will follow. Groups that are successful in gaining control of the state are said to form **the government**. The term *government* refers to the group of leaders in charge of directing the state. States and governments are often treated as equivalent expressions, but they need to be distinguished from each other. The state, as we argued, refers to a set of organizations imbued with sovereignty over a given area, whereas the government refers to the people who run those organizations. The state is the car; the government is the driver.

Although states are often powerful, they are not all-powerful. Indeed, some states are not powerful at all. "One law" and "one gun" are aspirations that states often find difficult to achieve. Their rule may be challenged by other institutions

The State

A state has four qualities: (1) It is an organization, that is, it has a specific administrative form; (2) it is sovereign, meaning it has ultimate power over people under its control; (3) it exerts this power through its control over the means of violence; (4) it extends this power over a bounded territory that defines the limits of its rule.

The Government

The *government* refers to those who run, or are in control of, the executive branch of the state. It alludes to those who occupy executive leadership positions within the state.

In-Depth: Somalia—The Weightlessness of Statelessness

If you are a libertarian or an anarchist who believes that states are a threat to freedom, you should consider moving to Somalia, which has had no permanent national government since 1991. The criteria we use to define a state—one government, one land, one law, and one gun—are absent there. Instead of the state enjoying a monopoly of violence, the country is ablaze with competing armies. Instead of the state ruling over a bounded territory, the country's borders are porous, with refugees and foreign troops crossing into its territory. Instead of the state being governed by one set of rules, many laws compete for supremacy. Finally, instead of the state being sovereign, the government's authority does not extend much beyond Mogadishu, the nation's capital. Elsewhere, whoever has the most guns rules. The Somali state has not simply failed; it has disappeared.

Without a state, "Somalia," according to *New York Times* reporter Jeffrey Gettleman, has returned to a Hobbesian "state of nature where life is nasty, brutish, and short."[13] Death comes frequently and randomly. Social conditions are deplorable. Infant mortality rates are among the highest in the world. Economically, the withering away of the state has unleashed entrepreneurial energy among Somalis to provide services, such as telecommunications and transport, in place of government, but the provision of services has been narrow in scope and dependent on remittances from Somalis living abroad because the lack of government discourages foreign investment. Without a state to promote development, the economy of Somalia depends on the charity of Somalis who have left.

For Further Discussion

1. Which is preferable: bad government, or no government?
2. Why hasn't Somalia without a state become the paradise that libertarians anticipate? Why hasn't statelessness enhanced the capabilities of Somalis and increased their life chances?

---

that want to enforce their own rules and have the resources with which to do so. Foreign governments may threaten their territorial rule, and groups inside their borders—clans, tribes, employers, property owners, and religious leaders—may threaten their sovereignty. Under such circumstances, states may find it difficult to govern, assert their authority, and implement their decisions. In general, then, the ability of states to govern—to process demands, develop policies, and implement them—cannot be taken for granted. In some countries, states are strong and effective; in others, they are weak and ineffectual.

The Origins of States

2.4 Evaluate different perspectives that explain the rise of states.

"As recently as 1500," Jared Diamond writes, "less than 20 percent of the world's land area was marked off by boundaries into states run by bureaucrats and governed by laws."[14] States had a hard time subduing their frontiers to which people could flee to escape taxes and obligations that states imposed.[15] "Even as late as the end of the 18th century," James C. Scott writes, "people who did not belong to any state inhabited a greater part of the world's land mass, rugged mountains, isolated steppes, hot deserts, cold polar regions, confusing marshes, and other inaccessible remote places."[16]

However, railroads and roads opened up previously isolated regions to state penetration. In addition, states now had more sophisticated weapons with which to subdue resistance and access to new technologies that could extend their administrative rule to distant outposts. Soon, there were no more zones to which people could flee beyond the reach of states. Just as the English peasant lost access to common lands that the nobility enclosed as their property in the eighteenth century, so did states enclose more territory until there were almost no places to which people could escape to avoid their rule.[17]

Today, virtually the entire world is organized into states. Choose any speck of land on a map, with the exception of Antarctica, and some state claims or exerts control over it. There are different views about why and how states emerged. Modernization theorists argue that states arose because of the increasing division of labor in society. As societies became more complex, they became more functionally specialized, requiring states to oversee the integration of their diverse parts. Modernization theorists see a parallel between the way states develop and how species evolve: As societies become more mature and differentiated, they require states to coordinate their more specialized parts. States emerge to solve coordination problems posed by society's increasing complexity.[18]

Modernization theory is helpful in drawing our attention to the coordination role that states play, but modernization theory perceives states as benign and stabilizing society, knitting its disparate parts together when, in fact, states can be malign and highly destabilizing. States can be corrupt and prey on society, and they can upset social routines instead of harmonizing them. In addition, modernization theory perceives the emergence of states occurring in a peaceful, rational fashion when, in fact, the process of state building has been filled with bloody turmoil. It was a process in which fragmented, local patterns of authority resisted state builders who wanted to centralize authority and promote coordination at local authorities' expense.[19]

Modernization Theory
A theory that held that modernizing traditional countries would follow the same developmental sequence as Western, more developed countries, which included industrialization, urbanization, specialization, and democratization.

Marxists take a different approach. Whereas modernization theorists saw states emerge as part of the requirements of society as a whole, Marxists perceive states emerging because of one of the interests inside them.[20] According to Marxists, the dominant class uses the state and its monopoly over the means of violence to impose its rule over subordinate classes. In *The Communist Manifesto*, Marx and Engels describe the modern state as "the executive committee of the bourgeoisie," by which they meant that the state reflects the general interests of the ruling, capitalist class. The state is not some neutral mechanism coordinating a complex society, as it is for modernization theorists. For Marxists, the state is much darker, representing the repressive apparatus that the dominant class wields against other classes to cement its rule and exploit them.

The Marxist theory of the state has the advantage of drawing us closer to the defining aspect of states based on violence and coercion than modernization theory. But the Marxist theory of the state too narrowly confines state-building to the requirements of class conflict. It ignores other actors with other motives from the story.

Finally, according to realists, "Wars made the state, and the state made war."[21] States defined by violence were forged in violence. According to these theorists, state building proceeded under pressure from external and internal rivals. Externally, states competed with each other to further their interests. No international law or organization regulated their behavior or sanctioned them. Consequently, states posed threats to each other. To protect themselves in such a lawless, threatening environment, states needed to create armies.But provisioning and maintaining an army was expensive, placing a heavy burden of requisitions, taxes, and conscription on the populace. It also required the state to develop new bureaucracies and administrative innovations to perform these tasks. States, in this view, developed in response to the extractive necessities of war, whose possibility is always lurking in an unruly, unstructured international system of competing states. "Without war," the German historian and politician Heinrich von Treitschke wrote in the 1890s, "there would be no state."[22]

This perspective hews closely to the genetic origin of states in coercion and violence. It also includes some elements of both the modernization and Marxian arguments. It incorporates the coordinating role that modernization theorists discuss by alluding to the state's attempt to bring order to society so it can increase the resources it needs to wage war.[23] It also includes the notion of interests that Marxists present but offers a different interpretation of them. According to this perspective, states pursue their own interests in a threatening international environment, as opposed to the interests of the ruling class. While including key elements of alternative explanations, the idea that states developed from the requirements of war has the added advantage of drawing attention to the role that the international system played in state-building. The other explanations perceive states as emerging wholly to solve domestic problems of order or domination. In contrast, this perspective explains the emergence of states by looking at relations between states as well as those within them.

Political Institutions

2.5 Compare the different ways states are organized.

Groups not only struggle for control of the state, but also tussle over what the state should look like. One need only recall the fierce debates in the United States between delegates from small and large states, and from slave and free states at the 1787 Constitutional Convention, as they debated how to construct the new American state. Small states, such as Delaware and Rhode Island, demanded the creation of a Senate in which each state would receive two votes as protection against the power that large states, such as New York and Massachusetts, wielded in the House of Representatives by virtue of their larger populations.

The distribution of power among the different levels and branches of the state is contested because groups have a stake in the outcome. A group may win or lose depending on which part of the state is making the decision. Whether policy is made by the executive, legislative, or judicial branch, or at the national or local level, influences the result. For example, Antonia Maioni attributes the failure of doctors to prevent the passage of national health insurance in Canada and their success in blocking similar legislation in the United States to different policy-making processes in the two countries. American doctors could exert influence on an independent and powerful Congress to block national health insurance in the United States, whereas the subordination of the legislature to the executive in Canada precluded doctors in that country from following that strategy.[24]

Groups with interests at stake seek to empower those parts of the state in which they have the most advantage. Levels and branches of the state rise and fall in power along with the groups whose interests they represent. In the United States, for example, the increasing power of the presidency in relation to Congress is often attributed to the rise of large corporations that shared the same national and international perspective of the president, whereas the influence of small business that shared Congress's more local and parochial perspective declined. The fact that different group interests are tied to different parts of the state accounts for conflict between them. Groups take an active interest in turf wars or jurisdictional conflicts within the state when it positions them better to advance their interests.

The way in which power is distributed within a state is presented in its constitution. **Constitutions** are blueprints that display the state's architecture. They are power maps that describe the internal distribution of power within the state and between the state and its citizens. First, constitutions depict how power is dispersed within the state; that is, they define the distribution of power within it. Second, they describe the rights of citizens or the limits of government. Some express this by describing rights that the government cannot infringe on, such as free speech, or by delineating rights the government must provide to its citizens, such as health and education. Finally, constitutions define the state and its goals. Some constitutions are brief, containing only 500 words; others are drawn out, extending to over 150,000 words.[25] The actual distribution of power often diverges from what is given in the constitution. Power depends on political factors as well as legal, formal, constitutional arrangements. For example, presidents elected by a landslide or with a legislative majority from their party will find it easier to govern than presidents who were narrowly elected or who must contend with an opposing majority in the legislature. In France, for example, the power of presidents has depended far more on whether the prime minister is also from their party than on what is legally stipulated regarding presidential

Constitutions
A constitution describes the powers and functions of the different parts of the state. It lays out how power is distributed within the state and between the state and its citizens.

powers in the constitution. Power is fluid and depends on circumstances; it is not static, as constitutions make it appear.

The constitutional distribution of power only maps what is included within the formal state. It does not include organizations outside the state that also influence officials, such as political parties, the media, and interest groups. We review below the different parts or components of the state that are featured in many constitutional maps. These include its legislative, executive, and judicial branches, subnational levels, and the state's bureaucratic and military arms.

Federal and Unitary Systems

Constitutions may divide power vertically between national and local levels and horizontally between the legislative, executive, and judicial branches. For example, some constitutions create **unitary systems** in which power is concentrated at the national level. Local levels of the state have little autonomous power to raise revenue, spend money, or make their own policies. They operate more as administrative arms of the central government than as independent authorities. In unitary systems, all sovereignty resides at the top, in the national government. Subnational units are created at the discretion of national governments and can be reorganized or abolished by them because they lack constitutional protection. China, France, and Japan are often cited as examples of unitary systems where regional and local governments lack significant policy-making powers and act largely as agents of the national government.

In **federal systems**, on the other hand, constitutions divide sovereignty between national and subnational levels of the state. "The essence of federalism," Brian Galligan writes, "is two spheres of government neither of which is sovereign but each of which has defined and limited powers."[26] Federal systems have a long tradition among developed countries, such as the United States and Switzerland, and are evident in developing countries, such as India and Brazil, as well. Authority in these countries is not concentrated at the national level but divided between national and lower, more local units of the state, with each level sometimes responsible for policy in a certain domain. For example, state governments in the United States play a leading role in education policy, the *Länder* in Germany play a prominent role in education and cultural policy, and the provinces in Canada have jurisdiction over the management and sale of public lands. In some countries, the specific tasks that the national and subnational levels of the state perform are neatly separated from each other as in a layer cake. In others, it more resembles a marble cake in which functions are interwoven and shared among the different levels.[27] Lower levels of the state in federal systems also have more fiscal independence than their counterparts in unitary systems. Local and regional governments can raise their own revenue, giving them resources with which to strike out on their own, independent of the central government. Finally, in federal systems, subnational political units also enjoy control over their own administrative agencies. A separate administrative apparatus controlled by local and regional governments exists to implement their policies.

Unitary Systems
Political systems where power is centralized at the national level in the federal government. Administrative units below the national level act as arms of the central government.

Federal Systems
Political systems where power is shared between national and regional governments that have their own independent authority to tax and make policy.

Unitary state forms are more common than federal systems. In most countries, the national government does not share power with other levels. Where federal systems do exist, they are often found among large countries, such as the United States and India, where the central government is challenged to extend its power over a large population spread across a large land mass.[28] They may also be found in smaller states with intense ethnic, religious, and linguistic cleavages that are territorially based. Federal systems offer such groups a stake in the larger, national government by giving them influence in a smaller, regional government, incorporating them into the wider polity by giving them a political space they can call their own. This, for example, is the case in Switzerland, where powerful regional governments called *cantons* reflect divisions among French, German, and Italian speakers as well as between Protestants and Catholics. It has also been the case in Canada, where powers guaranteed to the provinces have mollified to some extent the worries of French speakers in Quebec, who are concerned about losing their cultural identity in a predominantly English-speaking country.

Federalism is not only "designed to reconcile diversity wherever possible with union wherever necessary," but it also has economic consequences, affecting the distribution of resources.[29] Federal systems tend to be less redistributive, spending less on social programs than unitary political systems. Federalism leads competing local units to bid against each other, to reduce taxes on the rich and spending on the poor to attract business investment. Federalism also contributes to inequality by increasing the number of points in the legislative process at which bills can be blocked. When regions are empowered, it is harder to pass redistributive legislation a national majority supports.[30]

The Legislature

Political power is distributed not only vertically between national and subnational levels but also horizontally among the different branches of the state: the legislature, executive, and judiciary. **Legislatures** appear under different names in different countries. In the United States, the legislature is referred to

Legislature
An assembly that is a law-making body.

In Brief: Federal and Unitary Systems

In federal political systems:
- The central state shares sovereignty with lower political units.
- Regional governments can raise their own revenue and make their own policy.
- Lower state units have their own officials, agencies, and administrative integrity.

In unitary political systems:
- Political power is concentrated at the national level.
- Subnational levels of the state are primarily administrative arms of the central government.
- Lower levels of the state do not have the power to levy taxes or make policy.

as Congress, in Britain as Parliament, and in France as the National Assembly. Regardless of their different titles, they all do the same thing: They are assemblies that approve of policies on behalf of a larger political community that they represent.[31] This holds true in authoritarian states as well as in democratic polities. In authoritarian political systems, legislatures are tolerated because they provide the government with the fig leaf of public consent. They infrequently and only marginally influence policy. Their main function is simply to transmit local concerns to those actually in charge. For example, in China, the National People's Congress only passes those bills proposed by the government and not a single bill from an individual deputy has ever been enacted. Delegates to the National People's Congress lack the time and staff to evaluate bills and are under pressure to conform rather than challenge the ruling Communist Party.

In contrast to authoritarian political systems, legislatures in democracies are more than rubber stamps. They actually influence policy either by amending or rejecting executive proposals or by substituting their own measures for them. In addition, legislatures in democracies play an important role in overseeing the executive branch. They scrutinize the activities of the executive to make sure that laws are implemented effectively and appropriately.

Unicameral
A legislature that is composed of one chamber that debates and votes on bills.

Bicameral
A legislature that is composed of two chambers, consisting of an upper and lower house. These separate chambers often differ in terms of their powers and the types of constituencies they represent.

Most legislatures are **unicameral**, meaning that they have only one chamber. The **bicameral** structure of the United States Congress, with a House of Representatives and a Senate, is atypical. Where bicameralism occurs, each chamber is based on a different principle of representation. For example, the United States House of Representatives is based on population, whereas the Senate represents states. Larger countries tend toward bicameralism because the different principles of representation in each chamber can reflect the diversity of interests within them better. Bicameralism is also more common in countries with federal systems, where lower, regional political structures are represented by one of the chambers. This is true not only in the United States and Australia, where states are represented in the Senate, but also in Germany, where the *Länder* are represented in the upper house, or *Bundesrat*. This gives territorially based interests confidence that their interests will be reflected within the national government. The advantage of a unicameral legislature is that it is more efficient. There is no second chamber to delay, veto, or amend bills that the first chamber has already passed. The advantage of bicameralism is that it can offer a broader basis of representation than one chamber. This is especially valuable in large, diverse, and regionally divided countries.

Another comparative dimension to legislatures concerns their internal organization, especially their committee system. Even more than size—legislatures with fewer members tend to be more powerful than larger assemblies—a strong committee system is a good indicator of a legislature's ability to influence policy, demonstrating it is a work horse not a show horse. Legislative committees armed with clear jurisdictions and adequate resources permit their members to specialize. Legislators can develop expertise on narrow issues, which permits them to negotiate with the executive on an equal basis and knowledgably oversee its actions. Again, the United States Congress is unusual in this regard because its committee system is exceptionally strong. Compared with other legislatures, congressional committees have ample staff and budgets to collect information and draft legislation on their own. The strength of its committee system is a tip-off that the United States Congress is one of the most powerful legislatures in the world.

In practice, most legislatures today, at least in democracies, are reactive, not proactive; they reject and modify bills but do not often propose their own. They respond to the agenda—budgets and bills—proposed by the chief executive. Whereas previously members of the prime minister's Cabinet were recruited from the legislature, just a little more than half of all European ministers have any parliamentary background today. The legislature's subordination to the executive branch is attributed to the increasing significance of foreign policy, growth in the scope of government activity and the size of the bureaucracy to carry it out, the rising power of the media to portray politics in terms of personality, and the emergence of organized political parties that can deliver disciplined majorities for the government. However, it would be facile to regard legislatures as mere window dressing in democracies, despite their loss of power to the executive branch. At a minimum, legislatures in democracies retain "the capacity to influence, as opposed to determine; the ability to advise, rather than command; the facility to criticize but not to obstruct; [and] the competence to scrutinize rather than initiate."[32] At a maximum, they have the power to veto legislation, develop their own agenda and make policy, and even bring down the government itself.

Although legislatures have lost ground overall, they tend to be more powerful when they have a strong committee system, permitting legislators to build up expertise, and when parties are weak, depriving governments of disciplined legislative majorities to vote for their proposals. According to Kaare Strom and Torbjorn Bergman, legislatures tend to play larger roles in "parliamentary systems than in presidential systems, larger in unitary systems than in federal systems, larger in systems with relatively few veto gates than in those with many, and larger in states with a permissive constitution and weak judicial review than in systems with a restrictive constitution and strong institutions of judicial review."[33]

Finally, legislatures display more influence in some issue areas than in others. They generally exert little influence over foreign affairs or economic policy. These arenas tend to be dominated by the executive branch, whose perspective tends to be more national than the parochial view legislators take, reflecting the local constituencies from which they come. Although seemingly content to play background vocals on foreign and economic policy, legislatures are more apt to project their voice when it comes to social welfare policy, such as housing, health care, education, and pensions, which directly touch their constituents.[34]

The Executive

The **executive branch** is supposed to elaborate, coordinate, and implement the legislature's decisions. In fact, it does much more. The executive branch is often the energy center of the government, providing it with leadership. It sets the agenda of government, creating priorities and proposing bills. In most democracies, not only do a greater proportion of all bills that legislatures consider come from the executive, but those that originate there have a better chance of being approved.[35] We discuss three distinct parts of the executive branch: (1) the **core executive**, which includes the ruling government; (2) the bureaucracy, which is directly below the core executive and includes the different departments and agencies of the executive branch; and (3) the military, which includes the armed forces.

At the center of the executive branch is the core executive. The core executive includes all the significant policy-making and coordinating actors in the executive branch, such as the president or prime minister, members of their Cabinet, their personal advisors, and senior civil servants. The core executive pulls together and coordinates the diverse political and bureaucratic interests in a sprawling executive branch into a coherent and coordinated program to present to the legislature and the public. The core executive is at the apex of the executive branch, resolving disputes within it and setting priorities for it.

At the top of the core executive are its political leaders, the **head of state** and the **head of the government**. The former represents the country; the latter directs the executive branch. Sometimes these two positions are unified in the same office and person, as they are in the United States, where the president is both the head of state—the leader of the nation—and the head of the government—in charge of the federal bureaucracy. In many other countries, such as Great Britain, the two positions are separated. In Britain, the reigning monarch is the head of state, and the ruling prime minister is the head of the government. In such countries, the head of state usually plays only a ceremonial role, as the monarchy does in Britain, but there are countries, such as France, where power is shared between the head of state (the president) and the head of the government (the prime minister), and some rare cases, such as Jordan, where power resides in the head of state, who is the king, and not the head of the government, who is the prime minister.

As the executive branch has grown in size to keep pace with increasing state responsibilities, the central coordinating role that political leaders play has become more significant. Among developed countries, according to one study, "There is general agreement that over the last thirty to forty years there has been a steady movement toward the reinforcement of the political core executive . . . and, that within the core executive, there has been an increasing centralization of power around the person of the chief executive—President, Prime Minister, or both."[36] Their position at the top of government gives presidents and prime ministers a commanding view of the entire ground that other political actors

Executive Branch
That part of the government charged with executing the laws passed by the legislature. It is charged with implementing or carrying out policy.

Core Executive
Consists of the head of the government, often the president or prime minister, his or her closest advisors, and members of the Cabinet. The core executive is where power is concentrated within the executive branch.

Head of State
The official who represents the country and is considered its formal, symbolic leader.

Head of Government
The leader of the executive branch, often either the president or prime minister.

lack. In addition, political leaders can shape and manipulate public opinion through the media attention they attract. Presidents and prime ministers also now have more staff at their disposal to coordinate policy, provide expertise, manage their image, and help them develop political strategy. When Herbert Hoover was president of the United States (1928–1932), he was assisted by three confidential secretaries, a stenographer, and some clerks. Today, the Executive Office of the President—which didn't even exist as a formal office in Hoover's time—includes over 3,000 people who serve the president in all sorts of capacities. Finally, political leaders embody the national interest, which permits them to take charge of foreign policy. This policy domain is now more prominent because globalization has tied the fate of countries more closely together. As the world gets smaller, presidents and prime ministers get bigger. The result of these changes has been to personalize power and raise the profile of political leaders in relation to other political actors inside and outside the core executive.

The core executive includes not only political leaders such as the head of state and the head of the government but also those ministers who serve under them. These ministers direct state ministries or departments and are often members of the president's or prime minister's **Cabinet**. Jean Blondel estimated there are about 3,000 ministers throughout the world, with an average of twenty in each country.[37] In some countries, ministers serve on average for as long as five years, whereas in others there is quick turnover, and a minister's average tenure is as short as a year. Some are specialists who are familiar with the problems and issues of the department they lead, but others are amateurs who come to office with little specialized knowledge of the issues for which their department is responsible. Finally, some ministers may rotate among different posts within the government, whereas others fill only one post in the course of their ministerial career.

Cabinet
A group of officials in the executive branch that advise the head of the government and are in charge of various ministries within it.

Presidents and prime ministers are not simply first among equals in relation to their Cabinet; they are first without equal. That is, presidents and prime ministers set the direction of the government; the collective Cabinet does not. The Cabinet is more a collection of isolated ministers concerned with their particular departments than a cohesive group of political executives concerned with strategic planning for the government as a whole.[38] Although ministers might not enjoy much standing through their participation in the Cabinet, they often do so through the substantial discretion they have when it comes to managing their own departments. Ministers often manage their departments without much direction by presidents and prime ministers. Presidents and prime ministers cannot look everywhere at once and must practice "management by exception," given the pressures on their time and attention.

The Bureaucracy

The core executive directs the **bureaucracy**, or the different agencies and bureaus within the executive branch. The bureaucracy is supposed to be an extension of the government in power and its political leadership. The core executive makes

Bureaucracy
Part of the executive branch and supposed to administer policy in a neutral and professional way for whoever leads the government.

policy, and the bureaucrats or career civil servants below are supposed to execute it in an impartial and professional way. However, in fact, core executives often have a hard time imposing their will on bureaucrats. Political control of the bureaucracy is an aspiration, not a guarantee. Core executives have no choice but to delegate power to those below them to carry out policies, but doing so permits bureaucrats to shape policy in how it is administered. Policies can be altered subtly, as if in a game of telephone with multiple players, as it is passed down the chain of command.[39] President Harry Truman remarked ruefully as he was about to be replaced in office by former General Dwight D. Eisenhower, "He'll sit here and he'll say, 'Do this! Do that! *And nothing will happen.* Poor Ike—it won't be a bit like the Army. He'll find it very frustrating."[40] Policies can be thwarted by bureaucrats who have their own interests, separate from political executives, and their own sources of power with which to pursue them.[41] For example, bureaucrats can share their experience and knowledge with political executives to promote policies they like or withhold their cooperation in order to frustrate policies they oppose. Bureaucrats can also leak information that threatens their interests to the government's opponents. A notorious example of this occurred when FBI Assistant Director Mark Felt, known for decades only as Deep Throat, leaked information about White House efforts to cover up the Watergate break-in in 1972 because he believed President Nixon was trying to besmirch the reputation of his agency. Moreover, although bureaucrats are supposed to be neutral and impartial, they want to protect their own interests. They want to maximize their agency's budget and jurisdiction, which means higher pay and more career opportunities for them, and defend their professionalism from policies that threaten it.

Political leaders try to counter the bureaucracy's influence by strengthening their own personal staffs. Consequently, as we saw when we discussed the core executive, the number of people who work in the president's or prime minister's office has grown. They also try to increase the number of political appointees who work within the bureaucracy. The greater the number of political appointees, the more responsive the bureaucracy is to the administration in power. At one extreme are many African states where the bureaucracy is bloated with political appointees. Instead of being staffed by a permanent civil service selected on merit, rulers give state jobs to loyalists who then use their official

In Brief: Bureaucracy

According to Max Weber, an eminent German sociologist, the essential features of bureaucracies include:
- a division of labor in which people are given specific tasks to perform.
- a hierarchy in which there is a clear chain of command.
- a set of rules and regulations that govern the conduct of people in positions and limit their discretion.

posts to extract bribes and exploit the public they are supposed to serve. At the other end of the continuum are countries such as Great Britain. Its bureaucracy is staffed by a highly professional civil service that reaches up to the highest levels. A change in administration does not create turnover in a department's staff except at the very top for the ministers who run them and their assistants.

The Military

Seven Days in May, published in 1962, describes a military plot to take over the United States government. In the book, the Joint Chiefs of Staff are thwarted in their conspiracy to remove the president of the United States. *Seven Days in May* is fiction, a novel that became a Hollywood motion picture. It is a gripping political thriller because its plot is so plausible, but it is also far-fetched because civilian control of the military is such an intrinsic part of the American political tradition. It requires a novelist's imagination to conceive of a military coup occurring in the United States. Nevertheless, what novelists must invent regarding the United States is all too real elsewhere. Military takeovers are common in other countries. They are fact, not fiction.

The military is just one specialized department within the bureaucracy. We devote special attention to it because the military embodies the essence of the state. It is organizationally coherent, enjoying a centralized command structure; it has a corporate sense of purpose that binds it together; and it controls the armed forces, monopolizing the means of coercion. Consequently, the military needs to be treated differently than other parts of the state. The unique dilemma the military poses is who will guard the guardians? How can the state empower the military to protect and extend its influence and at the same time guard against the military turning its power against the state itself?

The relationship between the government and the military takes many forms. At one end of the spectrum is civilian control of the military's budget, command structure, and the promotion and assignment of its commanders. Civilian control also implies that the military does not intervene in political affairs. Politics is for civilians, not for military officers who take orders from democratically elected elites. Democracy is impossible without civilian control of the military. Barany writes, "Building democratic civic–military relations may be the most fundamental prerequisite of the transition to and consolidation of democracy."[42]

Nevertheless, civilian control of the military has its limits and is not absolute. In return for the military respecting the authority of the government, the government respects the autonomy and professionalism of the military. Of course, the boundary separating political from military issues is unclear, and civilians and the military often trespass on each other's domain. The military often injects itself into policy debates about national security and budget appropriations, and civilians often project their values on to the military and seek to use it for political advantage. Thus, even in countries where civilian control of the military is the norm, it still has to be negotiated.[43] Elected governments are careful to respect the professional norms of the military in order to receive respect from it in return.

Civilian control of the military is more likely to exist in those countries where both state and military institutions are strong. That is, the state has legitimacy and is capable of governing society, and the military has a strong ethos of professionalism and autonomy.[44] This is the case in much of the developed world. But in many developing countries, states are weak and unable to maintain order. Nor is the military highly professionalized. The army abuses its power to extort money from businesses and civilians, and officers give loyalty to their own ethnic group instead of to their commanders. When professionalism is low, military intervention in politics is more common.[45]

The military is also more apt to intervene to promote economic growth that could provide the wealth and technology that the army needs to improve its fighting capacity. The military believes that it must remove civilian governments that are too inept, corrupt, or unwilling to achieve these goals. Authoritarian rule quickly ensues in which political parties are banned, the news is censored, and protests are outlawed. The military tries to create the same sense of discipline in society that exists in the army as it pursues its program of economic modernization.

The Judiciary

Judiciary
A system of courts that interpret and apply the law.

The third branch of the state is the **judiciary**. It is a political institution that is, theoretically, above politics and outside of the policy-making process. The courts are supposed to be neutral and impartial, above the tug of sordid interests that sully legislators and executives. Their role is to interpret the laws, not make them. However, interpreting the law—settling disputes about its meaning and how it should be applied—requires courts to exercise power, to issue decisions that produce winners and losers. Consequently, courts are the object of intense conflict. Court jurisdictions, the manner in which judges are selected, and the content of judicial decisions are all political questions of the first order.

In authoritarian political systems, the powers of the judiciary are quite limited. Although laws and constitutions may exist, the judiciary is often too weak to uphold them. Dictators and tyrants do not want to be constrained by tedious and bothersome laws. The rule of law in authoritarian states is compromised because the judiciary lacks independence and is subordinate to the executive. Judges often owe their jobs to the ruler and can be removed easily if they decide a case "incorrectly." Although the rule of law may be weak under authoritarian regimes, they still subscribe to rule *by* the law. That is, authoritarian governments find it convenient to rule through the law. Consequently, they make great efforts to stage show trials of dissidents, ground their authority in emergency decrees that suspend the law temporarily, or use alternative forums outside the regular court system, such as military tribunals, to try cases and issue decisions.

Authoritarian regimes are not lawless. They have court systems and judges, but the courts are distinguished by their lack of independence in such countries.

By contrast, the judiciary enjoys more autonomy and political power in democracies. In some cases, the courts may even exercise the power of **judicial review**, which empowers courts to nullify and invalidate laws that they believe violate the constitution. Judicial review can be conducted through special constitutional courts set up for that purpose, as in France and Germany, or within the regular court system, as in Ireland and the United States. Regardless of where judicial review takes place, its practice is controversial. It has the same impact on policy as an executive veto and belies the claim that courts do not influence policy. For example, the U.S. Supreme Court in the 1954 case, *Brown v. Topeka Board of Education*, famously ruled that state laws requiring segregated schools were invalid because they violated the Fourteenth Amendment's equal protection clause of the Constitution.

Critics of judicial review believe that it is undemocratic for unelected judges to overturn laws passed by elected governments and thereby subvert the will of the people. Defenders respond that judicial review is necessary to prevent the majority from using the state to trample on the rights of the minority. They insist that constitutional limits need to be placed on what the majority may do.

Judicial review permits judges to influence policy by nullifying laws, but judges typically will not exercise this power unless their positions are secure. The independence of the judiciary depends on how its members are selected, how long they have tenure, and how difficult it is to remove them once they are on the bench. The United States, for example, safeguards the independence of federal judges by awarding them lifetime tenure. With their jobs secure, federal judges do not have to worry about shaping their decisions to suit either the president who nominated them or subsequent office holders. Moreover, once seated, they can only be removed from office by being impeached by Congress, which rarely occurs. Other countries seek to insulate the judiciary from political influences at the appointment stage. In Italy and Portugal, for example, the appointment and promotion of judges is taken out of the hands of voters, legislatures, and chief executives and given predominantly to judges themselves. Judges are insulated from political pressure by having control over their own career paths. An alternative strategy for ensuring the judiciary's independence is to appoint judges to nonrenewable terms, as is the practice in France. In still other countries, such as Canada and South Africa, appointments follow recommendations by special judicial selection commissions.

Political scientists have noticed a trend toward the **judicialization of politics**, in which political disputes are settled in courtrooms rather than legislatures. According to John Ferejohn, "Since World War II, there has been a profound shift in power away from legislatures and toward courts and other legal institutions."[46] Citizens are making increasing use of courts to "contest government decisions or to assert and defend their rights."[47] Alexis de Tocqueville's complaint that Americans frequently turn political issues into legal contests is becoming a common practice throughout the world.

Judicial Review
When courts have the power to overturn or invalidate laws that violate a country's constitution or basic law.

Judicialization of Politics
The increasing use of courts to raise and settle policy issues.

The judicialization of politics is also evident in the eagerness with which courts intervene in political thickets they previously avoided, such as struggles for power. In the 1990s, Italian judges brought down the Christian Democratic Party, which had been in the government from 1947 to 1994, on charges of corruption, and the United States Supreme Court issued rulings that decided the

Comparative Political Analysis: Does the Design of Political Institutions Make a Difference in People's Lives?

Problem: Do people live better under one set of political institutions than another? According to the political scientist Arend Lijphart, political institutions in democracies go together in consistent patterns that conform to either majoritarian or consensus principles. Majoritarian democracies have unitary systems, unicameral legislatures, weak courts, and strong core executives. Consensus democracies, on the other hand, operate on the principle that policies should be supported by broader agreement than a majority, which often involves sharing, dispersing, and limiting power in a variety of ways. Political institutions commonly found together in consensus democracies include federal systems, bicameral legislatures, courts with the power of judicial review, and weak core executives. Having distinguished between majoritarian and consensus democracies, Lijphart then asks the "so what" question: Do people live better under democracies with majoritarian institutions than they do in democracies with institutions that follow the principle of consensus?

Methods and Hypothesis: Lijphart ranked selected democracies according to the degree that their political institutions conformed to his models of majoritarian and consensus democracies and then statistically compared their economic, political, and social performance. He hypothesized that consensus democracies would produce better results because their policies have a broader base of support and are not as prone to abrupt policy shifts as typically occur in majoritarian democracies.

Operationalizing Concepts: To test his hypothesis, Lijphart measured the relative economic performance of majoritarian and consensus democracies, for example, by examining their average annual growth in GDPs. One of his measures of political performance was turnout rates in elections, and one of his indicators of social performance was welfare state expenditures.

Results: Lijphart found that consensus democracies performed better socially, devoting more money to the welfare state, and they performed better politically, with more citizens participating in elections. However, the form of democracy had little apparent impact on economic performance. Consensus democracies did not have more economic growth than majoritarian democracies.

For Further Discussion

1. Do you think Lijphart's indicators of economic, political, and social performance were appropriate?
2. Why did consensus democracies perform better than their majoritarian counterparts on political and social indicators but not on economic ones?

Source: Arend Lijphart, *Patterns of Democracy: Government Forms and Performance in Thirty-Six Countries*, 2nd edition (New Haven: Yale University Press, 2012).

outcome of the 2000 presidential election. However, the most stunning example of all might have been the role the judiciary played in the 2004 presidential election in the Ukraine. The Ukrainian Supreme Court nullified the results of that election and mandated new elections that produced a different winner. Remarkably, despite having so much at stake, Ukrainian politicians respected the power of the court to rule that electoral laws had been violated in a country not otherwise known to be so law abiding. The Ukrainian example shows how powerful courts have become, even in countries where one would least expect it.

Finally, judges are not only intervening more frequently in struggles for political power, but they are more aggressively using the power of judicial review to look over the shoulders of politicians and evaluate their decisions. The prospect that the courts might intervene forces public officials to anticipate the court's possible objections when they make laws and decisions. Policy makers increasingly legislate in the shadow of the courts.[48]

Weak States, Strong States, and the Good Society

2.6 Evaluate the performance of strong and weak states according to the standards of the good society.

States differ in how power is distributed within them. They also differ in their effectiveness. Some states are weak. They lack both autonomy and capacity. They are captured by narrow interests and lack the capacity to govern. They are corrupt and cannot translate their power into policy. This incapacity is not a small, innocent matter of inefficiency, such as when the postal service loses a package or pension checks are late but can have lethal results. Drinking water that is supposed to be clean carries dysentery, garbage that is supposed to be collected breeds deadly diseases. Millions of people in Africa die from AIDS not simply because antiretroviral drugs are expensive but because governments lack a public health infrastructure that could administer the complex protocols of AIDS prevention effectively.[49] The regulatory system is so poor in China that babies have died when their parents gave them infant formula they thought was safe but instead was filled with toxic poisons. The Chinese state is so weak and viewed with such distrust that parents now go abroad to buy baby formula to ensure its safety.

Strong states, on the other hand, display both autonomy and capacity. Strong states are not captured by social interests. Policy makers are insulated from social groups, which permit them to act independently. They also exhibit capacity, the ability to implement demands throughout their territory. They can defend their borders, maintain order within them, collect taxes, and execute policies with a minimum of slippage.

Strong states that exhibit both capacity and autonomy are not necessarily authoritarian states. In fact, many strong states are democracies, such as Sweden and Germany, whereas many authoritarian states, such as Pakistan and China, are weak. The governments in these countries have a difficult time insulating themselves from powerful social groups and implementing their policies.

Are stronger states better, in the sense of promoting people's capabilities, or does the quality of life for citizens improve when states are weak? To distinguish strong from weak states, we turn to the Failed States Index, developed by The Fund for Peace in conjunction with the journal, *Foreign Policy*. The Failed States Index that appears as Table 2.1 in the appendix used twelve indicators, including social factors such as demographic pressures; economic parameters such as poverty rates; and political indicators, such as the quality of public services, to assess state strength and weakness. States that performed the best on these indicators—what we would call the strongest—received the lowest scores on the Index; those that performed the worst, the weakest states, received the highest values. The Fund for Peace Failed States Index separated countries into four categories. Those countries that performed the best, such as Finland, which received the lowest score out of 177 countries, were labeled "sustainable." Only thirteen countries met these demanding conditions.

The index then proceeded to the next group, which included much of Western Europe and the United States. This was still a pretty select group that included only 48 states, which were labeled "stable." Not one African country, with the exception of the island nation of Mauritius, (profiled in Chapter 7) off the African coast in the Indian Ocean, qualified to join the elite group of strong states in the "sustainable" and "stable" categories.

The third group of states, which includes China and India, earned a "warning" because there was cause for concern about the quality of these states. This was the largest group of states, stretching from the worst performer, which was Guinea Bissau in Africa coming in at 15, all the way up to Bahrain in the Middle East that was rated 125. Finally, the Index issued an "alert" to the last and worst-performing group of states because it doubted their continuing viability or because these states had collapsed entirely. Somalia had the dubious distinction of being number 1, at the top of this list of 15 failed states.

In the following tables, we sorted states into five, not four groups as the Failed States Index did. We did so because it is not particularly useful to compare groups of such dissimilar sizes, with only 13 and 14 countries in our best and worst performing categories, respectively, and over 100 countries in the group labeled "warning." Consequently, we separated states that earned a "warning" in the Failed States Index—which included more than half the countries in the entire sample—into two similarly sized groups. We labeled roughly the top half of countries that the Failed States Index classified in the "warning" group as "moderate." They run from Bahrain at 125, the best performer from the warning category, down to Azerbaijan, which ranked 68. We then classified as "ominous" the remaining countries in the lower half of the Failed States Index warning category. This group included Ecuador in South America at 67 on the Failed States Index through Guinea Bissau, which ranked 15.

Physical Well-being

A good society, we argued, is one that meets the physical needs of its citizens. People should be fed, sheltered, and healthy, and the best way to measure this, we suggested, was to look at infant mortality rates. It is apparent from Figure 2.1 that infant mortality rates are highly correlated with state quality.[50] As we move along the horizontal *x* axis of Figure 2.1, from the weakest to the strongest states, the average infant mortality rate improves. The average infant mortality rate for states "on alert"—a group of failed or failing states—was 74 for every 1,000 babies that were born. The next worst performing group of states, those we classified as "ominous," did a bit better: Infant mortality rates dropped by about a third to an average of 46 babies out of 1,000 that died before their first birthday. Average infant mortality rates then drop precipitously—by more than 80 percent—as we move from states classified as "ominous" to those labeled "moderate," where the average infant mortality rate was only 8.3. They then decline by half again to an average of 3.5 babies in states categorized as sustainable, and then a bit lower to an average of 3.2 in the best-performing states, those that were deemed stable.

The quality of the state appears to matter when it comes to meeting people's physical needs. Strong states, which have the capacity to translate demands into effective policies and are not captured by social interests but enjoy some autonomy from them, are better able to meet the needs of their citizens than weak states.

Informed Decision Making

Good societies also equip their citizens with skills to make informed decisions regarding their lives. Citizens can read and write. When we look at literacy rates

---

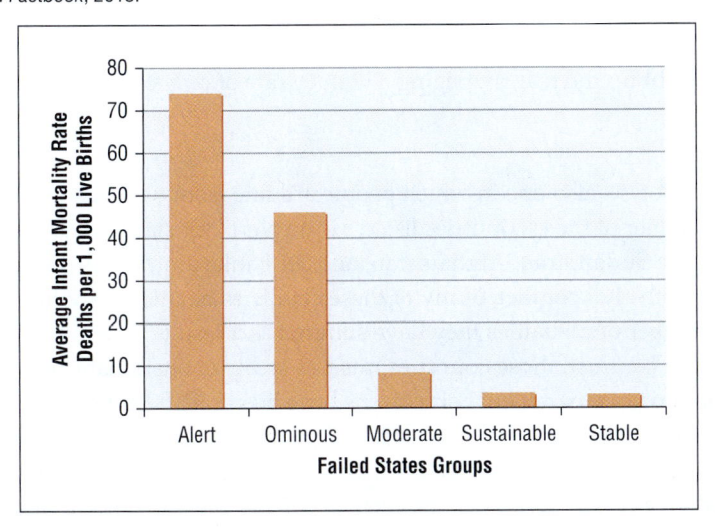

Figure 2.1 State Quality and Infant Mortality Rates

SOURCE: Failed States Index, 2013 and Country Comparison: Infant mortality rate data from the *CIA World Factbook*, 2013.

Figure 2.2 State Quality and Literacy Rates

SOURCE: Failed States Index, 2013. Adult literacy rates from the *Human Development Report*, 2011.

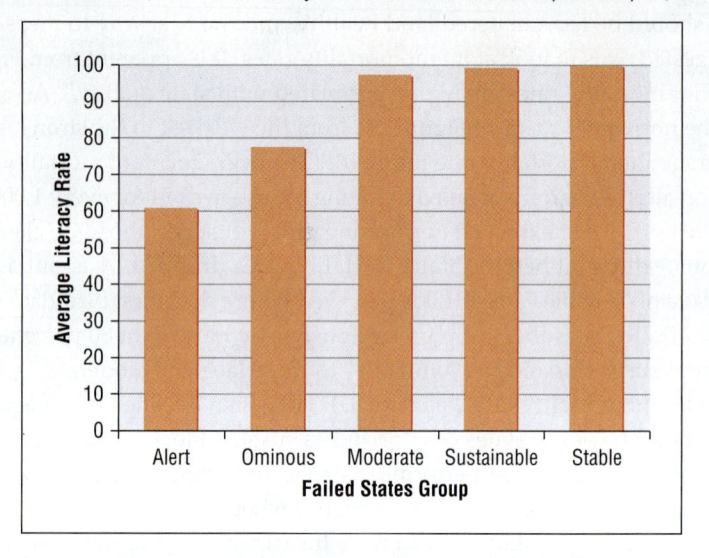

in Figure 2.2, we find again that the quality of the state matters. Most countries that scored well on the Failed States Index had high literacy rates, whereas those countries that were in danger of failing had lower ones. Every state in the stable category had a perfect, 100 percent, literacy rate. The average literacy rate for states regarded as sustainable was 99.1 percent; all but two countries among this group (Portugal and Singapore) recorded 100 percent literacy rates. States in the moderate group performed nearly as well, with an average literacy rate of 97.2 percent. However, as the quality of the state declines below those rated as moderate, literacy rates drop precipitously. Average literacy rates for those countries classified as ominous were 30 percent lower, only 77.4 percent, than those countries labeled as moderate. Then they decline by another 20 percent as we move to the next and lowest quality states, those in the "on alert" category. They brought up the rear, averaging a literacy rate of only 60.6 percent.

Safety

A good society is also one in which people are safe from violence. A disproportionate number of those countries listed as "on alert" for state weakness, such as Somalia, the Sudan, Iraq, Afghanistan, and Sri Lanka among others, have been wracked with civil conflict. Many of these countries have been in the headlines for the number of casualties they have suffered as a result of the wars they have endured. In contrast, those countries rated as stable or sustainable have experienced nothing comparable. Their citizens have been safe from political violence.

Homicide rates tell a similar story: Figure 2.3 shows that stronger, more efficient states perform much better than weaker, failing ones. Stable countries recorded an average of only 1.2 homicides per 100,000 citizens. Homicide rates

Figure 2.3 State Quality and Homicide Rates

SOURCE: Failed States Index, 2013.

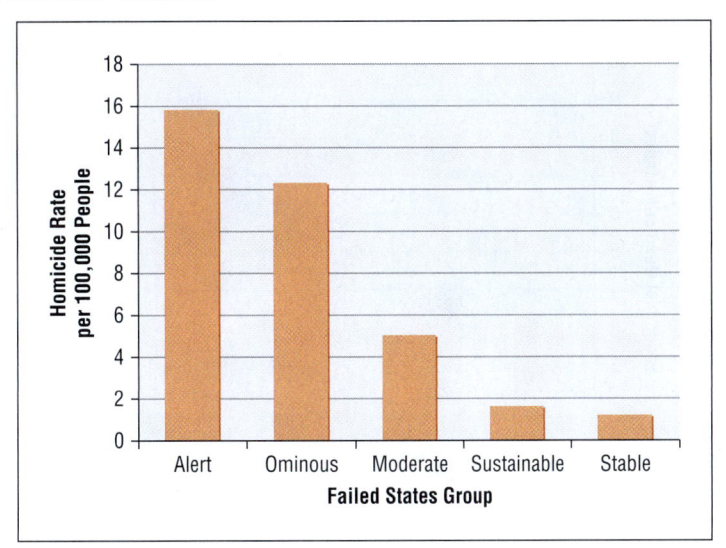

in countries classified as sustainable were about 25 percent higher, recording 1.6 homicides per 100,000 citizens, although the result for this group needs to be viewed suspiciously because an outlier drove up the average. The United States has a homicide rate of 5.0 per 100,000, which was almost twice the rate for the next-highest member of the group, South Korea. The median homicide rate for this group was only 1.2, meaning that half the countries in this group had homicide rates below that figure, whereas the other half were above it. The median, in this case, gives us a truer reading of how this group performed because it removes the distorting outlier of the United States, which pulled the average up.

States classified as "moderate" had an average homicide rate of 5.0 (which, coincidentally, is the U.S. homicide rate, meaning that the United States on this index performs at the average for countries in the "moderate" category). The average homicide rate for countries classified as "ominous," 12.3 per 100,000, was twice that of countries labeled as "moderate." (The median for states in this category was 9.5, so it appears there are outliers in this group, too, which are distorting and pulling up the average homicide rate.) Countries with the weakest states were the deadliest, most violent of all, with an average homicide rate of 15.8. Citizens in these states have the worst of both worlds: They suffer more from both political and everyday violence than citizens in other countries.

Democracy

Finally, the quality of the state also seems to be correlated with the form of government, the extent to which countries have democratic or authoritarian political systems. This correlation is illustrated in Figure 2.4. The strongest states were the most democratic. Countries classified as "stable" averaged 9.2 (out of

Figure 2.4 State Quality and Democracy

SOURCE: Failed States Index, 2013; The Democracy Index, *The Economist*, 2012.

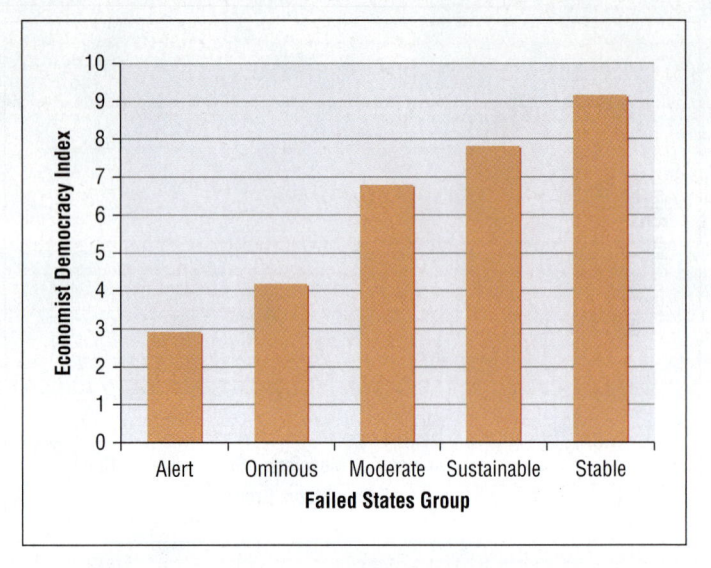

a possible 10) on the Democracy Index. Those labeled as "sustainable" averaged 7.8; "moderate" countries averaged 6.8; states regarded as "ominous" averaged 4.2; and states categorized as "on alert" took their customary position at the back of the pack, averaging only 2.9 on the democracy scale.

Contrary to those who applauded the Italian fascist dictator Benito Mussolini for making the trains run on time, it appears that democracies have stronger states than their authoritarian counterparts. The alleged benefit of authoritarianism, that it is more efficient than democracy, is a myth.

Conclusion

The state is the supreme sovereign authority within a country. The government, which controls the political institutions of the state, sets priorities and organizes society's resources in support of them. The modern state emerged in response to the insecurity of the international system. It required states to build up their administrative capacities to prepare for the ever-present danger of war. States come in a variety of shapes and forms as laid out in their constitutions. Some are unitary, with authority centralized at the national level; others have a federal structure in which subnational levels of the state can raise their own revenue and make their own policies. States also differ in how they arrange their essential building blocks, the legislative, executive, and judicial branches. In some states, the legislative branch is strong, with strong committee systems that permit members to build up expertise and propose their own bills, whereas in others, the legislature is weak and only rubber stamps what the core executive submits to it. In some states, the core executive can command the bureaucracy, including the military. In others, the bureaucracy and military can thwart the will of the core executive. Finally, in some states, the judiciary is independent and has the authority to overturn laws approved by the legislative and executive branches. In others, the judiciary is subordinate to the executive, although even here the government makes an effort to subscribe to rule by law, if not the rule of law.

The form states take—the manner in which power is divided within them—is not neutral or innocent in its effects. Some groups win and others lose, depending on these arrangements. As a result, the balance of power among the state's different levels and branches is constantly challenged. The distribution of state power is not frozen in law but changes subtly—and sometimes not so subtly—in response to political pressure. Political actors try to shape how power is distributed within the state because their success in influencing policy depends on it.

States not only differ in their institutional design but in their effectiveness, their ability to actually govern. Some states can process demands and implement policies, but others have trouble making their rules stick. We then found that strong states are more conducive to developing citizens' capabilities than weak states. Infant mortality rates are lower, literacy rates are higher, people are safer, and political systems are more democratic in strong rather than weak states.

Suggested Readings

Ludger Helms, *Presidents, Prime Ministers and Chancellors: Executive Leadership in Western Democracies* (New York: Palgrave, 2005). A good, comprehensive review of different political executive offices and styles.

Arend Lijphart, *Patterns of Democracy: Government Forms and Performance in Thirty-Six Countries*, 2nd edition (New Haven: Yale University Press, 2012). How certain executive, legislative, and judicial institutions have an affinity for each other in democracies.

Steven Lukes, *Power: A Radical View* (New York: Palgrave, 2005). Argues that there are three faces, or levels, of power: The first is associated with government decision making; the second is associated with agenda control and determining what issues are defined as political; and the third is ideological, which entails socialization to certain values and beliefs.

Gianfranco Poggi, *The State: Its Nature, Development and Prospects* (Stanford, CA: Stanford University Press, 1990). A short and rich analysis of the origins and future of the state.

James C. Scott, *Seeing Like a State: How Certain Schemes to Improve the Human Condition Have Failed* (New Haven: Yale University Press, 1998). How and why states seek to manage society.

Critical Thinking Questions

1. We argued at the beginning of the chapter that power takes three forms: economic, political, and ideological. Are these three forms of power equal? What claims for preeminence can be made about each of them?

2. Do states promote individuals' capabilities or restrict them?

3. If your country was just emerging and was writing a constitution, how would you organize your political institutions? What judicial, legislative, federal, and executive arrangements would you create and why?

4. Over time, the legislative branch has lost ground to the executive in almost all countries. Why has this happened and is this state of affairs constructive or harmful?

5. Because the military has all the guns, why doesn't it take over governments more frequently? Why does the military accept civilian control in some countries but is reluctant to consent to it in others?

Chapter 3
State and Society

Learning Objectives

3.1 Outline the role political participation plays as a bridge connecting the state to society.

3.2 Describe the different forms political participation takes and analyze why groups select different modes of political expression.

3.3 Distinguish political parties from other forms of political participation, describe why they emerged, and analyze the emergence of different types of party systems.

3.4 Define interest groups and distinguish between pluralist and corporatist interest group systems.

3.5 Illustrate the unique properties of social movements.

3.6 Describe patron–client relations and analyze the inequalities they perpetuate.

Introduction

3.1 Outline the role political participation plays as a bridge connecting the state to society.

It started with just one match, and soon an entire region was in flames. On December 17, 2010, Mohamed Bouazizi rose early in the morning to prepare for his job as a street vendor. He walked to the center of Sidi Bouzid, a small rural town in central Tunisia, where he carefully arranged the fruits and vegetables on his wheelbarrow. Later that morning, police approached Bouazizi to check whether he had the appropriate permits to do business. When Bouazizi could not produce the forms, the police confiscated Bouazizi's scale, overturned his cart, and reportedly beat him. Humiliated by his mistreatment, Bouazizi went to city hall to complain about police brutality and to retrieve his scales, but the mayor refused to see him or listen to his complaint. Bouazizi then purchased a can of gasoline from a nearby station and returned to the plaza in front of the mayor's office. There, less than an hour after the altercation with police at his cart, he doused himself with gas, lit a match, and set himself on fire. Startled locals tried to intervene and save him. Covered with burns over ninety percent of his body, Bouazizi fell into a coma and died two and half weeks later, on January 4, 2011.

Outraged citizens in Sidi Bouzid staged rallies condemning the government's arrogance and negligence that led to the incident. Protests spread rapidly throughout the country because Bouazizi's martyrdom reflected the frustration other Tunisians felt regarding their powerlessness and poverty. Efforts by police to quell the antigovernment protests only intensified them. With the army deserting him and citizens in revolt, President Ben Ali fled Tunisia on January 14, ending 23 years of dictatorial rule.

The fire that consumed a life in Sidi Bouzid's town square and grew to devour a cruel authoritarian regime in Tunisia headed east to Egypt. Two weeks after Ben Ali gave up power in Tunisia, youthful activists in Egypt called for a Day of Rage in Tahrir, or Liberation, Square, in the heart of Cairo. They were frustrated by the same lack of power and prospects in their country that led Bouazizi to immolate himself in Tunisia. Encouraged by the the fresh example of the successful revolution in Tunisia, more than 25,000 people showed up in Cairo, and another 20,000 appeared in Alexandria, Egypt's second largest city. The government led by the despot Hosni Mubarak for the past 30 years responded with force, arresting and brutalizing activists and shutting down phone and Internet services across the country.

The ruthlessness of the government's response backfired. A new call for demonstrations three days later brought out hundreds, instead of tens, of thousands of Egyptians, and they weren't simply calling for an end to corruption or for more government subsidies, as previous protests had demanded;

now they were insisting that Mubarak give up power. Instead of leaving Tahrir Square, the protesters occupied it. Fear and despair were replaced by hope and exhilaration. None of Mubarak's usual tactics and appeals that had been so effective in the past—that only he stood between Egypt and chaos, or promises to reshuffle his cabinet, or pledges of pay raises—worked anymore. When activists held the Square against efforts by security forces to remove them, Mubarak's days were numbered. He resigned on February 11, after 30 years of tyranny and decay.[1]

The fire continued to grow and to spread, igniting almost the entire Arab world. In Yemen, antigovernment activists confronted security forces over a period of nine months beginning in January 2011 until President Saleh finally resigned, setting the stage for the first transfer of power in Yemen in 33 years. In Libya, protests against the Qaddafi government began a month after the successful uprising in neighboring Tunisia and quickly escalated into civil war. Hostilities lasted for months until opponents of the regime finally routed government forces, killing Qaddafi in the process and ending 42 years of his tyrannical rule. In Syria, citizens braved tanks and torture to challenge the dictatorship of President Bashar al-Assad and demand an end to a state of emergency that had been in place for 26 years.

All across the Arab world, from Morocco on the Atlantic coast in the west to Bahrain on the Persian Gulf in the east, social movements emerged to challenge entrenched rulers. Collectively referred to as the Arab Spring, these protests reveal what can happen when the linkages connecting state and society fail. Demands from below for respect from officials, political reform, and economic opportunity can explode when the state ignores them. A routine act of arrogance by officials in a rural village, such as humiliating a simple street vendor, can become the basis for mass protest and revolution.

The previous chapter dissected the state to reveal its internal organs: the legislature, core executive, military, bureaucracy, and judiciary. This chapter examines political participation through which people express their values and convey demands to the state. Political participation is the bridge that connects society to the state, and people use different vehicles to cross it. Citizens express their values and convey demands by voting and choosing among candidates offered by political parties, by supporting interest groups that lobby policy makers, by joining social movements that are disruptive, and by engaging in patron–client relations in which citizens exchange their political support for material rewards.

Sometimes these linkages connecting the state and society work well. The wires connecting state to society are large enough to handle the amount of current pulsing through them. In other countries, such as Tunisia, Egypt, and Libya, the wires become overloaded. The level of political participation overwhelms the linkages designed to carry it and bursts forth in the form of protest and revolt.

Political Participation

3.2 Describe the different forms political participation takes and analyze why groups select different modes of political expression.

Political participation occurs in both democratic and authoritarian political systems. The former encourages citizens to influence policy; the latter promotes participation if only to register approval for what the government does. It can also take many forms. Where citizens fear for their lives, they engage in political activity furtively and anonymously by using satire to make fun of the powers that be, try to undermine rulers' legitimacy through rumor and innuendo, and carry out hidden acts of sabotage.[2] Political participation can also take the opposite form, in which citizens engage in open, violent revolt against their rulers. Citizens can yell from a soapbox or cast votes in a ballot box. Citizens use strategies they believe are appropriate given the resources they have and the opportunities that are available. Take the case, for example, of the environmental movement. Green parties that compete for votes are common and successful enough in some countries to become coalition partners in government, but Green parties have been unsuccessful in the United States, despite conditions as propitious in terms of public support for environmentalism as in Europe.

At the same time that Green parties are weaker in the United States, American environmental interest groups are more plentiful and powerful than they are in Europe. There are more than 10,000 environmentally oriented organizations registered as tax-exempt organizations in the United States, and they employ more staff and have bigger budgets than their European counterparts. The difference has to do with the opportunity structure for political participation in the two regions. In the United States, the decentralized, open structure of Congress is congenial to interest group activity. Interest groups can target their influence on congressional committees that have jurisdiction over their issues. At the same time, elections are not nearly as inviting. Third parties, such as the Greens, have a hard time competing in the United States due to winner-take-all electoral rules, obstacles to getting on the ballot, and a lack of media coverage given to minor parties. The **opportunity structure** is quite different in many European countries, leading environmentalists to mobilize electorally as opposed to through interest groups. Many European countries have proportional representation electoral systems in which small parties, such as the Greens, are awarded seats in the legislature based on the percentage of the vote they receive. This permits small parties to come away with some legislative influence so their voters do not feel they are wasting their vote as they would in the United States, where losing parties get nothing. In addition, parliamentary systems of government that exist throughout Europe deprive their legislatures of the kind of influence on policy that Congress enjoys. Consequently, environmentalist interest groups in Europe tend to be smaller and weaker than those in the United States. Groups engage in different forms of political participation, depending on the opportunities for influence that different political structures create.

Opportunity Structures
The relative openness of a political system to political participation. They refer to structural factors, such as the organization of the state or its appetite for repression, that facilitate or impede efforts to influence the state.

Of course, groups engage in different forms of political participation simultaneously, not one mode of participation at the expense or exclusion of another. Although environmentalists in Europe and the United States may not engage in interest group and electoral activity in equal proportion, they are both part of the movement's repertoire as they supplement and support each other. It is also the case that one form of participation may pave the way to another. Recent elections in Iran (2009) became the trigger for mass protests in which the initial mobilization for an opposition candidate later became the basis for mobilization against the state itself. One form of political participation, voting, morphed into another, street demonstrations. Groups can engage in different forms of political participation simultaneously, one form of political participation can change seamlessly into another, or groups can engage in different types of political participation sequentially. This, for example, was the case with the black civil rights movement in the United States. It shifted its strategy from protest to politics, from marches and demonstrations to voter registration and mobilization as the rewards of the former declined and opportunities for the latter increased. One can also see the same sequence occurring in terms of the history of the environmental movement. In Germany, the Green Party was the culmination of a process in which antinuclear peace activists shifted their focus from demonstrations to elections.

Like water trying to escape through the weakest part of a dam, political actors are always looking for the weakest point in the wall of power. They may engage in different forms of political participation simultaneously or move sequentially from one to another, depending on the resources they have and their opportunities to deploy them.

The early research on political participation found that voting was the most popular form of activism and that only a minority engaged in more demanding forms of participation beyond this, such as party work, and even fewer engaged in protests. People with more resources—more education, money, self-confidence, civic skills, and social contacts—were more likely to participate. Political activity was skewed to those who were most advantaged.[3] But levels of political activism are also affected by institutions, the rules of the game. Whether countries have proportional representation systems and schedule elections for nonworking days also affect turnout and who votes.[4] In addition, forms of political participation are expanding beyond traditional forms, such as voting. Turnout in elections may be declining in many countries, but new forms of civic and political action, such as petitioning, demonstrating, or participating in consumer boycotts are taking their place.[5]

Some political scientists found virtue in the limits of political participation, that so few engaged in it beyond the simple and infrequent act of voting. It was sufficient for democracy that citizens could choose among candidates in free and fair elections. Others believed that activism had virtue in itself, that it promoted social tolerance, interpersonal trust, political knowledge, and more responsive government. But few considered the inextricable link between political participation and people's capabilities, that improving people's capabilities only occurs through political activity. As Peter Evans notes, "my ability to choose the life I have reason to value often hangs on the possibility of my acting together with others who have reason to value similar things."[6] People cannot create the institutional structures they need on their own, by themselves, to promote their capabilities. They can only realize these goals through politics, which requires them to act collectively with others if they are to succeed. This is especially true for the underprivileged, who have few personal resources to develop their capabilities by themselves. They need to ally with others in political activity to create institutions that improve their lives. Individual capabilities depend on collective action, which occurs through parties, interest groups, social movements, and patron–client relations to achieve them. We review these forms of collective action.

Political Parties

3.3 Distinguish political parties from other forms of political participation, describe why they emerged, and analyze the emergence of different types of party systems.

Political Parties
Political parties first emerged with the development of democracy and are distinguished from other forms of political participation by putting forward candidates to run the government.

The Founders of the American Republic viewed **political parties** with contempt and believed they were a threat to liberty. Yet, even as the Founders condemned parties in theory, they helped create them in practice. Thomas Jefferson, who founded the Republican Party (the forerunner of today's Democratic Party), and Alexander Hamilton, who led the Federalist Party, both viewed political parties as "sores on the body politic." Two hundred years later, in 1986, Uganda tried to do what the Founders could not. The National Resistance Movement took power and tried to establish a no-party democracy. Although political parties were permitted, party activity on behalf of candidates running for office was banned. But the equivalent of party activity emerged in response to the very effort to limit it because those who opposed the ban on party activity ran against those who supported it.[7]

Political parties emerge even where they are ridiculed because people have diverse interests and values and find parties useful in expressing them to the state. Citizens turn to political parties to educate and mobilize voters, advocate policies that link voters to candidates, and connect elected officials from the same party to each other. But what distinguishes political parties most from other forms of political participation is that they recruit and nominate candidates for public office. Whereas interest groups seek to influence the state from the outside, political parties seek to influence it from the inside by offering candidates to form the government.

Political parties have often been condemned as baleful influences that threaten the unity and integrity of the political order. They "are *parts against* the whole," the political theorist Nancy L. Rosenblum writes, "not *parts of* the whole."[8] Other critics have attacked parties for being corrupt and corrupting; for pandering to special interests; or for serving the selfish, predatory needs of office seekers. But those who condemn parties for being divisive have a naïve view of politics. The unified political community that parties allegedly disrupt does not exist anywhere because people have diverse interests and values. Those diverse interests could not be denied within the new American state in 1787 any more than they could be ignored two hundred years later within Uganda's no-party democracy. Although parties may have vices, they also contribute to the political community by structuring conflict and organizing government. They play a creative role, Nancy L. Rosenblum suggests, that often goes unacknowledged in the way parties "stage the battle" by formulating issues and giving them political relevance. From the raw material of interests and grievances that exist in society, they create the practical art of governing by offering voters a choice of policies and candidates.[9]

Political parties emerged with democracy and the extension of voting rights in the nineteenth century. In some instances, they arose as extensions of factional disputes in the legislature. Legislators appealed to the people, organizing supporters among the broader public, to settle policy conflicts among themselves. Party in government gave birth to party in the electorate. This was the case in the United States, where opposing congressional factions, what became the Federalists and the Republicans, took their dispute outside the halls of Congress and appealed to the public for support. In other instances, the opposite occurred. Groups outside the legislature formed political parties to obtain more influence within it. An example of this occurred in Britain when the trade unions, frustrated with their lack of political representation in Parliament, gave birth to the Labour Party to increase their political influence. This was also the case in many developing countries where political parties formed to express the interests of particular castes, religious groups, and tribes.[10] For example, the Zulu tribe in South Africa found representation through the Inkatha Freedom Party, and the Bahujan Samaj Party emerged as the expression of lower-caste voters in northern India.

Parties play significant roles in democracies, competing to win elections and form governments. A crude sense of what the public wants is transmitted up to government through party competition in elections, but political parties are also common in authoritarian systems even in the absence of elections. Here they are used not to transmit demands from below up to government but to reverse the flow of information and convey government policies down to the people. Two political scientists suggested that parties in authoritarian regimes are used as "an instrument of political recruitment as well as a device for management of the public."[11] The party facilitates mass mobilization in support of the government to assert its legitimacy.

Beyond one-party authoritarian regimes, parties exist within **party systems** that entail enduring, stable forms of party competition. Party systems are distinguished by the number of parties they include. For example, people often refer to the American two-party *system* because electoral competition often takes the regular, patterned form of Democrats competing against Republicans. But

Party Systems
Party systems occur when party conflict takes a regular, stable form in terms of the number of parties competing, the relative vote share each party receives, and the types of interests they represent.

the American two-party system is actually quite rare. Multiparty systems are much more common, where the effective number of parties that compete for voters and win legislative seats is greater than two. In Israel, for example, 12 parties won enough votes in the 2013 elections to be represented in the Knesset, its legislature. Party systems are also distinguished by their ideological breadth. Some party systems are highly polarized due to the presence of extreme right- and left-wing parties.[12] Finally, party systems differ in their degree of institutionalization, the degree to which they function as a system at all. This, for example, is a dilemma faced in many new democracies in eastern Europe and Africa, where parties form and disappear quickly, party competition is highly unstable, and party organizations are weak, with few members or resilient local chapters.[13] Some party systems are characterized by strong parties that enjoy high memberships, loyal voters from one election to the next, and party discipline among their elected officials; other party systems give rise to weak parties with lots of volatility among voters from one election to the next, low party membership, and little unity or party-line voting among legislators.

Party systems reflect deeply rooted social divisions that are embedded in the history of a country. These cleavages give rise to group identities that find expression in political parties. Consequently, party competition assumes the characteristics of a system, with durable, recurrent patterns. According to two sociologists, Seymour Martin Lipset and Stein Rokkan, the party systems that emerged in Western democracies were the geological remains of violent economic and political conflicts from their pasts, specifically, the rise of industrial capitalism and the nation-state. The emergence of industrial capitalism gave birth to class and urban–rural conflicts; the development of the nation-state gave rise to church–state and national–local conflicts. Just as ice, water, and fire combined in unique ways to shape different regions of the earth, so did these four cleavages combine in distinctive ways to shape party competition in west European countries. The impact of these social divisions is still evident today in the form of socialist (class conflict), Christian democratic (church–state conflict), agrarian (rural–urban conflict), and regional parties (national–local conflict) in many European countries.

In Brief: Strong and Weak Political Parties

Characteristics	Weak Parties	Strong Parties
Membership	low	high
Party identification among voters	low	high
Electoral volatility	high	low
Party unity in the legislature	low	high

In-Depth: Iraq—From Bullets to Ballots (and Perhaps Back Again)

Following the American invasion, political participation in Iraq took the form of suicide bombings, civil strife, and ethnic cleansing. Kurds, Shiites, and Sunnis used bullets not ballots to influence the government and settle differences with each other. Political participation escaped the institutional channels designed to contain and express it.

In March 2010, legislative elections were held in which Kurds, Shiites, and Sunnis ran candidates and appealed for votes. Despite election-day violence that claimed 38 lives, 62 percent of eligible Iraqis cast their ballot, but Iraq's fragile institutions imperiled the election's success. A slow tallying of votes brought charges of vote tampering. When the election returns came in, they reflected the fragmentation of Iraq too well, yielding indecisive results.

A government finally emerged, but it is not clear it has earned the trust of Iraqis. The social conflicts in Iraq may be too powerful for electoral forms of political participation to contain. If elections cannot create effective governments, Iraqis may return to settling their differences with bullets instead of ballots.

For Further Discussion
1. Under what circumstances can elections help resolve conflicts instead of reflect them?
2. Although the capabilities approach argues that people are better off with civil and political rights, is it possible for democracy to be too much of a good thing in some places?

Party systems are also shaped by electoral laws. Different methods of counting votes, awarding seats in the legislature, and choosing presidents affect the shape of party systems. For example, the rules under which elections are held in the United States, where whoever gets the most votes wins, create a bias toward a two-party system. Under these rules, there are no rewards for losing. Consequently, voters do not want to waste their vote on parties that cannot win and strategically vote for the lesser of two evils between the two major parties that can. Under different electoral rules, such as proportional representation, where legislative seats are awarded to parties based on the percentage of the vote they receive, multiparty systems flourish. Parties receiving less than a plurality still receive some representation in the legislature. Voters can now vote their conscience without fear of throwing their vote away, as would be the case under winner-take-all rules. Electoral rules shape the nature of party competition by influencing the number of parties that compete and the ideological space between them.

However, not all parties and party systems are created equal. Some contribute more to developing citizens' capabilities than others. The quality of the link between state and society through political parties depends on the presence of well-organized, disciplined parties that articulate clear programs and appeal to a broad coalition of voters. Such parties can maximize the greatest asset of the underprivileged: their power of numbers. In their absence, when party systems are poorly institutionalized and parties appear and disappear rapidly—which is the case in many new democracies—it is hard for citizens to know what parties stand for and, thus, what they are voting for. Parties built around personalities tend to appear, and these party leaders are less likely to be constrained when they govern and to favor elites who have privileged access to them when they do. Programmatic commitments and organizational discipline that can limit wheeling and dealing by politicians and hold them accountable are absent.[14]

Parties built on **patronage** are as suspect as those that are weakly institutionalized and developed around personalities. Parties that are built around rewards in return for political loyalty divide the underprivileged into multiple, competing parties. The less fortunate form political ties with elites who offer them rewards instead of allying with each other. Where such parties exist, people with low capabilities have a difficult time making improvements in their lives because their power of numbers has been diluted. Developing their capabilities depends on political participation that flows through institutionalized and programmatic political parties that can harness their power of numbers and can appeal and unite a wide variety of voters around a common program.[15] **Programmatic parties** that link citizens to the state contribute to people's capabilities by providing more public services and engaging in less corruption.[16]

Patronage
Rewards offered to individuals in return for their electoral support. Citizens exchange their vote or other forms of political support for money, jobs, or access to public services.

Programmatic Parties
Parties that mobilize supporters on the basis of the party's platform that its representatives are committed to enact when in office.

Interest Groups

3.4 Define interest groups and distinguish between pluralist and corporatist interest group systems.

Political participation can also take the form of interest group activity, in which people with common interests organize to influence policy makers. **Interest groups** engage in many of the same activities as political parties: raising money, mobilizing voters, and supporting candidates. But unlike political parties, interest groups do not nominate candidates to run for office.

It may appear natural and easy for people with common interests to organize in pursuit of their shared goals, but interest group formation is not so simple and straightforward. Someone has to invest time, provide leadership, and commit resources to make it happen. Such skills and resources may not exist and are certainly not evenly distributed among groups. For this reason, interest groups that promote the interests of poor people, who lack time, money, and leadership skills, are very rare, whereas those of higher status groups, who have these resources, are more common. In addition, interest group formation faces the **free rider problem**. It is rational for people to try to gain the benefits that interest groups create without paying the costs of joining or participating in them. For example, it is rational not to contribute to

Interest Groups
An organized group that seeks to influence public policy.

Free Rider Problem
When services or goods are available that people can use without paying for them.

the Sierra Club and enjoy the benefits of clean air and water it helps promote while letting others pay dues to it. But if everyone acted rationally in this way, free riding on the activity of others, no interest groups would form. The Sierra Club would not exist.

Nevertheless, the Sierra Club and interest groups like it do exist because they offer a variety of incentives that entice people to join them. Some groups offer material incentives, some tangible reward for becoming a member, such as discounts on insurance or purchases. Other groups avoid the free rider problem by offering people an opportunity to feel fellowship in a common enterprise. They derive emotional satisfaction from joining others in an organization that seeks to realize their shared values.[17]

To some extent, the challenges of interest group formation and mobilization have been reduced by technological innovations such as the Internet. According to the political scientist Mark S. Bonchek, "electronic forms of communication reduce communication, coordination and information costs, facilitating group formation, group efficiency, membership recruitment and retention."[18] Organizers can recruit members, appeal for contributions, inform supporters, and coordinate their activity through a website, which is inexpensive to create and maintain. The expense of a bureaucracy to carry out basic functions of recruitment and coordination can now be avoided because these tasks can be done cheaper and more quickly through social media. The Internet permits interest groups to travel light because it reduces start-up costs.

The Internet has not only facilitated interest group formation but given impetus to professional advocacy organizations such as MoveOn.org. in the United States. These interest groups, in contrast to older ones, dispense with dues-paying members and local chapters and rely on foundations, direct mail, or Internet fund-raising appeals for money. They have a head but no body. Previously, members engaged in politics by participating in the life of the organization, developing civic values and leadership skills in the process. But these professional advocacy organizations do not need to involve their supporters in the life of the organization. They are creatures of their staff, who simply ask people to send a check to finance them.[19]

Some countries have a plethora of interest groups. In the United States, special interests proliferate. In other countries, interest groups are not as plentiful, even when one controls for population. The interest group universe is larger in some countries than others because their state structures are more conducive to pressure group influence. For example, the divided, decentralized political institutions of the United States create many access points at which groups can influence policy: at the state level, in the Senate, in the House of Representatives, and in the courts. The open, diffused, fractured structure of policy making in the United States invites groups with a stake in policy to lobby and exert influence. The more power is dispersed within the state, the more opportunities for special interests to apply pressure on it. In countries such as Sweden, where the state is unitary and policy making is centralized, there are not as many access points for interest groups to affect policy, and consequently, the incentive to form them is not as great.

Just as different types of party systems exist, so, too, are there different interest group systems. Groups in different countries that represent similar interests operate very differently, depending on the type of interest group system in which they are embedded. For example, even though the AFL-CIO in the United States and the LO in Sweden represent the interests of labor unions in their respective countries, they are organized and act differently because they are embedded in different interest group systems with distinctive characteristics.

Pluralist Interest Group Systems
Where large numbers of interest groups compete with one another for members and exert influence by lobbying the government.

Some countries have what is called a **pluralist interest group system**. Such systems are characterized by large numbers of interest groups that compete with each other for members and influence. Pluralist interest group systems have the following characteristics: First, groups have to compete for members to survive and expand. They all want to increase their market share and recruit members who can provide them with the money, staff, and resources they need to be influential. This is especially important because pluralist interest groups enjoy no special relationship with the government. They do not participate in policy making but have to exert influence from the outside through lobbying policy makers. Second, pluralist interest groups are less encompassing, only able to capture a small share of their potential market. Finally, pluralist interest groups tend to be decentralized. They lack the authority to sanction their members and tell them what to do. For example, the AFL-CIO cannot require its affiliated unions, such as the United Auto Workers or the Machinists union, to support the same bills and candidates it has endorsed. The AFL-CIO lacks sanctions short of expulsion to prevent affiliated unions from freelancing and ignoring its decisions.

Corporatist Interest Groups
When a few interest groups include a large proportion of potential members and are often given some official recognition by the state and included in the policy-making process.

At the other end of the spectrum are corporatist systems of interest group representation, in which there are fewer but larger interest groups. **Corporatist interest groups** are more encompassing. They recruit a higher percentage of those who are eligible to join because membership is often compulsory, not optional. They also enjoy a monopoly over their market, reducing competition for members. Finally, they are more hierarchically organized with the authority to sanction their members' behavior, and they are often invited to participate in policy making by the state as insiders, not outsiders. They are invited to negotiate directly with the government in return for complying with any agreement that is reached. In Table 3.1 which follows, countries that received high scores, such as Austria and Norway, have corporatist interest group systems, while countries with low scores, such as Canada and the United States, have pluralist interest group systems.

Corporatist and pluralist interest groups behave differently with consequences for people's capabilities. The pluralist interest group market is crowded with competing groups, which undermines their willingness to cooperate with each other. In addition, a lack of centralized control within pluralist interest

Table 3.1 Interest Group Systems

Corporatism	Scores	Corporatism	Scores
Austria	5.000	Ireland	2.000
Norway	4.864	New Zealand	1.955
Sweden	4.674	Australia	1.680
Netherlands	4.000	France	1.674
Denmark	3.545	United Kingdom	1.652
Germany (West)	3.543	Portugal	1.500
Switzerland	3.375	Italy	1.477
Finland	3.295	Spain	1.250
Japan	2.912	Canada	1.150
Belgium	2.841	United States	1.150

SOURCE: See Alan Siaroff, "Corporatism in 24 Industrial Democracies: Meaning and Measurement," *European Journal of Political Research* Vol. 36 (1999), p. 198.

groups prevents them from operating efficiently. Both, their competition and decentralization, sap the collective strength of pluralist interest groups. Corporatist interest groups, on the other hand, don't have to outbid other groups to attract members. They are not beset by organizational fragmentation. Nor do they suffer from as much organizational inefficiency due to a lack of centralized authority. Hierarchy within corporatist interest groups can resolve problems of internal coordination that plague their pluralist counterparts. Finally, their encompassing memberships require them to synthesize the diverse interests of their members and articulate only the most general interest among them. This broadens the appeal of these groups. All these qualities permit corporatist interest groups to unify and appeal to broader interests as well as use their limited resources more efficiently. For citizens who want to develop their capabilities and have to depend on their power of numbers to be politically effective, these are no small advantages. Fewer and bigger really is better.

In Brief: Pluralist and Corporatist Interest Groups

Characteristics	Pluralist	Corporatist
Number of interest groups	many	few
Internal organization	decentralized	hierarchical
Coverage	low density	encompassing
Relationship to government	lobbying	participates in policy-making

Social Movements

3.5 Illustrate the unique properties of social movements.

Americans and citizens around the world were all treated to the spectacle of a social movement in action in 2011 when "Occupy Wall Street" tent encampments appeared in downtown city plazas. People appropriated public space where they pitched tents, set up soup kitchens, and staged rallies to protest inequality and the political influence of the 1 percent at the expense of the 99 percent. From Mumbai in India to Madrid in Spain, protesters engaged in activities that disrupted normal routines and drew attention to their demands. Although each Occupy movement had its own local flavor, they all shared qualities that are typical of social movements. They lacked bureaucratic hierarchy, central coordination, and formal organization. Many of them emerged fairly spontaneously as people connected by social media converged on select locations. Another classic quality of social movements they exhibited was a high level of commitment from their supporters. People not only sacrificed comfort and routine to live in tents in the occupied zones, they also faced the threat of being arrested. Finally, like other social movements, the Occupy movement was disruptive and confrontational. Its tactics were designed to arouse awareness of inequality and corporate political influence among the public and to provoke a response from policy makers.

Social Movements
They are less formally organized than interest groups and engage in unconventional forms of political activism that require a higher level of commitment and sacrifice from their supporters.

Social movements engage in more unconventional and confrontational forms of political participation to influence policy makers than interest groups or political parties. They also tend to be less formally organized or hierarchical, tend to be more ideological and contentious, and move participation up to a more active and demanding level than other forms of political participation. Consequently, social movements tend to attract people with intense feelings about an issue who are more committed and willing to assume the increased risks that social movement activism entails. They often advance two kinds of claims, either to promote group acceptance in which outsiders want the same rights and privileges as insiders, or to demand some change in policy because the normal channels are blocked or unresponsive. The civil rights and feminist movements are examples of the first type of claim; the environmental and Occupy Wall Street movements exemplify the second. Although social movements are often identified with liberal and progressive goals, conservatives have also formed social movements to influence policy makers. The ideological commitment to participate in social movements is not the monopoly of any one tendency but can be found across the political spectrum.

The emergence of social movements was facilitated by the spread of democracy. Democracy contributed to this distinctive and innovative form of political participation by removing prohibitions against mass rallies and other repressive measures, providing convenient and accessible targets in the form of legislatures and representatives on whom social movements could focus demands, magnifying the political importance and respect given to sheer numbers, and increasing the significance of claims to represent "the people."[20] Where democracy flourished, so did social movements.

Many early social movements were formed by occupational groups around economic demands. Peasant, farmer, and labor movements proliferated, but as industrialism gave way to post-industrialism, new forms of domination became prominent alongside familiar forms of economic power. The landlord's domination of peasants, the merchant's power over farmers, and the employer's control over workers were now joined by male domination of women, straights of gays, whites of blacks, and settlers of indigenous people. Cultural domination, not simply economic domination, and quality of life issues, not simply redistribution, became new sources of social conflict as groups affirmed their way of life against traditional standards that devalued them. These social movements were as interested in legitimizing alternative lifestyles as they were in promoting their policy goals. Politics was personal in a way that was not true for participants in older, more traditional social movements. **New social movements** were also distinguished from their predecessors by their flatter and more decentralized structures. They were much more skeptical of bureaucracy, which they believed would compromise their ideals. When the 1997 Nobel Peace Prize was awarded to the International Campaign to Ban Landmines (ICBL) and Jody Williams, the ICBL had to wait nearly a year to receive its share of the money because it had no bank account or address to which the Nobel Committee could send it. New social movements believed that by avoiding bureaucracy and prefiguring their goals in the means they used to achieve them, they could avert being domesticated and co-opted like the economically based social movements that preceded them.

As the breadth of issues social movements covered increased, so did they expand in scope from the national to the international level. As the scope and power of international institutions grow, they create their own world of global social movements to shadow them. This is best exemplified by the formation of the World Social Forum. It brings together global activists to discuss issues and network among themselves and is modeled on the annual meetings of the World Economic Forum, which brings together political and economic elites to talk and network among themselves. Globalization from above represented by the World Economic Forum is replicated by globalization from below in the form of the World Social Forum. Globalization is also evident in the The Occupy movement that we profiled at the beginning of this section. The practice of occupying symbolic public spaces began in Egypt when opponents of President Hosni Mubarak occupied Tahrir or Liberation Square in the middle of Cairo. It was next appropriated by *Los Indignatos* in Spain, who encamped in *Puerto del sol* in the center of Madrid to protest spending cuts by the Spanish government and then crossed the ocean to the United States when activists occupied Zucotti Park in the heart of New York's financial district. From there, it went viral, across the country and across the globe.

Just as computer-mediated communication has made it easier to form interest groups by lowering the cost of recruiting and communicating with members, so has the Internet facilitated social movement formation and activity. Journalist

New Social Movements
Distinguished from their predecessors by their focus on issues of identity (feminism) and quality of life (environmentalism) as opposed to economic demands (redistribution) and by their belief that the internal organization of the movement should reflect its values.

Steve Coll argues that the many-to-many geometry of social media empowers individuals more than the one-to-many interaction of previous technologies.[21] When police in Egypt beat a protester, witnesses recorded it on their cell phones. When police claimed he died of drug use, outraged Egyptians posted contrary evidence on Facebook and YouTube. Wael Ghonem, an Egyptian Google marketing executive, created a Facebook page to protest the injustice and attracted hundreds of thousands of supporters in Egypt and throughout the Arab world. After the brutal Mubarak regime fell, Ghonem told a CNN correspondent, "I want to meet Mark Zuckerberg [Facebook's founder] one day and thank him. This revolution started on Facebook."[22] Social media are effective at coordinating and giving direction to leaderless challengers. It provides a free space where people can communicate with one another and can dramatize issues by posting pictures that circulate widely and attract attention.[23]

Comparative Political Analysis: Does Civic Engagement Contribute to Good Government?

Problem: Some political institutions perform better than others. In his book, *Making Democracy Work*, Robert Putnam asked why that might be so.[24] He compared the effectiveness and responsiveness of regional governments in Italy, each of which operated in their own milieu. Putnam likened the problem to a botany experiment in which genetically identical seeds—regional governments—were placed in different soil to compare whether their diverse settings made a difference in how the seeds grew.

Methods and Hypothesis: Putnam conducted interviews with officials and community leaders, surveyed voters, and, like an anthropologist, immersed himself in the various regions of Italy. He also supplemented his evidence with quantitative data. He hypothesized that the regional governemnts in Italy would be shaped by and reflect the social context in which they operated.

Operationalizing Concepts: Putnam developed indicators to assess the performance of regional governments. For example, he examined whether they met budget deadlines, implemented programs, and responded to questions he sent.

Results: Putnam found those regional institutions that performed best were located in areas where there was a great deal of civic trust and engagement that was cultivated by a rich array of local voluntary organizations, such as sports clubs and unions. He found that good citizens and good governments reinforced each other.

For Further Discussion

1. What circumstances contribute to a vibrant civic life that creates civic trust, which Putnam found is so essential to good government?
2. Can states create civic trust? Can states turn vicious circles of mutual suspicion among citizens into virtuous circles of mutual confidence?

Source: Robert D. Putnam with Robert Leonardi and Raffaella Y. Nanetti, *Making Democracy Work: Civic Traditions in Modern Italy* (Princeton: Princeton University Press, 1993).

Patron–Client Relations

3.6 Describe patron–client relations and analyze the inequalities they perpetuate.

The debt binding clients to patrons in the Philippines is greater than any exchange of money can expunge. In return for protection, which may take the form of a job, access to land, school tuition for children, or money for a medical emergency, sugar cane cutters give plantation owners their loyalty, gratitude, and respect. As one owner explained, "[plantation owners] control the community, because everybody is dependent on you, and you can have a say in everything they do."[25] When owners need political support, they simply call in their debt.

Patron–client relations, in which a patron offers or withholds some material benefit in return for political support, are another way in which citizens are linked to the state. Clients exchange their vote or participation in a rally for some tangible reward such as money, jobs, or better land to rent. As a party official in a rural part of Spain explained: "The citizen who is worried about resolving problems with the doctor or the school, or the problem of an unjust accusation before the courts, or of delinquency in paying taxes to the state, etc. . . . has recourse to an intermediary . . . who can intercede on his behalf, but in exchange for pledging his very conscience and his vote."[26] Patron–client relationships occur among those in deeply unequal relationships in which the haves are in a position to bargain for political support from the have-nots.

The bargain struck between patrons and clients is reinforced by **norms of reciprocity**, that people should help those who do favors for them. When patrons intercede on behalf of their clients or offer small loans to them, clients become obligated to their patrons. These feelings of obligation are powerful and cannot easily be dismissed or avoided because of the regular face-to-face contact that patrons have with clients daily. Moreover, exchanges create a sense of ongoing client dependence on patrons to ensure that they continue to provide gifts in the future. When a client was asked whether she was required to attend political rallies in return for free medicine she received from a party broker, she replied, "I know I have to go to her rally in order to fulfill my obligation to her, to show my gratitude. . . . [I]f I do not go to the rally, then, when I need something, she won't give it to me."[27] Of course, clients can always cheat and not go to the rally, but patron–client relations are embedded in local social networks that provide feedback about whether clients deliver on their end of the bargain. According to Susan C. Stokes, this turns the normal meaning of democratic accountability, in which parties are held accountable by voters, into its opposite, in which voters are held responsible for their actions by parties.[28]

Clientelism generates poverty, and poverty, in turn, breeds clientelism. Clientelism flourishes when people are desperate for handouts. Their vote and

Patron–Client Relations
An unequal exchange in which poor clients give their political support in return for some reward, such as money, land to farm, credit, protection, or access to services, from rich patrons.

Norms of Reciprocity
Favors that are given with expectation they will be repaid. When patrons do something on behalf of clients, it creates a sense of indebtedness and obligation, binding the client to the patron until the favor is returned.

Clientelism
When political parties attract support by buying it, offering rewards to voters, as opposed to appealing to them on the basis of shared values. Parties draw voters by dispensing favors as opposed to competing on the basis of principles or programs.

political support may not seem like much to exchange when people need food, a job, or medicine. The poor value benefits that patrons could deliver today more than the promises of redistribution others might promise tomorrow. Living so close to subsistence and vulnerable to abuse from powerful officials, clients appreciate the safety net that patrons offer and consider themselves luckier than those without one. Political parties that depend on patron–client networks for support provide targeted relief to individuals at the expense of providing public goods that might deliver bigger payoffs for all. Clientelist parties tend to forego developmental projects that contribute to economic growth and enhance the quality of life for everyone to provide private goods to their supporters.

Conclusion

Linkages such as political parties, interest groups, social movements, and patron–client relations, which connect citizens to the state, are important because they convey demands to the government. These wires carry the electrical current from the base of society to policy makers. But these linkages do not simply carry the current; they manage and transform it. The way in which they are structured, clientelistic or programmatic parties, pluralist or corporatist interest groups, affects which demands get through and which are discouraged, giving advantage to some groups at the expense of others.

Suggested Readings

Samuel P. Huntington, *Political Order in Changing Societies* (New Haven, CT: Yale University Press, 1968). A classic work in comparative politics that argues the greatest challenge for developing states is creating the institutional capacity to manage increasing rates of participation.

Mancur Olson, *The Logic of Collective Action: Public Goods and the Theory of Groups* (Cambridge: Harvard University Press, 1971). A look at the obstacles interest groups face in forming and the strategies they take in overcoming them.

Nancy L. Rosenblum, *On the Side of Angels: An Appreciation of Parties and Partisanship* (Princeton: Princeton University Press, 2008). A spirited defense of political parties and their contributions to democracy.

Charles Tilly and Lesley J. Wood, *Social Movements, 1768-2008* (Boulder, CO.: Paradigm Publishers, 2009). A primer on social movements.

Critical Thinking Questions

1. Is more political participation by citizens always better? Can there be too much of a good thing when it comes to political participation?

2. Can democracy exist without political parties?

3. What are some of the differences distinguishing political parties, interest groups, social movements, and patron–client relations as forms of political participation? Under what circumstances do people use one as opposed to another form of participation?

Chapter 4
Political Culture and Identity

Learning Objectives

4.1 Explain how Malala Yousafzai's experience exemplifies the ways in which identity and political culture can affect individuals' capabilities.

4.2 Define political culture and state the basic assumption of those using the concept to study politics.

4.3 Compare and contrast the civic culture and self-expression approaches to political culture.

4.4 Apply the concept of social capital to explain why some democracies do a better job than others of promoting citizens' capabilities.

4.5 Describe three identities that can become the basis of identity politics.

4.6 Apply primordial, instrumental, and constructivist approaches to explain how identity can lead to violent conflict.

4.7 Explain the advantages of scatter diagrams, identify the independent and dependent variables in a scatter diagram, and summarize the findings.

Introduction

4.1 Explain how Malala Yousafzai's experience exemplifies the ways in which identity and political culture can affect individuals' capabilities.

The same person can identify herself as a college sophomore, a Catholic, and a Hispanic-American. These identities give her a sense of who she is and how she relates to others. As a woman, she has things in common with other women that distinguish her from men. As a college sophomore, she has things in common with other sophomores that distinguish her from first-year students. As a Catholic, she has some things in common with other Catholics that she does not share with non-Catholics. As a Hispanic-American, she has some things in common with other Hispanic-Americans that distinguish her from Irish-Americans. Although she might never become politically active based on any of these identities, it is possible that some might become politically significant. This is more likely to happen if people like her are threatened or demeaned by others.

In 2012, Malala Yousafzai identified herself as a Muslim, a resident of northern Pakistan's Swat Valley, a girl, and a student. Her identities as a girl and a student are the ones that became politically salient for her. Malala's advocacy of female education led *Time* magazine to designate her as one of 2013's "100 Most Influential People in the World," but her activism also nearly cost her life when, in October 2012, she was shot in the head by a Muslim militant, barely surviving after being rushed to England for surgery. The Taliban who ordered the attack on Malala vowed to kill her if she ever returned to Pakistan.

Malala's offense was criticizing the Pakistani Taliban for its treatment of females, especially its efforts to deny girls the benefit of an education. The Taliban blew up more than 100 schools for girls in the area of Pakistan where she lived and subsequently banned girls from attending classes. Malala's critique of the Taliban began when she was only 11 years old, after a British reporter asked her to write a diary about life under the Taliban for the British Broadcasting Corporation. She did so under an assumed name, but by the time she was 14, she was pressing her case for girls' education openly. Because her outspoken demands offended the Taliban's interpretation of Islamic laws and local cultural values, they attempted to silence her.

Malala's experience exemplifies the ways in which identity and political culture can affect individuals' capabilities. Pakistan contains deep divisions among ethnic, nationalist, and religious groups. For decades, the majority Punjabi ethnic group has used its control of the state to benefit its own members and to foment distrust and tension among other groups to weaken their ability to unite against Punjabi dominance. Some groups living in border areas of Pakistan have even tried to break away and form an independent state in which they could observe their own customs without repression.

Religious identity is yet another source of conflict in Pakistan. Sunni Muslims form a large majority of the country's population. The government is dominated by Sunni officials, who encourage extremists to attack members of the smaller Shia sect. For example, in June 2013, a Sunni suicide bomber detonated explosives hidden in his vest during religious services at a Shiite mosque, killing 15 worshippers.

In addition to the division between Sunni and Shia, there are divisions within the Sunni Muslims. Militant, fundamentalist Sunnis such as the Pakistani Taliban threaten and attack more moderate and secular Sunnis such as Malala and her family. Malala is hardly the only female student to have been victimized. In June 2013, Sunni militants bombed a bus full of women university students, killing 10. Wounded students were taken to a hospital, which the militants invaded in an effort to finish their bloody mission.[1]

The consequence of such ethnic and religious conflict is a political culture characterized by extreme distrust among citizens, suspicion of state officials, and readiness to use violence to settle political disagreements. These circumstances have led to chronic political instability. Military officers often have seized political power from civilians, but even when they do not control the government directly, they represent a continuing threat to elected governments.[2]

This chapter examines issues of identity and political culture and why some countries can sustain stable democracies, whereas others cannot. The chapter is divided into five sections. The first defines political culture and cautions about traps to avoid in studying it. The second looks at the kind of political culture conducive to democracy. The third defines social capital and how it is related to capabilities. The fourth explores how ethnic, national, and religious identities can divide countries, how these divisions can give rise to violent conflicts, and how such outbreaks of violence can be explained. The final section of the chapter assesses how political culture and identity promote or frustrate citizens' capabilities.

Political Culture

4.2 Define political culture and state the basic assumption of those using the concept to study politics.

Political Culture
A society's widely shared beliefs, values, and orientations toward politics.

The term *culture* denotes a society's widely shared values, beliefs, norms, symbols, and orientations toward the world. It provides individuals with a sense of "what is the good life, what is possible, what is just, who counts, and who doesn't."[3] It acts as a kind of road map that gives people a sense of who they are and instructs them how to interact with others. **Political culture**, in contrast, is a narrower concept that refers to a society's values, beliefs, and norms, and orientations toward politics specifically. A society's political culture shapes how citizens regard their government and its decision-making process. It determines whether they feel proud or ashamed of their country, hopeful or cynical about its politics, and politically influential or impotent. The basic assumption of this approach to the study of politics is that political culture is a "crucial determinant of the type of political system by which a population is governed."[4]

Before turning to examine the specific ways political scientists study political culture, it is useful to keep in mind two traps to avoid. First, we should rely on evidence about what people believe rather falling back on stereotypes. For example, one common stereotype is that Muslims are hostile to democracy, but this is not supported by research data. A 2008–2012 Pew Foundation study of Muslim opinion in 39 countries and territories found "broad support for democracy," with majorities in many countries preferring democracy to alternative forms of government.[5] Several other studies have reached similar conclusions. Second, we should not assume that people of a certain ethnic or religious background all have similar political beliefs. Muslims do not all share the same political culture any more than Christians do. Even within predominantly Muslim societies, considerable individual differences can be found.

Two Approaches to Political Culture

4.3 Compare and contrast the civic culture and self-expression approaches to political culture.

In this section, we examine two approaches to political culture and how they have been used to explain why some countries have democracies that promote citizens' capabilities while others do not. They are the civic-culture and the self-expression approaches.

The Civic Culture Approach

The basic assumption of the **civic culture approach** is that congruence, or a match, between a country's political culture and its political institutions is necessary for political stability. That is, democratic political institutions require a democratic political culture in order to function properly, whereas authoritarian political institutions require an authoritarian political culture.[6] For example, according to supporters of the civic culture approach, the Nazis were able to take power in Germany in 1933 mainly because of the mismatch between the Weimar Republic's democratic institutions and widespread authoritarian attitudes within the German public. As one author put it, "democracy failed in Weimar Germany because it was 'a democracy without democrats.'"[7]

Some political scientists using the civic culture approach have focused on the kind of political culture necessary to maintain democracies. The pioneering study in that regard is Gabriel Almond and Sidney Verba's *The Civic Culture*, which was published in 1963. This was just eighteen years after the end of World War II, when the horrors of the Nazi regime were still fresh in people's minds. The authors' goal of discovering what kind of political culture was needed to sustain stable democracies was thus not just a matter of academic curiosity; that knowledge was vital to prevent democracies from collapsing into tyranny.[8]

In an attempt to answer that question, a team of researchers surveyed citizens' political attitudes in five democracies: Great Britain, the United States, Germany,

Civic Culture Approach
An approach to the study of comparative politics, which suggests that congruence, or a match, between a country's political culture and its political institutions is necessary for political stability, and that a mix of citizens with different levels of participation and interest in politics helps maintain a balance between keeping governments responsive to citizens and allowing them to operate without undue disruption and instability.

Italy, and Mexico. They concluded that the United States and Britain most closely exemplified the kind of political culture most likely to sustain democracy. Almond and Verba called this pattern the "civic culture." Ironically, it did not exhibit the characteristics extolled in civics textbooks of the era. According to these textbooks, the democratic ideal was one in which every citizen is well informed and actively involved in politics. Almond and Verba found that this did not hold true, even in the United States and Britain. Although many of the citizens in the United States and Britain were politically astute and aware, they typically limited their activities to reading about politics and voting in elections. Less involved citizens were law-abiding and aware of how government policies affected their lives but otherwise paid little attention to politics and often did not even bother to vote. Finally, a small percentage of citizens had little or no political knowledge, involvement, or interest. Almond and Verba concluded that the "civic culture" of the United States and Great Britain, with their mixed levels of citizens' involvement in politics, was actually preferable to the "ideal" political culture of the civics textbooks. The coexistence of citizens with different levels of political participation and interest helped maintain a healthy balance between maintaining government responsiveness to citizens' concerns and allowing it to govern without undue disruption. The other essential component of a civic culture is a high level of social trust among citizens, which facilitates cooperation. In countries with civic cultures, citizens have an "emotional involvement in the outcome of elections," but "this does not mean complete rejection of one's political opponent."[9]

The Self-Expression Approach

Subsequent researchers have concluded that the kind of political culture Almond and Gabriel Powell thought necessary for preserving democracy is not helpful for creating democracy or making it responsive to citizens' needs and wishes. Ronald Inglehart and Christian Welzel propose the **self-expression approach** as offering a better explanation for why democracy emerges and why some democracies are more effective and responsive than others. Their central argument is that economic development and the social changes that accompany it lead to changes in people's values that result in demands for democracy. These changes occur along two dimensions. The first is change from traditional to secular values. In very poor societies, many people hold **traditional values**, which include strong religious beliefs and respect for the authority of political and religious leaders. As societies become wealthier, increasing percentages of people tend to adopt a more secular orientation. Those holding **secular values** put less importance on religion as a guiding force and are less willing to respect authority based on religious validation.[10] They no longer accept claims that rulers hold power because it is God's will or that men should enjoy more privileges than women because holy texts say they should. As a result, proponents of secular values become more likely to challenge the authority of religious and non-elected political leaders.

The second dimension of value change is the shift from preoccupation with survival to an emphasis on self-expression. **Survival values** concern the

Self-Expression Approach
An approach to the study of comparative politics, which explains that economic development and social change contribute to the emergence of self-expression values.

Traditional Values
Values, which include strong religious beliefs and respect for the authority of political and religious leaders.

Secular Values
Values, which put less importance on religion as a guiding force, and which are less respectful of authority based on religious validation.

Survival Values
Values concerning the requirements for staying alive, including food, clothing, and shelter.

requirements of staying alive. In very poor societies, many people struggle just to feed themselves and their families, relying extensively on relatives and, sometimes, powerful patrons for assistance. They tend to accept traditional ways of believing and behaving and to distrust outsiders who might threaten their livelihood. However, economic development causes the incomes of many people to rise, thereby enhancing their feelings of security. They tend to become more self-reliant and to adopt **self-expression values**, which emphasize personal satisfaction, freedom to choose one's own path in life, and political liberty.[11] Such people are also more inclined to value liberty for others, including those of different religions, races, ethnic groups, and sexual orientations.

Measurable changes in societal values are reflected in survey data such as the World Values Survey conducted by a research team led by Ronald Inglehart. That study examined dozens of countries over a period of decades and made it possible to locate individuals' attitudes along the two dimensions of value change. The answers that individuals provide to questions can be combined to provide country averages. For example, one of the questions that helps the researchers measure a country's location along the "traditional values" to "secular values" dimension is, "How important is God in your life?" Respondents can use a scale ranging from 10 to 1. Ten means God is very important, and 1 means that God is not at all important. In surveys conducted between 1999 and 2001, almost 70 percent of Pakistanis chose 10 as their answer. Only nine percent of Swedes did.[12] Researchers use several such questions to determine countries' placement along the two dimensions. By using the data, they can construct figures like Figure 4.1.[13]

Self-Expression Values
Values, which emphasize personal satisfaction, freedom of speech, freedom to choose one's own path in life, tolerance toward people with different lifestyles, political liberty, and willingness to challenge authorities.

Figure 4.1 Two Dimensions of Value Change

SOURCE: Data from Ronald Inglehart and Christian Welzel, The WVS Cultural Map of the World. http://www.worldvaluessurvey.org/wvs/articles/folder_published/article_base_54. Accessed June 21, 2013. Presenting the figure in this format was suggested by David J. Samuels, Comparative Politics (New York, Pearson Education, Inc., 2013), p. 194.

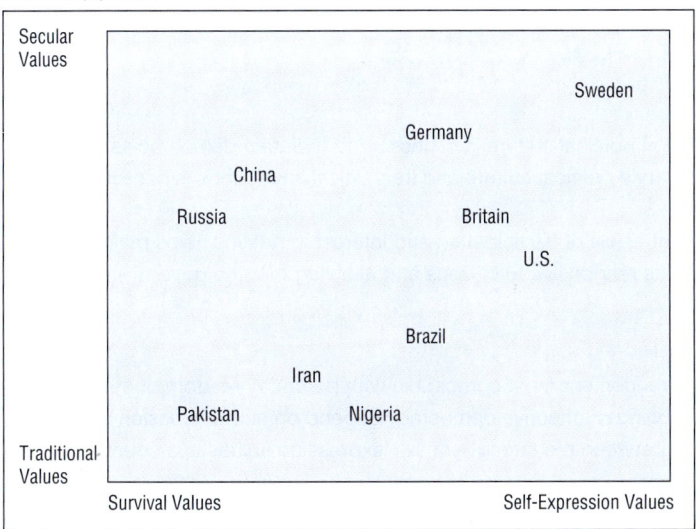

It is noteworthy that Pakistan, Malala Yousafzai's country, is located in the lower-left corner of the figure, indicating that a large proportion of people hold traditional and survival values. Sweden, at the upper right, exemplifies a country in which a large proportion of people hold secular and self-expression values. Interestingly, the United States ranks high on self-expression values but not on secular values, demonstrating that religion remains important for a much higher percentage of Americans (47 percent) than Swedes (9 percent).

One major consequence of rising self-expression values in a country is an increase in the number of individuals willing to challenge authoritarian rule through peaceful demonstrations, boycotts, sit-ins, and strikes. Self-expression values emphasize personal freedom of choice, with which democracy, of all existing political regimes, is most compatible. These values also enable individuals to join like-minded others to demand democratic reforms, and because self-expression values encompass trust in others, they continue to be important for consolidating democracy once authoritarian regimes have been overthrown and for sustaining democracy once it is established. In sum, citizens are likely to demand responsive, effective democracy in countries where high percentages of people hold self-expression values.

The self-expression approach is useful in explaining why people rise up to protest authoritarian rule and make demands of democratic leaders to be more responsive to their needs. Yet it has limitations. One is that there is nothing inevitable about a country becoming more democratic as it becomes more economically developed. Wealthy countries can lapse into authoritarian rule, as Germany did in the 1930s. Moreover, some of the wealthiest countries in the world today, such

In Brief: The Civic Culture and Self-Expression Approaches

Civic Culture Approach
- It seeks to explain what kind of political culture is necessary to maintain democracies.
- Congruence between a country's political culture and its political institutions is necessary for political stability.
- A mix of citizens with different levels of participation and interest in politics helps maintain a balance between keeping governments responsive to citizens and allowing them to govern without undue disruption and instability.

Self-Expression Approach
- Democracy is the political arrangement most compatible with personal freedom of choice.
- The development and functioning of effective democracy depend on self-expression values.
- There is a strong correlation between the strength of self-expression values in a country and its level of effective democracy.

as Kuwait, are not democratic. Another limitation is that self-expression values are not sufficient to ensure the overthrow of authoritarian rule and the establishment of democracy. In the absence of political parties ready to compete for power and offer coherent solutions for the country's problems, supporters of democracy are at a severe disadvantage vis-à-vis better organized groups such as the military or religious organizations. In addition, continuing strikes and demonstrations can sometimes overwhelm fragile new democracies. Finally, the self-expression approach does not directly address considerable differences in citizens' ability to make demands on governments based on income, education, gender and ethnic differences, and the inequalities in capabilities that result from these differences. In summary, the rise of self-expression values is not sufficient in itself to bring about the collapse of authoritarian regimes or create stable, responsive democracies.

Social Capital

4.4 Apply the concept of social capital to explain why some democracies do a better job than others of promoting citizens' capabilities.

Social capital has become an important concept in political science. It helps us address some questions left unanswered by the civic culture and self-expression approaches to political culture. One such question involves how individuals become coordinated for collective action such as demonstrations against authoritarian rule. It is not enough to possess self-expression values and the motivation to protest that those values provide. Their actions have to be coordinated with those of other individuals to meet at specific times and places for particular purposes. Another question is why some democracies do a better job than others of providing access to high-quality health care and education to their citizens. Self-expression values can contribute to the emergence of democracies, but some democracies have greater equality of access to good health care and education than others do. For example, Sweden does a better job than Great Britain of providing access to good education to students from low social and economic backgrounds.[14]

Social capital is the "ability of members of a group to collaborate for shared interests." It is based on "trust among people in a society and their ability to work together for common purposes."[15] The key assumption is that people who trust one another will be able to work together more effectively and share the burdens of achieving goals than people who do not.[16] Scholars using the **social capital approach** have focused on two particular factors that facilitate collaboration: social networks and social trust. **Social networks** are beneficial relationships among individuals rooted in reciprocity. Neighbors who look after each other, people who help a friend move to a new apartment, and alumni associations that assist graduates to find jobs are examples of social networks. Social networks can also enable individuals to work collectively to bring about political change. Black college students used social networks to organize sit-ins at lunch counters in Greensboro, North Carolina, to protest racial segregation during the American civil rights movement.[17] In 2013,

Social Capital Approach
This approach seeks to explain how people manage to collaborate to achieve goals, and why people often find it difficult to cooperate even when it would benefit them.

Social Capital
The ability of members of a group to collaborate for shared interests. It is based on trust among people and their ability to work together for common purposes.

Social Networks
Beneficial relationships among individuals rooted in reciprocity.

activists in Egypt used social networks to collect millions of signatures on petitions demanding the resignation of the Egyptian president.[18]

Online social networks have dramatically increased both the numbers of people who can be organized for collective action and the speed with which they can be mobilized. Facebook, Twitter, and smart phones enable individuals to connect with one another to organize demonstrations, launch protests against corruption, or send photographs of high-ranking officials engaging in corrupt and unethical behavior. For example, in China when the drunken son of a deputy police chief ran over two men in his car in 2010, and killed one of them, he yelled at onlookers, "Sue me if you dare. My father is Li Gang." In the past, he might have gotten away with such behavior. Sons of powerful and politically connected officials were used to escaping punishment. This time, however, networks of online activists all over the country picked up the story quickly and put so much pressure on the government that the son was sentenced to six years in prison.[19]

One caution is that there is a dark side to social networks: They can be used for destructive purposes as well as beneficial ones. For example, high school cliques are social networks used to bully and humiliate students who are not part of the network. The Nazis used networks of sympathetic organizations to orchestrate their rise to power. Social networks can be used to organize riots that kill hundreds of people. Al Qaeda uses online social networks to recruit followers.

Social trust, the other key concept in the social capital approach, helps explain why large numbers of individuals who do not know one another can act together for common goals. **Social trust** is trust that extends beyond one's own group or social network to include most people in a society. Because social trust leads people to take an interest in the well-being of others, the concept helps explain why some countries do a better job than others of providing nearly universal access to high-quality health care and education.[20] Citizens living in countries with high levels of social trust tend to "believe that various groups in society have a shared fate, and that there is a responsibility to provide for those with fewer resources."[21] Higher levels of social trust help make it possible to design public policies in ways to provide these resources and ensure that individuals have "their chances to reach their full potential as humans."[22]

The classic examples of countries with high levels of social trust are Denmark, Norway, and Sweden. These countries are characterized by relatively low levels of income inequality, public policies that promote equality of opportunity for citizens to develop their potential, and extremely low levels of government corruption. Income equality matters because when citizens are not divided by large income differentials, they are more likely to sympathize with one another's plight. Equality of opportunity matters because lower-income citizens can be optimistic about the future for themselves and their children. Honest governments matter because officials who treat citizens impartially reinforce social trust. Impartiality conveys the message that all are treated equally before the law no matter what their income, social class, ethnicity, religion, or gender. Citizens with more resources cannot bribe government officials to give them special privileges.[23]

Social Trust
Trust that extends beyond one's own group or social network to include most people in a society.

High levels of social trust increase citizens' willingness to pay the taxes necessary to support the public policies that provide high-quality health care and education for all. Sweden, which we will use as a case study in Chapter 9, exemplifies that attitude. It has one of the highest levels of social trust of any country in Europe and one of the least corrupt governments of any country in the world. Most Swedes believe government officials will use their tax money efficiently for public purposes and will not waste or steal it.[24] Ninety-eight percent of the taxes people are legally required to pay actually are paid. In contrast, Greece has one of the lowest levels of social trust in Europe, and its government is one of the most corrupt.[25] Many Greek citizens see no reason to pay their taxes

In-Depth: The Good Society—Getting to Denmark

By many measures, Denmark is one of the most successful countries in the world. It is prosperous with an effective democracy that is accountable to its citizens, who enjoy high capabilities. Denmark's infant mortality rate is among the lowest in the world, and its students do extremely well on international tests of educational skills. Homicide is rare, and citizens' civil and political liberties are effectively enforced.

Denmark is also one of the most successful countries in creating equality of opportunity for citizens. Children born into lower-income families have a better chance to achieve higher income levels than in most other prosperous countries, including the United States. One reason is that the students have access to high-quality education through the university level, regardless of family income.

Most Danes are willing to pay the taxes for education and other public services because they have high levels of trust in one another. They believe other Danes will pay their taxes. They trust state officials to be good stewards of public finances. When it has been necessary to make tough compromises on taxes and spending, Danish political leaders have been able to keep public spending in line with government revenues.[26] Moreover, Denmark has been able to sustain the economic performance needed to maximize tax revenues. It consistently ranks among the top countries in the world in economic innovation and competitiveness.[27]

Denmark's success is due to a combination of high income equality, honest government, high levels of social trust, and equality of opportunity. The four come as a package in which each reinforces the other. The result is a political culture in which most citizens see the state as an enabler of individuals' freedom of choice and capabilities, not as a threat to them.

Denmark's success does not mean it would be easy for other countries to follow it or, as political scientist Francis Fukuyama puts it, "to get to Denmark."[28] However, its success demonstrates that it is possible to combine effective and accountable democracy, high capabilities for citizens, and a highly competitive economy. Nor is Denmark alone in achieving these goals. The country's Nordic neighbors have done so, as have Germany and Switzerland.

For Further Discussion

1. Most Danes believe their government promotes individual liberty, whereas many Americans see government generally as a threat to liberty. Why are these perceptions so different?
2. How does social capital help explain Denmark's success? Is there anything else that might explain its success?

because they believe, with good reason, that other citizens are not paying theirs. Nor do they have confidence that tax officials will use their money efficiently or for the benefit of all citizens.

The lesson is that what people do is shaped in part by what they think others are doing. If they think their fellow citizens are cheating, they too are likely to cheat. If they think fellow citizens are honest, they are likely to follow suit. Once these patterns of behavior become established, it is very difficult to change them.

Politics of Identity

4.5 Describe three identities that can become the basis of identity politics.

We have discussed political culture, so far, without examining the ways in which people living in the same country can have very different ways of distinguishing between "us" and "them." This section begins with an analysis of three forms of identity that have played a significant role in politics: ethnicity, nationalism, and religion. These identities often form the basis for political organization and competition with other groups organized on a similar basis. In many cases, this competition is kept within the bounds of normal politics, but in others it leads to violent conflict.

Identity

Ethnicity, nationality, and religion provide people with a sense of place and meaning and a feeling of being part of a larger "us" that distinguishes them from others. These variables often drive political competition as groups vie for recognition and seek to influence how state policies affect people with whom they identify.

Many political scientists believed that ethnic, national, and religious identities would fade in political importance as countries modernized economically and socially. They assumed that as countries became wealthier and more urbanized, people would shift their allegiance to social class such as the working class, advocacy groups such as ones protecting the environment, or social movements such as the women's movement. Although millions of people around the world belong to these kinds of organizations, ethnic, national, and religious identities have not died out. If anything, they have become more significant in many countries.

Ethnicity

Ethnicity
Is a sense of belonging to a group having a common history, language, culture, religion, and geographic region.

Ethnicity is a sense of belonging to a group having a common history, language, culture, religion, and geographic region.[29] Examples of ethnic groups in the United States include Irish-Americans, Chinese-Americans, and Mexican-Americans. Very few countries are ethnically homogeneous. Japan and North and South Korea are the world's most ethnically homogeneous countries; at the other extreme, 20 sub-Saharan African countries rank among the world's most ethnically diverse countries.[30]

In Brief: Distinguishing between Race and Ethnicity

Individuals are usually assigned to different racial categories based on "observable physical characteristics that do not change over a lifetime," such as skin color, hair texture, and facial features. In the United States census, individuals can choose among the following racial categories: White, Black or African-American, American Indian, Alaska Native, Asian, Native Hawaiian or Other Pacific Islander.[31] By contrast, individuals are usually assigned to ethnic categories based on having a common language, culture, or religious practices. These are things that can and do sometimes change during a lifetime.

In large measure, racial and ethnic categories are arbitrary groupings with imprecise and fluid definitions that change over time. Often they have been used as weapons in a struggle for dominance and subordination. Persons in groups with the most power in society get to make such assignments.[32]

Ethnicity is, first and foremost, a social rather than a political identity. People can take pride in their ethnic background and celebrate ethnic food, customs, music, and holidays without linking those to politics. But although ethnic identity is not inherently political, in many countries it becomes politicized, both in wealthy democracies and in low-income countries. In most countries, identity politics is pursued in peaceful ways, using established political institutions. In fact, violent ethnic conflict is highly unusual, even in sub-Saharan Africa. Political scientists James Fearon and David Laitin found thousands of pairs of ethnic groups in Africa that could have been in conflict, but incidents of group violence have been "extremely rare."[33]

Nationalism

Political identity can also take the form of nationalism. Unlike ethnicity, nationalism is inherently political. A **nation** is a group of people sharing a common identity that derives from either having a state of their own or desiring one. Their sense of identity is usually based on a combination of cultural values, ethnicity, language, and living together in a geographical area that they consider their own. **Nationalism** is a sense of pride in one's nation and a desire to control a state representing that nation. This desire to have a state is driven by a population's wish to control its own destiny. Without a state, such people are subject to the authority of the state or states in which they live.

Nationalism can provide people with a strong sense of community, but in political scientist Benedict Anderson's famous definition, a nation is "an imagined political community." This is because "the members of even the smallest nation will never know most of their fellow-members, meet them, or even hear of them, yet in the minds of each lives the image of their communion."[34] Many Americans take pride in the achievements of an American team that wins a gold medal at the Olympics, even though they have never met its members. They are moved by seeing the American flag raised and the national anthem played.[35]

Nationalism has three main components. First, the members of a nation think of themselves as equals united by their common nationality. Whatever the

Nation
A group of people sharing a collective identity that desire to govern themselves through their own state.

Nationalism
A sense of pride in one's nationality and a desire to control a state representing that nationality.

income or social class inequalities among them, they are all equal as Americans, French, or Germans. Second, they see their nation as one among many in a world divided into sovereign nation-states. Finally, in each nation-state, legitimate authority is derived from the people, who should be able to determine their own policies and destiny.[36]

Nationalism does not evolve as part of a natural process. It is constructed by political elites. Historian Eugen Weber provides a classic description of how the French nation was constructed. In the mid-1800s, the lives of most people in France centered on local communities with few connections to the rest of the country. French was a foreign language for many of them, and they had no conception of being part of a French nation. That idea was limited mainly to certain members of the urban middle and upper classes.

French political elites set out to create a French identity among all people living within the country's borders. To accomplish this task, the state built roads and railways that linked villages and people. The state funded a national educational system and required every child to attend school. There they were taught the French language, French history, French literature, and respect for national symbols such as the flag.[37] The goal was to create emotional ties to other citizens and loyalty to the state. Nationalist feelings made them willing to pay taxes and to fight and die for their country.

African, Asian, and Latin American political leaders generated nationalist feelings to mobilize supporters to overthrow the colonial rule of the Dutch, French, Spanish, and British. Nationalism also has been a motivating force for ethnic minorities trapped within the boundaries of states dominated by more powerful ethnic or religious groups. Having their own sovereign state would give them the power to make their own decisions rather than having policies imposed on them by others.[38]

Religion

A third form of identity that plays an important role in politics is a sense of affiliation with others based on religion. Religion is not just about individuals' beliefs in a deity or an afterlife. It also provides them with a way to separate "us" from "them." Different ways of interpreting a sacred text such as the Bible or the Koran can issue in different identities, as in the case of Baptists versus Catholics or Sunni versus Shiite Muslims.[39] In some countries, there are two or more religions, such as Hindus and Muslims in India, but even where one religion predominates, citizens can be divided into separate sects or denominations that can be in conflict. For example, a large majority of citizens of Pakistan are Muslims, but tension exists between the majority Sunni Muslims and the minority Shiite Muslims, who are often the targets of violence.

Religious issues tend to be more salient in politics when a large percentage of a country's population regards religion as an important force in their lives. If religion does not matter much for people, they are not likely to be motivated to

Table 4.1 Importance of Religion in People's Lives, 2006–2008

Country	Percent Saying Religion Is Very Important in Their Lives
Egypt	95%
Iran	78%
Brazil	51%
United States	47%
Great Britain	21%
Russia	14%
Germany	11%
Sweden	9%
China	7%

SOURCE: World Values Survey, http://www.wvsevsdb.com/wvs/WVSAnalizeQuestion.jsp.

engage in political struggle about religious sentiments. There are significant differences among countries in this regard, as can be seen in Table 4.1.

Like ethnic identity, religious identity is not inherently political. Buddhists, Christians, Hindus, and Muslims can practice their faith without connecting it to politics. Nor do religious differences necessarily lead to political conflict. Christians and Jews live together peaceably in the United States, as do Catholics and Protestants in Germany.

Contentious Identity Politics

4.6 Apply primordial, instrumental, and constructivist approaches to explain how identity can lead to violent conflict.

Identity has been the source of contentious politics in many countries. Often, political conflict based on identity is contained within the bounds of normal politics. For example, this has been the case for immigration of Muslims from the Middle East into European countries. Their presence has led to increasing tensions between the immigrants and parts of the native-born majority in several countries. Some natives fear that immigrants threaten their jobs and national identity and believe that they are a drain on public finances. Immigrants typically respond by saying that natives have no appreciation of how hard it is to integrate in European societies or how much discrimination they face.[40]

Such cultural tensions are present even in the Nordic countries of Denmark, Finland, Norway, and Sweden. Many citizens of the Nordic countries hold self-expression values including equality of men and women, freedom of speech, and secularism. These values differ from those of many Muslim immigrants who come from poorer countries where traditional and survival values predominate. Some Scandinavians grumble about the costs of supporting immigrants and refugees. They contend that immigrants and refugees receive more in tax revenues than they contribute and are free-riding on the contributions of native-born citizens. These controversies raise the possibility than citizens of Denmark, Norway, and Sweden will be less willing to pay the taxes that sustain high levels of public services. The controversies are forcing governments to decide how much tolerance should be allowed for immigrants whose values sometimes vary significantly from those of native-born citizens. Governments also have to decide about whether to limit flows of immigrants as well as refugees from regions of the world torn by violence.[41]

Generally speaking, these controversies tend to be settled within the bounds of normal politics, but there are exceptions. Riots by young Muslim immigrants have occurred in several European cities. In 2011 a Norwegian extremist who claimed to be protecting Norwegian ethnicity, culture, and Christianity from Islamic immigration set off a bomb in the capital that killed eight people; he went on to slaughter 69 young people at a camp sponsored by the Norwegian Labor Party. The killer targeted them because he believed their party had been too sympathetic to Muslim immigrants.

Identity-based politics has led to much higher levels of violence in certain other parts of the world. This violence can take different forms. One is **mob violence**, in which members of one ethnic, nationalist, or religious group target people from another in response to a perceived grievance. Mob violence occurs suddenly and, although it can be intense while it lasts, it tends to die down just as quickly. Typically, it is limited to particular cities or regions rather than engulfing an entire country in violence. Another, much more deadly form of violence is **civil war**, defined as "fighting between agents of state and organized non-state groups who seek to take control of a government, take power in a region, or use violence to change government policies."[42] In the Democratic Republic of the Congo between 1998 and 2008, more than two and a half million people are estimated to have died as a consequence of civil war. Most victims were civilians rather than armed combatants. Finally, another destructive form is **genocide**, a state-sponsored policy to kill all members of a particular ethnic, nationalist, or religious group. The worst example of genocide in recent history occurred during World War II, when the Nazis tried to exterminate all European Jews as well as people of other ethnic groups deemed to be inferior. A more recent example occurred in Rwanda in 1994, when Hutu leaders incited members of their group to murder an estimated 800,000 Tutsis along with any moderate Hutus who tried to assist them.

Explaining Why Identity Leads to Violence

Thousands of ethnic, nationalist, and religious groups around the world live in close proximity without violence erupting between them. For example, there is no large-scale violence between Irish-Americans and Italian-Americans or between the Scottish and the English. In places where large-scale violence has

---

Mob Violence
Violence in which members of one ethnic, nationalist, or religious group target people from another in response to a perceived grievance.

Civil War
Fighting between agents of state and organized non-state groups who seek to take control of a government, take power in a region, or use violence to change government policies.

Genocide
A state-sponsored policy of deliberately and systematically killing all members of a particular ethnic group, nationality, or religion.

Comparative Political Analysis: Is Ethnic Diversity the Root Cause of Civil Wars?

Problem

In the past 65 years, many more people have died in wars fought inside countries than in wars fought between countries. Civil wars have devastating effects on human capabilities. They disrupt health care and agricultural production, typically causing more deaths from disease and famine than from combat. Education suffers as well. There are gross violations of civil and political rights, and rape is sometimes used to terrorize local populations. What causes these destructive wars?

Methods and Hypothesis

One popular hypothesis is that ethnic diversity is the root cause of civil wars. James Fearon and David Laitin have tested this hypothesis as well as the alternative hypothesis that attributes civil war to state weakness.

Operationalizing Concepts

The authors use three concepts to test the competing hypotheses:

1. Civil war is defined as "fighting between agents of state and organized non-state groups who seek to take control of a government, take power in a region, or use violence to change government policies." To count as a civil war, the conflict must result in at least 1,000 deaths with a yearly average death toll of at least 100, and at least 100 persons must have been killed on each side.
2. Ethnic diversity is defined using an index of ethnic fractionalization based on the probability that two randomly selected individuals in a country come from different ethnic groups.
3. State weakness is defined using per capita income as a proxy for state weakness. The assumption here is that the poorer the country, the more likely it is to have a weak state.

Results

The authors find no support for the hypothesis that ethnic diversity is the root cause of civil war. They acknowledge that ethnic grievances may motivate people to rebel, but their goal is not to explain what motivates rebellion but, rather, to find out "what factors distinguish countries that have tended to have civil wars from those that have not."[43] There is no consistent relationship between a country's degree of ethnic diversity and the outbreak of civil war once levels of income are taken into account. Among countries at the same income level, more ethnically diverse countries have no greater likelihood of civil war than less diverse countries. State weakness turns out to be a better explanation for the outbreak of civil war. Weak states do not have the administrative, military, and policing abilities to control all areas of a country and suppress rebels.

For Further Discussion

1. This Comparative Political Analysis box and the final section of chapter 2 both use "weak states" as a variable, but they use different operational definitions of the concept. Why? Is one preferable to the other?
2. Based on the authors' findings, what would be the best way for states to prevent civil wars and the devastating consequences they have on citizens' capabilities?

Source: James D. Fearon and David D. Laitin, "Ethnicity, Insurgency, and Civil War," *American Political Science Review* 97 (2003), 75–90.

Primordialism
This approach to understanding identity assumes that group identities emerge naturally as a result of differences in race, nationality, and religion, can be traced far back into the past, and tend to persist with little change once formed.

Instrumentalism
This approach to identity assumes that self-seeking political elites manipulate political identity for personal advantage.

Constructivism
This approach to political culture assumes that identities are not simply found ready-made but are socially constructed; they are continually refined and redefined.

broken out, the groups involved have often lived close to each other for decades without violence. This raises the question of why identity differences lead to violence in some instances but not others.

One approach to explaining violence among groups is known as **primordialism**. This approach assumes that violent conflict between ethnic, nationalist, or religious groups is the result of hostilities with roots that can extend back to time immemorial. Some scholars who favor this approach assume that intergroup conflict is inherent in human nature. One of them is Harvard political scientist Samuel Huntington, who argued in *The Clash of Civilizations* that "for self-definition and motivation people need enemies. . . . They naturally distrust and see as threats those who are different and have the capability to harm them."[44] Once groups are defined in this way, conflict between them becomes inevitable. However, this argument does not explain fully how Croats and Serbs in Yugoslavia, Hutus and Tutsis in Rwanda, and Christians and Muslims in Nigeria were able to live alongside each other peacefully for decades. Primordial explanations of identity conflict also do not explain fully why violent conflict breaks out in certain regions of a country or certain cities rather than in others.

Another approach to explaining why conflict arises is **instrumentalism**. Its proponents argue that violence is provoked by political leaders who manipulate symbols and beliefs to set groups against each other for political gain. This approach has been used to explain cases of violence between ethnic groups in Rwanda. Hutu leaders initiated genocide against the Tutsi in 1994 to consolidate their hold on power, whipping up ethnic hatred to achieve their goal. The instrumentalist approach has proved useful for explaining why ethnic and religious violence breaks out in some areas of a country or city and not in others, but it has its limits. Political leaders cannot manipulate people's identities in any way they desire at any time. Nor can they construct entirely new identities to suit their purposes. They must work within the framework of identities that already exist.

The final approach used to explain how identities are formed and why they sometimes lead to violence is known as **constructivism**. It points out that the criteria we employ to draw boundaries between ethnic and racial groups are not obvious or inherent. They are socially constructed and can differ considerably from one society, or one historical period, to another. Identities do not derive from time immemorial and remain fixed ever after, as some have argued. Instead, they change over time in a continuing process of refinement and redefinition.[45] Societies tend to have one socially constructed master cleavage, such as that between whites and blacks in the United States, Hutus and Tutsis in Rwanda, and Muslims and Hindus in India. Extremists can use an incident that happens spontaneously, or manufacture one, to start violence by placing the incident into the larger context of that master cleavage. The social constructivist approach suggests both that cultures change more than primordialists assume and that cultures are less easily manipulated than instrumentalists believe. Although the social constructivist approach does a better job than the other two of explaining identity formation, it does not explain why ethnic, national, or religious conflict occurs at specific times in specific locations.

Political Culture, Identity, and the Good Society

4.7 Explain the advantages of using scatter diagrams, identify the independent and dependent variables in the following scatter diagram, and summarize the findings.

We conclude the chapter with an examination of how political culture and political identity affect citizens' capabilities, testing a hypothesis suggested by the social capital approach. That hypothesis contends that citizens living in countries with high levels of social trust are more likely to be willing to help those with fewer resources achieve "their full potential as humans."[46] We will divide the hypothesis into four hypotheses, which we will test using **scatter diagrams** rather than the bar charts of previous chapters. The strength of bar charts is their ability to present a great deal of data in an easily understood manner; a glance at the height of the bars conveys relationships among variables quickly. This simplicity, however, comes at a cost. Bar charts do not allow us to compare individual countries or to determine whether they fit the relationship a hypothesis predicts. Scatter diagrams do. When countries do not fit the expected pattern, we are led to ask why. That question becomes the basis for further research that will help us gain a better understanding of the relationships among variables. Neither bar charts nor scatter diagrams offers the ideal way to test all hypotheses across the board, and each has its strengths and weaknesses. In the case of the following scatter diagrams, it is useful to keep in mind that the findings are correlations. They do not show causation.[47]

Scatter Diagram
A method of examining the relationship between two variables. The values of the independent variable are plotted on the X axis and the values of the dependent variable on the Y axis. The pattern of points formed by where the X and Y values intersect reveals whether there is any relationship between the two variables and how strong it is.

Physical Well-being

Our first hypothesis is that the higher the level of generalized social trusts in a country (independent variable), the lower the rate of infant mortality (dependent variable). We operationally define the level of social trust by using revised and updated data from the 2005–2008 World Values Survey. In the survey, participants were asked whether they agreed with the statement that "Most people can be trusted." The responses vary from a high of 49.9 percent agreement in Norway to only 1.96 percent in Trinidad and Tobago.[48] Infant mortality rates as a proxy for well-being are taken from our data set used in previous chapters.

The independent variable, level of social trust, is on the horizontal (or x) axis in Figure 4.2. The dependent variable, infant mortality rate, is on the vertical (y) axis of the figure. Each point in the figure represents a country.

As the scatter diagram shows, there is modest support for the hypothesis. Infant mortality tends to be lower in countries where there are higher levels of trust.[49] The straight line that appears in the scatter diagram helps us see this relationship. Called a regression line, it is drawn so that it fits the points in the scatter diagram as closely as possible. In this particular scatter diagram, it slopes downward from left to right, showing that the higher the value of the independent

Figure 4.2 Social Trust and Infant Mortality Rates

SOURCES: Data Source for Social Trust: Jan Delhey, Kenneth Newton, and Christian Welzel, "How General Is Trust in 'Most People'? Data supplied by Christian Welzel, March 13, 2012.

Data Source for Infant Mortality: Word Bank, World Development Indicators. http://databank.worldbank.org/ddp/home.do?Step=12&id=4&CNO=2.

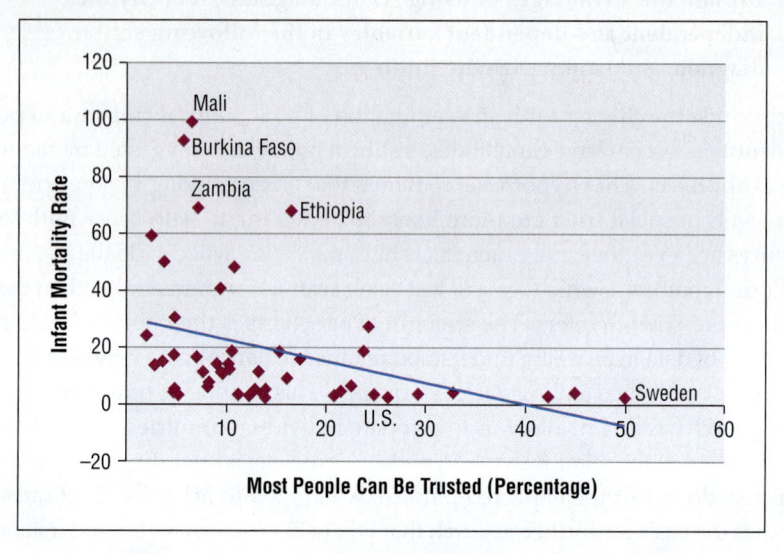

variable (trust), the lower the value of the dependent variable (infant mortality). Such a pattern is called a negative correlation. It is important to keep in mind that negative correlation does not mean there is no relationship between the variables. Rather, it means that as the value of the independent variable (trust in this case) increases, the value of the dependent variable (infant mortality) decreases.

The distribution of countries in the figure suggests other variables are at work in addition to social trust. For example, there are four countries at the top left corner of the figure, Zambia, Mali, Burkina Faso, and Ethiopia, that stand apart from the others, having extremely high infant mortality rates of over 60 per 1,000. One of the main advantages of using scatter diagrams is how they help us identify **outliers**, or countries that stand far apart from others. Why are their infant mortality rates so much higher? The outliers encourage thinking about other variables that might affect infant mortality in addition to social trust. Zambia, Mali, Burkina Faso, and Ethiopia are all extremely poor countries in sub-Saharan Africa. This suggests that another important variable in explaining levels of infant mortality is a country's per capita income.

Outliers
Countries that do not fit an expected pattern in a scattergram.

Informed Decision Making

The literature on social trust suggests that people living in countries with higher levels of social trust are more willing to provide all citizens with the opportunities to develop their capabilities. If this is the case, then they should be willing to provide everyone with the opportunity to become literate. This leads to

Figure 4.3 Social trust and Literacy Rates

SOURCE: Data Source for Adult Literacy: United Nations Development Program. *International Human Development Indicators*, http://hdrstats.undp.org/en/indicators/101406.html

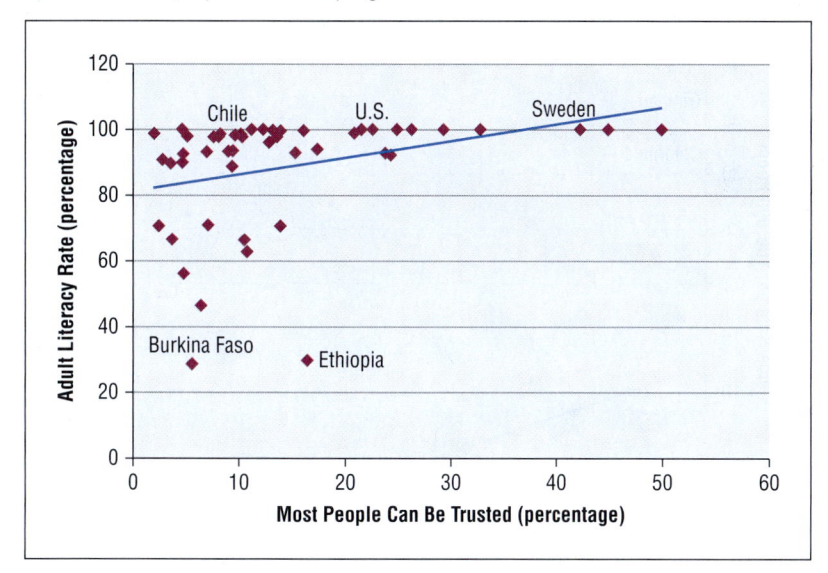

the hypothesis that the higher the level of social trust in a country, the higher the levels of adult literacy. The results of testing this hypothesis can be seen in Figure 4.3.

There is a modest relationship in the expected direction: The higher the level of social trust, the higher the literacy rate. However, a number of countries do not fit the expected pattern. There are several countries with low levels of social trust that have very high levels of literacy. One of them is Chile, where 98.6 percent of adults are literate, yet only 8 percent of people say most people can be trusted. There are also countries with very similar levels of trust that vary dramatically in the level of literacy. Burkina Faso and Ethiopia are outliers with literacy rates below 40 percent. They are two of the five outliers we identified in Figure 4.1. They are extremely poor countries with limited resources to spend on education.

Safety

It seems reasonable to expect that countries with high levels of trust among people will have lower levels of homicides than those with low levels of trust. We can test the validity of this hypothesis by using data on trust and operationally defining homicide rates per 100,000 people from the data set for *The Good Society*. The results can be seen in Figure 4.4.

There is modest support for the hypothesis that the higher the level of trust in a country, the lower the murder rate. For example, Sweden has the highest level of trust and one of the lowest homicide rates, whereas the United States

Figure 4.4 Social Trust and Homicide Rates

SOURCES: Data Source for Homicide Rates: *UNODC Global Study on Homicide*, 2011, http://www.unodc.org/unodc/en/data-and-analysis/homicide.html.

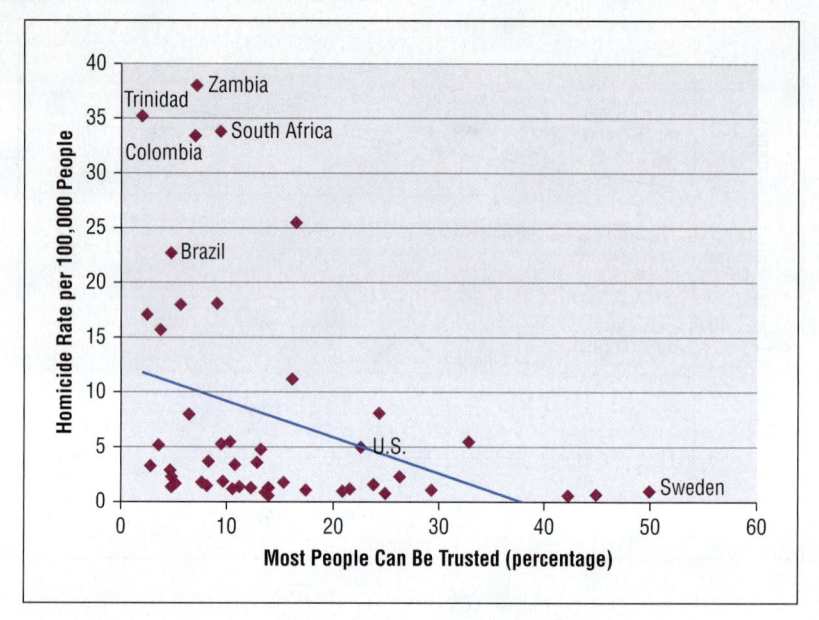

has lower trust and a higher homicide rate. However, as we have seen in tests of the other hypotheses, there are numerous exceptions. Four countries have exceptionally high homicide rates of over 30 per 100,000, and there is no clear, single variable that explains why their homicide rates are so high. Colombia's rate is explained in large part by conflict between government paramilitary forces and rebels funded by cocaine trade and by ongoing gang warfare to control the trade.

Democracy

Finally, we test the hypothesis that the higher the level of social trust in a country, the higher its level of democracy is likely to be. A country's level of democracy is operationalized using the *Economist* Democracy Index 2012. The highest democracy score in the index is ten, with a score of zero indicating the most extreme level of authoritarianism.[50] The results of the test can be seen in Figure 4.5.

The scatter diagram shows generally strong support for the hypothesis. The higher a country's level of social trust, the higher is its democracy index. Norway, Sweden, and Switzerland have the highest levels of social trust and very high democracy scores. Countries with lower levels of social trust also have lower scores on the democracy index. South Korea's location in the scatter diagram demonstrates that it is possible to have a relatively high level of

Figure 4.5 Social Trust and Democracy

SOURCES: Data Source for Democracy: *Economist* Democracy Index 2012.

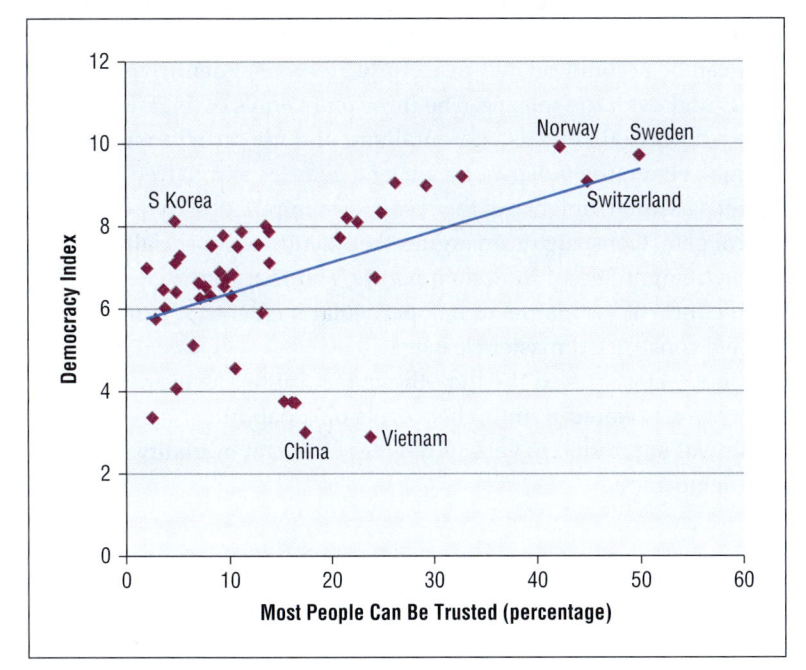

democracy despite a low level of social trust. China and South Vietnam, two countries with communist party leadership, are outliers with medium levels of social trust but very low democracy scores.

Conclusion

We began by defining political culture and then discussed two approaches to using political culture in the study of comparative politics: the civic culture and self-expression approaches. The civic culture approach suggests that a mix of citizens with different levels of participation and interest in politics helps maintain a balance between keeping governments responsive to citizens and allowing them to operate without undue disruption and instability. The self-expression approach explains that economic development and social change contribute to the emergence of self-expression values. These values motivate individuals to challenge authoritarian rule and demand democracy. They also motivate citizens to demand effective and accountable government once democracy is established. We also examined the concept of social capital. It explains how social networks and social trust enable individuals to engage in collective action to challenge authoritarian rule. The approach also helps explain how high levels of social trust enable people to work together. It is correlated with more effective and accountable democratic government and with more equal distribution of capabilities in countries.

The chapter focused next on three of the most important forms of political identity: ethnicity, nationalism, and religion. In many countries, these political identities can be accommodated peacefully. In others, identity politics has led to tensions and even to violence. The three main ways of explaining such violence are primordialism, instrumentalism, and constructivism. Primordial explanations blame the violence on ancient rivalries and hatred. Instrumental explanations assume violence is the result of manipulation by political leaders for political gain. Constructivism argues that identities are socially constructed, rather than being inherent in human nature, and that conflict results from the successful efforts of instigators to link particular incidents or rumors to a country's socially constructed master cleavage.

The final section tested the hypothesis that higher levels of social trust in a country are associated with higher levels of capabilities. We found that the hypothesis was supported to various degrees for infant mortality, literacy, homicide, and democracy.

Suggested Readings

Benedict Anderson, *Imagined Communities: Reflections on the Origins and Spread of Nationalism* (New York: Verso, 1991). A classic exploration of how concepts of nation and nationalism emerged, changed over time, and gained so much emotional attachment that people are willing to die for them.

Peter A. Hall and Michelle Lamont (eds.), *Successful Societies: How Institutions and Culture Affect Health* (New York: Cambridge University Press, 2009). Successful societies are defined as the ones that enhance people's capabilities to lead the kinds of lives they have reason to value. The authors focus on how culture and institutions interact to shape peoples' opportunities to lead healthy lives.

Samuel P. Huntington, *The Clash of Civilizations and the Remaking of World Order* (New York: Touchstone, 1997). Argues that in the twenty-first century, the fundamental source of conflict in world politics will be cultural conflict between different civilizations.

Ronald Inglehart and Christian Welzel, *Modernization, Cultural Change, and Democracy: The Human Development Sequence* (New York: Cambridge University Press, 2005). The authors argue that social and economic modernization lead to cultural change emphasizing self-expression values and demands for democracy.

Bo Rothstein, *The Quality of Government: Corruption, Social Trust, and Inequality in International Perspective* (New York: Cambridge University Press, 2011). Examines how the quality of government affects the quality of life and the emergence of social capital.

Critical Thinking Questions

1. Why do political scientists make a distinction between culture and political culture? Why not simply use culture and dispense with the concept of political culture?

2. Has civic culture in the United States deteriorated? How could you tell and why would it matter for politics?

3. The United States and Sweden have similar percentages of citizens holding self-expression values, but Sweden has a much higher percentage holding secular values (Figure 4.1). How might this difference in secular values shape differences in which issues become politically important in the two countries?

4. Which other variables, in addition to social trust, might explain differences in infant mortality, literacy, and homicide among countries with similar levels of income such as Sweden and the United States?

5. For some people, it is simple to understand why violence occurs among groups of people with different identities: It is part of human nature to behave this way. What are the problems with this explanation of violence among identity groups? Does it have any merit?

Chapter 5
Political Economy

Learning Objectives

5.1 Distinguish between state and market systems for producing and allocating goods and services.

5.2 Explain how economies that rely on markets require states to work and are alternatives to them.

5.3 Identify the advantages of market systems.

5.4 Identify the shortcomings of market systems.

5.5 Summarize historical swings in the balance between states and markets.

5.6 Define globalization and evaluate whether it contributes to or thwarts the good society.

5.7 Describe the different ways states intervene in the economy.

5.8 Evaluate the performance of state and market systems according to the standards of the good society.

Introduction

5.1 **Distinguish between state and market systems for producing and allocating goods and services.**

The good society depends on institutional arrangements that enhance people's capabilities. In Chapter 2, we saw that people who live in strong states that can translate demands into effective policies enjoyed greater life chances than those who lived in weak states that could not produce order or deliver on their policy commitments. In Chapter 4, we observed that some cultures, such as those that promoted generalized trust, led to better results than those in which people were suspicious and felt no sense of obligation to each other. In this chapter, we consider the proper sphere or range of state activity. Take the case, for example, of the former Soviet Union, which demonstrated the perils of too much state intervention. State control of the economy, the media, the arts, and civic life in the Soviet Union came at the expense of freedom, initiative, prosperity, and justice. The planned economy led to economic ruin, state censorship led to uninspiring art, political control of the media led to propaganda, Communist Party domination led to bureaucratic inertia, and state control of civic associations led to a spiritless public life.

If the Soviet Union was a cautionary tale about the evils of too much state intervention, then the introduction of capitalism into post-Soviet Russia is a moral tale about the perils of too little state involvement. People lived in fear of thugs and racketeers because the state was unable to protect them, much as they had previously lived in fear of the secret police under communism. Prosperity and enterprise were no longer foreclosed by a command economy run by the state but were now beyond reach because the state had difficulty upholding contracts; preventing fraud and extortion by criminal syndicates; or creating a stable, predictable environment for production and exchange. Court decisions that were for sale were as arbitrary and unfair a way of dispensing justice as when the state told judges how to decide cases. Bribes were as effective as Communist Party orders had once been in motivating state officials. Thus, Russia's second marriage, in which it suffered at the hands of a negligent and unfaithful state, was no better than its first, when Russia suffered at the hands of a domineering and abusive one.[1]

How much state activity is enough, we might ask, to produce the good society? This question applies most with regard to the role of the state in the economy. "Fundamentally," the economist Milton Friedman writes, "there are only two ways to coordinate the economic activities of millions. One is central planning by the government; the other depends on the voluntary cooperation of individuals—the technique of the marketplace."[2] According to the economist Joseph E. Stiglitz, the struggle between these two alternatives is the defining political question of our age. Stiglitz points out that "The battle of ideas between those who advocate a minimalist role for the state and those who believe that there is a greater need for government . . . is being fought in country after country, in the developing world no less than in the developed, [and] on both sides of the Atlantic and Pacific."[3] What balance between states and markets most enhances people's capabilities and contributes to the good society? Under communism, as we just saw, citizens in the former Soviet Union suffered from too much state power and not enough markets. When communism fell, Russians suffered from the opposite disorder, too much market and not enough state control.

According to political economist Charles Lindblom, markets have always been with us, but market *systems* have not. Records of people, cities, and states engaging in exchange go back to antiquity, but most pre-modern economic activity was not organized for the market. Households were self-sufficient, producing for their own use, and they infrequently engaged in exchange with others. Today, by contrast, almost all countries use market systems to organize and coordinate production. The term **market system** refers to an economy in which production for profit is intended for and coordinated through private exchanges between buyers and sellers.

European states were intent on shifting from household production to production for the market because the latter was more efficient and would produce more taxable wealth. However, the change was fraught with conflict because peasants at home and natives in the colonies resisted producing for the market. They saw market production as a threat to their welfare because it exposed them to more risk and uncertainty than subsistence production. States interested in increasing their revenue brought their subjects who were interested in defending their security into the market system at the point of a gun.[4]

Since then, the market system has become more extensive in terms of its global reach. Today, countries are engaged in more trade with one another than ever before. Exports and imports make up a larger proportion of their GNP than in the past. Foreign direct investment, in which firms invest outside of their own economies, has risen even faster than foreign trade. The growth in trade and foreign direct investment, however, pale in comparison to the growth in international financial transactions. International borrowing and lending, as well as currency trading, have increased spectacularly.

The market system has become not only more extensive, diffusing over the entire globe, but more intensive, involving more social transactions. In developed societies, and increasingly in developing societies as well, people rely on the market to satisfy their needs. Goods and services that families previously provided for themselves, such as caring for their children or cooking their own food, are now outsourced to the market in the form of day care centers and eating at McDonalds. We now go to the market to meet needs that people once satisfied in other ways.

States determine how extensive markets are. For example, they can discourage foreign trade by placing taxes on imported goods or encourage it by permitting imports to compete with domestic goods on a level playing field. Similarly, states can pass laws that discourage foreign investment or adopt laws

Market Systems
Market systems exist where productive assets are privately owned and employed to earn profits for their owners. Production is geared to produce goods for sale, and prices are set by market forces through supply and demand.

that encourage it. They can place strict controls on their currency or allow it to move freely across borders. In addition, states sign treaties and join international organizations that set the rules for exchange between countries. These rules can either promote or inhibit the **extensive growth of markets**.[5]

Similarly, states also determine how intensive markets are. They can restrict what is for sale, allowing some exchanges but blocking others, such as the sale of sexual favors or body parts.[6] In effect, states can say that there are some things money should not buy. They make these decisions based on competing pressures they receive from those who benefit from the extensive and **intensive growth of markets** and those who do not.

In this chapter, we first examine the relationship between states and markets. At the same time that states provide an alternative to markets, markets require states in order to thrive. States set the ground rules without which markets cannot work. We then describe the advantages and disadvantages of market systems. Next, we examine some of the ways states try to manage market systems. Finally, we review whether market-oriented or state-directed forms of political economy contribute most to people's capabilities.

In Brief: Market Systems

- Goods are produced for sale through commodity production.
- Productive assets are privately owned and employed to earn profits for their owners.
- Prices are not administered but set through supply and demand.

Extensive Growth of Markets
Refers to the broader geographic reach of market systems to include more people and places.

Intensive Growth of Markets
Refers to the broader range of activities that become part of, or are included within, the market system. People satisfy more of their needs through the market.

States and Markets

5.2 Explain how economies that rely on markets require states to work and are alternatives to them.

The triumph of market systems, their extensive and intensive growth, has been lauded as the triumph of freedom. In this view, states are about rules and compulsion; market systems are about choice and individual expression. In fact, although markets may lack the coercive apparatus of courts, jails, and police that states possess, their disciplinary power is just as great. "Like the state," Lindblom writes, "the market system is a method of controlling and coordinating people's behavior."[7] In market systems, production is coordinated not by a central plan but "through the mutual interaction of buyers and sellers."[8] The price at which firms sell their goods or what workers receive in wages obey the unseen imperatives of the market, like iron filings caught in an invisible magnetic force field. The magnet at one end of the force field is called "supply," and the magnet at the other end is called "demand."[9] People respond to shifts in the market, in the balance between supply and demand, but no one controls it. Producers have no choice but to reduce prices when demand is slack and to increase prices when demand is high if they want to remain in business. Those who misread or respond too late to market signals do so at their peril.

Public Goods
Goods that cannot be withheld from those who don't pay for them.

Market systems however, require states to function and cannot exist without them. Market systems need states to create a common currency to facilitate trade and exchange; to enforce contracts; and to supply **public goods**, such as transportation networks and police protection that markets cannot furnish themselves.[10] The state makes capital viable and promotes economic growth by creating and structuring markets in such a way that creativity and investments pay off. The visible hand of the state supplements the invisible hand of the market. Market freedom requires state compulsion to thrive.

Economist John McMillan uses the metaphor of the Internet to explain how markets require states to work. Instead of connecting buyers and sellers to each other, the Internet connects computers to other computers without any centralized agency directing its operation, but the anarchic, unplanned quality of the Internet rests on a foundation created by the state. The United States subsidized the Internet's initial development, created common technical standards so that computers could communicate with one another, managed the assignment of names so that each web address would be unique, and created and enforced laws against the spread of computer viruses.[11]

Markets, political economist John Zysman offers, "do not exist or operate apart from the rules and institutions that establish them." Such rules "structure how buying and selling, the very organization of production, takes place."[12] Thus, states make market systems possible, establishing the ground rules that permit markets to work at all. Consider, for example, the board game "Monopoly," which is intended to replicate a market in real estate that stretches from the low-rent district of Mediterranean and Baltic Avenues to the expensive properties of Park Place and Boardwalk. Players are given money and the opportunity to buy, sell, and trade different properties. Now, consider playing "Monopoly" if there were no rules stipulating what happened if you landed on someone else's property, no rules about how you could mortgage your property to raise cash, and no rules about how you could build houses and hotels to increase the value of your property. "Monopoly" is unplayable without rules. Markets are only as good as the rules states make to support them. The historian Jacques Barzun attributed the emergence of Venice as the center of international trade in the mid-seventeenth century to the quality of its regulatory, or rule-making, political institutions,[13] and historian Niall Ferguson made a similar point in explaining why London, rather than Paris, emerged as the epicenter of world capitalism in the eighteenth century. Ferguson writes, "The key difference between France and Britain in the eighteenth century, then, was not a matter of economic resources. France had more. Rather, it was a matter of institutions."[14] The reason some countries prospered while others did not is explained, economist John McMillan argues, "by the quality of their institutions," the rules that states design for them.[15] The economists Daren Acemoglu and James Robinson reinforce this point in their magisterial book, *Why Nations Fail*, when they argue that "getting the institutions right" determines why some countries prosper while others do not. According to these authors, "Institutional differences play the critical role in explaining economic growth through the ages."[16] They found some states create "inclusive institutions" that offer incentives that encourage people "to put their talents and skills to best use and . . . promote technological innovation that leads to greater productivity,"[17] whereas other states have "extractive institutions" that do not create incentives for people to save, invest, and innovate. Countries with inclusive institutions—secure property rights, the rule of law, public services, political pluralism, and political capacity—display the prosperous harmony depicted in Lorenzetti's fresco of Good Government that we described in the preface; those with extractive institutions exhibit the ugly stains of Bad Government represented in his other fresco.

The balance between political and market forces within a country, or what is referred to as its **political economy**, is critical in determining whether it will meet the minimal conditions of the good society. As Jacob S. Hacker and Paul Pierson explain, "the debate should not be over whether government is involved in the formation of markets. It always is. The debate should be over whether it is involved in a manner conducive to a good society."[18] For example, as we saw previously, Russia first suffered from too much state control and then from markets that were not sufficiently regulated. Both forms of economic management failed to produce results that permitted Russians to enjoy flourishing lives.

Political Economy
The manner in which states influence the economy and, reciprocally, how the economy affects states; the mutual influence of politics and economics.

The Advantages of Market Systems

5.3 Identify the advantages of market systems.

Security was surprisingly haphazard on July 25, 1959, for a meeting in Moscow between leaders of the two superpowers, the United States and the Soviet Union. Reporters and camera operators jostled with one another amid workers still preparing for the opening of the American National Exhibition. The Exhibition, the first of its kind in the Soviet Union since the Communists took power in 1917, would display the achievements of American capitalism. More than 800 corporations donated exhibits, including color televisions and a model home, extolling the American way of life. Vice President Richard M. Nixon had arrived to cut the ceremonial ribbon officially opening the Exhibition while his host, Soviet premier Nikita S. Khrushchev, looked on with satisfaction.

This trivial effort to build understanding between Cold War rivals quickly took an ominous turn. The two leaders began to argue and debate the relative merits of capitalism and communism. They chided each other as they passed through a model kitchen. Khrushchev complained about its affordability and workmanship. Nixon lauded its durability and technology. The confrontation climaxed when Nixon led Khrushchev into an exhibit of a working television studio and invited him to make some remarks. Khrushchev threw down the gauntlet. He claimed that the United States was three times older than the Soviet Union, but that the Soviet Union, despite its late start, would soon out-produce its rival. Communism would win the battle of the standard of living over capitalism. The Soviet Union would soon surpass the United States in productivity and production and look in its rearview mirror to wave as it sped by.[19]

The kitchen debate, as this small episode from the Cold War was called, had no apparent winner at the time, but fifty years of subsequent history has given a clear, unequivocal answer to the issue the leaders debated at the opening of the American Exhibition in Moscow. The Soviet model of the planned economy was no match for the dynamism of American capitalism. Far from overtaking the American economy as Khrushchev confidently predicted, the Soviet Union fell further and further behind, until it collapsed completely. In 1990, the average Soviet living standard was only one-third that of the average American. The Soviet Union lost the Cold War not on the battlefield but in the war of production between planned economies and market-based economic systems. Market systems were nimble, while planned economies were all thumbs; the former was innovative, the latter was immobile. "When it comes to the question of which system today is the most effective at generating rising standards of living," *New York Times* columnist Thomas A. Friedman writes, "the historical debate is over. The answer is free-market capitalism."[20] "There Is No Alternative," according to former British prime minister Margaret Thatcher. Societies either adopt market systems or suffer—as happened with the Soviet Union—being left behind in poverty and stagnation.

Market systems have many advantages. First, they are extraordinarily dynamic, promoting the development of new products and more efficient production methods and technologies. Competitive pressures and the thirst for profits give entrepreneurs strong incentives to produce goods and services that consumers want as cheaply as possible. Firms that fail to innovate and become more productive lose market share and profits to those that do. The Austrian economist Joseph Schumpeter described the unceasing transformation that market systems create as a process of "creative destruction." New products and more efficient technologies and production methods sweep away old firms, goods, skills, and even whole industries. What is new today will be seized on for revision and improvement tomorrow as firms continue to innovate under the pressure of competition and their desire for profits.

Second, market systems are enormously productive. As Marx and Engels acknowledged in *The Communist Manifesto* more than 150 years ago, capitalism developed "more massive and more colossal productive forces than have all the preceding generations put together."[21] The application of science to industry, advances in communication and transportation, and the development of more efficient ways to deploy and motivate labor all contributed to higher levels of labor productivity. Half the number of workers employed could now turn out twice as much as before. The result has been unimaginable wealth: rising per capita incomes, higher standards of living, and larger gross national products.

Finally, it appears that market systems enhance the prospects of democracy and political rights. Michael Mandelbaum writes, "The key to establishing a working democracy, and in particular the institutions of liberty, has been the free-market economy."[22] In contrast to planned economies, in which the state determines what is produced, what people are paid, where production takes place, and where profits are invested, the reach of the state within market systems is limited. The potential threat of an all-powerful state is stymied by removing such decisions from the state's purview. Market systems separate economic power from political power, permitting them to offset each other. In contrast, planned economies combine economic and political power in the hands of the state, foreclosing the development of countervailing economic power to it.[23] Although market systems are no guarantee of democracy and political freedom—one need only recall how well capitalism functioned in Nazi Germany or how well the introduction of markets has fared in Communist China—liberal democracy has had the most success in societies with market systems and has been absent from societies without them.

The Dark Side of Markets

5.4 Identify the shortcomings of market systems.

The American economic model, based on low taxes, weak unions, and small government, produced results that were the envy of the world in the 1990s. The economy grew, creating new jobs and new wealth. With credit cheap and banks anxious to lend, many people took out mortgages to purchase homes, causing prices to rise. The housing boom attracted more buyers anxious to take advantage of rising property values, pushing up housing prices even more. The market was feeding on itself. Then the music stopped. Investors who provided seed money for housing loans became skeptical of the values underlying the mortgage securities they bought. As the money to finance new mortgages dried up, housing prices began to plummet. In Fort Myers, Florida, the median price of a home, which had risen to $320,000 in 2005, fell to an astonishing $106,000 three years later. People who had taken out mortgages when prices were going up now could not pay their debt as housing prices started to fall. In some cases, prices had fallen so low that people's debt was greater than the value of their home. New homes that had been constructed in anticipation of the boom now stood empty and were joined by an inventory of foreclosed homes, which depressed prices even more. Just as rising demand for housing had pushed prices higher, so did the increasing supply of unsold homes drive prices lower, creating its own momentum in the opposite direction.

Previously, homes sales had contributed to the country's prosperity, filling bank coffers with profits. Now foreclosures threatened lenders with bankruptcy as people failed to repay their loans. As quick as they were to loan money in good times, banks were reluctant to do so when the economy soured. Banks would not extend credit, which threatened the entire economy, making it difficult for firms to pay suppliers, meet payrolls, or purchase goods. The economy entered its worst recession since the Great Depression. In a period of 18 months, from the last quarter of 2007 through the first quarter of 2009, about $12 trillion of wealth evaporated as housing prices collapsed and the stock market tumbled. Unemployment rose above 10 percent, the highest it had been in 26 years.

As this example shows, although market systems promote innovation, productivity, and provide a hospitable environment for democracy and personal freedom, they are also highly volatile. Markets do not remain in a stable equilibrium but are susceptible to periods of boom and bust. In the former, the economy is buoyant with investment, jobs, and commerce; in the latter, the economy is depressed with bankruptcies, layoffs, and declining sales. The volatility of markets would not be so worrisome if its disconcerting shifts were not so socially destructive. When the economy contracts, plants are idle and workers are unemployed. Vital resources are wasted that could be engaged productively.[24] Market instability also has more personal, more intimate costs. When markets move capriciously, they leave people with a sense of powerlessness and insecurity, the feeling that they do not control their own fate.

Market systems, as we have seen, generate extraordinary wealth, but they also generate extraordinary inequality. As the market's range expands, increasing competition for jobs, it tends to depress the bargaining power and hence the earnings of those without valued skills. The growth of the market, however, has the opposite effect on those who enjoy market power. Those who control scarce resources, such as skills or capital, now can apply their advantage over a much wider field and thereby recoup bloated rewards from it.[25] Able to extend their market advantage over a bigger playing field, they can capture commensurately bigger rewards. The result of these dynamics is increasing inequality because the market position of low-skill workers declines while those with market power increases.

Harmful Spillover Effects
Costs the public, or third parties, suffer as a result of others' transactions; when the damaging consequences of market activities are externalized, or placed on others who bear their costs.

Finally, market systems create **harmful spillover effects** or externalities. In market systems, participants tend to perceive their interests narrowly. They only consider the consequences of their decisions that fall on them, although others may be adversely affected. If people can avoid the costs of their decisions and pass them on to others, they are that much better off—although the society onto which the costs have been displaced may not be. For example, firms acting in a self-interested manner will not clean up the pollution they create because it would hurt their profits to do so. Instead, the costs of pollution will be borne by everyone in the form of dirty air and impure water. The firm's financial statement will look better as a result, but society's balance sheet will look worse.[26] Another example of harmful spillover is global warming. The prices people pay to drive their cars or heat their homes do not reflect their true costs in terms of the greenhouse gases they release. These gases create global warming that may be the greatest, most costly harmful spillover of all in terms of its catastrophic costs on future generations. One report estimated the real, unpaid cost of global warming to be in the area of $7 trillion, which is what it will take to respond to the extreme weather disasters and coastal flooding that global warming causes.

In Brief: The Advantages and Disadvantages of Market Systems

Advantages of Market Systems
- Promotes efficiency and productivity.
- Promotes innovation.
- More conducive to democracy than command economies.

Disadvantages of Market Systems
- Subject to volatile and destructive swings between recession and prosperity.
- Promotes inequality.
- Social costs of production are ignored.

The Shifting Balance Between States and Markets

5.5 Summarize the historical swings in the balance between states and markets.

Market systems, we argued previously, require rules enforced by the state to work at all. Rules reduce uncertainty that contracts will be honored, that money will retain its value, and that consumers will not be cheated. However, states do more to assist market systems than simply reassure participants that others will play fair. They try to steer economies to certain goals, actively intervening in the market to alter its results. For example, states try to counteract the three drawbacks of market systems we just reviewed. They create welfare systems to neutralize the natural tendency of markets toward inequality; they create regulations, such as pollution controls, to minimize harmful spillover effects; and they use their budgetary powers and control over the money supply to reduce the swings in the business cycle.

The degree to which states should intervene in the marketplace and impose their priorities on it is a source of tremendous conflict within most societies. To what degree should the welfare state alter market outcomes? To what degree should the state create regulations that require firms to limit harmful spillovers? To what degree should the state use its budgetary powers and control over the money supply to reduce the cycle of boom and bust? The boundary between what should be left to markets and what should be determined by states shifts constantly in response to political pressure. Following World War II, state intervention was accepted practice, whether this took the form of nationalized industry in Britain, indicative planning in France, the welfare state in Sweden, state-regulated business in India, or state-owned companies and marketing control boards in Africa. Everywhere, the state extended its reach into the economy "powered by the demands of the public in the industrial democracies for greater security, by the drive for progress and improved living conditions in the developing countries—and by the quest for fairness and justice."[27]

State interference was necessary to correct the all too apparent deficiencies of markets during the Great Depression, which left millions unemployed. After World War II, the benefits of state intervention were perceived to be just as obvious as the market's failures had been in the 1930s. States led the reconstruction effort in Europe following the war, laying the groundwork for a new golden age of prosperity in the West. They created welfare systems that protected people from the ravages of unemployment, sickness, and old age. They managed their budgets and money supply to tame the business cycle so that it would not be so disruptive, and they nationalized industries to ensure the production of essential goods and services. The growth of the welfare state, public enterprise, and state efforts to guide private investment were regarded as essential to a prosperous, public-spirited economy.

Working-class voters were the driving force behind the rise of the mixed economy of state intervention and private enterprise. Workers appreciated the security the welfare state offered as opposed to the precariousness of markets. They valued efforts to smooth out the business cycle as a way to avoid the massive unemployment of another depression, and they supported efforts to nationalize firms and regulate corporate behavior to assert public priorities. As a result of these policies, workers' standards of living in the West improved, unemployment declined, the average work day shrank, and unions grew.

State intervention became the new gospel not only in the developed world but in developing countries as well. Nation-building elites in Africa and Asia assumed that only the state could harness the resources necessary to transform traditional, agrarian societies into modern, industrial ones. The developing countries needed infrastructure—transportation and communication networks, electrical power, water and sewer lines—to lay the foundations for development, and only the state could raise the capital and assume the risk for such investments. Private sources of capital, it was believed, were too small and too concerned with narrow self-interest to get the job done. Thus, nationalistic elites in developing countries looked to the state to propel industrialization. They became the advocates of states over markets. In India, this took the form of creating national champions, public enterprises that could meet the consumer needs of a soaring population. In Africa, it took the form of state-run marketing boards to which growers sold their produce at fixed prices, and in Asia, it took the form of states encouraging firms to cooperate rather than compete.[28] The borders of the market were being rolled back.

However, the tide began to shift beginning in the 1970s. Economic growth in the West stalled as developed societies were ravaged by rising energy prices, increasing unemployment, and galloping inflation. Recession created the opportunity for new groups proposing new ideas to challenge the orthodoxy of the mixed economy. Backed by the business community, market supporters such as Prime Minister Margaret Thatcher in Britain (1979–1991) and President Ronald Reagan in the United States (1981–1989) took power, arguing that prosperity was being strangled by state intervention. Previously, advocates of states had pointed to systematic market failures as the reason state intervention was required. Now, promoters of markets pointed to systematic political failures as the reason markets needed to be restored. It was argued that growth had slowed because the welfare state had undermined the work ethic, that regulations had constrained entrepreneurial energies, that taxes had diverted too much income, and that public enterprises were inefficient. Market inequalities based on capital and wealth had simply been replaced by new inequalities based on power and privilege, and instead of looking out for the public good, public officials managing the economy looked out only for themselves.

Management of the economy changed to reflect this new consensus. States now tried to balance their budgets, lower their tax rates, reduce regulations, privatize state-owned firms, and curb the power of unions. Although the effort to roll back the state did not actually shrink it—states continued to grow in terms of budgets and activities—their purpose changed because states were now less inclined to direct markets than to support them. The shift was more qualitative than quantitative. Making markets work better required states to do new things, not fewer things. For example, supporting markets did not mean reducing the welfare state as much as it meant reorienting the welfare state so that it was more employment-friendly, encouraging work. Supporting markets did not mean less regulation but new types of regulations that encouraged competition.[29]

Nevertheless, the global recession of 2007 that began in the United States—the paragon of the market approach—cast doubt on the tilt toward markets. The financial crisis in the United States spread like a virus throughout the world, forcing governments to rescue failing banks and pump money into their economies to prevent them from collapsing. Faith in the recuperative power of the market gave way to a new belief in the restorative power of states. The United States, first under Republican president George W. Bush and then under his Democratic successor, Barack Obama, intervened dramatically in the economy, bailing out banks, buying shares in car companies, and investing in markets to prop them up. Other governments quickly followed suit. The market model was in retreat. In 2010, the *Economist*, a sober and respected newsweekly magazine, acknowledged that just when it seemed that "the great debate about the proper role and size of the state had been resolved. . . . Big Government is back with a vengeance: not just as a brute fact, but as a vigorous ideology."[30] With the world economy teetering on the brink and governments providing life support to bankrupt companies and banks, it was hard to argue otherwise. In the 1980s, advocates of markets silenced critics by asserting "There Is No Alternative" (or what came to be known as TINA) if the mistakes of the previous period were to be avoided. But in a startling about-face, the critics of markets now invoked TINA against those who had once used it

In-Depth: India—From States to Markets

After India gained independence in 1947, its rulers embarked on policies that called for a large degree of state intervention in the economy. Statist economic policies included high tariffs that limited imports to protect domestic producers from foreign competition; public ownership of the commanding heights of the economy; and heavy regulation of industry through licensing.

However, India abandoned statist economic policies in the wake of the economic reversals that it suffered in the 1980s. The industrial licensing system was abolished, nationalized firms were sold, and tariffs were cut. Because of this shift from state to market, foreign trade and foreign direct investment grew dramatically, as did GDP. Incomes rose for all groups, including the poor. But the reforms exaggerated the income gap between urban and rural India. More than 60 percent of all Indians derive their livelihoods from agriculture, which experienced little growth. Thus, although the reforms greatly improved the life chances of many urban Indians, they increased inequalities, especially rural–urban differences.

For Further Discussion

1. How can market reforms that have such unequal effects, leaving out the bulk of the population in the countryside engaged in agriculture, obtain popular support in a democracy such as India?
2. Without jeopardizing or undermining the impact of market reforms, what can states do to make their consequences fairer so that they enhance the capabilities of a larger number of citizens?

---

against them. Advocates of more government intervention now claimed there was no alternative if countries were to avoid falling off the precipice to which the free market model had brought them.

Shifting paradigms between states and markets reveal that economic models diffuse across the globe. As countries adopt similar policies, their economic fortunes are tied more closely together. Both are evidence of what social scientists refer to as globalization, which we review next.

Globalization

5.6 Define globalization and evaluate whether it contributes to or thwarts the Good Society.

Globalization
Refers to the greater integration and worldwide exchange of ideas, goods, currencies, investments, and culture.

The concept of **globalization** can be captured by looking at a map of the world that compares the number of commercial intercontinental flights in 1960 and 2000. The number of flights per year is displayed as lines of various widths. The map for 1960 shows relatively thin lines connecting the various continents, indicating that there were very few intercontinental commercial flights. In contrast, the map for 2000 shows so many lines that the continents themselves are nearly obscured. What is true of commercial airline flights is also true for trade, investment, labor, technology, and ideas. A few thin lines connecting countries and even continents have been replaced by many thicker ones.

Map 5.1 Airline Map circa 1960 and 2000

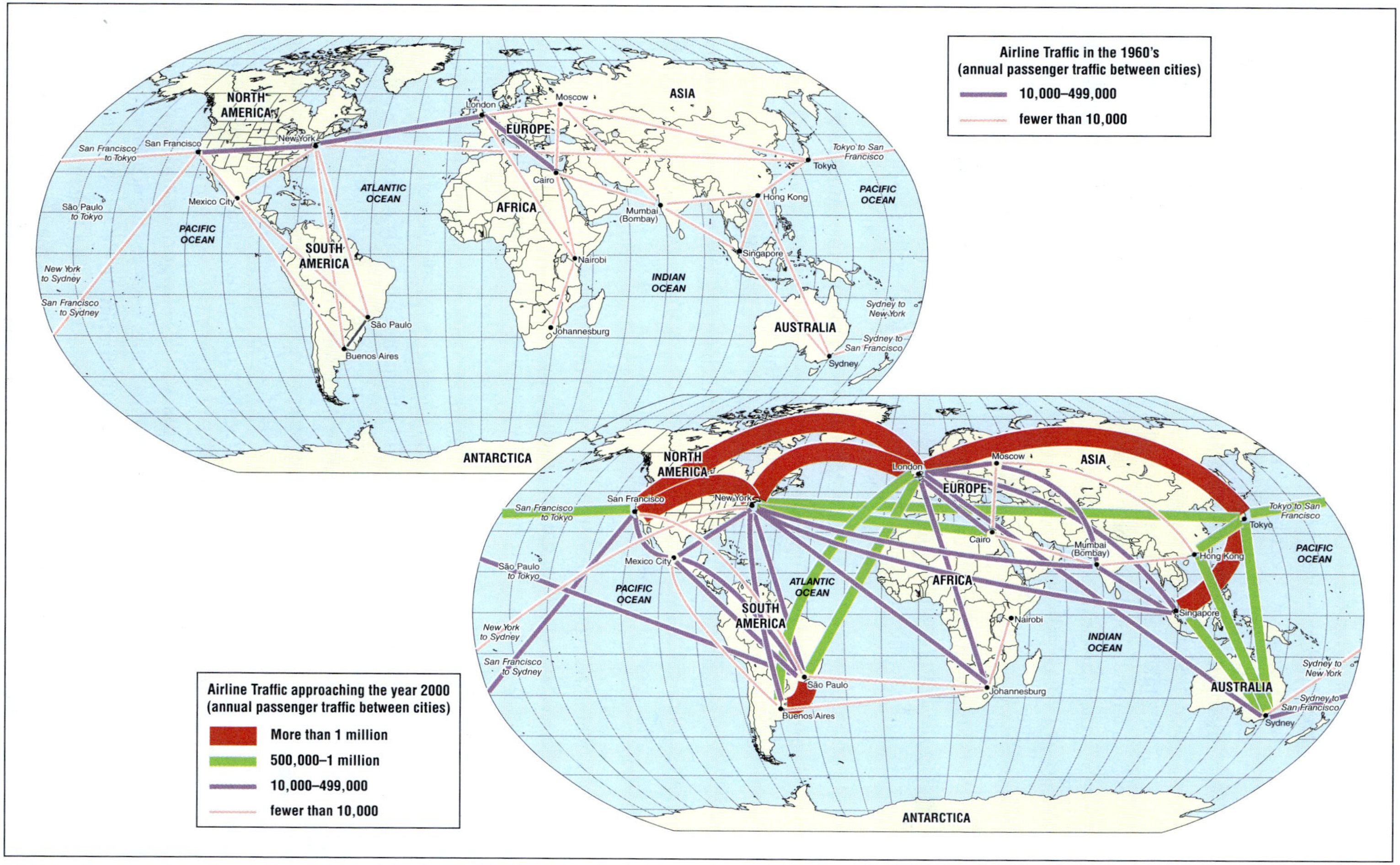

Global Supply Chains
Where different parts of an interconnected production process are outsourced to different firms that may even be located in different countries.

Washington Consensus or Neoliberalism
A diagnosis promoted by many Western governments and international economic agencies that attributed poor economic performance to too much state regulation and prescribed free trade, balanced budgets, and competition as the cure.

The World Bank
Established in 1944 and headquartered in Washington, D.C., the World Bank provides loans, credits, and grants to low- and middle-income countries to promote development.

Globalization refers to the increasing flow of money, people, skills, ideas, and goods across borders. Until the recent global recession, trade between countries grew as they lowered trade barriers, opening up their markets to foreign competition. Foreign direct investment, in which businesses invest outside their home countries, also increased. That is, firms were both selling more goods outside their home market and manufacturing more products abroad. Indeed, globalization has proceeded so far that different steps in the manufacturing process may now take place in different countries. For example, Barbie dolls, which are sold all over the world, are the product of a **global supply chain**. The United States provides the cardboard packaging, paint pigments, and molds; Taiwan refines the oil into plastic for the body; Japan contributes the nylon hair; all these parts are then assembled in China, where Barbie's clothes are also produced; and the final product is shipped out of Hong Kong. The iPod is also the product of a global supply chain, with its computer chips produced in Taiwan, its display modules made in Japan, and its memory chips manufactured in Korea.[31] Not only is there more economic exchange between countries, but there is also more cultural traffic. Curry has replaced fish and chips in Britain as the most common lunch, and kids in China dress like homeboys, listen to rap music, and do the worm.

There has always been trade, investment, and cultural exchange across borders. What is different today is the volume of international exchange, the breadth of the connections, and the speed with which they occur. Globalization is, in part, the result of technological change. For example, the dramatic increase in intercontinental flights is unimaginable in the absence of powerful jet engines that permit planes to fly long distances in a short amount of time. Huge cargo ships that ply the oceans have reduced transportation costs for goods at the same time the Internet has increased the cross-national flow of ideas.

Nevertheless, globalization is not simply the result of impersonal forces. It has been actively promoted by multinational corporations, governments, and international agencies. Globalization proceeded because states created international organizations and trade agreements that created rules to encourage the process. Nor does globalization necessarily imply the eclipse of the state or come at the state's expense. As David Marquand impishly argues, try entering a country without a passport by explaining to an immigration official that globalization has made states and national borders irrelevant.[32]

Prior to the 1980s, many states exercised a great deal of control over their trade through high tariffs, over foreign investment by restricting entry, and over their currency by limiting its movement abroad. But the 1970s recession saw the emergence of a new paradigm to restore growth based on markets, called the **Washington consensus** by its supporters and neoliberalism by its critics. This policy package required countries to balance their budgets by cutting spending, open their markets to foreign trade and investment, and sell off nationalized industries to private investors. The Washington consensus was supported by large multinational corporations; the United States; such international agencies as the **World Bank**, which provides loans and grants to countries for development projects; and the **International Monetary Fund** (IMF), which loans money to countries that cannot pay their bills.[33] The World Bank and IMF required countries in financial difficulty to adopt the policies of the Washington consensus as a condition for receiving aid from them.

Critics charged that the Washington consensus hurt the poor by requiring cuts in social services to achieve balanced budgets, increasing unemployment and driving out native businesses by requiring countries to open up their markets to imports and foreign competition, and weakening democracy by requiring countries to conform to IMF and World Bank conditions to obtain assistance from them.[34] Critics claimed that what they disparagingly referred to as neoliberalism merely rationalized policies that justified exploitation of less-developed countries by multinational corporations and their political allies. In response, supporters of the Washington consensus accused their critics of espousing "economic rubbish that jeopardizes . . . [advancing the] egalitarian causes" that critics said they valued.[35] Neoliberals argued that balanced budgets were necessary to stabilize a country's currency, that removing trade and investment controls was needed to attract foreign capital, and that privatizing state businesses was vital to increase their competitiveness and efficiency. Those who support the Washington consensus often attribute the lack of growth in developing countries to political failure, especially corruption, whereas its critics assign the blame to market failure, especially unfair competition. The former perceive Africa as the poster child of what went wrong to support their views; the latter point to the Asian tigers (Taiwan, South Korea, Thailand, Singapore, and Malaysia) as evidence of what went right.[36]

The debate between critics and supporters of the Washington consensus captured in microcosm a larger debate between the skeptics and advocates of globalization. In many ways, it reprises the argument between those who only see the benefits of markets and those who only see their disadvantages. Proponents perceive the economic openness that accompanies globalization as creating the conditions for a race to the top. Firms in less-developed countries that participate in global supply chains can make profits, pay workers more than they would have earned as farmers, and give them an opportunity to learn new skills.[37] From that point, these firms can grow, and employment and wages can increase. For example, Giant Manufacturing in Taiwan began as a low-wage manufacturer, producing bicycles for the Schwinn Corporation, an iconic brand based in the United States. When Schwinn found a new supplier, Giant began to produce bikes under its own name. It is now on the cutting edge of high-tech racing and mountain bikes, sold 6.3 million bicycles in 2012, and is the largest bike manufacturer by revenue in the world, with sales of $1.8 billion, whereas Schwinn's fortunes receded and it had to file for bankruptcy.[38]

Detractors of globalization argue that it actually creates a race to the bottom in which each country competes to have the lowest wages, lowest taxes, and fewest regulations to attract foreign investors who now have the whole world to choose from.[39] For example, corporations such as General Electric and General Motors were attracted initially to Mexico because of its low wages and access to American

International Monetary Fund (IMF)
Created at the same time as the World Bank, the IMF's purpose is to provide a safety net for countries when they experience financial crisis, which may occur when they cannot pay their debts.

markets but then moved their businesses to China where production costs were even lower.[40] Countries compete in prostituting themselves, repressing labor, driving down wages, and removing regulations to attract capital investment.

The record of countries that followed the development strategy of the Washington consensus has been uneven at best. The economist Dani Rodrik contends that if Martians were to arrive and compare predictions of the Washington consensus with actual growth performance since 1960, they would find that many Asian countries that diverged from its prescriptions by directing credit, subsidizing exports, and protecting their markets performed very well, whereas many Latin American countries that followed its instructions by deregulating their economies, balancing their budgets, and pursuing free trade did not.[41]

If embracing globalization was no magic elixir, there is also little evidence that globalization leads to a race to the bottom by depressing living standards and eliminating jobs in less-developed countries. Workers in several Asian countries that are deeply enmeshed in the global economy, including South Korea, Taiwan, and Thailand, have seen their standard of living improve. Hundreds of thousands of well-educated, young workers in India's information technology industry have dramatically increased their incomes since the country opened this sector to foreign investment and trade. Critics assume that employers are only looking to invest in countries that offer the lowest labor costs and taxes. In fact, investors are often less interested in countries that offer low wages than in those that offer political stability, good infrastructure, and a skilled labor force able to deliver higher levels of productivity. Far from creating a race either to the top or to the bottom for developing countries, globalization has increased the difference between the top and bottom. Some developing countries have profited enormously from globalization, whereas others have been victimized by it. Globalization has been the source of wealth and success for some developing countries and the cause of ruin and poverty for others.

Globalization has such varied outcomes because it is refracted through different institutions and governing coalitions. Countries that invite globalization by opening their economies to foreign trade and investment will profit only if they have supportive institutions and governing coalitions in place that can take advantage of its benefits and ameliorate its costs. What matters is not how much state activity there is but its quality. As Tina Rosenberg wrote of Haiti, which followed the Washington consensus and saw its economy contract in the 1990s, "If you are a corrupt and misgoverned nation with a closed economy, becoming a corrupt, misgoverned nation with an open economy is not going to solve your problems."[42] Reaping the benefits of globalization may be less a question of too much state and not enough market, as the Washington consensus imagined it, than a question of how effective states are at putting in place the foundations that enable markets to work well. Such prerequisites include educating workers, constructing a reliable infrastructure, and enforcing the rule of law. What matters are the different tools states use to influence the allocation of resources in the economy and how well they use them. We examine this issue next.

Comparative Political Analysis: Does Globalization Help or Hurt Workers in the Developing World?

Problem: Layna Mosley and Saiko Uno ask whether globalization contributes to or compromises workers' rights in developing countries. Leftists frequently assert that globalization hurts workers' rights because it leads to a race to the bottom. Others argue that globalization contributes to workers' rights by attracting companies that bring their best practices with them and care more about the quality of their labor than its cost.

Methods and Hypothesis: Mosley and Uno hypothesize that the impact of globalization on workers depends on the way countries participate in global production networks. Workers will benefit when countries attract more foreign direct investment, but they will suffer when countries engage in more trade. Foreign direct investment is benign because multinationals urge governments to improve infrastructure and the skills of the native workforce. Trade, on the other hand, compromises workers' interests because low wages are the key to increasing exports and winning business for local subcontractors.

Operationalizing Concepts: The authors operationally define workers' rights, their dependent variable, by counting the number of labor rights violations that countries committed.

They operationalize one of their independent variables, foreign direct investment (FDI), by looking at annual changes in FDI and the overall level of FDI as a percent of GDP. They operationalize their other independent variable, trade, by looking at the ratio of imports and exports to GDP.

Results: Statistical analysis confirmed Mosley and Uno's hypothesis: The higher the level of FDI as a percentage of GDP, the greater the respect for labor rights. Conversely, trade openness was shown to be detrimental to workers. Countries with higher levels of imports and exports treated their workers less well. Workers' rights improved in developing countries that attracted foreign direct investment, but deteriorated in those countries that engaged in more trade.

For Further Discussion

1. What other criteria aside from labor rights might the authors have investigated to see whether globalization hurts or helps workers in developing countries?
2. What sorts of controls do you think Mosley and Uno should have used in their analysis?

Source: Layna Mosley and Saiko Uno, "Racing to the Bottom or Climbing to the Top," *Comparative Political Studies* (August 2007), vol. 40, no. 8, pp. 923–948.

Forms of State Intervention

5.7 Describe the different ways states intervene in the economy.

Fiscal Policy

States try to influence economic conditions through **fiscal policy**, which involves juggling their budgets, their overall levels of revenues and expenditures. On the one hand, states can stimulate the economy and reduce unemployment by running budget deficits, which occur when the state spends more than it receives in revenues. Budget deficits put money into circulation

Fiscal Policy
Governments make fiscal policy, which uses the budget—government revenues and expenditures—to manage overall demand in the economy. Fiscal policy can run budget deficits to stimulate demand and run budget surpluses to reduce it.

that increases the demand for goods that, in turn, encourage businesses to invest and put people to work. On the other hand, states can dampen an economy that suffers from inflation by running a surplus, taking in more money than they spend. A surplus withdraws money from circulation, which depresses spending and discourages investment, thereby reducing inflationary pressures in the economy.

States differ greatly in the proportion of their economy devoted to taxes and state expenditures. Americans complain frequently that taxes in the United States are too high and the government spends too much. In fact, Americans enjoy a lighter tax burden than citizens in other rich democracies, and the American government is lean compared to others. As Table 5.1 reveals, taxes are a lower proportion of GDP in the United States than in any other country, and state expenditures in the United States are relatively low as well. Only Korea recorded lower state spending as a percentage of its economy than the United States. At the opposite end of the spectrum is Denmark, where state spending amounts to more than half of GDP. The fact that the Danish government collects almost half the national income in the form of taxes and diverts an even larger proportion in the form of spending gives it enormous power to determine how money is used and distributed within society.

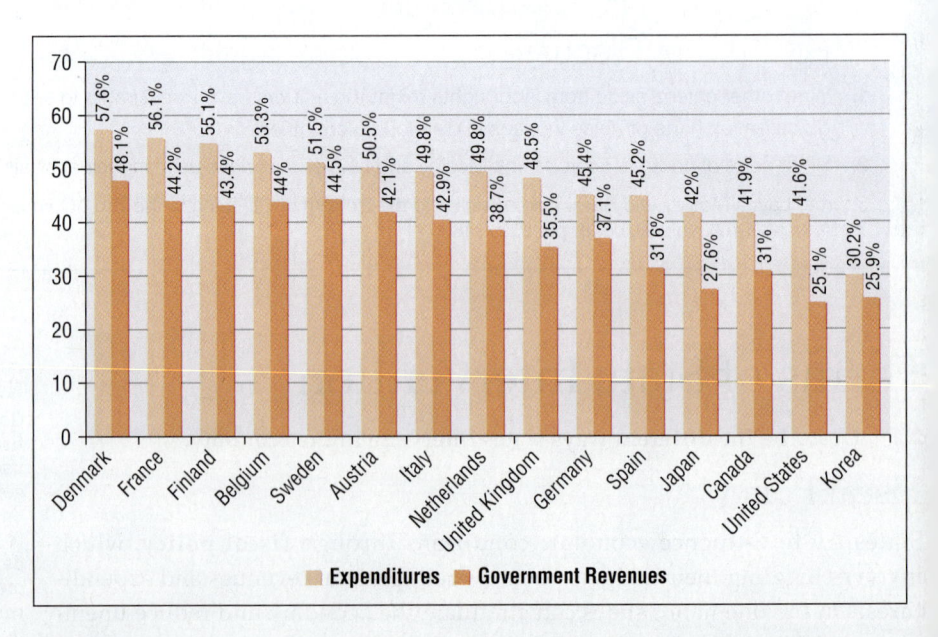

Table 5.1 Government Expenditures and Revenues as a Percentage of GDP, 2011.

Country	Expenditures	Government Revenues
Denmark	57.6%	48.1%
France	56.1%	44.2%
Finland	55.1%	43.4%
Belgium	53.3%	44.0%
Sweden	51.5%	44.5%
Austria	50.5%	42.1%
Italy	49.8%	42.9%
Netherlands	49.8%	38.7%
United Kingdom	48.5%	35.5%
Germany	45.4%	37.1%
Spain	45.2%	31.6%
Japan	42.0%	27.6%
Canada	41.9%	31.0%
United States	41.6%	25.1%
Korea	30.2%	25.9%

SOURCES: For expenditures as a percent of GDP, see OECD (2012), Annex Table 25, General Government Total Outlays, in *OECD Economic Outlook, Volume 2012 Issue 1*, OECD Publishing. doi: 10.1787/eco_outlook-v2012-1-table181-en. For revenues as a percent of GDP, see http://www.oecd-ilibrary.org/taxation/total-tax-revenue_20758510-table2.

Monetary policy

Another means by which states influence economic conditions is through **monetary policy**, by manipulating interest rates. Just as the state tries to fine-tune the economy by adjusting its budget, so does it try to manage the economy by regulating how much it costs to borrow money. High interest rates tend to discourage borrowing and spending and are used to counteract tendencies toward inflation. In contrast, low interest rates encourage borrowing and spending by making loans cheap and are employed to fight recessions.

Interest rates are largely determined by **central banks** that issue currency and manage its value in foreign exchange. One measure of the control that states exert over the economy is the influence they have over their central bank. In some countries, central banks are purposely insulated from political control, and states have little leverage over their policies. The central bank of the United States, for example, is the Federal Reserve Bank. Neither the president nor Congress has much leverage over the Federal Reserve Bank's policies. For those European countries that have adopted the Euro as their currency, interest rate targets are set by the European Central Bank (ECB), which is even less transparent and accountable than the U.S. Federal Reserve Bank. The European Central Bank's decisions are not reviewable by any external body, and it does not publish minutes of its meetings, divulge how members voted, or even have to explain its decisions when it announces them.

In other countries, governments enjoy more power over central banks. For example, the People's Bank in China is simply an administrative organ for carrying out decisions made by the governing Chinese Communist Party. Changes in the interest rate or the money supply require the approval of the government, and the central bank enjoys little independence.[43]

Monetary Policy
Monetary policy manages the money supply through which the government influences interest rates to promote economic stability and growth. Reducing the money supply increases interest rates, which depresses economic activity; increasing the money supply lowers interest rates, which stimulates spending.

Central Bank
Central banks control the money supply in each country. They set monetary policy.

Regulations

States manipulate budgets, and central banks manage interest rates with the intent of stabilizing prices and sustaining employment, but states can also use a more direct means to influence economic actors: They can issue **regulations** that set explicit rules of behavior that firms must follow. States engage in regulation and compel firms to behave in certain ways to manage competition, set industry standards, and require or forbid certain business practices. For example, states may set minimum pay rates to prevent firms from profiting by paying substandard wages, mandate environmental quality standards to prevent firms from polluting the air and water, and require firms to meet certain product standards to prevent them from selling unsafe or unreliable goods.

Some states are more committed to regulation than others. The number of procedures and days it takes to start a new business is a standard measure used to compare the thickness of the regulatory environment from country to country. According to the World Bank, it takes 9 interactions, taking an average of 45 days, to obtain the necessary licenses and permits to start a business

Regulations
Policies that compel economic actors to act in certain ways, setting explicit rules that firms and workers must follow.

in Germany and 17 steps, lasting 152 days, in Brazil as compared to just 5 steps, lasting 5 days, in the United States.[44] Another gauge of the regulatory environment is available if we examine labor relations. In many European countries, managers are required to negotiate with workers' councils in their shops, companies must follow a tedious and lengthy process prior to firing workers, and employees are entitled to seats on the board of directors. Employers in the United States do not have to adopt any of these practices because there are no laws requiring them. They do not have to negotiate with their employees or let them participate in setting corporate strategy, and they can fire any worker for any reason, except discrimination, without justifying their decision legally. As two labor relations specialists acknowledged, "By most international standards, American employers . . . are confronted with fewer direct regulations of employment conditions than employers in other countries."[45] Despite frequently heard complaints about big government and its obtrusiveness, American entrepreneurs are less burdened by regulations and have more autonomy to manage their businesses than their counterparts elsewhere.

Nationalization

Finally, states try to influence economic activity by nationalizing industries in which states own and control public enterprises. Nationalized industries permit the state to influence the economy through its control of strategic assets. For example, the state owns and controls the oil industry in Mexico, Venezuela, and Saudi Arabia, where oil is a major export. Public enterprises also help the state inject social criteria into the economy. Although state-owned enterprises in China may be inefficient, the government continues to subsidize them because they provide jobs and services to millions who would be poor and jobless without them.

States differ in the degree to which they nationalize industry. In socialist countries, such as Cuba and North Korea, the state owns and controls all the means of production, but with the demise of the Soviet Union, such socialist outposts are now few, small, and insignificant. At the opposite end of the spectrum are countries such as the United States and Chile, where the few public enterprises that exist contribute a very small percentage to the GDP. Some countries that once had a substantial nationalized sector have divested and sold off their holdings to private investors. By 1992, more than 80 countries had sold off as many as 6,800 public companies. In Britain, the list of privatizations since 1979 has included such industries as gas, coal, electricity, water, steel, telecommunications, and rail. This sweeping privatization reduced the workforce in British nationalized industries by 83 percent, from 1.8 million workers in 1979 to fewer than 350,000 twenty years later.[46]

Fiscal policy, monetary policy, regulation, and nationalization hardly exhaust the tools states use to influence the economy. In Japan, the state once intervened by promoting mergers and cooperation among firms to create businesses that were large and efficient enough to compete in world markets, and in Germany, intervention takes the form of the state brokering agreements among union and employer organizations. Each country works out, through political struggle, its own balance between states and markets, and the mix of policy tools that states adopt is different from country to country. Some have a preference for regulation, whereas others rely more on monetary policy to influence the economy. Where markets play a greater role, we expect to find that (1) states do not redirect as much of the country's income through taxes and expenditures, (2) states do not exert much influence on central banks that set interest rates, (3) state regulations are not as copious or intrusive on managers, and (4) public enterprises contribute little to the GDP. The opposite is the case where states play a powerful role in determining who gets what. The state redirects a larger proportion of the country's income through its budget, states exert great influence over central bank policies, state regulations are profuse and pervasive, and public enterprises control the economy's strategic industries.

The political economies of different countries can be placed on a continuum that stretches from the most market-oriented to the most state-directed. The Fraser Institute of Canada has developed a scale—what it calls the Economic Freedom Index—that evaluates political economies according to their degree of market control. Table 5.2 in the appendix gives the results of the Fraser Institute's survey. The higher a country's rankings, the more its economies are governed by markets, with the most market-oriented economies receiving the highest score of 10 and the most state-directed economies receiving the lowest score of 0. The index classified countries into four groups. We labeled the first group "free market." These countries relied on markets the most to coordinate and organize production. Next were "market-oriented" countries, where markets still dominated but were more balanced by state intervention than the previous group. The third group, which we labeled "mixed," involved even more state intervention in the economy. The final group was categorized as "statist," because states played a preponderant role in their economies.

States, Markets, and the Good Society

5.8 Evaluate the performance of state and market systems according to the standards of the good society.

Do countries in which market systems prevail do a better job of enhancing people's capabilities than countries where states intervene heavily in the economy? Which form of political economy is most compatible with the good society: meeting people's material needs, helping them make educated choices about their lives, protecting them from harm, and promoting democracy?

Figure 5.1 Capitalism and Infant Mortality Rates

SOURCE: Economic Freedom Index and infant mortality rates.

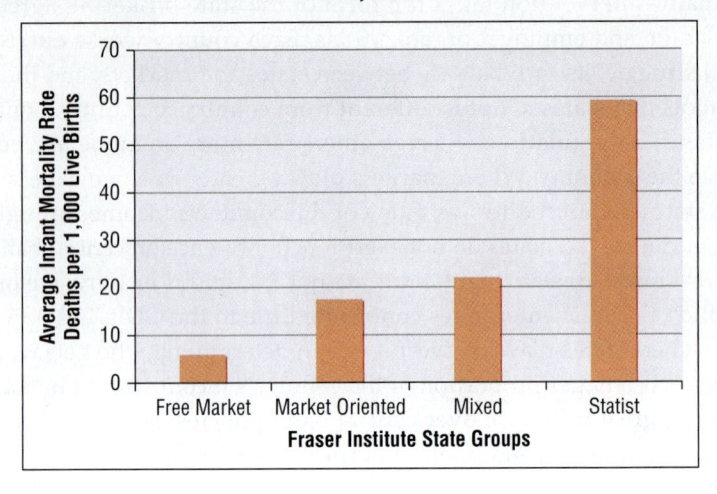

Physical Well-being

The good society requires citizens' basic material needs to be met, which we operationally defined in terms of infant mortality rates. As is apparent from Figure 5.1, countries that scored high on the Fraser Institute free market index tended to have lower infant mortality rates. As scores on the economic freedom index went down, infant mortality rates tended to go up. The average infant mortality rate for states in the free market category was 6.0. Average infant mortality rates rose by almost 300 percent for states with market-oriented economies, with an average of 17.5 babies dying before their first birthday for countries in this group. States with mixed economies performed even worse, recording an average infant mortality rate of 22, and countries with statist economies did worst of all, averaging an infant mortality rate of 59.

Informed Decision Making

Another attribute of the good society is the ability of its citizens to make informed decisions. The good society does not stipulate how people should live but ensures that people can make knowledgeable choices about how they want to live. As we argued earlier, literacy enhances people's ability to do that. According to Figure 5.2, literacy rates—like infant mortality rates—appear to be highly correlated with the degree of market freedom. Free-market economies performed the best, with an average literacy rate of 97.7 percent. Literacy rates declined to 92.2 percent for countries with market-oriented economies, although the median for this group was a more respectable 96. Average literacy rates then drop to 88.9 percent for countries with mixed economies and then drop even more for countries in the last group, those with statist economies. They performed worst of all, recording an average literacy rate of only 67 percent.

Figure 5.2 Capitalism and Literacy Rates

SOURCE: Economic Freedom Index and literacy rates.

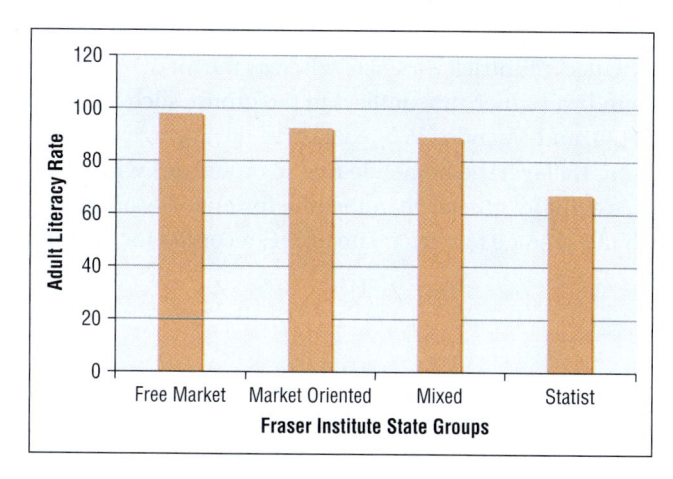

Safety

Warfare poses the greatest threat to citizens' safety, and, as we noted in Chapter 2, wars are far more likely to occur within states than between them. Studies show that the type of political economy a country has is virtually irrelevant in determining its risk of war. Countries with market-led economies are no less likely to be engaged in hostilities with other countries or erupt into civil war than those where states play a greater allocative role. Unlike democracies, which normally do not fight each other, countries with market-driven economies and those with state-led economies will fight with their own kind and any other kind. The type of political economy in place has no effect on levels of state aggression.[47]

Aside from warfare, safety can also be assessed by comparing homicide rates. Figure 5.3 portrays the relationship between homicide rates and type of

Figure 5.3 Capitalism and Homicide Rates

SOURCE: Economic Freedom Index and homicide rates.

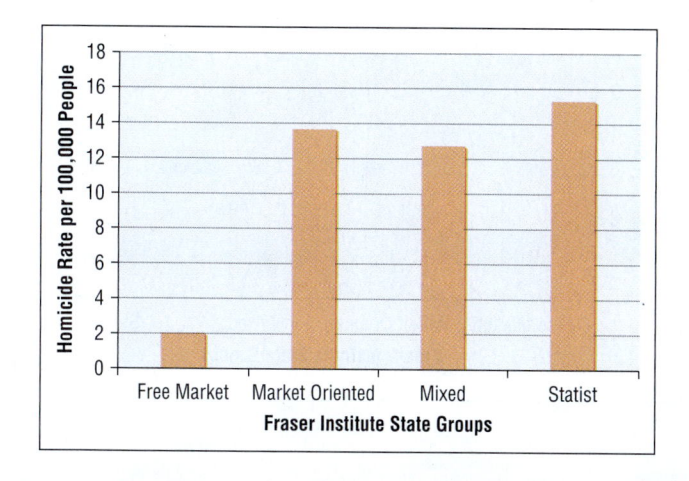

political economy as measured by the Economic Freedom Index. Free-market economies performed best of all, separating themselves from the pack, averaging just 2.0 homicides per 100,000 citizens, but political economy did not seem to have much impact on how the other groups fared. The average homicide rate for market-oriented countries was 13.6, whereas the median for this group was only 5.1. This indicates there are outliers in the group, such as Honduras (82.1), Guatemala (41.4), and Uganda (36.3), that drive the average up compared to the median. Indeed, the average homicide rate for countries with market-oriented economies was actually greater than the rate for mixed economies (12.9) and a bit lower than the average homicide rate of 15.2 recorded for countries with statist economies.

Democracy

A quick look at the Economic Freedom rankings finds robust democracies among the free-market group of countries and repressive dictatorships among the countries with statist economies. These results are reflected in Figure 5.4, which shows an apparent correlation between democracy and free markets. Countries with free-market economies averaged 7.3 on the Democracy index. This was followed by states with market-oriented economies that averaged 6.5 on the Democracy scale and then the same percentage decline to countries with mixed economies that averaged 5.8 on the Democracy index. Countries with statist economies took their customary position at the back of the pack, averaging just 4.1 on the Democracy measure.

There are some reasons to view these results skeptically due to striking anomalies in the rankings. The free-market group includes a number of

Figure 5.4 Capitalism and Democracy

SOURCE: Economic Freedom Index and Democracy Index.

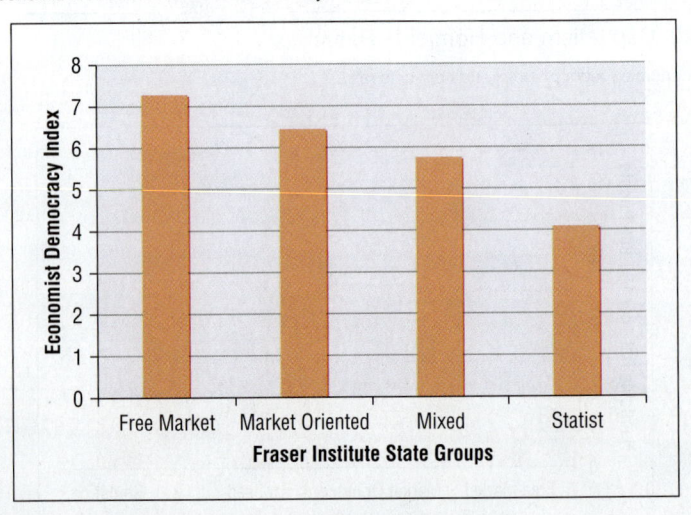

countries in Europe that rank very high on the Democracy Index, such as Finland and Switzerland, and some Middle Eastern countries, such as Bahrain and Oman, that rank very low. The range of where free-market countries fall on the democracy scale is very wide. For example, the United States is sandwiched on the Economic Freedom Index by Qatar just above it and Kuwait just below. The United States is a democracy, whereas both Qatar and Kuwait in the Middle East are not, receiving very low scores on the Democracy index. Iceland and Saudi Arabia, which appear in the next cohort of market-oriented economies, received the same score on the Economic Freedom Index (7.06), but Iceland was virtually at the top of the Democracy Index, whereas Saudi Arabia was nearly at the bottom.

Given these anomalies, the best we can say with some certainty is this: Capitalism may not guarantee liberal democracy, but there are no liberal democracies that are not capitalist. Although more markets do not translate automatically into more political freedom, the lack of a strong market system does seem to preclude it. Although democracies are monogamous and are faithful only to capitalism, capitalism is not so loyal and can be found in bed with all sorts of political systems.

These comparisons tell us that organizing economies more along market lines is correlated with higher capabilities but not consistently so. Although democracy may be weak among countries that do not rely on markets to organize production, it is not necessarily strong among those that do. Democracy may require markets, but markets do not require democracy. Capitalism was compatible with right-wing dictatorships in the past, such as Chile under the military rule of General Pinochet (1974–1990) and under contemporary left-wing dictatorships such as China, where the Communist Party rules without opposition. There does appear to be a correlation between market-based systems, on the one hand, and higher literacy and lower infant mortality rates on the other. Except for the performance of countries in the free-market group, capitalism did not seem to have much impact on homicide rates.

Conclusion

Market systems require states to ensure that property is safe, contracts are enforced, and vital goods that the market cannot supply are available. Laws and regulations set the ground rules that undergird markets, making exchanges predictable, secure, and easy.

Following World War II, the balance between states and markets tilted toward states as developed countries relied on them to manage postwar reconstruction, and developing countries looked to states to promote economic growth following independence. But in the 1970s, states began to concede more space to markets. Although there was a strong disposition toward markets leading to a more global economy, countries have moved in that direction to different degrees and in some cases are even swinging back in the other direction. The global recession that struck in the last quarter of 2007 has revived people's faith in states as a necessary and important defense against the volatility of capitalism. In some countries, states continue to have a powerful influence over the economy through levels of taxation and expenditures, central banks, regulations, and public enterprises. In other countries, states are more reluctant to use these levers to interfere with the market.

We then inquired whether market-oriented political economies perform better in increasing people's capabilities than those in which the state plays a larger role. We found that moving up the scale of market economies does not guarantee liberal democracy, although virtually all the countries ranked low on the scale are without it. We also found that people's basic material needs tend to be met more successfully in countries with market-oriented economies and that literacy rates in these countries tend to be higher. Homicide rates did not seem to correlate much with the type of political economy. . We also found, albeit with some qualifications, that people in countries with more market-oriented economies tend to be safer and have a greater ability to make informed decisions.

Markets are not a panacea; they must be supplemented to increase people's capability. As one economist famously advised, "The market has a place but must be kept in its place." The issue, then, is how to develop a balance between states and markets that promotes the best qualities of markets, such as innovation and productivity, while avoiding their worst effects, such as instability and inequality.

Suggested Readings

Thomas L. Friedman, *The World Is Flat: A Brief History of the Twenty-First Century* (New York: Farrar, Straus and Giroux, 2005). The most accessible treatise in support of globalization. The title reflects Friedman's idea that globalization has leveled the playing field, making the good things in life available to more people.

Robert Kuttner, *Everything for Sale: The Virtues and Limits of Markets* (New York: Knopf, 1997). A critical view of markets that acknowledges both their virtues and shortcomings.

Charles E. Lindblom, *The Market System: What It Is, How It Works, and What to Make of It* (New Haven: Yale University Press, 2001). An overview of markets that, like Kuttner's book, assesses the strengths and weaknesses of markets.

John McMillan, *Reinventing the Bazaar: A Natural History of Markets* (New York: W. W. Norton, 2002). An engaging, even entertaining, analysis of markets that examines why they are good, under what conditions they function well, and why limits to markets are necessary.

Joseph Stiglitz, *Globalization and Its Discontents*, (New York: W. W. Norton, 2002). A critical analysis of globalization that serves as a good counterpoint to Freidman's celebration of it.

Daniel Yergin and Joseph Stanislaw, *The Commanding Heights: The Battle between Government and the Marketplace That Is Remaking the Modern World* (New York: Simon & Schuster, 1998). A dutiful history of how the competing paradigms of states and markets have slipped in and out of fashion.

A good website for additional information about globalization is www.globalization101.org.

Critical Thinking Questions

1. Why do countries differ in their balance between states and markets? What factors determine why some countries depend more on markets, whereas others depend more on states?
2. What sort of activities should be left to the marketplace and what should be insulated from it? What criteria should determine where it is appropriate and where it is not for markets to operate?
3. Why have some developing countries benefited from globalization, whereas others have been victimized by it?
4. Many central banks that set monetary policy and influence interest rates are independent of government and, in effect, unaccountable to the people their policies affect. Should central banks be more democratically accountable?
5. We noted that although there are no democracies that are not also capitalist, many capitalist economies operate within authoritarian political systems. Why does democracy seem to require capitalism, but capitalism does not require democracy?

Chapter 6
Authoritarianism

Learning Objectives

6.1 Explain the characteristics of an authoritarian regime

6.2 Describe the two main political problems authoritarian rulers must address.

6.3 Explain how the four types of authoritarian regimes manage the problems of authoritarian power sharing and authoritarian control.

6.4 Evaluate explanations of authoritarian persistence in the Middle East and North Africa.

6.5 Explain the reasoning supporting the hypothesis that regime type affects capabilities and evaluate the way in which that hypothesis is tested.

Introduction

6.1 Explain the characteristics of an authoritarian regime.

In 1994, members of the Hutu ethnic group in Rwanda slaughtered approximately 800,000 ethnic Tutsis. In the aftermath of the killings, Rwanda faced a grim future. Because the Hutu and Tutsi feared and distrusted one another, it seemed unlikely that a stable government could be established, but despite these gloomy prospects, the government of President Paul Kagame, which came to power in 2000, has made considerable progress. It has promoted economic growth, reduced corruption, cut infant mortality, improved children's chances of getting an education, and promoted equality for women. The government generally has succeeded in improving capabilities—with one crucial exception: It has restricted civil and political liberties and retained power by authoritarian means. Critics charge that in the guise of preventing divisionism that might lead to renewed ethnic violence, the government has stifled criticism of its policies and intimidated its political opponents. It decides when opponents are practicing divisionism and can jail them when they cross the fuzzy line between what they are permitted to say and what they are not.[1]

President Kagame's success in improving citizens' capabilities raises uncomfortable questions for supporters of democracy. Is democracy appropriate for all countries? Is it possible that in some circumstances, such as those that prevail in Rwanda, authoritarian rule is necessary? Is it sometimes necessary to limit civil and political rights to achieve improvements in education, health, and safety? If so, are some kinds of authoritarian rule more successful than others at improving capabilities?

Authoritarianism is a type of political system in which a single individual or small elite rules without constitutional checks on its use of power. It can change rules when it is to its advantage and decide who can participate in politics. It can also set the penalties for breaking the rules it has made. Citizens in authoritarian systems cannot hold rulers accountable. They have no recourse to independent courts of law or constitutional guarantees to free and fair elections.[2]

Authoritarianism has been the main form of government through most of recorded history. Czars, emperors, kings, and sultans have assumed the right to rule without restraints on their power from ordinary people. Louis XV, the absolute monarch of France from 1715 to 1774, proclaimed without any hint of humility:

> In my person alone resides the sovereign power . . . and it is from me alone that the courts hold their existence and their authority. That . . . authority can only be exercised in my name. . . . For it is to me exclusively that the legislative power belongs. . . . The whole public order emanates from me since I am its supreme guardian. . . . The rights and interests of the nation . . . are necessarily united with my own and can only rest in my hands.[3]

Authoritarianism
a type of political system in which a single individual or small elite rules without constitutional checks on its use of power.

Although absolute monarchs such as Louis XV have disappeared, new forms of authoritarianism have taken their place. Like their pre-modern predecessors, modern forms of authoritarianism continue to concentrate state power in the hands of a small elite. What is new is that authoritarian leaders feel obliged to make a show of ruling with popular support. They live in an age in which democracy has become widely valued, even though it is not universally practiced.[4]

Authoritarian governments have declined in number since the mid-1970s, whereas the number of democracies has grown.[5] The collapse of the Soviet Union in 1991 was especially encouraging for supporters of democracy. In its wake, many political scientists came to believe there was no credible alternative to democracy. In their view, it was only a matter of time until democracy triumphed in countries still under authoritarian rule. Admittedly, the transition to democracy would take longer in some countries than in others, but democracy eventually would become "the final form of human government."[6]

More recently, however, that sort of optimism has ebbed. One reason is that authoritarian governments have displayed impressive staying power. The first decade of the twenty-first century actually saw a small decline in the number of democracies in the world.[7] Authoritarianism is prevalent in parts of Africa, Asia, and the Middle East, and China, the world's most populous country, remains under authoritarian rule. To make matters worse, some countries that once appeared to be on their way to democracy have slipped back into authoritarianism. Russia is the most significant example of this trend, but there has also been similar backsliding in Venezuela.[8]

Another reason for ebbing optimism about authoritarian decline is that some authoritarian regimes actually have thrived, and their leaders boast that they have done more to improve the lives of their citizens than could have been achieved under democratic rule. Most notably, China's Communist Party leaders take credit for rapid economic growth since 1980 that has raised more people out of extreme poverty in a shorter time than in any country in history. They attribute their success to their ability to make decisions quickly and institute policies for the long run. In their view, politicians in the United States and Western Europe tend to get bogged down in endless arguments and to think no further into the future than the next election cycle. Democracies, they charge, are reluctant to change ineffective and outdated policies supported by entrenched interest groups in fear of losing votes.

This chapter begins by summarizing the main features of authoritarian politics. It then turns to a description of four kinds of authoritarian governments: monarchical, military, one-party, and personal rule. It examines who selects the leader of each type, how leaders deal with problems of power sharing among the political elite, and how they manage problems of controlling society. The chapter next turns to the puzzle of how leaders of numerous authoritarian regimes have managed to remain in power in an age of democratization. This section focuses on the Middle East and North Africa, the region of the world most dominated by authoritarian rule. The chapter ends with a comparison of how different types of authoritarianism fare in promoting capabilities.

Authoritarian Politics

6.2 Describe the two main political problems authoritarian rulers must address.

Political scientist Milan Svolik writes that "authoritarian politics has always been a ruthless and treacherous business." "There is no independent authority able to enforce agreements among key political players,"[9] so leaders struggle to keep other members of the ruling group from seizing power and the population from rising up against them. These threats create two big political problems for authoritarian rulers. The first is the **problem of authoritarian power sharing**.[10] Chief executives in democracies do not have to worry about military officers or cabinet members seizing power through violent and nonconstitutional means. By contrast, leaders of authoritarian regimes do. Since 1945, far more authoritarian leaders have been overthrown by insiders than by mass uprisings.[11] One of their main problems involves working out ways of sharing power with other members of the leadership group to retain their support. Authoritarian leaders can win that support by including them in decision-making councils, making them heads of important state agencies, and giving them opportunities to enrich themselves. If the leader cannot trust certain members of the leadership group, the alternative to sharing power with them is eliminating them. This can be accomplished by dismissals from the leadership group, arrests, or executions.

In democratic regimes, citizens who do not like leaders can vote them out of power. In authoritarian regimes, removing rulers from power is usually not possible for citizens, at least not in the absence of a massive popular uprising, such as those that overthrew several authoritarian regimes in the Middle East in 2011. The possibility of mass uprisings creates the **problem of authoritarian control**, which involves keeping populations supportive and acquiescent.[12] Rulers use three strategies to do so. One is to win the support of some groups in society with policies that favor them in return for their loyalty. Another strategy that has been used with increasing frequency in recent decades is to hold multiparty elections. In these elections, opposition political parties can campaign for seats in the legislature and even nominate challengers to the leader of the country. Although these elections are neither free nor fair, they channel discontent onto a playing field in which the regime establishes the rules. When its candidates win election, the regime can claim to rule with popular support. The final strategy is repression. One level of repression is to limit citizens' civil and political liberties. Shutting down free speech and the right of assembly limits citizens' ability to organize against the regime. A harsher kind of repression is to target potential leaders of protests for intimidation, whether by means of arrest, imprisonment, rape, torture, or execution.[13]

As we shall see in the final section of the chapter, the ways in which different types of authoritarian regimes solve the problems of power sharing and control have an impact on citizens' capabilities. Some regimes do so in ways

Problem of Authoritarian Power Sharing
The problem faced by authoritarian leaders, of working out ways of sharing power with other members of the leadership group to retain their support and avoid being overthrown through violent and nonconstitutional means.

Problem of Authoritarian Control
The problem faced by authoritarian rulers of how to counter challenges from the masses of the population, and keep them supportive and acquiescent.

that lead to lower infant mortality, higher literacy, and lower homicide rates. They may even boast better performance on infant mortality, literacy, and homicide than in democracies such as the United States. Many other authoritarian regimes, however, solve the problems of power sharing and control in ways that result in extremely low capabilities for their citizens.

Types of Authoritarian Regimes

6.3 Explain how the four types of authoritarian regimes manage the problems of authoritarian power sharing and authoritarian control.

In this section, we examine how four types of authoritarian regimes manage the problems of authoritarian power sharing and authoritarian control: monarchical, military, one-party, and personal rule.

Monarchy

Monarchy
A regime in which the ruler is a person of royal descent, who inherits the position of head of state in accordance with accepted practice or the constitution.

Dynastic Monarchy
A type of monarchy in which the monarch is selected by leading members of the royal family and is accountable to them.

Monarchy is a regime in which the ruler is a person of royal descent, who inherits "the position of head of state in accordance with accepted practice or the constitution."[14] In some monarchies, the ruler's oldest son automatically inherits the throne. The most resilient monarchies have been **dynastic monarchies**, in which the monarch is selected by leading members of the royal family and is accountable to them.[15]

It is important to distinguish between ceremonial and ruling monarchs. Ceremonial monarchs serve a symbolic function and do not actually govern a country. Britain provides an example. Ruling monarchs, on the other hand, are the leaders of their countries and have power to appoint heads of government ministries and make important policy decisions. The largest number of ruling monarchies is found in the Middle East.

It may seem surprising that ruling monarchies still exist in an era when democracy has become so widespread. The number of monarchies remained relatively steady between 1980 and 2010, a period when many military regimes collapsed.[16] A major reason for monarchies' survival has been their effectiveness in handling the twin problems of power sharing and control.

Monarchs use several methods to manage the problem of power sharing. One is to establish deliberative councils that give leading members of the royal family a voice in policy making. Another is to allocate important state offices among the leaders of factions within the royal family. Here the most qualified senior members of the royal family hold the most important posts in the cabinet, civil service, and military. Dividing state revenues among members of the royal family is still another means of sharing power. The family members of monarchical states with large oil revenues have become some of the richest individuals in the world.[17]

To maintain control of society, monarchs use various tactics, which include building coalitions of supporters in society, providing social benefits for citizens, and using repression. In Jordan and Saudi Arabia, tribal leaders who are linked to the royal family by marriage are a key base of monarchical support.[18] Another key group in the Saudi coalition of supporters is Islamic religious leaders who adhere to a very conservative version of their faith.[19] In return for state patronage, these religious leaders encourage their followers to support the monarchy. Jordan's king also uses religion to shore up his legitimacy by reminding citizens that he descends from the Prophet Muhammad, the founder of Islam. Several monarchies have also built a base of support among members of the educated middle class. Monarchies need citizens who are competent to manage state bureaucracies and handle the complexities of managing revenues effectively.[20] These people are the main beneficiaries of state-provided education, and many of them work in the civil service and in state-owned enterprises. In times of political crisis, monarchies with large oil revenues can use the revenues to maintain popular support. In 2011, mass uprisings in several North African and Middle Eastern countries toppled authoritarian regimes. The Saudi government helped tamp down unrest by spending billions of dollars to increase salaries for government employees, build new housing, and expand unemployment benefits.[21]

Monarchies have been less likely to use elections as a means of control than other types of authoritarian regimes.[22] Monarchies never allow competition among political parties to determine who becomes monarch, but some do allow multiparty elections for parliaments. These parliaments generally have very limited powers.

Monarchies stay in power not just by mobilizing support but also through repression. Civil liberties such as free speech are restricted. In some monarchies, even mild criticisms of the ruler can result in arrest and imprisonment. Monarchies have provided generous funding for militaries and security agencies and have used both to suppress criticisms and demonstrations.

A final way monarchies survive is by seeking foreign support. The United States has been the most important source of support for monarchs in the Middle East. One reason for supporting them is that they help maintain the flow of oil from the region that is vital to the U.S. economy. Another reason is that several monarchies in the Middle East are strategically important. They provide military bases, have helped the United States in its fight against al Qaeda, and support its efforts to counter Iranian influence in the Middle East.

Military Regimes

In **military regimes**, the leader of the country is chosen by military officers. Military regimes were one of the most common forms of authoritarian rule in the 1960s and 1970s. During these decades, the military led nearly two-thirds of the countries of Africa, Asia, Latin America, and the Middle East. The number of military regimes has fallen dramatically, however, since the 1980s.[23]

Military Regime
A regime in which a group of military officers chooses the leader of the country, and participates in policy making. Key leadership positions in the state are staffed by military officers.

Coup D'état
A form of regime change in which force is used, often by military leaders, to seize control of a state illegally from its civilian leaders.

Junta
A decision-making council that shares power with an authoritarian ruler, made up of officers who participated in the *coup d'état*.

Military officers come to power by using force illegally to seize control of the state from civilian leaders. Such a seizure of power is known as a **coup d'état**, French for a "blow against the state." (Coup is pronounced "koo."). One common reason officers give for overthrowing a civilian government is that it has interfered in decisions they believe should be left to the military. Another of their rationales for seizing power is the alleged incompetence of civilian governments. Several coups have taken place in countries where economic decline and growing unemployment caused increasing criticism of a civilian government by citizens. The combination of economic woes and weakening political support provided officers with an opportunity to take power. Coups made in these circumstances often have widespread public support. Officers often take power by claiming they are the only ones capable of cleaning up the mess, and they promise to return control of the country to a more competent, civilian democratic government after they have succeeded. The coup d'etat by the Egyptian military in 2013 provides an example.

One of the first challenges confronting officers after they take power is resolving the problem of authoritarian power sharing. The main way they have done so is to form a decision-making council in which officers who participated in the coup share power. Such a council is known as a *junta* (pronounced "hunta"). Leaders of military regimes also share power by distributing control of important government ministries and agencies among *junta* officers. These positions often offer many possibilities for making the officers and members of their family wealthy. When the leader of a *junta* cannot trust other members and believes they are a threat to his power, he can dismiss them and send them into exile or even have them jailed or killed.

In addition to resolving the problem of power sharing, leaders of military regimes must address the issue of authoritarian control. One way of doing so is to build a coalition of supporters who benefit from having military officers in power. In South America, military regimes in the past often relied on a conservative coalition of plantation owners, leading industrialists, and bankers. They also sought the support of conservative, high-ranking clergy in the Catholic Church. In sub-Saharan Africa, military officers have tended to rely on narrow coalitions composed of relatives, business cronies, and members of their own ethnic group. In a small number of cases, military regimes have pursued policies that benefited a large cross section of the population. The military regime that ruled South Korea in the 1970s and 1980s had industrialists as its main supporters and harshly repressed labor unions, but it also enacted land-reform policies that helped poor farmers, and its educational policies helped the sons and daughters of workers.

Leaders of military regimes have used elections to manage the problem of authoritarian control more frequently than monarchies have but less frequently than one-party or personalist regimes.[24] When they have chosen that path, they typically established a political party that has considerable advantages over its civilian counterparts. The most important advantage is that "the incumbents have guns, whereas the opposition does not."[25] However, like other authoritarian regimes, the military's party also holds many other trump cards. These include a monopoly on media coverage, the ability to determine who is eligible to run for office, and control of the election commission that counts votes.

Not surprisingly, given their control over troops and weapons, military regimes have also made extensive use of force to repress opposition. One way of controlling opponents is to declare **martial law**. Martial law gives military rulers the authority to set curfews and ban protests and any other kind of public assembly. Military regimes have also made strong efforts to restrict civil liberties such as free speech and right of assembly. Doing so makes it more difficult for citizens to organize protests. In addition, military regimes have imprisoned, tortured, and killed large numbers of citizens. Military regimes in Argentina, Brazil, and Chile committed numerous murders, never informing the victims' friends and relatives they had been killed or where they were buried. Similarly, the Indonesian military was responsible for the deaths of hundreds of thousands of people in the two years following its seizure of power in 1965.

Finally, like monarchies, some military regimes have received support from the United States. The United States substantially aided military regimes in Brazil, Chile, Egypt, Indonesia, South Korea, Thailand, and elsewhere during the Cold War, and it continued to provide economic aid to the Egyptian military in 2013 even after it carried out a coup d'état against an elected government.

Martial Law
Law applied by military forces, which gives them the authority to set curfews, ban public gatherings and demonstrations, and forbid any other kind of public assembly in the name of maintaining public order and safety.

One-Party Regimes

In **one-party regimes**, high-ranking members of the ruling political party select the country's leader from among its senior personnel. There are two main kinds of one-party regimes. First are those in which the ruling party does not allow elections in which other political parties can compete against it. Current examples include Communist Party–led regimes in China, Laos, and Vietnam. The other kind of one-party regime is those in which the ruling group allows multiparty elections to determine who becomes the country's leader and who earns seats in the legislature. Examples include the regimes in Cambodia, Malaysia, Tanzania, and Zimbabwe.

Like monarchs and leaders of military regimes, the leaders of one-party regimes must be concerned with threats to their rule from within the party's top ranks. One of the most effective ways of limiting such threats is to establish committees in which elite party members can have a say in determining public policy. The other way of limiting threats is to establish rules about how transitions from one set of leaders to another are made. Such rules may stipulate that a leader cannot hold power for life but must step down after a set term in office and give other candidates a shot at leadership. In the absence of such rules, the struggle for power at the top ranks of the party can be ruthless and bloody. In the Soviet Union in the 1920s and 1930s, and in China in the 1960s and 1970s, struggles over policies and leadership were marked by brutal competition, ending in the imprisonment and deaths of thousands of members of the party elite.

One-Party Regime
A regime in which high-ranking members of the ruling political party elect the country's leader from among its senior personnel, control access to political office, and control policy-making.

Another way that one-party regimes handle the problem of authoritarian power sharing is to give high-ranking party members special benefits and privileges. These include appointments to powerful positions in the state bureaucracy and state-owned corporations, which provide numerous opportunities for cutting deals with domestic entrepreneurs and foreign investors. Holding a high-ranking position in the country's leadership provides opportunities for wealth for both the individual and his or her extended family. For example, between 2003 and 2013, family members of China's prime minister amassed a fortune estimated at $2.7 billion.[26]

One-party regimes also seek to win support among groups in society at large. They have a built-in base of support composed of party members and their families. In China, approximately one of every twelve adults is a party member. This is a sizable minority of the population that has a very strong stake in having the party remain in power.[27] In addition to relying on party members and their families, one-party regimes build coalitions among people who are important for their regimes' survival. Communist parties in China and Vietnam have increasingly sought the support of business people and well-educated professionals whose knowledge and skills are essential to maintaining the economic growth that creates jobs and raises incomes. Party leaders hope that these results will generate support.

Communist Party regimes do not hold elections in which multiple parties can compete for power. By contrast, nearly all other one-party states hold elections for the same reason that motivates leaders of other forms of authoritarian government, namely to draw opponents into electoral competitions that are rigged to favor the regime.[28] By winning elections, ruling parties can claim to rule with popular support. In addition, elections often have the side benefit of splitting opponents of the regime into those who take part in the elections in hopes of influencing policies and those who believe that such participation is naïve and only strengthens the regime. Elections also help regimes identify effective leaders in the larger society who need to be co-opted or suppressed.

Leaders of one-party regimes use the same kinds of sticks to solve the problem of authoritarian control that their monarchical and military counterparts do: curtailment of civil liberties, arrests, imprisonment, torture, and executions. One-party regimes vary considerably, however, in the extent to which they use certain means of repression. The governments of Singapore has relied more on threats, lawsuits, and arrests to intimidate critics. Other regimes, such as the one in Zimbabwe, have been much more willing to use violent repression.

Contemporary one-party regimes tend to rely less on foreign patrons than monarchies and military regimes do, unlike many of their counterparts from the past. In the 1950s China received extensive support from the Soviet Union, as did Cuba from the 1960s through the 1980s.

In-Depth: Zimbabwe—How to Wreck an Economy and Weaken Capabilities

During the 1970s, Robert Mugabe was one of the main leaders of an armed rebellion against white rule in the sub-Saharan Africa country of Rhodesia. In 1979, Great Britain arranged a negotiated settlement to end the fighting, and Mugabe was elected leader of the country the following year. Rhodesia was renamed Zimbabwe and was one of the most economically promising countries in Africa. Mugabe was still in power in 2013, but the means he used to achieve that status wrecked the economy and weakened citizens' capabilities.

Mugabe came to power as the party leader of the Zimbabwe African National Union (ZANU). He solved the problem of power sharing by giving party allies control of key state agencies and by appointing allies to executive positions in companies owned by the party or the state. His allies received millions of dollars illegally taken from state-owned diamond mines.[29]

Mugabe solved the problem of authoritarian control by mobilizing support, rigging elections, and using repression. In the 1990s, he won the support of thousands of former veterans of the war for independence by backing their violent seizure of white-owned farms. Likewise, he gained support from black business-people by approving a law requiring black majority ownership of large business firms.

Mugabe also used rigged elections as a means of control. Government-controlled media favor his party, and the national elections commission, which was packed with his appointees, manipulated names on voting rolls and rigged vote totals to ensure his victories.

Mugabe also used repression. In the 2008 presidential election, his opponent won enough votes to force Mugabe into a run-off. Security forces and hired thugs used beatings, rapes, amputations of hands and arms, and murders to intimidate his opponent's supporters. His opponent withdrew from the election.

Mugabe's economic policies led to astronomic levels of inflation. In 2007, a beer cost one million Zimbabwean dollars. By 2013, inflation was under control but growth was slowing and capabilities languished. The United Nations publishes an annual index of countries' performance on health, education, and standards of living. In 2013, only two countries in the world had a lower index score in 2012 than they had in 1990. One was Zimbabwe.[30] Yet Mugabe won the 2013 presidential election, which granted him another five years in power.

For Further Discussion

1. Why have the ways in which Mugabe solved problems of authoritarian power sharing and control resulted in so little improvement in capabilities?.
2. Mugabe has rationalized letting war veterans seize farms owned by white farmers by saying white settlers seized the best farm land in the country from Africans during the era of British colonialism. Is this rationale justified ?

Personalist Regimes

The leaders of monarchies, military, and one-party regimes are accountable to their respective supporters in the royal family, military officers, and high-ranking party members. There have been numerous cases, however, when leaders have been able to concentrate power in their own hands and loosen organizational

Personal Rule
A type of authoritarian rule in which a leader is able to concentrate power in his or her own hands to control policy making and selection of state personnel without effective constraints from an organization or the public.

restraints on what they can do. They accumulate so much power that they can impose their views without significant constraints from other leading members of the regime. The result is **personal rule**.[31] Personalist rulers gain control over appointment of personnel and policy. They tend to stay in power for life because the allies who helped them gain power no longer can seriously challenge them, and the persons they appoint to positions in the state depend completely on them.[32] The latter tend to be very loyal because if they offend the leader and are dismissed, they lose power, prestige, and the opportunity to share in the plunder of the country's economy. Most cases of personal rule occur in very poor countries with weak political and economic institutions. These countries are concentrated in two regions of the world: sub-Saharan Africa and Central Asia.[33]

Personalist rulers do not have to share power with others, but they do have to worry about ambitious individuals seeking to overthrow them. The biggest threat is from military officers. Personalist rulers try to neutralize this threat in two ways. First, they fill officer ranks with relatives and cronies and create personally loyal forces that are not part of the regular military. Second, they use surveillance and spies to inhibit cooperation among dissenting officers. Those suspected of plotting against them may be imprisoned or executed.

Personalist rulers rely on narrow coalitions of supporters in society and make extensive use of repression. Their links to society usually consist of cliques of relatives, friends, and crony entrepreneurs. State revenues are used mainly for enriching the ruler, the ruler's family members, and supporters rather than for improving the lives of citizens. Many use rigged elections that give opponents no chance to win as a strategy for holding on to power and claiming to rule with popular support.

Like other authoritarian leaders, personalist rulers have used foreign support to maintain their power. During the Cold War, many courted either the United States or the Soviet Union. The United States supported a number of personalist rulers, including Joseph Mobutu, who ruled the sub-Saharan nation of Zaire from 1965 until 1997. The United States backed Mobutu both to keep the

In Brief: Types of Authoritarian Rule

- Monarchy: rule by someone of royal descent who is made head of state in accordance with accepted practice or the constitution. Saudi Arabia is an example.
- Military: rule by a military officer or group of officers backed by a country's military. Examples include Brazil and Chile in the 1970s and 1980s and Egypt in 2014.
- One-party: rule by the leader of a dominant political party. In some cases, the dominant party allows no electoral competition. China is an example. In other cases, the dominant party allows multiparty elections in which the rules are tilted in favor of the dominant party. Singapore is an example.
- Personalist: rule by a single leader who makes political decisions without organizational constraints. Muammar Gaddafi of Libya was an example.

Comparative Political Analysis: Why Do Elections Lead to Democratization in Some Authoritarian Regimes but Not Others?

Problem: Many authoritarian regimes hold elections, but these elections are used as a means of authoritarian control rather than a means to give voters a political voice. In several countries, however, elections in authoritarian regimes have resulted in transitions to democratic politics. Why has this happened in some countries but not others? Steven Levitsky and Lucas A. Way suggest in *Competitive Authoritarianism: Hybrid Regimes after the Cold War* that international as well as domestic variables influence whether elections lead to democratization.

Hypothesis and Method: Levitsky and Way focus on a particular category of authoritarian regimes, which they label competitive authoritarian regimes. They hypothesize that when such regimes have strong links to Western democracies, they are likely to democratize. Western governments and human rights organizations are more likely to provide support for opposition groups in such countries. Moreover, these countries often have extensive trade with the West and therefore are vulnerable to trade sanctions. Finally, they tend to have many citizens who benefit from close ties to the West and want to maintain them. In these circumstances, authoritarian rulers are likely to allow democratic transitions.[34] The authors test their hypothesis by using comparative case studies of competitive authoritarian regimes in 35 countries between 1990 and 2008.

Operationalizing Concepts: The authors operationalize their key concepts as follows:

- Competitive authoritarian regimes are regimes in which democratic institutions are used to select leaders, but authoritarian rulers make it extremely difficult for opposition candidates to win elections.[35]
- Linkage, the independent variable, is the extent of trade, travel, telephone and internet traffic, and governmental ties between the country and Western Europe or the United States.[36]
- Democracy, the dependent variable, is defined as having "free, fair, and competitive elections; full adult suffrage; broad protection of civil liberties; and governing power in the hands of elected officials."[37]

Results: The comparative case studies of the 35 competitive authoritarian regimes provide strong support for the hypothesis. Competitive authoritarian regimes in countries having strong links to the West democratized. Where linkage with Western democracies was weak, competitive authoritarian regimes with strong state coercive capacity and governing political parties were likely to remain in power.[38]

For Further Discussion

1. Why do close links with Western countries make transitions to democracy likely in competitive authoritarian regimes?
2. How can Levitsky and Way's analysis help explain Robert Mugabe's long tenure in power in Zimbabwe?

country out of Soviet hands and to ensure access to the country's valuable mineral wealth. For his part, Mobutu used the aid to enrich himself and to help maintain the patronage network he relied on to control the state and society. He accumulated a personal fortune estimated at $5 billion in one of the poorest countries in the world during his years in power.

Explaining Authoritarian Persistence

6.4 Evaluate explanations of authoritarian persistence in the Middle East and North Africa.

The late twentieth century was particularly auspicious for democracy. Between 1974 and 1995, the number of democracies rose from 40 to 117, but authoritarian regimes were more likely to survive in some regions of the world than in others. Although democracy swept away numerous authoritarian regimes in Latin America, Africa, Asia, and Eastern Europe, the Middle East and North Africa resisted that trend.[39] This resistance seemed to be crumbling in 2011, when massive popular uprisings toppled authoritarian regimes in Tunisia, Egypt, Libya, and Yemen and challenged several other authoritarian regimes in the region.

The uprisings were fueled by unemployment, anger at corrupt officials, growing income inequality, and political repression. New social media such as Facebook and Twitter helped individuals communicate their anger. The Internet and smart phones helped organizers mobilize huge crowds in protests, which resulted in the collapse of authoritarian regimes.

Demonstrators' success in overthrowing authoritarian rulers in the region, and challenging several others, led to optimism that a wave of democracy would sweep through the Middle East. This optimism faded, however, as the remaining regimes in the region managed to hold on to power. Moreover, prospects for democracy crumbled in Egypt, Libya, Syria, and Yemen. In 2013, the Egyptian military seized power in a coup d'état, and large areas of Libya and Yemen were controlled by local strongmen and militias. Tunisia remained the sole country where establishing a democratic regime seemed possible, but prospects for democracy there remained uncertain.[40] In summary, in 2013, most countries in the Middle East remained under authoritarian control despite hopes the Arab Spring raised.[41]

Political scientists divide explanations of why authoritarianism persists into two categories: international and domestic. International explanations include both weak linkages to Western democracies, as detailed by Levitsky and Way, and the willingness of Western democracies to support particular authoritarian regimes for strategic purposes. The United States approved the overthrow of authoritarian regimes in Libya and Tunisia in 2011 but continued to back monarchies in Saudi Arabia and Bahrain. Saudi Arabia helps ensure the flow of Middle Eastern oil to the United States and cooperates in the struggle against al Qaeda. The monarchy in Bahrain provides the United States with a major naval base.

Map 6.1 Countries of the Middle East and North Africa

SOURCE: http://www.lefo.ro/iwlearn/www.worldbank.org/depweb/english/maps/men1.htm

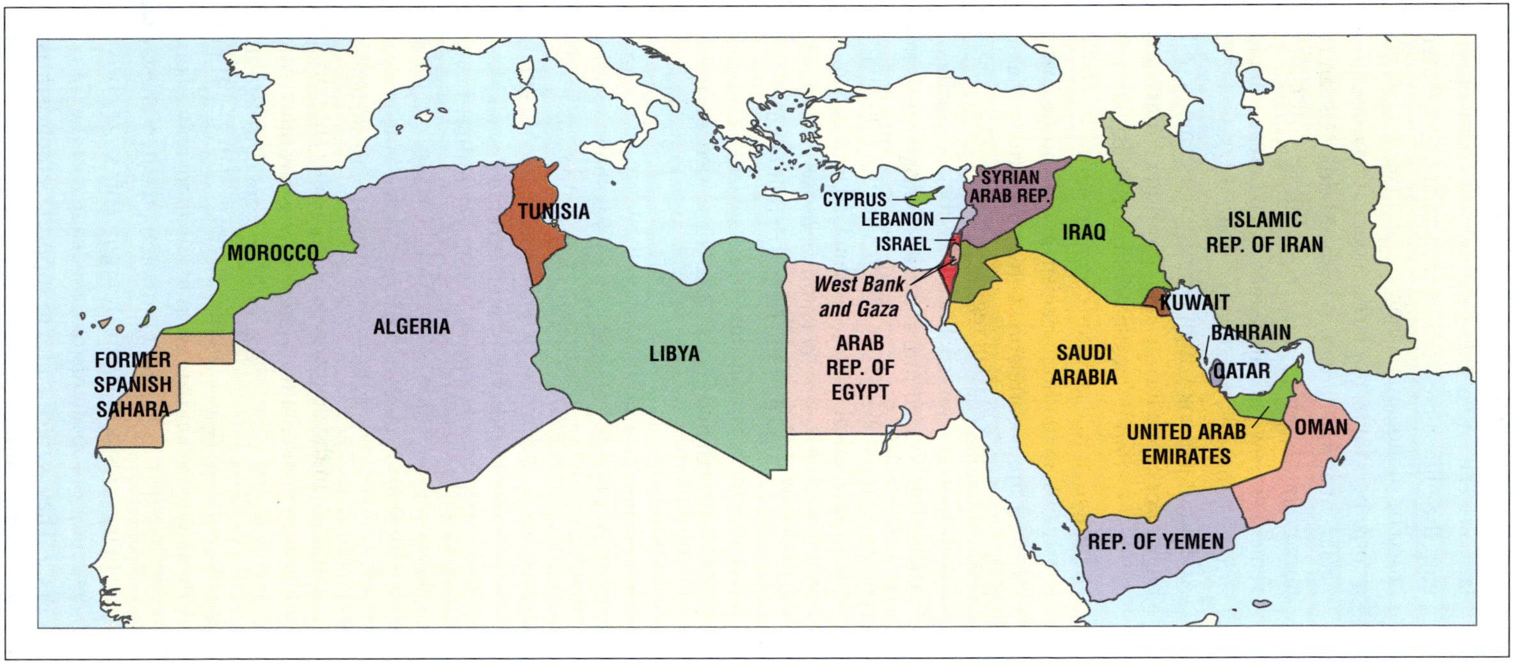

There are four main domestic explanations of the persistence of authoritarian rule. The first of these is a country's level of economic development. In general, the higher the level of economic development, the more likely countries are to be democratic. One way of measuring economic development is to use income per capita, but income per capita does not help much in understanding persistent authoritarianism in the Middle East and North Africa, where authoritarian regimes govern countries with very different levels of per capita income. Yemen has low per capita income, whereas Iran, Jordan, and Syria are middle-income countries, and Qatar,[42] Bahrain, Kuwait, Saudi Arabia, and the United Arab Emirates enjoy high per capita income. In 2012, Qatar ranked as having a higher per capita income than any other country in the world.[43]

The second domestic variable political scientists use to explain persistent authoritarian rule is culture. Some political scientists argue that Islamic culture is responsible for authoritarianism in the Middle East and North Africa, and there is indeed a strong correlation between the two variables. Although not all the countries with authoritarian regimes in the region have low per capita income, they are all Islamic. Some political scientists go further, arguing that the connection between Islamic culture and authoritarian rule is more than just a correlation; in their view, it is actually a cause. The best-known proponent of this position was Harvard political scientist Samuel P. Huntington, author of *The Clash of Civilizations and the Remaking of World Order*, who asserted bluntly that "Islamic culture explains in large part the failure of democracy to emerge in most of the Muslim world." One reason for this, he argued, is that Islam does not provide for the separation of church and state. The consequence is little tolerance for the pluralism of ideas that is essential for democracy.[44] Moreover, there is widespread belief that laws come from God and that, therefore, religious law rather than laws devised by democratically elected legislatures should be the foundation for states.[45]

Many scholars challenge Huntington's assertion that Islamic culture explains the failure of democracy to emerge in the Muslim world. They point out that no single interpretation of Islam is accepted by all Muslims. Individual Muslims differ in their attitudes toward political authority, rights for women, and even the status of Islamic law itself. Malala Yousafzai, the advocate for girls' education in Pakistan, discussed in Chapter 4 is a Muslim, yet her views are very different from those of the Pakistani Taliban. There are also significant differences among countries in the degree to which citizens support making Islamic *sharia* law the basis for their country's laws. **Sharia law** offers Muslims "moral and legal guidance for nearly all aspects of life—from marriage and divorce, to inheritance and contracts, to criminal punishments."[46] In Iraq, 91 percent favored making *sharia* the law of the land, whereas in Lebanon, only 29 percent did.[47]

Another reason for questioning the hypothesis that Islam is a major obstacle to democracy is that similar arguments were once made about Catholicism. For much of European history, the leaders of the Catholic Church opposed democracy. They wanted states to support Catholicism as "the one true faith"[48] and to deny non-Catholics the freedom to express their views and recruit others to their

Sharia Law
Muslim law based on the Qur'an and the teachings of the Prophet Muhammad, which offers Muslims moral and legal guidance for nearly all aspects of life.

beliefs. As recently as the 1970s, several countries where Catholics constituted a large majority of the population had authoritarian rule, including Spain, Brazil, and Argentina. These countries are now democracies. As political scientist Jay Ulfelder notes, predictions that democracy will not take root in a region because it is not compatible with the region's predominant religion do not have a good track record.[49]

A final reason for challenging the assertion that Islam is a major obstacle to democracy is that several surveys find substantial support for democracy in many Muslim societies. A Pew Foundation survey in 2012 reported that majorities in Egypt, Jordan, and Tunisia believed democracy was preferable to any other form of government.[50] Similar findings in other surveys contradict assertions that Islamic publics are hostile to democracy.[51] Even more important, in 2010, six predominantly Muslim countries were classified as democracies. These countries have not achieved the same standards of democracy as democracies in Western Europe or North America, but they are rated as democracies by respected organizations that rank countries' degree of democracy, such as the Polity IV Project.[52] One of them is Indonesia, the fourth most populous country in the world and by far the most populous Muslim country.[53] The existence of democratic countries where Muslims comprise a majority of the population is evidence that Islam is not an insuperable obstacle to democracy.

It is true that Islamic beliefs can be obstacles to democracy. The ways in which they do so, however, have less to do with a primordial, unchanging Islamic culture than with ways in which rulers and their allies interpret Islamic texts to justify their rule, and divisions in Islamic culture and the ways political leaders use these divisions for political advantage. As constructivist interpretations of culture and identity suggest, societies often have master cleavages that divide them. In Islamic societies, two master cleavages exist: between Islamic fundamentalists and moderate Muslims and between Shia and Sunni Muslims. These differences have served as fault lines for intense conflicts in Iraq, Egypt, and Libya, dampening prospects for the establishment of stable democracies. Leaders in these countries have often used these cleavages to fuel conflicts for political advantage. As this intensity escalates, it becomes harder to sustain democratic politics and easier to justify authoritarian rule.

Explanations using income per capita and Islamic culture do not provide satisfactory explanations for the persistence of authoritarian rule in the Middle East and North Africa. Explanations based on these variables also have difficulty explaining why most authoritarian rulers survived popular uprisings during the Arab Spring from late 2010 into 2012 while some did not. Oil wealth also has difficulties explaining authoritarian persistence for decades because several regimes in the region had no oil wealth. Oil wealth does a better job, however, of explaining the differing outcomes of the Arab Spring.

Oil exports provided the surviving regimes with extraordinarily high revenues. Rulers used the revenues to buy support from their citizens by providing large numbers of government jobs and generous public services. These

In Brief: Domestic Explanations for Authoritarian Persistence

Hypothesis

Per Capita Income	The higher a country's per capita income, the more likely it is to be a democracy.
Culture	Islam is responsible for the failure of democracy to emerge in most of the Muslim world because it does not separate religion and state and legitimates authoritarian, top-down rule.
Oil Revenue	High oil revenues help sustain authoritarian rule because they enable rulers to buy support and pay for repressive coercive forces to maintain their power.
Hereditary Rule	Hereditary rule helped rulers without oil wealth survive the Arab Spring.

expenditures helped a number of these regimes avoid large scale popular uprisings completely. The revenues also funded powerful security agencies and sizeable militaries that could be used to repress dissent if needed. The only oil-wealthy ruler who was overthrown was Libyan dictator Muammar Gaddafi. There was a massive popular uprising against him, but he was driven from power only after prolonged air strikes against his air force and troops by far superior European air forces. Oil revenues help explain why all the authoritarian regimes with large oil and gas revenues, remained in power with the exception of Gaddafi.[54] Oil revenues cannot be the full explanation of authoritarian persistence during the Arab Spring, however, because autocratic governments endured in three countries without large oil revenues: Jordan, Morocco, and Syria.[55]

Their survival can be explained by a fourth variable, hereditary rule in which a ruler's power can be transferred "smoothly from one member of the ruling family to another."[56] These rulers had loyal military commanders willing to use whatever force was necessary to suppress popular uprisings.

In summary, rulers with large oil wealth and hereditary rulers who lacked oil wealth, but had loyal officer corps, survived the Arab Spring. Non-hereditary rulers who lacked large oil revenues to buy support from the population, and loyal, united militaries to defend them against popular uprisings, were overthrown in Egypt, Tunisia, and Yemen.[57]

Authoritarianism and the Good Society

6.5 Explain the reasoning supporting the hypothesis that regime type affects capabilities and evaluate the way in which that hypothesis is tested.

Political leaders pay attention to the needs of those who put them in power and can remove them from power.[58] Capabilities tend to be higher in democracies than in authoritarian regimes because large numbers of voters participate in electing leaders. Leaders in democracies thus have strong incentives to choose policies that improve citizens' lives. In authoritarian regimes, only a very small percentage of the population has any say in selecting the leader. Nevertheless, there are considerable differences in levels of capabilities among authoritarian regimes. Why do some authoritarian regimes do more to improve the capabilities of citizens than others? We propose that those differences are due in part to the different ways in which authoritarian regimes select leaders and how leaders resolve problems of power sharing and control. Our first hypothesis is that monarchies will provide higher levels of capabilities than other types of authoritarian regimes.[59] Our second hypothesis is that personalist regimes will display the lowest capabilities.

The most successful monarchies are Middle Eastern dynastic monarchies in oil-rich countries. In these regimes, the ruler is selected by leading members of the royal family and is accountable to that group. To obtain support, the ruler must assure leading family members that they will be appointed to high-ranking positions in the state bureaucracy. They must also guarantee family members property rights to oil revenues and convince family members that they will promote their long-term interests.[60]

The ways in which dynastic monarchs are selected and required to share power give them incentives to adopt policies that produce sustained revenues for the long run. The policies are designed to increase the size of the economic pie to be divided among powerful members of the royal family. These policies include strong support for property rights and reliance on well-educated and skilled officials to manage economic policy.[61] Although members of the royal family are the main beneficiaries, the policies provide side benefits for citizens generally. The need for well-educated and skilled officials gives monarchs incentives to improve education, and the large, sustained revenues provide them funds to pay for education and health care without taxing citizens. These policies enable monarchs to portray themselves as benevolent rulers and help them gain citizens' acquiescence to their rule.

Personalist rulers differ from dynastic monarchs in every respect. They do not have to share power with other powerful elites, so they have free rein to plunder their economies for personal benefit. Although they need lieutenants to help them rule, they can buy their support by giving them a share in the plunder. They achieve authoritarian control by building a narrow base of support among relatives, cronies, and leaders of some ethnic groups. Under personal rule, property rights are weak; independent entrepreneurs have few incentives to develop businesses because they might be confiscated or taxed into bankruptcy. The consequences of personal rule tend to include low economic growth, poverty, and low capabilities.

We test our hypothesis by using the categories of authoritarian regimes we have used for the chapter: monarchical, military, one-party, and personal rule.[62] We exclude countries that are hybrids of different regime types. For example, Cuba is left out of our one-party category because it combines single-party and personal rule. Column charts are used to present our results. We do not include military regimes in the charts because our source for data on how long regimes were in power coded only two countries for that category for the years we are examining: Algeria and Myanmar (Burma). Column charts presenting average scores for just these two countries would result in a misleading summary of numerous military regimes' performance in Africa, Asia, and Latin America in previous decades. We rely on the work of others to summarize the effects of military regimes on capabilities. Our categories include 10 monarchies, 11 one-party regimes, and 17 personalist regimes. We selected all of the regimes in each category that had been in power for at least 15 years consecutively prior to 2010. We assume that regimes in power for this long have had sufficient time to have an impact on capabilities.

Physical Well-being

As can be seen in Figure 6.1, monarchies have the lowest infant mortality rates. One-party regimes have the next lowest rate, with personalist regimes lagging far behind.

Raw averages, however, hide considerable differences within each regime type. Oil-rich Middle Eastern dynastic monarchies such as Saudi Arabia, Qatar, and the United Arab Emirates had much lower infant mortality rates than poorer, non-dynastic monarchies. There are also large differences among one-party regimes. High-income Singapore had an infant mortality rate of only

Figure 6.1 Authoritarian Regime Type and Infant Mortality Rate per 1,000 in (2011)

SOURCES: Regime Type: Barbara Geddes, Joseph Wright, and Erica Frantz, *Global Regimes Codebook*, November 21, 2011, http://dictators.la.psu.edu/data/GlobalRegimesCodebook.pdf; Infant Mortality: World Bank. World Development Indicators 2011, http://data.worldbank.org/data-catalog/world-development-indicators.

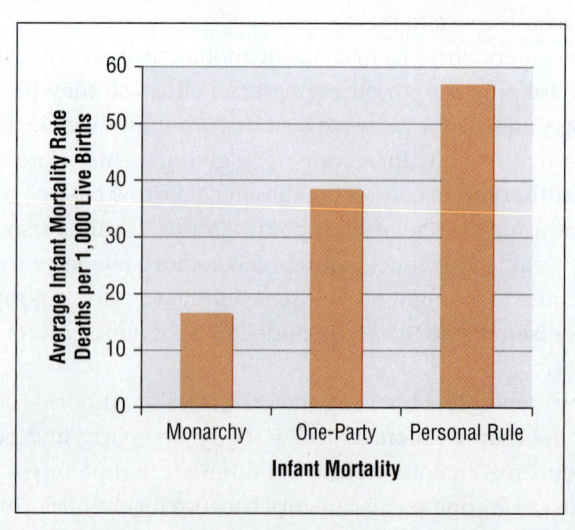

2 per 1,000 in 2011, much lower than the rate in the United States. On the other hand, impoverished Angola had 96 infant deaths per 1,000 births. A small number of countries with personalist regimes, such as Russia and Belarus, also had relatively low infant mortality rates. Most personalist regimes, however, are in very poor countries with extremely high infant mortality rates. We do not have comparable data for a significant number of military regimes, but data from earlier decades suggest that they fall between monarchies and personalist regimes with regard to infant mortality. As with the other regime types, there were significant differences among military regimes. Several in Asia and Latin America reduced infant mortality rates substantially. The Chilean military regime (1973–1990) rapidly reduced Chile's infant mortality rate between 1973 and 1984.[63] On the other hand, military regimes in poor countries had much worse records. The military regimes that controlled Nigeria from the early 1970s until the late 1990s had no success in reducing infant mortality rates, which hovered around 120 per 1,000 from 1975 until 1995.

Examining *levels* of infant mortality alone, as we did in the previous paragraph, may create the impression that no progress has occurred in personalist regimes, but that impression would be mistaken. Although many personalist regimes had very high *levels* of infant mortality in 2011, several of them made considerable advances in reducing the number of infant deaths while they were in power. This can be seen by examining *changes* in mortality rates.[64] In the 20-year span from 1990 to 2010, the average annual decline in infant mortality was 2.47 percent in monarchies, 2.29 percent in one-party regimes, and 1.55 percent in personalist regimes.[65] Monarchies still come out on top and personalist regimes on the bottom, but personalist regimes in very poor countries nevertheless achieved reductions in infant mortality between 1990 and 2010. A few achieved reductions of 40 percent or more. Examining changes in mortality rates also reveals countries that have failed to make progress. Robert Mugabe's Zimbabwe was one of the worst performers. Infant mortality rates in Zimbabwe, which stood at 52 per 1,000 in 1990, declined to only 51 per 1,000 in 2010.

Informed Decision Making

The same pattern between regime type and infant mortality rates holds for adult literacy. Monarchies were the most successful in promoting literacy, followed by one-party regimes. Personalist regimes had the worst record. See Figure 6.2.

As with infant mortality, there were big differences within the same regime type. Several Middle Eastern monarchies had rates of adult literacy exceeding 90 percent, whereas the North African monarchy of Morocco did much worse, with only 56 percent in 2012.

There are also significant disparities among one-party regimes. Ruling communist parties in China and Vietnam could boast literacy rates of over 90 percent by 2011, but Laos, another communist regime, lagged behind. Other kinds

Figure 6.2 Regime Type and Adult Literacy (2009–2011)

SOURCES: Regime Type: Barbara Geddes, Joseph Wright, and Erica Frantz, *Global Regimes Codebook*, November 21, 2011, http://dictators.la.psu.edu/data/GlobalRegimesCodebook.pdf; Adult Literacy: World Bank World Development Indicators, http://data.worldbank.org/data-catalog/world-development-indicators; and United Nations Human Development Programme, http://hdrstats.undp.org.

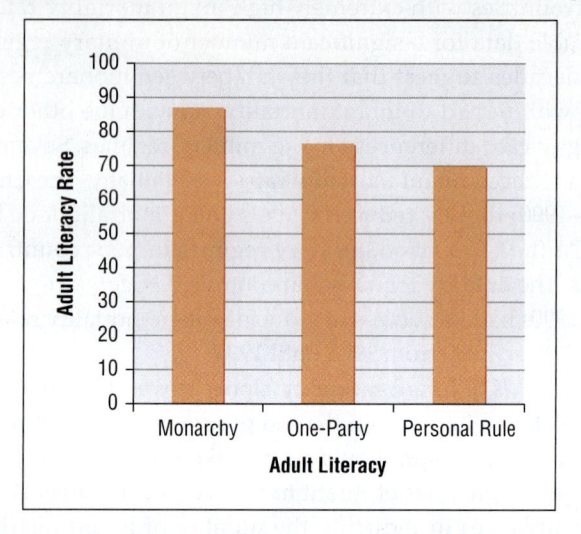

of one-party authoritarian regimes also vary greatly along this dimension. One-party regimes in extremely poor countries tended to have low literacy rates.

Personalist regimes again came in last, but there were dramatic differences within this category. The five personalist regimes in countries that were formerly part of the Soviet Union had literacy rates of 100 percent, largely. because of the emphasis the Communist Party of the Soviet Union placed on literacy. At the other extreme are poor countries in sub-Saharan Africa, which have extremely low rates of adult literacy. Chad's rate was a mere 34 percent.

The record of military regimes regarding literacy echoed their infant mortality. Some were quite successful in increasing literacy; others failed in that regard. South Korea, which already had a relatively high literacy rate at the beginning of military rule in 1961, made impressive gains by the time the military surrendered power in 1987. Military regimes in Brazil and Chile also raised literacy rates, but their counterparts in sub-Saharan Africa military regimes lagged well behind, as they did with infant mortality. When military rule ended in Nigeria in the late 1990s, literacy rates stood at only 55 percent.

Safety

Homicide rates can be a misleading indicator of citizens' safety in authoritarian regimes. In many of these regimes, the main threat to individual lives come not from fellow citizens but from officials of the state. One-party leaders sometimes

Figure 6.3 Regime Type and Homicide Rates per 100,000 (2011)

SOURCES: Regime Type: Barbara Geddes, Joseph Wright, and Erica Frantz, *Global Regimes Codebook*, November 21, 2011; Barbara Geddes, Joseph Wright, and Erica Frantz, "New Data on Autocratic Regimes," (September 8, 2012), http://dictators.la.psu.edu; Homicide Rates: *UNODC Global Study on Homicide 2011*, http://www.unodc.org/unodc/en/data-and-analysis/homicide.html.

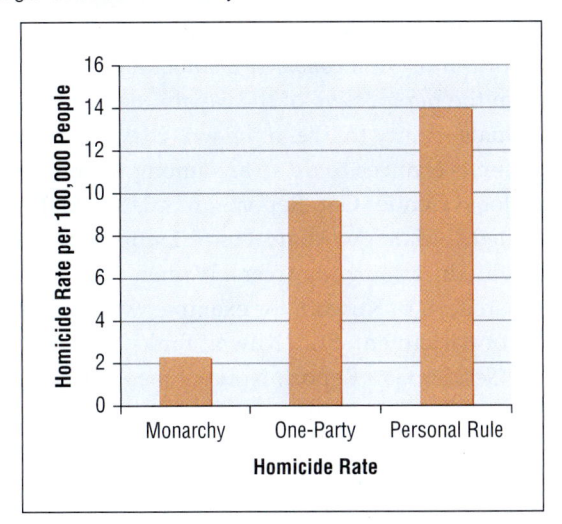

have initiated political campaigns that killed large numbers of people. Likewise, the seizure and consolidation of power by military regimes often have resulted in mass deaths. Homicide rates, however, still provide a useful way of measuring citizens' safety on a day-to-day basis.

As revealed in Figure 6.3, monarchies are once again the clear winners. Most Middle Eastern monarchies have homicide rates equal to, or lower than, those of high-income European democracies. The average homicide rate for the ten monarchies is only 2.3 per 100,000.[66]

One-party authoritarian regimes tend to have either unusually low or unusually high homicide rates. Some, such as Singapore and Tunisia, had homicide rates lower than 2 per 100,000. Others, such as Ethiopia and Tanzania, had homicide rates over 20 per 100,000, among the highest in the world.

The homicide rates found in personalist regimes also vary greatly. Several personalist regimes in countries that were formerly republics in the Soviet Union had low rates in 2011. In contrast, other personalist regimes, including Uganda and the Ivory Coast, had extremely high homicide rates.

Military regimes have had some of the lowest and highest homicide rates of any type of authoritarian regime, but homicide rates, as noted previously, can be a misleading indicator of citizen safety in these regimes. Military rulers in Brazil and Chile murdered thousands of suspected opponents, whereas in the 1960s, the Indonesian military murdered hundreds of thousands.

Democracy

Although monarchies, as we saw, have the lowest infant mortality and homicide rates and the highest literacy rates, they come in last in democracy rankings. See Figure 6.4. Some monarchies, such as Saudi Arabia, impose severe restrictions on civil and political rights, thereby weakening citizens' capabilities. It ranked near the bottom of the *Economist* Democracy Index in 2012 at 163 of 167 countries. From the perspective of the capabilities approach, good societies expand individuals' ability to live in the way they have reason to value. In Saudi Arabia, women's chances to do so are among the most restricted in the world. The 2012 Global Gender Gap Report ranks Saudi Arabia 131 among the 135 countries studied.[67] Male guardians control women's finances and make decisions about their education and careers. Women are not quite so restricted in other Arab monarchies. In Kuwait, for example, women can drive cars and serve as members of parliament. Still, Kuwait ranks 109 among the 135 countries in the Global Gender Gap Report. None of the Arab monarchies score in the top 100 in terms of gender equality. And it is worth noting that foreigners living in the Arab monarchies face even more severe restrictions than women. Foreign males work as laborers in the oil industry and at construction sites; females are employed as maids and personal servants. They receive none of the benefits that citizens do.

In democracy rankings, one-party regimes can be divided into two categories. Communist one-party regimes are highly repressive. China, Vietnam, and Laos receive lower scores on the *Economist* democracy index than most other one-party regimes. The exception is Zimbabwe, which was rated as even more authoritarian than China and Vietnam despite allowing multi-party elections.

Figure 6.4 Regime Type and Democracy Index (2012)

SOURCES: Regime Type: Barbara Geddes, Joseph Wright, and Erica Frantz, *Global Regimes Codebook*, November 21, 2011, http://dictators.la.psu.edu/data/GlobalRegimesCodebook.pdf

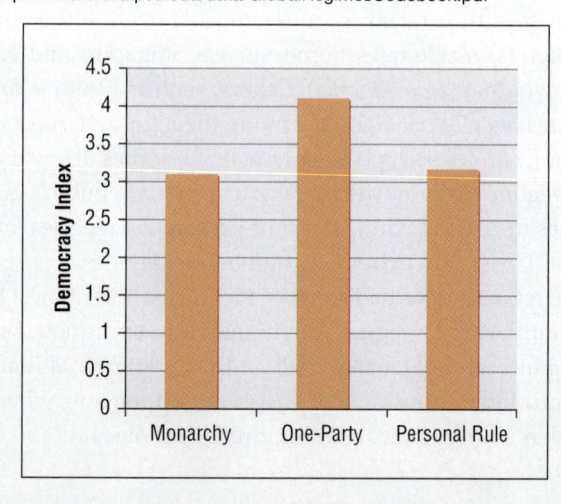

Personalist regimes have democracy ratings similar to those of monarchies, with two sub-Saharan African countries, the Central African Republic and Chad, standing out from the others regarding repressiveness. Military regimes in recent decades have varied in levels of authoritarianism.

In summary, four themes stand out in this comparison of regime type and capabilities. First, as we hypothesized, monarchies have the highest capabilities, and personalist regimes have the lowest. Second, there is considerable diversity in capabilities within regime types. All monarchies do not provide higher capabilities than all one-party or military regimes. Nor do all one-party regimes and military regimes provide higher capabilities than all personalist regimes. Third, a country's level of economic development matters a great deal for capabilities. Within regime types, wealthier countries tend to have higher capabilities than poorer ones. Finally, and surprisingly, even poor countries led by personalist rulers have made progress. Many of these countries still have very high infant mortality levels, but several have reduced infant mortality substantially. Our hypothesis did not anticipate this outcome.

These findings are tentative for several reasons. First, they are correlations rather than fully developed causal explanations. Also, there are different ways of categorizing authoritarian regimes than the one that we used. Using an alternative way of categorizing regimes might alter the results, as might examining a larger number of countries. Finally, variables could account for the differences among regimes that we missed. Nevertheless, the findings are in line with those of several other authors who have examined why some types of authoritarian regimes do better than others at promoting capabilities.[68]

Conclusion

The resilience of authoritarian regimes has forced political scientists to reassess their assumption of the 1990s that authoritarian regimes were relics that would soon be replaced by democracies. In the past two decades, political scientists have devoted considerable attention to explaining why such regimes have survived.[69] Their findings lead to five conclusions. First, some of the kinds of authoritarian regimes that have survived have done so by making big changes in policies. Communist one-party regimes have either collapsed, as in the case of the Soviet Union, or have been forced to make substantial changes, as in the case of China. China's leaders have shifted from economic models based on state ownership and central planning to allowing a significant role for markets. They have also given their citizens greater freedom to decide where to live, what to buy, and what to believe. Leaders of nearly all authoritarian regimes, excepting North Korea and Cuba, assume that the only effective economic system is one that relies extensively on markets.

Second, democracy today is the only widely accepted way of gaining political legitimacy. Nobel Prize–winning economist Amartya Sen writes, "While democracy is not yet universally practiced, nor indeed universally accepted, in the general climate of world opinion, democratic governance has now achieved the status of being taken to be generally right."[70] Even in the Middle East and North Africa, where authoritarian regimes have been especially tenacious, large majorities of citizens favor democracy over other forms of government.

Third, no ideologies comparable to Marxism hold appeal for masses of people in different parts of the world. Fundamentalist forms of Islam might gain traction in some countries outside the Middle East and North Africa, but even if regimes based on Islamist principles can be established, it remains to be seen how effective and enduring such regimes can be. The Islamist political party whose candidate won the presidential election in Egypt in 2012 was ousted a year later by a military coup that had the support of millions of Egyptians. In Indonesia, the world's most populous Muslim country, Islamist parties calling for the implementation of Sharia law have lost ground since 2004 in the percentage of vote they have received in competition with more moderate Islamic parties and secular parties.[71].

Fourth, although authoritarian rulers of various types have become more skillful in using elections as a means of staying in power, the strategy of electoral authoritarianism does not ensure authoritarian persistence. Political scientist Andreas Schedler suggests that electoral authoritarianism represents a last and weakening "line of authoritarian defense in a long history of struggle that has been unfolding since the invention of modern representative institutions."[72] Some regimes that have strong party and state institutions with militaries and security forces loyal to state leaders will be able to remain in power for the foreseeable future, but without strong party and state institutions, these regimes are vulnerable to the kinds of mass uprisings that overthrew several seemingly entrenched regimes in 2011. Although authoritarian regimes proved more resilient than many political scientists predicted in the 1990s, others—including Middle Eastern monarchs—may be more vulnerable than they appear.[73] Middle East specialist Marc Lynch suggests monarchical persistence in the region is due less to unique institutional features than to oil wealth and international support. Several monarchies have experienced large political protests in recent years, and such protests are likely to increase.[74]

Finally, there is growing evidence that new democracies born following the collapse of authoritarian regimes often fail. Political scientist Jay Ulfelder found that a majority of the democracies that emerged in the past 50 years were replaced with some form of authoritarian rule. It is not surprising, therefore, that democracy struggled to find a foothold in Egypt, Libya, and Yemen after the Arab Spring. On the other hand, countries in which democracy has failed are more likely to see further attempts to achieve democracy than ones in which democracy was never tried. This seems to be the case "because the organizations and expectations born from earlier tries do not evaporate when democratic institutions are dismantled." They provide the basis for achieving democracy in the future.[75]

Suggested Readings

Paul Brooker, *Non-Democratic Regime*, 2nd ed. (New York: Palgrave Macmillan, 2009). Good overall introduction to the types of authoritarian regimes and how they consolidate power and seek legitimacy.

Larry Diamond, "Why Are There No Arab Democracies?" *Journal of Democracy* 21:1 (January 2010), pp. 93–104. A brief, clear examination of the competing explanations of why there are no Arab democracies.

William J. Dobson, *The Dictator's Learning Curve: Inside the Global Battle for Democracy* (New York: Anchor Books, 2012). A readable and instructive guide to how authoritarian regimes have become more sophisticated in retaining power and how those wanting democracy effectively can challenge authoritarian rule.

Steven Levitsky and Lucas Way, *Competitive Authoritarianism: The Origins and Evolution of Hybrid Regimes in the Post–Cold War Era* (New York: Cambridge University Press, 2010). Outstanding example of how to use comparative analysis. Finds that competitive authoritarian regimes with close links to Western countries are most likely to democratize. In those without such links, democratization is most likely where regimes lack strong governing party and state organizations.

Milan W. Svolik, *The Politics of Authoritarian Rule* (New York: Cambridge University Press, 2012). Argues that authoritarian politics centers on problems of power sharing and control. Clearly written, with many examples.

Critical Thinking Questions

1. Why are rulers of authoritarian regimes more hopeful about their prospects today than they were in the 1990s?

2. Is authoritarian rule justified if a leader can achieve improvements in citizens' capabilities, as President Paul Kagame has done in Rwanda?

3. Why do citizens of personalist regimes tend to have worse capabilities than citizens of other types of authoritarian regimes?

4. In which ways, if any, does Islam block the emergence of democracy. How would you substantiate your answer?

5. Can Saudi Arabia's leaders legitimately justify their restrictions on women by appealing to Islamic teachings?

Chapter 7
Democracy

Learning Objectives

7.1 Describe the popularity and growing moral legitimacy of democracy.

7.2 Summarize the three waves of democracy and analyze the conditions that are conducive to its success.

7.3 Distinguish between parliamentary and presidential forms of democracy and assess their relative advantages.

7.4 Describe different electoral rules and assess their effects.

7.5 Evaluate whether democratic states economically outperform their authoritarian rivals.

7.6 Evaluate the performance of democratic and authoritarian states according to the standards of the good society.

Introduction

7.1 Describe the popularity and growing moral legitimacy of democracy.

It was official. The Guinness Book of Records recognized Belgium as the undisputed champ. Previously, in 2011, Belgium had earned recognition from Guinness for the world's largest cheese sculpture, weighing in at 2,330 pounds and the longest continuous stint serving beer when a bartender in the city of Ghent lasted 102 hours. However, the record Belgium set on April 20, 2011, put it in a class by itself. It now held the world record for the longest period any democracy had ever gone without a government, without selecting a prime minister and Cabinet, following elections. It broke the record of futility and dysfunction previously held by Iraq when it could not form a government following its first election after the American invasion. Iraq was beset by sectarian violence between Sunnis, Shiites, and Kurds and was hardly a model to follow or feel accomplished in surpassing.

Back in June 2010, Belgium held elections, which the New Flemish Alliance (NVA) Party won with just 17 percent of the vote and 11 other parties winning seats. But the NVA was an extreme party that advocated breaking up Belgium and separating 6.5 million Dutch-speakers in Flanders in the north from 4.5 million Francophones (French-speakers) in Walloon in the south. Belgium offered a richer blend of political conflict than just linguistic–regional differences in its legislature. Protestant and Catholic parties were represented, socialist and capitalist parties competed, and environmental parties—each in their Dutch-speaking Flemish and Francophone Wallonian versions—all added to the toxic mixture. Trying to form a majority coalition that could agree to support a prime minister and Cabinet from such a medley of parties was hard. King Albert II appealed to six party leaders to try to form a government, and all failed.

When Belgium eclipsed the record held by Iraq, celebrations occurred throughout the country to draw attention to the absurdity of the situation. Two hundred forty-nine students stripped to their underwear to signify the new record of 249 days without a government since the last election. In Dutch-speaking Leuven in the north, free french fries were distributed, and bars in French-speaking Louvain-de-Neuve in the south dispensed free beer. Whereas young people in the Arab world were using social media to bring down governments, students in Belgium were using it to organize flash mobs to express their desire to have one. One woman suggested that spouses withhold sex from legislators until they agree on a government. An entertainer proposed that men not shave until a prime minister was chosen.

The Iraqis were amateurs. By June 2011, Belgium had gone well beyond a mere 249 days without a government to its first anniversary since the last election without a government in place. Finally, after almost two years without a government since elections were held, external events forced accommodation. With Belgium's total debt surpassing its GDP, Standard & Poor's, the rating agency, downgraded Belgium's bonds, causing it to borrow money at higher interest rates. A budget deal was necessary. After 541 days, Elio di Rupo, the leader of the French-speaking Socialist party, told King Albert II that he was ready to lead a six-party coalition government. di Rupo was the first French speaker to become prime minister in three decades and the first socialist prime minister since 1974.

Belgium's recent surreal experience confirms Winston Churchill's famous comment that "democracy is the worst form of government, except for the others that have been tried." As the preceding chapter made clear, authoritarianism still exists and displays both vigor and variety, but democracy is now the dominant form of government throughout the world. "For the first time in history," the Institute for Democracy and Electoral Assistance noted in 1998, "more people are living in democracies than under dictatorships."[1] According to political scientist Valerie Bunce, "mass publics today have a higher probability than they ever had of living in a democratic system."[2] The allure of democracy has been so great that even governments that were not democratic needed to justify themselves by reference to it. For example, the so-called Democratic People's Republic of Korea—or what we are familiar with as North Korea—is a ruthless police state in which opposition is not tolerated and the ruler, Kim Jong-un, has absolute authority. The Democratic People's Republic of Korea has as much to do with real democracy as the National Socialist Party—the Nazis—had to do with real socialism.

This chapter will first review the remarkable growth of democracy. It will examine the transition to democracy and the reasons behind it. Next, it will survey the two predominant forms democracy takes, parliamentary and presidential democracy. Third, it will review electoral rules and the different ways party competition is organized in democracies. Finally, it will assess whether Winston Churchill's conviction that democracy is the worst form of government except for all the others is true. Do democracies have a better record of promoting people's capabilities than their authoritarian counterparts?

Transitions to Democracy

7.2 Summarize the three waves of democracy and analyze the conditions that are conducive to its success.

Democracy
Rule by the people, in which the government reflects the will of the people and is accountable to it.

The term **democracy** is derived from the Greek word *demokratia*, from the roots *demos* (people) and *kratos* (rule). Democracy, then, means rule by the people. Some take this quite literally. In classical times, democracies were states in which people participated directly in making the laws that governed them. Although direct democracy is still practiced within intimate group settings, such as local town meetings, it is unworkable for large, complex societies. Because the scale of states today makes direct democracy impossible, modern democracies depend on our interests and views being represented by others. Direct democracy must, of necessity, give way in contemporary societies to representative democracy.

According to economist Joseph Schumpeter, a realistic standard of democracy is one in which virtually all citizens are eligible to vote in free, fair, and periodic elections. The role of citizens in this version of democracy resembles that of consumers in an open marketplace. Just as consumers can choose among competing products offered by firms, citizens can choose among competing candidates offered by political parties[3] and, after they select their rulers, according to Schumpeter, citizens should avoid the temptation to become backseat drivers and leave the governing to their elected representatives. Although Schumpeter's standard is less demanding than direct democracy, some countries still have not met it, and those that have done so have found it surprisingly hard to achieve.

The transition from autocracy to democracy proceeded in three waves, according to political scientist Samuel P. Huntington.[4] The first wave had its roots in the American and French revolutions of the 18th century. The United States and some countries in Europe gradually began to expand the vote to citizens who previously had been excluded, and chief executives and their Cabinets became responsible to elected assemblies. By 1930, about thirty countries worldwide could be categorized as representative democracies. Barrington Moore, Jr., attributed the transition to democracy during this period to the presence of an independent, self-confident, vigorous, commercial middle class. The formula was plain, according to Moore: "No bourgeois, no democracy."[5] Where the middle class was weak, its members feared that democracy would empower the lower classes to take their property and redistribute their wealth. Believing that authoritarian governments would better serve their interests, they tended to ally with property owners and aristocrats, who shared their qualms about the lower orders' latent power under democracy. For example, in Germany, where commercial and manufacturing interests were small and late in developing, they allied with the landed upper class and royal bureaucracy. By contrast, where the urban, moneyed middle class was strong and assured, according to Moore, members did not find it necessary to join with antidemocratic elites to achieve political power. Instead, the middle class allied with the lower orders to press for democracy, which it believed it could control to serve its own interests. Thus, the size, independence, and vigor of the middle class explain why some countries took the democratic road during this first wave when others did not.

The first wave began to recede in the 1930s. The newest democracies were the first to crumble. Military coups in Latin America, fascism in Germany, and communism in the Soviet Union reversed the democratic tide, but the defeat of fascism in World War II inaugurated a second wave of democratization. Germany, Austria, and Japan emerged from Allied occupation as democracies, and many former European colonies in Africa and Asia adopted democratic constitutions when they achieved independence. The fight against fascism in World War II provided the rhetoric and ideology that independence movements used to make democratic claims against European colonial rule. As the Ghanaian nationalist Kwame Nkrumah explained, "All the fair brave words spoken about freedom that had been broadcast to the four corners of the earth took seed and grew where they had not been intended."[6]

Social scientists were optimistic about the democratic future of these newly independent countries in Africa and Asia. They argued that modernization, in the form of increasing education and urbanization, and the weakening of traditional loyalties to tribe and village would result in more tolerant attitudes and more democratic expectations,[7] but the second wave began to recede in the 1960s. Military coups beset countries in Latin America, and one-party dictatorships emerged in many African and Asian countries. Some social scientists attributed the turn to authoritarianism to the realities of Cold War politics, in which the United States supported dictators so long as they were sufficiently anticommunist. Others turned the conventional wisdom on its head and saw authoritarianism, not democracy, as the natural product of modernization. Guillermo O'Donnell argued that modernization activated lower-class groups, whose economic policies led to inflation and budget deficits that required authoritarian intervention to resolve.[8]

In-Depth: Mauritius—A Democratic Enigma

Mauritius, an island nation of over one million located off the southeast coast of Africa, hardly seemed ripe to be the poster child for democracy in the developing world. The country has been a stable democracy since gaining independence in 1968. The rule of law obtains, elections are free and fair, citizens enjoy civil and political rights, and parties alternate in power.

Scholars attribute Mauritius's democratic success to a "vibrant and healthy civil society that cuts across ethnic cleavages."[9] The island nation boasts an extraordinary number of civic organizations for a country its size, everything from soccer clubs to seniors groups to trade unions. Many of these are bridging organizations that cross religious and ethnic boundaries. They connect Chinese, Indians, creoles, whites, Christians, Muslims, and Hindus to one another, "creating transethnic 'common denominators' that solidify national unity," according to political scientist William F. S. Miles.[10]

The bridging role that civic organizations play in helping people transcend exclusive ethnic identities is supplemented in Mauritius by political institutions that promote the inclusion of all groups. Checks and balances proliferate, making it hard for any one group to obtain too much political power. There is no standing army, the judiciary is independent, the civil service is professional, constitutional changes require supermajorities, all of the constitutionally recognized ethnic and religious groups (Hindus; Muslims; Chinese; and the general population, composed of whites and creoles) are guaranteed seats in parliament, and the Constitution even provides for an office of Leader of Opposition, whom the president must consult on some issues. In other words, political institutions are designed so that no group is left out and policy making requires groups' broad inclusion.

Democracy is no panacea. Mauritius has ethnic conflict and suffers from corruption, but its democratic record is the best in Africa and among the best in the developing world.

For Further Discussion

1. The case of Mauritius suggests that a robust civil society is vital to the success of democracy. How can a vigorous civil society be promoted or created?
2. Why haven't Mauritius's political rules that divide power, so that no group can ever attain too much, led to stalemate and deadlock as opposed to successful governance?

The third wave of democracy appeared even before the second fully receded. In 1974, Portugal emerged from a half century of dictatorship, followed soon after by the collapse of the ruling military regime in Greece and of despotism in Spain. The democratic wave then crossed the ocean to Latin America, where democratic civilian governments replaced military *junta*s in Ecuador, Peru, Bolivia, Argentina, and Brazil. Asia also felt its effects as democracy was restored in India and the Philippines, and new elections were held in Korea, Turkey, and Pakistan. The global tide of democracy next touched down in Eastern Europe as the Berlin Wall fell and one country after another—Poland, Hungary, Czechoslovakia, Bulgaria, Romania, and finally the Soviet Union itself—deposed their ruling Communist parties and held democratic elections. Even Africa felt its effects. When the third wave began in 1974, there were only three democracies on the continent; by 2005, about half of Africa's 48 states were popularly elected. By the end of the third wave, Larry Diamond writes, "democracy became the only legitimate form of government in the world, the principal form of government in several regions of the world, and a viable option in every region except the Middle East."[11]

However, the progress of democracy has not been so linear since the dawn of the 21st century, as is evident in the following Global Trends in Governance chart (Figure 7.1), with the blue line representing democracy no longer ascending steadily but flat-lining. On the one hand, democracy continued its ascent into the only region that had resisted it. The Arab Spring saw popular demands

Figure 7.1 Global Trends in Governance, 1946–2012

SOURCE: Polity IV Country Reports, 2012 http://www.systemicpeace.org/polity/global2.htm.

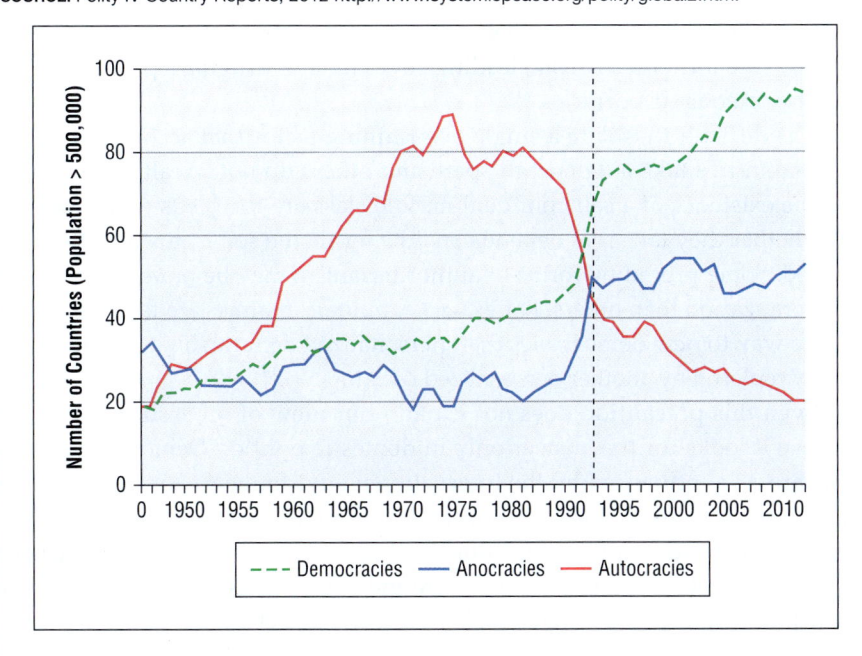

for democracy topple dictators in Libya, Egypt, and Tunisia, but the jury is still out on whether the Arab Spring will be the midwife to new democracies or new despots in the Middle East.

According to Dan Slater, the third wave of democracy has not been followed by a reverse wave of authoritarism as has happened with previous democratic surges. But there has not been much democratic consolidation, either. He argues the current period is not one of consolidation or collapse but of "careening" in which "democracies are lurching back and forth . . . between the forces of populism" or popular mobilization, "and the forces of restraint," who worry that populists will take power and rule through a despotic executive.[12] The current period of "careening" reflects the conflict between, on the one hand, the democratic principle of popular power and, on the other hand, the equally democratic principle of holding that power accountable.

Why did some countries succumb to the appeal of democracy while others resisted it? Some analysts offered cultural explanations that are hard to sustain today. For example, they argued that countries with large Muslim populations are less likely to be democratic because Islam's theology is not conducive to it, but Muslim youth who braved soldiers and tanks during the Arab Spring to depose dictators and demand democratic reforms put such claims to rest.

Other analysts proposed economic explanations, arguing that only certain kinds of economic development foster democratic government. For example, oil-producing countries in the Middle East are wealthy but not democratic. They suffer from the so-called curse of oil, with authoritarian rulers using oil revenues to pacify their citizens with low taxes, subsidized essentials, and reinforced security forces. Still other scholars argued that economic development promotes democratic stability, not democratization. They contend that rich democracies are simply more stable than poor ones. Poor democracies are more likely to collapse into authoritarianism, leading "over time to a high proportion of rich countries among democracies."[13]

It is difficult to isolate a single determining factor that accounts for why some countries take a democratic path and others do not. Wealth, education, and the existence of a self-confident middle class are the seeds of democracy, but whether they take root depends on how fertile the soil is in which they are planted. Some preceding forms of authoritarianism may be more amenable to democratization than others. For example, military regimes are far more likely to give way to new democracies than personalized dictatorships that are often simply replaced by another personalized dictatorship.[14]

Even this precaution does not expand our view of the issue far enough because it looks for the answer only in domestic politics. Democratic transitions are also influenced by the international environment. For example, the European Union has helped promote and consolidate democracy among countries that want to join it. In addition, political scientists have also noticed a **diffusion effect** in which countries surrounded by democracies find it in their interest to emulate their neighbors. The diffusion effect was certainly apparent

Diffusion Effects
Describes how what happens in one country spreads or is adopted by neighboring countries.

Comparative Political Analysis: Does Diversity Undermine Democracy?

Problem: Is it true that diversity poses an obstacle to democracy? Do ethnic, religious, and linguistic differences make compromise and consensus more difficult? Authoritarian leaders often claim that if they did not rule with an iron fist over ethnically divided societies, the countries would collapse in civil conflict. Is this argument valid or does it simply provide an excuse for authoritarian leaders to deprive people in diverse societies of their rights?

Methods and hypothesis: M. Steven Fish and Robin S. Brooks used Freedom House rankings (similar to our use of the Democracy Index discussed in Chapter 1) to scale countries from democratic to authoritarian and thereby establish their dependent variable. They then used another data set for their independent variable that assessed the fractionalization, or degree of diversity, within each country. Next, they did a statistical analysis to determine whether fractionalization affected the type of regime.

Results: The authors found that, contrary to prevailing wisdom, diversity did not hinder democracy.

For Further Discussion

1. How is it possible for democracy to survive ethnic conflicts when it gives free rein to their expression? How can democracies contain centrifugal forces that threaten to tear them apart?
2. If Fish and Brooks are correct in claiming that diversity does not reduce people's capabilities in terms of democracy, might it reduce their life chances in other ways, such as posing increased risks to their safety?

Source: M. Steven Fish and Robin S. Brooks, "Does Diversity Hurt Democracy?" *Journal of Democracy* (January 2004), vol. 15, no. 1, p. 164.

---

in the course of the Arab Spring, when demands for democracy raced across borders. As two political scientists report: "There is a strong association between a country's institutions and the extent of democracy in the surrounding regional context."[15] External circumstances can promote or discourage the transition to democracy as much as internal conditions.

Presidential and Parliamentary Democracy

7.3 Distinguish between parliamentary and presidential forms of democracy and assess their relative advantages.

"Democracy," the British political essayist David Marquand writes, "is plural not singular."[16] Like authoritarianism, democracy comes in many flavors. According to Adam Przeworski, "Systems of representation, arrangements of division and supervision of powers, manners of organization of interests, legal doctrines, as well as bundles of rights and obligations associated with citizenship differ significantly across regimes that are generally recognized as democratic."[17] The

> ## In Brief: Presidential Systems
>
> Presidential systems have some of the following properties:
> - Sovereignty is shared between the legislature and the president, creating checks and balances between them.
> - Presidents are directly elected by the people.
> - Presidents serve for fixed terms in office.
> - Presidents do not owe their jobs to the legislature.

Presidential Systems
Where sovereignty is shared between the legislature and the president. Where both the legislature and president share power and are elected independently by the people.

Parliamentary Systems
Where sovereignty resides in the legislature, which selects the executive. The executive is responsible to the legislature, which, in turn, is responsible to the voters.

different models of democracy can be arrayed along a continuum of presidential and parliamentary forms, with all sorts of hybrids in between. The United States is an example of a **presidential system**. In presidential systems, the executive and legislative branches are separated from each other.[18] That is, presidents do not owe their office to the legislature and do not require supportive legislative majorities to continue in it. Presidents are popularly elected, and they serve for a fixed term. In addition, presidents often have substantial lawmaking authority; otherwise, they would be mere figureheads.[19]

In contrast, in **parliamentary democracies**, the legislature is the only institution directly elected by voters. As a result, the legislature embodies the will of the people and its power is supreme. Legislatures then delegate power to the executive, which they elect. Governments, which are composed of prime ministers and their Cabinets, are elected committees of the legislature. The legislature and executive are not separate branches, as in the presidential model, but are fused, with the former empowering the latter.

The leader of the government in parliamentary systems is the prime minister, who is indirectly elected by the legislature. The prime minister's job is to form and direct the government: that is, to select a Cabinet composed of ministers to run the various executive departments, and direct and coordinate the government's activities. Rather than serving for a fixed term, prime ministers govern for as long as they maintain support in the legislature to do so. They may be removed from office and forced to resign when their party loses its parliamentary majority in national elections, when they no longer enjoy support among parliamentary members of their own party, or when coalition partners that helped them create a legislative majority defect.

Relations of power between the executive and legislative branches are a bit different in parliamentary and presidential regimes. In the former, the government is much more confident of having its proposals accepted by the legislature whose support it enjoys. Unlike presidents, prime ministers don't need to worry much about having their policies rejected by the legislature because they have a majority within it. On the other hand, presidents don't have to fear the legislature dismissing them from office as prime ministers do. The nature of legislative power is also different between the two models. In presidential systems, the legislature is more likely to develop its own bills and alter those proposed by the president, but it cannot make or break governments, as legislatures in parliamentary systems can do. The legislature in a parliamentary regime wields power through the government that it elects, as opposed to checking governments that are elected independently.[20]

The dispersion of power within democratic states occurs in presidential systems through checks and balances between the legislative and executive branches. Presidents and legislators are elected independently, and because each branch can check the other, the passage of bills requires the consent of both. In parliamentary systems, the fusion of the executive and legislative branches tends to concentrate power in the prime minister. But prime ministers are not all-powerful because they must constantly look over their shoulders to ensure that they retain the confidence of the legislature. In addition, the checks and balances that exist between the legislative and executive branches in presidential systems may take the form of negotiations among the different parties that comprise the ruling coalition in parliamentary systems. Prime ministers may not have to bargain with obstreperous legislatures, but they may have to negotiate with defiant parties in their ruling coalition that can block policies they propose.

Most new democracies created in the third wave chose to take a presidential, as opposed to parliamentary, form. Did they make the right choice? Presidential systems are said to suffer from gridlock that results when the legislative and executive branches, which are independent of one another, disagree. According to political scientist Juan Linz, their impasse may be so paralyzing that it undermines support for democracy itself.[21] Alfred Stepan and Cindy Skatch found new democracies that chose the presidential model were more likely to break down than those that chose the parliamentary form.[22] In addition, presidential systems are often criticized for delivering decisive winners, leaving losers upset, which may also lead them to withdraw support for democracy. The president

In Brief: Parliamentary Systems

Parliamentary systems have some of the following qualities:
- The legislature is directly elected by the people and is sovereign.
- Prime ministers are selected by the legislature.
- Prime ministers can be removed when a majority of the legislature no longer supports them.
- Although prime ministers rule only with the approval of the legislature, that support also assures them of legislative support for their policies.

may have only won a narrow plurality of the vote but assumes all the power. Critics claim that presidential systems are unrepresentative because election results are divisible, whereas executive power is not.

Although presidential systems may offer less in terms of representation than parliamentary regimes, they may offer more in terms of accountability. Voters can hold presidents accountable for their performance because they elect them directly, in contrast to parliamentary systems, in which the chief executive is selected by the legislature. In addition, voters have a more difficult time in parliamentary systems assigning responsibility for performance. The core executive in parliamentary systems is often composed of a ruling coalition of officials from different political parties, whereas the core executive in presidential systems is typically drawn from one party, thus making it easier for voters to assign credit and blame. Finally, voters in presidential systems can more easily target their vote in support of, or in opposition to, a particular candidate because control of the executive in parliamentary systems often depends on postelection negotiations among political parties. Voters in presidential systems can take better aim at their intended target, making their vote a more potent weapon than in parliamentary regimes.

Electoral Rules and Party Systems

7.4 Describe different electoral rules and assess their effects.

Electoral Systems
Describes the system by which votes are counted to yield a winner, such as majority or plurality rule. The rules by which winners in an election are chosen.

Single-member districts
Districts in which only one legislator is elected.

Multimember Districts
A district from which more than one representative is elected.

Democracies differ not only in how power is distributed between the legislative and executive branches but in their **electoral systems**, which determine how elections are conducted. For example, democracies differ in the average number of seats or representatives they assign per election district. Some countries, such as the United States, have **single-member districts** where only one legislator is elected from each district. Other countries, such as Sweden, have **multimember districts**, in which the number of legislators from each district depends on its size. The voting district that includes Stockholm County, the country's capital, has 36 seats to represent 800,000 residents, but the less-populated Gotland County, an island in the Baltic Sea with just 44,000 people, is accorded only two seats. In Israel and the Netherlands, the entire country is one multimember electoral district. In single-member districts, there is only one winner. The losing candidates return to the obscurity of their former line of work. Not so in multimember districts. Not only is the winner who is selected from a list of candidates that parties submit to voters seated, but so is the runner-up—and so on down the line, depending on the percentage of the vote that party received. For example, if there are 36 seats in the Stockholm election district, parties submit a list of 36 candidates, and citizens vote for one of the party lists. Legislative seats are then awarded to parties, depending on the percentage of the vote they receive. If a party wins 50 percent of the vote in the Stockholm election district, then the first eighteen candidates on the party's list would be seated; the next party receiving 25 percent of the vote would be permitted to seat the first eight candidates on its list, and so on.

Electoral systems also differ in the way votes are allocated, that is, how votes obtained by candidates and parties in elections are translated into legislative seats. Some countries run elections according to plurality—whoever gets the most votes wins—rules. Such rules govern federal elections in the United States and Canada, where the candidate receiving the most votes in a voting district is declared the winner. Although these voting rules may seem appropriate to Americans, Nepal is the only democracy without a significant British past to adopt them for legislative elections.

Americans tend to confuse pluralities, in which candidates receive the most votes, with majorities in which candidates receive more than 50 percent of the vote because the two major parties in the United States virtually monopolize political competition. In a two-party race, the candidate who receives the most votes must necessarily receive a majority, but countries that use plurality voting rules may have more than two effective parties. In this circumstance, it is unusual for the candidate who wins the most votes also to achieve a majority. In Canada and the United Kingdom, where the two major parties are not as dominant as in the United States, it is unusual for the winning candidate who obtains a plurality also to win a majority. In the 2010 election in Britain, not one candidate elected to Parliament won a majority of the vote in his or her voting district.

Other countries, such as France, guarantee that candidates must have majority support to prevail by running **double-ballot elections** in which candidates must receive a majority of votes to prevail. If no candidate wins a majority in the first election, a run-off is held between the two candidates who received the highest number of votes in the first round. In the 2012 French presidential election, for example, ten candidates competed in the first round, with the Socialist Party candidate, Francoise Hollande, placing first with 28 percent of the vote and the incumbent conservative Nicholas Sarkozy finishing second with 27 percent. Two weeks later, when the top two candidates faced off against each other, Hollande obtained an absolute majority of 52 percent against Sarkozy's 48 percent.

Double-ballot Elections
If no candidate receives a majority in the first election, a second, run-off election is then held between the two candidates who received the most votes.

Double-ballot electoral rules are not unique to France but have been adopted by many formerly communist countries in Eastern Europe as well as some countries in Africa, such as Chad, Gabon, and Mauritania.[23] They are even used in the United States, where many southern states require candidates to win a majority of the vote. In the 2008 election for a Senate seat in Georgia, a third-party spoiler candidate attracted enough votes to prevent both the Democratic and the Republican candidates from obtaining a majority on Election Day in November. This precipitated a run-off four weeks later, when the Republican was finally able to obtain the majority required for election.

A third alternative is to run elections according to **proportional representation** (PR) rules. Once parties attain a certain threshold of votes, they are awarded seats in the legislature based on the percentage of the vote they receive. For example, in the Netherlands, 21 parties competed in the 2012 parliamentary election with nine parties winning seats. The largest party, the Christian

Proportional Representation
Seats in the legislature are awarded to parties based on the percentage of the vote they received.

Democratic Appeal, won 27 percent of the vote and received 27 percent of the seats in Parliament; Labour, the next largest party, garnered 25 percent of the votes and was awarded 25 percent of the seats, and so on down to the Reformed Political Party, the smallest party, which received 2 percent of the vote and was given 2 percent of the legislative seats. Advocates of proportional representation argue that it is preferable to district-based, single-member, plurality, winner-take-all electoral rules because it offers voters "a broader range of candidates who have a real chance of being elected, and who talk about a greater breadth of issues that attract more voters to the polls."[24]

Electoral rules matter greatly. How votes are counted matters as much as how many votes candidates receive. Winners can become losers and losers turn into winners, depending on how votes are counted. In the 2010 election in Britain, Liberal Democratic candidates received 23.6 percent of the vote nationwide but only won 9 percent of the seats in Parliament. The Liberal Democrats were disadvantaged because their voters are geographically dispersed and unable to reach a plurality in many districts that would permit them to win that seat. If Britain awarded seats based on PR, the Liberal Democrats would have received 162 parliamentary seats instead of the 57 they actually won. In contrast, Labour candidates received 29 percent of the vote nationwide—just 6 percent more than the Liberal Democrats—but won 258 seats—400 percent more than the Liberal Democrats in Parliament! The electoral system benefits Labour because its voters are geographically concentrated and are thus more likely to attain a winning plurality in many district contests. The electoral rules make Labour efficient at translating votes into seats, giving it more weight in Parliament than their nationwide vote would warrant.

Political actors began to think strategically about electoral rules as democracy took root and the franchise was extended to working-class voters. Groups and parties wanted rules that worked to their advantage. For example, ethnic and regional minorities that could win elections locally supported proportional representation as a way to ensure that their interests were represented in the national legislature, but the most powerful supporters of PR were elites who were frightened by the prospect of working-class mobilization that might propel socialist parties to victory. Elites feared that bourgeois parties would suffer if elections were decided by plurality or majority rules in single-member districts. According to Andrew McLaren Carstairs, because "universal suffrage rendered it increasingly likely that the social democrats would achieve the status of a major or dominant party, it was bourgeois and non-socialist parties which inclined towards a reform of the electoral system."[25] Elites believed that proportional representation would blunt the power of socialist parties, requiring them to share power to govern.

Electoral rules are not neutral. All else being equal, PR systems tend to be more redistributive than rules that elect officials by plurality in single-member districts. PR systems are more redistributive because they are more likely to lead to results in which left-wing parties that support such policies are included in the government. In addition, PR systems are less likely to lead to geographically targeted spending, which is less redistributive than programs that are more universal. Politicians in single-member plurality voting systems have an incentive to target spending geographically to their home districts. The incentives are different under PR, in which officials are more apt to spread the wealth around since the nationwide vote matters.[26]

Electoral rules also give advantage to some parties at the expense of others, as we saw in the different fates of the Liberal Democrat and Labour parties under British electoral rules. With so much at stake, parties sometimes try to change the electoral system to compete under electoral rules that are more advantageous to them. In Britain, when no party received a majority in Parliament following the 2010 elections, the Liberal Democrats, for whom the electoral rules had been a disadvantage, made it a condition of their parliamentary support to reconsider them. Similarly, in France, the ruling Socialist Party anticipated defeat in the 1986 legislative elections and sought to minimize its losses by changing electoral laws. They switched from double-ballot electoral rules to proportional representation, believing the latter would give a radical right-wing party a better chance to draw off votes and seats from the Socialists' chief opponent, the Republican Right. When the Republican Right coalition took office following the election, it switched rules back to the old electoral system that offered them more protection. A popular, radical, right-wing party that could obtain enough votes to earn seats in the legislature under PR would have a harder time obtaining a majority in any district under double-ballot election rules.

Even though parties have an incentive to manipulate electoral rules to maximize their advantages, electoral systems rarely change. Winners under existing rules are unlikely to alter a system under which they succeeded. In the 1970s, the Parti Quebecois (PQ) in Canada held only a handful of seats in the provincial legislature, even though it received about 25 percent of the vote. Feeling cheated of the seats it deserved by plurality electoral rules, the PQ promised to enact proportional representation if elected. But when the PQ came to power in 1976, it failed to carry out its promise because PR might jeopardize the success the party now enjoyed. PQ deputies thought they stood a better chance of winning in the district where they were well known than competing as part of a party list in a proportional representation election.[27]

Electoral rules shape party systems or recurring patterns of party behavior resulting from political competition. The number of legislative seats accorded to each district and the way votes are translated into seats affect the number of effective parties that compete. Single-member districts in which winners are selected by simple plurality voting rules create a bias toward two-party systems. Voters fear wasting their votes on small third parties that cannot win and tend to choose candidates from those that can, a calculation that works to the advantage of the two largest parties. By contrast, countries with multimember districts selected by proportional representation tend to have multiparty systems. Voters can vote their conscience for minor parties that will lose, knowing they will be awarded some seats anyway.

Just as electoral rules have a ripple effect on the number of parties, so does the number of parties influence other aspects of the political system. The advantage of multiparty systems is that they accurately reflect the diversity of opinion within the country. The disadvantage is that they may be so representative of diverse opinions that countries become ungovernable—as we saw occur in Belgium. If, for example, many parties compete and receive seats, it becomes difficult to construct a majority coalition and form a government, and such governments are not likely to last: The smaller the share of seats held by the largest party, the more fragile the government will be.

Britain provides a dramatic example of the effect electoral rules have on party systems because rules differ for elections to the Welsh, Scottish, and European parliaments from those that pertain to the British Parliament. Elections in Wales, Scotland, and to the European Parliament are run according to versions of PR. As a result, a multiparty system has emerged for these elections, whereas single-member plurality rules create a dominant two-party system for elections to the British Parliament. Given different rules in Scottish, Welsh, and European Parliament elections, British voters supported a wider range of parties than ever before. Different electoral rules reveal how single-member plurality elections in British national elections suppress the party choices voters desire.[28]

Party Discipline
When legislators from the same party display unity in how they vote on bills. When legislators from the same party vote together as a block.

Electoral systems affect not only the degree of party competition but the internal life of parties as well. For example, **party discipline** in the legislature is greater in PR systems. Legislators want to increase their chances for reelection and move higher on the party list by proving their loyalty to party leaders who make those lists. Electoral rules also influence the number of female legislators. Plurality-based, single-member electoral systems tend to reinforce the effects of incumbency, which is often held by men. With only one candidate to offer for each seat, underrepresented groups, such as women, find it difficult to get into the game. In contrast, in multimember PR systems, in which there are more seats to fill in each election district, parties have greater scope to offer more women as candidates. In addition, more parties use quotas under these rules to reserve a certain number of spots for women on their lists. Consequently, women comprise a higher proportion of legislators under PR than they do in other electoral systems.

No electoral system is perfect. Economist Kenneth Arrow developed a set of requirements that any reasonable voting system should satisfy and found that none could meet them all. When the Royal Swedish Academy of Sciences gave Arrow a Nobel Prize for this work in 1972, it called his result "a rather discouraging one as regards the dream of a perfect democracy."[29] Electoral systems require one to choose your imperfection because none is flawless. Some promote accountability at the expense of choice. Others do the opposite. Although some may find it disheartening that no election system is perfect, a flawed election system is still better than having no elections at all.

Democracy, Authoritarianism, and Economic Development

7.5 Evaluate whether democratic states economically outperform their authoritarian rivals.

When it comes to soccer, past performances in the World Cup indicate that teams from fascist countries have better records than those governed by party dictatorships, teams representing military dictatorships have a higher winning percentage than those ruled by fascists, and teams fielded by West European democracies have the best record of all.[30] But that's soccer. Do democracies perform as well at enhancing the capabilities of their citizens as they do on the soccer field? Are they better at meeting their citizens' basic physical needs, ensuring their safety, and promoting their ability to make informed decisions than authoritarian political systems? Are people better off under democracy than under authoritarianism? In Chapter 1, we described democracy as one of the elements that comprise a good society, but we also warned that all good things do not necessarily go together. Perhaps the provision of health care, safety, education, and democracy are at odds, so that some conditions that permit people to lead lives they value come at the expense of others.

One of the indices that is frequently used to compare the performance of different types of states is economic growth. But as we argued in Chapter 1, economic growth is not a good indicator of how well states perform because all, or even most, citizens may not benefit from it. The fruits of economic growth may flow disproportionately to a rich few while the living standards of the majority decline. Still, although economic growth is hardly a panacea, it is a necessary, though not a sufficient condition to reduce poverty in extremely poor countries. Redistribution from the rich to the poor will not do much good where there is little wealth to redistribute. Growing the economy, increasing the wealth it produces, is the only way to raise the standard of living in countries that are very poor.

Is democracy or authoritarianism more conducive to generating economic growth? According to some political scientists, authoritarian regimes can invest society's limited resources better where they will do the most good. They will not succumb to the temptation of democracies to invest in low-yield projects in return for votes. Another alleged benefit of authoritarianism is that it permits the government to ignore demands to spend money that will be consumed immediately (bigger pensions, better schools, and more health care) and instead direct the country's limited savings toward investments that will pay off in the future. Party competition, it is argued, makes democracies susceptible to expensive bidding wars in which candidates try to win elections by pandering to citizens' short-term welfare needs at the expense of long-term investments that are the key to future growth. Finally, authoritarianism supposedly can create a more consistent, stable, orderly environment that is more favorable to investment and long-term growth. Whereas democracies are beset by racial, tribal, religious, and ethnic conflicts that result in stalemate or worse, authoritarian regimes are decisive and strong enough to rise above such conflicts and get things done. In brief, the argument is that authoritarian states produce better economic results because their policies are not distorted by crass political concerns.

Other political scientists challenge this account. They argue that democracy is an advantage, not a handicap, in promoting economic growth. Democracies, they claim, enjoy the rule of law that creates a predictable environment that encourages investment. Where the state wields power arbitrarily, insecurity discourages entrepreneurs. In addition, democracies benefit from more debate, more access to information, and more responsiveness, enabling them to act effectively when things go wrong. The openness and adaptability of democracies permit them to recognize and reverse policy mistakes more quickly and easily than authoritarian regimes. Finally, democracies give their citizens more freedom, which encourages them to be more creative and innovative.

When evaluated according to the standard of promoting economic growth, the record of democracies and dictatorships is quite mixed. In the ranks of democracies and dictatorships, we can find countries that are remarkable economic successes and others that are massive failures. For example, in the 1970s and 1980s, many Latin American countries experienced stagnant and even negative growth rates following their transition from military rule to democracy. Some authoritarian regimes have performed no better. Many African economies went into free-fall following their transition to one-party states. On the other hand, supporters of democracy and authoritarianism can both boast of economic successes. Supporters of democracy can celebrate the prosperity of the West compared to the collapse of Communist one-party states; admirers of authoritarianism can point to the superior growth of the People's Republic of China's compared to democratic India. Indeed, it is difficult to attribute better or worse economic performance to either democracy or authoritarianism. As Nobel prize–winning economist Amartya Sen puts it, "The selective anecdotal evidence goes in contrary directions, and the statistical picture does not yield any clear relationship at all."[31] Another analysis, by Adam Przeworski and Fernando Limongi, confirmed Sen's judgment. They write, "It does not seem to be democracy or authoritarianism per se that makes the difference but something else. What that something else might be is far from clear."[32]

Although neither democracy nor dictatorship can take credit for economic growth, democratic systems do have two important advantages. The first has to do with the greater range of choices open to women under democracies. When women have more opportunities, they tend to have fewer children. As the fertility rate falls, so does the number of citizens competing for the national income. Although the pot itself may not be any bigger in democracies, it is divided among fewer people, thereby raising the country's per capita income. Second, democracies have a better record of steady economic performance and avoiding calamitous outcomes. "Democracies," Halperin and his associates found, "regardless of income level, rarely let the bottom fall out of their economies."[33] When economic disaster strikes in the form of hyperinflation or massive unemployment, people have to sell off their assets to survive. Because democracies are more likely to avoid economic catastrophes, their citizens are better able to accumulate assets over time than their counterparts in dictatorships.

Overall, the results of our inquiry about which type of state promotes economic growth are inconclusive, with democracies, perhaps, earning the benefit of the doubt. Regardless of the outcome, higher economic growth does not translate automatically into higher capabilities for citizens, which is our standard for measuring state performance. How do democracies and authoritarian political systems compare when we look at capabilities?

Democracy, Authoritarianism, and the Good Society

7.6 Evaluate the performance of democratic and authoritarian states according to the standards of the good society.

Physical Well-being

We used the *Economist*'s Democracy Index, which grades countries on a scale of 0 to 10, to distinguish democratic from authoritarian countries. The higher the score on the Democracy Index, the more democratic a state's political system was judged to be. Norway, for example, was ranked the most democratic country in the world with a grade of 9.93, whereas North Korea shamefully brought up the rear as the most authoritarian, with a grade of only 1.08. Countries were classified into four groups by the Index, with the best performers referred to as "full" democracies. The next set of countries was labeled "flawed democracies," the third group was called "hybrid regimes," and the Index labeled the fourth and lowest-performing set of countries "authoritarian regimes."

To assess the relative ability of democracies and authoritarian countries to meet their citizens' basic physical needs, we will again look at infant mortality rates. As we noted previously, experts often use this indicator to gauge material well-being because it "reflects a multitude of conditions, from access to food, health care, and housing to the availability of schools for girls."[34] According to Figure 7.2, infant mortality rates appear to be highly correlated with a state's form of government, with more democratic countries recording lower infant mortality rates. Average infant mortality rates among countries that qualified as full democracies were only 4.32. Flawed democracies performed much worse, recording average infant mortality rates that were almost five times (19.8) the rate of full democracies. This was due to the inclusion of some African countries, such as Lesotho (62.6), Zambia (52.7), and Benin (67.9), that drove up the

Figure 7.2 Democracy and Infant Mortality Rates

SOURCE: The Economist Intelligence Unit, Democracy Index 2012, "Democracy Index 2012: Democracy at a Standstill," https://portoncv.gov.cv/dhub/porton.por_global.open_file?p_doc_id=1034.

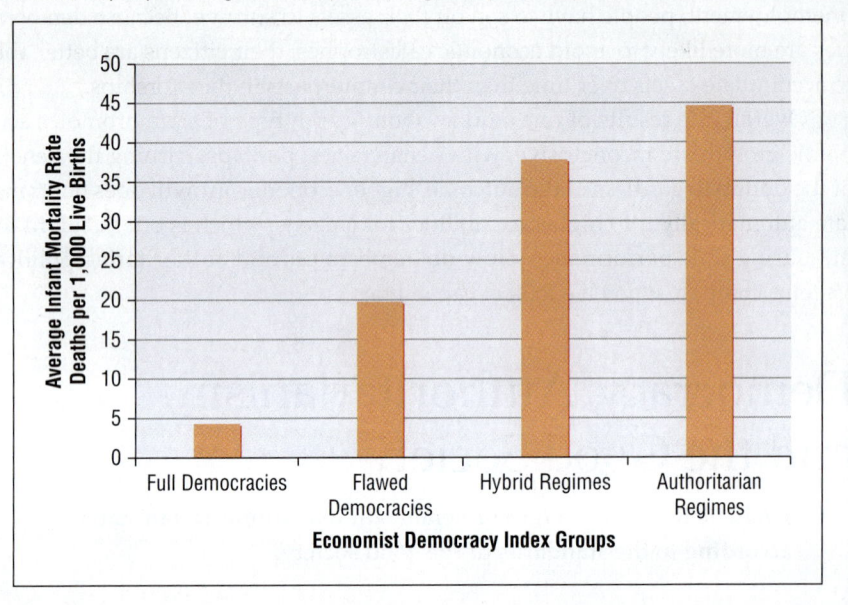

average for the group as a whole, whose median was a more respectable 13.6. Hybrid regimes did worse still (37.8), averaging almost double the rate of flawed democracies, and authoritarian regimes performed worst of all, registering an average infant mortality rate of 44.7.

Informed Decision Making

The performance gaps between democratic and authoritarian regimes that were so evident in infant mortality rates are much more muted when it comes to literacy rates, as Figure 7.3 shows. Almost all citizens in full democracies are literate. The average literacy rate for these countries was 99.2. Flawed democracies did less well, again primarily due to the presence of some African countries that had much lower literacy rates than the group as a whole. But flawed democracies still recorded a respectable average literacy rate of 91.1, and the median for the group (95) was better still. Surprisingly, authoritarian regimes (81.4) outperformed hybrid regimes (76.2) when it came to average literacy rates. That is, the most authoritarian countries, which composed the bottom grouping of the Democracy Index, did better than the countries in the next group above them. Nor was this the result of outliers driving down results for hybrid regimes, whose median literacy rate (78) was ten points lower than that for authoritarian regimes.

Safety

Finally, as Figure 7.4 reveals, full democracies again performed better than their peers. The average homicide rate for countries in this group was just 2.1. The

Figure 7.3 Democracy and Literacy Rates

SOURCE: The Economist Intelligence Unit, Democracy Index 2012.

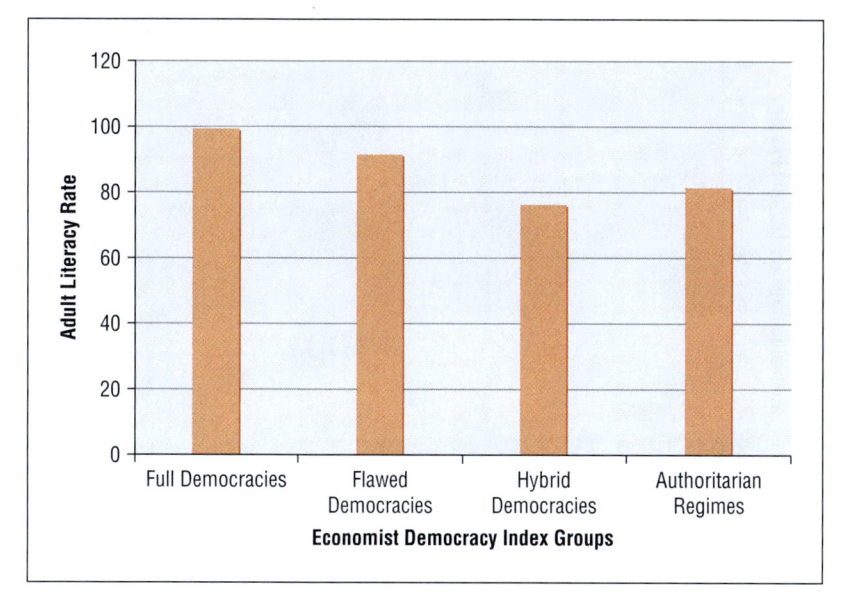

average homicide rate for flawed democracies was almost six times worse (12.0) and was even higher than the average homicide rate found in authoritarian regimes (10.8), which performed second-best among our four groups. Hybrid regimes again brought up the rear, just as they did in literacy rates, averaging 13.9 homicides. Although authoritarian regimes enjoyed lower average homicide rates than flawed democracies and hybrid regimes, its median was higher. The median homicide rate for authoritarian regimes was 9.2 but only 7.7 for hybrid regimes and 6.6 for flawed democracies. Lower medians but higher average homicide rates for hybrid regimes and flawed democracies were probably the result of a number of outliers at the low end of the scale for authoritarian regimes. Authoritarian regimes included many Middle East countries, such as Qatar (0.9), Jordan (1.8), and Bahrain (.06), which typically had very low homicide rates. The homicide rates for many of these Middle East countries that were included within the set of authoritarian regimes would have even compared favorably to those recorded by many full democracies. The inclusion of these countries within the set of authoritarian regimes explains why its average homicide rate is lower and its median is higher than that found in flawed democracies and hybrid regimes.

Although the most democratic states scored best on all our tests, democracy seemed to make less of a difference the more it declined, that is, the lower on the Democracy Index scale you go. Authoritarian states had lower average homicide rates than both flawed democracies and hybrid regimes and enjoyed higher average literacy rates than the latter. Thus, it does not appear that democracy by itself is the answer for all public problems. Some democracies have a

Figure 7.4 Democracy and Homicide Rates

SOURCE: The Economist Intelligence Unit, Democracy Index 2012.

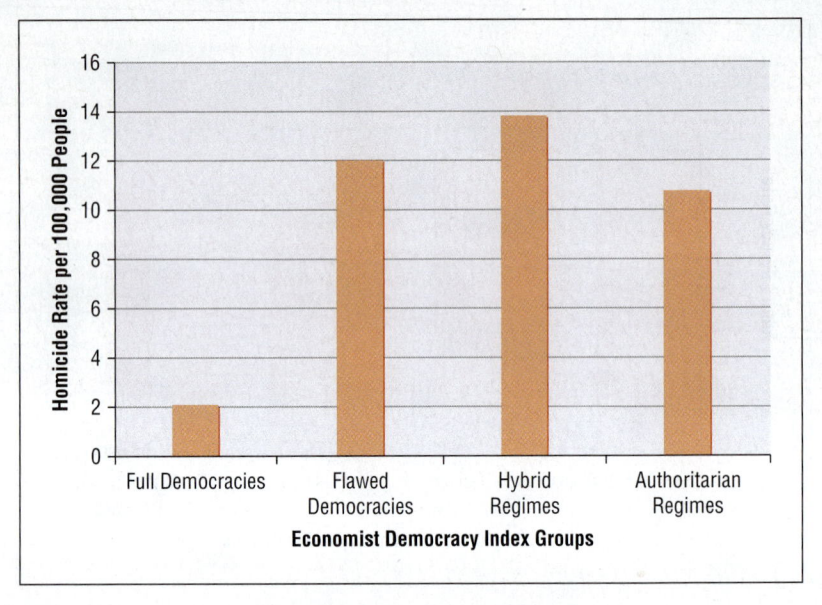

relatively poor record. After more than a half-century of democratic rule, India had an infant mortality rate of 47.2 deaths for every 1,000 live births, a literacy rate of 63 percent, and a homicide rate of 3.4 per 100,000 citizens. In contrast, some authoritarian regimes performed remarkably well on certain indices. It is hard to think of a country that has been more successful than China at reducing poverty, that has done more to wipe out illiteracy than Cuba, or that is safer than the United Arab Emirates. All of them are closed societies. The results of our tests thus confirm our earlier warning that all good things do not go together. It seems that more democracy only improves people's life chances at the highest level, among those countries that scored high on the Democracy Index as "Full Democracies." Otherwise, it does not appear to increase people's life chances very much in terms of making them safer, healthier, or more literate. Of course, this says nothing about whether democracy should be valued for its own sake as opposed to the effect it may or may not produce on other aspects of life.

Conclusion

We saw in this chapter that the prevalence of democracy rose unevenly but inexorably over the course of the 19th and 20th centuries. Political scientists attributed the rise of democracy to domestic factors, such as economic development, and to external forces, such as regional diffusion effects. The American and French revolutions launched the first wave, in which monarchies were overthrown and replaced by republican forms of government. Voting rights were extended to workers, and chief executives and their Cabinets were now responsible to elected assemblies. The second wave occurred following World War II as many former colonies in Africa and Asia drafted democratic constitutions when they became independent. The third wave began in 1975, with democratic transitions occurring first in Portugal, Spain, and Greece and then traveling across the ocean to remove military dictatorships in Latin America, passing through Asia, where elections were held in formerly autocratic countries, and finally cresting in Eastern Europe, where Communist parties were forced to give up their monopoly of power.

As democracy spread, it took two predominant forms, presidential and parliamentary democracy. In the former, presidents are directly elected for fixed terms and serve independently of the legislature. In the latter, the legislature selects and empowers the executive. Democracies differ not only in how authority is distributed between the legislative and executive branches but in how elections are conducted. Countries use different formulas to translate votes into legislative seats. These election rules, in turn, shape party behavior and competition.

Democracy seems to have plateaued and even receded a bit, however, in the 21st century, despite promising offshoots such as the Arab Spring. It appears to be stuck in a new equilibrium that is referred to as careening. Popular movements bring charismatic leaders to executive power, which elicits frantic efforts by their opponents to check and hold them accountable through the courts and legislature. Finally, the chapter examined whether democracies have a better record of improving people's life chances than authoritarian political systems. We found that only at the highest levels does democracy actually improve the quality of people's lives in terms of safety, subsistence, and literacy. Authoritarian regimes performed worse than all the others when it came to average infant mortality rates, but they did better than hybrid regimes when it came to literacy rates, and they did better than both flawed democracies and hybrid regimes when it came to homicide rates.

Suggested Readings

Andrew McLaren Carstairs, *A Short History of Electoral Systems in Western Europe* (London: George Allen & Unwin, 1980). As the title suggests, a good introduction to the origins and effects of different electoral systems.

Morton H. Halperin, Joseph T. Siegle, and Michael M. Weinstein, *The Democratic Advantage: How Democracies Promote Peace and Prosperity* revised edition (New York: Routledge, 2009). A careful analysis that argues democracy produces beneficial economic and social results.

Samuel P. Huntington, *The Third Wave: Democratization in the Late Twentieth Century* (Norman: University of Oklahoma Press, 1993). A concise history that probes the cycles of democratization and how each new wave leaves more democracies before receding again.

Michael Meyer, *The Year That Changed the World: The Untold Story behind the Fall of the Berlin Wall* (New York: Scribner, 2009). One of the best narrative histories of the end of communism in Eastern Europe.

Fareed Zakaria, *The Future of Freedom: Illiberal Democracy at Home and Abroad* (New York: W. W. Norton, 2003). An accessible and lively argument that democracy depends on the level of economic development.

Critical Thinking Questions

1. How would you define democracy? Should democracy be judged simply by process without regard to results?
2. Why has democracy been so elusive for developing countries? Why have so many developing countries adopted authoritarian political systems?
3. What social conditions are conducive to democracy?
4. Did many emerging democracies make the right choice in adopting presidential as opposed to parliamentary democratic forms?
5. What are the advantages and disadvantages of different electoral rules? Which set of electoral rules are most compatible with democracy?
6. If democracy is so beneficial, why didn't it appear to enhance people's capabilities when we ran our tests? Although the most democratic countries performed better, more democracy did not correlate with higher capabilities outside this select group of countries.

Chapter 8
Economic and Human Development

Learning Objectives

8.1 Understand how a country's overall wealth or poverty can affect the lives of its citizens.

8.2 Distinguish between economic development and human development.

8.3 Describe the criteria used for assigning countries to different levels of development.

8.4 Explain the difference between extreme poverty and relative poverty and identify which regions of the world have the highest numbers and percentages of people living in extreme poverty.

8.5 Identify the regions of the world with the highest percentages and numbers of people with low capabilities.

8.6 Compare and contrast rates of economic growth and the consequences for incomes between countries with high and low levels of development.

8.7 Explain why weak states have difficulty promoting sustained economic development.

8.8 Evaluate the strengths and limitations of the main explanations for why some countries are more economically developed than others.

8.9 Analyze the results of testing the hypothesis that higher income per capita is associated with higher capabilities.

Introduction

8.1: **Understand how a country's overall wealth or poverty can affect the lives of its citizens.**

In Luanda, the capital city of the sub-Saharan African country of Angola, a popular activity for children living in slums is to slide down garbage dumps on sleds made of sheet metal. In some places, they splash into creeks flowing through the garbage dumps. The creeks are "soaked with rivulets of human waste," because the city of 4.5 million lacks adequate sewage disposal. The creeks flow into the Bengu River, which is the main source of water for Luanda's poor. Slum dwellers use the untreated water for drinking, cooking, and bathing. In 2006, the water harbored the bacteria that cause cholera. The result was one of the worst cholera outbreaks in a decade, killing 1,400 people and making more than 40,000 sick.[1]

Cholera is not the only disease caused by untreated water. The World Health Organization estimates that unsafe water is responsible for 80 percent of the sickness in poor countries, causing the deaths of an estimated 1.8 million children per year.[2] Although cholera and other waterborne diseases can easily be prevented by building sewer systems that prevent human waste from flowing into lakes and rivers and by providing citizens with clean water for drinking and cooking, many low-income countries fail to take such measures. This is not so much for lack of money but, rather, because political elites have chosen to allocate government revenues for other priorities, including enriching themselves and their cronies. Angola is an oil-producing country that earns billions of dollars a year in export sales—funds that largely end up lining the pockets of the ruling elite.[3]

The cholera epidemic in Angola exemplifies how differences in per capita incomes and degrees of government accountability among countries can have enormous consequences for people's lives. Being born in a wealthy country such as Sweden awards an infant a high probability of surviving to adulthood, receiving an advanced education, being safe from violence, exercising civil and political rights, and enjoying both excellent health and a long life. Being born in a poor country such as Angola gives infants much poorer life chances, especially if their parents are not among the tiny elite that has benefited from the bonanza in oil revenues. Almost one in ten Angolan children dies before reaching his or her first birthday. If children manage to survive, they are likely to have poor health care and to die before they are 55 years old. Angola's homicide rate in 2011 was 19 times that of Sweden's. In addition to homicide, thousands of citizens were killed during Angola's lengthy (1975–2002) and brutal civil war, in which several thousand children were forced to become combatants. Under the authoritarian single-party regime that has been in power since 1976, Angolans have few civil and political rights. These differences between Sweden and Angola raise one of the biggest questions in the social sciences: Why do some countries have so much more wealth and capabilities to offer their citizens than others?

The first section of the chapter discusses the distinction between economic development and human development. The next sections of the chapter examine how wealthy and poor countries differ in terms of income, capabilities, economic growth, and state strength. Then it turns to the puzzle of why there are vast differences in development among countries. We examine five major explanations: geography, culture, colonialism, institutions, and political leadership. The chapter ends with a discussion of how differences in levels of economic development affect citizens' capabilities.

Economic Development and Human Development

8.2 Distinguish between economic development and human development.

Social scientists distinguish between economic development and human development. **Economic development** is the process of increasing a country's wealth by diversifying the goods and services it produces and making that production more efficient. In poor countries, the path to economic development often leads from production of a few major crops to the production of a greater range of crops and the development of industries outside the agricultural sector. As countries continue to develop economically, agriculture begins to make up a smaller percentage of the economy, and manufactured goods become more important. Countries gradually shift from products that involve relatively simple manufacturing processes, such as textiles and garments, to products that require more sophisticated production methods, such as steel and automobiles. As countries move up the development ladder, skilled labor replaces unskilled labor, complex technologies replace simple machines, and quality replaces quantity as the standard of production. Per capita income and the standard of living rise as countries become wealthier. Eventually, industrial production

Economic Development
The process of increasing a country's wealth by diversifying the goods and services it produces and increasing the efficiency with which it produces them.

becomes a smaller percentage of the country's GDP, losing ground to service, professional, and managerial activities. Such economies are described as postindustrial economies.

Most of today's high-income countries began this process in the middle to late 1800s. By the middle of the 20th century, they became industrialized countries and subsequently completed their postindustrial transformation by the end of the century. The roster of postindustrial countries includes the United Kingdom, Germany, and France in Western Europe; Canada and the United States in North America; and Japan, Singapore, and South Korea in East Asia.

Less economically developed countries in Africa, Asia, Latin America, and the Middle East got a much later start in the economic development process. Most of them were colonies of industrialized countries, and their economic development was stunted by the policies of their colonizers. Typically, the main products the colonizers extracted from them were agricultural goods or minerals. Most colonies had little, if any, industrialization, becoming engaged in the world economy as sources of raw materials for their colonial masters. Real industrialization did not get underway in many of these countries until the 1950s and 1960s after they won their independence and still has been slow to get underway in a number of them. The exceptions were countries in Latin America that achieved independence and began to industrialize much earlier.

Singapore and South Korea are former colonies that have had extraordinarily successful economic growth since becoming independent countries. When adjusted for purchasing power, the per capita income of Singapore is higher than that of the United States, and that of South Korea is higher than that of Spain or Italy. The majority of former colonies fall into a middle range of incomes. Most of the Latin American, Middle Eastern, North African, and Asian countries fall into this range. Most low-income countries are in sub-Saharan Africa, but a small number of countries located elsewhere, such as Afghanistan and North Korea in Asia and Haiti in Central America, fall into this group.[4]

Human development is "the process of expanding the choices people have to lead lives that they value."[6] To determine progress on that score, the United Nations Development Programme has developed a **Human Development Index (HDI)**. The index has three components: how healthy people are in a country, as measured by life expectancy at birth; how knowledgeable they are, as measured by adult literacy rates and school enrollments; and whether they enjoy a decent standard of living, as measured by their purchasing power. The value of the index ranges from 0 to 1. In 2012, Norway had the highest HDI score (0.955), whereas Mozambique in sub-Saharan Africa had the lowest (0.313.).[7] It is noteworthy that although the indicators used to create the HDI overlap with the criteria used in the capability approach to determine good societies, they are not identical. The HDI index includes indicators for meeting physical needs and making informed decisions but does not include indicators of being able to live in safety or exercise democratic rights.

Human Development
The process of expanding the choices people have to lead lives they value. These include being well-fed and healthy; being safe from violence; being literate and numerate; and enjoying political participation.

Human Development Index (HDI)
This index has three components: health, as measured by life expectancy at birth; knowledge, as measured by adult literacy rates and school enrollments; and standard of living, as measured by income purchasing power.

In-Depth: South Korea—From Least Likely to Succeed to Most Successful in Its Class

In the 1950s, South Korea was "a terribly depressing place where extreme privation and degradation touched everyone." The Korean War had just ended, and much of the country's infrastructure had been destroyed. Beggars roamed city streets, "often traveling in bunches of maimed or starved adults holding babies and searching through garbage dumps to find food."[5] An American official referred to South Korea as an economic "basket case." Yet by 2005, South Korea was among the World Bank's high-income countries. No other country has managed to come so far so fast.

The military regime that assumed power in 1961 set out to industrialize South Korea as rapidly as possible. In contrast with military regimes in other less-developed countries, it succeeded at this task. Government-controlled banks funded the development of privately owned industrial conglomerates, enabling them to become competitive in international markets. The puzzle is why this way of building an industrial society did not result in the creation of large numbers of inefficient firms and the massive theft of state funds. Several factors come into play here. First, because South Korea's very existence was threatened by two hostile neighbors, North Korea and China, its leaders believed the country had to industrialize rapidly to survive. Second, the military needed capitalist support to achieve this goal. Militaries cannot build dynamic industrial economies, but capitalists can. Third, the government inherited a relatively competent state bureaucracy and a good infrastructure of roads and electricity from South Korea' years as a colony of Japan. Finally, the country received considerable economic aid from the United States.

Although the military government placed less emphasis on developing citizens' capabilities, it turned out to be successful in that endeavor as well. The educational system was expanded, improving basic literacy and numeracy and increasing the numbers of engineers and scientists. Health care was expanded, too, although mainly for the benefit of the regime's political allies. On the negative side of the ledger, the regime restricted citizens' civil and political rights and, at the behest of corporate elites, ruthlessly suppressed the rights of workers.

After the fall of the military regime in 1987 and the emergence of democracy, the government began to expand civil and political rights and pushed for broad-based improvements in capabilities. In 2012, South Korea had lower infant mortality rates, longer life expectancies, and better scores in international tests of literacy than the United States.

For Further Discussion

1. Why has South Korea been so much more successful than many other poor countries?
2. Why didn't military officers in South Korea focus on enriching themselves regardless of the consequences for industrialization?

The authors of the Human Development Index emphasize that the Index measures "the potential human development that could be attained if achievements were distributed equally among residents." However, since, in practice, achievements tend not to be distributed equally, the authors also created an **Inequality-Adjusted Human Development Index**, which is "the actual level of human development (accounting for inequality)."[8] In countries such as India,

Inequality-Adjusted Human Development Index
The actual level of human development in a country taking inequality among citizens into account.

where there are big differences in access to health care and education between citizens with high and low incomes, there can be a significant difference between a country's HDI score and its inequality-adjusted HDI score. Whereas India's HDI score is .554, its inequality-adjusted HDI is only .392. Similar disparities also exist in many high-income countries. For example, in 2012, the United States had the third best HDI score in the world of 0.937, but its inequality-adjusted score was 0.821, dropping it to sixteenth place.[9]

In the best of circumstances, economic development and human development reinforce each other. Economic development and rising incomes can give people more choices about the kinds of lives they want to live. Economic development can also provide governments with increased revenues that can be used to pay for safe water, clinics and hospitals, schools, and universities. In turn, better-educated, healthier people can perform better as workers, which promotes economic development. Generally speaking, the more economically developed a country is, as measured by GDP per capita, the higher is citizens' capability, as measured by HDI scores. Norway and the United States are wealthy countries with very high HDI scores, whereas the HDI score of Niger in sub-Saharan Africa reflects the fact that it is one of the world's poorest countries, but the correlation between income per person and HDI scores is not perfect. Countries can have nearly identical per capita incomes and very different HDI scores. For example, both Barbados in the Caribbean and Equatorial Guinea in Africa had per capita incomes of approximately $26,000 in 2012, yet the former's HDI score was 0.825; the latter's was only 0.554.[10]

The gap between economic achievement and improvement in capabilities in places like India reminds us that although economic growth is important for improving citizens' capabilities, one does not necessarily lead to the other. Improving capabilities "requires active public policies to ensure that the fruits of economic growth are widely shared." It also requires making good use of the public revenue generated by fast economic growth for social services, especially for public healthcare and public education."[11]

In Brief: Economic Development and Human Development

- Economic development is the process of increasing a country's wealth by diversifying the goods and services it produces and increasing the efficiency with which it produces them. The progress of economic development is measured in two ways: (1) changes in the predominant economic structure from agriculture, to industry, and to services and (2) increasing per capita income.
- Human development is the process of "expanding the choices people have to lead lives that they value." These choices depend on whether the society in which they live gives them the opportunity to be well fed and healthy, safe from violence, literate and numerate, and able to participate effectively in politics.

Differing Levels of Development Among Countries

8.3 Describe the criteria used for assigning countries to different levels of development.

Having discussed the meaning of both economic development and human development, and the relationship between them, we can now turn to the ways in which countries differ in the levels of development they have attained. Any attempt to categorize countries on that basis requires some degree of arbitrariness. Countries with very similar per capita income and HDI scores often end up in different categories of development. We follow the lead of the World Bank and the United Nations Development Programme in assigning countries to four categories of development. The World Bank classifies countries based on their per capita income: high, upper-middle, lower-middle, and low-income countries. The United Nations Development Programme classifies countries based on their HDI scores: very high, high, medium, and low human development. In Table 8.1, we assign countries that are in both organizations' highest development category a label of High. Countries in both organizations' second-highest category are placed in our Upper-Middle category. The third set of countries goes into our Lower Middle category, and the countries that are in the lowest category for both organizations end up in our Low category.

Table 8.1 lists representative countries for each category, listed from the highest HDI score to the lowest. We have included (in boldface type) all the countries we use for case studies in Chapters 9 through 11 and several countries featured in the In-Depth boxes. Although most countries fit into one of the four categories, a few do not. For example, Saudi Arabia is in the World Bank's top income category but is in the United Nations Development Programme's second-highest category. This suggests that Saudi Arabia has not done as good a job as other high-income countries of converting its income into capabilities for

Table 8.1 Countries Compared by Level of Economic and Human Development

High	Upper Middle	Lower Middle	Low
1. Norway	55. **Russia**	100. Jordan	145. Kenya
3. US	55. Saudi Arabia	101. **China**	146. Pakistan
5. Germany	61. Mexico	103. Thailand	153. **Nigeria**
7. **Sweden**	62. Costa Rica	112. Egypt	161. Haiti
12. South Korea	76. **Iran**	119. Botswana	167. Rwanda
26. **UK**	80. Mauritius	131. Iraq	173. Zimbabwe
29. Greece	85. **Brazil**	136. India	175 Afghanistan

SOURCE: United Nations Development Programme, Human Development Report 2013: The Rise of the South, http://www.undp.org/content/undp/en/home/librarypage/hdr/human-development-report-2013/, pp. 144–146.

citizens. Nigeria is the other country that exhibits this divergence. In the cases of Saudi Arabia and Nigeria, we let their HDI score be the decisive factor in determining where they belong in Table 8.1.

In the following section, we will focus on countries with High and Low levels of development, comparing them in terms of income, capabilities, economic growth rates, and state strength.

Comparing Incomes Between Countries with High and Low Levels of Development

8.4 Explain the difference between extreme poverty and relative poverty and identify which regions of the world have the highest numbers and percentages of people living in extreme poverty.

One way of getting a sense of how different incomes are in high-income countries and low income countries is to ask whether it is better to be a poor person with an income in the bottom ten percent of a rich country or a rich person with an income in the top ten percent of a poor country. For the purposes of the question, a rich country is one whose average per capita income puts it in the top ten percent of countries in the world, and a poor country is one defined as having an average per capita income in the bottom ten percent. It turns out that poor people "in a rich country have it much, much better than the rich in the poor country." Poor people in rich countries typically "earn three times more than the average rich person in a poor country" when purchasing power is taken into account.[12]

Extreme Poverty
Poverty so dire as to be life threatening.

Unlike their counterparts in the developing world, poor people in rich countries are also unlikely to experience extreme poverty. **Extreme, or absolute poverty**, is defined as poverty so dire as to be life threatening. The World Bank defines this condition as having to live on less than $1.25 a day, adjusted for purchasing power. The extremely poor struggle to buy food to keep them nourished and medicine to combat disease. Unable to afford adequate housing, they often live in squalid shacks made of tin or cardboard. They often lack access to clean water and proper sanitation, and they cannot afford school fees for their children. The United States has poor people, but their poverty is usually not so severe that it endangers their lives. They are poor in relation to other people; thus, they experience **relative poverty**.

Relative Poverty
Poverty relative to other people's income and wealth, usually not so severe as to be life-threatening.

There are two ways of describing the extent of extreme poverty. One is to deal in *percentages*. According to World Bank estimates, 21 percent of the residents of developing countries lived on less than $1.25 a day in 2010—a major improvement over 1990, when that figure stood at 43 percent. From this perspective, the world's extreme poverty rate had been halved in just 20 years.

The other way to look at extreme poverty trends is to deal in raw *numbers* of people. In 2010, 1.22 billion people lived on less than $1.25 a day—again, a big drop from the 1990 figure of 1.91 billion. Even with these improvements, however, the World Bank estimates that approximately a billion people still will be suffering from extreme poverty in 2015.[13]

These figures for the world population conceal big regional differences in extreme poverty reduction. China has had the greatest success in reducing the percentage of its population living in extreme poverty. In 1981, 84 percent of its population did, but by 2008, the percentage had dropped to 13 percent. This accounted for almost three fourths of total world reduction in poverty during these years.[14] Other regions have had less success. In sub-Saharan Africa, there has been progress in reducing the percentage of extreme poverty, but the number of absolutely poor people went up because of population increase. As a result, there were substantially greater numbers of absolutely poor people in sub-Saharan Africa in 2008 than there were in 1981.[15]

Although sub-Saharan Africa has the highest *percentage* of extremely poor people, the region with the largest *number* of absolutely poor people is South Asia. The countries in this region with the largest numbers of poor people are Bangladesh, India, and Pakistan. India has more malnourished children than sub-Saharan Africa.[16] Each of these countries has a higher per capita income than many sub-Saharan African countries, but they have not been able to address the problem of extreme poverty effectively despite more financial resources.[17]

Comparing Capabilities Between Countries with High and Low Levels of Development

8.5 Identify the regions of the world with the highest percentages and numbers of people with low capabilities.

The wealthier a country, the higher the level of citizens' capabilities tends to be. The difference in capabilities is particularly stark between the highly developed and the least developed countries, as evidenced in Table 8.2. Although there are big differences in each category, the difference in infant mortality levels is particularly striking.

As is the case with extreme poverty, most of the countries with low capabilities are located in sub-Saharan Africa. For example, in Niger, 119 out of every 1,000 children died before reaching their first birthday in 2011. Adult literacy stood at 42 percent.[18] Whereas sub-Saharan Africa contains the highest percentage of citizens with low capabilities, South Asia has the highest number.

Table 8.2 Capabilities in the Top 20 Countries and Bottom 20 Countries ranked by HDI (2010)

	Infant Mortality 2010	Life Expectancy 2010	Adult Literacy 2005–2010
Top 20 Countries	3.5	81.5	89
Bottom 20 Countries	83	54	53.6

SOURCE: United Nations Development Programme, Human Development Report 2013, pp. 146–173.

Capabilities are improving, however, in both regions. The mortality rate for children under five in sub-Saharan Africa dropped from 197 per thousand in 1980 to 109 per thousand in 2011. Studies show that the rate of decline accelerated in the first decade of the 21st century in what one researcher calls "the biggest and best story in development."[19] There was also a rapid drop in infant mortality in South Asia, from 154 per 1,000 in 1980 to 62 in 2011. Although these statistics are still shockingly high from the perspective of high-income countries, halving the infant mortality rate nevertheless is a major achievement.[20]

Comparing Economic Growth Rates Between Countries with High and Low Levels of Development

8.6 Compare and contrast rates of economic growth and the consequences for incomes between countries with high and low levels of development.

Low-income countries differ not only in levels of income per capita but in rates of economic growth. Sustained economic growth during the 19th and 20th centuries was the major reason for falling poverty levels and rising capabilities in today's high-income countries. Over the past 20 years, economic growth can also be credited with decreasing poverty in low- and middle-income countries in Asia and Latin America. In contrast, many countries in the Low development category had difficulty reducing extreme poverty rates because they enjoyed little sustained growth from the 1960s through the 1990s.

The encouraging news is that a number of those countries have experienced rapid growth since the turn of the 21st century. This was particularly the case for many sub-Saharan African countries. In 2000, the editors of *The Economist*, a respected British magazine, labeled Africa "the hopeless continent." Thirteen years later, several sub-Saharan African countries boasted some of the fastest growth rates in the world, leading the editors of *The Economist* to call Africa "the hopeful continent." In the last decades of the 20th century, African countries depended heavily on exports of commodities such as oil, copper, and other raw materials for growth. When commodity prices were high, their economies grew rapidly, but when those prices dropped, growth collapsed. Current growth is less dependent on commodities and more driven by domestic investments in commerce and industry.[21]

Nevertheless, some observers remain skeptical about these countries' future. Although commodity sales account for only a third of the growth, some of the fastest growing countries remain heavily dependent on commodities, so that a fall in oil or copper prices would impair their growth. Even with the recent burst of growth, sub-Saharan Africa remains at the bottom of per capita income tables, along with a few countries in Asia. Furthermore, even if African countries' current high growth rates continue, an estimated 25 percent of its people will still be living in extreme poverty in 2030.[22]

States and Development

8.7 Explain why weak states have difficulty promoting sustained economic development.

Countries with high levels of human development typically have strong, effective states. Strong states can defend their territory from outside attack, maintain order within their borders, and implement policies effectively throughout the country. They can collect the taxes necessary to pay for defense, health programs, and education. Almost all children are inoculated against infectious diseases. Systems are constructed to provide safe water and proper sanitation; schools are built and staffed with teachers who can teach children to read and write. Strong states can do these things in part because they have competent, well-trained state bureaucracies. Civil servants typically are recruited based on merit and generally have a strong sense of professionalism. They normally implement decisions impartially by defined rules and responsibilities.

Countries with high levels of development have strong infrastructural and authoritative power. **Infrastructural power** is the power to implement state decisions effectively in a country. **Authoritative power** is the power to get citizens to comply with those decisions.[23]

Although some countries with low development have states with strong infrastructural and authoritative power, many do not. In the least-developed countries, many states cannot even satisfy the minimal task of maintaining law and order. Some extremely weak states have little authority beyond the immediate vicinity of the capital city. Local strongmen, criminal gangs, or warlords rule large parts of such countries. Afghanistan provides an example. The United States was able to crush the Taliban government that ruled the country between 1996 and 2001, but the U.S.-backed government that replaced the Taliban has little control of much of the country, and the Taliban have actually reasserted control over large areas. In short, the state in Afghanistan lacks infrastructural and authoritative power.

Infrastructural Power
The power to implement state decisions effectively in a country.

Authoritative Power
A state's power to get citizens to comply with state decisions.

In further contrast to states in countries with high development, officials in low-development countries often ignore official rules and statutes. Economists Lant Pritchett and Erik Werker write that perhaps the key feature distinguishing between these two types of countries is the gap between what formal rules and regulations say should happen and "what actually happens." In many countries with low development, "the stated 'rules of the game' have near zero predictive power for what will actually happen."[24] Every rule is up for negotiation between the official responsible for enforcing it and the person who is affected by the rule. The question is simply how much the affected person has to pay to avoid the rule.

The process of getting a driver's license in Delhi, India, provides an example. The official rules for getting a driver's license in India are similar to those in the United States. In India, however, one can avoid having to take a road test by paying men who specialize in bribing officials in the licensing office. In one experiment, researchers found that only 12 percent of those who hired such an intermediary had to take the driver's examination, as compared to nearly all who did not hire one.[25] In the United States, it can be frustrating to get one's first driver's license, but the frustration is offset by the freedom and mobility that the license provides. Nevertheless, a system of drivers' examinations that actually works creates an additional kind of freedom, namely, the freedom from fear that many other drivers lack demonstrated competence and therefore pose a hazard on the road.

Corruption
Behavior by government personnel that deviates from the formal duties of their public role, for the sake of private gain for themselves, their friends, family members, or political allies. The use of public office for private gain.

Bribe-taking by officials in Delhi highlights the problem of corruption that afflicts many developing countries. **Corruption** is behavior by government personnel "which deviates from the formal duties of a public role" for the sake of private gain for oneself or for one's friends, family members, and political allies.[26] Such activity takes many forms. For example, presidents, prime ministers, and other high-ranking officials sometimes become wealthy by confiscating foreign aid. Corruption percolates all the way down from the government in the capital city to teachers, clinic workers, and police officers in villages. The consequences are felt most strongly by poor citizens who cannot afford to pay bribes or who lack the power to defend themselves from officials' arbitrary actions.

Table 8.3 provides a more precise way of measuring relative levels of corruption. It ranks selected countries from the least to the most corrupt. The number to the left of the country is its position in the rankings. Countries that are used as case studies in subsequent chapters are represented in bold face.

Economic development can coexist with corruption. China has achieved rapid economic growth since 1980 despite considerable corruption within its government. Likewise, the United State enjoyed a high growth rate between the early 1870s and 1928, during which period its per capita income was similar to that of China between 1996 and 2009. In the 1870s, the United States actually might have had higher levels of corruption than China did in 1996.[27] The key to whether rapid growth can coexist with corruption has to do with who benefits from corruption. In some countries, although officials demand payments from businesspeople to get permits or to overlook regulations, they still have an interest in businesses succeeding. This has been the case in China for the past several

Table 8.3 Corruption Perceptions Index 2012

Rank	Country
1 (least corrupt)	Denmark
4	**Sweden**
13	**Germany**
17	**United Kingdom**
19	United States
45	South Korea
48	Costa Rica
50	Rwanda
66	Saudi Arabia
69	**Brazil**
80	**China**
94	Greece
94	India (tied with Greece)
118	Egypt
133	**Iran**
133	**Russia** (tied with Iran)
139	**Nigeria**
139	Pakistan (tied with Nigeria)
163	Zimbabwe
174 (most corrupt)	North Korea
174	Somalia (tied with North Korea)

SOURCE: Transparency International, "The 2012 Corruptions Perceptions Index," http://cpi.transparency.org/cpi2012/results/.

decades. Many high-ranking officials have grown wealthy, but so have businesspeople, and China's economy has boomed. In other countries, officials simply squeeze whatever they can out of businesspeople even if this practice destroys prospects for growth.[28] Although countries can have corruption along with bursts of growth, sustained growth of the sort that lifts countries permanently into the ranks of those with very high incomes is not compatible with high levels of corruption. Corruption tends to decline with rising per capita incomes.[29]

Poor countries' states also tend to be less democratic than their high-income counterparts. Although there was a dramatic increase in the number of low- and middle-income countries that ostensibly became democratic between 1974 and 1995, many are democracies in name only in the sense that they lack fair elections in which candidates compete for votes. Candidates who do not belong to the ruling party are intimidated along with voters who would like to support them. In extreme cases, candidates have even been murdered. This has been a substantial problem in some parts of India as well as in other less-developed countries, including Iraq. In addition to this kind of intimidation, landlords, business owners, and local strongmen can make meaningful citizenship impossible for extremely poor citizens who depend on them for their livelihood.[30] Landless peasants who rent land from a landlord, and impoverished workers who depend on wages from a business owner to feed their family, are often compelled to vote for the candidate of the landlord or business owner.

Why Did Some Countries Become More Economically Developed Than Others?

8.8 Evaluate the strengths and limitations of the main explanations for why some countries are more economically developed than others.

In the 16th, 17th, and 18th centuries, knowledgeable Europeans believed that South America's economic prospects were better than those of North America. Mexico's per capita income was nearly identical to that of the 13 colonies that would become the United States. Even more surprisingly, in 1790, Haiti was possibly "the richest society in the world on a per capita basis."[31] Yet by 2012, the per capita income of the United States, adjusted for purchasing power, was 3.2 times that of Mexico and 39 times that of Haiti. Similarly, at the start of the industrial revolution, the income gap between the richest and the poorest countries was about 2:1, whereas in 2013 that gap exceeded 80:1.[32] Economist Lant Pritchett calls this widening gap between high- and low-income countries "divergence, big time."[33] This section examines five ways of explaining that divergence: geography, culture, colonialism, institutions, and leadership.

Geography

A number of authors suggest that geography is the most important variable in explaining differences in levels of economic development. Jared Diamond's book, *Guns, Germs, and Steel*, proposes that some regions of the world became much more powerful and wealthy than others because of advantages conferred on them by their location. The most favored continent was Eurasia, the huge landmass that extends from Western Europe across the Middle East to China. Eurasia had a climate that allowed for the development of many species of domesticated plants, including wheat and rice. Its east–west orientation meant that there were only limited differences in growing conditions between regions, which allowed crops developed in one area to spread rapidly to others. For example, wheat, which was originally domesticated in Southwest Asia, eventually arrived in Europe, where it flourished. The continent was also the home of large mammals, such as horses, cows, and pigs, that could be easily domesticated. Cows gave milk, meat, and manure for fertilizer; pigs supplied meat and manure; and horses provided power for pulling plows and mobility for warfare.

The combination of these advantages in crops and animals led to food surpluses, which in turn favored the development of "large, dense, sedentary, stratified societies."[34] Although many people remained farmers, these societies could also support spiritual leaders who founded religions and political leaders who founded kingdoms and empires. They could also support artisans and fund the development of new technologies, including steel, swords, guns, cannons, and oceangoing ships.[35] These advantages contributed to Western Europe's eventual dominance of other societies in Latin America and Africa. By the early 1500s, European innovations in ship design helped European explorers reach Latin America, and superior weapons helped them conquer that continent.

According to Diamond, germs were the other advantage European conquerors had over the native peoples of Latin America. Living in close proximity to domestic animals for thousands of years had given Europeans immunity to many diseases spread by animals. The native peoples of the Americas had no such immunity, and more natives were killed by diseases carried by Europeans than by their weapons.[36]

Other authors believe that geography continues to explain why many less-developed countries have difficulty making progress. Some countries have rich natural resources; others have none. Some have fertile soils, and large parts of other countries are deserts. Some have access to ocean seaports or navigable rivers that enable them to produce goods and trade them with other countries. Others lack navigable rivers and are landlocked, with no access to the ocean. Such a geographical location creates several obstacles to development. They therefore must ship goods across the territory of other countries that often lack adequate road and railway networks. When those countries are bad neighbors wracked by civil wars or predatory governments, transportation across them is problematic. The high cost of transportation makes it difficult for landlocked countries to develop. These conditions help explain the number of very poor countries in Africa, a huge continent comprising many countries with no access to the sea. They are "condemned to small internal markets, an inefficient division of labor, and continued poverty."[37] Finally, some countries have to deal with deadly and debilitating diseases. Their climates are ideal for the spread of malaria, which kills large numbers of people every year. Endemic diseases, along with small local markets and poverty, discourage foreign trade and investment.[38]

Geography alone, however, does not work as an all-purpose explanation for why some countries have achieved much greater economic and human development than others. Jared Diamond's explanation does not account for why countries in the vast region of Eurasia have very different levels of economic development. For example, Pakistan and Afghanistan are part of Eurasia, but they are poorer than Western European countries. The Asian countries of Myanmar (formerly known as Burma) and Bangladesh remain very poor despite the fact that neither is landlocked. Nor is access to the sea a guarantee of success. Several African countries with access to the sea are among the poorest countries in the world. More tellingly, countries with similar geographical locations sometimes exhibit different levels of economic development. For example, South and North Korea are part of the same peninsula and were a single country for hundreds of years, but since their division in 1953, South Korea has experienced extraordinary economic growth while North Korea remains poor.

Culture

Another group of scholars attributes the success of the highly developed countries not to the hard materialism of geographic endowment but to the soft intangibles of cultural values. These scholars argue that the progress of different societies is determined by what is in people's heads rather than what is under their feet. The presence of certain values and beliefs is said to dispose people in some societies to be exceptionally productive. The eminent German social scientist Max Weber contended that the Protestant ethic's emphasis on steady, disciplined hard work, thrift, honesty, and effective use of time helps explain why economic development took off in northern Europe, where Protestant virtues were most prevalent. Weber argued that, contrary to popular belief, the capitalist spirit at its inception was not motivated by greed or by a desire for comfort or pleasure.[39] Instead, what fueled economic development in northern Europe was a mindset that promoted industrious work habits and the reinvestment of earnings into one's business rather than spending them on immediate gratifications. Weber did not claim the Protestant ethic was the sole cause of northern Europe's success. Rather, he argued that it was one in a constellation of factors that interacted to support dynamic, sustained economic growth.[40]

A number of contemporary authors have drawn on Weber's work to try to explain why some countries are wealthier than others. The Harvard historian David Landes wrote, "If we learn anything from the history of economic development, it is that culture makes almost all the difference."[41] Landes acknowledges the importance of geography and institutions in explaining economic development.[42] Nevertheless, he believes that in the end the key to European economic success was "the making of a new kind of man—rational, ordered, diligent, productive—and making good use of time."[43] Landes notes that this ethic does not have to be Protestant. He attributes Japan's success in catching up to Europe to a Japanese version of the work ethic.[44]

Whereas some scholars explain economic development in terms of character traits and culture, others emphasize the importance of trust. Political scientist Francis Fukuyama argues, "A nation's well-being, as well as its ability to compete economically, is conditioned by a single, pervasive cultural characteristic: the level of trust inherent in the society."[45] Economic activity, from running a factory to international trade, depends on social cooperation. If a factory depended mainly on penalties to prevent workers from stealing, and if firms depended mainly on lawsuits to enforce contracts, economic transactions would be very inefficient.[46] Trust "acts like a kind of lubricant that makes any group or organization run more efficiently."[47]

Like geography, culture cannot serve as an all-purpose explanation of why some countries have more economic and human development than others. Cultural explanations have a difficult time explaining why countries with similar cultural backgrounds such as South and North Korea can have very different records of economic performance. Cultural explanations also don't fully explain sudden changes in economic performance. Some theorists blamed China's failure to develop in the 19th and early 20th centuries on its Confucian culture. Yet in the late 1970s, China began one of the most remarkable bursts of economic development in history.

Colonialism

Still another explanation attributes the huge differences in incomes among countries to Western colonial exploitation. **Colonialism** is the formal political rule of one country over another. Colonial powers define the boundaries of their colonies, set up administrations to manage them, and exercise sovereign power within them.[48] European countries began to exert their control over larger and larger parts of the world in the 16th and 17th centuries, when the Spanish and the Portuguese established colonies in Latin and Central America. By the 18th century, Britain and France had colonies in North America and the Middle East, and in the 19th and early 20th centuries, they established colonies throughout Asia. China was never colonized, but European powers managed to divide it into spheres of influence. Sub-Saharan Africa was the last major area to be colonized in the late 19th century. The United States and Japan joined in the rush for colonies around the turn of the 20th century, with the United States taking control of the Philippines and other Pacific islands and Japan colonizing Taiwan and Korea.

Colonialism
The establishment of formal political control of one country over another.

Some scholars argue that the American and European powers exploited their colonies to fund their own economic development. In doing so, they stripped colonies of wealth and blocked their potential for economic growth. Haiti provides an example. As noted previously, Haiti was perhaps the richest society in the world in 1790 on a per capita basis, thanks to its lucrative sugar exports, but almost all the profits went to the French colonialists, not to the African slaves who grew and harvested the sugarcane. Haitian slaves won their independence from France in 1804 after an uprising that lasted 12 years. In exchange for independence, France demanded reparations that went on for decades. By one estimate, Haiti was still spending 80 percent of its national budget on those reparations as recently as 1900.[49] These reparations increased France's income while impoverishing Haiti. Some critics of Western colonialism argue that the Haitian case is representative of what happened elsewhere. European countries enriched themselves by using forced labor to grow lucrative cash crops or extract valuable minerals for sale in world markets. These profits funded their economic development while impoverishing their colonies and leaving them with overwhelming economic and political problems that persisted even after independence.[50]

Colonial powers also created other obstacles to development for newly independent countries. They often set the economy on a course that was highly vulnerable to market fluctuations because of its dependency on a single export crop. They drew the borders of countries arbitrarily to encompass many ethnic, linguistic, and religious groups. Such extreme diversity creates strains that even strong political institutions would have difficulty handling. Finally, colonial powers sometimes introduced racial cleavages. This was particularly the case in Latin America and the Caribbean countries, where most workers in the sugar plantations were African slaves or their descendants. During Brazil's "first 250 years, roughly 70 percent of the immigrants to this Portuguese colony arrived in chains."[51] The consequence of all these effects of colonialism is a world in which former colonies remain at an enormous economic disadvantage.

Those who disagree with the argument that colonialism is the main reason for the disparity between rich and poor countries advance three main criticisms. First, they believe there is evidence that the profits European countries made from colonialism were too small to account for why these countries became so much wealthier than the rest of the world.[52] Second, not all former colonies are poor today. Indeed, some are among the wealthiest countries in the world, including Australia, Canada, the United States, Singapore, and South Korea. In addition, a number of former colonies have achieved substantial economic growth even though they have not equaled the income levels of today's high-income countries. They include Botswana in sub-Saharan Africa, Malaysia in Southeast Asia, and Chile in Latin America. A successful explanation of the differences in income among countries must be able to account for their varying levels of development. Finally, and most important, the argument that colonial exploitation is the main cause of the gap between rich and poor countries does not explain why revenues from colonialism were put to such productive use in Europe. Wealth, in and of itself, does not ensure sustained economic growth. Nigeria has earned billions of dollars from oil sales in recent decades, yet it remains poor. A satisfactory explanation of "divergence, big time" should be able to account for low incomes in poor countries, high incomes in wealthy countries, and the wide range of incomes in between.

Institutions

Inclusive Economic Institutions
Institutions that enable citizens access to a wide range of economic opportunities and occupations instead of restricting access to a select few. They include private property rights, universal legal enforcement of those rights, and rules encouraging economic competition among businesses.

The fourth way of explaining differences in economic performance among countries makes institutions the key.[53] The basic assumption is that institutions matter for development because they affect individuals' incentives to invest in businesses, factories, and new technologies and to hire more workers—or fail to do so. Economist Daron Acemoglu and political scientist James A. Robinson, in their book, *Why Nations Fail*, distinguish between inclusive and extractive economic and political institutions. The former promote development, whereas the latter obstruct it. **Inclusive economic institutions** include private property rights, universal legal enforcement of those rights, and rules encouraging economic competition among businesses. Legally enforceable property rights assure entrepreneurs that they will be able to reap what they sow. They will be loath to invest in countries where rulers or warring factions indiscriminately seize property and earnings. Rules encouraging competition promote investments in new businesses and technologies because entrepreneurs see opportunities to make profits by creating better products than existing ones. Without such rules, owners of existing businesses can stifle competition. The results of inclusive economic institutions are economic growth, increases in productivity, and higher standards of living.[54]

Although economic institutions "are critical for determining whether a country is poor or prosperous, it is political institutions that determine what economic institutions a country has."[55] In other words, inclusive economic institutions are the product of inclusive political institutions. **Inclusive political institutions** include effective constitutional restraints on executive power and free and fair elections with universal suffrage and protection of civil and political rights to ensure that power is distributed broadly in society rather than being monopolized by a small elite.[56] Acemoglu and Robinson add that a strong, centralized state is essential to enable inclusive economic and political institutions to promote economic growth. Only strong states can provide law and order, enforce legal guarantees of private property, and finance the infrastructure of transport and universal education needed to underpin economic growth.[57] The result of inclusive institutions is broadly based distribution of the fruits of economic development.

In contrast, **extractive economic institutions** transfer income and wealth from most of the people in a country to a small elite. They are underpinned by **extractive political institutions**, which enable political leaders to concentrate power in their hands for their economic benefit. Haiti under French rule, discussed earlier, exemplified extractive institutions. Robert Mugabe's Zimbabwe provides a more recent example. During his tenure as president, he established state enterprises to control valuable diamond mines, which funneled profits to him and his cronies. At the same time, his political party passed legislation enabling supporters to seize control of white-owned farms and businesses. As a result, Mugabe and his inner circle became extraordinarily wealthy while most of the population remained poor, with a low quality of life.[58]

Inclusive institutions emerged first in northern Europe. The puzzle is why there and not somewhere else? Acemoglu, Johnson, and Robinson suggest that the type of economic institutions that emerge in a country "depends on who is able to get their way—who has political power."[59] In their view, the distribution of political power in a country is the main determinant of the kind and the quality of economic institutions that arise there. They hypothesize that inclusive institutions emerged first in certain European countries bordering the Atlantic Ocean that were heavily engaged in trade and colonialism. Profits from trade gave their merchants the economic and political power "to demand and obtain the institutional changes necessary for economic growth." Changes in economic institutions offered "secure property rights to a broad cross-section of society" and made it possible for citizens freely to enter a wide variety of businesses. Changes in political institutions restricted the power of monarchs and "groups allied with the monarchy" to monopolize whole sectors of the economy and stifle competition.[60]

The institutional approach also helps explain the large differences in incomes among former colonies of European countries. Canada and Nigeria were both British colonies, but the former is now a wealthy democratic country whereas the

Inclusive Political Institutions
Institutions that include effective constitutional restraints on executive power, free and fair elections with universal suffrage, and protection of civil and political rights to ensure that power is distributed broadly in society rather, than being monopolized by a small elite.

Extractive Economic Institutions
Institutions that transfer income and wealth from most of the people in a country to a small elite.

Extractive Political Institutions
Institutions which enable political leaders to concentrate power in their hands for their economic benefit.

latter is poor and semi-democratic. What accounts for the difference? Institutionalists argue that the fate of a colony depended heavily on whether Europeans were a majority in the colony. Colonies in which European settlers became the majority of the population adopted growth-promoting inclusive economic and political institutions from their home countries. By contrast, colonies in which Europeans were few in number and relied primarily on slave or forced labor to support them established extractive institutions. European elites in those colonies employed extractive economic institutions to funnel wealth into their hands and extractive political institutions to protect their privileges. Land-holding laws ensured that they maintained profitable rights to mines or plantations. Voting laws allowed them to monopolize their stronghold on political power. Education was restricted to the children of the elite and denied to the broad masses of the population.

This is not to say that the colonies in which Europeans constituted the majority were necessarily democratic or egalitarian. For example, in the United States, the franchise was limited to white men with significant property holdings until the early 1800s. However, meaningful voting rights emerged much earlier in the United States and Canada than they did in Central and South America. So did public primary schools. Although Canada and the United States were not societies of equals, they were generally more egalitarian than societies in Latin America, with the major exception being the American South before the Civil War. The key point is that once extractive institutions are in place, they tend to persist because privileged groups defend institutions that benefit them. Former colonies with institutions that were designed to sustain the economic and social privileges of a small elite continue to exhibit extreme economic and political inequality.[61]

Two factors, above all others, determined whether Europeans settled thickly or thinly in colonized areas. One was disease. Europeans were less inclined to live in places where they were vulnerable to tropical illnesses such as malaria, typhus, and yellow fever. The other factor was the suitability of soils and climates for growing cash crops such as tobacco and sugarcane that could be grown profitably with forced labor. In summary, although institutionalists affirm that geography matters in shaping nations' wealth or poverty, they insist that it is not the main determinant of wealth and power. Colonialism mattered more than geography, not so much because of the wealth that Europeans took from their colonies, but because of the legacy of economic and political institutions that they left behind.

The institutional explanation of the gap between rich and poor countries has many strengths, but some countries do not fit its explanation. China presents a particular challenge for the institutionalist approach. Its economy has developed very rapidly since 1980 without strong legal protections for property rights and inclusive political institutions. Acemoglu and Robinson acknowledge this rapid economic growth but believe it cannot be sustained. The Soviet Union also enjoyed several decades of rapid economic growth in the absence of inclusive institutions, but without innovations in products and technology encouraged by competitive markets, that growth began to falter in the 1970s. The Chinese government's growth model gives markets much more importance than the Soviet Union did, but that model falls far short of the inclusivity that Acemoglu and Robinson believe are necessary for sustained economic growth. The test of their hypothesis will be whether China can continue to grow with its present extractive institutions and achieve per capital income levels of Spain and Portugal.[62]

Comparative Political Analysis: Institutions as the Main Cause of Development and Underdevelopment

Problem
The citizens of wealthy countries have a much higher probability of developing their human potential than their counterparts in poor countries. Social scientists disagree about why some countries are rich while others are poor. Economist Daron Acemoglu and political scientist James A. Robinson believe the answer lies in differences in economic and political institutions.

Hypothesis and Method
The authors hypothesize that economic institutions protecting property rights and relying on markets are most likely to sustain economic growth. They use the comparative case studies method to test their hypothesis by comparing the development experiences of North Korea and South Korea. These countries were chosen because they were one political entity for hundreds of years. They have the same geography, culture, and experience of being a Japanese colony. They differ in economic and political institutions of being separated after World War II.

Operationalizing Concepts
The authors operationalize their central concepts as follows:
- The independent variable is the presence of private property rights and market incentives.
- The dependent variable is economic growth defined as GDP growth per capita.

Results
The Communist party that ruled North Korea abolished private property and markets and introduced a state-planned economy. The military government that ruled South Korea from 1961 to 1987 chose a different approach based on secure private property rights. The government also made improvements in education and infrastructure. All these achievements depended on a centralized state capable of providing law and order, enforcing contracts, providing good education, and building roads and bridges. The state also provided low interest loans and credit to promising firms to help them become competitive in world markets. The result was rapid economic growth. South Korean entrepreneurs had incentives to invest in firms, knowing that their profits would not be expropriated and that they could profit from investments and improve their standard of living. Sustained economic growth was aided by the development of inclusive democratic institutions after the late 1980s,

The results confirm the authors' hypothesis. South Korean institutions generated rapid economic growth and improvements in citizens' lives. North Korea's economy fell further and further behind that of South Korea. By 2010 South Korea ranked among the World Bank's high income economies while North Korea remained a low income country.[63] South Korea's institutions made the difference.

For Further Discussion
1. If private property, markets, and political institutions that constrain political elites are essential for creating sustained development, how can the authors explain China's development success, since it has extensive involvement in the economy and weak protection of property rights?
2. What are the limits of using the comparative cases method to confirm the hypothesis?

Source: Daron Acemoglu and James A. Robinson, *Why Nations Fail: The Origins of Power, Prosperity, and Poverty* (New York: Crown Publishers, 2012), pp. 70–76.

Leadership

None of the four explanations for development and underdevelopment that we have considered—geography, culture, colonialism, and institutions—addresses the issue of leadership. Yet leadership clearly plays a role in promoting or hindering economic development. Leaders of some less-developed countries face particularly difficult obstacles. For example, Paul Kagame took power in the very poor country of Rwanda just a few years after a horrific genocide. Yet, development is determined not only by a country's past and its position in the international division of labor but also by its leaders' skills in choosing successful policies, constructing coalitions of supporters for these policies, and establishing effective economic and political institutions.[64] Although South Korea had advantages that most sub-Saharan African countries lacked, it is unlikely that it would have achieved its current level of development as rapidly as it did without the leadership provided by General Park Chung Hee. Likewise, President Paul Kagame has made a difference in Rwanda. On the one hand, he is authoritarian, but he has achieved reductions in government corruption, lifted large numbers of citizens out of poverty, established universal health insurance and primary education, and achieved high growth rates. Leaders of countries such as Mauritius and Costa Rica have managed to improve the capabilities of many citizens while sustaining effective democracies.

In Brief: Five Explanations for Different Levels of Development Among Countries

- Geography favored countries in Eurasia over those in Africa and Latin America by providing native plant and animal species that were suitable for domestication and adaptable to different environments. Today, geography inhibits trade and development in poor landlocked countries with bad neighbors.
- Cultures that emphasize disciplined work and investment over self-gratification contribute to economic development. So do ones with high levels of social capital and trust.
- Colonialism increased the wealth of European countries and impoverished colonies. It also created numerous obstacles for newly independent countries, including reliance on a single crop for export earnings, extreme ethnic diversity, and racial cleavages.
- Institutions can create or destroy incentives for productive investment. Western European countries outpaced the rest of the world in development because they were first to establish economic and political institutions that support sustained growth.
- Leadership matters because of the policies leaders choose, the kinds of coalitions of supporters they build, and the quality of institutions they help create.

Development, Underdevelopment, and the Good Society

8.9 Analyze the results of testing the hypothesis that higher income per capita is associated with higher capabilities.

Economic development can make a big difference in people's capabilities. Wealthier countries have more revenue to spend on health care, education, and safety for their populations. Higher incomes give individuals more choices about what they can do and who they can become. Higher levels of income per capita are also associated with higher levels of democracy. In this section, we test the hypothesis that higher income per capita is correlated with higher capabilities.

Physical Well-being

We begin with the hypothesis that higher income per capita is linked to lower infant mortality rates. We use income per capita data adjusted for purchasing power in 2011 from the CIA World Fact Book[65] and draw on statistics for infant mortality from the database for *The Good Society*. We test the hypothesis for the 31 countries featured in Chapter 1, Figure 1.1.[66] The findings are displayed in Figure 8.1 below.

The relationship is generally what we expected to find: higher-income countries tend to have lower infant mortality rates than low-income countries, but it is not the case that each increase in income per capita results in a corresponding

Figure 8.1 Income per Capita and Infant Mortality Rates

SOURCES: CIA World Fact Book, https://www.cia.gov/library/publications/the-world-factbook/; World Bank, World Development Indicators, http://data.worldbank.org/data-catalog/world-development-indicators.

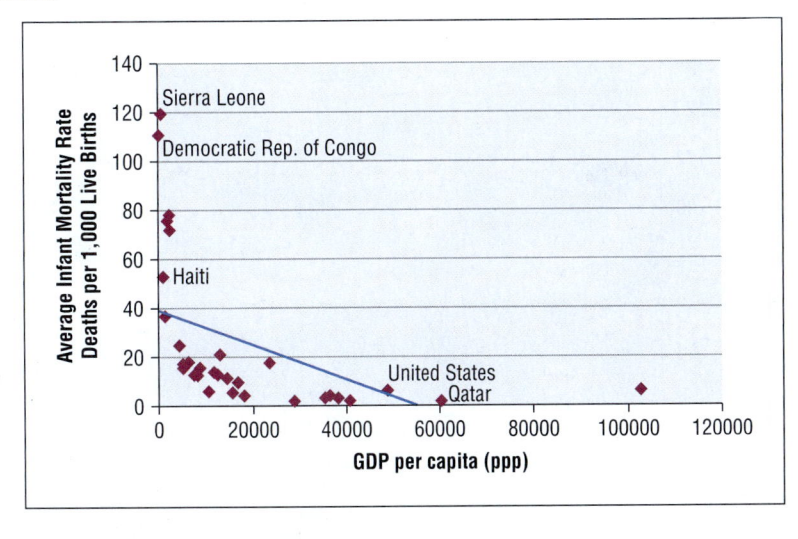

decrease in infant mortality. Countries with per capita incomes ranging from $15,000 to $60,000 can have nearly identical infant mortality rates. For example, Malaysia, with an income per capita of $15,800, averages 5.6 infant deaths per 1,000 births, whereas the United States, with a per capita income of $50,000 has a higher rate of 6.4. Thus, the data in the scatter diagram demonstrate that it is possible to achieve low levels of infant mortality even in the absence of high per capita incomes. A second conclusion is that very poor countries differ profoundly along this dimension. Sierra Leone, located at the top of the vertical axis in the scatter diagram, with an infant mortality rate of 119 per 1,000, had a per capita income in 2011 of $900. Haiti, with a per capita income only $400 higher than that of Sierra Leone, achieved the much lower infant mortality rate of 53. This is still a tragically high figure, but it demonstrates that Haiti performs better in converting meager resources into fewer infant deaths.

Informed Decision Making

The second hypothesis we test, using the same sources as for Figure 8.1, is that higher-income per capita is associated with higher rates of adult literacy.[67] The results are shown in Figure 8.2.

Here again, the hypothesis is borne out. Higher income per capita countries do tend to have higher adult literacy rates, but the results resemble those for the relationship between income per capita and infant mortality. Countries at very different levels of income can achieve nearly 100 percent literacy. Armenia, the country at the far left of the x axis, has achieved 100 per cent literacy with a per capita income of only $5,500. This rate matches that of the United States

Figure 8.2 Income per Capita and Adult Literacy Rates

SOURCES: CIA World Fact Book, https://www.cia.gov/library/publications/the-world-factbook/; World Bank, World Development Indicators, http://data.worldbank.org/data-catalog/world-development-indicators, and United Nations Development Programme, http://hdrstats.undp.org.

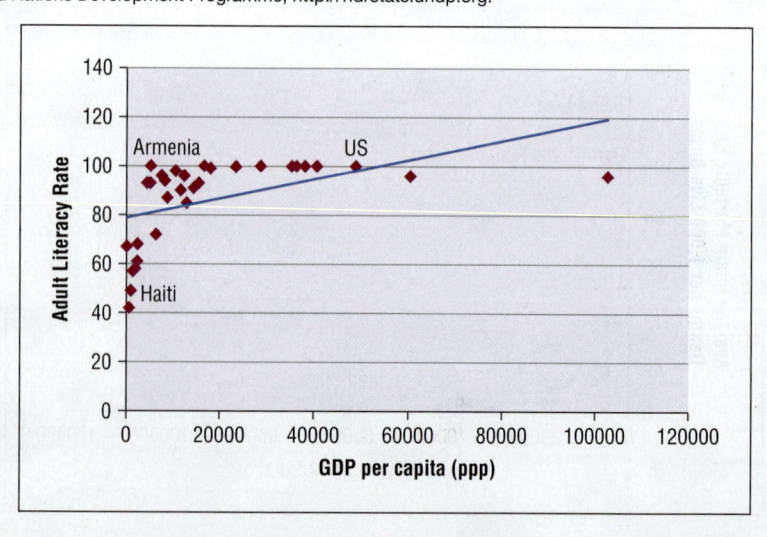

and several other countries, which have much higher per capita incomes. On the other hand, poor countries with roughly similar incomes differ considerably in literacy rates. Haiti has one of the lowest literacy rates of any country in the scatter diagram, but other countries with higher rates have similar incomes.

Safety

The next hypothesis we test is that higher per capita income is associated with lower homicide rates. Admittedly, homicide rates can be a misleading gauge of citizens' feelings of safety. In sub-Saharan Africa, some very poor countries are embroiled in civil wars in which civilians die and combatants often perpetrate mass rapes. The Syrian civil war that began in 2012 had taken more than 100,000 lives by mid-2013. Deaths in civil wars are not included in the homicide date. Focusing only on homicide rates can also miss many reasons citizens might not feel safe. Iraq is a case in point. Although its reported homicide rate is lower than that of Costa Rica, it is highly unlikely that citizens feel safer from physical violence in Iraq than in Costa Rica. Despite this caveat, we include a test of the hypothesis that higher income is associated with lower rates of homicide to determine whether a relationship exists between per capita income and that particular threat to safety. The results are in Figure 8.3.

Homicide rates tend to be lower in higher-income countries, but the scatter diagram reveals several discrepancies from this pattern. All the countries with an income per capita over $30,000 have homicide rates lower than 5 per 100,000 except for the United States. A cluster of countries at the lower left corner of the diagram with per capita incomes ranging from Armenia at $5,500 to Croatia at $18,300 also have lower homicide rates than the United States, which had a per

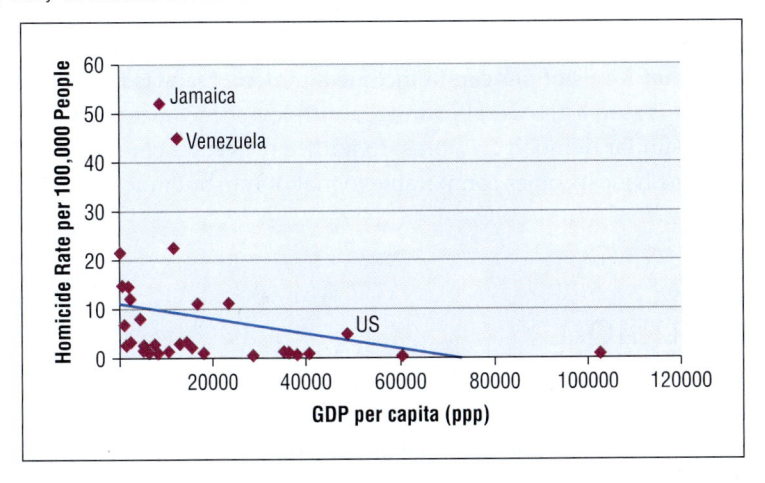

Figure 8.3 Income per Capita and Homicide Rates

SOURCES: CIA World Fact Book, https://www.cia.gov/library/publications/the-world-factbook/; UNODC Global Study on Homicide, 2011, http://www.unodc.org/unodc/en/data-and-analysis/statistics/crime/global-study-on-homicide-2011.html.

Figure 8.4 Income per Capita and Democracy Index

SOURCES: CIA World Fact Book, https://www.cia.gov/library/publications/the-world-factbook/; the *Economist* Intelligence Unit, *Democracy Index 2012*, https://portoncv.gov.cv/dhub/porton.por_global.open_file?p_doc_id=1034.

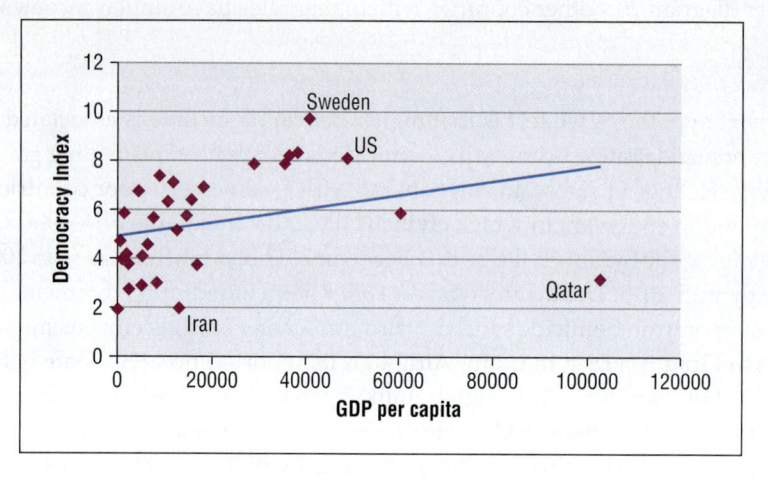

capita income of $50,000 measured by purchasing parity. The scatter diagram also shows that poor countries vary wildly in outcomes. Jamaica and Venezuela both display extremely high homicide rates.

Democracy

The final hypothesis we test is that higher per capita income is associated with higher levels of democracy. Income per capita is from the same source as the previous tests. The data for the level of democracy is from the the *Economist* Intelligence Unit, *Democracy Index 2012: Democracy at a Standstill*.[68] The results are shown in Figure 8.4.

The results confirm the hypothesis. With the exception of the outlier of Qatar, an oil-rich monarchy in the Middle East, there is a modest relationship between GDP per capita and level of democracy. However, the relationship between higher levels of per capita income and democracy is far from perfect. As shown in Figure 8.4, several countries with lower incomes than the United States have similar democracy scores. In addition, several countries above the regression line have incomes comparable to that of Iran but much higher democracy scores.

Conclusion

This chapter has focused on economic and human development gaps between countries. It began by distinguishing between these two types of development and suggesting that they often, but not always, go together. Some countries have much more success in promoting human development than might be expected from their level of economic development; in others, human development lags well behind. Furthermore, there can be big differences in human development in countries with similar per capita incomes. These differences show up countries' Inequality-Adjusted Human Development Index scores.

The chapter then discussed four main ways in which countries with high economic and human development differ from those with low levels of attainment. The latter have much higher levels of extreme poverty, much lower capabilities for citizens, less sustained economic growth, and weaker states. One of the most encouraging trends over the past decade has been quickening economic growth in many of the poorest countries in the world. The results have been dramatic declines in extreme poverty and dramatic improvements in literacy and infant mortality rates.

The next section of the chapter examined five explanations for differences in development among countries. The first emphasizes the effects of geography, which gave Eurasia advantages over Africa and South America and continues to hamper countries that lack access to ports and trade routes. The second suggests that some cultural values are particularly conducive to economic development. The third asserts that colonialism was the main cause of the gap: European countries grew wealthy by exploiting and impoverishing their colonies. The fourth focuses on institutions as the main cause of developmental disparities among countries. In this context, we identified those institutional differences that appear to be most important and tried to show why they first emerged where they did. Finally, we suggested a fifth explanation: Leadership can make a difference. People can act as agents of their own destinies, although this is much easier in some times and places than in others. Some leaders are successful in using new policies and approaches to build coalitions of supporters that set their countries on favorable paths.

Suggested Readings

Daron Acemoglu and James A. Robinson, *Why Nations Fail: The Origins of Power, Prosperity, and Poverty* (New York: Crown Publishers, 2012). Readable, excellent introduction to an institutional way of thinking about why some countries develop and others fail to do so. The authors reject geography and culture as explanations.

Katherine Boo, *Behind the Beautiful Forevers: Life, Death, and Hope in a Mumbai Undercity* (New York: Random House, 2012). Extremely well written, powerful account of the lives of individuals living in a slum in India's largest city. One of the best books available on what it is like to be poor in a developing country.

Jared Diamond, *Guns, Germs, and Steel: The Fates of Human Societies* (New York: W. W. Norton and Company, 1999). A Pulitzer Prize–winning best seller explaining why geography determines the economic fate of nations.

Lawrence E. Harrison and Samuel P. Huntington, *Culture Matters: How Values Shape Human Progress* (New York: Basic Books, 2000).

Includes chapters by several well-known scholars who believe culture makes all the difference in determining whether a country develops.

Charles Kenny, *Getting Better: Why Global Development Is Succeeding—And How We Can Improve the World Even More* (New York: Basic Books, 2011). Readable, excellent presentation of the thesis that those who focus on failures of development miss the main story of the past several decades, which have seen major improvements in health, education, and civil and political liberties in most countries, even some of the poorest ones.

Critical Thinking Questions

1. What is the difference between economic development and human development?
2. Why are there sometimes discrepancies between a country's level of economic development and its level of human development?
3. How do differences in state strength between developed and less-developed countries make a difference for citizens' capabilities?
4. How would supporters of colonial, geographical, cultural, and institutional explanations, respectively, explain why Haiti changed from being one of the richest societies in the world in 1790 to one of the poorest today?
5. What variables might account for the differences in homicide rates between the United States and other countries at its income level in Figure 8.3? What hypotheses do the variables generate and how could you test them?

Chapter 9
Developed Countries and the Good Society

Learning Objectives

9.1 Describe what affluent democracies have in common and introduce the three models found among them.

9.2 Summarize the main features of the social democratic model.

9.3 Describe the history, political culture, political economy, political institutions, and party system within Sweden.

9.4 Summarize the main features of the extreme market model.

9.5 Describe the history, political culture, political economy, political institutions, and party system within the United Kingdom.

9.6 Summarize the main features of the Christian democratic model.

9.7 Describe the history, political culture, political economy, political institutions, and party system within Germany.

9.8 Compare capabilities in Sweden, the United Kingdom, and Germany.

Introduction

9.1 Describe what affluent democracies have in common and introduce the three models found among them.

Eric Johannson lives in Stockholm, Sweden. When he was a teenager, he was a striker for the Swedish Junior Football (soccer) team. His team was knocked out of the Union of European Football Associations (UEFA) Under-17 Football Championship in the qualifying round when it was defeated by Germany led by their best player, Lukas Meyer. Germany went on to defeat the United Kingdom in the finals when Meyer put the winning goal past Britain's goalkeeper, Jack Williams. Injuries, not enough talent, and burnout short-circuited the soccer careers of all three players, and they coincidentally ended up working on the shop floor in automobile plants back in their native countries. Johannson assembled Volvos in Torslanda on the outskirts of Gothenburg, Sweden. Meyer worked in Volkswagen's German facility in Hannover, and Williams built Aston-Martin sports cars at its U.K. assembly plant in Warwickshire. Each of them earned the average hourly pay for manufacturing workers in their country. Johannson earned $24.78 per hour at the Volvo plant in Sweden, Meyer received almost a dollar more, collecting $25.80 at Volkswagen, and Williams was paid almost three dollars less, receiving just $21.16 per hour on the Aston-Martin assembly line in Britain.[1] However, Williams retained more of his wages because he paid lower taxes on his earnings than his former soccer rivals. The effective tax rate, which included income taxes and social security contributions, was just 31.5 percent on earnings in the United Kingdom in 2012; it was 35 percent in Sweden and 43 percent in Germany.[2]

Then the recession struck, and all three were laid off from work. Each applied for and received unemployment insurance. Johannson in Sweden received 80 percent of his weekly earnings for the first 9 months he was unemployed and 70 percent after that. Meyers's unemployment benefits covered about 60 percent of his former earnings. Unemployment benefits were much stingier in Britain, replacing only 10 percent of Williams's former wages, and although both Johannson and Meyer were eligible to collect unemployment benefits for about ten months, Williams was entitled to receive them for only six.[3]

Johannson, Meyer, and Williams are fictitious. They do not exist, but a comparison of their circumstances highlights differences among citizens in Sweden, Germany, and the United Kingdom. All three countries are capitalist economies. Production is privately controlled and carried on for sale or profit in each country. All of them use market systems to coordinate production, but all three differ in important ways, as we saw from the wages Johannson,

Meyer, and Williams earned, the taxes they paid, and the unemployment checks they received.

Sweden, Germany, and the United Kingdom represent different types of political models, or families of nations, found among affluent democracies. By the term *political model*, we mean countries that share similar institutions, politics, and policies. Certain forms of politics, particular kinds of political institutions, and specific types of policies have an elective affinity for one another; they tend to fit together in predictable ways to form distinctive political models. For example, rich democracies in which social democratic parties are dominant (politics) also tend to have proportional representation electoral systems (institutions) and be high welfare state spenders (policy).[4] We can thus speak of political models in which countries cluster together in terms of their politics, institutions, and policies, which reinforce and complement one another.

Affluent democracies include the countries of Western Europe, such as Sweden, Germany, and the United Kingdom; North America, including the United States and Canada; as well as Japan, Australia, and New Zealand.[5] Politically, they are all democracies. Elections are regular, competitive, and open in the sense that citizens are free to organize, express, and exchange their views. Economically, they are all fairly wealthy, with high per capita GDP. Wealth is a result of high levels of labor productivity, which has been supported by large infusions of capital and technology. Sociologically, these countries have moved furthest along the path of a **postindustrial** occupational structure. Industrial jobs in manufacturing have been replaced by the growth of white-collar service, professional, and managerial sector jobs.

This is a select group of countries. Some countries, such as the oil sheikdoms in the Middle East, may be wealthy and have high per capita GDPs but are not democratic, postindustrial, or even industrial, for that matter. Other countries, such as those in Eastern Europe, may be democratic but are not rich. What separates this group, which is sometimes referred to as the West, from the rest are greater labor productivity, higher per capita incomes, more technologically advanced production methods, a higher percentage of postindustrial service workers in the labor force, and a democratic political system. Some countries outside the West may have some of these qualities, but only the affluent democracies rank high on all these measures.

This chapter outlines the characteristics of the social democratic, extreme market, and Christian democratic political models found among Western countries and then offers case studies of countries that represent each of them. Sweden exemplifies the social democratic model; the United Kingdom embodies the extreme market prototype; and Germany exhibits many typical Christian democratic features. Finally, we compare which of these countries performs best in meeting the criteria of the good society.

Postindustrial
A society in which more than 50 percent of the labor force is engaged in service occupations as opposed to industry and agriculture.

Social Democracy

9.2 Summarize the main features of the social democratic model

Social democracy first emerged in the 19th century to represent the political interests of a growing and newly enfranchised working class. Although many of these parties had radical Marxist origins, they quickly shed them in favor of an electoral road to socialism. Socialism, they argued, could be achieved through the ballot box by means of a working class majority. To attract voters, these parties dropped all revolutionary pretenses and instead proposed reforms, incremental improvements that would ameliorate the worst aspects of capitalism. Socialism would be reached gradually as each elected socialist government built on reforms of those that preceded it.

The social democratic model is exemplified best in the Scandinavian countries of Denmark, Norway, and Sweden, where social democratic parties are dominant: larger than their rivals, frequently part of the ruling coalition, and often at the head of the government. Social democratic parties have been unusually successful in Scandinavia because their opponents on the right have been divided; working-class identification is strong because, until recently, these societies have been ethnically, religiously, and linguistically homogenous; and these parties have been able to attract middle-class voters because they receive welfare state benefits these parties offer.

Despite their reputation as socialist countries, Scandinavian societies are thoroughly capitalist. Private ownership of the means of production prevails. The state does not dictate prices or production levels, nor does it own and control many firms. Governments adopt free trade rules and don't try to protect themselves from world markets. They let iconic companies such as Saab go bankrupt and Volvo to be sold to the Chinese. Although Scandinavian countries are not socialist, their reputation for big government is well deserved. Taxes and state spending each account for around 50 percent of total GDP, the highest percentage among all affluent democracies. In addition, public sector employment is high, with over 20 percent of the workforce employed by the state. The public sector workforce is so large because it delivers an array of welfare state services.

The social democratic welfare state is distinctive in many respects. First, eligibility for welfare state programs is universal, available to all citizens. Second, the welfare state is comprehensive, providing cradle-to-grave protection. Third, it is generous. Replacement rates for income lost due to pregnancy, sickness, injury, and unemployment are high. By way of comparison, income replacement ratios for the unemployed varied between 80 percent for up to 260 weeks in Denmark and 85 percent for up to 60 weeks in Sweden, as opposed to just 60 percent for only 26 weeks in the United States.[6] Fourth, not only does the welfare state set high benefit levels, but it also provides an extensive array of services such as health care, day care, elder care, job training, and after-school programs. Finally, social democratic welfare states are redistributive, reducing inequality between the rich and the poor. The effect of these policies is to detach a citizen's quality of life from his or her job. The presence of a large, generous, universal, service-oriented, redistributive welfare state means that a citizen's standard of living does not depend so much on how well he or she performs in the labor market and the paycheck drawn from it. The social democratic welfare state does more to negate the inequalities of the market than Christian Democratic welfare states found in Germany or extreme market welfare states that exist in Britain.[7]

Critics contend that social democracy needs to be rethought because its program of high taxes, large welfare states, and deficit spending to support employment no longer work. High taxes punish entrepreneurial risk-taking. Large welfare states undermine the work ethic. The decline of unions and industry subverts the working-class base of the party, and the introduction of new issues, such as immigration and environmentalism, threaten to crosscut and weaken class identification.

Social democracy has been resilient despite these challenges. The economist Martin Wolf reports, "There is no sign that highly taxed countries [such as those in Scandinavia] . . . suffer from a huge unrequited outflow of corporate capital. . . . The conclusion is that lack of competitiveness is nowhere to be found in these highly taxed countries. Particularly important is the finding that they are not suffering a hemorrhage of capital or of skilled people."[8]

Large welfare states may actually contribute to economic success in Scandinavia by permitting women to enter the workforce in unprecedented numbers, and far from shirking work, Scandinavian societies have some of the highest labor force participation rates among all affluent democracies. Detaching workers' standard of living from the labor market makes them less fearful of change since society socializes these costs and they do not fall directly on workers themselves. Consequently, there is less resistance to technological innovation and moving resources from declining sectors to rising new industries in response to shifting markets. The welfare state also helps moderate wage demands by offering compensating benefits in place of higher wages that might hurt competitiveness, and **active labor market policies** offer retraining, job placement, and relocation assistance to unemployed workers to assist their transition back into the labor force. Scandinavian welfare states offer employment security as opposed to job security.

The result is highly competitive economies alongside large and redistributive welfare states. Far from acting as a drag on economic growth, the welfare state has contributed to it by encouraging labor force participation by women, moderating wage demands, improving workers' skills and productivity, and aligning the interests of workers with economic change by removing the threats it poses to workers' standard of living. As former Swedish prime minister Goran Persson explained, the size of the Scandinavian welfare state is presumed to prevent the economy from growing just as the bumblebee "with its heavy body and frail wings shouldn't fly. Yet it does. . . . We have high taxes and a big public sector—and yet Sweden flies. And we fly in a way that many look

Active Labor Market Policies
Government programs designed to move the unemployed back into the labor market by giving them additional training, creating jobs, subsidizing employment, or helping them with their job search.

upon with envy."[9] At the very moment when the virtue of markets was taken for granted, between 1992 up to the recession of 2008, Sweden refuted the common wisdom by combining high taxes, high state spending, high unionization rates, and an egalitarian income distribution with low unemployment, high labor force participation, low deficits, little poverty, and high rates of innovation and competitiveness. In 2011, the World Economic Forum, a group of world business and political leaders, ranked Sweden third, Denmark eighth, and Norway sixteenth most competitive economies in the world. Sweden has more billionaires on a per capita basis than the United States and is the home to such successful firms as H&M, Ikea, and Tetra Pak.[10] Welfare states have made Scandinavian economies more, not less, competitive. Instead of being undermined by globalization, the welfare state has eased adjustment to it.

The Scandinavian countries perform so well on international comparisons, from global competitiveness to government efficiency and from educational performance to life satisfaction polls, that they have been lauded as the next supermodel. Their accomplishments have been so notable that other countries now hold out the goal "of getting to Denmark or to Sweden" for themselves.[11]

Sweden

9.3 Describe the history, political culture, political economy, political institutions, and party system within Sweden.

Historical Background

Sweden has nine million people, one million more than the population of New York City, who live in a country of 174,000 square miles, about the size of California. Although Sweden is small in size and has few strategic assets, it attracts considerable attention. The mainstream press has lampooned it as the country of sex, suicide, socialism, and spirits (the alcoholic kind), but within the field of comparative politics, Sweden has received disproportionate attention because nowhere else has the working class been so successfully organized economically through labor unions and politically through the Swedish Social Democratic Party (SAP). Sweden boasts the highest proportion of workers who belong to unions among all affluent democracies and, according to the political scientist Goran Therborn, the SAP "has occupied a position of parliamentary power during this [20th] century without parallel in the history of modern democracy."[12] Political analysts have ranked Sweden first, where the working class has been able to attain the most power, among all affluent democracies.[13]

Sweden got a late start on the road to working-class power. Industrialization did not begin until the 1880s, but its growth and development from that point was speedy and thorough. From 1870 to 1914, the value of manufactured goods in Sweden increased twenty-fold, and the industrial workforce quadrupled.[14] Farmers, who comprised about three-quarters of the workforce in 1870, comprised less than half by the end of World War I, and the number of persons engaged in manufacturing and commerce grew during that period from 20 to 50 percent. With industry advancing rapidly, proletarianization of the workforce proceeded faster in Sweden than anywhere else in Europe.

Democracy also got a late start in Sweden. It was not until the end of World War I, when the government was threatened by disturbances at home and the example of the Russian Revolution abroad that universal suffrage was granted and parliamentary democracy was established.

The State

According to the political scientist Arend Lijphart, Sweden is an example of a "consensual democracy," whose political institutions promote "inclusiveness, bargaining and compromise."[15] The consensual character of Swedish democracy is evident, first, in the extent to which governing requires sharing power. Coalition governments are the norm, requiring even dominant parties, such as the Social Democrats, to obtain the support of other parties to enact their policies. Second, consensus is apparent in the inclusiveness of the policy-making process. Interest groups are routinely invited to comment on and suggest amendments to bills under consideration. Third, the views of nongovernmental parties are often taken into account in parliamentary committees, where compromises are forged to obtain these parties' support. Finally, proportional representation electoral rules ensure that parties with only modest support win some parliamentary seats, permitting even small currents of opinion to be represented.[16]

Sweden is a parliamentary democracy. Prime ministers and their Cabinets are accountable to the *Riksdag*, the country's unicameral legislature. Elections to the *Riksdag* are held every four years unless parliament is dissolved before then, which is rare. Elections are conducted according to proportional representation rules in Sweden's 29 multimember election districts, with larger election districts being awarded more seats. Parties, however, must cross the threshold of receiving either four percent of the national vote or 12 percent of the vote in a single constituency to be seated. The *Riksdag* engages in policy making through a strong committee system. Committees review and amend bills, and their recommendations often prevail. But the *Riksdag* has been especially active recently in terms of performing oversight of the executive. It is in session longer and deputies are asking and submitting more written questions to government officials to elicit information. Further, oversight is performed through the office of the parliamentary ombudsman. The ombudsman investigates state agencies for malfeasance, either in response to complaints by citizens or on its own initiative.

The executive branch in Sweden is separated between the head of state and the head of the government. The reigning monarch, currently King Carl Gustaf XVI, is the head of state, but the monarch merely performs ceremonial duties, such as opening parliament and awarding Nobel prizes. Real power resides with the core executive, prime ministers and their Cabinets, who administer and direct executive agencies and set the agenda of government. They develop and submit bills to the *Riksdag*, almost all of which become law due to the way the government builds

Map 9.1 Sweden

Country	Population	Infant Mortality	Life Expectancy	Adult Literacy	Capital City	GDP Per Capita (PPP)	Labor Force by Occupation
Sweden	9,700,000 (2013)	2.2 deaths under 1 year old per 1,000 live births (2013)	81.9 (2013)	99% (2013)	Stockholm	40,900 (2013)	Agriculture: 1.1% Industry: 28.2% Services: 70.7% (2013)

consensus for them. Before proposing a bill, the government will often seek advice from Commissions of Inquiry composed of academic experts, interest group representatives, *Riksdag* deputies, and administrative officials and then, when a bill is prepared, will invite interest groups to comment on it. As is true in all parliamentary democracies, the larger the parliamentary majority the government enjoys, the more power it has relative to the *Riksdag*. The opposite also holds true: when parliamentary majorities are unstable or absent and the government rules as a minority, the more power shifts away from the executive to the legislature.

Many prime ministers and high ministers with important portfolios followed similar recruitment paths. They previously had parliamentary experience "and proved their loyalty to the party prior to being appointed."[17] The core executive dominates policy making in Sweden, as it does in all parliamentary democracies, and within the core executive there is some evidence of presidentialization. The staff of prime ministers has grown, giving prime ministers more ability to initiate policy and monitor ministerial activities. The European Union has also increased the stature of prime ministers who negotiate and sit with other heads of state on behalf of Sweden. While the core executive takes the lead in policy-making, the process is more inclusive and permeable than it is in other European parliamentary democracies. Executive power is tempered by a limited form of judicial review. A similar type of balance is evident when we examine Swedish federalism. The Swedish state is unitary, with political power concentrated at the national level. For example, the Cabinet appoints the governor to each of Sweden's 24 regional, provincial units. Provincial and municipal governments largely carry out policies decided at the top, delivering such services as health care, childcare, and education. But regional and local governments now enjoy an increasing amount of discretion in how they perform these tasks. One Swedish political scientist notes that "the autonomy of local and regional governments has increased dramatically" so that the services they provide can be more responsive to their users' demands.[18] Decentralization has given provincial and municipal governments more discretion in how they deliver public services.

State and Society

Following democratization, the Swedish Social Democratic Party (SAP) emerged as the single largest party in the 1920s but "was unable to govern for more than brief and typically traumatic interludes."[19] To break through politically, the SAP dropped its image as a workers' party and instead began to promote itself as the "people's home," which implied reaching out to other social groups and building broad coalitions. To appeal to groups beyond its working-class base, the party dropped its program of nationalization, which frightened potential allies, and instead began to articulate a more reformist program. The new strategy, which replaced demands to socialize production with appeals to socialize its distribution, propelled the SAP into power and made it the dominant, governing party in Sweden for the rest of the 20th century and beyond.

The new orientation was first evident in response to the Depression of the 1930s, when the SAP formed a government with the Agrarian Party. Relations with the Agrarian Party, however, began to wane in the 1950s because farmers were losing political influence, replaced by a burgeoning white-collar, salaried middle class. To attract middle-class support, the SAP proposed to add a second-tier pension, which would be related to earnings, to the very modest pensions already in place. The supplementary pension bound middle-class voters to the SAP, transforming it from a party based on workers to a modern, wage-earners party based on traditional blue-collar and new middle-class voters.[20]

The new wage earners' coalition of blue- and white-collar workers permitted the Social Democrats to form majority governments from 1958 to 1976. The SAP, which captured about 70 percent of the working class vote, was also able to attract voters beyond this solid proletarian base, but this was the high-water mark of Social Democratic success. Inflation in the 1970s undermined faith in the party's management of the economy. Citizens also began to question the safety and appropriateness of the party's energy policy based on nuclear power. Finally, business devoted vast resources to defeating the Social Democrats following its proposals to give workers more power at work and the state more power over investment. In the 1976 elections, support for the Social Democrats slipped to its lowest level since 1932, and they were thrown out of office for the first time in 44 years. A coalition government composed exclusively of nonsocialist parties took power for the first time since the establishment of democracy in Sweden at the end of World War I.[21] But when the new government was beset by unemployment, budget crises, and instability among the nonsocialist coalition parties, voters returned the Social Democrats to power in 1982.

Although the Social Democrats returned to their accustomed place as head of the government, the ground had shifted permanently. Social Democratic support became more volatile in ensuing elections, reflecting a general instability in the Swedish party system. New parties emerged, and the balance among existing parties shifted. The Social Democrats still remained the dominant, governing party, but they were no longer able to achieve either a majority of votes in elections or of seats in the legislature. The Social Democratic vote fluctuated at around 40 percent and was concentrated among women, public-sector employees, and a declining blue-collar proletariat. Consequently, the Social Democrats had to depend on the cooperation of other parties to govern. From 1994 through 2006, the Social Democrats ruled as a single-party minority government. They relied on the Left and Ecology parties' votes in the legislature but ruled them out as formal coalition partners with seats in the Cabinet because of these parties' opposition to Swedish participation in the European Union (EU).

Most of the change within the Swedish party system has occurred among the nonsocialist or right-wing bloc of parties. The Agrarian Party changed its name to the Centre Party, signaling its intent to shift its shrinking base among farmers and appeal instead to the growing middle class. But rebranding could not forestall the party's decline from what had once been the largest nonsocialist party to what is now one of the smallest. Its losses have been captured by the rising fortunes of the Moderate and Christian Democratic parties. The former denounces the tax-and-spend policies of the Social Democrats and wants to reduce the size of the public sector; the latter is critical of the Social Democrats' social policies and wants to defend family values. A populist right-wing, anti-immigrant party, New Democracy, was able to pass the 4 percent barrier required for parliamentary representation in 1991, but it quickly passed from the scene. However, in the 2010 elections, its successor, the Sweden Democrats, received 5.7 percent of the vote, and then in the 2014 elections more than doubled that total to become the third largest party, with 49 seats in the legislature.

Politically, Sweden exhibits much change without change. New parties, such as the Ecology Party on the left and the Sweden Democrats on the right, have emerged, and the distribution of votes among all the parties has shifted. The Social Democrats and the Centre Party, for example, have lost votes, with other parties on the left and the right picking them up. Class voting has declined and new issues, such as immigration, relations with the European Union, family values, and ecology, are now represented within the party system. While the traditional left-right cleavage reflective of class divisions is still dominant, it no longer exclusively defines the party system.[22] The party system has fragmented from a stable 5 party system to 7 or 8 parties, making government formation more uncertain and complex. Alongside fragmentation, the party system also shows signs of weakening. Voters are less loyal, and membership in political parties and turnout at elections have declined, although the latter is still high by international standards.

But even with the introduction of new bases of cleavage and more electoral instability among voters, the balance between the right (Conservative/Moderate, Liberal, Christian Democrat, and Center parties) and left (Social Democratic, Left, and Green parties) blocs has not changed much. Until the recent 2014 election, most vote switching has occurred within the two blocs not outside of them.

In 2010, for the first time in nearly a century, a right-leaning government finished a full term in office and was reelected by the voters. The Conservative/Moderates won 30 percent of the vote, pulling even with the Social Democrats, who continued to decline and suffered their worst result since 1914. In the 2014 election, the left bloc did not win as much as the governing center-right coalition lost. The left bloc emerged victorious with only 43.7 percent of the vote, failing to improve much beyond its 2010 totals, one of its worst results ever. But the center-right bloc won only 39.3 percent of the vote, losing voters to the surging, far right, xenophobic Sweden Democrats. With neither the center-left nor the center-right able to obtain a majority, the Sweden Democrats hold the balance of power. But that party is considered such a pariah that other parties won't ally with it. Winners by default in 2014, the Social Democrats and their allies on the left will have a hard time putting together a majority in order to govern. Recent Swedish election results are provided in Table 9.1.

Table 9.1 Sweden Votes[23]

Parties	2002 Seats %	2002 Votes %	2006 Seats %	2006 Votes %	2010 Seats %	2010 Votes %	2014 Seats %	2014 Votes %
Social Democrats (S)	41.3	40.2	37.2	35.2	32.3	30.9	32.4	31.2
Conservative/Moderates (M)	15.8	15.2	27.8	26.1	30.6	30.0	24.1	23.2
Liberals (FP)	13.8	13.3	8.0	7.5	6.8	7.1	5.4	5.4
Christian Democrats (KD)	9.5	9.1	6.8	6.6	5.4	5.6	4.9	4.6
Left Party (V)	8.6	8.3	6.3	5.8	5.4	5.6	6	5.7
Centre Party	6.3	6.2	8.3	7.9	6.3	6.6	6.3	6.1
Greens (MP)	4.9	4.6	5.4	5.2	7.1	7.2	6.9	6.8
Sweden Democrats (SD)	–	–	–	–	5.7	5.7	14	12.9
Others	0	3.1	0	2.7	–	1.4	0	4.1
Turnout	–	80.1	–	82.8	–	82.1	–	83.3

Political Culture

When a Russian expressed admiration for Sweden, he despaired that his own country could ever achieve the same results because Russia did not have "enough Swedes" to make it work there.[24] Sweden was a compelling but unattainable goal to this Russian observer because his own country lacked the trust, democratic values, pragmatism, and egalitarianism that characterize Swedish political culture.

Swedish political culture is, paradoxically, one in which individualism and statism are not only respected but perceived as augmenting one another. Since Swedish peasants were never serfs, Swedes believe individualism, democracy, and freedom are birthrights, part of their history as a people. But these precious legacies can only be realized through the state, not against it. The state creates an egalitarian community that protects its members from the injustice of social inequality and liberates them from degrading ties of dependency.[25] "The state is popular," one journalist writes, "not because it is big but because it works."[26]

Alongside what Lars Tragadh referred to as "statist individualism," Swedes are also quite equalitarian. For example, Swedes are less tolerant of wage differentials between high and low earners that citizens in other countries find morally acceptable. Surveys find that Swedes believe the highest-paid occupations should receive no more than 250 percent more than the lowest-paid jobs, whereas the British and Germans were willing to accept almost twice as much inequality between what the top and bottom were paid than the Swedish ideal.[27] Not only are Swedes less tolerant of gross inequality but they are more approving of government efforts to reduce it. Public opinion is more supportive of government programs that redistribute income than in most other affluent democracies.

In addition, Swedish political culture values consensus and pragmatism, that policy making should be inclusive, and that broad consultation will yield solutions to problems. The consensual and pragmatic aspects of Swedish political culture are reflected in the policy-making process through Commissions of Inquiry. These commissions routinely include members from opposition parties as well as affected groups to review the government's legislative proposals. According to Thomas J. Anton, broad consultation occurs through the commissions, where "finding workable solutions to specific problems structures a consensual approach to policy-making."[28] The inclusion of political opponents and affected interests in the policy-making process builds consensus for its results. Pragmatism and consensus are attributed to Sweden's homogeneity and a historical pattern of collaboration among elites who have forged successful compromises.

Finally, Sweden is considered a high-trust society in which citizens act virtuously because they believe their fellow citizens will act virtuously, too. Put another way, in high-trust societies, people are not afraid of being considered a chump, for not trying to game the system. They don't cheat on their taxes and instead pay their fair share because they are confident that others are not cheating and are paying their fair share as well. High trust is attributed to a vibrant associational life. Swedes are joiners. Whereas organizational life in many affluent democracies has declined, "voluntary organizations" in Sweden "have been growing in size, level of activity, and financial resources."[29] "In terms of membership, activity, and financing," the Swedish political scientist Bo Rothstein writes, "the voluntary sector in Sweden is as large, or larger than those in most other Western industrialized democracies."[30] The average Swede belongs to 3.2 private organizations, and only 6 percent of Swedes belong to none. Far from displacing or crowding out trust and voluntary work, the universal welfare state promotes it. Where everyone is included within the welfare state, citizens don't stigmatize those who receive support from the government as "others," and since programs are not means-tested to decide who is eligible, people are less likely to suspect others of cheating to qualify for benefits they don't deserve.[31] Universal welfare states take issues off the table that could potentially breed distrust.

Nevertheless, social trust in Sweden is being challenged today by the arrival of immigrants who share different values and customs. Sweden has been transformed from one of the most homogeneous countries in Europe to one of its most diverse, with 17.8 percent of all Swedes being either first- or second-generation immigrants. About one-quarter of these immigrants are Muslims from the Middle East, Asia, or the Balkans who are much less integrated than Danish and Norwegian nationals who resemble native Swedes. Maureen A. Eger found that immigration and the proportion of foreign born in Sweden has reduced support for the Swedish welfare state.[32] As one Swedish union official explained, "Sweden is a small country. . . . Up to 10 years ago it was a very homogenous country. Everything was very alike. Up until then all Swedes looked the same; almost all thought the same. Because we are all so equal, we can share the pain of the problems. . . . As Sweden gets more divided, it's more difficult to keep this idea of sharing the pain."[33] Einhorn and Logue explain that because many new immigrants' families were larger, poorer, and included fewer working women, they also received a disproportionate share of welfare state benefits, which produced a backlash among natives.[34] Only 51 percent of non-Europeans have a job in Sweden compared to 84 percent of native Swedes, and first-generation immigrants make up a disproportionate percentage of prisoners, the poor, and the unemployed. In 2010, the median household income of non-European immigrants was 36 percent lower than for native-born Swedes, a much greater difference between immigrants and natives than existed in 1991. Immigrants threaten to become an underclass, cut off from mainstream society, which—in a vicious circle—reduces the level of trust and support native Swedes are willing to extend to them. All of these issues came to the fore in 2013 when the immigrant suburbs around Stockholm erupted in violence. Immigrant youth burned cars, vandalized schools, and attacked police stations. Some native Swedes reacted with resentment to the violence, perceiving immigrants as ungrateful, while others viewed the riots as evidence that Sweden needs to do more to confront the intolerance and racism that many immigrants encounter.

Political Economy

The Swedish Social Democratic Party wage earners' coalition of blue- and white-collar workers made it the "the most successful political party in the world," having governed until 2006 for 61 of the past 70 years, "a record without equal among democratic societies."[35] The SAP was so successful because it developed a generous, universal, service-oriented welfare state that both middle- and working-class citizens had a stake in defending. Good policy turned out to be good politics. About 50 percent of all Swedish citizens are said to derive their income from the state as either clients who depend on welfare state programs or as public-sector workers who deliver them. Both these groups, public-sector clients and workers, have an incentive to vote for the Social Democrats to protect their benefits or jobs.[36]

A welfare state that was originally designed in the 1930s to eliminate poverty and squalor was transformed in the 1960s into one that would "provide a lifelong middle class standard of living for all" and redistribute income. Income lost due to sickness, disability, and unemployment was raised from "roughly 30 to 40 percent to about 60 to 90 percent of average workers' wages."[37] Maintaining generous, high-quality welfare state programs was possible only as long as full employment and steady growth could generate the tax revenue to pay for them.[38] Each increase or decrease in unemployment has a much greater effect on budget balances in Sweden than it does in many other European countries or in the United States. Evidence of this became clear in 1990 when Sweden experienced the sharpest recession in its history. The economy contracted by 6 percent, and unemployment soared from 2 to 12 percent, creating a severe budget deficit. The budget crisis required Sweden to trim unemployment compensation, sick pay and parental leave benefits, and to charge health care and day care clients higher fees. In response to an explosion in the number of workers receiving sick pay benefits in a country that is one of the healthiest in the world, eligibility rules were tightened to rein in costs, and pensions were tied more closely to contributions, making them less redistributive. Finally, privatization and markets were introduced. Individuals could now invest some of their pension contributions into individualized accounts that they managed themselves, and there was now market competition in the field of education. Instead of a public school monopoly, parents were free to choose whether to send their child to a public school or have the state pay tuition for their child to attend an independent school (which, unlike American private schools, cannot charge private tuition or select their students).[39]

Despite these reforms, one analyst notes, the Swedish welfare state's "major attributes when compared to other countries—e.g., its generosity, universality, and developed welfare state services—are almost as prominent as before."[40] Sweden continues to make more welfare effort than other countries, which produces egalitarian results to offset market-generated inequalities.

Economically, Sweden has also undergone some adjustment. Although people mistakenly describe Sweden as socialist because of its large welfare state, its economy is thoroughly capitalist. The means of production are privately owned, and the market rules. Economist Mike Marshall writes, "Public ownership of industry has always been very rare in Sweden, economic planning has never been undertaken, [and] state intervention in production has not taken place."[41] State-owned firms account for less than 10 percent of GDP. Not only is Sweden capitalist, but it has also developed a very successful model of capitalism based on three precepts: full employment, **centralized wage bargaining**, and **wage solidarity**. Full employment not only sustains workers' incomes but also keeps the welfare state afloat financially. When people are employed, they require less from the welfare state in the form of benefits, and they contribute more to it in the form of taxes on their earnings. But full employment also has a tendency to encourage inflation, which is restrained by centralized wage bargaining. Centralized bargaining prevents workers from bidding up wages that could price goods out of the market. Consequently, the federation of blue-collar unions, the LO, and the employers' organization, the SAF, negotiated wage agreements for basic industry, which then set the pattern for white-collar and public-sector workers.[42]

The third principle of the Swedish model, wage solidarity, was embedded within centralized bargaining. At first, the concept of wage solidarity was captured in the principle of equal pay for equal work: that workers doing the same job at different firms should be paid the same. Over time, however, the concept of wage solidarity was redefined from standardizing pay across industries to equalizing pay within them, that is, narrowing pay differences between high- and low-wage workers. Alongside the old wage solidarity principle of "equal pay for equal work" was now the new principle of "equal pay for all work."[43]

Centralized Wage Bargaining
When there is a high degree of inter-union and inter-employer cooperation in wage setting; when wage agreements by the peak organizations of unions and employers set the framework for lower-level bargaining.

Wage Solidarity
The principle that workers doing similar work should be paid similarly and that wage differentials between the top and the bottom should be reduced as much as possible.

Like the Swedish welfare state, the Swedish model fell on hard times. Full employment, the first pillar of the model, collapsed in the recession of the early 1990s, when unemployment hit 12 percent. Centralized bargaining also eroded. In 1990, SAF simply closed its bargaining department, signaling that employers were no longer interested in peak-level negotiations with the LO. Employers instigated a shift to decentralized bargaining at the industry and even firm level to disrupt the model's third pillar, wage solidarity. "Equal pay for all work," the more radical meaning of wage solidarity, had inflationary consequences that were unacceptable to Swedish firms that competed in world markets. Compensating less-productive service- and public-sector workers in tandem with wage increases offered to highly productive skilled workers in Swedish industry tended to ratchet up wages. Swedish exporters in manufacturing needed relief from wage hikes that included workers in other sectors of the economy who could not sustain them with higher rates of productivity.[44]

The current Swedish model may only be a shadow of its past, but it produces very similar results. Since the deep recession of the early 1990s, Swedish rates of unemployment have been among the lowest in Europe. Labor force participation rates remain high at 70 percent of all working-age adults, and long-term unemployment rates remain low. Although both unions and employers retreated from decentralized bargaining and the wage spiral it might have precipitated, national-level bargaining that prevailed before has not returned. Instead, sector-level bargaining predominates. Wage bargaining between labor and capital in the export manufacturing sector no longer sets the framework for bargaining between unions and employers in the sheltered, or public sector of the economy.[45] Even with the demise of pattern bargaining and wage solidarity, pay differentials between the top and the bottom are still the smallest within all of Western Europe.[46] Nor have smaller wage differentials undermined incentives to achieve and enjoy social mobility. Strivers have a better chance of realizing the American dream in Sweden than they do in the United States, Germany, or Britain.[47]

The Swedish model has had to adapt to address new challenges. In doing so, it has shown that economic growth and social equality can go together. It can offer the best of both worlds: dynamism and productivity as well as security and equality. The resiliency of the Swedish model was particularly evident in its ability to weather the recent recession. An open economy, with over 50 percent of GDP dependent on exports, growth declined by 4.9 percent in 2009 in wake of the Great Recession. The Swedish government responded with a very aggressive combination of lower taxes and higher spending to stimulate the economy. The fact that this typically social democratic response was undertaken by a nonsocialist government in Sweden indicates how powerful the pull of social democracy remains within it. Consequently, the increase in unemployment was lower in Sweden than in the Eurozone, the increase in public debt was milder, and balance of payments accounts were more favorable.

In foreign policy, Sweden has continued to follow a policy of neutrality and internationalism. Sweden was neutral in both World War I and World War II, profiting from both conflicts because Swedish industry emerged from both wars in much better shape than other European countries whose manufacturing bases were destroyed. Sweden continued its policy of non-alignment in the Cold War that followed. Unlike its Nordic brothers, Norway and Denmark, Sweden never joined the North Atlantic Treaty Organization (NATO), the military alliance created in response to the Soviet Union. It also moved hesitantly in the direction of European integration, finally joining the European Union in 1995. But Sweden's caution about tieing itself further to Europe was on display in 2003 when it voted by referendum to reject adopting the euro, the European currency, in favor of retaining its own money, the krona.

Sweden jealously guards its independence and neutrality. At the same time, it is an advocate of internationalism. It is an avid supporter of stronger international organizations, such as the United Nations (U.N.), the World Trade Organization (W.T.O.), and the International Monetary Fund (I.M.F.). Sweden tries to leverage whatever influence it has through international organizations and a generous foreign aid program. As a small country that doesn't have much weight to throw around, it regards international law as the best way to promote peace and prosperity.

Extreme Market Democracy

9.4 **Summarize the main features of the extreme market model.**

The price of a cup of coffee reveals differences between social democratic and extreme market countries. Coffee costs $5 in a cafe in Stockholm, Sweden, whereas it is one-third that price in Stockholm, Maine. Higher taxes and wages make a simple cup of coffee cost three times more in Sweden than it sells for in the United States. However, the cost of affordable coffee comes in the form of a lower standard of living for coffee servers and fewer public services for them.[48]

Extreme market democracies are found predominantly in the Anglo-American democracies, that is, in Britain and her former colonies, such as Canada, the United States, Ireland, Australia, and New Zealand. These countries possess roughly similar politics, institutions, and policies. Politically, leftist political parties are either completely absent in these countries, as is the case in the United States; are rarely in government, as is the case in Canada and Ireland; or are not the natural party of government, which is true of the Labor Party in Australia and Britain. Part of the reason these parties have not fared well is because **class voting** is so weak within them. Working-class voters are more likely to betray their class and cast their ballots for bourgeois parties. Not only are working-class voters more disloyal, but they are less likely to vote. Class differences in turnout are higher in these countries than in our other two models. Consequently, business has been politically dominant in extreme market democracies. Politicians appeal to core wealthy voters who are more likely to vote and ignore the demands of peripheral, working-class voters who are less likely to do so.

Class Voting
When citizens vote for parties aligned with their class position. That is, workers vote for parties of the left while capitalists vote for parties of the right.

Extreme market democracies also share a distinctive policy profile that distinguishes them from social and Christian democrats. They are more likely to leave the production and allocation of goods to the market than is the case in either social democratic or Christian democratic countries. The public sector is relatively small among extreme market democracies with these countries clustered near the bottom when it comes to state spending and revenues as a proportion of GDP. Extreme market democracies also rank low in terms of **welfare effort**, the proportion of GDP devoted to social spending. Social democratic countries devote about a third of their spending to welfare; Christian democratic countries spend about 30 percent; and extreme market democracies expend around 25 percent. Welfare state programs tend to be targeted to the poor, and benefit levels tend to be stingy. Consequently, people's standard of living is tied closely to their job. Their fate is more at the mercy of market forces.

Extreme market democracies exhibit a diversity of state institutions. Canada and the United States are federal systems, whereas Ireland is a unitary state. Australia and Britain are parliamentary democracies; the United States is presidential. Ireland has a form of proportional representation, whereas all the rest use pluralities to elect candidates in single-member districts. However, their interest group structures are quite similar. They all have pluralist systems in which interest groups compete for members, membership is voluntary and highly fluid, and power within them is decentralized. Although unions loom large in the institutional landscape of social and Christian democracy, they are peripheral in extreme market democracies. **Union density** is relatively low, and unions are decentralized, making coordination among them difficult. The same is true of employer organizations. Many businesses are unaffiliated, and employer organizations lack the power to direct their members.

Welfare Effort
A measure that divides welfare spending by GDP to compare different countries' relative commitment to the welfare state.

Union Density
The proportion of the workforce that belongs to labor unions.

The United Kingdom of Great Britain and Northern Ireland

9.5 Describe the history, political culture, political economy, political institutions, and party system within the United Kingdom.

Historical Background

It is hard to imagine that such a small country—about the size of Minnesota—once could have had such an oversized influence on world affairs. After World War I, at the height of the British Empire, the United Kingdom ruled more than a fifth of the world's population, spread over a quarter of the globe. It was the largest empire in history, with the Union Jack, the British flag, firmly planted on all seven continents.

The United Kingdom (U.K.) of Great Britain and Northern Island is a multinational state composed of four parts: England, Wales, and Scotland—which together comprise Great Britain—and Northern Ireland, which includes the six northern counties that remained under British rule when Ireland became independent in 1922. England accounts for about 84 percent of all U.K. citizens, with 9 percent living in Scotland, 5 percent in Wales, and the remainder in Northern Ireland.

Britain claims, with much justification, to be the birthplace of democracy. The absolute power of kings was first challenged when feudal barons forced King John to sign the Magna Carta in 1215, thereby establishing the rule of law in England. However, the Magna Carta was only the beginning of a power struggle between the crown and the aristocracy that was not settled until the Glorious Revolution of 1688. The result of this nearly bloodless revolution was to create a constitutional monarchy that required the monarchy to rule with the consent of parliament.

As Britain paved the way to parliamentary democracy, it also took the lead in economic development. Industrial capitalism emerged earlier and advanced faster in Britain than elsewhere. The annual rate of growth between 1815 and 1861 was 3.5 percent, which was extraordinary by the standards of the time. Coal output doubled between 1800 and 1830, pig iron production tripled, and industrial production increased by more than 200 percent. Technological innovation and the commercialization of agriculture combined to create tremendous wealth, but it also generated profound social dislocations. Peasants who lost access to land and artisans who could not compete against mechanized production were turned into wage laborers. Cities grew and class divisions became more evident and intense. The poet, William Blake, saw "dark satanic mills"; the novelist Charles Dickens described "wretched, abject, frightful, hideous, [and] miserable" children working in factories; and the socialist Frederick Engels found working-class slums in "which the filth and tottering ruin surpass all description." Laborers began to form unions to improve their wages and working conditions, and they began to press for the right to vote, which was restricted to those with substantial property. Their demands gradually bore fruit. Beginning in 1832, the franchise was extended in measured doses until almost all adults were granted voting rights by 1928.

As the electorate expanded, parties began to organize more deliberately to appeal to new voters. The party system in the second half of the 19th century was dominated by the Tories, or the Conservative Party, supported predominantly by devout Anglicans, rural villagers, and property owners. It stood for the traditional virtues of property, the Church of England, and the Crown. The Liberal Party drew its voters from both the new urban middle class and the working class. It advocated new principles of free trade and social reform. However, in the early years of the 20th century, policies and judicial decisions that threatened trade union security prompted workers to break their ties to the Liberal Party. They allied with smaller, leftist parties to form the Labour Party in 1906. The new party was so successful in cutting into Liberal Party support that by the 1920s, the Labour Party replaced the Liberals as one of the two dominant parties in Britain.

The United Kingdom entered World War I "as the dominant force on the world stage."[49] It still had a strong domestic industrial base and ruled over a vast empire, but the years between the two world wars marked the beginning of the country's long decline. The work force losses from World War I were staggering, and in the war's aftermath, exports fell and the national debt increased. At the same time, turmoil erupted across the Irish Sea. Irish nationalists declared a Catholic Republic in Dublin, demanding independence. Unable to quell the bloody disorder in the streets, Parliament granted Ireland its independence in 1922, with six counties in Northern Ireland remaining part of the mother country.

In 1929, the Depression struck hard as markets for British exports dried up. Ten years later, World War II erupted, with Hitler's Nazis poised to invade the only European adversary they had not conquered, but in its finest hour, the United Kingdom resisted and helped defeat fascism in Europe.

The postwar years, which we take up in the rest of this chapter, have been years of trial and decline. The United Kingdom lost its empire and its eminence. As it begins the 21st century, it faces sobering choices and demanding challenges. Its political system may be entering a new era. The 2010 election resulted in a hung parliament, defined as one in which no party enjoyed a legislative majority. The last time this happened was in 1974. The indecisive election results were resolved when the Conservatives and Liberal Democrats formed the first peacetime coalition government since 1931.

British society is also in flux. The United Kingdom is now a diverse country, with nonwhites and foreign-born residents comprising about 10 percent of the population. Not only is Britain more multiracial and multiethnic, but its multinational character is also more in evidence. Welsh and Scottish demands for autonomy or even independence have led Parliament to devolve authority to governments in Scotland, Wales, and Northern Ireland. In 2014 Scotland held a referendum on whether to secede from the United Kingdom, with a majority voting to retain their 307 year old union. Britain faces tough foreign policy choices because it is no longer capable of wielding global influence by itself. On the one hand, it can look across the English Channel and seek to project power as part of Europe. It can invest in the European Union. Alternatively, it can look across the Atlantic Ocean and exert influence by building on its special relationship with the United States. Either way, as a mid-level power, it now needs to work through others to have global influence.

The State

Like other states, Britain has a Constitution, but unlike most other countries, you can't read, distribute, or display it because no copies exist. The British Constitution does not take the form of a single, formal, collected, codified document.[50] Rather, it is composed of a blend of parliamentary laws, judicial precedents, and accepted conventions. Together, along with the laws of the

European Union (EU) to which Britain subscribes as a member, these various sources compose the British Constitution. Because there is no separate formal document, there is no need for a special process to amend or change it as there is in the United States. Instead, Constitutional change entails altering the laws, court decisions, and traditions that comprise it. The lack of a codified, single document gives the British constitution a certain political flexibility in the sense that it doesn't put clear limits on what government can do. It also presumes a certain amount of good faith that political actors will not abuse its imprecision and that governments will act within the constitution's vague limits.

British parliamentary democracy is often referred to as the Westminster model, in deference to the Palace of Westminster where the British Parliament, the British legislature, is located. In the British system, parliament is supreme. The legislature can make and unmake any laws, and its decisions cannot be set aside or overridden. There are no checks and balances on parliament. Unlike the United States, there are no courts to nullify parliamentary acts by claiming they violate the constitution, or presidents to veto them. This has led some to criticize the Westminster model as an elective dictatorship because there allegedly is nothing to prevent any government from passing any law so long as it has a legislative majority to vote for it. This critique overlooks the fact that Parliament must act within the constraints of not one constitution but two. First, it must still act within the common-law decisions and conventions of the Constitution. They may be legally thin, but they are politically potent. Parliament must also abide by the rules and limits set by European Union laws and treaties, which Britain agreed to follow when it joined the organization in 1973. If British and EU laws are in dispute, the former may be nullified if the European Union's supreme court, the European Court of Justice, finds they are in violation of EU law.

Parliamentary supremacy is not unique to Britain; it is also found in many other European countries. Presumably, they too should be worried about the absence of checks and balances on their governments, but the Westminster model differs from other European parliamentary democracies in ways that make this concern especially relevant. Many parliamentary democracies in Europe conduct their elections according to proportional representation rules in which seats are awarded to parties according to the percentage of the vote they receive. As we explained in Chapter 7, these rules tend to create multiparty systems in which no party can achieve a legislative majority, often requiring parties to form coalition governments. The need to ally with other parties and share power with them is in its own right a form of checks and balances, one that prevents coalition governments from becoming too aggressive.

Britain does not use proportional representation to decide elections. Instead, its electoral rules are similar to those in the United States, where the candidate who receives the most votes in each district is the winner. These rules create

Map 9.2 United Kingdom

Country	Population	Infant Mortality	Life Expectancy	Adult Literacy	Capital City	GDP Per Capita (PPP)	Labor Force by Occupation
United Kingdom of Great Britain and Northern Ireland	63,700,000 (2013)	4.4 deaths under 1 year old per 1,000 live births (2013)	80.4 (2013)	99% (2013)	London	37,100 (2013)	Agriculture: 0.7% Industry: 20.5% Services: 78.9% (2013)

a bias toward a two-party system in Britain or, at least, away from the multi-party systems found in the rest of Europe. The result is that British elections frequently deliver clear parliamentary majorities for one party as opposed to the coalition governments encouraged by proportional representation (PR) rules. Whereas parties that belong to coalitions have to appease their partners, a party with a parliamentary majority can legislate freely. Consequently, the threat of parliamentary supremacy becoming an elective dictatorship is greater when one party commands a legislative majority—as is typically the case in the United Kingdom.

The British Parliament contains two chambers: The House of Lords comprises the upper house, the House of Commons is the lower house. Although supreme authority is invested in Parliament, it only has a modest influence over policy. It would be unkind but not totally inaccurate to belittle Parliament as a rubber stamp for the executive, which has more access to information to develop policy, more staff to work on it, and can depend on party discipline to pass it. Prime ministers and their Cabinets determine the legislative agenda, and although televised debate in the House of Commons on their proposals may make for good theater, the outcome of parliamentary votes is rarely in doubt. Still, despite the fact that parliamentary assent is virtually assured because the government has a majority within it, the legislature nevertheless serves a useful purpose in requiring the government to explain and defend its proposals.

The House of Lords is the weaker of the two chambers because it fits awkwardly in a democracy in which none of its members are elected. It can only delay bills, not veto them. Until quite recently, hereditary peers—nobles such as barons and earls who held their seats based on inherited titles—were the majority in the House of Lords. This gave the upper chamber a conservative bias that led to efforts to reduce its powers. There are few hereditary peers any longer in the House of Lords. Most of its members are life peers, appointed by the monarch on the recommendation of the government. They retain their seat, or lordship, until they die, in contrast to heredity peers whose seats are passed down to their descendants. The shift from hereditary to lifetime peers has not made the House of Lords more powerful, though it has made the institution more assertive. Lifetime peers tend to take their jobs more seriously and to be more conscientious in scrutinizing and offering amendments to legislation.

In 2010, the House of Commons was composed of 650 Members of Parliament (MPs), each of whom was elected from a particular constituency, just as every district in the United States elects one member to serve in the House of Representatives. As part of the unwritten constitution, parliamentary terms are set at a maximum of five years, at which point the government must call for new elections if it has not done so already. Most MPs today are professional politicians, although they do not receive as much compensation and administrative support as their American counterparts. Although MPs ostensibly represent the district that elected them, they really represent the party that nominated them. They depend on their party for support, voters elect them based on their party's program, and if MPs want to further their political career by ascending to the Cabinet, they need to display party loyalty. It is an overstatement, but not much of one, to describe the government as the ventriloquist and parliament as the puppet through which it speaks. The ruling party absorbs so much of the legislative timetable that individual members have little opportunity to introduce their own bills. Less than 10 percent of all bills passed in Parliament come without government sponsorship. Amendments to bills that the government opposes are rarely approved, and legislators are unlikely to vote against their party because of the influence it has over their career, from being re-nominated at the next election to being considered for a leadership post in the next government.

However, parliamentary deference can also be overdrawn. The puppet sometimes finds its own voice. Recently, backbenchers—members of the governing party who do not also have a government post—have displayed more backbone. For example, many Labour Party backbenchers defected in 2003 rather than support the government's policy committing British troops to Iraq. The Conservative Party faced a similar rebellion in its ranks in 2011, when backbenchers defied the leadership by voting to approve a referendum on whether Britain should remain within the European Union.

The British monarchy plays a neutral and neutered role in politics. It stands above the sordid and divisive fray of partisan conflict, representing the dignified parts of the constitution. The greatest power still vested in the monarchy is its authority to choose the prime minister. This usually just entails asking the leader of the party that received a majority in parliament to form a government. This has posed few problems in the past because elections usually delivered clear majorities for either the Labour or Conservative parties, but today, there is less assurance that parties can consistently deliver a majority in parliament as they once did. If they fail to win a parliamentary majority, the reigning monarch has an opening to exercise discretion in choosing which party leader to select as prime minister and form a government. Even when such opportunities arise, the monarchy is careful to be deferential and circumspect in using its powers. For example, following the 2010 elections, when no party won a parliamentary majority, Queen Elizabeth accepted the advice of the outgoing prime minister and asked Conservative Party leader David Cameron, whose party won a plurality of seats, to form a government.

Today, the executive—specifically prime ministers and their Cabinets—dominate policy making in Britain. In theory, they turn their party's program into policy, assured of a parliamentary majority to support it, but the real world that prime ministers encounter is not as frictionless as this description implies. They have to satisfy public opinion, appease members of their party in parliament, defend their program in parliamentary debate, create consensus within their Cabinet, placate interest groups, attend to European Union commitments, and consider new regional governments and old national identities.

Prime ministers are elected to the House of Commons and are leaders of their party within it. They are first among equals in their Cabinet, which is composed of about 20 to 25 ministers who run various executive ministries

(Defense, Education, Northern Ireland, Transport, etc.) as well as some ministers who serve without portfolio, meaning without official ministerial responsibilities. Members of the British Cabinet differ from their American counterparts in that the former also serve as members of Parliament, whereas the latter do not serve in Congress; however, the Cabinets in the United States and the United Kingdom are similar in two important ways. First, members of the American Cabinet are appointed and can be dismissed by the president, just as members of the British Cabinet serve at the pleasure of the prime minister. The power to hire and fire their colleagues makes prime ministers very much first among equals.

Second, members of the official Cabinet in each country have been eclipsed by the chief executive's kitchen Cabinet, the informal network of personal advisors on whom prime ministers and presidents rely. Prime ministers, like presidents, have more confidence in the policy advisors who work in their executive offices than they do in the collective wisdom of their Cabinets. Consequently, they prefer to develop policy within their expanded offices rather than depend on the Cabinet and the ministries they lead to do so. This has led some analysts to describe a creeping presidentialization of British prime ministers in which the staffing and administrative resources of the prime minister's office have grown, and policy making is increasingly concentrated within it; in which prime ministers increasingly use the media to personalize power at the expense of their parliamentary party and Cabinet; and in which British elections are now more candidate-centered, based on the appeal of the party leader and not on the draw of the party's program. For example, presidentialization was evident in the 2010 parliamentary election when, for the first time in British history, party leaders held televised debates, just as American presidential candidates do.

Unlike the United States, however, the United Kingdom is a unitary state, with authority concentrated at the national level, formally in Parliament. Even though subnational levels of government lack independent, legal rights derived from the constitution, as individual states do in the United States, they still wield powers that Parliament is willing to grant them. For example, readers will recall that the United Kingdom is composed of four nations with their own identities and cultures. Despite centuries of unification, demands for Welsh and Scottish autonomy persist. In 1997, Parliament responded and permitted voters in Scotland and Wales to schedule referenda, in which both Scots and Welsh approved the creation of their own governments. Both new governments were given authority over domestic issues, such as health, education and the environment, with the British Parliament in Westminster reserving authority for itself over defense, immigration, and foreign affairs. The U.K. minister of health is now, in practice, only the minister of health for England because the governments in Wales and Scotland have their own heath ministries. In the 2014 referendum on Scottish independence, British party leaders promised to devolve even more authority to Scotland in order to attract wavering voters who were considering secession. Devolution has created an awkward situation in which people in Scotland and Wales can vote on matters that affect England, but citizens in England cannot vote on matters affecting Scotland and Wales.

State and Society

Britain emerged from World War II victorious but depleted. Food had to be rationed, housing was scarce, more than a quarter of its productive capacity was destroyed, and people were exhausted by the sacrifices the war imposed on them. The end of the war also brought an end to the coalition government that ruled during hostilities, with normal conflict resuming between the Conservative and Labour parties when the Nazis were defeated. Class position continued to determine party support, with the Labour Party appealing predominantly to manual workers and the Conservatives attracting a broader, more national electorate.

The Labour Party won the 1945 elections in a landslide and proceeded to repay citizens for their wartime sacrifices by increasing the welfare state, creating the National Health Service, building public housing, and nationalizing some industries. However, the 1950s were a period of ominous decline for Labour because Conservatives won three elections in a row, leading two electoral analysts to publish a book in 1960 with the portentous title, *Must Labour Lose?* Considerable soul searching within Labour followed as some called into question its formula of gradual socialism, in which short-term reforms build toward the long-term goal of common ownership of the means of production.

The ruling Conservative Party left in place much of the policy legacy it inherited from the postwar Labour Party, including both the welfare state and nationalized industries. However, the British economy did not perform well in the postwar years compared to more dynamic economies in Europe. What had been the workshop of the world and the birthplace of the industrial revolution could no longer compete. British trade and investment had been directed toward the remote corners of the Empire instead of being focused at home. As former colonies gained independence, the crutch of the Empire was gone. Economic growth lagged, inflation grew, and unemployment swelled. A sign of Britain's economic decline was that Italy, which the British had viewed condescendingly as a warm and charming vacation venue, was now wealthier than it was!

Voters in the 1970s turned to the Labour Party in the hope that it could revive economic growth. Labour pledged to restore British competitiveness by negotiating a social contract with the unions, its natural allies. The government offered to redistribute income and increase welfare state spending in return for wage restraint by the unions, but neither party was a faithful partner to the social contract. Unions found it difficult to restrain wages as workers struck to maintain their living standards, and the government failed to deliver on its promises. The Winter of Discontent in 1979, when public-sector strikes immobilized London, proved to be the last straw.

The policy paradigm to which both parties subscribed—economic management plus the welfare state—seemed exhausted. In 1979, the Conservatives won a majority of seats in Parliament, and their parliamentary leader, Margaret Thatcher, promised a bold departure. As prime minister, Thatcher curbed the unions, sold off nationalized firms, raised interest rates to snuff out inflation, and cut back the welfare state. In place of the sins of collectivism, she promised the rewards of thrift, competition, and individual responsibility. Thatcher was a polarizing figure throughout her term, even within her own party. Conservative members of her Cabinet and parliamentary party bristled at her dismissiveness, and the unpopularity of some of her policies convinced them to make a change. Thatcher had served as prime minister more consecutive years than any British parliamentary leader in the 20th century until she was ousted in 1990 by members of her own party and replaced by John Major.

In the 1950s and 1960s, the two major parties captured about 90 percent of the total vote between them, but policy failure by both the Labour and Conservative parties led voters to look for alternatives. The Liberals, who previously had been limping along, received 19.3 percent of the vote in the 1974 elections. Nine years later, the Alliance, which merged the Liberals and Social Democrats (right-wing Labour Party defectors), received 25 percent of the vote. Although Margaret Thatcher could count on large majorities in the House of Commons throughout her tenure, the Conservatives never received a majority of the vote nationally in any of the three elections (1979, 1983, and 1987) that elevated her to prime minister. Alternatives to the two major parties continued to poll well into the next century. In 2010, Labour and the Conservatives together won less than two-thirds of the vote—their lowest combined total since 1922—the first election that followed the partition of Ireland.

Third-party success at the polls—first in the guise of the Liberals, then by the Alliance, and then the Liberal Democrats—did not translate into a proportional number of seats in Parliament. Previously, in the 1950s and 1960s, when Labour and the Conservatives monopolized the vote, the percentage of the vote a party won was closely aligned with the percentage of seats it received, but as third parties began attracting voters in the 1970s, the correlation between votes and seats was broken. This occurred at the expense of third parties that consistently won a smaller percentage of seats in the House of Commons than their percentage of the national vote would suggest. Although third parties had become increasingly popular, their voters were too geographically dispersed to win pluralities in many election districts, and thus take seats in Parliament. For example, in the recent 2010 elections, the Liberals received 23.6 percent of the vote nationally but won only 8.9 percent of the seats in Parliament. In contrast, as the comparison of votes and seats in Table 9.2 reveals, the Conservatives, and especially the Labour Party, were very efficient in turning votes into seats. Labour received only about 6 percent more votes nationwide than the Liberal Democrats in 2010 but won 400 percent more seats in Parliament!

The revitalization of third parties, and even smaller fourth and fifth parties, such as the anti-immigrant British Nationalist Party, the anti-EU UK Independent Party, the ecologist Green Party, and the nationalist parties in Scotland, Wales, and Northern Ireland, signaled the dealignment of the British party system. The hung Parliament and coalition government that emerged from the

Table 9.2 British Election Results

	1997 Votes	1997 Seats	2001 Votes	2001 Seats	2005 Votes	2005 Seats	2010 Votes	2010 Seats
Labour	43.2	63.4	40.7	62.5	35.2	35.0	29.0	39.8
Conservative	30.7	25.0	31.7	25.2	32.4	30.7	36.1	47.2
LibDem	16.8	7.0	18.3	7.9	22.0	9.6	23.0	8.8
Others	9.3	4.6	9.3	4.4	10.4	4.7	11.9	4.2
Turnout		71.3%		59.4%		61.4%		65.1%

SOURCE: www.politicalresources.net/area/uk/uktable.htm

2010 election was no fluke but rather the culmination of long-term, dealigning trends in British politics. Party identification with the Labour and the Conservative parties has declined, and voters are less inclined to vote for them. Tribal loyalties that connected manual workers to the Labour Party and middle-class voters to the Conservative Party still exist but are not as powerful as they once were. British voting analysts found that by the end of the "twentieth century, class had come to play a very limited role in determining the vote preferences of the British electorate." [51] Alongside the diminished influence of class, region, and race now also structured the vote. Voters in the south of England were more likely to vote Conservative, while the growing number of ethnic minorities were more likely to vote Labour. In addition, new issues, such as immigration, the European Union, and Scottish and Welsh nationalism, have emerged to upset and complicate the old left–right spectrum and create opportunities for new parties to arise outside of it.

Political Culture

In their 1963 classic book on political culture, *The Civic Culture* (see Chapter 4 for more discussion of the book's approach), Gabriel Almond and Sidney Verba described British political culture as "deferential."[52] The British, according to Almond and Verba, had confidence and faith in the government. They trusted political elites to be responsive and competent, which may explain why the British did not feel they needed a codified, formal constitution. Citizens believed that only informal limits were necessary because they assumed the government would not abuse its authority.

That was 1963. Since then, confidence and faith in the government has declined, but political alienation has increased in all Western democracies, with the British still recording higher levels of trust in their government than citizens in many advanced democracies.[53] Moreover, trust in government is related to trust in one's fellow citizens, which also still remains comparatively high in Britain. The British have adjusted well to becoming a multiracial and multi-ethnic society in which people pursue different lifestyles. Public opinion polls indicate that the British exhibit more tolerant attitudes toward gay rights, gender equality, and people of different races than they did in the past.[54] And they are more tolerant than their European peers. Surveys indicate the British are more at ease with the idea of a non-white political leader—their own equivalent to President Obama—than citizens are across the English Channel. Tolerance is not only evident in surveys but in behavior. The gap in unemployment rates between natives and immigrants is less than it is in Sweden and intermarriage rates among whites with Asians as well as Caribbean blacks have increased.[55]

Finally, the British value what is effective and pragmatic over what is ideological and principled. This may explain why right-wing fascist and left-wing communist parties have never had much appeal to British voters. It also may explain why retaining such an archaic institution as the monarchy continues to receive broad support among the British public. They value it not because they are royalists but because it seems to work.

Political Economy

The British Empire was both a blessing and a curse for the mother country. It secured access to foreign markets and raw materials, but it also diverted investment from domestic industries and promoted complacency at home. By 1900, both Germany and the United States eclipsed British manufacturing because they were more innovative, more efficient, and more capital-intensive. In the ensuing years, cataclysmic events that included two world wars and the Great Depression concealed how much Britain had slipped, but the return to normalcy at the end of World War II put the country's lack of dynamism into sharp relief. Its average annual rate of growth from 1950 to 1973 was less than half what Italy, France, and West Germany achieved. Unemployment was higher, productivity was lower, and Britain routinely ran trade deficits.

As noted earlier, a succession of Labour and Conservative governments came to power in the 1970s. Each promised to stimulate growth, and each failed miserably. At the end of the decade, Margaret Thatcher became prime minister, promising to break with the failed policies of her predecessors. She was determined to let markets rule and reduce state intervention in the economy. The economy dipped into recession at first but then, beginning in 1983, it grew at an impressive rate of 4 percent before going into recession again by 1990, when Thatcher left office. The best that could be said after Thatcher's harsh medicine was that Britain was no longer a laggard; its economy's growth rate was now on par with other European countries through the 1990s.

Thatcher's policies transformed Britain in many ways. She moved Britain closer to her ideal of the ownership society in which more people owned property, which would allegedly make them more sympathetic to Conservative party values. She transformed renters into homeowners when she sold off public housing units to tenants, and turned workers into capitalists when she sold off nationalized firms, inviting the public to invest and purchase stock in them. She thrashed the unions so thoroughly, restricting their ability to organize and to strike, that they never recovered. Union membership dropped from 55 percent of the workforce in 1979 when Thatcher took office to less than half that, just 26 percent, in 2011. She also oversaw a large rise in regional inequality. Industrial regions in the north were hollowed out while a service sector boom attracted money to the south, around London. Last, income inequality increased alongside regional inequality. Thatcher cut tax rates for the rich and made it more difficult for the needy to access welfare state benefits by tightening eligibility standards.

The Thatcher years had such a powerful influence that when Labour returned to power in 1997, it did so as a chastened party. Prime Minister Tony Blair agreed with Thatcher's premise that Labour's stale program of deficit spending, a large public sector, and income redistribution would no longer work. In its place, Blair proposed a New Labour agenda that he marketed as a third way between the inefficiency of Labour's previous reliance on the public sector and the callousness of Thatcher's reliance on markets. Blair followed Thatcher's lead in macroeconomic policy. He believed that governments need to create favorable conditions for business to compete globally by lowering the tax burden, removing regulations, reducing the public debt, and keeping inflation and interest rates low—all very Conservative virtues. He also made no effort to restore union prerogatives but was an advocate of Thatcher's goal of increasing labor flexibility. However, contrary to Thatcherism, Blair oversaw increases in welfare state spending, especially on education and health care. Between 1995 and 2007, Labour governments also made tax and benefit changes that increased the real disposable income for the poorest of the poor by 20 percent.[56] Blair argued that the state should do more to prepare people to work and to respond to their plight when they were out of work. This is where New Labour's policies and Thatcher's faith in markets diverged: Blair believed that only the state could give people the resources they needed to be productive citizens, something markets would not and could not do on their own.

The economy performed admirably as Britain turned the corner on a new century in 2000. No longer the "sick man of Europe," Britain's average growth rate was not only higher than the G7[57] from 1994 to 2006 but less volatile. Unemployment fell throughout the period, and inflation stabilized at a comfortable 2 or 3 percent. Nevertheless, much of the prosperity was built on consumer debt, mostly for housing mortgages, which banks made available on cheap and easy credit terms. This debt, in turn, fed the growth of the finance sector of the economy (insurance companies, banks, and investment houses), which accounted for a larger share of the United Kingdom's total output and profits. The U.K. finance sector grew at 4.7 percent per year from 1987 to 2007, whereas the overall economy grew at just 2.6 percent, and although finance accounted for 1.5 percent of total profits in 1978, it now accounted for 15 percent of all profits in 2008.[58]

When the housing market burst in the United States in 2007, its contagious effects were magnified in Britain because of the size and global integration of its financial sector. After housing prices collapsed in Britain, people were left with debt they could not afford, and banks that were themselves overextended would not offer new credit lines. Demand collapsed and unemployment rose. The deep recession that began in 2008 imposed added costs on the government at the same time that it reduced revenues, creating the largest peacetime deficit—11 percent of GDP—in 2010.

When the Conservative–Liberal Democrats coalition took power in 2010, it inherited the unenviable task of actually tackling these problems. The new government proceeded to slash spending across the board, up to 25 percent in some instances—"the largest spending cuts ever seen in Britain outside of wartime emergency planning," according to British political scientist Colin Hay.[59] Prime Minister David Cameron hoped that such dramatic cuts, as well as increasing the value added tax and freezing most public sector employee salaries for two years, would signal markets that Britain was serious about getting its fiscal house in order and in attracting investors.

However, austerity has failed to entice suitors. Worse, the lack of demand in the absence of government stimulus seems to be driving them away. By the end of 2011, the British economy was still 4 percent smaller than it was four years ago, when the recession started. Despite budget cuts, the government's debt is bigger compared to the economy than when Cameron first took office. Whether the government will be rewarded for its austerity program will be measured at the polls in the next election scheduled for 2015.

Christian Democracy

9.6 Summarize the main features of the Christian democratic model.

Christian democracy is "the most successful western European political movement since 1945," according to the respected magazine *The Economist*.[60] The Christian democratic family of nations includes Austria, Belgium, the Netherlands, and Germany, where Christian democratic parties are often the largest though not dominant political party. However, these parties' influence is not due to their popularity as much as to their frequency in government. Their size and location in the middle of the political spectrum make them frequent partners in any ruling coalition.

Christian democratic parties first arose in the 19th century in reaction to state efforts to take over activities such as education and family policy, which churches believed properly belonged to them. Today, Christian democratic parties have only the most extenuating links to the church. They are now fairly secular parties and present themselves more as defenders of Christian values than of Church dogma.[61] They seek to moderate class cleavages at the same time they defend class differences, but they are most concerned with safeguarding the strength of the family and the moral authority of the Church from threats posed to them by divisive class conflict, an intrusive market, and an encroaching state.[62]

Christian democracy believes in capitalism but also wants to mute its inegalitarian effects. It supports the welfare state, which compensates for market failure, and favors unions because they promote social order through class reconciliation. Christian democratic countries tend to be high tax-and-spend states due to their welfare effort, which is almost as big as that found in social democratic states. But Christian democratic welfare states do not offer the array of collective services as social democrats do but, instead, provide generous **transfer payments** to provide income security to families. Although the state sector is large, its purpose is limited. Christian democracy is distrustful of too much state intervention that threatens to rule over the moral lives of their citizens and displace civic institutions through which Christian principles are instilled. State intervention should "repair society, not replace it."[63]

Transfer Payments
When the government distributes money to individuals as specified by law, such as issuing checks to those who qualify for unemployment insurance.

Institutionally, Christian democratic countries are all parliamentary democracies in which legislative majorities empower the executive, but there are still notable differences among them. All of them have bicameral legislatures, but only Germany invests its second chamber, the *Bundesrat*, with real power. Although the Netherlands has no judicial review, and Belgium and Austria only mild forms of it, the German Federal Constitutional Court can nullify laws it finds unconstitutional. Finally, Germany is a federal state in which powers are reserved to the *Länder*, or states, which elect their own officials and raise their own revenue. Belgium also has a high degree of federalism, followed closely by Austria and then the Netherlands.

Nevertheless, the most important institutional feature of Christian democratic countries, with the exception of Belgium, is the degree of corporatism found within them. Austria, for example, "is widely regarded as the 'paradigm' case of corporatism."[64] Groups are organized into a limited number of hierarchically structured associations, and these organizations are recognized by the state and invited to participate in the policy-making process affecting their interests. The state, for its part, plays an unobtrusive role, content to provide a broad legal framework in which social partners could find mutually agreeable settlements.

Germany

9.7 Describe the history, political culture, political economy, political institutions, and party system within Germany.

Historical Background

Germany has had a volatile history. In the space of 100 years, it has been beset by victory and defeat, scarcity and prosperity, and its state has taken a variety of forms, including fascism, Communist Party dictatorship, and parliamentary democracy. In addition, its borders have been in flux. They have expanded and contracted, been divided and united. It is the biggest country in Europe, with

82 million people, and it has the fourth largest economy in the world, one-third larger than its nearest European competitor.

Germany got a late start politically when the Prussian military leader Otto von Bismarck united small independent principalities in central Europe to form the modern German state in 1871. Germany also had to play catch-up economically. At the beginning of the 19th century, Germany was largely an agrarian feudal society that bore few marks of industrial capitalism. However, by the end of the century, Germany rivaled such leading economic powers as Britain, France, and the United States. Germany's rapid transformation has been attributed to Bismarck's strategy of imposing high tariffs to protect German producers, capturing colonies to open new markets and obtain raw materials, and creating welfare-state programs to co-opt workers and bind them to the state. Germany's economic ambitions clashed with those of more established European powers, leading to World War I. Defeat in the greatest mass slaughter the world had seen to that point brought an end to the Second Reich.

With defeat, the authoritarian Second Reich was replaced by Germany's first democracy, the Weimar Republic, named after the city in which Germany's new constitution was drafted. But the fledgling Republic lacked legitimacy in the eyes of many Germans. Right-wing parties blamed defeat in the war on democrats who had allegedly stabbed Germany in the back; left-wing Communists attacked Weimar as a devious attempt to restore German capitalism on a new democratic basis. In addition, onerous war reparations, hyperinflation, and growing unemployment further eroded Weimar's legitimacy. The Nazi Party, led by Adolf Hitler, emerged during this time of crisis, and as its electoral fortunes rose, President Hindenburg appointed Hitler as chancellor in 1933. When the *Reichstag*, the home of the German legislature, was destroyed by fire under suspicious circumstances, Hitler was given broad powers by emergency decree that he used to suspend civil liberties, ban political parties, and eliminate political opponents.

World War II began when German armies invaded Poland in 1939. Initially, the German army experienced rapid and stunning success, occupying much of Europe. But by May 1945, with Soviet troops advancing from the east and American, British, and Canadian troops from the west, German hopes of creating the Thousand Year Reich lay in rubble and defeat. With its surrender, Germany was occupied, and the Allies—Britain, France, the Soviet Union, and the United States—partitioned it into four zones. As the Cold War heated up, the four zones were reduced to just two. The area occupied by the Soviet Union became the German Democratic Republic (GDR) or what was known colloquially as East Germany, and the three zones occupied by France, Britain, and the United States became the Federal Republic of Germany (FRG), or what was commonly called West Germany. The front lines of the Cold War, the line separating capitalism from communism, now ran right through Germany, dividing it between West and East, respectively.

Map 9.3 Germany

Country	Population	Infant Mortality	Life Expectancy	Adult Literacy	Capital City	GDP Per Capita (PPP)	Labor Force by Occupation
Germany	81,900,000 (2013)	3.30 deaths under 1 year old per 1,000 live births (2013)	80.5 (2013)	99% (2013)	Berlin	$39,200 (2013)	Agriculture: 0.8 Industry: 30.1 Services: 69.0 (2013)

The State

In 1987, political scientist Peter Katzenstein described Germany as a "semisovereign state" in which authority is so divided and shared among institutions that the national government actually finds it hard to govern.[65] Katzenstein attributes the semisovereign character of the state to, first, its federal character, in which authority is divided between the central government and 16 federal states, or *Länder*. The *Länder* not only raise their own taxes and elect their own governments but select members to the *Bundesrat*, the upper house of the national legislature, which has veto power over bills that affect their jurisdictions. The constitutional powers granted the *Lander* and their responsibility for policy areas such as education and security make Germany the most decentralized state in Europe.

The authority of the national government is not only constrained from below in the form of sharing power with the *Länder* but is also squeezed from above in the form of the **European Union** (EU). The government has ceded power to the European Union in some policy arenas, such as trade, environmental policy, and border controls. In addition, monetary policy is now performed by the **European Central Bank**, fiscal policy is constrained by EU agreements, and laws are subject to judicial review by the European Court of Justice.

European Union
An economic and political union of 28 European countries committed to regional integration of the region.

European Central Bank
The central bank for those countries that are members of the European Union and use the euro as their currency.

Third, the semisovereign nature of political power in Germany is also reflected in the power of judicial review granted the Federal Constitutional Court. The Constitutional Court is similar to the U.S. Supreme Court in that it has the power to nullify laws passed by the government that it regards as contrary to the Basic Law, Germany's constitution. The Court has not been shy about using its powers of judicial review, requiring German governments to make policy in its shadow as they try to anticipate and take its reactions into account.

Fourth, policy making by the central government is constrained by powerful and encompassing interest groups that cannot be ignored. This is particularly true of labor and employer organizations that expect to be consulted on policy if the government wants their cooperation on its implementation.

Finally, the power of the government is stymied by bicameralism. As we already mentioned, the upper chamber, the *Bundesrat*, represents the interests of the *Länder*. Each *Land* is given votes in the *Bundesrat* based on its size, with larger states awarded more votes than smaller ones. Deputies to the *Bundesrat* are appointed by their state legislature and vote as a block on instruction from their government. Thus, if one party has a majority in state governments but another holds a majority in the national government, the former can appoint deputies to the *Bundesrat* who can block bills favored by the latter. **Divided government**, in which different parties enjoy a majority in the two legislative houses, is becoming more prevalent, limiting the decision-making capacity of the government.

Divided Government
When different parties enjoy a majority in different parts of the state's elected institutions, such as its executive and legislative branches.

The *Bundestag*, the lower house of the legislature, selects the government. Elections to the *Bundestag* are held every four years, although early elections can also be called, as happened in 1983, following the no-confidence vote that elevated Helmut Kohl to Chancellor. Citizens cast two ballots in electing deputies to the *Bundestag*. On the left-hand side of the ballot, candidates are listed by name with their party affiliation. Voters select the candidate they want to represent their election district. On the right-hand side of the ballot is a list of the major parties within each state. Here, voters select which party they prefer. These rules permit voters to select the candidate they want to represent them and to apportion seats among the parties in the *Bundestag* according to proportional representation. Each party keeps the seats its candidates won in the first vote, and then each party is awarded additional seats so that the percentage of seats it holds is equivalent to the support it received on the second, party list, vote. To prevent small, extremist parties from gaining seats through proportional representation, Germany requires parties to win at least 5 percent of the vote before they are awarded representation.[66]

As in other parliamentary democracies, the *Bundestag* elects and controls the government. Parties loom large within the lower chamber where the *Fraktion*, parliamentary party caucuses, organize its work. Leaders of each *Fraktion* hand out committee assignments and even office space to individual deputies who offer their loyalty in return if they want to develop their political careers. Committees within the legislature have become more scrupulous in considering bills. They cannot pigeonhole bills but are now more emboldened to offer suggestions and amendments to them. Still, four out of five bills submitted by the government emerge from committees with favorable reports.

The head of state is the president, who performs ceremonial functions and selects a party leader to form a government. Although the president is supposed to represent Germany with dignity, two recent appointees have had to resign in disgrace, damaging the office that is expected to provide a moral compass for the nation. The head of government is the chancellor, who commands majority support in the *Bundestag*. Although chancellors are the most powerful position in the German political system, they are less powerful than chief executives in other countries. Their powers are limited by coalition treaties they negotiate with their partners in government and by ministers they appoint who are pretty independent in managing their departmental responsibilities.[67] Chancellors can usually count on the support of parliamentary majorities throughout their term in office. Party discipline within parties is tight and coalition governments are stable because they have been composed by just two parties.

The semisovereign state has been a great success in terms of building a "political and party system that would prove more stable than the Weimar Republic had been, while avoiding the centralization and lawlessness of the Nazi dictatorship."[68] The constraints on the exercise of power by the national government that we just described have fostered consensual decision making and incremental change. Mild reform of current policies is all that can be achieved when so many players have to be accommodated., This may be an asset when

Germany confronts problems that require just mild adjustment. But the consensual nature of the semi-sovereign state becomes a liability when Germany needs to make dramatic policy changes in response to serious problems.

State and Society

Like the rest of Eastern Europe during the Cold War, East Germany was a one-party state under the control of the Communist Party. It was a "people's democracy" under which the people experienced very little democracy. The state provided substandard living conditions and, in return, workers produced substandard goods. People pretended to work, and the state pretended to pay them. Social life was dreary and spiritless, and the political system was rigid and coercive.

While East Germany strained under the inefficiencies of the planned economy and Communist Party domination, West Germany thrived under capitalist democracy. The first election put a coalition consisting of the Christian Democratic Union (CDU), its sister party in the south the Christian Social Union (CSU); and the centrist party, the Free Democrats (FDP), into power, which it maintained until 1966. Germany prospered under Chancellor Konrad Adenauer of the CDU and its pro-West, pro-welfare, and pro-market orientation. Between 1950 and 1961, the economy grew at a rapid average rate of 8.3 percent. The social democrats (SPD) were reduced to perpetual opposition. To expand their appeal, they became more reformist, now advocating "as much competition as possible, as much planning as necessary" and adopting a more pro-Western foreign policy in the hope of attracting middle-class voters.

Reinvention brought revival. The SPD became a junior partner in government when it participated in the Grand Coalition with the CDU in 1966 and then took power for the first time in 1969 in coalition with the Free Democrats. Under the SPD leadership of Chancellors Willy Brandt (1969–1974) and Helmut Schmidt (1974–1982), the FRG established diplomatic ties with its Eastern bloc neighbors. However, the two-and-a-half party system, composed of the CDU, FDP, and SDP that had dominated German politics to that point, was showing signs of erosion. Party membership, party identification, turnout, and support for all three governing parties declined. New groups articulating new issues, such as highly educated young people concerned about ecology, emerged to form the Green Party, which finally broke through to be represented in the legislature in 1983.

In 1982, the SPD lost a vote of confidence in the legislature when FDP deputies switched sides and gave their support to the CDU. The new parliamentary majority selected CDU leader Helmut Kohl as Chancellor, who then called for early elections and was confirmed by the voters the following year. Chancellor Kohl ruled Germany from 1982 to 1998, the longest tenure of any elected European leader in the postwar period. German unification occurred in 1990 under his chancellorship as the former East Germany was incorporated into

Dealignment
When voters' identification with political parties weakens and their preferences become more fleeting and volatile.

the FRG as five new federal states. Unification accelerated **dealignment** of the party system as new parties representing new groups identified with new issues emerged. The Greens became a permanent fixture in the legislature, and the Left Party, composed of disgruntled SPD voters in the west and disenchanted former Communists in the east, also found its way into the *Bundestag*. Dealignment was not only evident in the emergence of new parties at the expense of support for the CDU-CSU and the SPD, but in declining "trust" for the parties that surveys revealed, and in declining party memberships.

In 1998, the CDU–FDP ruling government that Kohl led was finally defeated by a coalition of the SDP and the Greens. The SPD–Green coalition headed by Chancellor Gerhard Schroeder (1998–2005) did not substantially depart from policies followed by Kohl except that it charted a more independent course in foreign policy because Schroeder was critical of the U.S. war in Iraq. The September 2005 election results between the CDU and SPD were so close that pundits declared nobody won. Angela Merkel of the CDU emerged as Chancellor, but not before she had to make many policy concessions and appoint many Social Democrats to Cabinet posts in her government. The inconclusiveness of the 2005 elections was resolved in the 2009 elections when the CDU outpolled the SPD and allied with the FDP to form a government. The SPD polled only 23 percent of the vote in 2009, its worst showing since 1893.

Dealignment disrupted the crusty and incestuous two-and-a-half party system in which the CDU on the right and the SDP on the left competed for the affections of the FDP in the center. (See Table 9.3 below for recent German election results.) In fact, in the 2013 elections, the FDP failed to clear the 5 percent barrier and was voted out of the *Bundestag* for the first time in Germany's postwar history. The 2013 election was, paradoxically, a resounding victory for the largest party on the right, the CDU–CSU but not for the right wing as a whole. The CDU–CSU, led by Chancellor Angela Merkel, won 311 seats, just five short of a majority in the *Bundestag*, but the failure of the FDP—or any other non-leftist party to win seats—meant that even as the CDU–CSU won 72 more seats than it did in 2009, the right bloc in the legislature actually declined. The 2013 elections seated four parties in the legislature, three of them parties of the left: the SPD, the Greens, and the Left. The CDU–CSU achieved a remarkable triumph in the 2013 elections. It won 42 percent of the vote, a level of support it had not received since 1990, when Germans rewarded it at the polls for reunification. However, the CDU–CSU success came at the expense of its allies, not its opponents on the left, whose bloc of votes and seats remained pretty steady. Consequently, even though the CDU–CSU did much better than any other party in 2013, it still fell short of a majority and had to form a coalition government with the Social Democrats.

Political Culture

Defeat in war and the crimes of the Holocaust required Germans to "create a new life, not just materially, but also intellectually and spiritually."[69] A new

Table 9.3 Germany Votes

	2002 % of Vote	2002 % Seats	2005 % of Vote	2005 % Seats	2009 % of Vote	2009 % Seats	2013 % of Vote	2013 % Seats
SDP	38.5	41.6	34.2	36.2	23.0	23.5	25.7	30.7
CDU/CSU	38.5	41.1	35.2	36.8	33.8	38.4	41.5	49.6
GREENS	8.6	9.1	8.1	8.3	10.7	10.9	8.4	9.5
FPP	7.4	7.8	9.8	9.9	14.6	15.0	4.8	0
PDS	4.0	0.3	–	–	–	–	–	–
LEFT	–	–	8.7	8.8	11.9	12.2	8.6	10.0
OTHERS	3.0	–	3.0	–	6.0	–	11.8	–
TURNOUT	79.1%		77.7%		70.8%		71.5%	

SOURCE: www.electionresources.org/de/bundestag.php?election=2002;2005;2009;2013.

German political culture that repudiated a past glorifying militarism, nationalism, and anti-Semitism would have to be constructed. This occurred as much through contrition—Germans deciding to repudiate their shameful past—as it did through imposition, the Allied occupying forces preventing any effort to revive the ideological foundations of Nazism. Germans were anxious to absorb the lessons of defeat as a way of moving beyond the crimes of the Nazis, but the occupying powers were also intent on making sure that those were the only lessons that would be available. For example, Allied efforts to outlaw militarism dovetailed with the sense Germans now had that all war was futile, and Allied efforts to ban Nazis and other antidemocratic elements fit well with German feelings of guilt over Nazi war crimes.

The new postwar political culture articulated a different set of values from the previous one. First, German culture was demilitarized. Defeat had tarnished the luster of war, and the barbarism with which the Nazis waged it had stained the reputation of the military. The demilitarization of German society succeeded so well that subsequent attempts at rearmament were opposed by the public, "even to the extent of deploying German troops under the multilateral leadership of the U.N. or NATO." A new "culture of anti-militarism," in which peace "is an absolute, incontestable, and always valued good," has replaced the old culture in which the military was respected and war was glorified.[70]

Similarly, German nationalism was delegitimized as thoroughly as German militarism. German nationalism was suspect because of how the Nazis had used it to justify racism and deceive Germans to follow them. The Fatherland was no longer a source of pride but of shame. In response, Germans became postnationalist and willing to endorse European unity. They became enthusiastic supporters of the European Union as an alternative to a national identity that was burdened by a disreputable past.

Finally, the reorientation extended to the new respect given to democracy. The Basic Law, or German Constitution, guaranteed civil and political rights, political parties rotated in office, and government responded to grievances and processed demands successfully. At the beginning, after World War II, Germans were ambivalent about democracy. They did not identify with the Basic Law, which was essentially drawn up by the Allied occupying powers, and they simply wanted to get on with their private lives and put politics, which had brought so much shame and grief, behind them. Today, in contrast, there is a substantial consensus in favor of parliamentary democracy. The success of democratic values could be attributed to the comparison between the negative example of East Germany's dictatorship and the attractive model the West provided in which democracy and economic success went together. Germans came to believe in democracy because it proved itself in practice.

The greatest challenge to the reorientation of German political culture took the form of unification and immigration. East Germans learned different lessons of defeat under the rule of the Communist Party in the German Democratic Republic than West Germans absorbed who lived in the Federal Republic of Germany. The cultural walls separating East and West Germans were harder to bring down than the physical ones that separated them. Immigration posed similar dilemmas when workers from Turkey and other foreign countries came to Germany to relieve labor shortages. They were followed by their dependents and then by asylum seekers from foreign countries who were allowed to settle in Germany as victims of political persecution. By 2011, about 9 percent of the people living in Germany were foreign residents. Their different values, religions, and cultural practices tested the tolerance of native Germans who sometimes responded with racist attacks and xenophobic outbursts. As in other European countries, immigrant subcultures have developed in which a toxic mix of discrimination and a reluctance to assimilate have led to higher crime and unemployment rates and lower mobility and education levels among immigrants than native Germans. The new German political culture will be tested by how it responds to the cultural challenge that unification and immigration pose to it.

Political Economy

German revival following World War II was nothing short of extraordinary. Germany enjoyed steady and fast economic growth, high wages, low inflation, and generous welfare benefits. It became renowned as a producer of high-quality manufactured goods that competed in world markets. For example, the 2012–2013 Global Competitiveness Index ranked Germany the 6th most competitive economy in the world.[71] It is the world's largest exporter, after China and the United States, which flatters Germany because the two countries ahead of it are much larger and bigger.

The postwar German model of the **social market economy** called for "as little state intervention as possible" and "as much state intervention as necessary."[72] The state's role was not to intervene in competitive markets but to promote cooperation among its different actors. It would provide broad guidelines

Social Market Economy
An economic model that combined capitalism with a good deal of government regulation and welfare state spending.

and empower private groups, such as employers and unions, to administer programs as opposed to performing those tasks itself or giving them detailed instructions on how to do so. In addition, the state would ensure that people's needs were met by creating a generous welfare state and that their demands were heard by requiring the formation of works councils within firms.

The German model—Modell Deutschland—of the social market economy delivered high-quality products, high wages, high fringe benefits, high levels of worker representation, and high levels of time off work.[73] The model rested on the consensus and coordination of well-organized and powerful private actors, including employer associations, unions, and banks, that the state helped bring together. Banks provided patient capital that permitted managers to think about the long-term welfare of their businesses. Employer associations underwrote vocational training, increasing the skills and productivity of the workforce, which no single firm would have done on its own. Unions bargained on behalf of the workforce, moderating wage claims and resolving disputes with employers.

Nevertheless, growth rates began to decline from 2.3 percent in the 1980s to 1.3 percent in the 1990s. As growth rates waned, so did the economy's ability to create new jobs. The German labor market was increasingly divided between insiders who had good jobs that paid good wages and benefits and outsiders composed of the long-term unemployed for whom there were no job prospects because the economy was not robust enough to create them. Rising social expenses for pensions, health care, and unemployment insurance, as well as the costs associated with the unification of East Germany—about 1 billion euros ($1.34 billion) invested in East Germany per year—created budget deficits so large that Germany was in violation of the European Monetary Union's deficit (3 percent of GDP) and debt rule (60 percent of GDP).

What were previously perceived as the advantages of the German model—consensus, patience, coordination, and incremental change—were now regarded as the source of its poor performance. As the economy's performance declined, the model began to show signs of erosion. Banks became less patient in seeking a return on their domestic investments, and industry became less willing to pay high payroll taxes that funded the welfare state. Both unions and employer associations became less encompassing as union membership declined and firms defected. Union density fell from about one-third of the workforce in 1990 to less than 20 percent by 2010. Employer associations also lost members as more firms chose to go it alone. The destabilization of unions and employer associations undermined their ability to negotiate industry-wide collective bargaining agreements. Whereas almost three-quarters of all workers were covered by industrywide collective bargaining agreements in 1995, only 59 percent of all employees were covered ten years later.[74] Both employers and works councils that represent workers within firms have sought more labor flexibility by ignoring industrywide agreements and adjusting wages to suit local conditions.

Government policy also shifted course. The Social Democrats reduced tax rates, increased co-payments, tightened eligibility rules, and cut welfare benefits to revive growth. In addition, German wages stagnated. From 1990 to 2010, median per capita income has risen only 7.5 percent. In other words, part of Germany's economic success has come at the expense of German workers' living standards. Increasing economic growth has not been reflected in rising wages.[75]

The previous round of reforms and wage restraint positioned Germany well when the 2008 recession hit. It did not face budget deficits to the same extent as other countries in Europe, which meant that it had more room to implement expansionary policies in response to the slowdown. This permitted the government to engage in higher levels of deficit spending to stimulate the economy than many other countries could afford. Germany also kept unemployment low by subsidizing firms' wage costs. In return for firms retaining workers, keeping them working on short time, the government would make up the difference of workers' full-time paycheck. As a result, workers retained their skills and were ready to work when trade and orders resumed. Consequently, Germany came out of the recession in far better shape than many of its fellow EU member-states. Germany now accounts for almost one-third of the output of the entire Eurozone, which includes 17 European Union member states that use the Euro as their currency. While Germany's low unemployment rate is the envy of its neighbors, most of the positions created in Germany since the recession have been in new entry level, lower wage jobs for part-time and contingent workers who lack many of the protections and benefits that more traditional workers receive. Germany's prowess as an exporter of sophisticated manufactured goods has depended to some extent on importing some of the worst aspects of flexible labor markets found in extreme market democracies: the use of low wage workers who lack legal and union protection.

Germany has struck a new bargain, for better or worse, that has paid dividends. It enjoys lower unemployment and higher growth than almost any other EU country, and can afford to contribute billions of euros to bail out EU countries needing financial assistance. However, the price of receiving German economic assistance has been austerity, requiring governments to reduce spending and raise taxes to balance their budgets. The effect of such policies on receiving countries, such as Greece and Ireland, has been to aggravate their debt and unemployment problems, not relieve them. The Germans take a hard line because they don't want their money used to reward what they regard as irresponsible policies and profligate governments—even if the policies they impose make the problem worse. Harsh German conditions have reopened old fears and wounds about German power that go back to World War II.

Economic success has also had domestic costs. Wage stagnation has increased inequality. In addition, most of the new positions created in Germany since the recession have been in new entry level, lower wage jobs for part-time and contingent workers that lack many of the protections and benefits that more traditional workers receive.

The passage of time and Germany's economic success have permitted it to shed its reputation as an economic giant and a political dwarf in the realm of foreign policy. Previously, Germany was reluctant to assert itself in world affairs in fear of the suspicions this would provoke given its past. It was an advocate of European integration to show that it wanted to be a good neighbor, and it was a dependable ally of the United States in return for the protection it provided during the Cold War. However, a new generation of leaders has emerged who have no direct memory of the Nazi era and feel less constrained by it. In addition, the end of the Cold War freed Germany from its dependence on the military protection of the United States. As a result, it has begun to pull its weight. Germany is the largest member of the European Union and feels it is entitled to influence within it that matches its size. In addition, it no longer feels that it has to defer to the United States and was clear in opposing the U.S.-led war in Iraq. At the same time, Germany is still reluctant to seize the initiative. It abstained from the 2011 U.N. vote endorsing military intervention to remove Qaddafi when Libyan rebels were trying to overthrow his brutal disctatorship. It initially responded meekly when Russian president Vladimir Putin invaded the Crimea in 2014.

Germany is too big to avoid responsibilities and too held down by the past to face them. Foreign policy is a delicate balancing act requiring Germany to disarm the suspicion neighbors have of it based on the past; at the same time, it confronts new expectations that Germany will use its size and power to solve regional problems.

Comparing Capabilities Among Sweden, the United Kingdom, and Germany

9.8   Compare capabilities in Sweden, the United Kingdom, and Germany.

We profiled Sweden, the United Kingdom, and Germany because they each typify different political models found among affluent democracies. Sweden represents the social democratic model, the United Kingdom is an archetype of extreme market democracies, and Germany typifies the Christian democratic model. A comparison of how these countries perform in terms of our criteria for the good society is important because it provides clues about which of these models best meets the standards of the good society. However, comparing capabilities among developed countries is more difficult than comparing capabilities between developed and less-developed countries. The gap between developed and developing countries is often glaring. That is not the case with Sweden, the United Kingdom, and Germany. They are all democracies, literacy rates are high, and infant mortality rates are low. To compare capabilities meaningfully among our three countries that represent different models, we need more subtle and discerning measures than those commonly used to compare developed and less-developed societies.

Physical Well-Being

We have used infant mortality rates to assess physical well-being in previous chapters. Since we are not worried about finding a measure that applies to such a large number of countries here, we can use poverty rates that provide a better, more discriminating, more accurate measure. Poverty rates measure the percentage of households who fall below some income threshold. For example, the poverty line for a family of four in 2014 in the United States was $23,850. We will take the income threshold the United States uses to define who is poor, estimate what the poverty rate would be in Sweden, the United Kingdom, and Germany if they adopted the same threshold and then equalize purchasing power among them. The figures are given in Table 9.4.[76]

Sweden and Germany, representing the social democratic and Christian democratic models, respectively, performed similarly, and each performed better than the United Kingdom, which typified extreme market democracies when it came to meeting the physical needs of its citizens. Differences between the two top performers and the United Kingdom are actually greater than they appear at first. Poverty rates only measure income and do not include public services or welfare benefits available to the poor. Since these are greater in social democratic and Christian democratic models, Sweden and Germany perform even better than appears in comparison to the United Kingdom when one looks only at income.

Table 9.4 Poverty Rates

Poverty Rates	
Sweden	7.5
U.K.	12.4
Germany	7.6

Informed Decision Making

We require a more demanding measure of this standard than literacy rates since 99 percent of all citizens in Sweden, the United Kingdom, and Germany are literate. Consequently, we will use the more discerning International Adult Literacy Survey (IALS), which examines the ability of citizens "to understand and employ printed information in daily activities, at home, at work and in the community—to achieve one's goals, and to develop one's knowledge and potential."[77]

The IALS assessed literacy skills, and then citizens were graded according to five levels, with level one including people who were functionally illiterate and levels four and five including respondents who were very proficient at processing information. Table 9.5 gives the proportion of citizens in Sweden, the United Kingdom, and Germany whose average scores placed them into either level one or two, the lowest-performing groups.[78]

Table 9.5 Literacy Skills[79]

Literacy Proficiency among 16–65-year-olds	
Sweden	42%
U.K.	50%
Germany	52%

According to these results, Sweden does a better job than either the United Kingdom or Germany of providing adults with the skills they need to realize their potentials.

Safety

Unlike some developing societies, where political violence and civil war pose real threats to safety for their citizens, Sweden, the United Kingdom, and Germany do not suffer from such turbulence. Citizens in our sample of countries have little to fear from political persecution or civil strife on a massive scale. Physical safety remains an issue nonetheless, due to the prevalence of violent crimes, such as homicides, sex offenses, and serious assaults. We will again use homicide rates, which are the most reliable statistic, to assess performance on this criterion. Homicide rates for Sweden, the United Kingdom, and Germany are given in Table 9.6.

From one perspective, differences among our countries are not great. All have pretty low homicide rates, and only a meager two tenths of a percent sets them apart as one goes from the best to worst performer. However, from another perspective, Germany's homicide rate is one-third less than that of Britain's, with Sweden's located midpoint between the two of them. From this angle, Christian democracies performed best, social democracies took the middle position, and extreme market democracies brought up the rear.

Table 9.6 Safety[80]

Homicide Rates per 100,000	
Sweden	1.0
U.K.	1.2
Germany	0.8

Democracy

Aside from meeting the basic physical needs of citizens, helping them gain the ability to make informed decisions about their lives, and protecting them from harm, the good society, we argued, also guarantees political and civil rights. These are available in all our countries—all of them were rated 10, the highest possible score as democracies in the Polity IV data set that measures democracy. We need more-nuanced measures that compare the quality of these rights within them, not whether they exist. We propose to do so by measuring the quality of their democratic practice as Table 9.7 shows.

According to this measure, the quality of democracy is better in Sweden than in Germany or in the United Kingdom, and between those two countries, it is better in the former than in the latter. Social democracy, represented by Sweden, outperformed Christian and extreme market democracies, and in the loser's bracket, Christian democracy performed better than extreme market democracy.

In conclusion, some political models among rich western democracies are better able to create conditions that enhance the capabilities of their citizens more than others. Specifically, social democracy, in the form of Sweden, generally performed

Table 9.7 Quality of Democracy[81]

Democracy Scores	
Sweden	9.73
U.K.	8.21
Germany	8.34

better in meeting the standards of the good society than either Christian or extreme market democracies, represented by Germany and the United Kingdom, respectively. The quality of democracy was higher in Sweden, and its citizens were more likely to possess the skills they need to make informed decisions about their lives. Sweden and Germany performed similarly when it came to meeting the physical needs of their citizens, and both performed much better than the United Kingdom. Finally, Germany performed better than Sweden, which, in turn, did better than Britain when it came to safety, although the differences in homicide rates among the countries were not great.

Conclusion

This chapter described three types of political models, or families of nations, found among affluent democracies: social democratic, extreme market, and Christian democratic. They differ in their politics, institutions, values, and policies. We then provided case studies, using countries that serve as paradigmatic models of each model: Sweden as representative of social democracy; the United Kingdom as emblematic of extreme market democracies; and Germany as an example of Christian democracy. Finally, we examined which of these countries—and thereby the models they represent—came closest to meeting the criteria of the good society: promoting their citizens' capabilities. According to our tests, Sweden, representing social democracy, generally performed better, followed by Germany, and then the extreme market model represented by the United Kingdom.

Suggested Readings

Gosta Esping-Andersen, *Social Foundations of Postindustrial Economies* (New York: Oxford University Press: 1999). A good elaboration and extension of the regime-centered approach to Western democracies.

Eric S. Einhorn and John Logue, *Modern Welfare States: Scandinavian Politics and Policy in the Global Age*, 2nd ed. (Westport, CT: Praeger, 2003). Offers comprehensive coverage of Scandinavian politics.

Pol O'Dochartaigh, *Germany since 1945* (New York: Palgrave, 2004). A short text covering German politics.

Jonas Pontusson, *Inequality and Prosperity: Social Europe vs. Liberal America* (Ithaca: Cornell University Press, 2005). Offers interesting comparisons among Western democracies.

Critical Thinking Questions

1. How would you operationalize the four criteria we use to assess regime performance? Using your measures, which countries enhance the capabilities of their citizens most and come closest to the standard of the good society?

2. Do you think the different regimes among Western democracies are converging, becoming more alike, in any of the areas we investigated—politics, political institutions, political culture, and political economy—or have their differences in all of these arenas remained profound?

3. What do you believe is the greatest challenge social democratic, liberal democratic, and Christian democratic regimes face today? In what respect are their challenges similar to one another or specific to each model?

4. What do you see as the strengths and weaknesses of each political model?

Chapter 10
Less-Developed Countries and the Good Society

Learning Objectives

10.1 Explain why there are more regime types in less developed countries than in Western Europe and North America.

10.2 Summarize the main features of flawed democracy.

10.3 Describe the history, state, relations between state and society, political culture, and political economy of Brazil.

10.4 Summarize the main features of semi-democracy.

10.5 Describe the history, state, relations between state and society, political culture, and political economy of Nigeria.

10.6 Summarize the main features of electoral authoritarianism.

10.7 Describe the history, state, relations between state and society, political culture, and political economy of Iran.

10.8 Compare capabilities in Brazil, Nigeria, and Iran.

Introduction

10.1 Explain why there are more regime types in less developed countries than in Western Europe and North America.

Many less-developed countries do not have democratic governments, and most of those that do have a kind of democracy that is very different from that found in Western Europe and North America. India, for example, is the world's most populous democracy, but its elections are frequently marred by violence. Vote-buying is common, and voters are often intimidated by supporters of opposing parties. Candidates who have been charged with rape and murder run for office and win. In 2012, 162 of the 545 members of the lower house of India's national legislature won election despite being charged with crimes.[1] Civil servants, including public school teachers, are often corrupt. Many teachers do not bother to come to class, sell rice meant for children's lunches for personal profit, and fail to teach basic skills in reading and arithmetic.[2]

The countries of Western Europe and North America have several economic and societal features in common. They are all high per capita income, predominantly urbanized societies with postindustrial occupational structures. They also have high percentages of citizens with secular and self-expressive values. In contrast, less-developed countries in Africa, Asia, Central and South America, and the Middle East are extremely diverse. They vary dramatically in income level, degree of urbanization, and occupational structure. Many of them have much greater ethnic diversity than any Western European or North American country. They also include a wide variety of religions and cultures, and substantial percentages of the population may hold traditional and survival values.

It is not surprising that with all this economic, social, and cultural diversity, less-developed countries are also politically diverse. Some have authoritarian regimes governed by monarchs, military *junta*s, single parties, or personalist rulers. Others are governed by democratic regimes. A few of these democracies meet very high standards: Uruguay, Mauritius, and Costa Rica are examples, but most do not. Even when countries do have democratic governments, they tend to be more like democracy in India than democracy in Sweden.

This chapter examines three common types of regimes found in developing countries with different degrees of democracy: flawed democracies that share some of the same features as democracies in high-income countries but fall short on others; semi-democracies that exist in a gray area between democracy and authoritarianism; and regimes that use the trappings of democracy to maintain authoritarian control. The chapter summarizes the characteristics of each type and offers a case study of a country that typifies each type: Brazil exemplifying a flawed democracy, Nigeria exemplifying semi-democracy, and Iran exemplifying how authoritarian regimes use elections to help maintain control of the population.

We have chosen these particular countries for four reasons. First, they have large populations, so their governments' policies affect the capabilities of tens of millions of people. Brazil has the largest population in Latin America, Nigeria has the largest in Africa, and Iran has the second-largest population in the Middle East. Second, they represent different levels of economic development: Brazil and Iran are upper-middle-income countries whereas Nigeria is lower-middle income. Third, they are from different regions of the world. Finally, they are important to the United States and other high-income democracies. Nigeria supplies oil to the United States and is influential within its region. The rapid growth of a violent, anti-Western Muslim organization in northern Nigeria has created security concerns for the United States. Brazil is important commercially for the United States and Europe and may become a major oil exporter when recently discovered offshore oil fields come on line. Finally, Iran is located in a part of the world of strategic interest to the United States and is strongly suspected of working to develop nuclear weapons.

Flawed Democracy

10.2 **Summarize the main features of flawed democracy.**

Flawed Democracy
A democracy sharing some features of full democracy but marred by voter fraud, uneven enforcement of civil and political rights, patronage politics, and corruption.

The first prevalent type of democracy in developing countries is **flawed democracy**. Flawed democracies occupy an intermediate realm between full democracies and semi-democracies. On the one hand, they have universal suffrage for all citizens and hold regularly scheduled elections in which multiple political parties compete. Citizens have access to information from various media, including radio, television, print, and the Internet. Elections are conducted using secret ballots. On the other hand, elections are often marred by voter fraud. Flawed democracies have freer and fairer elections and better enforcement of political and civil rights than semi-democracies such as Nigeria, but elections are not as free and fair as those of full democracies. Nor is their enforcement of civil and political rights as effective. Citizens' rights are frequently violated by local strongmen in both urban slums and remote rural areas.

The quality of democracy depends on the kinds of political parties countries have as well as on whether elections are free and fair. Political parties in flawed democracies tend to rely heavily on patronage, or on appeals to racial and ethnic identity to win votes, rather than presenting policy alternatives that appeal to broad categories of voters.

Flawed democracies also have stronger states, with higher autonomy and capacity, than semi-democracies do. Although many officials have clientelist ties with individuals or groups in society, substantial numbers of officials are also recruited on the basis of merit and insulated from direct partisan political pressure. These officials serve the public with a sense of professionalism. States in flawed democracies also have greater capacity to implement their decisions throughout their territory than do those of semi-democracies. Finally, flawed democracies have stronger societal foundations than semi-democracies. They tend to be located in lower- and upper-middle-income countries having a strong private business sector, organized labor unions, and numerous civil society organizations.

It can be difficult, nevertheless, to make substantial improvements in capabilities for low-income citizens in flawed democracies. Many of them are wracked by large inequalities in wealth and political power. Wealth tends to be concentrated in the hands of bankers, high-level executives, and owners of large farms and businesses. Economic inequality is reinforced by inequalities based on ethnicity and race. When countries are extremely diverse, it can be difficult to establish broad-based interest associations and political parties. In the absence of broad-based movements that can successfully unite citizens with diverse identities for collective action, politicians tend to be more responsive to the interests of upper-income groups.[3] Even though lower-income citizens are more numerous than their upper-income counterparts, their ability to use their numbers effectively is diluted by clientelism and ethnic and religious divisions.

The *Economist* Democracy Index lists Brazil, Mexico, India, and Indonesia as examples of flawed democracies.[4] In the following section, we provide a case study of a flawed democracy in Brazil.

Brazil

10.3 Describe the history, state, relations between state and society, political culture, and political economy of Brazil.

"Brazil is the country of the future, and always will be." For decades, this cynical witticism reflected Brazil's failure to live up to its considerable potential. The world's fifth most populous country and fifth largest in area, it has the world's seventh largest economy. It has a strong manufacturing sector that exports steel, airplanes, and a wide range of industrial products. In addition, Brazil is a major exporter of iron ore and agricultural products. Between 2000 and 2010, the country seemed to be finally ready to deliver on its promise. It enjoyed strong economic growth during these years, and the discovery of large offshore oil fields in 2007 promised to make it a major oil exporter. It also received international recognition: Brazil was selected to host both the 2014 World Cup of soccer, and the 2016 Summer Olympics.

In several respects, however, Brazil remains "the country of the future." To begin with, income inequality is extreme, even though it has begun to decline. Violent crime is rampant, and homicide rates are among the highest in the world. Two weeks after Rio de Janeiro was awarded the 2016 Summer Olympics, drug traffickers shot down a police helicopter a mile from the stadium where the Olympic Games opening and closing ceremonies are planned to take place.[5] Its public education system is woeful, and citizens routinely complain about the low quality of health care and public transportation. Economic growth has slowed dramatically since 2010.

Historical Background

Brazil's path to its current status as a flawed democracy began with its colonization by Portugal in the 1500s. The population was divided between a small European elite that owned vast sugar plantations and a much larger number of slaves brought from Africa to work on them. Independence from Portugal in 1822 brought little change to the social structure; the same landowning elite continued to dominate Brazil's politics for several decades. By 1900, however, the sugar barons were eclipsed politically by cattle ranchers and coffee growers. This shift in power among landed elites was accompanied by a change in the locus of power from the northeast, where the sugar plantations were based, to the southeast, where ranching and coffee growing predominated. The change made little difference to most Brazilians, who remained poor, illiterate, and powerless.[6]

When Getulio Vargas became president in 1930, he built a new governing coalition based on industrialists, workers, the middle class, and the military rather than on landed elites. At the same time, he initiated policies to promote rapid economic development through **state-led industrialization** as opposed to relying on private entrepreneurs. Vargas's imperious style eventually produced growing discontent, and the military forced him out in 1945, but Vargas left a legacy of state-led industrialization that continues to influence Brazilian leaders.

The 1960s were marked by rapid industrialization but also by growing economic and political polarization between social classes. Peasants began to seize land from large landowners, and industrial workers initiated strikes against businesses. In 1964, President João Goulart sided with the peasants and workers and proposed major reforms that alarmed wealthy owners of plantations and companies. In 1964, the military once again overthrew the government, this time with the backing of agricultural and business elites and parts of the middle class.

The *junta*'s leaders promoted rapid economic development by using state-led industrialization. They offered businesses tariff protection, subsidies, and tax benefits; created hundreds of state-owned enterprises; repressed labor unions; and reduced social spending. Left-wing political parties were banned, and their leaders were either driven out of the country or arrested, imprisoned, and tortured.

State-Led Industrialization
Industrialization relying heavily on funding from state-owned banks and state-owned firms to develop industries selected by the state instead of relying mainly on privately owned banks and firms.

Less-Developed Countries and the Good Society 255

Map 10.1 Brazil

Country	Population	Infant Mortality	Life Expectancy	Adult Literacy	Capital City	GDP Per Capita (PPP)	Labor Force by Occupation
Brazil	202,657,000	13.9 deaths per 1,000 live births	73 years	90%	Brasilia	$12,700 (2013 est.)	Agriculture: 15.7% Industry: 13.3% Services: 71%

Military leaders assumed that a rising standard of living would generate legitimacy for their rule. Between 1968 and 1974, the economy grew at more than 10 percent a year, and admirers began to refer to a Brazilian miracle, but in the early 1980s, Brazil plunged "into a prolonged period of economic stagnation" known as "the lost decade."[7] As economic difficulties mounted, criticism of the *junta* grew, even among business people and middle-class Brazilians who had formerly supported it. Under pressure, the army finally allowed a return to civilian rule in 1985. In 1988, a new constitution went into effect, and a year later, there was an election for a president.

The State

The Brazilian state is relatively strong compared with those in other developing countries. It can exercise its authority throughout Brazil, collect taxes needed to fund government programs, and implement many policies effectively. Recent presidents have had notable successes, including ending chronic inflation and indebtedness and improving capabilities of lower-income citizens. Brazil also has one of the most effective anti-HIV/AIDS programs in the world. In other respects, however, the Brazilian state has not performed well. It has not equaled other countries at its income level in promoting literacy, improving health care, or controlling crime and violence.

Brazil has a presidential form of government. Presidents are directly elected by voters to four-year terms and are limited to two consecutive terms. In 2010, Dilma Rousseff was chosen as Brazil's first woman president, succeeding her mentor, Luiz Inácio Lula da Silva. Lula, as he is commonly known, was not only the most popular president in Brazilian history, but one of the most popular leaders in the world, ending his two terms in office in 2010 with an approval rating of 80 percent.[8] He anointed Rousseff, his chief of staff and former minister of energy and mines, as his successor and campaigned energetically on her behalf. Rousseff, who had never run for any elective office, owed her victory to Lula's support.[9] She won a second term in office in 2014.

Brazilian presidents have considerable constitutional power; they can initiate legislation, appoint numerous state officials, and issue temporary emergency measures that have the effect of law,[10] but these formal constitutional powers are weakened by a fragmented legislature that impairs their ability to pass legislation.

Members of Brazil's bicameral legislature are directly elected. The upper house is the 81-member Senate consisting of three senators from each state and the federal district. Senators hold eight-year terms. The lower house is the Chamber of Deputies, whose 513 members are elected for four-year terms. In the October, 2014, elections for the Chamber of Deputies, 28 political parties won seats. None of them came close to having a majority. This kind of fragmentation in the Chamber of Deputies is common, and it forces presidents to rely on support from a coalition of parties to pass legislation. Coalition members typically demand favors in return for their votes. These favors can include seats in the president's Cabinet, government spending for projects in their districts, and even direct cash payments. When President Rousseff took office, she made strong efforts to end this pattern of institutionalized corruption, but accomplished only limited progress. Legislators refused to support her legislative initiatives if she pushed too hard for reform.

State and Society

Social class long has been the most politically important cleavage in Brazilian politics, but in recent years, race has emerged as another significant source of division. We begin with social class and then turn to race.

Brazil is one of the world's most economically unequal societies. Social scientists measure income inequality in two ways. One is to compare the ratio of a country's total income that goes to the top 20 percent of income earners (top quintile) to the percentage that goes to the bottom 20 percent (bottom quintile). This is called the quintile ratio. The other is the **Gini Index**, which ranges from 0 to 100. A Gini Index value of 0 means that "everyone has the same income," whereas a value of 100 means that "one person has the entire income of a country."[11] In real life, no country reaches either extreme, but the closer a country's Gini Index is to 100, the greater is its income inequality. See Table 10.1.

Wealth—which includes ownership of homes, businesses, land, and stocks and bonds—is even more unequally distributed in Brazil than income. Two percent of landowners own approximately 50 percent of the country's farmland.[12] This highly unequal distribution of income and wealth results in considerable inequalities in health care, access to education, and safety.

For most of its history, Brazil has lacked the sorts of interest groups and political parties that could enable poor citizens to improve their well-being by taking advantage of their large numbers. In many other countries, trade unions are one of the main organizations that workers have used to advance their interests. In Brazil, however, workers are divided into those in the economy's formal

Gini Index
The Gini Index is used to measure the extent of income inequality in a country. A Gini Index value of 0 equals perfect equality of income in which everyone receives the same share of a country's income while a value of 100 equals perfect inequality.

Table 10.1 Brazil's Income Distribution in Comparative Perspective

Country (2000–2010)	Quintile income Ratio (2000–2010)	Gini Index
Haiti	26.6	59.2
Brazil	**20.6**	**54.7**
Costa Rica	14.5	50.7
Nigeria	12.2	48.8
United States	8.4	40.8
Germany	4.3	28.3
Sweden	4.0	25.0

SOURCE: United Nations Human Development Programme, *Human Development Report 2013*, pp. 152–153.

sector who work for state-owned firms and large private firms and a much larger number who work in the informal sector, such as day laborers at construction sites and garment workers in small firms. Workers in the formal sector are more likely to be unionized and to have some benefits, but unions do not represent workers in the informal sector.[13]

Brazil's fragmented political parties also have hampered efforts to reduce inequalities in access to health care and education. Fragmented parties make it much easier for upper- and middle-class citizens to maintain government programs that help them than for poorer citizens to make changes that would improve their lives. To keep their privileges, members of the upper and middle classes need only to maintain existing institutions and policies, whereas the poor need broad-based political parties that can take advantage of their larger numbers to change institutions and policies.[14] For decades, no large political party promised to represent them. Most political parties in Brazil are patronage machines whose leaders win office by doing favors for influential individuals and groups in their constituencies. These parties won votes from poor, uneducated Brazilians by paying them a small amount to vote for the party and promising paying jobs.[15] Although cash payments and jobs brought some benefits, they went only to those who voted for the party, and they failed to provide lasting improvements in people's lives. Better education and access to health care for all poor Brazilians was a much better alternative, but poor Brazilians needed a political party that would work on their behalf to achieve such goals.

Workers' Party
The dominant political party in Brazil since 2000 which has pursued programs aimed at improving the lives of poor Brazilians while seeking to reassure middle and upper class Brazilians it will not threaten government programs that benefit them.

The **Workers' Party** (Partido dos Trabalhadores) became that party. It emerged during the years of military rule and built a strong coalition of supporters at the municipal and state levels among union members, poor farmers, landless workers, community activists, and radical academics. Its leader, Luiz Inácio Lula da Silva, came from a very poor family and worked in a factory before becoming involved in politics.

In its early years, the Workers' Party called for greater state direction of the economy with an emphasis on lowering income inequality. It advocated the empowerment of workers and unions and radical land reform that would take land from owners of large plantations and give it to poor or landless farmers. To win the presidency, however, Lula had to win a broader constituency than workers and peasants. Toning down his anti-capitalist rhetoric, he reached out to middle-class voters and reassured domestic and foreign business interests that he would pursue pro-market policies. Lula acknowledged that he needed the support of capitalists to sustain economic growth, which was essential to create jobs and provide revenue for his programs. He promised to maintain a budget surplus, restrain state spending, and keep interest rates high enough to attract investors and control inflation.

Bolsa Familia (family grant) program
A social welfare program in Brazil giving cash payments to poor families in return for keeping their children in school and making sure that they receive medical care.

While reassuring the business community and foreign investors, Lula also made strong efforts to win support from poor Brazilians. Once in office, he implemented programs that would bring them quick benefits. One of the most successful was the *Bolsa Familia* **(family grant) program**, which gives cash payments to poor families in return for keeping their children in school and making sure that children have medical check-ups and vaccinations for diseases. The criteria for receiving the cash payments are clear, and the payments go to all who meet the criteria. No patron is needed to get payments, and all eligible receive payments, even if they vote against the Workers' Party.[16]

In addition to initiating a program that reduced infant mortality, improved children's health, and raised the incomes of poor families, Lula expanded spending on education and made it easier for low-income students to attend college. He also increased the minimum wage for workers.[17] The economic gap between poor and rich Brazilians narrowed between 2000 and 2010 because of these policies in combination with strong economic growth.

Brazil has also made some progress in improving the lives of Brazilians of African descent. Between the 16th and 19th centuries, many more African slaves were shipped to Brazil to work on Brazil's sugar plantations and in mines than were shipped to the United States. Brazil only abolished slavery in 1888, the last country in the Americas to do so. Today, Brazilians of African descent outnumber those of European descent.

Brazil's racial politics differ in significant ways from those of the United States. Unlike the United States, where historically there were sharp distinctions between black and white citizens, racial categories in Brazil have been "fluid and ambiguous."[18] That is, there are many intermediate categories between black and white. Brazil never banned interracial marriage, as several states in the United States did, and never had state-imposed racial segregation. In fact, Brazilian constitutions since the 1930s have upheld racial equality. The 1988 constitution actually defines racism as a crime.[19] Many Brazilians believe themselves to be citizens of a "racial democracy."

Nevertheless, despite constitutional guarantees of racial equality, Brazil remains "profoundly stratified by color."[20] Citizens of African descent are more likely than whites to live in poverty, have less schooling, and be illiterate.[21] These inequalities did not become a significant political issue until the 1990s. Before then, politicians saw no advantage in raising the issue of racial inequalities, and no large and well-organized Afro-Brazilian groups pressed the issue. Constitutional guarantees of equality, the fluidity of racial identity, and the absence of legalized segregation made it more difficult for Brazilians of African descent to organize around racial issues than it was for African-Americans in the United States.[22]

It was not until the administration of President Fernando Henrique Cardoso in 1995 that a Brazilian government directly addressed the problem of racial inequality. Since then, presidents Lula and Rousseff have supported efforts to improve the lives of Afro-Brazilians. One of the main initiatives has been the adoption of racial quotas in several dozen Brazilian universities. The percentage of Brazilians of African descent attending universities has increased as a result.[23]

These quotas have initiated an intense debate. Critics argue that quotas will result in polarizing Brazilians along black-and-white lines. They also argue that quotas undermine equality of opportunity based on merit. On the other side of the debate, supporters of quotas contend that Brazil is already divided into blacks and whites. In their view, racial democracy is a myth. They maintain, furthermore, that merit is not the main criterion for gaining admission to many universities, and that there is little equality of opportunity. Admission is granted disproportionately to white students who have wealthy parents and attended private high schools.

Some Brazilians suggest that a way around these polarized positions is to use social class rather than race as the criterion for university admission. Many Afro-Brazilian students come from poor families. Using social class as the basis for affirmative action would benefit both poor black and poor white students while avoiding the drawbacks of racial quotas.[24]

Political Culture

The United States and Brazil are the two largest democracies in the Americas, but they have very different political cultures. Some of the main themes of the United States' political culture have been distrust of state intervention in the economy, individualism, equality of opportunity, and equality before the law.

Brazil's political culture differs from that of the United States on each point. Most Brazilians accept the need for a strong state that plays an active role in the economy. Through most of the 20th century, the state played a leading role in promoting industrialization in Brazil, and Brazilians continue to be much more sympathetic toward a large state role in the economy than Americans are. In a 2006 survey, 43 percent of Brazilians expressed some degree of support for the idea that government ownership of business should be increased. In the same survey, only 14 percent of Americans expressed any support for that policy.[25]

This difference in views concerning the proper role of the state in the economy carries over to beliefs about the state's role in promoting citizens' welfare. In the United States, a major theme of political culture is that individuals should take responsibility for their lives. In Brazil, there is much greater approval for the idea that government should help provide for them. In the 2006 survey, only 9 percent of Americans believed government should take more responsibility to ensure that everyone is provided for, as compared to 27 percent of Brazilians.[26]

There is much more backing in the United States for equality of opportunity and equality before the law than in Brazil. Brazil's history of extreme income inequality among social classes contributed to a culture in which elites have not valued political equality. To the contrary, for most of Brazil's history, elites believed in a hierarchical society in which some people are inherently better and therefore deserved to rule. Well into the 20th century, the political elite in Brazil thought of themselves as a "political class" with "unique rights and privileges."[27]

Brazil's extreme income inequality has also made its citizens more class conscious than Americans are. The most successful Brazilian party in recent years has been the Workers' Party—a party whose name makes it clear that it is representing a social class. Moreover, in its early years, party leaders defined its goal as representing the interests of workers against capitalists. Even in its more moderate present-day form, the Workers' Party is not simply a Brazilian version of the Democratic Party of the United States.

Brazilians are also much less likely than Americans to believe that individuals' hard work brings success. Instead, they tend to believe that success is more a matter of luck and connections.[28] Finally, compared to citizens of the United States, Brazilians are much less trusting of others. In a recent survey, 39 percent of Americans believed that most people could be trusted, whereas only 9 percent of Brazilians did.[29] Few countries in the world have such low levels of social trust.

Brazilian political culture has changed significantly in recent decades. There is now more support for democracy and representative government, more emphasis on equal rights for all, and greater acceptance of markets. Economic growth, the development of a sizable middle class, and a decline in poverty have reduced the appeal of radical political ideas. New associations and political movements have emerged to press for improvements in the lives of the poor, women, Afro-Brazilians, and indigenous peoples. Yet the distinctive features that separate Brazilian political culture from the United States remain, albeit in a more muted form.

Political Economy

From the 1930s through the 1980s, Brazil pursued a strategy of state-led industrialization. State officials, and economists who advised them, believed that local capitalists could not catch up to their counterparts in developed industrial countries without state help. Brazilian leaders allocated credit to industry through state-owned development banks and used tax incentives, subsidies, and wage and price controls to promote industrialization. Tariffs on imported goods were used to protect the domestic market from foreign competition.[30]

Although state-led industrialization led to rapid growth, it had two major drawbacks. One was recurrent economic crises. Brazil's strategy for industrialization required oil imports and high levels of foreign borrowing. When oil prices increased dramatically in 1973 and 1979, Brazil paid for its imported oil by borrowing from abroad, which led to high levels of indebtedness and raging inflation that Brazil struggled to control in the early 1980s. Another shortcoming of state-led industrialization was a disregard for the welfare of the country's poor. Industrial development was not accompanied by significant reductions in poverty or economic inequality.

President Fernando Henrique Cardoso (1995–2003) implemented changes in economic policy that laid the base for improved economic performance in the first decade of the 21st century. Cardoso sold off a number of state-owned enterprises to private investors to increase efficiency and productivity and introduced policies to keep inflation under control.

The decade from 2000 to 2010 was exhilarating for Brazilians. After suffering through prolonged periods of inflation and unemployment, Brazil seemed to have entered a phase of sustained growth. Lula maintained many of Cardoso's policies, and the country benefited from booming prices in world markets for its agricultural and industrial exports.

President Rousseff came into office in 2011 intent on building on Lula's achievements. One of her main goals was to end poverty. She set a national poverty line and promised to raise all Brazilians above that level by 2014. She reasoned that reducing poverty was not just a matter of helping poor Brazilians; raising poor people's incomes would increase demand for goods and services, which would promote economic growth. Her ambition to end poverty reflected the belief that improving people's lives is a key public policy objective, and that economic growth is a means to that end.[31]

Rousseff's other major goal was to make Brazilian industries more competitive. She recognized that sustained economic growth depended on having products that could be sold in world markets. She believed that the state could be used to advance Brazil's economic competitiveness. Soon after taking office, Rousseff targeted specific industries for assistance from the state development bank.[32] She also gave the state-owned oil company the responsibility of developing newly found offshore oil deposits.[33]

Her ambitious proposals ran into difficulty, however, when Brazil's growth rate slowed after 2010. Rapid economic growth is needed to fund both the social programs that Lula initiated and the ones that Rousseff sought to add to the mix. This is in part because the new programs were instituted without cutting expensive benefits for the middle class and retirees, groups that possess substantial political clout.[34]

The other major problem facing Rousseff was that previous governments' success in increasing economic growth and raising incomes produced a burgeoning middle class that had high expectations for government performance. Journalist Nicholas Lemann warned in 2011 that if the president failed to satisfy these expectations, the middle class citizens who had profited from past policies were likely to become the government's most vocal critics.[35]

Precisely this scenario played out in June 2013. A proposal to raise bus fares by ten cents in the city of Sao Paulo sparked protests that eventually spread to other cities and came to encompass other government policies. Hundreds of thousands of people, many of them members of Brazil's growing middle class, joined in these protests demanding better education, health care, and public transportation as well as safer streets. Their anger was driven in part by the increasing taxes they had to pay as their incomes rose and the low quality of services they received in return. It was also driven by the government's decision to spend billions of dollars on sports facilities for the soccer World Cup and the Olympics, which was perceived to be a bonanza for politicians and their cronies at the expense of ordinary citizens.[36]

The protests marked a potential change in Brazilian political culture. Protestors were demanding not only better public services but also that their leaders be less corrupt and more accountable,[37] but their protest lost momentum because there was no interest group, social movement, or political party to represent them. Although Rousseff has expressed sympathy with their demands, it is not clear how far she could go in converting that sympathy into action. For decades, her own political party has focused on improving the lives of workers and poor people rather than on meeting the demands of the urban middle class. Furthermore, Rousseff, and subsequent presidents, will have to deal with the obstacles presented by Brazil's fragmented political parties and the difficulties they present in passing legislation. Much slower economic growth has made the challenge even greater.

Semi-Democracy

10.4 Summarize the main features of semi-democracy.

Semi-democracies are neither fully democratic nor fully authoritarian but, rather, a mix of both. They hold regularly scheduled elections in which leaders of political parties compete to hold public offices. These elections do matter because incumbents can be defeated by challengers. Still, democracy in these regimes is weakly institutionalized. Personal relationships and winning office often matter more than following formal rules.[38] In many semi-democratic regimes, democracy was introduced relatively recently, and political elites are not firmly committed to its values, as witnessed by their tendency to buy votes, stuff ballot boxes, and intimidate supporters of other candidates.

Semi-Democracy
A system of government which is neither fully democratic nor fully authoritarian, but mixes the characteristics of democracy and authoritarianism.

Political parties in semi-democracies tend be based on personality and patron–client relationships rather than on strong organization and well-defined positions and programs. Instead of devising policies that appeal to broad cross-sections of the population, leaders of political parties endorse policies that benefit individuals and narrow groups of supporters.

Semi-democracies also tend to have weak states with little autonomy or capacity. They lack autonomy because many state officials work on behalf of clients rather than for broader publics. Recruited on the basis of personal connections rather than merit, they neither work in accordance with formal rules nor serve the public interest with a sense of professionalism. The temptation to behave corruptly is strong because the rewards can be large and the chances of being punished are small. These generalizations, of course, do not apply to all officials in semi-democracies. Some do display professional integrity and a desire to serve the public. They tend, however, to be in the minority.

The lack of state capacity makes it difficult for semi-democratic regimes to improve health, education, and safety. Typically, the central government is unable to implement decisions effectively throughout its territory. In many areas, local political bosses, landlords, criminal gangs, or insurgents may hold effective control.

Semi-democracies also have weak foundations in society. The countries lack the essential raw materials for building strong opposition parties and civil society organizations that can support democracy. Patron–client ties tend to be the main links between the state and the society. Semi-democracies usually are located in low-income countries in which most citizens are poor and therefore cannot offer much funding for opposition parties. Civil society organizations that champion civil and political rights are small and limited mainly to cities. Political elites, many military officers, and leaders of influential groups in society are only weakly committed to democracy as a means of winning and holding power. Finally, the political culture generally has high percentages of people identifying with their own ethnic or religious group rather than with the nation; relatively high levels of support for strong leaders who are not responsible to parliaments; significant percentages of citizens holding traditional and survival values; and low levels of trust in others.

Examples of semi-democracies include Bangladesh, Pakistan, and Nigeria, which we examine in the following section.[39]

Nigeria

10.5 Describe the history, state, relations between state and society, political culture, and political economy of Nigeria.

When Nigeria gained independence from Britain in 1960, many people expected it to become a success story. Africa's most populous country, Nigeria is the seventh most populous country in the world. It is among the world's top ten oil exporters, and it boasts valuable mineral resources and large areas of arable soil. Yet for decades, it remained a poor country. In 2010, 62 percent of its people lived below the extreme poverty level of $1.25 per day.[40] Approximately 40 percent of adults are illiterate, and 78 out of every 1,000 newborns die before their first birthday.[41] These failures are attributable to both the complexity of ethnic and religious divisions in Nigeria and the inadequacy of its political institutions for meeting the challenges that these divisions present. In 1999, the country became democratic after years of military rule and since has improved its economic performance and made some headway in enhancing citizens' capabilities.

Historical Background

Nigeria is an artificial country created by British colonialism. The colonial borders enclosed more than 250 ethnic groups that never before had been ruled by the same state. Thus, Nigeria lacked a history of common political institutions to which its people had some degree of loyalty. There was no agreement among its multiple ethnic groups over the rules of politics.[42] Nor did the British attempt to create such rules. They governed their colony on the cheap, relying on local leaders to maintain order and collect taxes. The northern part of the country was left in the hands of Islamic rulers, or emirs, under loose British supervision, with a legal system based on traditional Muslim shari'a law. By contrast, chiefs in the southern part of the country were under direct British control. The British made little effort to recruit and train a professional Nigerian civil service.[43]

Colonialism left four damaging legacies for Nigeria's politics. One was a country divided by major ethnic and religious differences. The Hausa-Fulani, Nigeria's largest ethnic group, dominate the north; the Yoruba, the second largest, live mainly in the southwest; and the Igbo, in third place, occupy the southeast. These ethnic divisions are overlain by religious differences. The Hausa-Fulani are predominantly Muslim, whereas the Igbo and Yoruba are predominantly Christian. The center of the country is a mix of Muslims, Christians, and practitioners of traditional faiths.

A second damaging colonial legacy was the **divide and rule** tactic that the British employed to pit ethnic groups against one another. The policy heightened ethnic awareness and helped ensure that ethnicity would be a main line of political cleavage after Nigeria became an independent country.

Divide and Rule
A strategy that pits groups against each other so they are unable to act collectively.

The third unfortunate legacy was a system of rule based on personal relationships rather than on formal institutions.[44] The chiefs who worked with the British colonial state did so "in the name of tradition" but without the checks on their power provided by traditional norms, and they used personal relationships with British field administrators to accumulate wealth and power.[45] This form of rule relied on a hierarchy of local big men linked to superiors through personal connections and held together by a strong executive at the top. It became the model for politics in independent Nigeria.[46]

The final damaging legacy was the creation of an increasingly active and interventionist state during World War II, which persisted up until independence in 1960. The fragmented Nigerian elite who took over Nigeria at independence found this state well suited for their patronage needs. They used the state as an employment agency for clients and a source of funding for projects in their regions. The ambition was to strengthen their political base, not to achieve broader goals of economic and human development that would benefit all Nigerians.[47]

The State

Nigeria has a weak state that has difficulty maintaining law and order, supplying adequate education, safety, and health care, and providing secure civil and political rights. One major cause of state weakness is the use of patronage appointments, as opposed to civil servants selected based on merit, to staff state agencies. Political leaders reward followers with government jobs and increase the number of civil service positions to raise the number of jobs they can dole out. In the main, politics in Nigeria is a competition among powerful **big men** and their clients. Clients help big men get elected and, in return, are rewarded with jobs, contracts for construction projects, or simply a share in the theft of government funds. In a setting where corruption is rampant, it makes little sense for officials to be the only honest persons in their agencies. Although there are a few pockets of effectiveness in the Nigerian state, creating and sustaining these kinds of agencies is very difficult.[48]

Big Men
Politically powerful leaders in Nigeria.

Map 10.2 Nigeria

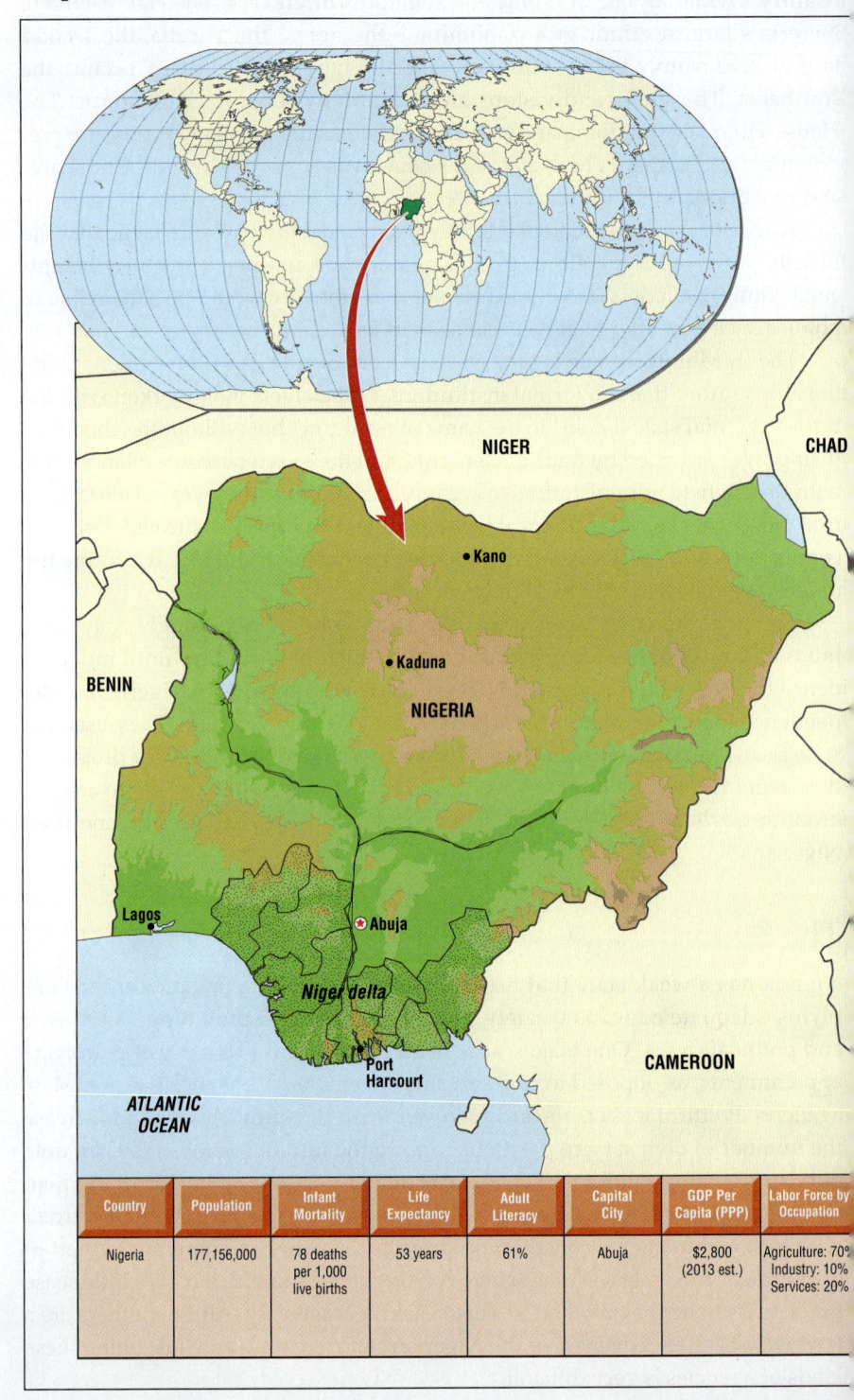

Country	Population	Infant Mortality	Life Expectancy	Adult Literacy	Capital City	GDP Per Capita (PPP)	Labor Force by Occupation
Nigeria	177,156,000	78 deaths per 1,000 live births	53 years	61%	Abuja	$2,800 (2013 est.)	Agriculture: 70% Industry: 10% Services: 20%

The Nigerian state is weak also because no constitutional arrangement has lasted long enough to become fully institutionalized. Whereas the United States has had a single constitution since 1789, Nigeria has had four since 1960. Its political history as an independent country has been marked by a civil war, failed democracies, and long periods of military rule. The first democratic period, which lasted from 1960 until 1966, collapsed into a devastating civil war when the large Igbo ethnic group in the southeastern part of the country tried to secede and form an independent country they called Biafra. The war caused an estimated one million deaths, many from starvation, before the Nigerian army finally defeated the rebels in 1970.

Military officers ruled Nigeria from the end of the civil war until 1979, when Nigerians made a second attempt at democratic governance. This time, military officers waited only four years before seizing power. The *junta* pointed to massive corruption and mismanagement to justify the coup. Although it promised a quick return to civilian rule, it stayed in power for the next two decades. Rather than reducing corruption and mismanagement, the military rulers became increasingly predatory. General Sani Abacha, who served as president from 1993 until 1998, was the worst of them all. Nobel Prize–winning author Wole Soyinka predicted that Abacha would be Nigeria's "last despot," because he was such a bad leader that he discredited military rule.[49] When he died of a heart attack in 1998, there was widespread rejoicing.

Nigeria's present constitution came into effect in 1999. It is the most recent in a long line of attempts to craft an arrangement of state institutions that can hold together an ethnically and religiously diverse country. It provides for a federal system, with power divided between the central government, with its capital in Abuja, and 36 states. The balance of power is tilted heavily toward the federal government.

The most powerful office in the central government is the presidency. The president is elected by voters every four years and can serve for no more than two terms. He or she serves as both head of state and head of the executive branch of government and appoints a Cabinet, the Federal Executive Council. To satisfy the diversity of regions, ethnicities, and religions in Nigeria, the president must have at least one Cabinet member from each of the 36 states.

The legislature, or National Assembly, has two chambers, a House of Representatives and a Senate. The 360 members of the House of Representatives are elected based on states' population; three senators are elected to the Senate from each state, and one represents the capital city of Abuja. Even though the president and legislative majorities in both houses have been from the same political party since 1999, there have been struggles over budgets and legislation between the two branches. A watershed moment in this power struggle occurred in 2006, when the Senate rejected a constitutional amendment proposed by President Olusegun Obasanjo that would have allowed him a third term in office.[50]

The judicial system includes a Supreme Court, a Court of Appeal, and a system of state courts. In the first decades after Nigeria became independent, courts were highly regarded as independent institutions that decided cases based on the law. Although they lost a great deal of their independence during the years of military rule, they have begun to regain some of it since the return of civilian government in 1999.

One of the unusual features of the Nigerian legal system is the presence of **shari'a law** courts in 12 northern states with large Muslim populations. Such courts existed for hundreds of years prior to British colonial rule and continued to handle family law and criminal cases during the colonial period, but their right to adjudicate criminal law cases ended with the transition to Nigerian independence in 1960. In 1999, some northern politicians saw political advantages in appealing to Muslim voters by reinstating shari'a courts' rights to decide criminal law cases.[51] Although the courts' decisions apply only to Muslims, the expanded authority of shari'a courts alarmed Christians and secular Muslims. Shari'a allows for severe corporal punishment, including amputating a hand for theft and stoning adulteresses to death. Such punishments attracted international attention in 2002 when a shari'a court sentenced a young, unmarried woman to be stoned for having a child. Concerns about the courts have declined in recent years, however, because the most draconian penalties are seldom applied. Amputations for theft have been rare, and an appeals court overturned the ruling that the unmarried woman should be stoned.[52]

Shari'a Law
Muslim law based on the Qur'an and the teachings of the Prophet Mohammed, which offers Muslims moral and legal guidance for nearly all aspects of life.

State and Society

Nigerian political parties do a poor job of linking citizens to the state and enabling them to choose among alternative sets of government policies. Party leaders fail to offer competing programs to address social and economic problems that will be implemented once they are in power. Instead, they compete for votes by winning over local ethnic and religious leaders who can mobilize blocs of votes. It is more cost-effective for party leaders to use public money to build patron–client relationships than to provide effective services. Once in office, they can use their positions to build personal fortunes and accumulate funds for future campaigns. The total amount of state funds siphoned off by politicians adds up to billions of dollars. In 2011, the "speaker of the lower house of parliament was investigated for 'misappropriating' $140 million, and in 2014 the governor of the central bank reported that as much as $20 billion from oil sales by the state-owned Nigerian National Petroleum Corporation was missing. He was subsequently dismissed from his position by the President."[53]

The most successful political party has been the People's Democratic Party (PDP). Until the contentious presidential election, in 2011, it was based on a power-sharing arrangement in which the presidency alternated between a Muslim from the north and a Christian from the south. In the 2011 election, however, the party selected Goodluck Jonathan, a southerner, as its candidate. His election resulted in rioting by northern Muslims, who claimed Jonathan had stolen the presidency. International observers found, to the contrary, that the election was actually much cleaner than the previous presidential contest.

Yet the riots were evidence that religious identity is becoming a cause of violent conflict in Nigeria. Many Muslims have become insecure as economic and population trends have turned against them. The north has fallen further and further behind economically, and increasing numbers of evangelical Christians have moved into areas once considered Muslim strongholds.[54]

Mainstream northern politicians began to seek votes by playing on Muslim identity and insecurities. They promised to jump-start economic growth in the north, provide more jobs, and otherwise improve citizens' lives, but they failed to deliver. Corruption continued, and the northern economy produced little growth and few jobs. These problems created the opening for a violent Islamic radical movement—**Boko Haram**—to offer a completely different analysis of the north's difficulties and a proposal for overcoming them. Boko Haram, translated into English, means "Western learning is forbidden." The movement's leaders attribute the north's economic and social woes to attempts to impose on it Western economic and political institutions and Western values. Their proposed solution is to create a society based on fundamentalist Islam that would eliminate corruption and injustice and restore morality and order under their own leadership.[55] Boko Haram militants initially targeted police officers and Nigerian soldiers for assassination. In 2013, they began killing school teachers and students in government schools as well. By mid-2013, the militants were estimated to have killed over 3,000 people.[56] The goal is to cripple the power of the Nigerian state and replace it with an authoritarian religious government.[57]

Boko Haram
A violent Islamic radical movement active in Nigeria.

Fortunately, most Nigerians are not embroiled in the violence initiated by Boko Haram. Nor are political parties the sole agencies of participation. Both interest groups and patron–client relationships also play key roles. Among interest groups, business owners stand out. Business associations demand less government corruption, better roads, more reliable electricity, and fewer obstacles to starting new companies. All too often, however, their attempts to act collectively have been undercut by individual entrepreneurs going directly to influential politicians and civil servants to make requests. Attempts to coordinate businesses nationally are also hampered by ethnic and regional differences. Trust is in short supply between business and the government and among entrepreneurs themselves.

Trade unions have also emerged as links between society and state, although their rights are tightly restricted. Unions have worked within these restrictions to improve factory conditions and raise wages and sometimes have gone on strike to stop proposed cuts in government services. Although they have had some success achieving improvements for their members, ethnic and religious differences among workers have limited their influence. Moreover, some union victories have had ambivalent results. An example was their success in 2012 in forcing President Jonathan to back down on a proposal to end government subsidies that kept the price of gasoline low for consumers. Eliminating that subsidy would have raised the cost from $1.70 a gallon to $3.50 a gallon, saved the state an estimated eight billion dollars, and encouraged consumers to use gas more efficiently. The initiative failed when two unions led a strike against the price increase.[58] Many other citizens joined the unions' protest, including car-owning middle-class citizens and truck drivers who resisted paying substantially more at the pump. Although the strike protected citizens from price increases, it left the wasteful subsidy in place.

Political Culture

Despite all the problems confronting Nigeria, a 2012 survey found that 75 percent of its citizens said it makes them "proud to be called a Nigerian while only 14 percent said it did not."[59] Moreover, a much higher percentage said they identified themselves as both Nigerian and a member of their ethnic group than those who identified only with the latter.[60]

Nigerians also support democracy, although with less enthusiasm than in 2000, just after Nigeria had returned to civilian rule. In a survey taken in 2000, 81 percent of Nigerians agreed that "democracy is preferable to any other form of government." By 2005, high levels of government corruption, poor delivery of services, and ethnic and religious conflicts had caused this figure to drop to 65 percent, but by 2012, it had rebounded to 69 percent. Despite difficulties with democracy, very few Nigerians want a return to military rule. On the other hand, a majority of Nigerians regard their country as a democracy facing major problems.

Many Nigerians take an interest in politics and how it affects their lives. Substantial numbers of citizens make an effort to stay informed about government activities.[61] A majority agree that it is proper for citizens to question the actions of government officials rather than simply to go along with their decisions.[62] As we saw earlier, a willingness to challenge officials is a key self-expression value. Although the percentage of Nigerians holding such values remains well below that found in upper-income democracies such as Great Britain, Germany, and Sweden, it is higher than in other upper- and lower-middle income democracies, including Indonesia, Turkey, South Africa, and Chile.[63]

Although the previously mentioned aspects of political culture are promising for the future of democracy in Nigeria, the lack of trust in political institutions is not. With good reason, Nigerians have low levels of trust in government institutions, including the presidency, national assembly, courts, and police. Unfortunately, officials' corrupt behavior and poor performance takes a toll on social capital. As we saw in Chapter 4, the behavior of government officials can affect citizens' willingness to trust one another. When government officials treat people impartially and can be trusted, citizens are more likely to exhibit trust.

When government officials treat citizens badly, or treat some differently from others, citizens are more likely to exhibit distrust. It is therefore not surprising that in 2012, only 16 percent of Nigerians believed most people could be trusted, whereas 80 percent believed "you must be very careful in dealing with people."[64]

Political Economy

The struggle among political elites to gain access to revenues produced by the country's abundant oil wealth is the central theme of Nigerian political economy.[65] Nigerians refer to the federal budget as the "national cake," and politics is largely about getting the biggest slices. Oil revenues provide a classic example of profits in the form of **rents**. Rents are revenues from natural resources or businesses greater than normal profits which could be made in competitive markets.[66] The major source of rents is the oil industry, and much economic activity in Nigeria takes the form of **rent seeking**, or attempting to gain access to the rent provided by oil revenues. One of the easiest ways to do so is to get state contracts for constructing roads, bridges, or schools. State officials pay developers exorbitant sums for these projects, and in return get kickbacks from the entrepreneurs who received the contracts. Most of the oil revenues go to a small number of people. In 2007, the World Bank estimated that 80 percent of the billions of dollars Nigeria has earned from oil exports "are controlled by 1 percent of the population." [67]

One reason for all this rent seeking is that Nigeria has not created institutions that provide incentives for business people to invest in industry. Although there are bustling markets in Nigerian cities for consumer goods and food, industrial development has lagged. Sustained industrial development requires relatively secure property rights, rules promoting economic competition, and modern infrastructure, including reliable electricity supplies and good roads. Astonishingly, Nigeria even suffers from unstable fuel supplies, despite being a major exporter of oil. Its state-managed refineries have antiquated equipment and produce well below capacity. Most petroleum products are imported, and the state-managed distribution system is riddled with corruption, inefficiency, and mismanagement.[68]

There has been progress in recent years. The transition to democracy has created greater political stability, which has made people more confident about investing in new businesses. In addition, presidents have initiated economic reforms in the banking and financial sector that have strengthened banks and increased transparency so that business people have more accurate economic information. Governments have also enforced sounder fiscal policy. Competitive bidding on state contracts has been introduced, which has reduced the cost of projects "by an average of 40 percent."[69] Finally, more than 100 inefficient state enterprises have been privatized. These reforms contributed to GDP growth rates of over 7 percent per year between 2003 and 2012 and made Nigeria one of

Rents
Artificially high revenues greater than the normal profits that could be made in competitive markets derived from scarce natural resources such as oil, or ability to gain protection from competition.

Rent Seeking
Seeking profits by lobbying government officials for protection from competitors instead of making better products for customers and improving productivity.

the fastest growing economies in the world. It now has the largest economy in Africa. Some of this growth was the result of rising oil prices in world markets, but most of it was in wholesale and retail trade, telecommunications, and manufacturing sectors.[70] Nigeria has a long way to go, however, in creating institutions that can sustain industrial growth over the long term.

Moreover, this growth did little to improve the well-being of many Nigerians. Poverty reduction lagged in most of Nigeria, with the number of poor people increasing in half of its states. The highest poverty rates are in the Muslim-dominated north. Job creation has lagged behind population growth, which means unemployment numbers have increased. As the World Bank warns, "with a median age of 14 and population growth at close to 3%, the very stability of the country depends on a major acceleration in the creation of jobs, opportunities and basic social services for the population."[71]

Electoral Authoritarianism

10.6 Summarize the main features of electoral authoritarianism.

Electoral Authoritarianism
The use of elections to mask the reality of authoritarian rule, in which the ruling party holds regularly scheduled elections and allows multiple political parties to participate in them but the elections are not free and fair, and election rules are tilted strongly in favor of the ruling political party.

Electoral authoritarianism is the use of elections to "mask the reality of authoritarian domination."[72] Under electoral authoritarianism, chief executives and legislators are chosen by voters and several political parties are allowed to nominate candidates to compete for the positions. The electoral rules are tilted so strongly in favor of the ruling party or faction, however, that opposition parties or movements have little chance of taking power. Political and civil rights are frequently denied to the leaders and members of opposition parties, even when such rights are guaranteed in the constitution.

Many regimes using electoral authoritarianism have a strong ruling political party. Such parties generally have procedures for selecting the country's leaders and provide a setting in which disputes among different party factions can be resolved. Ruling parties are also important for organizing campaigns for the party's candidates in elections. Finally, parties provide an institutionalized means for recruiting new members and making the change from one leader to another. Regimes using electoral authoritarianism that govern without benefit of a ruling political party have to find other ways of selecting leaders and balancing the interests of competing factions.

Authoritarian regimes that allow multiparty elections also need strong security and military forces. If large-scale protests erupt, security and military forces are necessary to subdue them. Officers and troops must have both the ability and the will to suppress demonstrations, even if doing so requires killing large numbers of people.

Political scientists have used Iran, Venezuela, and Zimbabwe as examples of regimes using electoral authoritarianism.[73]

Iran

10.7 Describe the history, state, relations between state and society, political culture, and political economy of Iran.

The presidents of Brazil, Nigeria, and Iran are all elected by popular vote in elections in which several candidates compete for office, but two features make Iranian elections very different from those in Brazil and Nigeria. One is that the president is not the most powerful leader in Iran. Ultimate power is held by the Supreme Leader, who is not elected by popular vote. Second, candidates for the presidency must be approved by a council whose members are appointed by the Supreme Leader. Only candidates committed to the Iranian regime are permitted to run for office. These restrictions do not make elections meaningless. Although the candidates must stay within boundaries set by the Supreme Leader, they have different approaches to economic, social, and foreign policy. Moreover, the candidate favored by the Supreme Leader sometimes loses, as happened in the 2013 presidential election. Iran has a higher degree of political competitiveness than other authoritarian Middle Eastern regimes.[74]

Historical Background

For most of its 2,500-year history, Iran was known as Persia. In the sixth century BC, the Persian Empire controlled territory that extended well beyond Iran's current borders, but eventually the empire began to lose influence, and it was invaded first by Arabs, who brought Islam to the area, and then by Turkic invaders, who ruled from 1501 until 1722. These invaders converted Persians to **Shiite Islam**. This is the smaller of the two major branches of Islam, Sunni Islam being the other. Of the more than one billion Muslims in the world, less than 20 percent are Shiites. The split between the two dates back to the 7th century and stems from arguments over who should succeed the Prophet Muhammad as the religion's leader. Shiites believe that this authority should have passed to his hereditary successors known as imams. The 12th of the Imams is known as the **Mahdi**, who Shiites believe did not die but was hidden by God in 941 to ensure his safety. They further believe the Mahdi will reappear again as a messiah to establish just rule on earth. The clerics who now rule Iran consider themselves the legitimate rulers of Iran until the Mahdi returns.

When imperial powers Great Britain and Russia extended their influence over Persia in the 19th century, the ruling Turkic dynasty remained nominally in power. In fact, however, the British controlled large parts of the economy and financial system and sought control of Persia's oil. In 1921, Colonel Reza Khan carried out a coup d'état against the Turkic rulers and began to build an independent state that could stand up to Western powers. He established the Pahlavi Dynasty in 1925 and tried to westernize Persia, building a modern army and bureaucracy. It was Reza Khan who, in 1935, changed the name of the country

Shiite Islam
The smaller of the two major branches of Islam. Sunni Muslims are the other. The split between the two branches dates back to the seventh century over who should succeed the Prophet Mohammed as the leader of Islam.

Mahdi
The Mahdi is the twelfth Shiite Imam. Shiites believe he did not die, but went into hiding in 941 and will reappear again as the messiah to establish just rule on earth.

from Persia to Iran. After his removal from power by the British and Russians in 1941, he was succeeded by his son, Mohammed Reza Shah Pahlavi.

After World War II, Iran experienced a brief period of democratic politics. In 1951, Mohammad Mossadegh was elected prime minister. He tried to take control of Iran's oil industry from the British, with the intent of using oil revenues for national development. His efforts were thwarted by the British government and the United States Central Intelligence Agency, which backed a revolt of military officers and clerics against Mossadegh in 1953 and returned the Shah to power.[75]

Subsequently, the Shah became a strong ally of the United States and pursued policies aimed at modernizing Iran. He introduced Western legal principles, increased the number of schools, strengthened the rights of women, and implemented land reforms transferring property from large landowners to farmers with small holdings. His rule was brutal and authoritarian, however, sustained by a ruthlessly effective security service and backed by one of the largest armies in the world.

The Shah's goal was to make Iran an economically developed, modern country, but the means he used to achieve these goals angered many Iranians. They included shopkeepers and merchants in Iran's traditional bazaars, who resented his neglect of their interests; workers who derived few benefits from his policies; intellectuals and middle-class Iranians who resented his oppressive authoritarianism; and conservative Islamic clerics who opposed westernization and Western cultural values. The Shah's close ties to the United States guaranteed that anger aimed at the Shah was also directed at the United States, which was providing him with economic and military aid.

In 1979, the Shah was overthrown by a revolution led by an Islamic cleric, Ruhollah Khomeini. Ayatollah Khomeini built a broad coalition of supporters by appealing to anti-Shah elements in the population. He condemned Western capitalism as exploitative, advocated social justice for the poor, and called for a return to Islamic values. He portrayed the Shah not only as a tyrant but as a tool of Western imperialism.

After the Shah was forced into exile, there was an intense struggle among the elements of Khomeini's coalition for control of the state. The fundamental divide was between Khomeini and his followers and those who wanted a secular democracy. Khomeini's key political concept was *velayat-e-faqih*, or "guardianship of the jurist." This meant that a cleric should be the leader of the country, and Khomeini should be that cleric. His rationale was that "the shari'a, or divine law, was handed down to lead the community on the right path, and since the clergy had the expertise to understand, interpret and implement the shari'a, it followed that they should guide the state."[76] In short, Khomeini wanted a **theocracy**, or a state ruled by leaders who are divinely guided. Others who participated in the revolution preferred a secular, democratic state in which elected legislators, not religious clerics claiming to speak for God, would make laws.[77] Khomeini prevailed in the struggle over who would inherit the Iranian revolution.

Velayat-E-Faqih
The guiding principle of the Islamic Republic of Iran. It is translated into English as "guardianship of the jurist," and holds that the clerics most trained in Islamic jurisprudence should rule and that a cleric should be the leader of the country.

Theocracy
A regime in which religious leaders rule.

Less-Developed Countries and the Good Society 275

Map 10.3 Iran

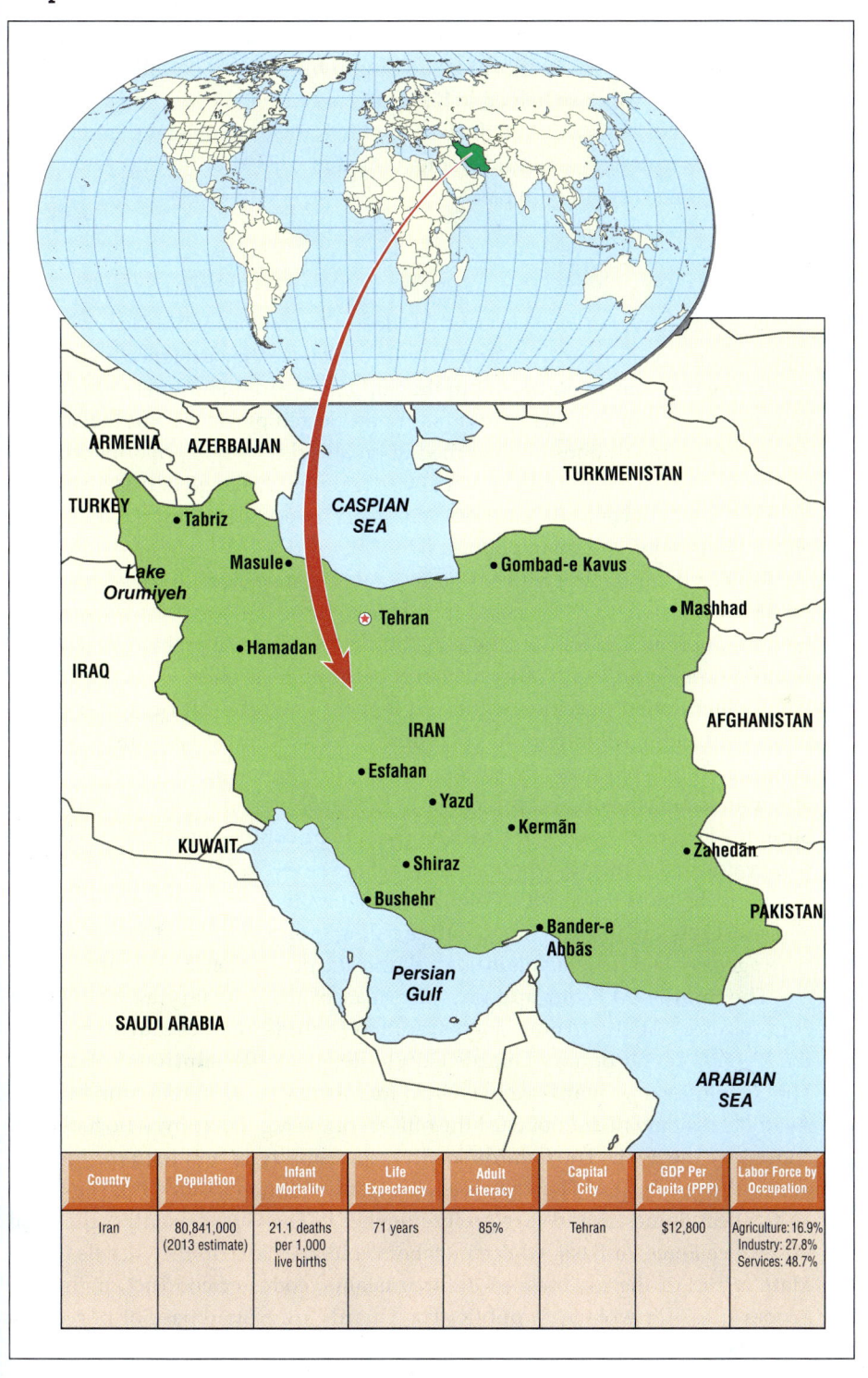

Country	Population	Infant Mortality	Life Expectancy	Adult Literacy	Capital City	GDP Per Capita (PPP)	Labor Force by Occupation
Iran	80,841,000 (2013 estimate)	21.1 deaths per 1,000 live births	71 years	85%	Tehran	$12,800	Agriculture: 16.9% Industry: 27.8% Services: 48.7%

Iranian students' seizure of the American Embassy in Tehran in November 1979 helped Khomeini win support from large parts of the population. The students held U.S. diplomats hostage for 444 days, showing the world, as Khomeini put it, that Iran could stand up to the country he called the Great Satan. Khomeini was also helped in his efforts to consolidate his power by Iraq's attack on Iran in 1980. He used the war to rally Iranians to defend their country and his new regime. Although Khomeini died in 1989 after the war ended, by then his regime was firmly in place.

The State

To make sure that his vision survived his death, Khomeini and his close advisers devised state institutions to ensure the rule of clerics. They designed a constitution that gave ultimate authority to the Supreme Leader and unelected offices held by clerics, but they also provided for an elected president and legislators. These elected institutions are hemmed in on all sides by unelected institutions that keep them in check and prevent any substantial challenge to rule by clerics, but this "inherent contradiction between theocracy and democracy" has created enduring tensions in Iranian politics.[78]

We begin this section with a description of the state institutions whose leaders are not elected by citizens and then turn to those that are. We next examine how the Supreme Leader uses these institutions to solve the problem of authoritarian power sharing with other members of the political elite.

As mentioned previously, the single most powerful office is that of the **Supreme Leader**. All important government decisions must have his approval. The constitution requires him to ensure that government agencies "function in line with Islamic tenets and principles of the revolution of 1979."[79] The current Supreme Leader is Ayatollah Khamenei (not to be confused with his predecessor, Ayatollah Khomeini), who assumed that post in 1989. Although the Supreme Leader is the most powerful official, he is not omnipotent; he cannot rule alone and must rely on other members of the ruling group of clerics to manage key state agencies and help maintain control over the population. See Figure 10.1

The Supreme Leader appoints the head of the judiciary as well as the commanders of the armed forces, which include the regular army and the Iranian Revolutionary Guards Corps (IRGC), or **Revolutionary Guards**. The Revolutionary Guards were created following the 1979 revolution because Ayatollah Khomeini did not trust the officers of the regular army, who had been chosen by the Shah. The Guards' main responsibility is to safeguard the legacy of the revolution. They suppress protests, command Iran's missile force, and collect domestic and foreign intelligence.[80] The Guards control the Basij Resistance Force, or Basij, whose members volunteer to help the Guards intimidate critics of the regime and enforce Islamic codes of conduct, including proper dress for women in public. The Guards are a main base of power for Ayatollah Khamenei.

Supreme Leader
The most powerful political leader in Iran charged with safekeeping the legacy of the Islamic Revolution of 1979.

Revolutionary Guards
An all-volunteer elite military force who are responsible to the Supreme Leader and are supposed to defend the Islamic Revolution.

Figure 10.1 Iranian Political Institutions

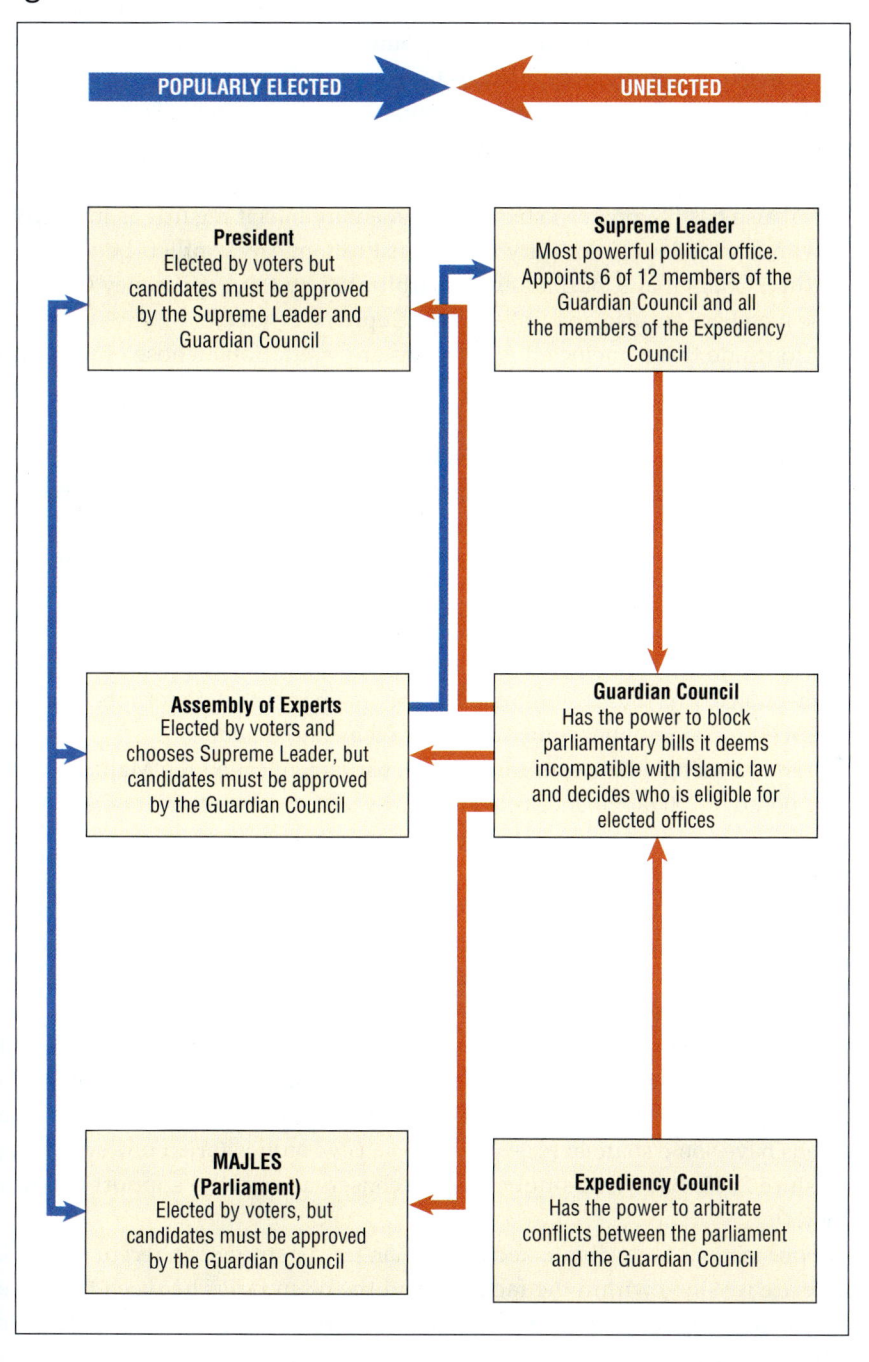

POPULARLY ELECTED → ← UNELECTED

President
Elected by voters but candidates must be approved by the Supreme Leader and Guardian Council

Supreme Leader
Most powerful political office. Appoints 6 of 12 members of the Guardian Council and all the members of the Expediency Council

Assembly of Experts
Elected by voters and chooses Supreme Leader, but candidates must be approved by the Guardian Council

Guardian Council
Has the power to block parliamentary bills it deems incompatible with Islamic law and decides who is eligible for elected offices

MAJLES (Parliament)
Elected by voters, but candidates must be approved by the Guardian Council

Expediency Council
Has the power to arbitrate conflicts between the parliament and the Guardian Council

Guardian Council (Iran)
An advisory council to the Supreme Leader, with power to select who can run for the presidency and parliament, and to block parliamentary bills it regards as incompatible with Islamic law or contrary to the constitution.

The Supreme Leader also appoints the six religious members of the 12-member **Guardian Council (Iran)**. The other six are legal scholars selected by the Chief Justice, who himself is appointed by the Supreme Leader.[81] The Guardian Council screens candidates for the presidency and parliament. Any candidates deemed threatening to the regime are disqualified. Thus, although there are elections for president and the legislature, voters are allowed to choose only from among candidates approved by the top leadership. The Guardian Council also has the power to block parliamentary bills it regards as incompatible with Islamic law or contrary to the constitution. Any conflicts between the Guardian Council and parliament are arbitrated by the Expediency Council, whose members are also appointed by the Supreme Leader.

Alongside these unelected institutions are institutions whose officials are elected by citizens. One such institution is the Assembly of Experts, which has the authority to select the Supreme Leader and supervise his activities, but it would be wrong to infer that citizens have an indirect voice in choosing him. Candidates for seats in the Assembly of Experts are carefully vetted by the Guardian Council, which is, once again, appointed by the Supreme Leader.

The president, who heads the executive branch of government, is elected by popular vote for a four-year term. Presidents are limited to two consecutive terms. Only men are eligible to run. Candidates must receive prior consent from the Guardian Council, and after the election, the Supreme Leader must ratify the voters' choice. Presidents nominate Cabinet members and governors of provinces, whose appointments must be approved by parliament.

Majles
Iran's unicameral legislature.

Iran has a single-house, or unicameral, parliament called the **Majles**, which is composed of 290 members elected for four-year terms by popular vote. Unlike the office of president, women can serve as members of the Majles. The Majles has the authority to confirm the president's nominees for his Cabinet, question Cabinet members about their ministries' policies, and pass legislation. It must approve the government's budgets and is at liberty to reject presidential budget proposals. However, like presidential power, legislative power is hedged in on all sides by unelected officials.

These state institutions are the main prizes in the struggle for political power in Iran, among leaders of factions in the ruling group. The Supreme Leader is the arbiter of these struggles. He has made sure that leaders of the factions have some share in state power to achieve authoritarian power sharing but, since 2005, has increasingly favored conservatives who support his own views.

Four factions have dominated the Iranian power struggle in recent decades. There are tensions within the factions, and the boundaries between them are not clearly defined, but they are the basic units of politics in Iran. The leaders of the first three factions are all influential Muslim clerics who graduated from Islamic seminaries and were followers of Ayatollah Khomeini during the revolution. Ever since, they have held a variety of powerful political positions and are now quite elderly. The leaders of the fourth faction come from a younger generation of non-clerics, but like the other three, they support the principle of *velayat-e-faqih*. In this sense, the leaders of all four factions are all insiders who want to maintain the present regime, but they differ about the best ways of doing so. The main points of difference concern the appropriate balance of power between elected and unelected institutions, economic policy, cultural policy, and Iran's relations with the United States.

The most powerful is the **conservative faction**, headed by the current Supreme Leader, Ayatollah Khamenei. Its members believe "the essential purpose of the Iranian state is the realization of God's will on earth" and that they understand best what God's will is.[82] Accordingly, they resist movement toward more democracy and popular participation in politics and have little tolerance for individual rights or ideological pluralism. Conservatives insist on strict dress codes for women, tight control of the media to block decadent Western influences, and a ban on the sales of alcohol. They repeatedly reaffirm their commitment to improving the lives of the poor. For example, they decided to provide state subsidies for bread, sugar, and other essentials, but these subsidies also went to the middle class, costing the state billions of dollars. While professing support for economic justice, many members of the conservative faction have become quite wealthy. In foreign policy, conservatives regard the United States as an imperial power that seeks to dominate the entire Middle East. Iran, in their view, must vigilantly resist the United States, and one of the main means of doing so is to increase Iran's nuclear capability.

Conservative Faction
The conservative faction strongly supports theocracy and minimizing the power of voters to choose leaders or policies.

The **pragmatist faction** has much less power than the conservatives do. They believe that conservatives' economic policies have been too state-oriented and that their dismissive view of elected institutions endangers the long-run stability and legitimacy of the regime. Pragmatists want to develop a competitive industrial economy, and they think that opening Iran to foreign investment will further that goal. Better relations with the West are a necessary step in this direction. They maintain that economic growth will do much more to improve the lives of poor citizens than government subsidies. Professionals, some members of the business community, highly educated technocrats in the bureaucracy, and portions of the urban middle class comprise their main constituency. Politically, the pragmatists would like to see more power given to democratic institutions. Culturally, they are less restrictive than the conservatives, contending that the conservatives' rigid codes of conduct are causing the regime to lose the support of Iran's younger population. The pragmatists' best-known leader is Hashemi Rafsanjani. The members of this faction had their greatest influence from 1989 to 1997 when Rafsanjani served as president.

Pragmatist Faction
The pragmatist faction puts primary emphasis on improving economic growth by relying more on market forces.

The **reformist faction** has gone the furthest in inching toward democracy, but they are weaker than the other two. In their view, Islam and democracy can coexist, and religious leaders cannot claim special insight into God's will to rationalize their monopoly of political power. Reformists contend that the Supreme Leader "must defer to the elected branches of the government."[83] They support economic policies similar to those of the pragmatists but want to go further in

Reformist Faction
The reformist faction wants to give more authority to elected institutions and permit more cultural freedom.

loosening cultural controls and improving relations with the West. Their best-known leader is a mid-level cleric, Mohammed Khatami. This faction had its greatest influence when Khatami was president, from 1997 to 2004, but has lost a good deal of its influence since that time.

Finally, there is the **principlist faction**. It had its greatest influence during Mahmoud Ahmadinejad's first term as president, from 2005 to 2009. Most of the men around him were from a younger generation of leaders than those in the other three factions. Many had served in the Revolutionary Guards. They criticized the leaders of the older generation for abandoning the goals of the revolution, becoming corrupt, and focusing on personal power and wealth rather than on social justice and helping the poor. Ahmadinejad presented himself as a leader who spoke for ordinary people and stood up to the rich and powerful. He was re-elected president in 2009 with the backing of Supreme Leader Khamenei, the Revolutionary Guards, and the Basij but had a falling out with Khamenei toward the end of his second term over policy differences. Without control of the presidency and the patronage opportunities that position offers, this faction has little power.

Supreme Leader Khamenei has acted as an arbiter in these power struggles. Although he has favored the conservative faction, he has allowed leaders of the others to hold important state posts. As noted already, Rafsanjani (pragmatist), Khatami (reformist), and Ahmadinejad (principlist) have all been president of Iran. Leaders of the first three factions have at one time or another also headed the Assembly of Religious Experts, served as speaker of the Majles, and chaired the Expediency Council.

Elections for president provide another means of sharing power among the factions. Although the Guardian Council screens out any presidential candidates it deems too critical of the regime, it typically includes at least one pragmatist or reformer. These candidates have won presidential elections, including the election of 2013. The winner, Hassan Rouhani, was supported by leaders of the pragmatist and reformist factions. He was not the person favored by Khamenei, and his victory demonstrates to the leaders of the pragmatist and reformist factions that they still have influence. Thus, there is reason for them to continue as insiders rather than taking their disagreements with Khamenei and the conservatives outside the regime as leaders of protests.

State and Society

The Iranian regime has been in power since 1979. Its present leaders have used three main strategies to maintain authoritarian control. One has been to build support for the regime by implementing policies and programs targeted to benefit certain groups. For example, Supreme Leader Khamenei and his conservative faction have built a large following among the urban poor, religious conservatives, and large parts of the rural population by appealing to conservative moral values and promising social justice. To that end, they have created

---

Principlist Faction
The principlist faction is composed of a younger generation of leaders who believe many of the older leaders have become corrupt and abandoned the principles of the Islamic Revolution. They are hard-line conservatives on cultural policy and confrontational toward the United States, Europe, and Israel.

an "**interventionist-redistributive social contract**."[84] Its terms are that the state will provide benefits to a wide variety of groups in exchange for their acceptance of clerical rule. These benefits have included state subsidies to offset the cost of basic necessities. Poor families receive additional payments to increase their income from the state and state-supported charities. Middle-class Iranians also benefited from this social contract in the form of subsidized gasoline prices, "public education, generous state pensions, or low health care costs."[85]

In addition to the subsidies that many groups of Iranians receive, conservatives provide targeted benefits to organizations with links to their faction. One example is semi-public charitable organizations known as ***bonyads***. After the 1979 revolution, Iran's new rulers funded the *bonyads* with assets seized from the Shah. The *bonyads* used that money partly to help poor Iranians but also to invest in various sectors of the Iranian economy, including real estate, construction, transportation, and automobile companies. They now control assets worth billions of dollars, and some of their directors are multimillionaires.[86]

Another organization that has gained from conservative policies is the Revolutionary Guards. Like the *bonyads*, they have extended their activities well beyond their original mission. They are now involved in a wide range of commercial activities from mining to the construction and defense industries. President Ahmadinejad made a special effort to win support from the officers of the Revolutionary Guards after he became president in 2005, approving hundreds of construction and petrochemical contracts worth billions of dollars for companies owned by the Guards.[87]

The second way that the regime tries to win support is to hold regularly scheduled elections for the presidency and members of parliament. The elections enable citizens to choose from among competing candidates representing different factions in the ruling group that have different policy positions. Elections have often displayed high voter interest and strong partisanship in favor of one candidate over others. In the late 1990s and early 2000s, the leaders of the moderate and reformist factions controlled the presidency. In 2005, Ahmadinejad emerged victorious, to the dismay of citizens wanting greater personal freedoms and institutions that were more democratic. In the 2013 election, however, Hassan Rouhani, who was supported by leaders of the reformist and moderate factions, won a stunning victory over four conservatives. Those who voted for Rouhani know that the Supreme Leader still has ultimate power in Iran, but Rouhani's victory gives them reason to believe that their votes matter and that they can have some impact on public policies. It provides hope that change is possible and thereby encourages playing by the regime's rules rather than taking to the streets.

Another reason for not taking to the streets is that the regime does not rely solely on winning support by providing benefits and holding contested elections to stay in power. It also uses repression to maintain control over the organizations that link state and society. Iran's political parties are formed to champion individual candidates and do not have enduring organization, a large membership, or

Interventionist-Redistributive Social Contract
The contract is that the state will provide benefits to a wide variety of groups in exchange for their acceptance of clerical rule.

Bonyads
Semi-public charitable foundations in Iran that receive state and private funding. They own numerous firms in various sectors of the Iranian economy.

strong roots in society.[88] They must be approved by the Ministry of the Interior, which can deny them permits if officials deem them anti-Islamic. This measure guarantees that no party can advocate significant change in the regime. Party leaders accused of doing so risk punishment. During the fall of 2009 and spring of 2010, leaders of the three largest reformist parties were arrested and imprisoned.[89] The presidential candidate who ran against Ahmadinejad in 2009 was still under house arrest in 2013 for challenging the results of the election.

The heavy hand of the state also extends to unions. Unions are tightly controlled by labor laws and independent unions are not permitted. Workers can establish Islamic Labor Councils, but their leaders must be approved by a state agency. Union leaders who lead strikes can be imprisoned. In recent years, conservative governments have cracked down on them with increasing harshness out of concern that they might join with other regime opponents to work for political change.

Social movements are also tightly controlled. Iran has a strong women's movement, which has worked to eliminate systematic gender discrimination against women in Iran. Conservative hard-liners have strengthened strict dress codes that are enforced by the Basij paramilitary group. Women also face discrimination in marriage and divorce laws. They have made progress despite tight controls by the state and have profited from the regime's educational policies. A majority of university students are women, and there are many women professors. These educated women helped provide leadership for the women's movement. One of them, Shirin Ebadi, won the Nobel Peace Prize in 2003 for her work on behalf of human rights in general and the rights of women in particular.

Other social movements that regime leaders perceive as more threatening to their political power have been repressed brutally. One example is what happened to the Green Movement that emerged during the 2009 presidential campaign to oppose Ahmadinejad's election. After his victory was announced, leaders of the Green Movement challenged the vote count, asserting that Ahmadinejad had stolen the election, and organized huge, peaceful demonstrations to protest his victory. Governmental leaders responded violently to stop the protests. More than a hundred protestors were murdered, and thousands were imprisoned.

Political Culture

In a World Values Survey compiled in 2005, 91 percent of Iranians told interviewers that they were "very" or "quite" proud of their country. These figures were almost identical to the survey responses of Americans. Iranians have a strong sense of nationalism and resent the humiliations they have suffered at the hands of other countries during their history, including the United States. Iran's leaders draw on and stoke these resentments to build support for their goal of enhancing Iran's influence in the Middle East. Likewise, they play on nationalistic feelings to defend Iran's right to develop a nuclear program without interference from the United States and Western Europe.

In domestic politics, a large majority of Iranians say that they want a democratic political system. A 2005 World Values Survey found that over 92 percent agreed that having a democratic political system was either a "very good" or "fairly good idea." On the other hand, self-expression values that are important for creating and sustaining democracy are in short supply. For example, only 11 percent of Iranians agreed that most people could be trusted, whereas 89 percent believed one "can't be too careful" in dealing with others. In addition, many Iranians long for a strong leader; in the 2005 survey, 74 percent agreed that having a strong leader is "good" or "very good."[90]

Attempts by political elites to garner support by using subsidies have led many Iranians to believe that it is the government's responsibility to provide for them economically. As previously noted, Ayatollah Khomeini repeatedly promised justice for poor Iranians, and his way of fulfilling that pledge was to subsidize incomes and to guarantee low prices for necessities. The current Supreme Leader, Ayatollah Khamenei, former President Ahmadinejad, and other leaders have echoed these promises. In the 2005 World Values Survey, Iranians were asked to locate themselves on a ten-point scale, with 1 representing the view that "people should take more responsibility to provide for themselves" and 10 favoring the position that "the government should take more responsibility." The answers tilted strongly in the latter direction.

Many Iranians also express distrust of private ownership of business, especially of large industrial corporations. The survey found that a higher percentage of respondents believed that government ownership of business should increase than those who thought private ownership should increase. These values stem from decades of experience with the Shah's version of crony capitalism as well as attacks by Khomeini and subsequent clerical leaders on the exploitative nature of capitalism.

Political Economy

The interventionist–redistributive political economy that Iranian leaders used to build support in society was expensive and inefficient. Many state-owned enterprises were used by political leaders for patronage purposes and had low levels of productivity. By 2010, however, leading members of all four political factions had come to the conclusion that major economic reforms were necessary. Economic growth was stalling out, and subsidies for gasoline and electricity were costing the state billions of dollars and causing wasteful use of resources.[91] In 2010, President Ahmadinejad cut the subsidies, replacing them with monthly cash payments for citizens. Despite warnings that the change would cause large protests, it was made relatively smoothly. The plan ran into difficulties in 2012, however, when soaring inflation rates dramatically reduced the purchasing power of the monthly payments. The Majles voted to halt planned "price increases in food, fuel, water, and electricity."[92] Hassan Rouhani, the president elected in 2013, promised to continue the system of payments but to make adjustments to ease financial burdens on citizens.

The other major economic reform, the privatization of many state-owned enterprises, also aimed at cutting government spending and improving economic efficiency. In 2010, more than 300 enterprises were privatized, including airlines, insurance companies, and car makers, but instead of simply selling these operations to independent private entrepreneurs, Iranian officials turned most of them over to banks, pension funds, endowed foundations, and military contractors linked to factions in the ruling group. Sociologist Kevan Harris describes the process as "pseudo-privatization." State officials in charge of the privatization program lacked sufficient independence from contending factions in the elite, and from the many groups in society who benefited from the Iranian welfare state, to enact thoroughgoing privatization.[93] The way the policy was implemented is not likely to improve firms' economic performance.

Iran's economic difficulties worsened in 2012 because of international economic sanctions imposed to deter its development of nuclear weapons. Some of the sanctions targeted sales of Iranian oil in world markets. Oil revenue produces 80 percent of government revenues, and by mid-2013, oil revenue had been cut in half. Others cut Iran off from global networks that allow banks to move money electronically from one country to another. As a result, Iranian entrepreneurs could no longer use electronic transfers of funds to pay for goods from foreign companies. Instead, they had to send "suitcases of cash through street-level money changers to shady bankers abroad."[94] Consumers have to pay much more for imported goods because of the falling value of the Iranian currency against the dollar.

Despite its economic difficulties, the Iranian regime succeeded in improving citizens' capabilities in education and health. Ayatollah Khomeini and his successors have made progress in achieving their goal of improving the lives of poor Iranians. Poverty rates have dropped considerably, and access to education and health care have improved for poor families. Life expectancy has increased. Access to educational opportunities have expanded for girls, especially for those from rural families, and a higher percentage of women than men now graduate from college. The Islamic Republic has also reduced infant mortality rates by focusing on providing clean water and health care services to villages, even in remote parts of the country.[95]

Despite these achievements, the regime is not assured of remaining in power. As we noted in the discussion of electoral authoritarian regimes, the most stable have a strong ruling party that has institutionalized means for making the transition from one leader to another. Iran does not have such a political party. This matters because the leaders of the three major factions are all aging veterans of the 1979 revolution. It remains to be seen whether the ruling group can make a smooth transition from one Supreme Leader to another. In addition, the Green Movement that emerged in 2009 demonstrated that millions of Iranians can be mobilized to press for political change. The 2011 Arab Spring showed that such uprisings can topple authoritarian regimes where military and security forces are not willing to suppress demonstrators by killing large numbers of them. In Iran, they were indeed prepared to do so in 2009, but a Supreme Leader who depends on the military and security forces to stay in power makes himself beholden to them.

Comparing Capabilities Among Brazil, Nigeria, and Iran

10.8 Compare capabilities in Brazil, Nigeria, and Iran.

We profiled Brazil, Nigeria, and Iran because they typify regimes with different degrees of democracy found in developing countries. Brazil is a flawed democracy, Nigeria a semi-democracy, and Iran an example of electoral authoritarianism. A comparison of how these countries perform in terms of our criteria for the good society provides clues to how the main features of each type of democracy promotes, or hinders, citizens' capabilities.

Physical Well-Being

In Chapter 1, we argued that infant mortality rates are the best indicator of well-being. All three countries achieved improvements in infant mortality between 1990 and 2010. In percentage terms, Brazil had the most success, with a 66 percent decline, followed by Iran with 56 percent and Nigeria with 30 percent. See Table 10.2.

The table indicates only a slight correlation between degree of democracy and decline in infant mortality. Brazil is the most democratic of the three and achieved the largest percentage decline, but authoritarian Iran had similar levels of success. Nigeria trailed both, in part because of its lower level of economic development.

Informed Decision Making

The pattern for literacy is similar to that for infant mortality, with Brazil having the best record, followed by Iran and then Nigeria. One of Brazil's biggest successes has been increasing school attendance and literacy among children

Table 10.2 Infant Mortality Rates per 1,000 Live Births

	1990	2000	2010	% Change
Brazil	50	29	17	66
Nigeria	126	107	88	30
Iran	50	28	22	56

SOURCE: Human Development Indicators, *Human Development Report 2013*, United Nations Development Programme, www.google.com/publicdata; and World Bank, Human Development Indicators, http://data.worldbank.org/indicator/SP.DYN.IMRT.IN?page=2.

Table 10.3 Adult Literacy Rates, 15 Years Old and Older, Selected Years

	2000–2003	2008–2010
Brazil	86%	90%
Nigeria	55%	60%
Iran	77%	85%

SOURCE: World Bank, World Development Indicators, http://data.worldbank.org/indicator/SE.ADT.LITR.ZS/countries.

from poor families, whereas one of Iran's biggest successes has been increasing educational access for girls. Nigeria, by contrast, has had very limited improvements in literacy. See Table 10.3.

Safety

Safety levels, as operationally defined by homicide rates, does not fit the previous pattern. Brazil has the highest level of democracy but also has the highest homicide level by far. Nigeria's is also relatively high. In Iran, however, the homicide rate is extremely low, comparable to that in several Western European democracies. See Table 10.4.

These data on homicide must be treated with caution because they do not provide a sense of how safety for individuals differs by region and social class. Nigerian Christians living in communities that border predominantly Muslim populations are not likely to feel as safe as those in the southern parts of the country. Poor Brazilians living in the huge urban slums known as *favelas* are not as likely to feel as safe as wealthy Brazilians, who dwell in exclusive neighborhoods. Nor can Iranians who have the courage to challenge the regime openly feel as safe as regime supporters.

Democracy

Individuals' ability to participate in political choices that govern their lives is essential for sustaining conditions that improve their health, education, and safety. Authoritarian governments can make decisions to improve these

Table 10.4 Homicide Rates in Brazil, Iran, and Nigeria, per 100,000 People, 2011

Brazil	22.7
Nigeria	12.2
Iran	3.0

SOURCE: UNODC Global Study on Homicide 2011, http://www.unodc.org/unodc/en/data-and-analysis/homicide.html.

Table 10.5 Democracy Ratings for Brazil, Nigeria, and Iran

Brazil	7.12
Nigeria	3.77
Iran	1.98

SOURCE: The Economist Intelligence Unit, *Democracy Index 2012: Democracy at a Standstill*.

capabilities, as they have in Iran, but without the right to political participation, free speech, and association, citizens cannot be assured that governments will continue along that pattern. There are considerable differences in the ability to participate effectively among Nigeria, Brazil, and Iran. See Table 10.5.

In the *Economist* Democracy Index for 2012, Brazil ranks highest of the three countries, with Nigeria in the middle and Iran a distant third.[96]

As is the case with safety, there are big differences within countries in citizens' ability to exercise their civil and political liberties. Although Brazil is a flawed democracy, its extremely high levels of income inequality give wealthier Brazilians greater ability to exercise their civil and political rights than poor Brazilians. In Nigeria, large numbers of citizens live in extreme poverty. These citizens have very limited ability to exercise civil and political rights. In Iran, all citizens have limited civil and political rights, but women have been singled out for discriminatory treatment.

In summary, with the exception of homicide, Brazil does a better job than Nigeria or Iran in creating conditions that enhance the capabilities of its citizens.

Conclusion

In this chapter, we have evaluated three countries with varying degrees of democracy in developing countries with a representative example for each. One main conclusion is that democratic regimes differ not only by type, whether presidential or parliamentary, but also by the degree of democracy they offer. A related point is that it is too simple to divide countries into democracies and authoritarian regimes. There are degrees of authoritarianism as well as degrees of democracy. Although Iran is clearly not as democratic as Brazil, it is more democratic than Saudi Arabia. Its presidential elections do present citizens with a choice of leaders who offer alternative policy choices. These elections can also result in surprise victories, as happened in 2013 when Hassan Rouhani defeated candidates preferred by the Supreme Leader.

The second conclusion is that authoritarian regimes do not have a clear advantage over democracies in decision making. Contrary to claims that authoritarian regimes can make decisions quickly and effectively because they do not have to be concerned about offending vested interests, we saw that the military in Nigeria and the clerics in Iran were clearly hampered in decision making by vested interests. The military in Nigeria was hampered by massive rent seeking by officials and businesspeople with ties to the officials. Clerics in Iran are hampered by factional struggles and the power of vested interests. Many leading clerics have personal interests in maintaining Iran's present economic policies and so do the constituencies with which they have close ties, such as the *bonyads* and Revolutionary Guards. In contrast, democratically elected governments in Brazil in recent decades have made decisions that eased the country's perpetual economic crises, contributed to economic growth, and raised millions of citizens out of poverty.

Finally, although the governments of Brazil and Iran both have brought down infant mortality rates and increased educational opportunities for the children of poor families, poor Brazilians have more opportunity to participate effectively in political choices that affect their lives than do their poor Iranian counterparts. The poor in Brazil form an important voting constituency of the Workers' Party. Leaders of the Workers' Party strive to improve their capabilities not just because of ideological commitments but because they need their votes to win office. Competitive elections are decisive in determining who holds the most powerful offices in Brazil, and they give the poor political leverage. In Iran, competitive elections are not decisive in determining who holds the most powerful political offices or in shaping regime policies.

Suggested Readings

Wendy Hunter, *The Transformation of the Worker's Party in Brazil, 1989–2009* (New York, Cambridge University Press, 2010). Excellent discussion of the Worker's Party; the rise of its leader, Lula, to become the most popular president in Brazil's history; and how Lula and party leaders adapted to the realities of governing Brazil.

Wendy Hunter and Natasha Borges Sukiyama, "Democracy and Social Policy in Brazil: Advancing Basic Needs, Preserving Privileged Interests" *Latin American Politics and Society* 51:2 (2009), pp. 29–57. A clear explanation of why improvements in the capabilities of poor Brazilians are difficult because politically influential groups can protect their entitlements and block efforts to reallocate resources to the poor.

Paul M. Lubeck, "Mapping a Sharia Restorationist Movement," in *Sharia Politics: Islamic Law and Society in the Modern World*, Robert Hefner, (ed.), (Bloomington, IN: University of Indiana Press, 2011), pp. 247–248. Insightful, well-informed explanation of why sharia politics has become so important in Nigeria. Available at http://escholarship.org/uc/item/436307k8.

Michael Axworthy, *Revolutionary Iran: A History of the Islamic Republic* (New York: Oxford University Press, 2013), Readable, insightful analysis of how Ayatollah Khomeini led a revolution in Iran and the clerical regime he established with vivid accounts of personalities and events.

The Iran Primer: Power, Politics, and U.S Policy. Robin Wright (ed.). (Washington, DC: United States Institute of Peace Press, 2010) A useful source for beginning to learn about Iran's politics, foreign policy, economics, and nuclear program with short well-written articles by experts on Iran. Each article is available in PDF format at http://iranprimer.usip.org/.

Critical Thinking Questions

1. Why has Nigeria had so little success in achieving economic and human development despite huge revenues from oil?
2. How would someone using the institutionalist approach (chapter 8) explain why Brazil is more developed than Nigeria?
3. Why are broad-based associations and political parties more important for the improvement of capabilities for poor Brazilians than for wealthier Brazilians?
4. If the goal is to improve capabilities, does it really make any difference whether poor families in Iran get better health care through authoritarian means or democratic ones?
5. Why has the reformist faction in Iran not been more successful in its struggles to liberalize politics and cultural policy?

Chapter 11
Communism, Postcommunism, and the Good Society

Learning Objectives

11.1 Understand the impact of the collapse of the Soviet Union on the remaining communist regimes.

11.2 Describe the two main features of communist regimes in the 20th century and explain the flaws of centrally planned economies based on state-owned firms.

11.3 Describe the history, state, relations between state and society, political culture, and political economy of Russia.

11.4 Describe the history, state, relations between state and society, political culture, and political economy of China.

11.5 Compare and contrast capabilities in Russia and China.

Introduction

11.1 Understand the impact of the collapse of the Soviet Union on the remaining communist regimes.

In 1986, a participant at a conference of specialists on the Soviet Union asked "whether the Soviet Union would collapse" during their lifetimes. Other participants laughed out loud at the apparent absurdity of the question. To them, the Soviet Union was an international superpower whose leaders were firmly in control of the population.[1] Just five years later, the Soviet Union broke apart into several independent countries. The largest of these is Russia.

Many in the United States and Europe rejoiced over the collapse of the Communist Party's rule in the Soviet Union and hoped that democratic politics and market economics would emerge in Russia. These hopes, however, have been dashed. Russia has become an authoritarian regime with an economy dominated by state-owned corporations and business empires owned by wealthy oligarchs.[2]

The leaders of the world's remaining communist regimes had a very different reaction to the Soviet collapse. They were shocked by its fall and left with the task of trying to understand what went wrong so that they did not follow their Soviet counterpart into oblivion. This chapter examines how leaders of Russia shaped a new regime, how the leaders of China adapted to the Soviet collapse, and how these changing circumstances affected their citizens' capabilities.

The chapter is divided into four parts. The first describes the institutional features that defined communist regimes for much of the 20th century. The second examines Russia's personalist regime, and the third examines China's one-party regime. Section four compares capabilities in the two countries.

The Institutional Basis of Communist Regimes

11.2 Describe the two main features of communist regimes in the 20th century and explain the flaws of centrally planned economies based on state-owned firms.

For most of the 20th century, communist regimes shared two features that distinguished them from other types of authoritarian regimes, namely Communist party control of the state and state-owned, centrally planned economies.

Communist Party Rule

Communist Party
A political party based on Marxist beliefs and organized as a vanguard party to lead workers and peasants in revolution to overthrow capitalism and build socialism and communism.

Communist parties are vanguard parties led by an elite who claim to speak on behalf of the working class. They believe they understand the long-term interests of workers better than workers themselves. From their perspective, workers tend to focus on short-term issues such as working conditions, pay, and hours of work and are unable to grasp that the only way they can permanently improve their lives is by overthrowing capitalism and building a communist society. The role of a Communist party is thus to provide direction in achieving these goals.

In countries ruled by Communist parties, the party and state have separate organizational hierarchies with the party in charge of the state. Major policy decisions are made by the top party leadership and subsequently implemented by government agencies. During the 20th century, the party in these countries also tended to exercise tight control over all aspects of society. No competing

In-Depth: Socialism and Communism

Socialism (Karl Marx)
The transitional period preceding communism, during which workers hold political power and use that power to expropriate private property.

Communism (Karl Marx)
The economic system that follows socialism. Communist societies have no division of labor, no social classes, and no state, along with no private ownership of banks, businesses, or factories. Communist societies were to be societies of abundance in which the criterion for the production and distribution of goods was to be "from each according to his ability; to each according to his needs."

According to Karl Marx, a German-born economist and philosopher, (1818–1883), all societies are based on the exploitation of one social class by another. Slave-holding, feudal, and capitalist societies all have in common economies in which one social class owns the means of production and lives off the surplus produced by others. Masters exploited slaves, feudal lords exploited serfs, and capitalists exploit workers. The state and legal system of each type of society are designed to reinforce these exploitative relationships.

For Marx, just as feudalism was replaced by capitalism, capitalism will be replaced by communism. Capitalism, in his view, produces a revolutionary working class that will overthrow it and institute a new order. The economic system established immediately after the overthrow of capitalism will be **socialism**. It will have a division of labor in which citizens are paid based on their contribution to society. Workers will be the dominant class, not capitalists, and the state will defend their interests, and prevent capitalists from returning to power. Socialism will evolve eventually into **communism**. In communist societies, there will be no division of labor, no social classes, and no state. Private ownership of banks, businesses, and factories will end. Communist societies will be societies of abundance in which the criterion for the production and distribution of goods will be "from each according to their ability; to each according to their needs."

Leaders of communist parties who seized power in the name of workers in Russia, parts of Asia, and Cuba made revolutions in the name of Marxism and typically described the societies they founded as socialist. The regimes found in these countries are commonly called communist, but this is because they are led by communist parties, not because they have become communist societies as defined by Karl Marx.

political parties or organizations were permitted. Labor unions, youth and women's groups, and even sports associations were all party-affiliated.

State-Owned, Centrally Planned Economies

The second main institutional feature of 20th-century communist regimes was the prevalence of state-owned firms whose production and sales were coordinated by **central planning**. Economic planners decided the type, quantity, and price of the goods that each factory produced. Farms were either owned by the state or collectively owned by farmers, but collective ownership was meaningless because the state determined what such farms would plant and what they would charge for their crops. Communist party leaders defined socialist economies based on this conjunction of state ownership and central planning.

Although such economies can produce rapid growth for a few decades, they eventually tend toward economic stagnation because state-owned, centrally planned economies lack incentives for managers and workers to improve efficiency, productivity, and innovation. They can be good at achieving **extensive growth**, which entails mobilizing large amounts of labor and material to build or produce things, but they are not adept at promoting **intensive growth**, which rests on technological improvements and economic innovation. To avoid stagnation, it is necessary to make the transition from the former to the latter. The difference between extensive and intensive growth can be illustrated by ditch digging. Two men working with shovels can dig a ditch faster than one man, and ten men can do so faster than two. Similar logic applies to factory production. Adding workers and raw materials can increase a factory's output. However, this kind of growth has limits. Although ten men might be more productive at digging a ditch than two, 10,000 would simply get in each other's way. Similarly, 100 workers in a factory might produce twice as much as 50, but 1,000 won't necessarily produce 10 times more than 100.

Another flaw of centrally planned economies is that they create few incentives for being smarter about how to use resources. Workers have little incentive to work hard because they know they will never be fired. Managers have little incentive to raise productivity because their firms have no competition and will never go bankrupt. They are paid for meeting their factory's quota, not for producing higher-quality products. The best way to achieve quotas is to use time-tested production methods.

Central Planning
An economic model in which decisions about what is produced, how much is produced, and at what price it is sold, are made by a state planning agency.

Extensive Growth
Economic growth achieved by mobilizing large amounts of labor and material to build or produce products.

Intensive Growth
Economic growth achieved by using labor and material more efficiently, resulting mainly from technological improvements and economic innovation.

Russia

11.3 Describe the history, state, relations between state and society, political culture, and political economy of Russia.

In this section, we examine Russia as a case study of a postcommunist regime. It is no longer ruled by a Communist party, but past Communist party rule continues to affect its political and economic situation in significant ways.

President Vladimir Putin, shaping his image as a tough, personalist ruler.

Its first president, Boris Yeltsin, was one of the highest-ranking members of the Communist Party of the Soviet Union. Its second president, Vladimir Putin, was a lieutenant colonel in the KGB, the state security agency of the Soviet Union. Russia's current state security agency is a direct descendant of its Soviet predecessor and is President Putin's most important power base. President Putin's vision of a highly centralized state with power in the hands of a single leader at the top draws heavily on the Soviet model, and although the economy now has many privately owned firms, state-owned firms dominate important sectors of the economy, especially the all-important oil and gas industries.

Russia, formally known as the Russian Federation, has the largest land area of any country in the world. Its population of approximately 142 million is 45 percent that of the United States' population. Russia is one of the two largest oil-producing countries and the second largest producer of natural gas. Its other natural resources include coal, copper, diamonds, and gold. Approximately 80 percent of the population is ethnically Russian, but close to 100 ethnic groups make up the rest of the population. The North Caucasus region in southern Russia has a large Muslim population.

Historical Background

The autocratic czarist regime that had ruled Russia since the 16th century collapsed in 1917. World War I revealed the regime's poor civilian and military leadership. Russian troops were poorly equipped and led. As defeats accumulated and central authority weakened, soldiers deserted the army, peasants seized land owned by nobles, and workers took over factories. The czar was forced to abdicate, and a provisional government was formed to lead the country.

By late 1917, Vladimir Lenin, the leader of a wing of the Russian Social Democratic Labor Party known as the Bolsheviks, believed that the weaknesses of the provisional government provided an opportunity to seize power in the name of workers, even though Russia did not meet the standard criteria for a socialist revolution. Peasants constituted 80 percent of the population, workers were but a small minority, and capitalism was poorly developed.

No one was more surprised at the success of the 1917 October Revolution in Russia than many of the Bolsheviks. They came to power without a blueprint for how to build socialism and communism, and much of what they did was in reaction to the rush of events. The new government was beset by domestic and foreign enemies intent on defeating it. The Bolsheviks responded forcefully. Lenin eliminated all opposition political parties, giving the Communist Party a monopoly of power. He created an internal security force to collect intelligence and arrest opponents.

The Bolsheviks adopted what they called the New Economic Policy (NEP) in 1921. The state assumed control of banks and major businesses but left small firms in the hands of owners. Peasants were allowed to keep land they had seized from their landlords. The NEP recognized private property and included a place for market exchange. Many party members and most citizens assumed the NEP would be in place for a long time.

However, when Joseph Stalin came to power, he initiated dramatic economic changes that created the characteristic institutions of Soviet socialism.

The economic revolution of the 1920s and 1930s had three parts. First, Stalin collectivized agriculture. Collectivized agriculture gave the state control over supplies of grain, which were used both to feed urban workers and earn foreign exchange required to develop Soviet industry. When farmers resisted collectivization, Stalin ordered security and military forces to crush them and ordered food to be withheld from peasants to weaken their defiance. This decision caused a famine that killed millions.[3]

The second part of Stalin's "revolution from above" was the creation of a state-owned, centrally planned economy. Stalin chose to invest in power plants, steel, railroads, infrastructure, and military equipment at the expense of consumer goods.

In addition to transforming the economy, Stalin increased the use of terror to annihilate his opponents in the party, government, and military. Party leaders who had worked with Stalin since the revolution of 1917 were falsely accused of collaborating with foreign spies, prosecuted in elaborate show trials, forced to confess their guilt, and then executed. Thousands of other party members were also killed. As many as 700,000 perished in these purges.[4] Ordinary people also were terrorized. Hundreds of thousands were executed. Others were arrested and sent to labor camps in Siberia.[5] Scholars debate the number of people who died because of Stalin' policies. The estimates range from one million upward.[6]

After Stalin died in 1953, his personal rule was replaced by a system of power sharing. The party leader's personnel and policy choices were constrained by other high-ranking party members. Soviet politics became more stable, and the economy continued to grow. In the 1960s and 1970s, most people in the United States viewed the U.S.S.R. as a superpower and a formidable military threat.

Beneath this impressive appearance, however, the Soviet Union was in serious economic trouble. By 1980, extensive economic growth had reached its limits, and central planning discouraged efficient production and the development of new technologies, but many Communist party members, government officials, and factory managers continued to live well and had no incentive to make changes. A new generation of leaders that emerged in the 1980s acknowledged that the Soviet Union was falling further and further behind the West and that it was essential to reform the system to save it.

In 1985, Mikhail Gorbachev became head of the Communist Party and began reforms aimed at renewing economic growth. The reforms led instead to the collapse of the Soviet Union. Gorbachev pursued three strategies: *glasnost, perestroika,* and *demokratizatsiia.* **Glasnost**, or openness, encouraged freer expression of opinion. Gorbachev hoped reducing censorship and letting information flow more freely would enable citizens to express their criticisms of economic shortcomings. This would create momentum for reform by placing the obstructionist wing of the Communist Party on the defensive and build support for Gorbachev's reform program. **Perestroika**, usually translated

Glasnost
Used to describe Soviet leader Mikhail Gorbachev's policy in the late 1980s of "openness," in which freer expression of opinion was encouraged within the Soviet Union.

Perestroika
Policy followed by Soviet leader Mikhail Gorbachev in the 1980s to describe his policy of restructuring, or loosening state control of the economy and creating more freedom for firms to respond to consumer demand.

as restructuring, aimed at loosening state control of the economy and creating more freedom for firms to respond to demands from consumers. Finally, *demokratizatsiia* shifted some power from the Communist Party to the government by creating new legislative institutions and allowing competitive elections. Gorbachev hoped candidates supporting his program would form a majority in the legislature.

Gorbachev's ambitious reforms divided the Communist Party. For the party's conservative elements, the reforms went too far too fast; for progressives, they went neither far nor fast enough. In a classic example of insiders overthrowing a leader, conservatives struck first. Hard-liners in the party, military, and state security led a coup d'état against Gorbachev in August 1991. The effort collapsed after only a few days, discrediting opponents of reform, but it also weakened Gorbachev when it became known that some of the coup leaders had been members of his government.

The winner in this struggle was Boris Yeltsin. Yeltsin had been a protégé of Gorbachev, but the reforms went too slowly for him, and he became increasingly critical. Gorbachev dismissed him from the inner ranks of the Communist Party, but Gorbachev's efforts to introduce a degree of democracy in the Soviet Union had created institutions that gave Yeltsin an alternative route to power. In June 1991, he was elected President of the Russian Republic and won popular acclaim for his leadership in thwarting the conservatives' coup effort against Gorbachev in August. Yeltsin realized that the way to defeat Gorbachev was to cause the collapse of the U.S.S.R. With no Soviet Union, Gorbachev would have no country to govern. Thus, Yeltsin schemed with presidents of the other republics to withdraw from the Soviet Union and become independent countries. It was a winning strategy. In December 1991, the Soviet Union came to an end. Its 15 republics all formed independent countries, with Russia being the largest.

The State

Russia's constitution provides for a strong **president**. The president is elected by popular vote, and as of 2012, presidents could remain in office for two consecutive six-year terms. Presidents have authority to appoint and dismiss the prime minister and members of the Cabinet and to issue decrees that have the force of law so long as they do not violate the constitution. The president determines Russia's overall domestic and foreign policy, is commander-in-chief of the armed forces, and controls the Russian Security Council, which coordinates Russia's security agencies as well as government ministries with responsibility for foreign affairs and defense. The most powerful of these agencies is the **Federal Security Service (FSB)**. Responsible for internal security, counter-terrorism, and control of Russia's borders, it collects information on Russian citizens and intelligence on other countries.

President (Russia)
The most powerful political office in Russia. The president was elected by voters for four year terms, but beginning in 2012, the term is six years.

Federal Security Service (FSB)
Government agency responsible for internal security, counter-terrorism, and control of Russia's borders.

Map 11.1 Russia
SOURCE: CIA World Fact Book

Country	Population	Infant Mortality	Life Expectancy	Adult Literacy	Capital City	GDP Per Capita (PPP)	Labor Force by Occupation
Russia	142,470,000 (2013 estimate)	9.8 deaths/ 1,000 live births	70	100%	Moscow	$18,100 (2013 estimate)	Agriculture: 9.7% Industry: 27.8% Services: 62.5% (2013)

The **prime minister** must be approved by the lower house of parliament, the State Duma, but unlike prime ministers in parliamentary systems, such as Great Britain's and Sweden's, the prime minister requires the president's support, not the parliament's, to stay in office. Prime ministers are responsible for managing the day-to-day business of the government and focus primarily on economic and social policy.

The bicameral legislature, or **Federal Assembly**, is weak and has no power to challenge presidential policies. Its upper house, the **Federation Council**, represents Russia's 83 regional governments and has 166 members—two from each region regardless of population. A region's governor chooses one of the representatives and the region's legislature chooses the other.

The lower house, the **State Duma**, has 450 deputies directly elected by voters to four-year terms. Constitutionally, the State Duma is the more powerful of the two chambers. The constitution gives it an influential role in shaping legislation, but in practice, it has little influence. Almost all the legislation it passes is written by advisers to the president and is approved as written. United Russia, a political party supporting President Vladimir Putin, has held a majority of seats in the Duma since 2003.

Russia has a Constitutional Court to decide controversies among political institutions and to rule on the constitutionality of laws. The Court has been

Prime Minister (Russia)
Head of the cabinet appointed by the president and in charge of day to day government operations.

Federal Assembly
Russia's bicameral legislature composed of the Federation Council and the State Duma.

Federation Council
Russia's upper house which represents Russia's regional administrative divisions.

State Duma
Russia's lower house whose members are elected by proportional representation.

Figure 11.1 Russian Political Institutions

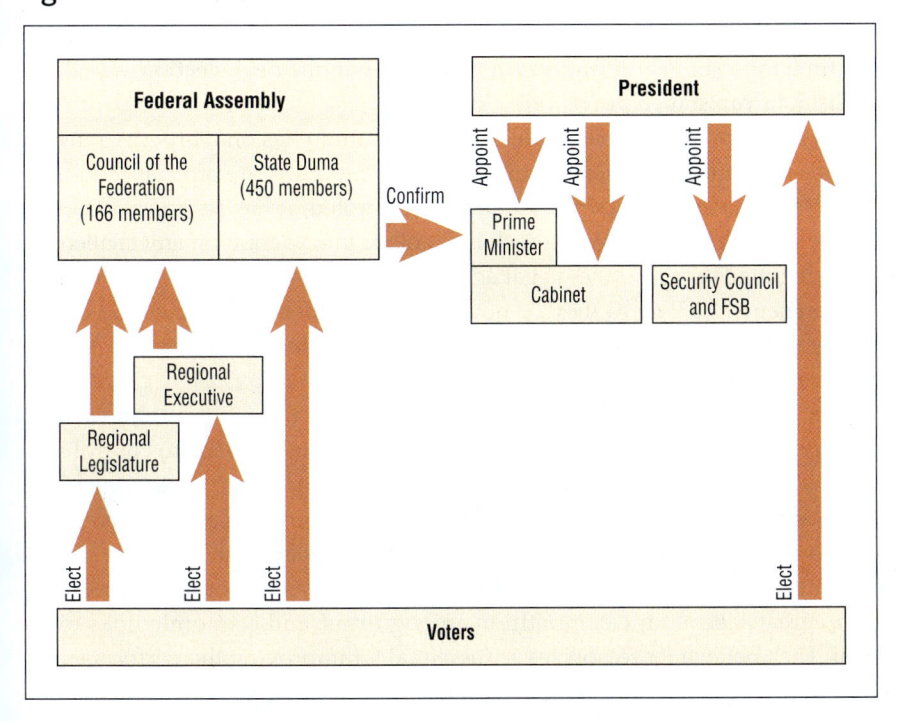

cautious about challenging the president. In addition to the Constitutional Court, a system of courts handles civil and criminal cases, with the Supreme Court at the top of the hierarchy. These courts have a reputation for corruption and susceptibility to political influence.

One of President Putin's main goals upon being elected president in 2000 was to reassert central government control over regional governments. During the Soviet years, regional units of government had been tightly controlled from Moscow by the Communist Party, but the collapse of the Soviet regime gave regional leaders opportunities to build power and accumulate wealth. President Yeltsin's strategy was to share power with them, hoping to hold the country together and construct a federal system of government. Putin reversed this approach, gaining control over how governors are selected and subordinating them to his wishes. The result of these changes was to create what Putin terms "the power vertical," or the "hierarchical subordination of sub-national authorities by the ruling elite."[7]

President Putin has created a system of personal rule in which he is the ultimate authority. He governs with the help of an inner circle of trusted advisers. Personal relationships rather than constitutional rules determine who has power.[8] The discrepancy between what the constitution says and how power is actually exercised is illustrated by the way President Putin circumvented term limits on his presidency. After serving his allotted two terms as president from 2000 to 2008, he switched positions with his prime minister between 2008 and 2012. Despite the constitution's directive that the president has ultimate authority, there was no question that Putin reigned supreme while he was prime minister. In 2012, he became eligible to run for president again and won the election, this time for a six-year term. If he manages to win the next election, scheduled for 2018, he can stay in power until 2024.

In addition to his inner circle, President Putin relies on a broader range of officials to maintain political control. The most important are officials in the FSB, Russia's state security agency. As previously noted, it has responsibilities for internal security, and part of its task is to collect information on any challengers of the regime, including the illegal activities of other state officials and wealthy entrepreneurs. As long as they do not threaten President Putin, they can engage in illegal activities with impunity, but otherwise, Putin can use any dirt the FSB uncovers to prosecute and imprison them.

Politics in Russia is largely about competition among rival networks, comprising wealthy business people allied with state officials, to control state offices. Two large networks have dominated the struggle for power. One is centered on the Federal Security Service (FSB) and has links to officials managing state enterprises and conservative leaders of the Russian Orthodox Church. The other network includes officials and business people who support private enterprise, greater economic competition among firms, and economic links to the West. They believe these policies are essential for improving the performance of the stagnating Russian economy. The networks' main goals are to accumulate wealth and expand their influence over state policies.[9] Russia lacks institutionalized means for resolving this competition. Instead, President Putin serves as the arbiter among competing networks, determining how billions of dollars of state revenues are allocated. For most of his time in power he has tried to balance power between the two main networks so that neither became dominant, but since returning to the presidency in 2012 has favored the FSB network.[10]

Although Putin successfully centralized state power in his hands, the state itself remains relatively ineffective as measured by "the quality of the civil service, its independence from political pressures," and its ability to implement policies.[11] According to the World Bank, the Russian state is less effective than those of China and Brazil and far less effective than those of Sweden, Germany, and Great Britain.[12] There are highly capable, dedicated civil servants in some Russian ministries and government offices. For example, officials responsible for fiscal and monetary policy did an admirable job of managing economic policy between 2000 and 2010. On the other hand, in many agencies, the unwritten contract among officials and President Putin is that loyalty to him gives them "a license to steal."[13] The more powerful the officials, the higher the bribes they can demand.[14] Corruption extends from top to bottom of the bureaucracy. Many officials are up for sale; they act in their individual interests, not to achieve the stated goals of their agency. These officials include judges, who take payoffs to decide cases in favor of the highest bidder. As a young lawyer explains the process, "I go to a judge and say, 'I really need to win this case.' He says, let's say, 100,000 rubles. I go to my client and tell him 130,000."[15] Airport security officers also accept bribes. In 2004, two women paid an airport security agent the equivalent of $170 to let them into the boarding area. They boarded separate airplanes, and soon after taking off, both airplanes exploded, killing 89 passengers. The two women turned out to be suicide bombers.[16] In 2012, Transparency International ranked Russia as more corrupt than several poor sub-Saharan African countries, including Uganda, Sierra Leone, and Mozambique. Of 174 rankings, in which some countries tied for the same ranking, Russia ranked 133.[17]

State and Society

Like other authoritarian rulers, Vladimir Putin has used three strategies to control society: provide benefits to win support, rig elections, and use repression. His main way of building support was to increase citizens' incomes after he became president in 2000. This stratagem was made possible by dramatic increases in the world price of oil, Russia's main export. Oil sales dramatically increased state revenues, and the administration funneled the revenues into the economy, "largely through state-led investment projects."[18] The incomes of middle-class Russian rose rapidly between 2000 and 2010. In addition to higher incomes, they benefited from "moderate inflation, affordable mortgages, access to higher education, satellite television, Internet connections, passports, foreign visas and—above all else—no economic shocks."[19] Putin did not cause the increase in world oil prices, but he did take credit for the economic benefits they brought.

United Russia
Russia's dominant ruling political party.

Allowing multiparty elections is a second strategy for maintaining control of society. The regime's political party is **United Russia**. It was created in 2003 to win presidential elections for President Putin and ensure victories in State Duma elections for candidates supporting President Putin.[20] Other political parties are allowed to compete; Putin and his advisers do not seek to eliminate competition entirely because it provides useful information about public preferences and grievances. The important point is that this competition is controlled. The authorities want "managed democracy" in which they are guaranteed to win elections.[21]

To ensure this, they tilt the playing field in favor of United Russia. One way of doing so is to restrict the number of political parties. Election regulations make it difficult for opposition parties to register and find financing. These regulations reduced the number of officially recognized political parties from 44 in 2003 to 10 in 2009.[22] In the 2011 State Duma election, only four parties won seats. Likewise, the authorities have also created political parties to give the appearance that there are viable alternatives to United Russia. The consequence is that "party competition is more nominal than real," and voters cannot have "meaningful choices over policy alternatives."[23] During elections, major media outlets give United Russia's candidates extensive coverage while denying it to other parties. Journalists critical of United Russia are harassed by tax authorities, sued in courts, and even arrested.[24]

Oligarchs
Extremely wealthy businesspeople in Russia who used political connections in the 1990s to establish banks, gain control of television stations, and become owners of valuable natural resources.

The third strategy President Putin and his advisers employ is outright repression. Their first targets after taking power were certain billionaires who came to be known as **oligarchs**. These men had used political connections and entrepreneurial skills to establish banks, gain control of television stations, and purchase oil companies. Although they enjoyed great influence over government policy when Boris Yeltsin was president, Putin had no intention of allowing that influence to continue during his presidency. After he took office in 2000, two of the oligarchs used their television stations to criticize his policies. Putin met with 20 of the oligarchs, telling them they could keep their wealth only if they stayed out of politics. Soon afterward, prosecutors announced legal charges against the two who had criticized President Putin. Stripped of their main assets, including their television stations, both went into exile.[25] In 2003, Mikhail Khodorkovsky, another oligarch, who owned the Yukos oil company and opposed some of Putin's policies for the oil industry, was arrested and sentenced to a nine-year prison term. Yukos was taken over by the state.[26] In 2010, Khodorkovsky was found guilty on dubious charges of embezzlement and sentenced to six more years in prison, although he was pardoned by Putin and released from prison in December, 2013. Other oligarchs have gotten the message and become more cooperative, fearing they will suffer a similar fate.

The regime has also suppressed human rights organizations and groups protesting environmental destruction, mainly by using laws and regulations rather than brute force. Authorities examine their tax records, find them guilty of nonpayment, and then charge exorbitant fines intended to bankrupt them. Building inspectors examine buildings where their offices are located and close them for failure to meet building codes. International organizations such as Amnesty International and Human Rights Watch have been closed temporarily, and many of their Russian counterparts have been closed permanently.

Putin has suppressed free media by taking control of television stations, newspapers, and magazines through which over 90 percent of Russians get their news about politics. When he came into power, the state owned only one of the television stations; the other two were the property of oligarchs, but the oligarchs' stations are now owned by the state. Not surprisingly, they heap praise on the government's accomplishments and portray Putin as a tough, decisive, and manly leader. He is shown demonstrating his judo skills, hunting shirtless in rugged terrain, riding a horse shirtless in Siberia, and arm wrestling a much bigger man.[27]

Independent sources of information and news do exist. Citizens can use the Internet to get access to news that is not controlled by the state. The authorities allow such access because it allows them to claim there is freedom of expression in Russia and because it provides them with intelligence about developments in society.[28] Recently, however, the authorities have become increasingly aggressive about closing access to websites banned by the government. They also use technologies that allow officials to read e-mails, track users, and monitor social networks.[29]

Finally, through its control of the police and the judicial system, the regime also uses arrests, trials, and imprisonment to silence critics. One example is that of Alexei Navalny, a Russian blogger with a large following, who exposes corrupt government officials. He is best known for labelling United Russia "the party of crooks and thieves." In retaliation, the government charged him with stealing several hundred thousand dollars from a timber company, and in 2013, a court found him guilty.[30] Navalny's sentence was subsequently suspended, but he was later banned from using the Internet. Other critics convicted of crimes have suffered worse fates. In the past decade, journalists critical of the regime have been threatened and beaten, and several have been murdered.

Despite these efforts, the regime's control over society appeared to be waning in 2011. Putin's approval rating had dropped, and United Russia was also losing support. By 2013, a majority of Russians agreed with Navalny's characterization of the party as "the party of crooks and thieves."[31] There are three main reasons for the reduced support. One was growing anger over corruption, especially among the educated, urban middle class and owners of private businesses. Motorists were tired of police stopping them and demanding bribes, and store owners resented having to pay safety inspectors or risk the closure of their businesses.

Another reason for growing discontent was the widespread feeling that nothing was going to change politically. Citizens had no way of holding officials accountable, and Putin seemed determined to hold on to power for years to come. A final reason was an increase in the numbers of citizens holding self-expression values. Many members of Russia's growing middle class, who no longer had to worry about scraping by economically, had begun to focus on personal well-being and political liberty.[32]

This discontent erupted in open protest after the rigged election for the State Duma a in 2011. United Russia failed to win a majority of votes for the first time, despite falsifying election results, and its number of seats fell from 315 to 238.[33] Demonstrators braved bitterly cold weather to demand political reforms and an end to suffocating corruption and abuses of power. It was by far the largest public protest in Russia since Vladimir Putin became president.[34] More large protests followed in the spring of 2012. Although President Putin won reelection that year, it was with a much lower percentage of the vote than he had received in previous contests.

Analysts agreed that the protests marked a change in Russian politics but differed about its significance. One reason for doubting that the protests represented a turning point was that most protestors did not belong to organizations capable of sustained, effective collective action.[35] As Maria Lipman, Russian specialist at the Carnegie Foundation, wrote, "Frustration and anger are a far cry from developing a collective voice and the bargaining power required for raising serious demands vis-à-vis the government."[36]

Furthermore, it is misleading to portray the Russian middle class as a vanguard of democracy. The middle class is not united in its political views. Instead, it comprises three distinct groups: entrepreneurs who support the rule of law and clearly defined property rights to protect them from corrupt officials; mid-level managers at large, state-owned companies and multinational corporations who care about their quality of life but have little interest in broader political issues; and finally, state officials, many of whom support the status quo. As political scientist Sam Greene points out, these groups "are not only not unified. They're often at cross-purposes."[37]

In 2014, Putin's approval ratings began to climb. One reason was increased Russian patriotism stemming from the success of Russian athletes at the Winter Olympics held in Sochi, Russia in January. They won the most medals of any country. The other, more important reason, was his decision to seize control of Crimea from the neighboring country of Ukraine in March 2014, In the aftermath of the invasion President Putin's approval ratings soared to 80 percent. Intensified patriotic feelings, and his increasing personal popularity, made it easier for him to suppress his critics. They were condemned for being anti-Russian and puppets of the United States.

Political Culture

Russian political culture has been shaped by Russia's history of authoritarian rule. Czars ruled for hundreds of years and Communist Party officials for most of the 20th century. Democratic institutions were not introduced until the 1990s. In 1991, a majority of Russians supported the change to multiparty democracy from Communist Party rule. Since that time, support for democracy has ebbed. In the 1990s, democracy for many Russians acquired the taint of unstable politics, economic disruption, and falling living standards. Many welcomed President Putin's strong leadership, which they associated with improvements in their standard of living, political stability, and increased Russian power and influence in the world.

A key dimension of political culture is citizens' level of pride in their nation and the political system as a whole. In 2006, when asked how proud they are of their nationality, 46 percent of Russians said they were very proud. This is lower than the 65 percent in the United States but much higher than Germany's 22 percent or China's 21 percent.[38] Pride in Russian nationality increased after the Winter Olympics and the seizure of Crimea.

It is useful, however, to go beyond general statements about pride to understand nationalism in Russia. There are competing versions of nationalism at play. One is imperial nationalism, which means nostalgia for the days when the Soviet Union was an empire and a superpower. In its current version, imperial nationalism supports rebuilding Russian prestige and power worldwide, and gaining influence over neighboring countries that were once part of the Soviet empire. This version of Russian nationalism was displayed in President Putin's seizure of Crimea in 2014. An alternative is xenophobic nationalism, which demands a Russia for Russians and is hostile to ethnic minorities. Supporters of this version of nationalism bitterly resent what they see as lenient government treatment of Muslims from the North Caucasus region and migrant workers from Central Asia. They accuse them of getting away with theft, murder, rape and taking jobs from Russians while the government does little to protect Russians. A 2013 poll found that "nearly 73 percent of Russians . . . favor the deportation of migrant workers. Some 66 percent agreed to some degree with the idea that 'Russia is for Russians'."[39] In recent years, President Putin has showed sympathy for this version of Russian nationalism, as have other political leaders.[40] There is also a moderate version of nationalism that denounces xenophobia and renounces Putin's expansionist ambitions and anti-Westernism. Supporters of this version of nationalism want a democratic Russia based on the rule of law, which is inclusive of citizens who differ from Russians in ethnicity and religion,[41] but this liberal, democratic type of nationalism has far fewer supporters than the other two. Although Russians disagree on nationalism, there is greater agreement about Russian political institutions, which are widely seen as benefiting wealthy, corrupt elites. In 2011, only 37 percent of Russians believed that "generally, the state is run for the benefit of all the people."[42] Officials' corruption and contempt for ordinary citizens has undermined support for political institutions.

A second dimension of political culture is citizens' view of their role in the political process. Many Russians believe they have little say in politics and see themselves as subjects of the state rather than citizens capable of choosing leaders or influencing policy. A poll conducted in 2011 by the Russian Public Opinion Research Center found that 61 percent of those questioned took "no interest in politics or public life."[43] Weak social capital is an obstacle to a more participatory political culture, making it difficult for citizens "to band together with strangers to further their common interest."[44]

Moreover, a majority of Russians said in 2012 that they "want a strong leader who does not have to bother with parliaments and elections." A number of commentators conclude that this means Russians want authoritarian rule, not democracy. Political scientist Henry Hale offers an alternative explanation. He suggests that although a majority of Russians wants a strong leader, they also want that individual to be elected in fair and free elections. His term for this kind of democracy is delegative democracy. Wanting this kind of democracy is not the same as believing that any form or authoritarian rule is better than democracy.[45]

The final dimension of political culture is what citizens expect from government. Many Russians say they want a paternalistic state that looks out for them. When asked in 2006 whether "people should take more responsibility to provide for themselves" or the "government should take more responsibility for ensuring that everyone is provided for," 43 percent of Russians opted for the latter. By contrast, in the United States and China, these figures were 9 percent and 15 percent, respectively. It is not surprising that Russians prefer a larger role for the government in this area than Americans do, but it is surprising so many more Russians than Chinese want the government to provide for citizens, since China is ruled by a Communist party.[46]

Since returning to office in 2012, President Putin has appealed to Russians who take a paternalistic view of the state. He has constructed a version of Russian political culture that focuses on winning the support of ethnic Russians by portraying himself as the protector of Russian national identity. He draws selectively on Russian culture and history to argue that obedience to the ruler and conservative social values as taught by the Russian Orthodox Church have always been part of the Russian identity. Putin's efforts to curry support for the Church was behind the government's arrest of several members of the feminist rock band Pussy Riot in 2012. The band members sang their protest prayer, "Mother of God Drive Putin Away," and danced in a Russian Orthodox cathedral in Moscow, outraging parishioners at the church. Three band members were sentenced to prison terms.

Putin asserts that Russian political culture is distinctive and needs to be protected from the encroachment of decadent Western self-expression values embodies by Pussy Riot, such as challenging authority, demanding responsive democratic government, and tolerating different lifestyles. In making these claims Putin has tried to construct a coherent rationale for his personalistic rule that goes beyond simply saying he deserves to rule because he has raised people's incomes. He has attempted to build support among large numbers of Russians and at the same time argue that those who criticize him are not really Russians.[47]

Political Economy

A country's political economy is defined by the way in which politics and economics interact to produce income and wealth and how income and wealth are distributed among the population. Russia made a transformation from a centrally planned, state-owned economy to a mixture of state and markets in the 1990s.

During the first decade of the 21st century, the balance shifted in favor of the state as it took control of the oil and gas industries. The way in which these changes have occurred give the state a large role in the economy and have resulted in high degrees of inequality, both between social classes and between different regions of the country. Russia depends heavily on oil and gas sales in world markets to achieve economic growth and fund government revenues. The prospect of declining oil revenues in the next few decades present major challenges for Russia.

Russia's present political economy originated in the attempts of President Boris Yeltsin's government to restore economic growth in the deteriorating economy it inherited from the Soviet Union. Both Yeltsin's own economic advisers and their counterparts from the International Monetary Fund and the United States convinced him that the only economic option for reviving the economy quickly was **shock therapy**, making a transition to a market economy as rapidly as possible. The goals of shock therapy were to let prices be set by the market rather than by government planners, to slash state spending to reduce budget deficits, to encourage foreign direct investment, and to sell state-owned firms to private investors.[48]

Shock Therapy
A term applied to Russia's attempt to make the transition from a centrally planned economy to a market economy as rapidly as possible.

For most of the 1990s, none of the four components of shock therapy worked as planned. Inflation skyrocketed once prices were allowed to be determined by market forces, with devastating consequences for millions of Russians living on fixed incomes. Old women stood in freezing winter weather hawking household items or cigarettes, and combat veterans tried to sell their war medals to survive. Nor was the state able to reduce deficits because economic recession reduced revenues and the government continued to subsidize ailing businesses. Finally, increased dependence on international investment and trade contributed to an economic crisis in 1998. World oil prices dropped, reducing revenues, and made it impossible for Russia to pay its debts.

Many state-owned firms were privatized, but instead of winding up in the hands of entrepreneurs intent on making them more efficient and productive, they typically were acquired by the same people who had managed them while they were state-owned firms or were bought by entrepreneurs with political connections. New owners sometimes sold off their firms' assets to make a quick profit instead of investing to make them more competitive. Other owners used political connections to establish banks, television stations, and construction companies. Some of them were given a chance to become even wealthier in 1995, when the government was desperately short of revenues, and President Yeltsin faced the prospect of losing the 1996 election to the leader of Russia's Communist Party. Yeltsin agreed to a proposal for leading oligarchs to make loans to the government, in return for shares in some of the world's largest oil, gas, and metals companies that were owned by the state.[49] By gaining control of these companies for a small fraction of what they were really worth, the oligarchs became extraordinarily wealthy and influential.

As we saw earlier, President Putin stripped the oligarchs who challenged him of their assets but allowed compliant ones to continue to run their businesses. These individuals have thrived. In 2000, Russia had only six billionaires,[50] but by 2012, there were 100. Most of their wealth comes from real estate, construction, the energy sector, and other commodities—industries where political connections are important for success.[51]

The greatest income gains since 2000 have gone to the highest income earners, resulting in increasing income inequality. Only three of the 35 member countries of the Organization for Cooperation and Development have higher income inequality than Russia, and only four have a higher poverty rate.[52] There are also extreme regional inequalities. The per capita income of the richest region in Russia is "24 times that of the poorest." In comparison, the gap between the richest and poorest regions in the Soviet Union prior to its breakup was only 6 to 1. Regional inequality is also much higher than in China, where the gap between the richest and poorest provinces is ten to one.[53]

Oil and gas exports have driven most of Russia's economic growth since 2000. It will find sustaining economic growth more difficult in future years. Yields from existing oil fields have begun to decline, and although Russia has extensive reserves, they are in Siberia and under the Arctic Ocean. Opening new fields in these areas will be extremely costly. In addition, other countries, including the United States, are using state-of-the-art technologies to produce oil and gas for their domestic use and to sell in world markets. As these new supplies come increasingly online, they doubtless will cut into Russian revenues.

President Putin and other Russian leaders are aware of these challenges and have emphasized the importance of changing from growth based on fossil-fuel extraction to one centering on technological innovation, but this change is likely to be difficult to effect. The interests of many high-ranking Russian leaders conflict with the requirements of economic modernization. They depend on revenues from oil and gas and their ability to make the government interfere in markets on their behalf. "Competition and the rule of law undermine this arrangement. Corruption holds it together, and ensures the loyalty of the bureaucracy."[54]

The prospect of declining revenues from oil and gas exports, and the inability to implement economic upgrading, present political difficulties for President Putin and whoever might succeed him. Large revenues from oil and gas made it easier to maintain political support of high-ranking government officials, military commanders, the government's security agencies and to balance the claims of competing networks, which in future years will likely struggle to maintain their shares of a smaller pie. Lower state revenues, along with any proposed cuts in spending, will also face opposition from state employees and pensioners. Out of Russia's total population of a little over 140 million people, 20 million work for the state, and another 40 million receive state pensions.[55] An effort to lower pension benefits in 2005 provoked demonstrations in numerous Russian cities. The regime is loath to see a repeat of that sort of unrest.[56] Finally, oil revenues help maintain social peace in poorer regions and in Muslim North Caucasus.[57]

In conclusion, a likely decline in state revenues will make it more difficult for the Russian government to solve the twin problems of power-sharing and authoritarian control. President Putin's continuation in power, as we have seen, depends on his ability to balance the interests of competing clans, but falling revenues will complicate that balancing act, jeopardizing his support. The seizure of Crimea and promises to protect the rights of ethnic Russians in Ukraine boosted his popularity, but long term economic trends are likely to lead to greater political struggles over declining government revenues and drops in his popularity. As political scientist Sam Greene notes, "When your power is based on your ability to balance, rather than on more sturdy foundations, the risks are high. . . . There is no backstop once the trust, leverage and fealty evaporate, as can happen remarkably quickly."[58]

A decline in world oil prices will also create problems of authoritarian control. Much of President Putin's support during his initial terms in office depended on the sustained, rapid economic growth that rising oil prices made possible. Lower revenues will weaken leaders' ability to maintain control by paying off various groups in society. At the same time, elections have lost their ability to win support for the regime as well. This leaves only suppression as a tool of authoritarian control, which is an expensive and ultimately unsustainable way to remain in power.

China

11.4 Describe the history, state, relations between state and society, political culture, and political economy of China.

China has the largest population of any country, with more than 1.3 billion people, and is the fourth largest in area. In 2012, it had the world's second largest economy as measured by purchasing power. Between 1980 and 2010, it had one of the fastest economic growth rates in history, averaging almost 10 percent per year, and raised millions of people out of poverty. Nevertheless, these successes have not come cheap. Inequality has increased dramatically among individuals and between regions. Rapid industrialization and urbanization have caused extensive environmental damage, with severe health costs.

Historical Background

In 1976, citizens of the United States proudly celebrated 200 years of independence. For Chinese citizens, 200 years is not much to brag about. The first Chinese empire emerged in 221 BCE. In subsequent centuries, Chinese emperors developed a centralized state that ruled over a country larger than the continental United States. When Europeans first came to China, they were impressed with the size of its cities, the dynamism of its economy, and the sophistication of its art. European access was limited to a few ports because there was little China needed from Europeans. By the middle of the 19th century, however, several European countries had pulled ahead of China economically and militarily and began to press its leaders to open their country to trade. This

Xi Jinping, center, the new leader of China's one-party regime

pressure increased at a time when the ruling dynasty was in decline. The British easily defeated the Chinese during the Opium War (1839–1843) and demanded reparations for the costs of the war as well as the opening of China to British products. Other European countries soon followed suit and divided China into spheres of influence, a humiliating sign of the country's weakness.

In 1911, a rebellion led to the collapse of the dynasty, and a year later Sun Yat-sen, a Western-educated nationalist, was named president of the new Republic of China. However, he was unable to establish a stable regime, and five years later, the country disintegrated into regions controlled by competing warlords. Two political parties emerged to lead the struggle to reunify China: the **Nationalist (or *Guomindang*) Party** and the Chinese Communist Party (CCP). The newly created Soviet Union threw its support behind the Nationalist Party and advised the smaller CCP to ally with it against the warlords. The Nationalists drew support mainly from landlords, wealthy farmers, and big business interests, whereas the Communists received their support from poor peasants and urban workers.

Chiang Kai-shek, who became leader of the Nationalist Party after Sun's death in 1925, decided the alliance with the Communist Party was unworkable. His troops massacred Communist Party members and proceeded to reunify the country, either by defeating warlords' armies or forming alliances with them. The Communist Party attempted to regroup in southern China but was forced to flee to a remote area in the northwest. This flight became known as the Long March, a journey of 6,000 miles that only 10 percent of the Communists survived. Mao Zedong became the party's leader during the march.

The turning point in the struggle between the Nationalist Party and Communist Party came in 1937, when Japan invaded China. The Japanese

Nationalist (Or *Guomindang*) Party
The political party that governed China from 1928 until its defeat by the Communist Party in 1949.

Map 11.2 China

SOURCE: CIA World Fact Book

Country	Population	Infant Mortality	Life Expectancy	Adult Literacy	Capital City	GDP Per Capita (PPP)	Labor Force by Occupation
China	1,356,000,000 (2013 estimate)	12.6 deaths/ 1,000 live births	75	94	Beijing	$9,800	Agriculture: 33.6% Industry: 30.3% Services: 36.1% (2013)

invasion forced the Nationalists into the interior of the country, where they waited for the United States to defeat Japan. In contrast, the Communists greatly expanded their support by enacting reforms that benefited peasants and by rallying Chinese to defend their country against the Japanese. After the Japanese defeat in World War II, civil war broke out between the Communists and the Nationalists, and by 1949, the Communists, with their formidable, battle-hardened army, had driven the Nationalists out of China to the island of Taiwan. On October 1, 1949, Mao Zedong announced the founding of the People's Republic of China.

In its first few years in power, the leaders of the CCP relied heavily on the Soviet model of socialism. They grouped peasants into collective farms, nationalized business enterprises, established a centrally planned economy, and focused on developing heavy industry. By the mid-1950s, however, Mao Zedong became increasingly critical of the Soviet model on both economic and ideological grounds, economically because it was not creating enough jobs, and food production was beginning to fall behind population growth, and ideologically because it empowered bureaucrats rather than peasants and workers.

Great Leap Forward (1958–1960)
Mass campaign initiated by Mao Zedong to catch up economically with the West within 15 years and create a new kind of socialism in the process.

Mao's first effort to create an alternative to the Soviet model was the **Great Leap Forward** (1958–1960). Its goal was to catch up economically with West European countries within 15 years and create a new kind of socialism in the process. The Great Leap Forward was based on the mass mobilization of peasants and workers, substituting "ideological fervor for material rewards" to motivate people.[59] Instead of focusing on developing heavy industry in the cities, Mao sought to balance rural and urban development. The Great Leap is now remembered for its spectacular failures. For example, peasants were encouraged to build millions of backyard furnaces for the manufacture of iron and steel, but the furnaces were crude affairs, and the metal they produced quickly fell a part. An even more spectacular failure was a famine that killed an estimated 36 million people between 1958 and 1962.[60]

Great Proletarian Cultural Revolution (1966–1976)
Mass campaign initiated by Mao Zedong to reshape citizens' thinking in line with Mao's version of socialism. Major goals of the Cultural Revolution were to purge the party of "capitalist roaders" and "class enemies" and rid the country of old culture, habits, ideas, and customs.

The failures of the Great Leap Forward caused Mao to withdraw from day-to-day decision making. Two senior party leaders, Liu Shaoqi and Deng Xiaoping, took the lead in restoring economic growth. They relied on careful economic planning and even used market incentives to encourage peasants to grow more crops. Deng's justification for trying different approaches to jump-start growth is reflected in his famous remark, "It doesn't matter if a cat is white or black as long as it catches the mouse."[61] Mao did not find the comment amusing and regarded Deng Xiaoping as a counter-revolutionary whose policies encouraged people to focus on making money and exploiting others to do so rather than building socialism. Mao believed that what China needed instead was a "**Great Proletarian Cultural Revolution** (1966–1976)" that would reshape people's thinking in line with his version of socialism. A major goal of the Cultural Revolution was to purge the party of capitalist roaders and class enemies such as Liu Shaoqi and Deng Xiaoping and to rid the country of old culture, habits, ideas, and customs. Mao charged the Red Guards, mainly high school and college students, with the task of rooting out capitalist influences by burning Western books and novels; purging universities, high schools, factories, newspaper offices, and local governments of class enemies; and brutalizing, even murdering, many former capitalists, landlords, and their children.

The Cultural Revolution "imposed great suffering on tens of millions."[62] It only ended when conflicts between Red Guard factions threatened to bring competing factions in the military into conflict. In 1969, a new party leadership restored a measure of political and social stability, but it was not until after Mao died in 1976 that a stable Party leadership finally came to power and set China on a new course.

Deng Xiaoping returned from his humiliation during the Cultural Revolution to become China's leader in 1978. With the aid of numerous officials who had been purged during the Cultural Revolution, he began to build a different socialism from that envisaged by Mao. Deng's policies aimed at strengthening the Communist Party and gaining legitimacy for it by promoting rapid economic growth that would improve citizens' lives. He reassured the Chinese there would be no more turmoil-inducing mass movements such as the Great Leap Forward and the Cultural Revolution. He initiated legal reforms that gave citizens some protection from arbitrary state policies. He also allowed more cultural diversity than had been permitted in the recent past.

The most far-reaching of Deng's reforms, however, were those that gave a greater role to markets and market incentives. He concluded that Soviet-style socialism was inadequate to develop China sufficiently to achieve wealth and international power. Nor could China rely on rich deposits of oil and gas to drive growth. The alternative was to rely more on markets and manufactured exports. They were summarized in the phrase "**reform and opening**," meaning reform of the domestic economy and opening to the world economy. Three economic reforms were particularly important. First was to end collective farming. Communes were broken up, and households were allowed to decide what crops to grow. The households were not given ownership of land—agricultural land is still not privately owned in China—but farmers could now make their own decisions and benefit from their efforts rather than having to plant what officials told them and share the benefits with other farm families. Because of this reform, agricultural output grew, and farmers' income rose.

The second economic reform was to open China to world markets. Initially, the opening was limited to special zones in coastal provinces and a few cities that gave foreign companies permission to invest, build factories, and export their goods. These areas experienced an economic boom that powered China's rapid export trade in the 1980s and 1990s.[63] The final reform was to allow privately owned businesses as well as businesses jointly owned by local governments and private investors called township and village enterprises (TVEs). In 1978, when the reforms began, state-owned enterprises accounted for 78 percent of industrial output, but by 2002, that figure had fallen to 41 percent. In the same

Reform and Opening
Policies initiated by Deng Xiaoping to introduce market forces and open the economy to foreign investment and trade.

period, the share of privately owned firms rose astronomically from 0.2 percent to 41 percent.[64] It is difficult to be precise about private firms' share of industrial output in recent years, but recent estimates place it at two-thirds.[65]

Although Deng Xiaoping approved of reducing state control of the economy, he had no intention of allowing it to threaten Party control. Indeed, Deng supported market-oriented reforms because he believed they would increase support for the Party. Although economic growth did indeed produce benefits for many, it also affected groups of people differently. For many urban Chinese, the reforms were too slow. Students also accused Party elites of using corruption to enrich their families. In 1989, student protesters filled Tiananmen Square in Beijing and spread to other major cities. As the protests spread, they attracted wider support from middle-class and working-class citizens, millions of whom joined the protests. For weeks, party leaders were divided about how to respond, until hard-liners who opposed any concessions prevailed. Early on the morning of June 4, 1989, soldiers cleared Tiananmen Square of protestors and shot and killed large numbers of students on streets near the square.

After the **Tiananmen Square protests**, the leaders of the Communist Party followed the basic strategy instituted by Deng Xiaoping: rely on markets and exports to drive economic growth while strengthening the power of the Communist Party so that it stays in power. Both parts of the strategy face challenges. Chinese leaders have decided that they cannot continue to rely on export-led growth, and although the Party remains firmly in power, it faces increased challenges from society.

Tiananmen Square Protests
Student-led protests in China in 1989 against corruption and government unresponsiveness. The protests lasted for weeks until they were suppressed brutally by the military.

The State

The Chinese Communist Party dominates Chinese politics, and within the party power is largely in the hands of the party's leader and high-ranking party members of the **Politburo** (short for Political Bureau) and the **Standing Committee of the Politburo**. In November 2012, the party chose the first new Politburo in a decade. It has 25 members, seven of whom are also members of the Standing Committee. The new leader of the Party is Xi Jinping who is first among equals rather than a dominating, personalist leader as Mao Zedong was.[66] Political scientist Cheng Li identifies two factions in the Politburo. One is the "elitist faction," whose members are from families that have had top party leaders in past decades. Because of this background, they are also known as "the princelings." Most of them began their careers in wealthy coastal cities. The elitist faction usually represents the interests of China's entrepreneurs and emerging middle class." Xi Jinping, the new leader of the Party, is the leader of this faction. The other faction is the "populist faction," whose members come from less-privileged backgrounds and have spent most of their careers in poorer inland provinces. They "often voice the concerns of vulnerable social groups such as farmers, migrant workers, and the urban poor."[67] Six of the seven members of the new Standing Committee of the Politburo are members of the elitist faction.

Politburo
Main policy-making institution of a Communist party.

Standing Committee of the Politburo
Seven-man committee consisting of the Politburo members who are the top leadership of the Chinese Communist Party.

This is a major shift in favor of this faction in the Standing Committee, but the two factions are more evenly balanced in the Politburo. Thus, power sharing is maintained.

The party leader is always the **General Secretary** of the party's **Secretariat**. This organization's power derives from its responsibilities for overseeing implementation of Politburo decisions and managing the party's personnel. The General Secretary has considerable influence over promotions and transfers of personnel to important positions in the party and government.

According to the party constitution, the members of the Politburo and Secretariat are elected by the **Central Committee**, an organization of around 200 full members. In reality, the selection process is the reverse of what the party constitution describes. The Politburo decides who gets into the Central Committee, and the Central Committee simply approves the names presented to it for Politburo membership. The party constitution also gives the Central Committee a major policy-making role, but this, too, exists more in theory than in fact. Although it is not powerful as a policy-making institution, its members have a good deal of political power as individuals. Some are heads of government ministries; others are governors of provinces that have bigger populations than many European countries.

Central Committee members are nominally elected by the **National Party Congress** according to the party constitution, but with over 2000 delegates who

General Secretary
Head of the secretariat and the most powerful position in the Communist Party.

Secretariat
Communist Party institution with responsibility for overseeing the implementation of politburo decisions.

Central Committee
Communist Party institution that approves appointments to the politburo and party policies. In theory it has a great deal of power but has little in practice.

National Party Congress
In theory it has supreme authority in the Communist Party, electing members of the central committee and approving party policy. In practice, it has little influence and approves what the party leadership presents to it.

Figure 11.2 Chinese Political Institutions

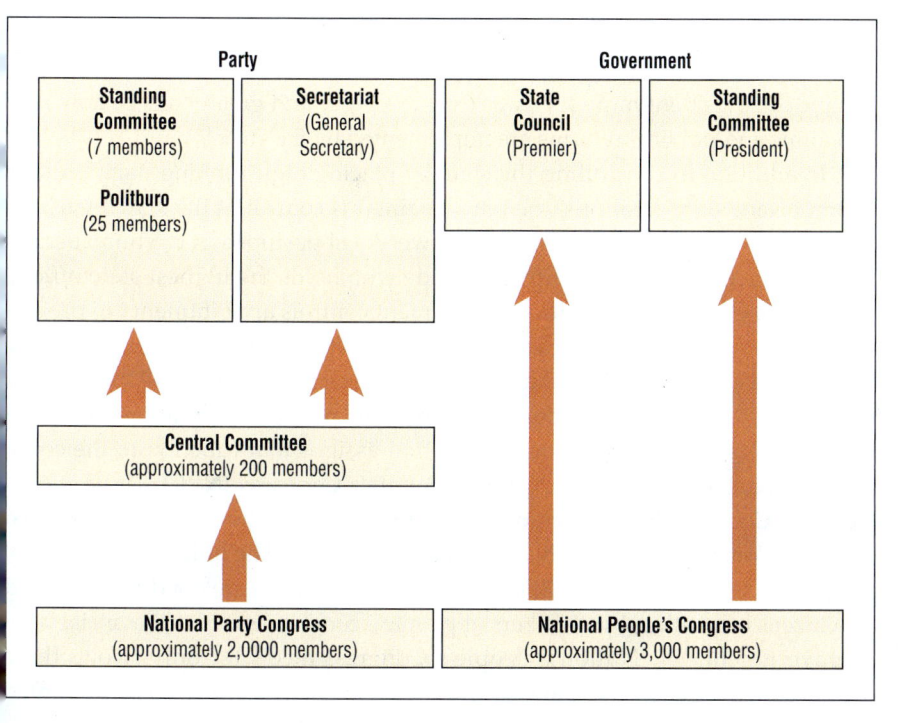

Party:
- Standing Committee (7 members)
- Politburo (25 members)
- Secretariat (General Secretary)
- Central Committee (approximately 200 members)
- National Party Congress (approximately 2,0000 members)

Government:
- State Council (Premier)
- Standing Committee (President)
- National People's Congress (approximately 3,000 members)

meet for one to two weeks every five years, it is largely a rubber stamp designed to approve the choices of the party leaders. It met last in 2012. Below these national party institutions are provincial, city, and county institutions.

As we explained in the opening section of the chapter, in countries ruled by Communist parties, the party and state have separate organizational hierarchies, with the party in charge of the state. The state's central function is to implement policies decided by leaders of the Communist Party. For example, although the Politburo determines the main goals of educational policy, the ministry of education implements the policy throughout the school system. Teachers are employees of the ministry of education, not of the Communist Party.

One of the key problems for any Communist party is how to ensure that the state does what the party wants it to do. One way of achieving this goal is to place top party leaders in leadership positions in the state. The **premier** of the government is always a member of the party's Politburo and its Standing Committee. The premier is the head of the government with responsibility for leading and coordinating its tasks. The premier heads China's Cabinet, the **State Council**, which includes many of the same kinds of ministries one finds in European countries, such as finance, foreign affairs, and national defense.

The **President** of China, who is the head of state, is always also the leader of the Communist Party. Communist Party General Secretary Xi Jinping became President of China in 2013. Until recently, the presidency has been mainly a ceremonial position, but it allowed the most powerful leader in China to have standing as a head of state who could meet with other heads of state. For example, when the Chinese leader meets with U.S. presidents, he is acting in his role as the President of China, not as Secretary General of the CCP. In 2013, the new president, Xi Jinping, announced plans to strengthen the presidency. His goal is to give the president more leverage over the party and greater say in how new economic and political reforms are implemented by the state.[68]

In addition to controlling the state by placing high-ranking party leaders in important state positions, the party maintains control of the state by deciding who is appointed to thousands of lower-level positions in the bureaucracy. Whereas members of the Politburo decide who holds the highest state offices, the party's Central Organization Department controls appointments of provincial governors, mayors of cities, judges, heads of state-owned corporations, presidents of major universities, and executives of television networks.[69]

Leaders of the party choose who becomes president, premier, and Cabinet ministers, even though the constitution assigns that function to the country's national legislature, the **National People's Congress (NPC)**. The National People's Congress is a government institution, which should not be confused with the Communist Party's National Party Congress. The unicameral National People's Congress has almost 3,000 members. Its members are not directly elected by citizens but, rather, by members of people's congresses at the provincial level of government. The National People's Congress meets for only two to three weeks each year and has little power. When it is not in session, it is represented

Premier
Head of government who oversees and coordinates the work of government ministries and agencies

State Council
It comprises the premier and cabinet, which is composed of vice premiers and ministers who head government ministries.

President (China)
Serves as head of state and represents China in meetings with other world leaders. The Chinese Communist Party's Secretary General is also the president.

National People's Congress (NPC)
China's unicameral legislature which is in session for only two or three weeks a year and has little power.

by a Standing Committee of approximately 150 members. For decades, the NPC was a rubber stamp for party policies, but its members have become more outspoken in their criticisms of party policies in recent years. Although the NPC has become more of a forum for debate over policies than in the past, it still lacks the ability to determine its own agenda independent of the Communist Party.[70]

China's judicial system is headed by a Supreme People's Court. There is no system of judicial review, and the court system is subordinate to the Communist Party. Many legal reforms have been implemented in recent decades, and the number of lawyers has increased dramatically. Lawsuits against businesses and government agencies have also increased. Despite these reforms, the Communist Party still exercises considerable influence over lawyers, prosecutors, judges, and court decisions.[71] Many lawyers are members of the Communist Party and are more responsive to it than to the rights of their clients. The party "is fundamentally unwilling to allow real judicial constraints on the exercise of its power."[72] To make matters worse, the judiciary has a reputation for being "one of the most corrupt government institutions."[73]

State and Society

Leaders of the Chinese Communist Party use the same three strategies to control society that that other authoritarian regimes do: provide benefits to win support, control elections, and employ repression. It can use them much more effectively than Russian leaders do, however, because the party penetrates so deeply into society.

The party's advantages over Russia begin with winning the support of groups in society. The CCP begins with a built-in base of support comprising party members and their families. It has approximately 83 million members, or one out of twelve adults in China, who have a strong vested interest in keeping the party in power. The party penetrates society all the way down to the neighborhood and village level with "four million grassroots branches."[74]

In addition to having the support of party members and their families, the CCP has built support among different social classes. In its first decades in power, the party focused on gaining the support of peasants and workers. In these years, capitalists were condemned as exploiters of the people, and during the Cultural Revolution, Red Guards targeted those who had been capitalists before the revolution for harassment and beatings. The party began to change its treatment of capitalists after Reform and Opening began. It needed entrepreneurs and professionals to achieve the rapid economic growth necessary to sustain popular support for the party. One way of winning their support was to scrap the party's identity as a party of workers and peasants and appeal to entrepreneurs and professionals. In 2000, Party leaders announced that the party represented "the advanced productive forces in society" and governs in the "interests of the vast majority of people."[75] "Advanced productive forces" included entrepreneurs, professionals, and intellectuals. The most striking evidence of this change in ideology was the party's effort to recruit entrepreneurs as members of the Communist Party. It also made efforts to co-opt professionals and intellectuals by subsidizing their research and appointing them to desirable positions.[76] The consequence of these changes was that by the first decade of the 21st century, the CCP was becoming the "party of elites, including commercial elites," and less a party representing the interests of workers and peasants.[77]

The party has also made efforts to win the support of China's emerging middle class. Rapid economic growth raised middle-class incomes, enabling its members to afford fashionable clothes, televisions, computers, and automobiles. In addition, they had much greater personal liberty than in the past. From 1950 until 1979, the Party tried to control almost every aspect of citizens' lives, from where they could live and work to which books they could read and how they should dress. Now middle-class Chinese have choices about where they live, their occupations, what they can read, and how they dress.

In recent years, party leaders have made greater efforts to win support from workers and peasants. These efforts were spurred by increasing numbers of strikes by workers over pay and working conditions and demonstrations by peasants against corrupt local governments. The Party's All-China Federation of Trade Unions (ACFTU) had traditionally been an organization for transmitting party policy to workers but began helping workers win concessions from foreign companies in 2010. In addition, every province and city in China raised the minimum wage for workers by 12 to 41 percent that year.[78] Party leaders have no intention of allowing independent trade unions to form or of making strikes legal. Their goal is to reduce unrest by improving working conditions and wages. In the words of China expert Mary Gallagher, the Party's goal is "helping workers so as not to empower workers."[79] China's leaders also initiated policies to help rural Chinese, including higher unemployment benefits and subsidies for food, education, and health care.[80] As with the case of workers, the efforts have been made to reduce unrest in the countryside.

In addition to building support among groups in society, party leaders have also used elections to control the population, although to much less extent than Russian leaders have. The party allows competitive elections only at the village, district, and township level. These elected governments are subordinate to higher levels of government whose officials are not elected. Furthermore, it is not clear whether elections have made local officials more accountable. Some China scholars have found that many local elections are won by local party members, clans, religious organizations, or organized crime groups, benefiting the members of these groups rather than villagers as a whole.[81] Other scholars find that the elections have made local officials more accountable. The introduction of elections resulted in more investment to improve health care, education, drinking water, and roads.[82] What is clear is that village elections were instituted as a means of ensuring social stability at the local level and that party leaders have no inclination to introduce competitive elections at the provincial or national level.

The party does not rely just on winning support and limited experiments with elections to maintain control. If citizens engage in any activity challenging party rule, it is quick to use repression. Repression increased after the Arab Spring when several authoritarian regimes were overthrown in the Middle East and North Africa. As a result, the government has increased spending to "maintain social stability" and now spends more on the police and public security than it does on national defense.[83]

Repression takes several forms, including constant surveillance, house arrest, sending citizens to labor camps without trial, prosecution and imprisonment, and executions. One way of intimidating citizens who are regarded as a threat to the party is to have security details follow them constantly so they know they are always being watched. Human rights activists are arrested and imprisoned. The most famous case of this is author and literary critic Liu Xiaobo, who won the Nobel Peace Prize for his efforts to improve human rights in China. Hundreds of thousands of citizens have been sent to reform through labor camps without benefit of trial as punishment for a variety of political and social offenses. They were forced to perform hard labor for hours a day, and torture was common. Investigative reporters and bloggers have highlighted cases of gross violations of justice, including one of a mother who was sent to the camps for staging a public protest to demand a death sentence for the man who raped her eleven-year-old daughter. Local police decided she should be punished for "seriously disturbing the public order." Under pressure from social media, and wanting to rein in abuses of power by police that have created unrest, new party leader Xi Jinping announced in 2013 that the camps would be closed.[84]

The party retains other means of repressing political dissent by using the legal system. Criminal cases in China are handled by the "people's procuratorate," which is controlled by the party. When prosecutors bring a case to trial, the accused is almost invariably convicted. Prison terms are long, and the death penalty is applied for a wide range of offenses, including certain economic crimes. Amnesty International estimates that China executes more people than all of the other countries in the world combined.[85]

Although the CCP has been successful in preventing mass uprisings large enough to threaten its hold on power in the past two decades, the number of protests has increased dramatically in recent years. Farmers have protested illegal seizure of land by local officials who then lease the land to developers, workers have protested against working conditions and nonpayment of wages, and middle class citizens have protested over rising air pollution and pollution of rivers. In 2013, there were, on average, 500 protests, or "mass incidents," as the party calls them, a day.[86] Increasing use of the Internet, social media, and smart phones have made it easier to organize protests and publicize them by sending messages and photos to the media. In one example from 2012, farmers demonstrated against a petrochemical plant and were joined by thousands of middle-class residents. The "residents held aloft smartphones and computer tablets and flooded microblog sites with images and vivid descriptions of the running battles with the police."[87] China specialist Elizabeth Economy suggests these new technologies have resulted in unprecedented levels of official accountability.[88]

The overriding concern of Party authorities is to prevent protests focusing on local issues from becoming broader mass movements. One way of doing so is to try to control Internet access and social media content. An army of Internet watchers quickly shuts down websites or blogs authorities deem threatening. The ones most likely to be censored are those that might mobilize citizens for mass movements.[89] Similarly, the government cracks down much harder on protests that have the potential to involve large numbers of factories or cities and make general demands, such as for workers' right to strike, than it does on protests about local issues.[90]

Political Culture

More than three-quarters of Chinese report that they are proud of their nation, and they have reasons to feel this way. China has a rich cultural legacy and, for most of its history, was the dominant country in Asia. More recently, it has had great economic success. Along with pride in these accomplishments is deep resentment over Western humiliation of China in the 19th and early 20th centuries and Japanese brutalities during World War II. This mix of pride and bitterness has produced what China specialist David Shambaugh calls "competing nationalisms." On the one hand, pride has contributed to a "confident nationalism" based on China's economic success and renewed role as a major power in international politics. This is the nationalism China showcased at the Summer Olympic Games in 2008. On the other hand, there is a resentful nationalism based on past treatment by Western powers and Japan.[91] This resentful nationalism can be seen in growing public hostility toward Japan in confrontations between China and Japan over islands claimed by both countries.[92]

Chinese citizens report remarkably strong support for their political system. In 2011, 76 percent of Chinese respondents to a national survey expressed pride in their political system and preferred it "over any possible alternatives."[93]

Many commentators think the high level of support is due to the regime's success in improving standards of living. Nevertheless, such a high level of support is puzzling given the thousands of protests that have occurred in recent years. How can support for the government be so high when there are so many protests? The answer seems to be that citizens blame local officials for illegal land seizures, polluted water, and unsafe food, not the central government.

Another puzzle of Chinese political culture is why 66 percent of Chinese surveyed in 2011 said they were "fairly" or "very satisfied" with the way democracy works in China.[94] Most citizens of the United States think of China as an authoritarian regime, not a democracy. Political scientist Tianjian Shi hypothesized that the answer to the puzzle might be that many citizens have a different conception of democracy than that used in the United States. In the United States most citizens equate democracy with **liberal democracy**, a system of governance

Liberal Democracy
A system of governance defined by open and competitive elections for selecting government leaders, well-established checks and balances, and institutionalized protection of liberty and assurance of political rights.

defined by "open and competitive elections for selecting government leaders, well-established checks and balances, and institutionalized protection of liberty and assurance of political rights." [95] In China by contrast, many citizens conceive of democracy as a government led by well-educated, virtuous politicians who act on behalf of citizens to make decisions for the public good. This conception of democracy is known as **guardianship democracy**.[96] It is how leaders of the Chinese Communist Party define democracy.

Guardianship Democracy
A government led by well-educated, virtuous politicians who act on behalf of citizens to make decisions for the public good.

Tianjian Shi and political scientist Jie Lu found strong survey evidence for the hypothesis. Approximately 46 percent of Chinese citizens have a liberal conception of democracy, whereas "around 44 percent" have a guardianship conception.[97] The remaining ten percent of those surveyed could not be placed in either category. Those holding a guardianship conception are the ones most likely to say they are "fairly" or "very satisfied" with the way democracy works in China. The ten percent in the survey who did not provide meaningful answers to the survey are also likely to say they are satisfied with the way democracy works. These two categories of respondents account for the otherwise puzzling finding that two-thirds of citizens say they are satisfied with the way democracy works in China.[98]

Although many Chinese citizens hold a guardianship conception of democracy, they are much less likely than Russians to expect governments to ensure that everyone is provided for or to desire a strong leader. Lengthy Communist Party rule in both countries might be expected to have shaped similar expectations of government, but it has not. Russians are far more likely to want the government to take care of them and to want a strong leader. See Table 11.1.

Political Economy

Chinese leaders describe China' economy as **socialism with Chinese characteristics** to distinguish it from the kind of socialism that was practiced in the Soviet Union and in the first decades of Communist Party rule in China. That earlier socialism featured state ownership of all business firms, central planning, and very limited engagement in international trade. Socialism with Chinese characteristics differs on each point. Market forces determine prices in many sectors of the economy, there is a large role for privately owned firms, and China engages extensively in world trade. Despite these changes, the leadership insists that

Socialism with Chinese Characteristics
Chinese concept for describing their current economy which will continue to be socialist despite a large role for private firms, markets, and integration into the global economy.

Table 11.1 Differing Chinese and Russian Political Values

Value	Russia (2006)	China (2007)
Governments should take more responsibility for ensuring that everyone is provided for.	43%	15%
Need a strong leader who does not have to bother with parliament or elections.	20%	5%

SOURCE: World Values Survey 2005–2008, www.worldvaluessurvey.org.

China's economy is, and will remain, socialist. It will do so by keeping a substantial state-owned enterprise sector and by retaining collective ownership of farmland.

Chinese authorities used these principles to justify a strategy of economic growth that achieved one of the fastest growth rates in history. This growth was driven mainly by exports of manufactured goods made by millions of low-income, relatively low-skilled workers who moved from rural China to cities. The state supported growth by investing vast amounts of money to build roads, railways, shipping ports, and airports. Although this export strategy achieved high rates of economic growth, lifted millions out of poverty, and vaulted China to the rank of second largest economy in the world, it also created numerous problems that have forced Chinese leaders to try to devise a new strategy to sustain growth. One of the biggest problems is that cheap labor is coming to an end. The flood of peasants moving into cities is slowing, and labor shortages are appearing. Labor shortages have increased workers' bargaining power to increase their wages and weakened China's competitiveness in the manufacture of textiles, clothing, toys, and home appliances.

Another problem is that reliance on exports left China vulnerable to economic downturns in its major markets. The world recession of 2008–2010 brought home the danger of relying so heavily on exports. A third economic problem is that state-directed investment in infrastructure was driven by political as well as economic motives. Managers of state-owned enterprises and high-level party members with personal connections to the enterprises pushed for more and more investment so they could take their cut. State-owned companies, local governments, and property developers borrowed funds that they cannot repay, leaving the government with a vexing debt problem.[99]

The export strategy also created political and social problems. The biggest political problem has been corruption. As discussed previously, one of the Chinese Communist Party's strengths is that it penetrates deep into society, but this penetration into society also creates opportunities for society to influence the party—party officials become susceptible to bribes. There was certainly corruption in China before the economic reforms of the late 1970s, but the extraordinary growth since then has generated great wealth and temptations for party officials to cash in on the wealth. High-ranking Party members and their families have been some of the main beneficiaries. Bloomberg News found that the family of China's current leader, Xi Jinping, is worth hundreds of millions of dollars. Close family members of China's former prime minister are estimated to have accumulated $2.7 billion.[100] Sons and daughters of high-ranking party members use their connections to start up new businesses and to go into partnerships with foreign investors in return for lucrative kickbacks and payoffs. This behavior works its way down to provincial and city levels. Party secretaries at these levels can become wealthy by selling government positions to the highest bidder. Individuals are willing to buy the offices because "almost all government offices can be a profit-making enterprise. Transportation officials take kickbacks for road projects. Planning directors cash in on their approval powers. Police chiefs dismiss cases for private payments. Judges accept bribes for lighter sentences."[101]

The growth model has also created social problems. One has been a dramatic increase in income inequality. China has gone from having one of the most equal income distributions in Asia to having one of the most unequal. The number of Chinese billionaires rose from 2 in 2005 to 64 in 2010,[102] and some studies find another big increase between 2010 and 2012.[103] There are also many millionaires and multimillionaires. Below these extremely wealthy citizens is a middle class comprising "smaller entrepreneurs, managers and other white-collar employees of foreign or large companies and professionals."[104] At the bottom are the urban poor, comprising workers, who have lost their jobs, and their family members,[105] and millions of peasant migrants to the cities looking for jobs who are part of the informal labor force. The urban poor now make up a "large portion of the average city's citizenry."[106] The combination of rich entrepreneurs who live in gated communities and drive luxury cars alongside the urban poor is reflected in data on increasing income inequality. The Gini Index, where zero equals perfect equality and 100 perfect inequality, rose from 33 at the beginning of the reforms in the late 1970s to around 42.1 in 2009, higher than Russia's 40.1 Gini index in the same year.[107]

The second major social division is between urban and rural dwellers. Deng Xiaoping's reforms began in the rural areas and led to rapid increases in most farmers' incomes in the 1980s. By the 1990s, however, the impact of these reforms on income growth had for the most part ended. Consequently, rural income growth stagnated in the 1990s, whereas in many cities, especially those along the east coast, per capita income grew rapidly. The gap between the richest and poorest provinces was ten to one by 2010.[108]

There are also sizable inequalities in access to education. Most rural schools are not as good as urban schools, and in urban areas, the children of rich parents go to better schools than children of poor parents. The gap between rich and poor has grown larger in cities in recent years because school administrators demand bribes upward of $16,000 for students to enroll in good middle schools. Having connections with Party or government officials also helps. Getting into a good middle school is essential for getting into a top high school, which in turn is necessary for doing well on China's college entrance examination.[109]

Children of migrant workers in the cities are particularly disadvantaged in education. They are penalized by China's household registration system, which divides Chinese into urban and rural residents. Migrant workers' registration papers identify them as rural dwellers, and their children are expected to attend schools in their parents' rural village. There are as many as 160 million migrant workers living in cities who are not classified as permanent residents of the cities.[110] As a result, "tens of millions of children of migrant workers are, in effect, forced to stay in the countryside for schooling looked after by other relatives."[111]

Finally, the breakneck pace of industrialization fueled by inefficient coal-burning power plants and permissive policies allowing factories to dump wastes into rivers produced perhaps the world's worst environmental problems.[112] Coal provides about 70 percent of China's energy and is a major reason that 16 of the world's 20 most polluted cities are in China. The rapid increase in automobile and truck traffic has made air pollution even worse. By 2013, major cities were covered in choking smog on a regular basis, and devices to measure particulates in the air are best sellers. Air pollution causes as many as 750,000 premature deaths a year. China has surpassed the United States to become the biggest producer of carbon dioxide. China's water supplies are becoming depleted because of increasing use of water for irrigation and rapidly growing cities. Much of the water supply is polluted, and contaminated water is a major cause of death among children under five in the rural population. Pollution is caused by industrial waste dumping into rivers and runoff from farm animal waste into rivers. In March 2013, even knowledgeable observers of China's water pollution problems were taken aback when approximately 14,000 dead pigs were found floating in the river that runs through Shanghai, China's largest city.

These problems led to a decision to change the growth strategy. In late 2013, Communist Party leader and Chinese president Xi Jinping introduced a new economic strategy designed to address the problems of the current growth model. The key economic elements of the proposal are to shift from growth based on exports to growth based on domestic consumption; to make more use of market criteria in making investment decisions; and to upgrade from an economy based on low-wage, low-skilled labor to one based on higher-wage, high-skilled labor, one capable of innovation and new-product development. Growth based on a higher-wage economy will permit increased domestic consumption and create more jobs for college graduates whose unemployment rate in 2013 was estimated at 25 percent.[113] Using market criteria to make investment decisions will cut wasteful spending and overinvestment and weaken the opportunities for party and government officials to inflate prices and demand kickbacks. Party leader Xi Jinping proclaims that this new strategy of growth will achieve "**the Chinese dream**"—a return to Chinese greatness in the world and better lives for its citizens.[114]

The Chinese Dream
The goal of returning China to a position of greatness in the world and providing better lives for its citizens.

These economic policies are to be complemented by more spending for health care and pensions. Such spending will reduce the need for citizens to save as much as they can to pay for unexpected health problems and have savings for old age. With better coverage for health care and larger pensions, citizens can spend more of their income on products made in China, thus complementing the strategy of shifting from export-led growth to growth based on domestic consumption.[115]

The party will retain its central leadership role, and Xi Jinping wants to strengthen the leadership's ability to implement his economic reforms over the resistance of those who benefit from the present political economy. The party has also cracked down on its critics in society. Some leading critics of the party have been arrested; others have been warned to avoid publicly advocating civil and political rights.[116]

Leading China experts disagree on the prospects for the reforms. Political scientist Minxin Pei argues that it will be extremely difficult for party leaders to implement the reforms. In an analysis that parallels the one Russian specialists make about Russia, he argues that China's political economy is based on "carving up the spoils of development." The higher ranking the Party member, the more wealth he or she can accumulate.[117] These party members will seek to prevent reforms aimed at changing present policies. He approvingly quotes a top Party leader who "summarized the dilemma in dealing with corruption. 'Corruption will kill the Party,' he supposedly said, 'but fighting corruption will kill it, too.'"[118] This is because party elites no longer share beliefs, values, or rules but get along with each other by using their political power to become wealthy.[119]

Political scientist Cheng Li, on the other hand, is more optimistic about the proposed reforms. He points to the removal of corrupt top executives from three major state-owned enterprises—railways, oil, and telecommunications—in 2013 as evidence that the new leadership can overcome resistance to its proposed reforms. He also suggests that party leaders have worked out ways of sharing power so that both major factions in the party are more or less evenly balanced in the Politburo, so that there is little danger of a falling out among them that would weaken party control over the population. All the leaders have a strong interest in maintaining party control.

Whichever expert is correct, the party leaders face a difficult time in pushing through the reforms and making a transition to a different kind of growth strategy. Reducing corruption will produce serious challenges, as will reining in abuses of local officials, which outrage villagers, and abuses of factory owners, which anger workers. Finally, even if the economic growth strategy succeeds, it is essential to reduce pollution, which is currently a major cause of protests by city dwellers. The danger to the party, of which its leaders are well aware, "is the successful organization of a civil-resistance movement calling for fundamental changes in China's political system."[120]

Comparing Capabilities Between Russia and China

11.5 Compare and contrast capabilities in Russia and China.

Despite its spectacular economic growth rates since 1980, China is a poorer country than Russia. In 2012, its per capita income was $9,300 in purchasing power parity terms. The corresponding figure for Russia was $18,000, almost twice that of China.[121] Russia has a considerable advantage in per capita income over China and leads China in some indicators of capability, but China is catching up in some areas where it lags.

Table 11.2 Infant Mortality Rates in Russia and China per 1,000 Live Births

	1970	1980	1990	2000	2012
Russia	33	28	23	20	9
China	83	46	37	30	12

SOURCE: World Bank, World Development Indicators at www.google.com/publicdata; World Bank, World Development Indicators, http://data.worldbank.org/indicator/SP.DYN.IMRT.IN.

Physical Well-Being

We have suggested that the best way of measuring whether governments meet the physical needs of their citizens is to look at infant mortality rates. If governments fail here, there is no chance for infants to develop other capabilities. Russia started off with a large lead over China in 1970, but China has reduced infant mortality rates much more rapidly than Russia since then and is approaching Russia's infant mortality rate with less than half Russia's per capita income. See Table 11.2.

In a little more than 40 years, China cut its infant mortality gap with Russia from 50 infant deaths per 1,000 to 3 per 1,000. It is notable that the Chinese infant mortality rate continued to fall, despite reductions in government-provided health care for many citizens after the economic reforms that began in 1978. This is because even though the government provided less health care, rapid economic growth raised incomes and enabled citizens to afford better health care.[122] Since 2009, China has dramatically expanded community health care centers and enrolled citizens in subsidized insurance plans. By 2012, an estimated 95 percent of citizens had insurance.[123]

Informed Decision Making

Both countries have done an excellent job of teaching literacy, as can be seen in Table 11.3.

The countries are almost identical in youth literacy rates, although Russia has a slight edge in adult literacy. This difference reflects lower literacy rates among older adults in China, many of whom live in rural areas. China has achieved these rates with a much lower income than Russia. Although China has done well in

Table 11.3 Youth and Adult Literacy Rates in Russia and China, 2010

	Youth Literacy % people 15–24 2010	Adult Literacy % people over 15 2010
Russia	99.7%	99.6%
China	99.4%	94.3%

SOURCE: World Bank, World Development Indicators, www.worldbank.org/indicator and Human Development Indicators, www.google.com/publicdata.

Table 11.4 Homicide Rates in Russia and China per 100,000 People (2011)

Russia	11.2
China	1.1

SOURCE: UNODC Global Study on Homicide 2011, http://www.unodc.org/unodc/en/data-and-analysis/homicide.html.

achieving basic literacy, it has not done well in getting students to finish high school. Only 20 to 30 percent of rural children go on from junior high school to high school. This has implications for students' capabilities but also for Ji Xinping's Chinese Dream. It will need to have a much higher percentage of students finishing high school than it does now to develop a more complex innovative economy.[124]

Safety

China is a much safer country than Russia as measured by homicide rates. See Table 11.4. China's homicide rate is lower than that of Scotland, Finland, Switzerland, and the United States. Russia's, on the other hand, places it among the most homicide-prone countries in the world.

The World Bank's World Governance Indicators provide an alternative method of comparing violence among countries. Its "rule of law" indicator measures "the quality of police and courts as well as the likelihood of crime and violence."[125] The scores range from 2.5 to –2.5, with more positive scores indicating higher quality of policing and courts and less likelihood of crime and violence. The percentages in the table indicate a country's ranking relative to other countries. The results for Russia and China can be seen in Table 11.5.

Based on this indicator, which includes the quality of justice as well as likelihood of crime and violence, neither country scores well. There is still a difference between Russia and China. Russia's rule of law ranking was better than that of only 28 percent of the other countries ranked by the World Bank, whereas China's ranking was better than 39 percent of the countries.

Democracy

Individuals' ability to participate effectively in political choices that govern their lives is essential for sustaining conditions that improve their health, education, and safety. For example, although the Chinese authorities have had considerable

Table 11.5 Rule of Law in Russia and China, 2012

	Score	Percentile Rank
Russia	–0.8	28%
China	–0.5	39%

SOURCE: World Bank, Worldwide Governance Indicators, http://info.worldbank.org/governance/wgi/index.

Table 11.6 Democracy Index, 2013

| Russia | 3.74 |
| China | 3.0 |

SOURCE: The *Economist* Intelligence Unit, *Democracy Index 2012: Democracy at a Standstill*.

Table 11.7 Voice and Accountability in Russia and China, 2012

	Score	Percentile Rank
Russia	−1.0	20
China	−1.6	4.7

SOURCE: World Bank, Governance Indicators 2012, http://databank.worldbank.org/data/views/reports/tableview.aspx.

success in raising citizens out of poverty and improving their health, they also threaten citizens' health by pursuing industrialization policies detrimental to health. Citizens have little ability to change these policies. Table 11.6 shows that Russia has a higher democracy rating than China.

Another way of measuring citizens' ability to express their views to governments and hold governments accountable is to use the World Bank's Governance Indicators Dataset for "voice and accountability." Countries were scored on a −2.50 to 2.50 scale in this index. The higher a country's score, the more its citizens were deemed to have "voice and accountability." The percentile rank shows the percentage of countries ranked below the country. See Table 11.7.

Measured this way, both countries perform poorly in providing voice and accountability for citizens, although Russia does better than China. Less than 5 percent of the countries in the world had lower voice and accountability scores than China.

Suggested Readings

Lilia Shevtsova, *Russia XXI: The Logic of Suicide and Rebirth* (Moscow, Russia: Carnegie Moscow Center, Carnegie Foundation for International Peace, 2013). Russia specialist argues that the personalist Putin regime is beginning to decay and discusses what the future might hold for Russia. She examines how the regime might lose power, what kind of regime might follow it, and whether the currently divided and weak liberal opposition can become a consolidated opposition with a broad social base.

Dmitri Trenin, Alexei Arbatov, Maria Lipman, Alexey Malashenko, Nikolay Petrov, Andrei Ryabov, and Lilia Shevtsova, *The Russian Awakening* (Moscow, Carnegie Moscow Center, Carnegie Endowment for International Peace, November 2012), http://

carnegieendowment.org/2012/11/27/russian-awakening/en9d. Argues that Russia faces political and economic crises that the present personalized political regime cannot accommodate. Excellent brief summary of politics, political economy, and possible futures for Russia.

Bruce K. Dickson, *Wealth into Power: The Communist Party's Embrace of China's Private Sector* (New York: Cambridge University Press, 2008). An excellent analysis of how and why the interests of China's Communist Party leaders and business elites have become intertwined and why China's capitalists have become one of the most important bases of support for the party.

Richard McGregor, *The Party: The Secret World of China's Communist Rulers* (New York: Penguin Books, 2010). The best general introduction to how the Chinese Communist Party is organized and how it controls the state and military as well as its relations with businesspeople. Extremely well written.

David Shambaugh, *China's Communist Party: Atrophy and Adaptation* (Washington, DC: Woodrow Wilson Center Press, 2009). An excellent explanation of how China's Communist Party used comparative analysis of the collapse of Communist regimes in Eastern Europe and the Soviet Union to make changes in China to avoid a similar fate.

Critical Thinking Questions

1. Why has China's Communist Party been able to survive the kind of political upheavals that toppled the Communist Party of the Soviet Union?

2. In what ways are the political cultures of Russia and China supportive of authoritarian rule, and is there any evidence that their political cultures might be changing to become more supportive of democracy?

3. Some China experts argue that China's leaders will not be able to implement the economic reforms successfully that they have announced because China's political economy depends on corruption. Some analysts make the same argument about the Russian regime. Does the argument apply equally to both, or is one more likely to make needed economic changes than the other?

4. Both China and Russia have high levels of corruption. Why has China grown much more rapidly in recent decades than Russia despite high levels of corruption?

5. China's government receives highly favorable ratings from its citizens. If citizens approve of the government, does it matter that China has an authoritarian regime rather than a democratic one?

Appendix

Table 1.1 Infant Mortality Rates

Country	Rank	Rate
San Marino	1	1.6
Iceland	2	1.7
Liechtenstein	3	1.8
Singapore	4	2
Slovenia	5	2.1
Sweden	6	2.2
Finland	7	2.3
Luxembourg	7	2.3
Japan	9	2.4
Cyprus	10	2.6
Norway	10	2.6
Portugal	12	2.7
Andorra	13	2.8
Estonia	13	2.8
Denmark	15	3.1
Czech Republic	16	3.2
Ireland	16	3.2
Italy	16	3.2
Monaco	16	3.2
Germany	20	3.3
France	21	3.4
Netherlands	21	3.4
Austria	23	3.5
Belgium	23	3.5
Israel	23	3.5
Spain	23	3.5
Greece	27	3.7
Belarus	28	3.9
Switzerland	29	4
Australia	30	4.1
Korea, Rep.	30	4.1

Country	Rank	Rate
Croatia	32	4.4
United Kingdom	32	4.4
Cuba	33	4.5
Lithuania	34	4.7
New Zealand	34	4.7
Canada	36	4.9
Poland	36	4.9
Malta	37	5.1
Hungary	38	5.4
Brunei Darussalam	39	5.6
Malaysia	39	5.6
United Arab Emirates	39	5.6
Serbia	42	6.1
St. Kitts and Nevis	43	6.1
Antigua and Barbuda	44	6.4
Qatar	44	6.4
United States	44	6.4
Montenegro	45	6.5
Slovak Republic	45	6.5
Bosnia and Herzegovina	47	6.7
Latvia	48	7.1
Oman	49	7.3
Chile	50	7.7
Saudi Arabia	51	7.9
Lebanon	52	8
Bahrain	53	8.6
Costa Rica	53	8.6
Macedonia, FYR	55	8.7
Ukraine	55	8.7
Uruguay	55	8.7
Maldives	58	9.2

Table 1.1 (Continued)

Country	Rank	Rate	Country	Rank	Rate
Kuwait	59	9.3	Jordan	96	18
Russian Federation	60	9.8	Cape Verde	98	18.2
Grenada	61	10.3	Honduras	98	18.2
Sri Lanka	62	10.5	Georgia	100	18.3
Bulgaria	63	10.6	Solomon Islands	101	18.4
Thailand	63	10.6	Paraguay	102	19.1
Dominica	65	10.7	St. Vincent and the Grenadines	103	19.5
Romania	66	10.8	Ecuador	104	19.6
Vanuatu	67	11.4	West Bank and Gaza	105	19.7
Turkey	68	11.5	Philippines	106	20.2
Seychelles	69	11.9	Botswana	107	20.3
Argentina	70	12.6	Dominican Republic	108	20.9
China	70	12.6	Iran, Islamic Rep.	109	21.1
Albania	72	12.8	Nicaragua	110	21.6
Libya	72	12.8	Marshall Islands	111	22.1
Mauritius	72	12.8	Guatemala	112	24.2
Venezuela, RB	75	12.9	Trinidad and Tobago	113	24.5
El Salvador	76	13.1	Indonesia	114	24.8
Syrian Arab Republic	77	13.2	Kazakhstan	115	25
Tonga	77	13.2	Tuvalu	116	25.1
Mexico	79	13.4	Mongolia	117	25.5
Moldova	80	13.8	Algeria	118	25.6
St. Lucia	80	13.8	Suriname	119	26
Brazil	82	13.9	Korea, Dem. Rep.	120	26.3
Tunisia	82	13.9	Kyrgyz Republic	121	27
Bahamas, The	84	14.1	Morocco	122	28.2
Fiji	84	14.1	Guyana	123	29.4
Peru	84	14.1	Namibia	124	29.6
Palau	87	14.3	Iraq	125	30.9
Belize	88	14.5	Micronesia, Fed. Sts.	126	33.5
Colombia	89	15.4	Lao PDR	127	33.8
Armenia	90	15.6	South Africa	128	34.6
Jamaica	91	15.7	Cambodia	129	36.2
Samoa	92	16	Bangladesh	130	36.7
Panama	93	16.7	Kiribati	131	37.7
Vietnam	94	17.3	Rwanda	132	38.1
Barbados	95	17.7	Azerbaijan	133	38.5
Egypt, Arab Rep.	96	18	Nepal	134	39

(Continued)

Table 1.1 (Continued)

Country	Rank	Rate	Country	Rank	Rate
Bolivia	135	39.3	Pakistan	163	59.2
Uzbekistan	136	41.5	Lesotho	164	62.6
Bhutan	137	42	Congo, Rep.	165	63.8
Madagascar	138	42.8	Niger	166	66.4
Zimbabwe	138	42.8	Benin	167	67.9
Turkmenistan	140	44.6	Swaziland	168	69
Papua New Guinea	141	44.8	Mozambique	169	71.6
Tanzania	142	45.4	Djibouti	170	71.8
Timor-Leste	143	45.8	Afghanistan	171	72.7
Eritrea	144	46.3	Togo	172	72.9
Senegal	145	46.7	Mauritania	173	75.6
India	146	47.2	South Sudan	174	76
Myanmar	147	47.9	Nigeria	175	78
Kenya	148	48.3	Guinea	176	78.9
Gabon	149	49.3	Cameroon	177	79.2
Ethiopia	150	51.5	Equatorial Guinea	178	79.6
Ghana	151	51.8	Cote d'Ivoire	179	81.2
Zambia	152	52.7	Burkina Faso	180	81.6
Tajikistan	153	52.8	Burundi	181	86.3
Haiti	154	52.9	Angola	182	96.4
Malawi	154	52.9	Chad	183	97.1
Sudan	156	56.6	Guinea-Bissau	184	98
Yemen, Rep.	157	57	Mali	185	98.2
Gambia, The	158	57.6	Central African Republic	186	108.2
Uganda	159	57.9	Somalia	187	108.3
Liberia	160	58.2	Congo, Dem. Rep.	188	110.6
Sao Tome and Principe	160	58.2	Sierra Leone	189	119.2
Comoros	162	58.8			

SOURCE: World Bank World Development Indicators
http://data.worldbank.org/data-catalog/world-development-indicators

Table 1.2 Adult Literacy Rates

Country	Rank	Rate
Armenia	1	100
Australia	1	100
Austria	1	100
Azerbaijan	1	100
Belarus	1	100
Belgium	1	100
Canada	1	100
Cuba	1	100
Czech Republic	1	100
Denmark	1	100
Estonia	1	100
Finland	1	100
France	1	100
Georgia	1	100
Germany	1	100
Iceland	1	100
Ireland	1	100
Israel	1	100
Japan	1	100
Kazakhstan	1	100
Korea Dem Rep	1	100
Korea Rep	1	100
Latvia	1	100
Lithuania	1	100
Netherlands	1	100
New Zealand	1	100
Norway	1	100
Poland	1	100
Russian Federation	1	100
Slovenia	1	100
Sweden	1	100
Switzerland	1	100
Tajikistan	1	100
Turkmenistan	1	100
Ukraine	1	100
United Kingdom	1	100
United States	1	100
Chile	38	99
Croatia	38	99
Hungary	38	99
Italy	38	99
Kyrgyz Rep	38	99
Moldova	38	99
Trinidad Tobago	38	99
Uzbekistan	38	99
Argentina	46	98
Bosnia Herzegovina	46	98
Bulgaria	46	98
Cyprus	46	98
Romania	46	98
Serbia	46	98
Spain	46	98
Uruguay	46	98
Aruba	54	97
Greece	54	97
Mongolia	54	97
Albania	57	96
Costa Rica	57	96
Qatar	57	96
Singapore	57	96
Venezuela	57	96
Philippines	62	95
Portugal	62	95
China	64	94
Equatorial Guinea	64	94
China	64	94
Kuwait	64	94
Paraguay	64	94
Panama	69	93.6
Colombia	70	93
Indonesia	70	93
Jordan	70	93
Malaysia	70	93
Mexico	70	93
Thailand	70	93
Vietnam	70	93

(Continued)

Table 1.2 (Continued)

Country	Rank	Rate	Country	Rank	Rate
Bahrain	77	92	Tanzania	112	73
Ecuador	77	92	Uganda	112	73
Myanmar	77	92	Laos	113	72.7
Zimbabwe	77	92	Egypt	114	72
Bolivia	81	91	Rwanda	115	71
Sri Lanka	81	91	Sudan	115	71
Turkey	81	91	Zambia	115	71
Brazil	84	90	Angola	118	70
Lesotho	84	90	Eritrea	119	68
Puerto Rico	84	90	Burundi	120	67
United Arab Emirates	84	90	Congo Dem Rep	121	67
Lebanon	88	89.6	Yemen	122	64
Libya	89	89	India	123	63
Mauritius	89	89	Liberia	124	61
Peru	89	89	Nigeria	124	61
Gabon	92	88	Nepal	126	60
South Africa	92	88	Mauritania	127	58
Ghana	94	87	Bangladesh	128	57
Jamaica	94	87	Togo	128	57
Kenya	94	87	Morocco	130	56.1
Saudi Arabia	94	87	Central African Rep	131	56
Swaziland	94	87	Cote d'Ivoire	131	56
Honduras	99	85	Mozambique	131	56
Iran	99	85	Pakistan	134	55
Botswana	101	84	Guinea-Bissau	135	54
Cape Verde	101	84	Gambia	136	50
El Salvador	101	84	Senegal	137	49.7
Syria	104	83	Haiti	138	49
Iraq	105	78	Benin	139	42
Nicaragua	105	78	Sierra Leone	139	42
Tunisia	105	78	Guinea	141	41
Comoros	108	75	Chad	142	34
Guatemala	108	75	Mali	143	31
Malawi	108	75	Niger	144	29
Cambodia	111	74			

SOURCE: World Bank World Development Indicators
http://data.worldbank.org/data-catalog/world-development-indicators
United Nations Development Programme
http://hdrstats.undp.org

Table 1.3 Homicide Rates per 100,000

Country	Rank	Rate	Country	Rank	Rate
Monaco	1	0	Andorra	40	1.3
Palau	1	0	Poland	40	1.3
Iceland	3	0.3	France	42	1.4
Austria	4	0.5	Hungary	42	1.4
Brunei Darussalam	4	0.5	Morocco	42	1.4
China, Hong Kong	4	0.5	Tajikistan	42	1.4
Japan	4	0.5	Algeria	46	1.5
Singapore	4	0.5	New Zealand	46	1.5
Bahrain	9	0.6	Serbia	46	1.5
Guam	9	0.6	Slovakia	46	1.5
Norway	9	0.6	Somalia	46	1.5
Slovenia	9	0.6	Maldives	51	1.6
Oman	13	0.7	Vietnam	51	1.6
Switzerland	13	0.7	Belgium	53	1.7
Germany	15	0.8	Bosnia and Herzegovina	53	1.7
United Arab Emirates	15	0.8	Cyprus	53	1.7
Czech Republic	17	0.9	Canada	56	1.8
Denmark	17	0.9	Jordan	56	1.8
Micronesia	17	0.9	Romania	56	1.8
Qatar	17	0.9	Bulgaria	59	1.9
Spain	17	0.9	China, Macao	59	1.9
Vanuatu	17	0.9	Sao Tome and Principe	59	1.9
Bhutan	23	1	Macedonia	59	1.9
Greece	23	1	Iraq	63	2
Italy	23	1	Azerbaijan	64	2.1
Malta	23	1	Israel	64	2.1
Saudi Arabia	23	1	Kuwait	66	2.2
Sweden	23	1	Lebanon	66	2.2
Tonga	23	1	Finland	68	2.3
China	30	1.1	Malaysia	68	2.3
Croatia	30	1.1	Afghanistan	70	2.4
Netherlands	30	1.1	Luxembourg	71	2.5
Samoa	30	1.1	Armenia	72	2.7
Tunisia	30	1.1	Bangladesh	72	2.7
Australia	35	1.2	Fiji	74	2.8
Egypt	35	1.2	Liechtenstein	74	2.8
Ireland	35	1.2	Nepal	74	2.8
Portugal	35	1.2	Albania	77	2.9
United Kingdom	35	1.2	Libya	77	2.9

(Continued)

Table 1.3 (Continued)

Country	Rank	Rate	Country	Rank	Rate
Republic of Korea	77	2.9	Guadeloupe	117	7
Iran	80	3	Kiribati	118	7.3
Syrian Arab Republic	80	3	Pakistan	118	7.3
Uzbekistan	82	3.1	Lithuania	120	7.5
Turkey	83	3.3	Mongolia	121	7.6
Cambodia	84	3.4	Bermuda	122	7.7
Djibouti	84	3.4	Mali	123	8
French Polynesia	84	3.4	Indonesia	124	8.1
India	84	3.4	Kyrgyzstan	124	8.1
Montenegro	88	3.5	Madagascar	124	8.1
Taiwan	89	3.6	Seychelles	127	8.3
Chile	90	3.7	British Virgin Islands	128	8.6
Solomon Islands	90	3.7	Senegal	129	8.7
Niger	92	3.8	Mozambique	130	8.8
Georgia	93	4.1	Bolivia	131	8.9
Palestine	93	4.1	Turks and Caicos Islands	131	8.9
Martinique	95	4.2	Nauru	132	9.8
Mauritius	95	4.2	Liberia	133	10.1
Yemen	95	4.2	Myanmar	134	10.2
Turkmenistan	98	4.4	Greenland	135	10.5
Cuba	99	4.6	Kazakhstan	136	10.7
Laos	99	4.6	Gambia	137	10.8
Sri Lanka	99	4.6	Togo	138	10.9
Latvia	102	4.8	Russian Federation	139	11.2
Ukraine	102	4.8	Barbados	140	11.3
Belarus	104	4.9	Costa Rica	141	11.3
United States	105	5	Grenada	142	11.5
Estonia	106	5.2	Paraguay	142	11.5
Peru	106	5.2	Cape Verde	144	11.6
Thailand	108	5.3	Cayman Islands	145	11.7
Philippines	109	5.4	Comoros	146	12.2
Argentina	110	5.5	Nigeria	146	12.2
Uruguay	111	6.1	Swaziland	148	12.9
Republic of Moldova	112	6.6	Papua New Guinea	149	13
Anguilla	113	6.8	Nicaragua	150	13.2
Antigua	113	6.8	Suriname	151	13.7
Haiti	115	6.9	Gabon	152	13.8
Timor-Leste	115	6.9	Zimbabwe	153	14.3

Table 1.3 (Continued)

Country	Rank	Rate	Country	Rank	Rate
Botswana	154	14.5	Brazil	181	22.7
French Guiana	155	14.6	Sudan	182	24.2
Mauritania	156	14.7	Tanzania	183	24.5
Sierra Leone	157	14.9	Dominican Republic	184	24.9
Benin	158	15.1	Saint Lucia	185	25.2
Korea, North	159	15.2	Ethiopia	186	25.5
Ghana	160	15.7	Puerto Rico	187	26.2
Chad	161	15.8	Bahamas	188	28
Rwanda	162	17.1	Central African Rep	189	29.3
Namibia	163	17.2	Congo	199	30.8
Eritrea	164	17.8	Colombia	200	33.4
Burkina Faso	165	18	Lesotho	201	33.6
Mexico	166	18.1	South Africa	204	33.8
Ecuador	167	18.2	Trinidad and Tobago	205	35.2
Guyana	168	18.4	Malawi	206	36
Angola	169	19	Uganda	207	36.3
Cameroon	170	19.7	Zambia	208	38
Montserrat	170	19.7	Saint Kitts and Nevis	209	38.2
Kenya	172	20.1	Virgin Islands	210	39.2
Guinea-Bissau	173	20.2	Guatemala	211	41.4
Equatorial Guinea	174	20.7	Belize	212	41.7
Panama	175	21.6	Venezuela	213	45
Burundi	176	21.7	Jamaica	214	52.2
Congo, Dem Rep	176	21.7	Cote d'Ivoire	215	56.9
St. Vincent	178	22	El Salvador	216	66
Dominica	179	22.1	Honduras	217	82.1
Guinea	180	22.5			

SOURCE: UNODC Global Study on Homicide 2011

Table 1.4 Democracy Index

FULL DEMOCRACIES

Country	Rank	Score	Country	Rank	Score
Norway	1	9.93	Germany	14	8.34
Sweden	2	9.73	Malta	15	8.28
Iceland	3	9.65	United Kingdom	15	8.21
Denmark	4	9.52	Czech Republic	17	8.19
New Zealand	5	9.26	Uruguay	18	8.17
Australia	6	9.22	Mauritius	18	8.17
Switzerland	7	9.09	South Korea	20	8.13
Canada	8	9.08	United States	21	8.11
Finland	9	9.06	Costa Rica	22	8.1
Netherlands	10	8.99	Japan	23	8.08
Luxembourg	11	8.88	Belgium	24	8.05
Austria	12	8.62	Spain	25	8.02
Ireland	13	8.56			

FLAWED DEMOCRACIES

Country	Rank	Score	Country	Rank	Score
Cape Verde	26	7.92	Trinidad Tobago	48	6.99
Portugal	26	7.92	Hungary	49	6.96
France	28	7.88	Croatia	50	6.93
Slovenia	28	7.88	Mexico	51	6.9
Botswana	30	7.85	Argentina	52	6.84
South Africa	31	7.79	Indonesia	53	6.76
Italy	32	7.74	Bulgaria	54	6.72
Greece	33	7.65	Lesotho	55	6.66
Estonia	34	7.61	Suriname	56	6.65
Taiwan	35	7.57	Colombia	57	6.63
Chile	36	7.54	Thailand	58	6.55
Israel	37	7.53	Romania	59	6.54
India	38	7.52	Dominican Republic	60	6.49
Jamaica	39	7.39	El Salvador	61	6.47
Slovakia	40	7.35	Peru	61	6.47
Cyprus	41	7.29	Hong Kong	63	6.42
Lithuania	42	7.24	Malaysia	64	6.41
Timor-Leste	43	7.16	Mongolia	65	6.35
Poland	44	7.12	Serbia	66	6.33
Brazil	44	7.12	Moldova	67	6.32
Panama	46	7.08	Papua New Guinea	67	6.32
Latvia	47	7.05	Philippines	69	6.3

Table 1.4 (Continued)

Country	Rank	Score	Country	Rank	Score
Zambia	70	6.26	Malawi	75	6.08
Paraguay	70	6.26	Montenegro	76	6.05
Namibia	72	6.24	Guyana	76	6.05
Macedonia	73	6.16	Ghana	78	6.02
Senegal	74	6.09	Benin	79	6

HYBRID REGIMES

Country	Rank	Score	Country	Rank	Score
Ukraine	80	5.91	Lebanon	99	5.05
Guatemala	81	5.88	Cambodia	100	4.96
Singapore	81	5.88	Liberia	101	4.95
Tanzania	81	5.88	Mozambique	102	4.88
Bangladesh	84	5.86	Palestine	103	4.8
Bolivia	85	5.84	Kenya	104	4.71
Honduras	85	5.84	Sierra Leone	104	4.71
Ecuador	86	5.78	Kyrgyz Republic	106	4.69
Turkey	87	5.76	Bhutan	107	4.65
Sri Lanka	88	5.75	Pakistan	108	4.57
Tunisia	89	5.67	Egypt	109	4.56
Albania	89	5.67	Mauritania	110	4.17
Nicaragua	92	5.56	Nepal	111	4.16
Georgia	93	5.53	Niger	111	4.16
Uganda	94	5.16	Iraq	113	4.1
Libya	95	5.15	Armenia	114	4.09
Venezuela	95	5.15	Morocco	115	4.07
Mali	96	5.12	Haiti	116	3.96
Bosnia Herzegovina	98	5.11			

AUTHORITARIAN REGIMES

Country	Rank	Score	Country	Rank	Score
Madagascar	117	3.93	Burkina Faso	127	3.52
Algeria	118	3.83	Cuba	127	3.52
Kuwait	119	3.78	Comoros	127	3.52
Nigeria	120	3.77	Togo	130	3.45
Jordan	121	3.76	Cameroon	131	3.44
Russia	122	3.74	Rwanda	132	3.36
Ethiopia	123	3.72	Angola	133	3.35
Fiji	124	3.67	Gambia	134	3.31
Burundi	125	3.6	Oman	135	3.26
Gabon	126	3.56	Côte d'Ivoire	136	3.25

(Continued)

Table 1.4 (Continued)

Country	Rank	Score	Country	Rank	Score
Swaziland	137	3.2	Eritrea	153	2.4
Qatar	138	3.18	Sudan	154	2.38
Azerbaijan	139	3.15	Myanmar	155	2.35
Yemen	140	3.12	Laos	156	2.32
Belarus	141	3.04	Central African Rep	157	1.99
China	142	3	Iran	158	1.98
Kazakhstan	143	2.95	Dem Rep of Congo	159	1.92
Vietnam	144	2.89	Equatorial Guinea	160	1.83
Congo, Brazzaville	144	2.89	Uzbekistan	161	1.72
Guinea	146	2.79	Turkmenistan	161	1.72
Djibouti	147	2.67	Saudi Arabia	163	1.71
Zimbabwe	148	2.67	Syria	164	1.63
United Arab Emirates	149	2.58	Chad	165	1.62
Bahrain	150	2.53	Guinea-Bissau	166	1.43
Tajikistan	151	2.51	North Korea	167	1.08
Afghanistan	152	2.48			

SOURCE: The Economist Intelligence Unit Democracy Index 2012

Table 2.1 Failed States Index

ALERT

Country	Rank	Score	Country	Rank	Score
Somalia	1	114.9	Yemen	8	104.8
Congo (D. R.)	2	111.2	Iraq	9	104.3
Sudan	3	109.4	Central African Republic	10	103.8
Chad	4	107.6	Cote d'Ivoire	11	103.6
Zimbabwe	5	106.3	Guinea	12	101.9
Afghanistan	6	106.0	Pakistan	13	101.6
Haiti	7	104.9	Nigeria	14	101.1

OMINOUS

Country	Rank	Score	Country	Rank	Score
Guinea Bissau	15	99.2	Kyrgyzstan	41	87.4
Kenya	16	98.4	Equatorial Guinea	43	86.3
Ethiopia	17	97.9	Zambia	44	85.9
Burundi	18	97.5	Lebanon	45	85.8
Niger	18	96.9	Tajikistan	46	85.7
Uganda	20	96.5	Solomon Islands	47	85.6
Myanmar	21	96.2	Laos	48	85.5
North Korea	22	95.5	Angola	48	85.1
Eritrea	23	94.5	Libya	50	84.9
Syria	23	94.5	Georgia	51	84.8
Liberia	25	93.3	Colombia	52	84.4
Cameroon	26	93.1	Djibouti	53	83.8
Nepal	27	93.0	Papua New Guinea	54	83.7
Timor-Leste	28	92.7	Swaziland	55	83.5
Bangladesh	29	92.2	Philippines	56	83.2
Sri Lanka	29	92.2	Comoros	57	83.0
Sierra Leone	31	90.4	Madagascar	58	82.5
Egypt	31	90.4	Mozambique	59	82.4
Congo (Republic)	33	90.1	Bhutan	59	82.4
Iran	34	89.6	Israel/West Bank	61	82.2
Rwanda	35	89.3	Bolivia	62	82.1
Malawi	36	88.8	Indonesia	63	80.6
Cambodia	37	88.7	Gambia	63	80.6
Mauritania	38	87.6	Fiji	65	80.5
Togo	39	87.5	Tanzania	66	80.4
Uzbekistan	39	87.5	Ecuador	67	80.1
Burkina Faso	41	87.4			

(Continued)

Table 2.1 (Continued)

MODERATE

Country	Rank	Score	Country	Rank	Score
Azerbaijan	68	79.8	Sao Tome	97	73.9
Nicaragua	69	79.6	Mexico	98	73.6
Guatemala	70	79.4	Peru	99	73.5
Senegal	71	79.3	Saudi Arabia	100	73.4
Lesotho	72	79.0	Cuba	101	73.1
Moldova	73	78.7	Armenia	102	72.2
Benin	74	78.6	Micronesia	103	71.9
Honduras	75	78.5	Guyana	104	71.4
China	76	78.3	Suriname	105	71.2
Algeria	77	78.1	Namibia	106	71.0
India	78	78.0	Paraguay	107	70.9
Mali	79	77.9	Kazakhstan	107	70.9
Bosnia and Herzegovina	79	77.9	Macedonia	109	69.1
Turkmenistan	81	77.4	Samoa	110	68.5
Venezuela	82	77.3	Malaysia	110	68.5
Russia	83	77.1	Ghana	112	67.5
Thailand	84	77.0	Ukraine	113	67.2
Turkey	85	76.6	Belize	113	67.2
Belarus	85	76.6	South Africa	115	66.8
Morocco	87	76.1	Cyprus	115	66.8
Maldives	88	75.1	Botswana	117	66.5
Serbia	89	75.0	Albania	118	66.1
Jordan	90	74.8	Jamaica	119	65.8
Cape Verde	91	74.7	Seychelles	120	65.1
Gabon	92	74.6	Grenada	121	65.0
El Salvador	93	74.4	Trinidad	122	64.4
Tunisia	94	74.2	Brazil	123	64.1
Dominican Republic	95	74.1	Brunei	123	64.1
Vietnam	96	74.0	Bahrain	125	62.2

STABLE

Country	Rank	Score	Country	Rank	Score
Romania	126	59.5	Panama	132	56.1
Antigua & Barbuda	127	58.9	Montenegro	133	55.5
Kuwait	128	58.8	Bahamas	134	55.1
Mongolia	129	58.7	Barbados	135	52.0
Bulgaria	130	56.3	Latvia	136	51.9
Croatia	130	56.3	Oman	137	51.7

Table 2.1 (Continued)

Country	Rank	Score	Country	Rank	Score
Greece	138	50.4	Japan	151	43.5
Costa Rica	139	49.7	Spain	153	42.8
United Arab Emirates	140	48.9	Uruguay	154	40.5
Hungary	141	48.3	Czech Republic	155	39.5
Qatar	142	48.0	South Korea	156	37.6
Estonia	143	47.5	Singapore	157	35.6
Slovakia	144	47.4	United Kingdom	158	35.3
Argentina	145	46.5	United States	159	34.8
Italy	145	45.8	Portugal	160	34.2
Mauritius	147	44.7	Slovenia	161	34.0
Poland	148	44.3	France	162	33.6
Lithuania	149	44.2	Belgium	163	33.5
Malta	150	43.8	Germany	164	31.7
Chile	151	43.5			

SUSTAINABLE

Country	Rank	Score	Country	Rank	Score
Australia	165	29.2	Luxembourg	172	25.5
Iceland	166	29.1	Norway	173	23.9
Netherlands	167	28.1	Switzerland	174	23.3
Austria	168	27.5	Denmark	175	23.0
Canada	169	26.8	Sweden	176	21.3
Ireland	170	26.5	Finland	177	20.0
New Zealand	171	25.6			

SOURCE: The Fund for Peace
http://ffp.statesindex.org/rankings-2012-sortable

Table 5.2   Economic Freedom Index

Country	Rank	Score	Country	Rank	Score
Hong Kong	1	8.9	Panama	37	7.4
Singapore	2	8.69	Bahamas	40	7.36
New Zealand	3	8.36	Belgium	21	7.35
Switzerland	4	8.24	Albania	42	7.34
Australia	5	7.97	Costa Rica	42	7.34
Canada	6	7.97	Georgia	42	7.34
Bahrain	7	7.94	Bulgaria	45	7.33
Mauritius	8	7.9	Rwanda	45	7.33
Finland	9	7.88	France	47	7.32
Chile	10	7.84	Poland	48	7.31
United Arab Emirates	11	7.83	Zambia	48	7.31
Ireland	12	7.75	Uganda	50	7.3
United Kingdom	12	7.75	Uruguay	51	7.29
Estonia	14	7.74	Honduras	52	7.24
Taiwan	15	7.72	Israel	52	7.24
Denmark	16	7.71	Nicaragua	52	7.24
Qatar	17	7.7	Guatemala	55	7.21
United States	18	7.69	El Salvador	56	7.2
Kuwait	19	7.66	Fiji	56	7.2
Cyprus	20	7.64	Cambodia	58	7.16
Japan	20	7.64	Czech Republic	58	7.16
Oman	20	7.64	Portugal	60	7.14
Jordan	23	7.63	Latvia	61	7.12
Peru	24	7.61	Philippines	61	7.12
Malta	25	7.57	Dominican Republic	63	7.09
Norway	25	7.57	Hungary	64	7.08
Austria	27	7.56	Iceland	65	7.06
Lithuania	28	7.54	Saudi Arabia	65	7.06
Montenegro	28	7.54	Botswana	67	7.03
Sweden	30	7.53	Papua New Guinea	67	7.03
Germany	31	7.52	Mongolia	69	7.01
Luxembourg	32	7.47	Kazakhstan	70	6.97
Slovak Republic	33	7.45	Ghana	71	6.96
Spain	34	7.43	Malaysia	71	6.96
Armenia	35	7.42	Barbados	73	6.94
Romania	36	7.41	Macedonia	73	6.94
Korea, South	37	7.4	Turkey	75	6.92
Netherlands	37	7.4	Indonesia	76	6.88

Table 5.2 (Continued)

Country	Rank	Score	Country	Rank	Score
Trinidad and Tobago	76	6.88	India	111	6.26
Kenya	78	6.87	Iran	111	6.26
Jamaica	79	6.84	Pakistan	111	6.26
Tunisia	80	6.81	Guyana	114	6.24
Greece	81	6.78	Benin	115	6.18
Paraguay	81	6.78	Azerbaijan	116	6.17
Italy	83	6.77	Mali	117	6.12
Croatia	84	6.76	Burkina Faso	118	6.09
Moldova	85	6.75	Syria	119	6.08
South Africa	85	6.75	Nigeria	120	6.07
Thailand	87	630	Sierra Leone	121	5.99
Belize	88	6.68	Ukraine	122	5.94
Kyrgyz Republic	88	6.68	Gabon	123	5.88
Malawi	88	6.68	Senegal	123	5.88
Mexico	91	6.66	Lesotho	125	5.81
Slovenia	92	6.63	Ecuador	126	5.8
Bosnia	93	6.61	Argentina	127	5.79
Namibia	94	6.59	Niger	128	5.78
Russia	95	6.56	Cote d'Ivoire	129	5.76
Vietnam	96	6.54	Central African Rep	129	5.73
Colombia	97	6.5	Ethiopia	131	5.72
Haiti	97	6.5	Mauritania	132	5.67
Egypt	99	6.49	Togo	133	5.59
Sri Lanka	100	6.48	Burundi	134	5.55
Madagascar	101	6.42	Mozambique	134	5.55
Morocco	102	6.41	Chad	136	5.41
Serbia	102	6.41	Algeria	137	5.34
Bolivia	104	6.39	Guinea Bissau	138	5.23
Brazil	105	6.37	Congo Dem Republic	139	5.18
Cameroon	106	6.36	Angola	140	5.12
China	107	6.35	Congo, Republic of	141	4.86
Tanzania	107	6.35	Zimbabwe	142	4.35
Bangladesh	109	6.34	Myanmar	143	4.29
Nepal	110	6.33	Venezuela	144	4.07

SOURCE: Economic Freedom of the World Annual Report 2012
http://www.freetheworld.com/2012/EFW2012-complete.pdf

Glossary

Active Labor Market Policies Government programs designed to move the unemployed back into the labor market by giving them additional training, creating jobs, subsidizing their wages, or helping them with their job search.

Authoritarianism a type of political system in which a single individual or small elite rules without constitutional checks on its use of power.

Authoritative Power A state's power to get citizens to comply with its decisions.

Authority When power is exercised in a way that people recognize as legitimate or appropriate.

Bicameral A legislature that is composed of two chambers, consisting of an upper and lower house.

Big men Politically powerful leaders in Nigeria.

Boko Haram A violent fundamentalist Islamic movement in Nigeria.

***Bolsa Familia (family grant)* program** A social welfare program in Brazil giving cash payments to poor families in return for keeping their children in school and making sure that they receive medical care.

Bonyads Semi-public charitable foundations in Iran that receive state and private funding.

Bureaucracy A part of the executive branch that is supposed to administer and implement policy in a neutral and professional way.

Cabinet A group of officials in the executive branch that advise the head of the government and are in charge of various ministries within it.

Capabilities Approach An approach for comparing and evaluating countries in terms of the freedoms citizens have to choose and act to develop their human potential.

Central Bank Central banks control the money supply in each country and manage its value in foreign exchange.

Central Committee Communist Party institution that approves appointments to the politburo and party policies in annual sessions. In theory it has a great deal of power but has little in practice.

Centralized Wage Bargaining When there is a high degree of inter-union and inter-employer cooperation in wage setting; when wage agreements by the peak organizations of unions and employers set the framework for lower level bargaining.

The Chinese Dream The goal of returning China to a position of greatness in the world and providing better lives for its citizens.

Civic Culture Approach An approach to the study of comparative politics which suggests that congruence, or a match, between a country's political culture and its political institutions is necessary for political stability.

Civil Rights Those rights guaranteed by the state to all individuals as citizens. These are equal rights that the state guarantees to all its citizens, such as the right to marry or the right to use public accommodations.

Civil War Fighting between agents of a state, and organized groups in society who seek to take control of a state, take power in a region, or use violence to change government policies.

Classical Definition of Democracy A form of participatory democracy in which the people are directly involved in making the laws that govern them.

Class Voting When citizens vote for parties aligned with their class position. That is, workers vote for parties of the left while capitalists vote for parties of the right.

Clientelism A method states and political parties use to win support by dispensing favors to individuals or small groups.

Colonialism The establishment of formal political control of one country over another.

Communism (Karl Marx) The economic system that follows socialism. Communist societies have no division of labor, no social classes, no state, and no private ownership of banks, businesses, or factories. Communist societies were to be societies of abundance in which the criterion for the production and distribution of goods was to be "from each according to his ability; to each according to his needs."

Communist Party A political party based on Marxist beliefs and organized as a vanguard party to lead workers and peasants in revolution to overthrow capitalism and build socialism and communism.

Comparative Political Analysis Forming and testing hypothesis in the study of comparative politics.

Comparative Politics A subfield of political science that studies similarities and differences among countries' politics, why they exist, and their consequences.

Conservative Faction This faction strongly supports theocracy and minimizing the power of voters to choose leaders or policies in Iran.

Constitution Describes the powers and functions of the different parts of the state. It lays out how power is distributed within the state and between the state and its citizens.

Constructivism Assumes that identities are not simply found ready-made, but are socially constructed; they are continually refined and redefined.

Control Variables When researchers hold other factors constant so they can determine if their independent variable, as opposed to some extraneous factor, was responsible for a change to their dependent variable.

Core Executive Consists of the head of the government, often the president or prime minister, their closest advisors, and members of their cabinet.

Corporatist Interest Groups When a few interest groups include a large proportion of potential members and are often given some official recognition by the state and included in the policymaking process.

Corruption The unlawful use of public office for private gain.

Coup D'état The forceful seizure of control of the state from civilian leaders by military officers.

Cultural Relativism The premise that countries should be evaluated according to their own cultural values, as opposed to being judged according to values out-siders impose on them.

Culture A society's widely shared values, beliefs, norms, and orientations toward the world.

Dealignment When voters' identification with political parties weakens and their preferences become more fleeting and volatile.

Democracy Rule by the people, in which the government reflects the will of the people and is accountable to it.

Dependent Variable What the analyst is trying to explain; what the independent variable acts upon.

Diffusion Effects Describes how what happens in one country spreads or is adopted by neighboring countries.

Divide and Rule A strategy that pits groups against each other so they are unable to act collectively.

Divided Government When different parties enjoy a majority in different parts of the state's elected institutions, such as its executive and legislative branches.

Double-ballot Elections If no candidate receives a majority in the first election, a second, run-off election is then held between the two candidates who received the most votes.

Dynastic Monarchy A type of monarchy in which the monarch is selected by leading members of the royal family and is accountable to them.

Economic Development The process of increasing a country's wealth by diversifying the goods and services it produces and making production more efficient.

Electoral Authoritarianism The use of elections to mask the reality of authoritarian rule.

Electoral Systems Describes the system by which votes are counted to yield a winner, such as majority, or plurality rule. The rules by which winners in elections are chosen.

Empirical Analysis A factual, objective presentation of material.

Ethnicity A sense of belonging to a group having a common history, language, culture, religion, and geographic region.

European Central Bank The central bank for those countries that are members of the European Union and use the Euro as their currency.

European Union An economic and political union of 28 European countries committed to regional integration.

Executive Branch That part of the government charged with executing the laws passed by the legislature. It is charged with implementing or carrying out policy.

Extensive Growth of Markets Refers to the broader geographic reach of market systems to include more people and places.

Extensive Economic Growth Economic growth achieved by mobilizing large amounts of labor and material to build or produce products.

Extractive Economic Institutions Institutions that transfer income and wealth from most of the people in a country to a small elite.

Extractive Political Institutions Institutions which enable political leaders to concentrate power in their hands for their economic benefit.

Extreme Poverty Poverty so dire as to be life threatening.

Federal Assembly (Russia) Bicameral legislature composed of the Federation Council and the State Duma.

Federal Security Service (FSB) Government agency responsible for internal security, counter-terrorism, and control of Russia's borders.

Federal Systems Political systems where power is shared between national and regional governments that have their own independent authority to tax and make policy.

Federation Council (Russia) Upper house which represents Russia's regional administrative divisions.

Fiscal Policy Governments make fiscal policy which uses the budget—government revenues and expenditures—to manage overall demand in the economy.

Flawed Democracy A democracy sharing some features of full democracy but marred by voter fraud, uneven enforcement of civil and political rights, patronage politics, and corruption.

Free Rider Problem When services or goods are available that people can use without paying for them.

GDP A country's economic output that includes the total amount of goods and services it consumes.

General Secretary of the Communist Party Head of the secretariat and the most powerful position in a Communist Party.

Genocide A state-sponsored policy of deliberately and systematically killing all members of a particular ethnic group, nationality, or religion.

Gini Index An index used to measure the extent of income inequality in a country. A Gini Index value of 0 equals perfect equality of income in which everyone receives the same share of a country's income while a value of 100 equals perfect inequality.

Glasnost Russian term used to describe Soviet leader Mikhail Gorbachev's policy of encouraging freer expression of opinion in the Soviet Union in the 1980s.

Global Supply Chains Where different parts of an interconnected production process are outsourced to different firms that are located in different countries.

Globalization Refers to the greater integration and worldwide exchange of ideas, goods, currencies, investments, and culture.

The Government The government refers to those who run, or are in control of, the executive branch of the state. It alludes to those who occupy executive leadership positions within the state.

Great Leap Forward (1958–1960) Mass campaign initiated by Mao Zedong in China to catch up economically with the West within 15 years and create a new kind of socialism in the process.

Great Proletarian Cultural Revolution (1966–1976) Mass campaign initiated by Mao Zedong to reshape citizens' thinking in line with Mao's version of socialism. Major goals of the Cultural Revolution were to purge the party of "capitalist roaders" and "class enemies" and rid the country of old culture, habits, ideas, and customs.

Guardian Council (Iran) An advisory council to the Supreme Leader, with power to select who can run for the presidency and parliament, and to block parliamentary bills it regards as incompatible with Islamic law or contrary to the constitution.

Guardianship Democracy A government led by well-educated politicians who act on behalf of citizens to make decisions for the public good.

Harmful Spillover Effects These are costs that the public, or third parties, suffer as a result of other's transactions or activities.

Head of Government The leader of the executive branch, often either the president or prime minister.

Head of State The official who represents the country and is considered its formal, symbolic leader.

Human Development Index (HDI) This index has three components: health, as measured by life expectancy at birth; knowledge, as measured by literacy rates and school enrollments; and standard of living, as measured by income purchasing power.

Human Development The process of expanding the choices people have to lead lives they value.

Hypothesis Proposed relationship among variables. An educated guess about how one thing affects something else.

Inclusive Economic Institutions Institutions that enable citizens access to a wide range of economic opportunities and occupations instead of restricting access to a select few. They include private property rights, universal legal enforcement of those rights, and rules encouraging economic competition among businesses.

Inclusive Political Institutions Institutions that ensure that political power is distributed broadly in a society. They include effective constitutional restraints on executive power, free and fair elections with universal suffrage, and protection of civil and political rights.

Independent Variable The agent of change in a hypothesis. What the analyst believes explains the change to the dependent variable.

Inequality-Adjusted Human Development Index The actual level of human development in a country taking inequality among citizens into account.

Infrastructural Power The power to implement state decisions effectively in a country."

Institutions Institutions refer not only to rules but to the organizations that make them. Institutions create patterns of behavior that give order to society.

Instrumentalism An approach to identity politics which assumes that self-seeking political elites manipulate political identity for personal advantage.

Intensive Economic Growth Economic growth achieved by using labor and material more efficiently, resulting mainly from technological improvements and economic innovation.

Interest Groups An organized group that seeks to influence public policy.

International Monetary Fund (IMF) Created in 1945, the IMF's purpose is to provide a safety net for countries when they experience financial crisis, which occurs when they cannot pay their debts.

Interventionist-Redistributive Social Contract (Iran) The contract is that the state will provide benefits to a wide variety of groups in exchange for their acceptance of clerical rule.

Judicial Review When courts have the power to overturn or invalidate laws that violate a country's Constitution or basic law.

Judicialization of Politics The increasing use of courts to settle policy issues.

Judiciary A system of courts that interpret and apply the law.

Junta A decision-making council of officers who lead a military government.

Legislature An assembly that is a law-making body.

Legitimacy The willingness of citizens to believe that rulers rightfully hold and exercise power and should be obeyed.

Liberal Democracy A system of governance defined by open and competitive elections for selecting government leaders, well-established checks and balances, and institutionalized protection of civil and political rights.

Mahdi The Mahdi is the twelfth Shiite Imam. Shiites believe he did not die, but went into hiding in 941 and will reappear again as the messiah to establish just rule on earth.

Majles Iran's unicameral legislature.

Market Systems Market systems exist where productive assets are privately owned and employed to earn profits for their owners. Production is geared to produce goods for sale, and prices are set by market forces through supply and demand.

Martial Law Law applied by military forces, which gives them the authority to set curfews, ban public gatherings and demonstrations, and forbid any other kind of public assembly in the name of maintaining public order and safety.

Medicare Government provided medical insurance in the United States for people 65 or older.

Military Regime A regime in which a group of military officers chooses the leader of the country, and participates in policy making. Key leadership positions in the state are staffed by military officers.

Mob Violence Violence typically limited to particular cities or regions which tends to occur suddenly and die down quickly.

Monarchy A regime in which the ruler is a person of royal descent, who inherits the position of head of state in accordance with accepted practice or the constitution.

Monetary Policy Policy through which governments manage the money supply in order to influence interest rates so as to promote economic stability and growth.

Multimember Districts A district from which more than one representative is elected.

Nation A group of people sharing a collective identity that desires to govern themselves through their own state.

National Party Congress In theory it has supreme authority in the Communist Party, electing members of the central committee and approving party policy. In practice, it has little influence and approves what the party leadership presents to it.

National People's Congress (NPC) China's unicameral legislature which is in session for only two or three weeks a year and has little power.

Nationalism A sense of pride in one's nationality and a desire to control a state representing that nationality.

Nationalist (or Guomindang) Party The political party that governed China from 1928 until its defeat by the Communist Party in 1949.

New Social Movements New social movements are distinguished from their predecessors by their focus on issues of identity (feminism) and quality of life (environmentalism) as opposed to economic demands (redistribution).

Oligarchs Extremely wealthy business people in Russia who used political connections in the 1990s to establish banks, gain control of television stations, and become owners of valuable natural resources.

Ombudsman Investigates complaints by citizens against a government agency or official.

One-party Regime A regime in which high-ranking members of the ruling political party elect the country's leader from among its senior personnel, control access to political office, and control policy making.

Operationalize Variables When we substitute specific, real-life, measurable alternatives in place of concepts that are too abstract and general for use in testing hypotheses.

Opportunity Structures The relative openness of a political system to political participation and influence.

Outliers Countries that do not fit an expected pattern in a scatter diagram.

Parliamentary Systems Where sovereignty resides in the legislature, which selects the executive. The executive is responsible to the legislature which, in turn, is responsible to the voters.

Party Discipline When legislators from the same party display unity in how they vote on bills. When legislators from the same party vote together as a block.

Party Systems Party systems occur when party conflict takes a regular, stable form in terms of the number of parties competing, the relative vote share each party receives, and the types of interests they represent.

Patronage Rewards offered to individuals in return for their electoral support.

Patron-Client Relations An unequal exchange in which poor clients give their political support in return for some reward, such as money, farm land, credit, protection, or access to services, from rich patrons.

Perestroika Term used by Soviet leader Mikhail Gorbachev in the 1980s to describe his policy of restructuring, or loosening state control of the economy and creating more freedom for firms to respond to consumer demand.

Personal Rule A type of authoritarian rule in which a leader is able to concentrate power in his or her own hands to control policy making and selection of state personnel without effective constraints from an organization or the public.

Pluralist Interest Group Systems Where large numbers of interest groups compete with each other for members and exert influence by lobbying the government.

Politburo Main policy-making institution of a communist party.

Political Culture A society's widely shared beliefs, values, and orientations toward politics.

Political Economy The manner in which states influence the economy and, reciprocally, how the economy affects states; the mutual influence of politics and economics.

Political Parties Political parties are distinguished from other forms of political participation by putting forward candidates to run the government.

Political Rights Those rights that pertain to participating in the establishment or administration of the government, such as the right to vote.

Postindustrial A society in which more than fifty percent of the labor force is engaged in service occupations, as opposed to industry and agriculture.

Power The ability to influence people's ideas and behavior; to influence others to comply with your wishes.

Pragmatist faction This faction puts primary emphasis on improving economic growth by relying more on market forces.

Premier Head of government who oversees and coordinates the work of government ministries and agencies

President (Russia) The most powerful political office in Russia who is elected by voters for six year terms

President (China) Serves as head of state and represents China in meetings with other world leaders. The president is always also the Chinese Communist Party's Secretary General.

Presidential Systems Where sovereignty is shared between the legislature and the president. Where both the legislature and president share power and are elected independently by the people.

Prime Minister (Russia) Head of the cabinet appointed by the president and in charge of day to day government operations.

Primordialism This approach to understanding identity assumes that group identities emerge naturally as a result of differences in race, nationality, and religion, can be traced far back into the past, and tend to persist with little change once formed.

Principlist faction The principlist faction is composed of a younger generation of leaders who believe many of the older leaders have become corrupt and abandoned the principles of the Islamic Revolution. They are hard-line conservatives on cultural policy and confrontational toward the United States, Europe, and Israel.

Privatize When state-owned firms are sold on the market to private business people.

Problem of Authoritarian Control The problem faced by authoritarian rulers of how to counter challenges from the masses of the population, and keep them supportive and acquiescent.

Problem of Authoritarian Power Sharing The problem faced by authoritarian leaders of working out ways of sharing power with other members of the leadership group to retain their support and avoid being overthrown through violent and nonconstitutional means.

Programmatic Parties Parties that mobilize supporters on the basis of the party's platform, or policy proposals, that its representatives are committed to enact when in office.

Proportional Representation Seats in the legislature are awarded to parties based upon the percentage of the vote they received.

Reform and Opening (China) Policies initiated by Deng Xiaoping to introduce market forces and open the economy to foreign investment and trade.

Reformist faction This faction wants to give more authority to elected institutions and permit more cultural freedom.

Regulations Policies that compel economic actors to act in certain ways, setting explicit rules they must follow.

Relative Poverty Poverty relative to other people's income and wealth, usually not so severe as to be life-threatening..

Religious Identity Identity based on religious beliefs.

Rent Seeking Seeking profits by lobbying government officials for protection from competitors instead of making better products for customers and improving productivity.

Rents Artificially high revenues greater than the normal profits that could be made in competitive markets derived from scarce natural resources such as oil, or ability to gain protection from competition.

Revolutionary Guards (Iran) An all-volunteer elite military force who are responsible to the Supreme Leader and are supposed to defend the Islamic Revolution.

Scatter Diagram A method of examining the relationship between two variables. The values of the independent variable are plotted on the X axis and the values of the dependent variable on the Y axis. The pattern of points formed by where the X and Y values intersect reveals whether there is any relationship between the two variables and how strong it is.

Secretariat Communist Party institution with responsibility for overseeing the implementation of politburo decisions.

Secular Values Values based on wordly rather than religious sources.

Self-Expression Approach An approach to the study of comparative politics asserting that economic development and urbanization give rise to secular and self-expression values.

Self-expression Values Values which emphasize personal satisfaction, freedom of speech, freedom to choose one's own path in life, tolerance toward people with different lifestyles, political liberty, and willingness to challenge authorities.

Semi-Democracy A system of government which is neither fully democratic nor fully authoritarian, but which mixes the characteristics of democracy and authoritarianism.

Shari'a Law Muslim law based on the Qur'an and the teachings of the Prophet Muhammad, which offers Muslims moral and legal guidance for nearly all aspects of life.

Shiite Islam The smaller of the two major branches of Islam. Sunni Muslims are the other. The split between the two branches dates back to the seventh century over who should succeed the Prophet Mohammed as the leader of Islam.

Shock Therapy A term applied to Russia's attempt to make the transition from a centrally planned economy to a market economy as rapidly as possible in the 1990s.

Single-Member Districts Districts from which only one legislator is elected.

Social Capital Approach This approach seeks to explain how people manage to collaborate to achieve goals, and why people often find it difficult to cooperate even when it would benefit them.

Social Capital The ability of members of a group to collaborate for shared interests. It is based on trust among people and their ability to work together for common purposes.

Social Market Economy An economic model that combined capitalism with a good deal of government regulation and welfare state spending.

Social Movements Social movements are less formally organized than interest groups and engage in unconventional forms of political activism that require a higher level of commitment and sacrifice from their supporters.

Social Networks Beneficial relationships among individuals rooted in reciprocity.

Social Trust Trust that extends beyond one's own group or social network to include most people in a society.

Socialism (Karl Marx) The transitional period preceding communism, during which workers hold political power and use that power to expropriate private property.

Socialism with Chinese Characteristics Official term describing the current Chinese economy which will continue to be socialist despite a large role for private firms, markets, and integration into the global economy.

Standing Committee of the Politburo (China) Seven-man committee consisting of the Politburo members who form the top leadership of the Chinese Communist Party.

The State A state has four qualities: (1) It is an organization that has a specific administrative form; (2) is sovereign, meaning it has ultimate power over people under its control; (3) exerts this power through its control over the means of violence; and (4) extends this power over a bounded territory that defines the limits of its rule.

State Corporatism Refers to state recognized and favored business and labor organizations that cooperate with the state to make public policy.

State Council (Russia) It comprises the premier and cabinet, which is composed of vice premiers and ministers who head government ministries.

State Duma Russia's lower house of parliament whose members are elected by voters to four year terms.

State-led Industrialization Industrialization relying heavily on funding from state-owned banks and state-owned firms to develop industries selected by the state instead of relying mainly on privately owned banks and firms.

Strong States States not captured by any social group and able to govern and make their rules stick.

Supreme Leader The most powerful political leader in Iran charged with safekeeping the legacy of the Islamic Revolution of 1979.

Survival Values Values concerning the requirements for staying alive, including food, clothing, and shelter.

Theocracy An authoritarian regime in which religious leaders rule.

Tiananmen Square Protests Studentled protests in China in 1989 against corruption and government unresponsiveness. The protests lasted for weeks until they were suppressed brutally by the military.

Traditional Values Values which include strong religious beliefs, and respect for the authority of political and religious leaders.

Transfer Payments When the government distributes money to individuals as specified by law, such as issuing checks to those who qualify for unemployment insurance.

Unicameral A legislature that is composed of one chamber that debates and votes on bills.

Union Density Rate The proportion of workers who belong to labor unions.

Unitary Systems Political systems where power is centralized at the national level in the federal government.

United Russia Russia's dominant ruling political party.

Velayat-e-faqih The guiding principle of the Islamic Republic of Iran translated into English as "guardianship of the jurist," and holding that the clerics most trained in Islamic jurisprudence should rule and that a cleric should be the leader of the country.

Veto Points Places in a decision-making or policymaking process at which proposals can be defeated or blocked.

Wage Solidarity The principle that workers doing similar work should be paid similarly and that wage differentials between the top and the bottom should be reduced as much as possible.

Washington Consensus or Neoliberalism A diagnosis promoted by many Western governments and international agencies that attributed poor economic performance to too much state regulation and prescribed free trade, balanced budgets, and competition as the cure.

Weak States States that have trouble making their laws effective or acting independently of social groups.

Welfare Effort A measure that divides welfare spending by GDP to compare different countries' relative commitments to the welfare state.

Workers' Party The dominant political party in Brazil since 2000 which has pursued programs aimed at improving the lives of poor Brazilians while seeking to reassure middle and upper class Brazilians it will not threaten government programs that benefit them.

The World Bank The World Bank provides loans, credits, and grants to low and middle-income countries to promote development.

Credits

Photo Credits

Chapter 1 Page 1: Ken Straiton/Encyclopedia/Corbis

Chapter 2 Page 26: Atef Hassan/Reuters/Corbis

Chapter 3 Page 55: Megapress/Alamy

Chapter 4 Page 74: Scott Houston/Alamy

Chapter 5 Page 98: Massimo Borchi/Atlantide Phototravel/Latitude/Corbis

Chapter 6 Page 74: Simon Maina/Getty Images/Newscom

Chapter 7 Page 152: Andrew Lichtenstein/Corbis

Chapter 8 Page 175: Red Luna/epa/Corbis

Chapter 9 Page 203: Jacques Demarthon/Getty Images

Chapter 10 Page 250: Jake Lyell/Alamy

Chapter 11 Page 290: Howard Sochurek//Time Life Pictures/Getty Images; 294: Alexei Druzhinin/RIA Novosti pool/AP Images; 310: Kyodo/Newscom

Cover zhu difeng/Shutterstock

Text Credits

Chapter 1 Page 02: President Johnson is quoted in Ira Katznelson, When Affirmative Action Was White: An Untold History of Racial Inequality in Twentieth Century America (New York: Norton, 2005), p. 175; 02: Alice Schroeder, The Snowball: Warren Buffet and the Business of Life (New York: Bantam, 2008), p. 43; 12: Jean Dreze and Amartya Sen, "Putting Growth in its Place," www.OutlookInida.com/printarticle.aspx?278843 accessed November 8, 2011; 13: Edward Wong, "The Cost of Environmental Damage in China Growing Rapidly Amid Industrialization," New York Times, (March 29, 2013); 13: Dickens is quoted in Martha Nussbaum and Amartya Sen, eds., The Quality of Life (New York: Oxford University Press, 1992), p. 1; 13: Paul Collier, The Bottom Billion: Why the poorest countries are failing and what can be done about it(New York: Oxford University Press, 2007), .p. 190; 14: Bok is quoted in Thomas Nagel, "Who is Happy and When," New York Review of Books (December 23, 2010), Vol. 57, No. 20, p. 48; 14–15: John F. Helliwell and Shun Wang, "The State of the World Happiness," in Part 1, Chapter 2 of World Happiness Report edited by John F. Helliwell, Richard Layard and Jeffrey Sachs. P. 21; 15: Sen, The Idea of Justice, (Cambridge: Hardward University Press, 2009), p. 283; 16: William C. Martel, "Formulating Victory and the Implications for Policy," Orbis 52:4 (2008); 16: Robert J. Samuelson, "The Global Happiness Index," Washington Post (April 16, 2012); 16: Bo Rothstein, "Creating a Sustainable Society: A Manual," Quality of Government Institute (September, 2011) QoG Working Paper Series 2011:7 (Gothenberg Sweden); 16–17: Bo Rothstein, "Creating a Sustainable Society: A Manual," Quality of Government Institute (September, 2011) QoG Working Paper Series 2011:7 (Gothenberg Sweden); 17: Martha Nussbaum, Creating Capabilities: The Human Development Approach (Cambridge: Harvard University Press, 2011), p. 14; 17: Martha Nussbaum, Creating Capabilities: The Human Development Approach (Cambridge: Harvard University Press, 2011), p. 18; 18–19: Lydia Polgreen, "Right-to Know Law Gives India's Poor a Lever," New York Times (June 28, 2010), p. 1; 19: James Surowieki, "Greater Fools," The New Yorker (July 5, 2010), p. 23; 19: Hugh Stephen Whitaker, "A New Day: The Effects of Negro Enfranchisement in Selected Mississippi Counties," Florida State University, Ph.D., 1965, p. 174; 20: Martha Nussbaum, Creating Capabilities: The Human Development Approach (Cambridge: Harvard University Press, 2011), p. 80; 22: Peter A. Hall, "A Capabilities Approach to Successful Societies," Perspectives on Europe (Spring 2010), Vol. 40, No. 1, p. 11; 22: United Nations Development Programme, Human Development Report 2002 (New York: Oxford University Press, 2002), p. 13; 22: Amartya Sen, The Idea of Justice (Cambridge: Harvard University Press, 2009), pp. 18–19; 23: Martha Nussbaum, Creating Capabilities: The Human Development Approach (Cambridge: Harvard University Press, 2011), p. 103; 10–11: Gary A. Haugan and Victor Boutros, The Locust Effect: Why the End of Poverty Requires the End of Violence (Oxford University Press, 2014); 13: Dani Rodrik, One Economics, Many Recipes: Globalization, Institutions, and Economic Growth (Princeton University Press, 2008); 14: Jean Dreze and Amartya Sen, An Uncertain Glory: India and its Contradictions (Penguin UK, 2013); 19: Amartya Sen quoted in Gary A. Haugan and Victor Boutros, The Locust Effect: Why the End of Poverty Requires the End of Violence (Oxford University Press, 2014); 19–20: World Bank's Voices of the Poor study quoted in Gary A. Haugan and Victor Boutros, The Locust Effect: Why the End of Poverty Requires the End of Violence (Oxford University Press, 2014); 24: Drèze and Sen, 2013:43, An Uncertain Glory: India and its Contradictions (Penguin UK).

Chapter 2 Page 27: James C. Scott, Seeing Like a State, (New Haven: Yale University Press, 1998); 27: James C. Scott, Seeing Like a State, (New Haven: Yale University Press, 1998); 28: Samuel P. Huntington, Political Order in Changing Societies (New Haven: Yale University Press, 1968), p. 1; 29: John Tierney, "A Baghdad Traffic Circle is a Microcosm for Chaos," The New York Times, September 12, 2003, p. 1; 29: James C. Scott, Seeing Like a State, (New Haven: Yale University Press, 1998). p. 7; 29: Daniel Rodgers, The Age of Fracture, p. 78; 32: Jeffrey Gettleman, "The Most Dangerous Place in the World," Foreing Policy (March/April, 2009), p. 63; 32: Jared Diamond, Guns, Germs and Steel: The Fate of Human Societies (New York: W.W. Norton, 1999), p. 266; 33: James C Scott, The art of not being governed: an anarchist history of upland Southeast Asia(New Haven, CT: Yale University Press, 2009), p. 10; 34: Charles Tilly, "The History of European State-Making," in The Formation of National States in Western Europe, Charles Tilly, ed. (Princeton, NJ: Princeton University Press, 1975), p. 42; 34: Von Treitschke is quoted in James J. Sheehan, Where Have all the Soldiers Gone (New York: Houghton Mifflin, 2008), p. 3; 36: Brian Galligan, "Comparative Federalism," in The Oxford Handbook of Political Institutions, edited by R A. W. Rhodes, Sarah A, Binder and Bert A. Rockman (New York: Oxford University Press, 2006), p. 268; 37: David Marquand, The End of the West: The Once and Future Europe (Princeton: Princeton University Press, 2011), p. 139; 39: Nicholas D. J. Baldwin, "Concluding Observations: Legislative Weakness, Scrutinizing Strength?," Journal of Legislative Studies Vol 10, No 2/3 (Summer/Autumn 2004), p. 302; 40: B. Guy Peters, R. A. W. Rhodes and Vincent Wright, "Staffing the Summit—The Administration of the Core Executive: Convergent Trends and National Specificities," in

353

Administering the Summit edited by B. Guy Peters, R. A. W. Rhodes and Vincent Wright (New York: St. Martin's Press, 2000), p. 7; 42: Truman is quoted in Richard E. Neustadt, Presidential Power: The Politics of Leadership (New York: Wiley, 1960), p. 9 emphasis in original; 43: Zolton Barany, The Soldier and the Changing State: Building Democratic Armies in Africa, Asia, Europe and the Americas (Princeton: Princeton University Press, 2012), p. 10; 45: John Ferejohn, "Judicializing Politics, Politicizing Law," Law and Contemporary Problems (2002), Vol. 65: No. 3, p. 41; 45: Paul Heywood, Erik Jones, and Martin Rhodes, "Introduction: West European States Confront the Challenge of a New Millennium," in Developments in West European Politics, 2nd edition, Paul Heywood, Erik Jones and Martin Rhodes, eds. (New York: Palgrave, 2002), p. 10; 46: Arend Lijphart, Patterns of Democracy: Government Forms and Performance in Thirty-Six Countries, 2nd edition (New Haven: Yale University Press, 2012).

Chapter 3 Page 60: Peter Evans, "Collective Capabilities, Culture, and Amartya Sen's Development as Freedom," Studies in Comparative International Development (Summer 2002), Vol. 37, No. 2, p. 56; 60: Nancy L. Rosenblum, On the Side of Angels: An Appreciation of Parties and Partisanship (Princeton: Princeton University Press, 2008), p. 12 (emphasis in original); 61: Myron Weiner and Joseph Lapalombara, "The Impact of Parties on Political Development," in Political Parties and Political Development by Joseph Lapalombera and Myron Weiner, eds., (Princeton: Princeton University Press, 1996), p. 403; 65: Mark S. Bonchek, "Grassroots in Cyberspace: Using computer Networks to Facilitate Political Participation," Paper presented at the Midwest Political Science Association, Chicago, Ill., (April 1995), p. 1; 70: Steve Coll, "The Internet, for Better or Worse," New York Review of Books, (April 7 2011); 71: Alan Berlow, Dead Season: A Story of Murder and Revenge (New York: Vintage, 1996), p. 81; 71: Quoted in Richard Gunther and Larry Diamond, "Types and Functions of Parties," in Political Parties and Demcoracy, edited by Larry Diamond and Richard Gunther (Baltimore, Md.: Johns Hopkins Press, 2001), p. 14–15; 71: Quoted in Susan C. Stokes, "Political Clientelism," in Carles Boix and Susan C. Stokes, eds., The Oxford Handbook of Comparative Politics (New York: Oxford University Press, 2007), pp. 609–10; 70: Robert D. Putnam with Robert Leonardi and Raffaella Y. Nanetti, Making Democracy Work: Civic Traditions in Modern Italy (Princeton: Princeton University Press, 1993).

Chapter 4 Page 76: Hazel Rose Markus, 'frontis peace to Successful Societies: How Institutions and Culture Affect Health edited by Peter A. Hall and Michele Lamont (New York: Cambridge University Press, 2009); 76: Christian Welzel, "Political Culture," in The SAGE Handbook of Comparative Politics edited by Todd Landman and Neil Robinson (Thousand Oaks, CA: Sage Publications, 2009) p. 300; 77: Cited in Christian Welzel and Ronald Inglehart, "Mass Beliefs and Democratic Institutions," in The Oxford Handbook of Comparative Politics edited by CarlesBoix and Susan C. Stokes (New York: Oxford University Press, 2009) p. 298; 78: Gabriel Almond and SidneyVerba, The Civic Culture: Political Attitudes and Democracy in Five Nations (Princeton, NJ: Princeton University Press, 1963), pp. 440, 475. The quotation is from page 440; 79: Data from Ronald Inglehart and Christian Welzel, The WVS Cultural Map of the World. http://www.worldvaluessurvey.org/wvs/articles/folder_published/article_base_54. Accessed June 21, 2013. Presenting the figure in this format was suggested by David J. Samuels, Comparative Politics (New York, Pearson Education, Inc., 2013), p. 194; 81: Kirk Hamilton, "Where Is the Wealth of Nations? Measuring Capital for the 21st Century."(Washington, DC: The World Bank, 2006), p. xvii; 82: Bo Rothstein and Eric M. Uslaner, "All for All: Equality, Corruption, and Social Trust," World Politis58:1 (October 2005), p. 42; 82: Bo Rothstein, "Creating a Sustainable Solidaristic Society: A Manual,")Goteburg, Sweden: University of Gothenburg, The Quality of Government Institute, September 2011), pages 3, 11–15. http://www.qog.pol.gu.se/digitalAssets/1357/1357838_2011_7_rothstein.pdf. Accessed October 21, 2013; 83: Francis Fukuyama,

The Origins of Political Order (New York: Farrar, Straus, and Giroux, 2011), pp. 13–18; 85: James Habyarimana, Macartan Humphries, Daniel Posner, and Jeremy Weinstein, "Is Ethnic Conflict Inevitable? Parting Ways Over Nationalism and Separatism," Foreign Affairs (July/August, 2008), p. 139; 85: Benedict Anderson, Imagined Communities: Reflections on the Origins and Spread of Nationalism (New York and London: Verso, 1991), p. 6; 88: James D. Fearon and David D. Laitin, "Ethnicity, Insurgency, and Civil War," American Political Science Review 97 (2003), 75–86; 89: James D. Fearon and David D. Laitin, "Ethnicity, Insurgency, and Civil War," American Political Science Review 97 (2003), 75–90; 89: David D. Laitin"Grievances and civil war," The Monkey Cage Blog, June 27, 2012.http://themonkeycage.org/blog/2012/06/27/grievances-and-civil-war/#more-19372. Accessed June 27, 2012/; 90: Samuel P. Huntington, The Clash of Civilizations and the Re-Making of World Order (New York: Touchstone, 1997), p. 130; 91: Bo Rothstein, "Creating a Sustainable Solidaristic Society," pp. 3, 11–15.

Chapter 5 Page 99: Friedman is quoted in Robert Kuttner, Everything for Sale: The Virtues and Limits of Markets (New York: Knopf, 1997), p. 33; 99–100: Joseph E. Stiglitz, The Roaring Nineties: A New History of the World's Most Prosperous Decade (New York: Norton, 2003), p. xi; 101: Charles E. Lindblom, The Market System: What It Is, How It Works, and What To Make of It (New Haven: Yale University Press, 2001), p. 7; 101: Charles E. Lindblom, The Market System: What It Is, How It Works, and What To Make of It (New Haven: Yale University Press, 2001), p. 3; 102: John Zysman, "How Institutions Create Historically Rooted Trajectories of Growth," Industrial and Corporate Change, Vol. 3, No. 1 (1994), p. 243; 102: Niall Ferguson, The Cash Nexus: Money and Power in the Modern World, 1700–2000 (New York: Basic Books, 2001), p. 174; 102: McMillan, Reinventing the Bazaar, p. 222; 102–103: Daren Acegmolu and James Robinson, Why Nations Fail: The Origins of Power, Prosperity and Poverty (New York: Random House, 2012), p. 124; 103: Acegmolyu and Robinson, Why Nations Fail, p. 77; 103: Jacob Hacker and Paul Pierson, Winner Take All Politics: How Washington Made the Rich Richer and Turned Its Back on the Middle Class, (New York: Simon & Schuster, 2010), p. 82; 104: Thomas L. Friedman, The Lexus and the Olive Tree (New York: Farrar, Straus, Giroux, 1999), p. 86; 104: Robert C. Tucker, ed., The Marx-Engels Reader, 2nd ed. (New York: Norton, 1978), p. 477; 104–105: Michael Mandelbaum, "Democracy without America: The Spontaneous Spread of Freedom," Foreign Affairs (September/October 2007), Vol. 86., No. 5. pp. 123–24; 108: Daniel Yergin and Joseph Stanislaw, The Commanding Heights: The Battle Between Government and the Marketplace That Is Remaking the Modern World (New York: Simon & Schuster, 1998), p. 11; 109: Economist, "The Growth of the State: Leviathan Stirs Again," (January 21, 2010); 113: John Williamson, "Democracy and 'Washington Consensus,'" World Development, 21:8 (1993), p. 1330; 114: Tina Rosenberg, "The Free Trade Fix," New York Times Magazine Section (August 18, 2002), p. 31; 115: Layna Mosley and Saiko Uno, "Racing to the Bottom or Climbing to the Top," Comparative Political Studies Vol. 40, No. 8, (August 2007), pp. 923–948; 118: Paul Osterman, Thomas A. Kochan, Richard Locke, and Michael J. Piore, Working in America: A Blueprint for a New Labor Market (Cambridge, MA: MIT Press, 2001), p. 47.

Chapter 6 Page 127: Quoted in David Held, Models of Democracy, 2nd ed. (Stanford: Stanford University Press, 1996), p. 71; 128: Francis Fukuyama, The End of History and the Last Man (New York: Simon and Schuster, 2006), p. xi; 129: Milan W. Svolick, The Politics of Authoriarian Rule, pp. 13–14; 130: Axel Hadenius and Jan Teorell, "Pathways from Authoritarianism," Journal of Democracy, 18:1 (January 2007), p. 146; 132–133: Richard Snyder, "Beyond Electoral Authoritarianism: The Spectrum of Nondemocratic Regimes," in Andreas Schedler, editor, Electoral Authoritarianism: The Dynamics of Unfree Competition (Boulder, CO: Lynne Rienner Publishers, 2006), p. 219; 137: Steven Levitsky and Lucan Way, Competitive Authoritarianism: The Origins and Evolution of Hybrid Regimes in the Post-Cold War Era (New York:

Cambridge University Press, 2010), pp. 5–6; 140: Samuel P. Huntington, The Clash of Civilizations and the Remaking of World Order (New York: Touchstone, 1997), p. 29; 140: Pew Research Center, The World's Muslims: Religion, Politics, and Society (Washington, DC: Pew Research Center's Forum on Religion and Public Life, 2013), pp. 17..http://www.pewforum.org/Muslim/the-worlds-muslims-religion-politics-society.aspx. Accessed July 21, 2013; 140: David Samuels, "Comparative Politics (New York: Pearson Education, Inc., 2013), pp. 179–180; 149–150: AmartyaSen, "Democracy as a Universal Value, ' Journal of Democracy 10 (July 1999), cited in Marc Plattner, "Populism, Pluralism, and Liberal Democracy," p. 82; 150: Andreas Schedler, "Authoritarianism's Last Line of Defense," Journal of Democracy 21:1 (January 2010), p. 69; 150: Jay Ulfelder, "Prospects for New Democracies in the Arab World," Monkey Cage Blog (April 26, 2011). http://themonkeycage.org/2011/04/26/prospects_for_new_democracies._/. Accessed April 27, 2011; 142: Lynette Mitchell, The Heroic Rulers of Archaic and Classical Greece (A & C Black, 2013).

Chapter 7 Page 154: Winston Churchill, rom a House of Commons speech on Nov. 11, 1947; 154: Quoted in Niall Ferguson, The Cash Nexus: Money and Power in the Modern World (New York: Basic Books, 2001), p. 353; 154: Valerie Bunce, "Comparative Democratization: Big and Bounded Generalizations," Comparative Political Studies (Aug.–Sept. 2000), p. 704; 155: Barrington Moore Jr., The Social Origins of Dictatorship and Democracy (Boston: Beacon Press, 1993), p. 418; 155: Quoted in Johann Hari, "The Two Churchills," New York Times Book Review (August 15, 2010), p. 11; 156: William F. S. Miles, "The Mauritius Enigma," Journal of Democracy 10.2 (1999), p. 99; 156: William F. S. Miles, "The Mauritius Enigma," Journal of Democracy 10.2 (1999), p. 99; 157: Larry Diamond, "Democracy's Third Wave Today," Current History, (November 2011), p. 299; 158: Barbara Geddes, "What Causes Democratization," in The Oxford Handbook of Political Science, edited by Robert E. Goodin (New York: Oxford University Press, 2009), p. 596; 159: Kristian Skrede Gleditsch and Michael D. Ward, "Diffusion and the Spread of Democratic Institutions," in The Global Diffusion of Markets and Democracy," edited by Beth A. Simmons, Frank Dobbin, and Geoffrey Garrett (New York: Cambridge University Press, 2008), p. 295; 159: M. Steven Fish and Robin S. Brooks, "Does Diversity Hurt Democracy?," Journal of Democracy, (January 2004), Vol. 15, No. 1., p. 164; 159: David Marquand, The End of the West (Princeton: Princeton University Press, 2011), p. 125; 159: Adam Przeworski, Sustainable Democracy (New York: Cambridge University Press, 1995), pp. 12–13; 164: Steven Hill, Europe's Promise: Why the European Way is the Best hope in an Insecure Age (Berkeley: University of California Press, 2010), p. 265; 164: Andrew McLaren Carstairs, A Short History of Electoral Systems in Western Europe (London: George Allen & Unwin, 1980), p. 215; 166: Quoted in Anthony Gottlieb, "Win or Lose," The New Yorker (July 22, 2010); 168: Amartya Sen, "Human Rights and Economic Achievements," in Joanne R. Bauer and Daniel A. Bell, eds., The East Asian Challenge for Human Rights (New York: Cambridge University Press, 1999), p. 91; 168: Adam Przeworski and Fernando Limongi, "Political Regimes and Economic Growth," Journal of Economic Perspectives, Vol. 7 (Summer 1993), p. 65; 169: Morton H. Halperin, Joseph T. Siegle and Michael M.Weinstein, The Democratic Advantage: How Democracies Promote Peace and Prosperity, (New York: Routledge, 2005), p. 34; 169: Morton H. Halperin, Joseph T. Siegle and Michael M.Weinstein, The Democratic Advantage: How Democracies Promote Peace and Prosperity, (New York: Routledge, 2005), p. 38.

Chapter 8 Page 179: Bruce Cumings, Korea's Place in the Sun: A Modern History (New York, W.W. Norton and Company, 1997), p. 303; 178: United Nations Development Programme, "What Is Human Development?" Human Development Report 2002, .org; 179: United Nations Development Programme, Human Development Report, 20013 p. 141; 180: Jean Dreze and Amartya Sen, "Putting Growth in Its Place."(November 7, 2011), OutlookIndia.com. http://www.outlookindia.com/article.aspx?278843. Accessed November 8, 2011; 182: This question is asked by Dani Rodrik, "The Past, Present, and Future Extreme poverty of Economic Growth," Global Citizen Foundation, Working Paper No. 1 (June, 2013). http://www.gcf.ch/?page_id=5758. Accessed August 15, 2013; 184: "The best story in development," The Economist (May 19, 2012). http://www.economist.com/node/21555571#footnote1. Accessed May 19, 2012; 185: Based on Peter Evans and Pattrick Heller, "Human Development, State Transformation, and the Politics of the Developmental State," in Stephan Leibfried, Frank Nullmeier, Evelyne Huber, Matthew Lange, eds, The Oxford Handbook of Transformations of the State (New York: Oxford University Press, 2013); 185: Based on Peter Evans and Pattrick Heller, "Human Development, State Transformation, and the Politics of the Developmental State," in Stephan Leibfried, Frank Nullmeier, Evelyne Huber, Matthew Lange, eds, The Oxford Handbook of Transformations of the State (New York: Oxford University Press, 2013); 186: Lant Pritchettt and Erik Werker, "Developing the guts of a GUT (Grand Unified Theory): elite commitment and inclusive growth, "Effective States and Inclusive Development, Working Paper Series 16/12 (Cambridge, MAHarvard Business SchoolDecember 7, 2012) p. 39. http://www.hbs.edu/faculty/Pages/item.aspx?num=44065. Accessed October 25, 2013; 188: Kenneth L. Sokoloff and Stanley L. Engermann, "History Lessons: Institutions, Factor Endowments, and Paths of Development in the New World," Journal of Economic Perspectives 14:3 (Summer 2000), p. 217; 188: Dani Rodrik, "The Past, Present, and Future of Economic Growth," Global Citizen Foundation, Working Paper 1 (June 2013). Pp. 14–15. http://www.gcf.ch/?page_id=5758. Accessed August 13, 2013; 189: Jared Diamond, Guns, Germs, and Steel: The Fates of Human Societies (New York: W. W. Norton and Company, 1999), p. 87; 189: Jeffrey D. Sachs, "Institutions Matter, but Not for Everything," Finance and Development 40:2 (June 2003), p. 39; 190: David S. Landes, "Culture Makes Almost All the Difference," in Lawrence E Harrison and Samuel P. Huntington, Culture Matters: How Values Shape Human Progress(New York: Basic Books, 2000), p. 2; 190: David S. Landes, The Wealth and Poverty of Nations: Why Some Nations Are So Rich and Some So Poor (New York: W. W. Norton and Company, 1998), pp. 217–218, 274–275; 190: Francis Fukuyama, "The Economics of Trust," National Review (August 14, 1995), p. 42; 190: Francis Fukuyama, "Social Capital," in Lawrence E. Harrison and Samuel P. Huntington, Culture Matters, p. 98; 192: David D. Ferranti, Guillermo D. Perry, and Fracisco Ferreira, Inequality in Latin America: Breaking with History? (Washington, D.C.: The World Bank, 2004), p. 110; 193: Daron Acemoglu and James A. Robinson, Why Nations Fail: The Origins of Power, Prosperity, and Poverty (New York: Crown Pubishers, 2012), pp. 73–79. The quotation is from page 43; 193: Daron Acemoglu, Simon Johnson, and James A. Robinson, "Institutions as a Fundamental Cause of Long-Run Growth," p. 446; 193: Daron Acemoglu, Simon Johnson, and James A. Robinson, "Institutions as a Fundamental Cause of Long-Run Growth," p. 446; 193: Daron Acemoglu, Simon Johnson, and James A. Robinson, "Institutions as a Fundamental Cause of Long-Run Growth," p. 446; 193: Daron Acemoglu, Simon Johnson, and James Robinson," The Rise of Europe: Atlantic Trade, Institutional Change, and Economic Growth." American Economic Review 95:3 (June 2005), pp. 549–551; 195: Daron Acemoglu and James A. Robinson, Why Nations Fail: The Origins of Power, Prosperity, and Poverty (New York: Crown Publishers, 2012, pp. 70–76.

Chapter 9 Page 207: Wolf is quoted in Andrew Glyn, Capitalism Unleashed (New York: Oxford University Press, 2006), p. 167; 207–208: Perrson is quoted in Jenny Anderson, "The People's Library and the Electronic Workshop: Comparing Swedish and British Social Democracy," Politics & Society Vol. 34, No. 3, (September 2006), p. 439; 208: See Special Report "Northern Lights" in The Economist (February 2, 2013), pp. 9–16; 208: Goran Therborn, "A Unique Chapter in the History of Democracy: The Social Democrats in Sweden," in Klaus Misgeld, Karl Molin, and Klas Amark, eds., Creating Social Democracy: A Century of the Social Democratic Labor Party in Sweden (University Park, PA: Pennsylvania State University Press, 1992), pp. 1–2; 209: Arend Lijphart, Patterns of Democracy: Government Forms and Performance in Thirty-Six Countries (New Haven: Yale University Press, 1999), p. 2; 211: Rune Premfors, "Reshaping the Democratic State: Swedish Experiences in a Comparative Perspective," Public Administration Vol. 76 (Spring 1998), p. 154; 211: Gosta Esping-Andersen, "The Making of A Social Democratic Welfare State," in Klaus Misgeld, Karl Molin, and Klas Amark, eds., Creating Social Democracy: A Century of the Social Democratic Labor Party in Sweden (University Park, PA: Pennsylvania State University Press, 1992), p. 41; 214: The Economist, "The Next Supermodel," (February 2, 2013), p. 9; 215: Thomas J. Anton, Policy-Making and Political Culture in Sweden," Scandinavian Political Studies Vol … p. 99; 215: Bo Rothstein, "Social Capital in the Social Democratic State," in Democracies in Flux: The Evolution of Social Capital in Contemporary Society, Robert Putnam, ed., (New York: Oxford University Press, 2002), p. 303; 215: Bo Rothstein, "Social Capital in the Social Democratic State," in Democracies in Flux: The Evolution of Social Capital in Contemporary Society, Robert Putnam, ed., (New York: Oxford University Press, 2002), p. 319; 215–216: Maureen A. Eger, "Even in Sweden: The Effect of Immigration on support for Welfare State Spending," European Sociological Review, Vol. 26, No. 2 (2010), pp. 203; 216: Robert Taylor, quoted in John T. S. Madeley, "'The Swedish Model is Dead! Long Live the Swedish Model,'" p. 165; 216: Gosta Esping Andersen, Politics Against Markets: The social Democratic Road to Power (Princeton: Princeton University Press, 1985). p. 197; 217: Anders Lindblom, "Dismantling the Social Democratic Welfare Model?: Has the Swedish Welfare State Lost its Defining Characteristics?," Scandinavian Political Studies, Vol. 24, No. 3, (2001), p. 17; 217: Mike Marshall, "The Changing Face of Swedish Corporatism: The Disintegration of Consensus," Journal of Economic Issues Vol. 30 (September 1996), p. 858; 217: Douglas A. Hibbs Jr. and Hakan Locking, "Wage Dispersion and Productive Efficiency: Evidence from Sweden," Journal of Labor Economics Vol. 18, No. 4 (2000), pp. 755–782; 221: Charles Dickens, A Christmas Carol, A&C Black, 2011; 222: Ellis Wasson, A History of Modern Britain, 1714 to the Present (Chichester: John Wiley & Sons, 2010), p. 210; 233: Colin Hay, "Britain and the Global Financial Crisis: The Return of Boom and Bust," British Politics 9 (New York: Palgrave, 2011) p. 239; 234: van Kersbergen, Social Capitalism, pp. 180–81; 234: Emmerich Talos, "Corporatism—The Austrian Model," in Volmar Lauber, ed., Contemporary Austrian Politics (Boulder: Westview Press, 1996), p. 104; 238: Simon Green and William E. Paterson, "Introduction: Semisovereignty Challenged," in Governance in Contemporary Germany: The Semisovereign State Revisited, edited by Simon Green and William E. Paterson, (New York: Cambridge University Press, 2005), p. 6; 240: Hans Fuchs, newly appointed president of the North Rhine province under the Allied occupation, quoted in Konrad H. Jarausch, After Hitler: Recivilizing Germans, 1945–1995 (New York: Oxford University Press, 2006), p. 20; 242: Pol O'Dochartaigh, Germany since 1945, (New York: Palgrave, 2004), p. 41; 246: Based on Timothy Smeeding, "Poor People in Rich Nations," Journal of Economic Perspectives Vol 20, No. 1 (2006), pp. 69–90. See Table 2: Absolute Poverty Rates Using Official US Poverty Standards in Nine Rich Countries at the Turn of the Century; 246: OECD/HRDC, Literacy in the Information Age: Final Report of the International Adult Literacy Survey " (Paris: Organization for Economic Cooperation and Development; and Ottawa: Human Resources Development Canada, 2000), p. x; 246: OECD Skills Outlook, 2013: First Results from the Survey of Adult Skills, (Paris, OECD: 2013), p. 75; 247: Economist Democracy Index, 2011; 211: Torbjörn Bergman, Kaare Strøm, The Madisonian Turn: Political Parties and Parliamentary Democracy in Nordic Europe (University of Michigan Press, 2011); 230: Geoffrey Evans, Nan Dirk de Graaf, Political Choice Matters: Explaining the Strength of Class and Religious Cleavages in Cross-National Perspective (Oxford University Press, 2013); 247: Based on UNODC Global Study on Homicide 2011.

Chapter 10 Page 256: Atul Kohli, State-Diredted Development: Political power and industrialization in the Global periphery (New York: Cambridge University Press, 2004) p. 171; 257: Branko Milanovic, "Inequality and Its Discontents: Why So Many Feel Left Behind," Foreign Affairs August 12, 2011, http://www.foreignaffairs.com/articles/68031/branko-milanovic/inequality-and-its-discontents?page=show. Accessed August 12, 2011; 259: Mala Htun, "From 'Racial Democracy' to Affirmative Action: Changing State Policy on Race in Brazil," Latin American Research Review 39:1 (February 2004), p. 61; 259: Mala Htun, "Racial Quotas for a 'Racial Democracy,'" NACLA Report on the Americas (January/February 2005), p. 20; 260: Ben Ross Schneider, "The Dessarollista State in Brazil and Mexico," in Meredith Woo-Cumings, The Developmental State (Ithaca, NY: Cornell University Press, 1999), p. 289; 268: A man and a morass," Economist (May 26, 2011). http://www.economist.com/node/18741606?story_id=18741606. Accessed May 27, 2011; 270: AFROBAROMETER, Survey of Results Afrobarometer Round 5 Survey in Nigeria, 2012 p. 54. www.afrobarometer.org; 271: AFROBAROMETER, Survey of Results Afrobarometer Round 5 Survey in Nigeria, 2012; 271: Paul M. Lubeck, "Nigeria: Mapping a Shari's Restorationist Movement," p. 248; 271: Paul Collier, The Bottom Billion, p. 49; 272: World Bank, "Nigeria Economic Report," (May, 2013) pp. 8 – 9; 272: Larry Diamond," Thinking About Hybrid Regimes," The Journal of Democracy, 13:2 (April 2002), p. 24; 274: Ervand Abrahamian, "Who's in Charge?" London Review of Books 30:21 (November 6, 2008). http://www.lrb.co.uk/v30/n21/ervand-abrahamian/whos-in-charge. Accessed April 5, 2011; 276: Ervand Abrahamian, "Who's in Charge?" London Review of Books 30:21 (November 6, 2008). http://www.lrb.co.uk/v30/n21/ervand-abrahamian/whos-in-charge. Accessed April 5, 2011; 276: Khamenei speech entitled "Reforms, Strategies, and Challenges" quoted in Karim Sadjadpour, "Reading Khamenei: The World View of Iran's Most Powerful Leader," (Washington, DC: Carnegie Endowment for International Peace, 2008), p. 8; 279: This discussion of the first three factions draws on Ray Takeyh, Hidden Iran pp. 31–57; 279: Ray Takeyh, Hidden Iran: Paradox and Power in the Islamic Republic (New York: Henry Holt and Company, 2006) p. 48; 281: The phrase is from T. Yousef, "Employment, Development and the Social Contract in the Middle East and North Africa." Technical report, Washington, D.C. 2004, cited in Dvjavad Salhehi-Isfahani, "Revolution and Redistribution in Iran: Poverty and Inequality 25 Years Later," Department of Economics, Virginia Tech University, August 2006, p. 4; 281: Kevan Harris," Subsidy Payments in Iran: Too Much or Not Enough?" http://www.kevanharris.com/post/9754508505/subsidy-payments-in-iran-too-much-or-not-enough. Accessed September 8, 2011; 283: Kevan Harris, "The Politics of Subsidy Reform in Iran," Middle East Research and Information Project, 254 (Spring 2010).http://merip.org/mer/mer254/harris.html. Accessed October 6, 2013; 284: Thomas Erdbrink, "Iran Staggers as Sanctions Hit Economy," New York Times (September 30, 2013. http://www.nytimes.com/2013/10/01/world/middleeast/iran-staggers-as-sanctions-hit-economy.html?hp&_r=0. Accessed October 1. 2013.

Chapter 11 Page 300: Vladimir Gelman, "Institutional Trap in Russian Politics: Still No Way Out? PONARS Eurasia Policy Memo No. 151. (May 2011), p. 2; 301: The World Bank, "Worldwide Goevernance Indicators," http://info.worldbank.org/governance/wgi/index.aspx#doc. r Accessed November 24, 2013; 301: Gideon Lichfield, "Survey of Russia: Watch Your Back," The Economist (May 20, 2004), www.economist.com, accessed June 30, 2010; 301: "Russia's Economy: The S Word," The Economist (November 9, 2013). http://www.economist.com/news/europe/21589455-will-stagnating-economy-bring-about-much-needed-structural-reform-s-word. Accessed November 8, 2013; 301: Stephen Kotkin, "Now Comes the Tough Part in Russia," New York Times (March 2, 2008). http://www.nytimes.com/2008/03/02/business/worldbusiness/02shelf.html?pagewanted=print&_r=0. Accessed November 6, 2013; 302: Thomas F. Remington, "Politics in Russia," in Comparative

Politics Today, 9th edition, ed. Gabriel A. Almond, G. Bingham Powell, Jr., Russell J. Dalton, and Kaare Strom (New York: Pearson Longman. 2008), pp. 392–393; 304: Maria Lipman at a fourm celebrating the publication of "Russia in 2020: Scenarios for the Future." Clifford Gaddy, Sam Greene, Maria Lipman, and Nikolay Petrov, "Russia in 2020: Scenarios for the Future," (Washington, DC: Carnegie Endowment for International 21, 2011, no page number http://carnegieendowment.org/files/0421_transcript_russia2020.pdf. Accessedd November 22, 2011.; 304: Sam Greene at a forum celebrating the publication of "Russia in 2010: Secnarious fo r the future. Clifford Gaddy, Sam Greene, Maria Lipman, and Nikolay Petrov, "Russia in 2020: Scenarios for the Future," no page number; 305: Peter Pomerantsey, " Russia for Russians," London Review of Books (November 5, 2013. http://www.lrb.co.uk/blog/2013/11/05/peter-pomerantsev/russia-for-russians/. Accessed November 7, 2013; 305: Andrew Kohut, "Confidence in Democracy and Capitalism Wanes in the Former Soviet Union," Pew Global Attitudes Project (December 5, 2011), pages 3, 21–23; 305: Amy Knight, "Putting the Watch on Putin, New York Review of Books, 58:7 (April 14, 2011). http://www.nybooks.com/blogs/nyrblog/2011/apr/14/russia-opposition-putin-corruption/. Accessed April 28, 2011; 305: Thomas de Waal, "An Anatomy of Apathy," The National Interest (April 29, 2011). http://nationalinterest.org/commentary/anatomy-apathy-5239. Accessed May 18, 2011; 308: Another great leap forward?, The Economist; 309: Sam Greene, "Putin in 2012."; 312: Frederick C. Teiwes, "Politics at the 'Core': The Political Circumstances of Mao Zedong, Deng Xiaoping and Jiang Zemin," China information: A Journal of Contemporary China Studies, Vol. XV, No. 1, p. 27; 313: Andrew Nathan, China's Transition (New York: Columbia University Press, 1997), p. 29; 314: Cheng Li, "Rule of the Princelings," The Cairo Review of Global Affairs (February 10, 2013), pp. 36–38. http://www.aucegypt.edu/gapp/cairoreview/Pages/articleDetails.aspx?aid=295. Accessed November 24, 2013; 317: Minxin Pei, China's Trapped Transition, p. 65; 317: Minxin Pei, China's Trapped Transition, p. 70–71; 317: Cheng Li, "China at the Tipping Point," Journal of Democracy 24:1 (January 2013), p. 45; 317: David Shambaugh, China's Communist Party:: Atrophy and Adaptation (Washington, DC: Woodrow Wilson Center Press, 2009), p. 111; 318: Andrew Higgins, "China trade union takes up new cause – workers," Washington Post (April 28, 2011. http://www.washingtonpost.com/world/asia-pacific/chinas-trade-union-takes-up-a-new-cause--workers/2011/03/01/AFMjIN5E_story.html. Accessed April 19, 2011; 319–320: Andrew Jacobs, Protests at Chemical Plant Forces Officials to Back Down," The New York Times (October 28, 2012). http://www.nytimes.com/2012/10/29/world/asia/protests-against-sinopec-plant-in-china-reach-third-day.html?hpw. Accessed October 29, 2012; 320: Jie Lu, "Democratic Conceptions and Regime Support Among Chinese Citizens," Asian Barometer: A Comparative Survey of Democracy, Governance, and Development: Working Paper Series Number 66 (2012), pp. 41–42; 321: Jie Lu, "Democratic Conceptions and Regime Support Among Chinese Citizens," pp. 45–47; 322–323: Didi Tang, "Plague of office-buying wears at China's Image." Yahoo News. (October 31, 2012) http://news.yahoo.com/plague-office-buying-wears-chinas-image-080904130.html. Accessed October 31, 2012; 323: An Chen, "The New Inequality," Journal of Democracy 14:1 (January 2003), p. 54; 323: Dorothy Solinger, "Path Dependence Re-examined: Chinese Welfare Policy in the Transition to Unemployment," Comparative Politics 38:1 (October 2005), p. 96; 323: "Invisible and Heavy Shackles," The Economist (May 6, 2010).www.economist.com, accessed May 10, 2010; 325: Minxin Pei, "The Politics of a Slowing China," Project Syndicate, (July 6, 2013), . http://www.project-syndicate.org/commentary/the-impact-of-slow-gdp-growth-on-chinese-politics-by-minxin-pei. Accessed July 9, 2013; 325: Jay Ulfelder, "Wny the Communist Party of China Is Right to Worry about Popular Protests," Dart Throwing Chimp Blog (August 9, 2012). http://dartthrowingchimp.wordpress.com/. Accessed August 10, 2012; 327: Daniel Kaufmann, Aart Kraay, and Massimo Mastruzzi, Governance Matters IV: Governance Indicators for 1996–2004 (Washington, D.C.: The World Bank, 2005), http://info.worldbank.org/etools/docs/library/206973/GovMatters_IV_main.pdf, accessed June 16, 2010; 325: Minxin Pei, Beijing fakes the good fight against its own corruption, November 2, 2012.

Tables

Page 246: Based on Timothy Smeeding, "Poor People in Rich Nations," Journal of Economic Perspectives Vol 20, No. 1 (2006), pp. 69-90. See Table 2: Absolute Poverty Rates Using Official US Poverty Standards in Nine Rich Countries at the Turn of the Century; 246: OECD Skills Outlook, 2013: First Results from the Survey of Adult Skills, (Paris, OECD: 2013), p. 75; 247: Based on UNODC Global Study on Homicide 2011; 247: Economist Democracy Index, 2011

Index

A

Abacha, Sani, 267
Absolute poverty, 182
ACFTU. *See* All-China Federation of Trade Unions (ACFTU)
Active labor market policies, 207
Adenauer, Konrad, 239
Adult literacy rates
    in Brazil, 285–286
    in China, 326–327
    in developed and less developed countries, 198–199
    in Iran, 286
    in Nigeria, 285–286
    in Russia, 326–327
Affluent democracies, 205–208, 214, 215, 245
    organizational life in, 215
    political model in, 205
Afghanistan
    girls education in, 23
    low income, 178
    Taliban government in, 23
AFL-CIO, 66
Africa. *See also* Less developed countries; Sub-Saharan Africa
    authoritarianism in, 128
    death from AIDS in, 47
    democratic future in, 156
    nation-building elites in, 108
    party systems in, 61, 62
Afro-Brazilians, 259, 261
Agrarian Party (Sweden), 212. *See also* Centre Party (Sweden)
Agrarian societies, 108
Ahmadinejad, Mahmoud, 280, 281, 282, 283
AIDS
    Brazilian strategies for, 256
    death in Africa from, 47
    weak states and, 47
Air pollution, in China, 319, 324
Ali, Ben, 56
All-China Federation of Trade Unions (ACFTU), 318
Almond, Gabriel, 77–78, 230
Al Qaeda, 82, 131, 138
American National Exhibition, 103
American Political Science Association, 22
Amnesty International, 303, 319
Anglo-American democracies, 219
Angola, infants in, 177
Anti-EU UK Independent Party, 229
Anti-immigrant British Nationalist Party, 229
Anton, Thomas J., 215
Arab world
    authoritarianism in, 138, 140–142
    vs. Middle East, 138
    oil revenue in, 141–142
Argentina, 133, 141, 157
Armed forces. *See* Military
Arrow, Kenneth, 166
Asia. *See also* specific countries
    authoritarianism in, 128
    democratic future in, 156, 157
    globalization and, 114
    nation-building elites in, 108
Assembly of Experts (Iran), 278
Australia, 38
Austria, 5, 7
    as Christian democracy, 233, 234
    corporatist interest group in, 66
Authoritarianism
    defined, 127
    and economic development, 167–169
    and good society, 142–149
    politics, 129–130
    problem of authoritarian control, 129
    problem of authoritarian power sharing, 129
Authoritarian leaders, 128, 129, 136
Authoritarian persistence, 138–142
    domestic, 138, 140–142
    international, 138
    Middle East, 138–141
    North Africa, 138–141
Authoritarian regimes
    democracy and, 148–149
    informed decision making, 145–146
    military regimes, 131–133
    monarchies, 130–131
    one-party regimes in, 133–134
    persistence, 138–142
    personalist regimes, 135–138
    physical well-being, 144–145
    safety and, 146–147
    types of, 130–138
Authoritative power, 185
Authority, 29
Autonomy
    judiciary and, 45
    of military, 44
    strong states and, 47

B

Bahujan Samaj Party (India), 61
Balance of power (Nigeria), 267
Bangladesh, 3, 5, 7, 183, 189
Barbie dolls, 112
Basij Resistance Force (Iran), 276
BBC. *See also* British Broadcasting Corporation (BBC)
Belgium, 233
Berlin Wall, 157
Biafra, 267. *See also* Nigeria
Bible, 86
Bicameralism, 38
Big Men (Nigeria), 265
Blake, William, 221
Blondel, Jean, 41
Bloomberg News, 322
Boko Haram, 269
Bolsa Familia (family grant) program, 258
Bolsheviks, 295
Bonchek, Mark S., 65
Bonyads (Iran), 281
Bouazizi, Mohamed, 56
Brandt, Willy, 239
Brazil
    African descent, 259
    anti-HIV/AIDS programs, 256
    Chamber of Deputies, 256
    children's health, 259
    colonization by Portugal, 254
    flawed democracy, 254
    fragmented political parties, 258
    historical background, 254–256
    income inequality, 257–258
    industrialization, 254
    military, 254, 256
    political culture, 260–261
    political economy, 261–263
    presidential form of government, 256
    racial politics, 259–260
    senators, 256
    society, 257–260
    as state, 256–257
    sugar plantations in, 254
    Workers' Party, 258
"Brazilian miracle," 256
Brazilians of African descent, 259
Bribery, 186
Britain
    bureaucracy in, 43
    cabinet, 226–227
    colonies, 191
    conservative party, 221, 222, 228
    "deferential" culture, 230
    difference between United States cabinet and, 227
    election 2010, 163
    electoral systems in, 164
    France compared with (eighteenth century), 102
    Glorious Revolution of 1688, 221
    Great depression, 231
    head of state in, 40
    House of Commons, lower house, 225
    House of Lords, upper house, 225
    industrial capitalism in, 221
    Labour Party, 221, 226, 228–230
    legislatures in, 38
    Liberal Party, 221, 222

Index

members of parliament (MPs), 225–226
multiracial and multiethnic, 222, 230
parliamentary democracy, 221, 223
political culture, 78, 230–231
political economy, 231–233
political parties in, 61, 164
privatizations, 118
right to vote in, 221
society, 228–230
as state, 222–227
third-party success, 229
trade unions in, 61
World War II, 228
British Broadcasting Corporation (BBC), 75
Brown v. Topeka Board of Education, 45
Buffet, Warren, 2
Bundesrat (Germany), 237
Bureaucracy, 41–43
in Iran, 273, 279
Burma. *See* Myanmar
Bush, George W., 109

C

Cabinet, 41
Cameron, David, 226
Canada
federal system in, 36, 220
homicide rate in, 20
interest groups in, 66
national health insurance in, 35
political parties in, 163
voting rights in, 194
Cantons (Switzerland), 37
Capabilities, 17–21
Russia and China, 325–328
Capabilities approach, 21–23
defined, 16
quality of life, 17–21
responding to criticisms, 21–23
Capitalism, 62, 103–105
Christian democracy and, 234
Cardoso, Fernando Henrique, 259
Carnegie Foundation, 304
Carstairs, Andrew McLaren, 164
Causation, 6
CCP. *See* Chinese Communist Party (CCP)
CDU. *See* Christian Democratic Union (CDU)
Central banks, 117
Central Committee (China), 315
Centralized wage bargaining (Sweden), 217
Centrally planned economies, 293
extensive growth in, 293
farms in, 293
intensive growth and, 293
Central planning, 293. *See also* Centrally planned economies
Centre Party (Sweden), 212. *See also* Agrarian Party (Sweden)
Chad, 146, 149
Chamber of Deputies (Brazil), 256
Cheng Li, 314, 325

Chiang Kai-shek, 310
Chile, 93, 118, 123, 133, 146, 147, 192, 270
China, 309–325
absolutely poverty, 183
access to education, 323
air pollution, 319, 324
corruption, 322
cultural revolution in, 312
economic development in, 186
economic reforms in, 313–314
globalization and, 114
health care in, 325
historical background, 309–314
income inequality, 323
industrialization, 323–324
Japan's invasion of, 310, 312
judicial system in, 317
legislature in, 316
legislatures in, 38
political culture, 320–321
political economy, 321–325
reforms, 325
regulatory system, 47
reliance on exports, 322
repression, 319
Russia compared with, 325–328
society, 317–320
as state, 314–317
urban and rural dwellers, division, 323
Chinese Communist Party (CCP), 6, 117, 310, 314, 316, 317, 321, 322
Cholera, 176
Christian democracy, 233–234
Christian Democratic Appeal (Netherlands), 163–164
Christian Democratic Union (CDU), 239, 240
Christian Social Union (CSU), 239
Civic culture approach, 77–78
Civil war, 88
Class voting, 219
Clientelism, 71–72
Collier, Paul, 13
Colonialism, 191–192
Commissions of Inquiry (Sweden), 211, 215
Communism
centrally planned economies, 293
institutional basis of, 291–293
party rule, 292–293
Communism (Karl Marx), 292
Communist parties, 292–293
concept, 292
leadership, 292, 293
policy decisions in, 292
role of, 292
Comparative political analysis, 4–10, 6, 9, 24
Comparative politics, 3
Congress (United States)
bicameral structure of, 38
committee system, 38
interest groups and, 58
Consensual democracy, 209
Conservative faction (Iran), 279

Conservative Party (Britain), 221, 222, 228
Constitutional Court (Germany), 237
Constitutional Court (Russia), 299–300
Constitutions, 35
Constructivism, 90
Control variables, 3
Core executive, 40–41. *See also* Executive branch
Corporatist interest groups, 66–67. *See also* Interest groups
Corruption, 186–187
Costa Rica, 18
Coup d'état, 132, 133, 138
Court system (Nigeria), 267–268
Criminal cases, in China, 319
CSU. *See* Christian Social Union (CSU)
Cultural power, 29. *See also* Power
Cultural relativism, 23
Cultural relativists, 23
Cultural Revolution (China), 313
Culture
defined, 76
and development, 190–191
Cyclone, 3

D

Dealignment, 240
Demand, 101
Democracy(ies)
in authoritarian regimes, 148–149
in Brazil, 286
Catholicism, 140–141
in China, 327–328
concept of, 154
in developed and less developed countries, 200
and economic development, 167–169
in Germany, 247
India, 251
informed decision making in, 170
in Iran, 286
Islam, 140–141
in Nigeria, 286
parliamentary, 159–162
physical well-being, 169–170
political economy and, 122–123
presidential, 159–162
in Russia, 327–328
safety and, 170–172
semi-democracies, 251–253, 263–264
social movements and, 68–69
social trust, 94–95
in strong and weak states, 51–52
in Sweden, 247
transition from autocracy to, 155
in United Kingdom, 247
Demokratia, 154
Demokratizatsiia, 296
Deng Xiaoping, 312, 314, 323
Denmark, good society, 83
Dependent variable, 4
Developed countries
citizens' capabilities and, 183–184
colonialism, 191–192
culture and, 190–191

Developed countries (*continued*)
different levels of development, 181–182
GDP per capita and, 180
geography, 188–190
informed decision-making in, 198–199
institutions, 192–195
leadership, 196
vs. less developed countries, 181–188
physical well-being in, 197–198
safety in, 199–200
Diamond, Jared, 32, 188–189
Dickens, Charles, 13, 221
Diffusion effects, 158
"Divide and rule" (Nigeria), 265
Divided government, 237
Double-ballot elections, 163
Duma (Russia), 299, 302, 304
Dynastic monarchy, 130

E

ECB. *See* European Central Bank (ECB)
Ecologist Green Party, 229
Ecology Party (Sweden), 213
Economic development, 177–180
concept, 177
and corruption, 186
and human development, 180
Economic Freedom Index, 119–123
Economic power, 30. *See also* Power
Eger, Maureen A., 215
Einstein, Albert, 16
Eisenhower, Dwight D., 42
Electoral authoritarianism, 272
Electoral systems, 162–166
in Britain, 164
in Canada, 163, 165
defined, 162
in France, 163, 165
in Netherlands, 163
party discipline and, 166
party systems and, 166
in United States, 162, 163
vote allocation in, 163
Engels, Frederick, 221
Ethnicity, 84
Ethnic violence, mob violence, 88
Eurasia, 188–189, 201
European Central Bank (ECB), 117, 237
European Union (EU), 24, 211–213, 219, 222–223, 226, 230, 237, 241, 245
EU. *See* European Union (EU)
Executive branch, 40–41
concept of, 40
Expediency Council (Iran), 278, 280
Extensive growth of market, 101
Extractive economic institutions, 193
Extractive political institutions, 193
Extreme market democracies, 219–220
diversity of state institutions, 220
Extreme poverty, 182

F

Facebook, 82
Failed States Index, 48, 50
Fascism, 155
FDP. *See* Free Democrats (FDP)

Federal Assembly (Russia), 299
Federal Executive Council (Nigeria), 267
Federalist Party (United States), 60, 61
Federal Republic of Germany (FRG), 235
Federal Reserve (United States), 117
Federal Security Service (FSB) (Russia), 297
Federal systems, 36, 37
Federation Council (Russia), 299
Felt, Mark, 42
Ferejohn, John, 45
Fiscal policy, 115–116
Flawed democracy, 252–253
Foreign Policy, 48
France
Britain compared with (eighteenth century), 102
colonies, 191
double-ballot elections in, 163
electoral systems in, 163, 165
legislatures in, 38
political parties, 165
power sharing in, 40
presidents's power in, 35, 40
Free Democrats (FDP), 239, 240
Free rider problem, 64–65
FRG. *See* Federal Republic of Germany (FRG)
Friedman, Thomas A., 104
Fukuyama, Francis, 190
Fund for Peace, 48

G

Gallagher, Mary, 318
GDP. *See* Gross domestic product (GDP)
GDR. *See* German Democratic Republic (GDR)
General Secretary (China), 315
Genocide, 88
Geography, 188–190
German Democratic Republic (GDR), 235
Germany, 234–236
demilitarization of, 241
economy, 242–245
historical background, 234–235
legislature in, 237–238
nationalism, 241
political culture, 240–242
society, 239–240
as state, 237–239
Germany, Green Party in, 59
Germs (Diamond), 188
Gettleman, Jeffrey, 32
Giant Manufacturing, 113
Gini Index, 257, 323
Glasnost, 296
Globalization, 110–114
Global supply chain, 112
Glorious Revolution of 1688, 221
GNH. *See* Gross National Happiness (GNH)
Good societies
authoritarian regimes and, 142–149
economic development and, 197–200
institutions, 28–30
markets and, 119–123

quality of life, 17–21
vision of, 10–17
wealth and happiness, 10–17
Good Society, 47, 49, 50
Gorbachev, Mikhail, 296–297
Goulart, João, 254
Government
defined, 31
military and, 43
Great Britain. *See* Britain
Great Depression, 108
Great Leap Forward (China), 312–313
Great Proletarian Cultural Revolution (China), 312
Greene, Sam, 309
Green Movement (Iran), 282, 284
Green Parties, 58
Gross domestic product (GDP), 5, 10–17. *See also* Gross domestic product (GDP)
Gross National Happiness (GNH), 10–17
Guardian Council (Iran), 278
Guardianship democracy (China), 321
Guns (Diamond), 188

H

Hacker, Jacob S., 103
Hall, Peter A., 21
Hamilton, Alexander, 60
Happiness, 10–17
Hard Times (Dickens), 13
Harmful spillover effects, 106, 107
Hausa-Fulani (Nigeria), 265
HDI. *See* Human Development Index (HDI)
Head of state, 40–41
Head of the government, 40
Hindus and Muslims, 86–87
Hitler, Adolf, 235
Hollande, Francoise, 163
Holocaust, 240
Homicide, 121–122
Homicide rates
in Brazil, 286
in China, 327
income per capita and, 199–200
in Germany, 247
in Iran, 286
in Nigeria, 286
in Russia, 327
in Sweden, 247
in United Kingdom, 247
Hoover, Herbert, 41
House of Commons, lower house (Britain), 225
House of Lords, upper house (Britain), 225
House of Representatives (Nigeria), 267
Human development
concept, 178
economic development and, 179–180
Human Development Index (HDI), 178, 180
Human Development Report, 22
Huntington, Samuel P., 90, 140
Hypotheses, 4

I

IALS. *See* International Adult Literacy Survey (IALS)
ICBL. *See* International Campaign to Ban Landmines (ICBL)
Identity
  politics of identity, 84
  violence, 88, 90
Igbo (Nigeria), 265, 267
Imams, 273
IMF. *See* International Monetary Fund (IMF)
Inclusive economic institutions, 192
Inclusive political institutions, 193
Independent variable, 4
India, 110
  democracy in, 251
  globalization and, 114
  homicide rate in, 172
  infant mortality rate, 172
  information technology in, 114
  literacy rate, 172
  religion in, 86, 90
  right to information law in, 18
  state intervention, 108
Inequality-Adjusted Human Development Index, 179
Infant mortality
  in China, 326
  income per capita and, 197–198
  in Iran, 284, 285
  in Nigeria, 285
  in Russia, 326
  in Somalia, 32
Informed decision-making, 18–19
  in authoritarian regimes, 145–146
  in Brazil, 285–286
  in China, 326–327
  democracy and, 170
  income per capita and, 198–199
  in Iran, 286
  in Nigeria, 285–286
  political economy and, 120
  in Russia, 326–327
  social trust, 92–93
  in strong and weak states, 49–50
Infrastructural power, 185
Inglehart, Ronald, 79
Inkatha Freedom Party (South Africa), 61
Institutions, 28–30, 192–195
  concept of, 28–29
Instrumentalism, 90
Intensive growth of market, 101
Interest groups, 64–67
  concept, 64
  corporatist, 66–67
  pluralist, 66–67
International Adult Literacy Survey (IALS), 246
International Campaign to Ban Landmines (ICBL), 69
International Monetary Fund (IMF), 113
"Interventionist-redistributive social contract" (Iran), 281
IPod, 112
Iran, 273–285
  conservative faction, 279
  historical background, 273–276
  political culture, 282–283
  political economy, 283–285
  pragmatist faction, 279
  principlist faction, 280
  reformist faction, 279
Iranian Revolutionary Guards Corps (IRGC), 276
Iraq, 63
  attack on Iran, 276
  homicide rate in, 199
Iraq War, 240, 245
IRGC. *See* Iranian Revolutionary Guards Corps (IRGC)
Islam
  compatiblity with democracy, 140–141
Israel
  legislature in, 62
  multimember districts, 162
  party system in, 62

J

James, LeBron, 16
Japan, invasion of China, 310, 312
Jefferson, Thomas, 60
Jie Lu, 321
Johnson, Lyndon Baines, 2
Jonathan, Goodluck, 268
Jordan, head of state in, 40
Judicialization of politics, 45–46
Judicial review, 45
Judiciary, 44–47
  in authoritarian regimes, 44
  and autonomy, 44
  China, 317
  in Nigeria, 267–268
  in South Africa, 45
  in Ukraine, 47
  in United States, 45, 46
Junta, 132
Junta leaders (Brazil), 254

K

Kagame, Paul, 127, 196
Katzenstein, Peter, 237
Khamenei, Ayatollah Ali, 276, 279, 280, 283
Khan, Genghis, 16
Khan, Reza, 273
Khodorkovsky, Mikhail, 302
Khomeini, Ayatollah Ruhollah, 274, 276, 278, 283, 284
Khrushchev, Nikita S., 103–104
King, Martin Luther, 29
"Kitchen debate, "104
Kohl, Helmut, 238–240
Kolbert, Elizabeth, 15

L

Labor market, Germany, 243
Labour and conservative governments, 231
Labour Party (Britain), 61, 165, 221, 226, 228–230
Länder (Germany), 234, 237
Landes, David, 190
Landlocked countries, 189

Latin America
  economic progress in, 178
  military regimes in, 131
Leadership, and development of countries, 196
Legislatures, 37–39
  in authoritarian states, 38
  bicameralism, 38
  in Brazil, 256–257
  in China, 38, 316
  committee system, 38
  in democracies, 39
  in France, 39
  in Germany, 237–238
  in Israel, 62
  Nigeria, 267
  unicameralism, 38
  in United States, 38
Lenin, Vladimir, 295
Less developed countries
  absolute poverty and, 182
  citizens' capabilities and, 183–184
  colonialism and, 191–192
  culture and, 190–191
  economic development in, 178
  economic status, 251
  geography and, 188–190
  high and low level of development, capabilities comparison, 183–184
  high and low level of development, income comparison, 182–183
  informed decision-making in, 198–199
  institutions and, 192–195
  leadership, 196
  physical well-being in, 197–198
  safety in, 199–200
Liberal democracy (China), 320–321
Liberal Democrats (Britain), 165
Liberal Party (Britain), 221, 222
Linz, Juan, 161
Lipman, Maria, 304
Literacy rates
  in Brazil, 285–286
  in China, 326–327
  in developed and less developed countries, 198–199
  in Iran, 286
  in Nigeria, 285–286
  in Russia, 326–327
  sub-saharan Africa, 146
Literacy skills
  in Germany, 246
  in Sweden, 246
  in United Kingdom, 246
Liu Shaoqi, 312
Liu Xiaobo, 319
Long March (China), 310
Louis XV, 127–128
Lula da Silva, Luiz Inácio, 256, 258, 259
Lynch, Marc, 150

M

Magna Carta, 221
Mahdi, 273
Maioni, Antonia, 35
Majles (Iran), 280
Major, John, 229

Index

Mandelbaum, Michael, 104
Mao Zedong, 310, 312, 314
Market systems, 101–103
  advantage of, 103–105
  disadvantages of, 105–106
Marshall, Mike, 217
Martial law, 133
Marx, Karl, 292
Mauritius, 156
  citizens' capabilities in, 196
  democratic success, 156
McMillan, John, 102
Members of Parliament (MPs) (Britain), 225–226
Merkel, Angela, 240
Mexico
  globalization and, 113
  oil industry in, 118
  per capita income in, 188
Middle East, 138
  authoritarianism in, 138–142
Miles, William F. S., 156
Military, 43–44
Military coups, 155–156
Military officers, in Nigeria, 267
Military regimes, 131–133
Ministers, 41
Minxin Pei, 325
Mob violence, 88
Modernization theory, 33
Monarchies, 130–131
Monetary policy, 117
Monopoly, 102
Moore, Barrington, Jr., 155
Moral judgment, 10
Mossadegh, Mohammad, 274
Mugabe, Robert, 135, 193
Muhammed (Prophet), 273
Multimember election districts (Sweden), 162, 209
Muslims and Hindus, 86–87
Myanmar, 189

N

Nargis (cyclone), 3
Nation, 85
Nationalism, 85–86
Nationalist (or *Guomindang*) Party (China), 310, 312
Nationalization, 118–119
National Party Congress (China), 315
National People's Congress (NPC) (China), 38, 316
National Resistance Movement (Uganda), 60
Navalny, Alexei, 303
Nazi Party (Germany), 235
Neoliberalism, 112
New Economic Policy (NEP), 295
New social movements, 69
New York Times, 29
Nicaragua, 3
Nigeria, 264–272
  Boko Haram, 269
  colonialism and, 264
  constitution in, 267
  democracy, 270

ethnicity in, 264
historical background, 264–265
infant mortality rate, 145
judicial system in, 267–268
legislature in, 267
military governments in, 264–265, 267, 269
political culture, 270–271
political economy, 271–272
presidency, 267
progress in recent years, 271–272
rent seeking, 271
semi-democracies, 252
shari'a law, 268
society, 268–270
as state, 265–268
trade unions, 269
Nixon, Richard M., 103
Nkrumah, Kwame, 155
Normative judgment, 10
Norms of reciprocity, 71
North America, economic status, 251
North Korea, 178, 190, 191
Norway
  corporatist interest group in, 66
  HDI in, 178
  physical well-being in, 91
  social trust, 94
Nussbaum, Martha, 16

O

Obama, Barack, 109, 231
Obasanjo, Olusegun, 267
Objective judgment, 10
O'Donnell, Guillermo, 156
Oligarchs, 302, 303, 307
Ombudsman, 209
One-party regimes, 133–134
Operationalize variables, 5
Opium War (1839–1843), 310
Opportunity structure, 58
Outliers, 92

P

Pahlavi, Mohammed Reza Shah, 274
Pahlavi Dynasty, 273
Pakistan
  malnourished children, 183
  religion, 86
  religious identity, 75–76
  Yousafzai , Malala, 75
Park Chung Hee, 196
Parliamentary democracies, 160
Parliamentary systems, 160
Parti Quebecois (PQ) (Canada), 165
Party discipline, 166
Party systems, 61–64, 166
  electoral laws and, 63
Patronage, 64
Patron–client relations, 71–72
People's Bank in China, 117
People's Democratic Party (PDP) (Nigeria), 268
"People's procuratorate" (China), 319
Per capita GDP, 5, 7, 8, 12
Per capita income
  China, 323, 325, 326

democracy and, 200
and HDI, 180
homicide rates and, 199–200
infant mortality rates and, 197–198
literacy rates and, 198–199
Mexico, 188
Qatar, 140
Russia, 323, 325, 326
United States, 188
Perestroika, 296
Persia. *See* Iran
Personalist regimes, 135–138
Personal rule, defined, 136
Persson, Goran, 207
Physical well-being, 17–18
  in authoritarian regimes, 144–145
  in Brazil, 285
  China, 326
  democracy and, 169–170
  income per capita and, 197–198
  in Germany, 246
  in Iran, 285
  in Nigeria, 285
  political economy and, 120
  Russia, 326
  social trust, 91–92
  in strong and weak states, 49
  in Sweden, 246
  in United States, 246
Pierson, Paul, 103
Pluralist interest groups, 66–67
Politburo (China), 314
Political analysis, 195
Political culture
  Brazil, 260–261
  Britain, 78, 230–231
  China, 320–321
  civic culture approach to, 77–78
  defined, 76
  Germany, 240–242
  Iran, 282–283
  Nigeria, 270–271
  Russia, 304–306
  self-expression approach to, 78–81
  social capital, 81–84
  Sweden, 214–216
  United States, 78
Political economy
  Brazil, 261–263
  China, 321–325
  concept, 103
  democracy and, 122–123
  Germany, 242–245
  informed decision making, 120
  Iran, 283–285
  market control and, 119
  Nigeria, 271–272
  physical well-being, 120
  Russia, 306–309
  safety and, 121–122
  Sweden, 216–219
  United Kingdom, 231–233
  United States, 123
Political model, 205
Political participation, 58–60
  in authoritarian regime, 58
  in democracy, 58

Political parties, 60–64
    in authoritarian regimes, 61
    democracies and, 60–62, 252
Political power, 30. *See also* Power
Politics of identity, 84–87
    contentious, 87–90
    ethnicity, 84
    identity, 84
    nationalism, 85–86
    religion, 86–87
Postindustrial, 205
Poverty rates
    in Germany, 246
    in Sweden, 246
    in United States, 246
Power
    concept of, 29–30
    in federal systems, 36
    forms of, 29–30
    in unitary systems, 36, 37
PPP. *See* Purchasing power parity (PPP)
Pragmatist faction (Iran), 279
Premier (China), 316
President, 40–41
    in Brazil, 254–257, 261–263
    China, 316
    in Iran, 273, 278, 280–281
    in Nigeria, 267
    in Russia, 297
Presidential election 2012, in France, 163
Presidential systems, 160
Prime Minister (Russia), 299
Primordialism, 90
Principlist faction (Iran), 280
Pritchett, Lant, 186, 188
Problem of authoritarian control, 129
Problem of authoritarian power sharing, 129
Programmatic parties, 64
Property rights, 192–195
Prophet Muhammad, 131
Proportional representation (PR) rules, 163–165, 205, 209, 220, 223, 225, 238
PR rules. *See* Proportional representation (PR) rules
Purchasing power parity (PPP), 7
Putin, Vladimir, 294, 299, 300–309

Q
Qatar, 140, 144
Queen Elizabeth, 226

R
Reagan, Ronald, 109
"Reform and opening" (China), 313
Reformed Political Party (Netherlands), 164
Reformist Faction (Iran), 279
Regulations, 117–118
Regulatory policy, 117–118
Reichstag (Germany), 235
Relative poverty, 182
Religion, 86–87
Rents, defined, 271
Rent seeking, 271
Republican Party (United States), 60, 61

Republican Right (France), 165
Revolutionary Guards (Iran), 276
Right to information law, in India, 18
Riksdag (Sweden), 209
Rio de Janeiro (Brazil), 254
Rodrik, Dani, 13
Rosenberg, Tina, 114
Rosenblum, Nancy L., 60
Rothstein, Bo, 6
Rousseff, Dilma, 256–257, 259, 262
Royal Swedish Academy of Sciences, 166
"Rule of law" indicator, 327
Russia, 293–309
    China compared with, 325–328
    corruption, 301
    czarist regime collapse, 295
    highest income earners, 308
    historical background, 295–297
    infant mortality in, 326
    NEP in, 295
    oil and gas exports, 308
    oil sales, 301
    political culture, 304–306
    political economy, 306–309
    politics in, 300
    population of, 295
    society, 301–304
    as state, 297–301
    United Russia, 302
Russian Orthodox Church, 300, 306
Russian Security Council, 297
Russian Social Democratic Labor Party, 295

S
Safety, 19–20
    in authoritarian regimes, 146–147
    in Brazil, 286
    in China, 327
    democracy and, 170–172
    income per capita and, 199–200
    in Germany, 247
    in Iran, 286
    in Nigeria, 286
    political economy and, 121–122
    in Russia, 327
    social trust, 93–94
    in strong and weak states, 50–51
    in Sweden, 247
    in United Kingdom, 247
SAP. *See* Social Democratic Party (SAP) (Sweden)
Sarkozy, Nicholas, 12, 163
Scandinavian societies, 206–207
    labor force participation in, 207
    welfare states, 206–208
Scatter diagrams, 91
Schmidt, Helmut, 239
Schroeder, Gerhard, 240
Schumpeter, Joseph, 154–155
Second Reich (Germany), 235
Secretariat (China), 315
Secular values, 78
Self-expression approach, 78–81
Self-expression values, 79–80
    civic culture and, 80

Semi-democracies, 251–253, 263–264
Sen, Amartya, 12, 14, 15, 16, 19, 22, 149
Senators (Brazil), 256
Seven Days in May, 43
Shambaugh, David, 320
Shari'a Law, 140, 268, 274
Shia Muslims, 76, 141
Shiite Islam, 11, 76, 86, 141, 153, 273
Shock therapy, 307
Sierra Club, 65
Singapore
    economic development in, 178
    homicide rates, 147
    per capita income, 6–7
Single-member districts (United States), 162
Skatch, Cindy, 161
Slater, Dan, 158
Slavery, defined, 10–11
Smart phones, 82
Social capital, defined, 81
Social capital approach, 81–84
Social democracy, 206–208
    socialism, 206
Social democratic parties, 205, 206
Social Democratic Party (SAP) (Sweden), 208, 211, 212, 216
Social Democrats (SPD) (Germany), 240
Socialism (Karl Marx), 206, 292
Socialism with Chinese characteristics, 321
Socialist Party (France), 165
Social market economy, 242
Social movements, 68–70
    democracy and, 68–69
Social networks, 81, 82
Social trust, 82, 83
Somalia, 32
    as weak state, 48, 50
South Africa
    judiciary in, 45
    political parties in, 61
South Asia, 183, 184. *See also* Bangladesh; India; Pakistan
    absolute poverty in, 183
South Korea
    economic development in, 178, 179
    military regime, 132, 146
Sovereignty, concept of, 32
Soyinka, Wole, 267
SPD. *See* Social Democrats (SPD) (Germany)
Stalin, Joseph, 295–296
Standing Committee of the Politburo (China), 314
State Council (China), 316
State-led industrialization, 254
State-owned, centrally planned economies, 293
State(s), 30–36
    bureaucracy, 41–43
    coercion and violence, 31
    defined, 31
    executive branch, 40–41
    federal systems, 36, 37
    judiciary, 44–47

State(s) (*continued*)
  legislature, 37–39
  Marxist theory of, 34
  military, 43–44
  modernization theory of, 33, 34
  origin of, 32–34
  powers of, 31–32
  realists on, 34
  unitary systems, 36–37
"Statist individualism," 214
Steel (Diamond), 188
Stepan, Alfred, 161
Stokes, Susan C., 71
Strong states, 47–49
Sub-Saharan Africa
  absolutely poverty, 183
  leadership and development, 196
  literacy rates, 146
  military leaders in, 132
  personal rule in, 136
  safety in, 199
Summer Olympic Games (2008) (China), 320
Summer Olympics 2016 (Brazil), 253
Sunni Muslims, 11, 75, 76, 86, 141, 273
Sun Yat-sen, 310
Supply, 101
Supreme Leader (Iran), 276
Surowieki, James, 19
Survival values, 78–79
Sweden
  as consensual democracy, 209
  economy, 216–219
  executive branch in, 209
  as high trust society, 215
  immigration and, 215–216
  infants in, 176–177
  political culture, 214–216
  political parties, 211–213
  society, 211–213
Swedish Model, 217–218

T
Tanzania
  homicide rates, 147
Taxes, 206
Territoriality, 31
Thailand, 113, 114
Thatcher, Margaret, 104, 109, 228–229, 231
The Chinese Dream, 324
The Civic Culture (Almond and Verba), 77, 230
The Clash of Civilizations and the Remaking of World Order (Huntington), 140
The Communist Manifesto, 33, 104
The Economist, 109
The Journal of Human Development and Capabilities, 22
Theocracy, 274
"There Is No Alternative" (TINA), 104, 109
The Winter of Discontent, 1979, 228
Tiananmen Square protests (China), 314
Tianjian Shi, 321

Tierney, John, 29
Time (magazine), 75
TINA. See "There Is No Alternative" (TINA)
Township and village enterprises (TVEs) (China), 313
Traditional values, 78
Tragadh, Lars, 214
Transfer payments, 234
Transparency International, 301
Truman, Harry, 42
Tsai, Kellee, 6
Tunisia, 56
TVEs. See Township and village enterprises (TVEs) (China)
Twitter, 82

U
Uganda, political parties in, 60, 61
Ukraine, judiciary in, 47
Unicameral legislature, 38
Union density, 220, 243
Unitary systems, 36–37. *See also* Federal systems
United Arab Emirates, 140, 144
United Auto Workers, 66
United Kingdom. *See also* Britain
  depression, 222
  and World War I, 222
United Kingdom of Great Britain and Northern Ireland, 220–233
United Nations Development Programme, 178, 181
United Russia, 302
United States
  federal system in, 36
  head of state in, 40
  interest groups in, 65, 66
  judiciary in, 45, 46
  legislatures in, 37–38
  national health insurance in, 35
  political culture, 78
  political parties in, 61
  voting rights in, 194

V
Vargas, Getulio, 254
Velayat-e-faqih (Iran), 274, 279
Verba, Sidney, 77–78, 230
Voice and accountability, 328
Von Bismarck, Otto, 235
Von Treitschke, Heinrich, 34
Voting rights, 173, 194

W
Wage Solidarity, 217
Wage solidarity, 217
Wage solidarity (Sweden), 217
Warfare, 121
Washington consensus, 112
"Washington consensus," 112
Weak states, 47–49
Weber, Max, 190
Weimar Republic (Germany), 235

Welfare effort, 220
Welfare state, 9
  Christian democratic, 234
  growth of, 108
  Scandinavian, 207–208
  social democratic, 206–208
  Swedish, 215–216, 217
  work ethic and, 109
Werker, Erik, 186
Western Europe
  economic status, 251
Williams, Jody, 69
Winter Olympics (Russia), 304
Wolf, Martin, 207
Women
  in Afghanistan, 23
  in Iran, 284
  literacy rate in Pakistan, 76
Workers, 118
  in Brazil, 254, 257–259, 261–263
  communist parties and, 292
  globalization and, 115
  in Iran, 274
  labor market policies and, 207
  in Sweden, 216–219
  welfare state and, 108
Workers' Party (Brazil), 258
World Bank, 181–183
  defined, 112
  on absolute poverty, 182
  World Governance Indicators, 327
World Cup of soccer 2014 (Brazil), 253
World Economic Forum, 69
World Governance Indicators, of World Bank, 327
World Social Forum, 69
World Trade Organization (WTO), 219
World Values Survey, 14
World War II, and Germany, 235
WTO. *See* World Trade Organization (WTO)

X
Xi Jinping, 314, 319, 322, 324

Y
Yeltsin, Boris, 294, 297, 302, 307
Yoruba (Nigeria), 265
Yousafzai, Malala, 75, 140
Yukos oil company, 302

Z
ZANU. *See* Zimbabwe African National Union (ZANU)
Zimbabwe
  economic wreckage, 135
  infant mortality rate, 145
  infant mortality rate in, 145
Zimbabwe African National Union (ZANU), 135
Zuberi, Dan, 5–6
Zulu tribe (South Africa), 61
Zysman, John, 102

Notes

Chapter 1

1. President Johnson is quoted in Ira Katznelson, *When Affirmative Action Was White: An Untold History of Racial Inequality in Twentieth Century America* (New York: Norton, 2005), p. 175.
2. Alice Schroeder, *The Snowball: Warren Buffet and the Business of Life* (New York: Bantam, 2008), p. 43.
3. Andrew C. Revkin, "The Dangers of the Deltas," *New York Times* (May 11, 2008).
4. Steve Lohr, "For Today's Graduate, Just One Word: Statistics," *New York Times* (August 5, 2009).
5. Ann Meier and Kelly Musick, "Is the Family Dinner Overrated?" *New York Times* (July 1, 2012).
6. Dan Zuberi, *Differences That Matter: Social Policy and the Working Poor in the United States and Canada* (Ithaca: Cornell University Press, 2006).
7. Kellee S. Tsai, *Capitalism without Democracy: The Private Sector in Contemporary China* (Ithaca: Cornell University Press, 2007).
8. United Nations Development Programme, *Human Development Report 2011- Sustainability and Equity: A Better Future for All*. http:hdr.undp.org/en/statistics/.
9. Bo Rothstein, *The Quality of Government: Corruption, Social Trust, and Inequality in International Perspective* (Chicago, IL: University of Chicago Press, 2011), pp. 193–206.
10. Adam Przeworski, "Institutions Matter," *Government and Opposition* vol. 39, no. 4, (Autumn, 2004), pp. 527–540.
11. Adam Przeworski, "Institutions Matter."
12. William Adema, "The Welfare State across Selected OECD Countries: How Much Does It Really Cost and How Good Is It at Reducing Poverty?" in *The Future of the Welfare State*, edited by Brigid Reynolds, Sean Healy, and Michael Collins, (Dublin: Social Justice Ireland, 2010), Chart 1, p. 31.
13. For social welfare spending in Sweden and the United States as a percent of GDP, see "Social Expenditure-Aggregated Data," OECD Statextracts. OECD, 2013. www.//stats.oecd.org?Index.aspx?QueryID=4549. Turnout data is from Rafael Lopez Pintor, Maria Gratschew, and Kate Sullivan, *Voter Turnout Rates from a Comparative Perspective*. See Figure 12, p. 78, at http://www.idea.int/publications/vt/upload/Voter%20turnout.pdf.
14. Gary A. Haugan and Victor Boutros, The Locust Effect: Why the End of Poverty Requires the End of Violence (New York: Oxford Uiversity Press, 2014), p. 68 (emphasis in original)
15. It is important to compare countries based on per capita GDP because otherwise a very large country such as China would appear to be wealthier than a small country such as Denmark. China's GDP is bigger, but its population is much bigger than Denmark's.
16. United Nations Development Programme. *Human Development Report 2011 – Sustainability and Equity: A Better Future for All*, http://hdr.org/en/statistics. These amounts show the actual purchasing power of citizens can buy when their currency is converted to dollars.
17. The group was called The Commission on the Measurement of Economic Performance and Social Progress.
18. Jean Dreze and Amartya Sen, "Putting Growth in its Place," www.OutlookIndia.com/printarticle.aspx?278843.
19. Edward Wong, "The Cost of Environmental Damage in China Growing Rapidly amid Industrialization," *New York Times* (March 29, 2013).
20. Sarah Dykstra, Benjamin Dykstra, and Justin Dandefur, "We Just Ran Twenty-Three Million Queries of the World Bank's Web Site," Center for Global Development, Working Paper 362 (April 2014), p. 9.
21. Dickens is quoted in Martha Nussbaum and Amartya Sen, eds., *The Quality of Life* (New York: Oxford University Press, 1992), p. 1.
22. Paul Collier, *The Bottom Billion: Why the Poorest Countries Are Failing and What Can Be Done about It* (New York: Oxford University Press, 2007), p. 190.
23. Dani Rodrik, *One Economics, Many Recipes* (Princeton: Princeton University Press, 2007), p. 2.
24. Jean Dreze and Amartya Sen, *An Uncertain Glory: India and its Contradictions* (Princeton: Princeton University Press, 2013), p. 38, 18.
25. Bok is quoted in Thomas Nagel, "Who Is Happy and When," *New York Review of Books* (December 23, 2010), vol. 57, no. 20, p. 48.
26. Eduardo Porter, "All They Are Saying Is Give Happiness a Chance," *New York Times*, November 12, 2007.
27. Seth Mydans, "Recalculating Happiness in a Himalyan Kingdom," *New York Times*, May 7, 2009, p. A8.

28. National Science Foundation, "Despite Frustrations Americans Are Pretty Darned Happy," Press Release 08-110 (June 30, 2008). http://www.nsf.gov/news/newsmedia/pr111725/pr111725.pdf
29. John F. Helliwell and Shun Wang, "The State of World Happiness," in Part 1, Chapter 2 of the World Happiness Report, edited by John F. Helliwell, Richard Layard and Jeffrey Sachs, p. 21.
30. Martha Nussbaum, "Poverty and Human Functioning: Capabilities as Fundamental Human Entitlements," in David B. Grusky and Ravi Kanbur (eds.), *Poverty and Inequality* (Berkeley: University of California Press, 2006), pp. 48–49.
31. Sen, *The Idea of Justice* (Cambridge: Harvard University Press, 2009), p. 283.
32. Martha Nussbaum, "Poverty and Human Functioning: Capabilities as Fundamental Human Entitlements," *Poverty and Inequality*, pp. 48–49.
33. Charles Kenny, "Bentham from the Crypt: Politicians in Pursuit of Happiness," Center for Global Development, (June 2011).
34. Elizabeth Kolbert, "Everybody Have Fun," *New Yorker* (March 22, 2010), p. 72–74.
35. William C. Martel, "Formulating Victory and Implications for Policy," *Orbis* 52:4 (2008), pp. 613–626.
36. Robert J. Samuelson, "The Global Happiness Derby," *Washington Post* (April 16, 2012).
37. Alberto Alesino, Raphael di Tella, and Robert MacCulloch, "Inequality and Happiness: Are Europeans and Americans Different?" *Journal of Public Economics* 88:9–10 (2004), pp. 2009–2042.
38. Bo Rothstein, "Creating a Sustainable Society: A Manual," Quality of Government Institute (September, 2011) QoG Working Paper Series 2011:7 (Gothenberg, Sweden).
39. Martha Nussbaum, *Creating Capabilities: The Human Development Approach* (Cambridge: Harvard University Press, 2011), p. 14.
40. Nussbaum, *Creating Capabilities*, p. 18.
41. Jon Gertner, "The Rise and Fall of the G.D.P.," *New York Times Magazine* (May 10, 2010).
42. World Bank, World Development Indicators. Appendix 1.
43. Lydia Polgreen, "Right-to-Know Law Gives India's Poor a Lever," *New York Times* (June 28, 2010), p. 1.
44. Carlotta Gall, "Long in Dark, Afghan Women Say to Read Is Finally to See," *New York Times* (September 24, 2002).
45. James Surowieki, "Greater Fools," *New Yorker* (July 5, 2010), p. 23.
46. Nussbaum, *Creating Capabilities*, p. 98–99.
47. Hugh Stephen Whitaker, "A New Day: The Effects of Negro Enfranchisement in Selected Mississippi Counties," Florida State University, Ph.D. dissertation, 1965, p. 174.
48. Haugan and Boutros, *The Locust Effect*, p. 31.
49. Sen and the World Bank *Voices of the Poor* study are quoted in Haugan and Boutros, *The Locust Effect*, p. 100–101.
50. Nussbaum, *Creating Capabilities*, p. 34.
51. Patrick Heller, "Deepening Democracy in India and South Africa," *Journal of Asian and African Studies*, 44:1 (2009), pp. 123–149."
52. The Economist Intelligence Unit, *Democracy Index 2012* can be accessed at: The Economist Intelligence Unit, "Democracy Index 2012: Democracy at a Standstill." https://portoncv.gov.cv/dhub/porton.por_global.open_file?p_doc_id=1034.
53. Adam Przeworski et al., *Democracy and Development: Political Institutions and Well-Being in the World*, 1950–1990 (New York: Cambridge University Press, 2000), p. 1.
54. Martha C. Nussbaum, *Women and Development*, p. 88.
55. Amartya Sen, *The Idea of Justice*, p. 238.
56. Peter A. Hall, "A Capabilities Approach to Successful Societies," *Perspectives on Europe* (Spring 2010), vol. 40, no. 1, p. 11.
57. Peter A. Hall and Michelle Lamont, *Successful Societies: How Institutions and Culture Affect Health* (New York: Cambridge University Press, 2009).
58. United Nations Development Programme, *Human Development Report 2002* (New York: Oxford University Press, 2002), p. 13.
59. Lew Daly and Sean McElwee, "Forget the GDP, Some States Have Found a Better Way to Measure our Progress," *New Republic* (February 3, 2014). The article can also be found at: http://www.newrepublic.com/article/116461/gpi-better-gdp-measuring-united-states-progress.
60. These criticisms have come from our students who have read drafts of this chapter. For examples of scholarly critiques, see G. A. Cohen, "Amartya Sen's Unequal World," *New Left Review* 203 (1994), pp. 117–129; Peter Evans, "Collective Capability, Culture, and Amartya Sen's "Development as Freedom," *Studies in Comparative International Development* 37:2 (Summer, 2002), pp. 54–60; and Nivadita Menon, "Universalism without Foundations," *Economy and Society* (February 2002) vol. 31, no. 1, pp. 152–169.
61. Charles Kenny, *Getting Better: Why Global Development is Succeeding—And How We Can Improve the World Even More* (New York: Basic Books, 2011), pages 71–92.
62. Amartya Sen, *The Idea of Justice*, pp. 18–19.
63. Andrew J. Nathan, "The Place of Values in Cross-Cultural Studies," in Andrew J. Nathan, *China's Transition* (New York: Columbia University Press, 1997), p. 200. See also Martha C. Nussbaum,

Sex and Social Justice (New York: Oxford University Press, 1999), p. 121.
64. Ibid., p. 122.
65. Martha Nussbaum, *Creating Capabilities*, p. 103.
66. Dreze and Sen, *An Uncertain Glory*, p. 43.

Chapter 2

1. James C. Scott, *Seeing Like a State: How Certain Schemes to Improve the Human Condition Have Failed* (New Haven: Yale University Press, 1998).
2. Scott, *Seeing Like a State*, p. 20.
3. Scott, *Seeing Like a State*, p. 21.
4. Samuel P. Huntington, *Political Order in Changing Societies* (New Haven: Yale University Press, 1968), p. 1.
5. John Tierney, "A Baghdad Traffic Circle Is a Microcosm for Chaos," *New York Times*, (September 12, 2003).
6. James C. Scott, *Seeing Like a State*, p. 7.
7. Robert A. Dahl, "The Concept of Power," *Behavioral Scientist* (July 1957), pp. 201–215.
8. King actually took the phrase from United Auto Workers President Walter Reuther. See Michael K. Honey, *All Labor Has Dignity* (Boston: Beacon Press, 2011), p. 177.
9. Daniel Rodgers, *The Age of Fracture*, (Cambridge: Harvard University Press, 2011), p. 78.
10. Gianfranco Poggi, *The State: Its Nature, Development and Prospects* (Stanford, CA: Stanford University Press, 1990), pp. 3–19.
11. Poggi, *The State*, p. 9.
12. Poggi, *The State*, p. 22.
13. Jeffrey Gettleman, "A New Approach to Bringing Order in Somalia," *New York Times*, (April 18, 2008).
14. Jared Diamond, *Guns, Germs and Steel: The Fate of Human Societies* (New York: W.W. Norton, 1999), p. 266.
15. James C. Scott, *The Art of Not Being Governed: An Anarchist History of Upland Southeast Asia* (New Haven: Yale University Press, 2009), p. 4.
16. Ibid. p. 10.
17. Ibid, p. 4.
18. Poggi, *The State*, pp. 86–93.
19. Sheri Berman, "From the Sun King to Karzai," *Foreign Affairs* (March–April, 2010) vol. 89, no. 2, pp. 2–9.
20. Poggi, *The State*, p. 94.
21. Charles Tilly, "The History of European State-Making," in *The Formation of National States in Western Europe*, Charles Tilly, (ed.) (Princeton, NJ: Princeton University Press, 1975), p. 42.
22. Von Treitschke is quoted in James J. Sheehan, *Where Have all the Soldiers Gone* (New York: Houghton Mifflin, 2008), p. 3.
23. James C. Scott, *Seeing Like A State*.
24. Antonia Maioni, *Parting at the Crossroads: The Emergence of Health Insurance in the United States and Canada* (Princeton: Princeton University Press, 1998).
25. Zachery Elkins, "Comparability and the Analysis of National Constitutions," *APSA Comparative Politics Newsletter* (Winter 2013), vol 23, no. 1, p. 9.
26. Brian Galligan, "Comparative Federalism," in *The Oxford Handbook of Political Institutions*, eds. R. A.W. Rhodes, Sarah A, Binder, and Bert A. Rockman (New York: Oxford University Press, 2006), p. 268.
27. Morton Grodzins, *The American System: A New View of Government in the United States* Daniel J. Elazar, (ed.), (Chicago: Rand McNally, 1966).
28. China is a major exception to this rule.
29. David Marquand, *The End of the West: The Once and Future Europe* (Princeton: Princeton University Press, 2011), p. 139.
30. Nolan McCarty and Jonas Pontusson, "The Political Economy of Inequality and Redistribution," in *Oxford Handbook of Economic Inequality*, eds. Wiemer Salverda, Brian Nolan, and Timothy N. Smeeding (New York: Oxford University Press, 2009), p. 677.
31. Nicholas D. J. Baldwin, "Concluding Observations: Legislative Weakness, Scrutinizing Strength?" *Journal of Legislative Studies* (Summer/Autumn 2004), vol. 10, no 2/3, p. 295.
32. Nicholas D. J. Baldwin, "Concluding Observations: Legislative Weakness, Scrutinizing Strength?" p. 302.
33. Kaare Strom and Torbjorn Bergman, "Parliamentary Democracies Under Siege?," in *The Madisonian Turn: Political Parties and Parliamentary Democracies in Nordic Europe*, edited by Torbjorn Bergman and Kaare Strom, (Ann Arbor: University of Michigan Press, 2011), p. 14.
34. Paul Heywood, "Executive Capacity and Legislative Limits," in *Developments in West European Politics 2*, eds. Paul Heywood, Erik Jones, and Martin Rhodes (New York: Palgrave, 2002), pp. 151–167.
35. Ludger Helms, *Presidents, Prime Ministers and Chancellors: Executive Leadership in Western Democracies* (New York: Palgrave, 2005), p. 5.
36. B. Guy Peters, R.A.W. Rhodes and Vincent Wright, "Staffing the Summit—The Administration of the Core Executive: Convergent Trends and National Specificities," in *Administering the Summit*, eds. B. Guy Peters, R.A.W. Rhodes, and Vincent Wright (New York: St. Martin's Press, 2000), p. 7.
37. Jean Blondel, *Government Ministers in the Contemporary World* (New York: Sage, 1985), p. 4.
38. Thomas T. Mackie and Brian W. Hopwood, "Decision-Arenas in Executive Decision-Making: Cabinet Committees in Comparative Perspective," *British Journal of Political Science* (July 1984), vol. 14, no. 3, p. 304.
39. Jeffrey L. Pressman and Aaron J. Wildavsky, *Implementation: How*

Great Expectations in Washington Are Dashed in Oakland: Or, Why It's Amazing That Federal Programs Work at All, This Being a Saga of the Economic Development Administration as Told by Two Sympathetic Observers Who Seek to Build Morals on a Foundation of Ruined Hopes (Berkeley: University of California Press, 1973).
40. Truman is quoted in Richard E. Neustadt, *Presidential Power: The Politics of Leadership* (New York: Wiley, 1960), p. 9, emphasis in original.
41. Max Weber, "Bureaucracy," in *From Max Weber: Essays in Sociology*, H. H. Gerth and C. Wright Mills, eds. (New York: Oxford University Press, 1958).
42. Zolton Barany, *The Soldier and the Changing State: Building Democratic Armies in Africa, Asia, Europe and the Americas* (Princeton: Princeton University Press, 2012), p. 10.
43. Huntington is quoted in Douglas L. Bland, "A Unified Theory of Civil–Military Relations," *Armed Forces & Society* 26:7 (1999), p. 11.
44. Robin Luckham, "A Comparative Typology of Civil-Military Relations," *Government and Opposition* 6:1 (1971), pp. 5–35.
45. Samuel P. Huntington, *The Soldier and the State* (Cambridge: Harvard University Press, 1957).
46. John Ferejohn, "Judicializing Politics, Politicizing Law," *Law and Contemporary Problems* 65:3 (2002), p. 41.
47. Paul Heywood, Erik Jones, and Martin Rhodes, "Introduction: West European States Confront the Challenge of a New Millennium," in *Developments in West European Politics*, 2nd ed., Paul Heywood, Erik Jones, and Martin Rhodes, (eds.), (New York: Palgrave, 2002), p. 10.
48. C. Neal Tate and Torbjorn Vallinder, eds., *The Global Expansion of Judicial Power* (New York: NYU Press, 1995).
49. Patrick Heller, *The Labor of Development* (Ithaca: Cornell University Press, 1999), p. 28. The examples are from Francis Fukuyama, *State Building* (Ithaca: Cornell University Press, 2004), p. x.
50. See Gary King and Langche Zeng, "Improving Forecasts of State Failure," *World Politics* (July 2001), pp. 623–658 for further support of the close fit between state quality and infant mortality rates.

Chapter 3

1. Max Rodenbeck, "Volcano of Rage," *New York Review of Books* (March 24, 2011).
2. James C. Scott, *Weapons of the Weak: Everyday Forms of Peasant Resistance* (New Haven: Yale University Press, 1985).
3. SidneyVerba, Kay Schlozman, and Henry E. Brady, *Voice and Equality: Civic Voluntarism in American Politics* (Cambridge: Harvard University Press, 1995).
4. Mark N. Franklin, *Voter Turnout and the Dynamics of Electoral Competition in Established Democracies since 1945* (New York: Cambridge University Press, 2004).
5. Bruce Cain, Russell Dalton, and Susan Scarrow, eds., *Democracy Transformed: Expanding Political Opportunities in Advanced Industrial Democracies* (New York: Oxford University Press, 2003).
6. Peter Evans, "Collective Capabilities, Culture, and Amartya Sen's *Development as Freedom*," *Studies in Comparative International Development* (Summer 2002), vol. 37, no. 2, p. 56.
7. Giovanni Carbone, *No Party Democracy: Ugandan Politics in Comparative Perspective* (Boulder, CO.: Lynne Reimer, 2008).
8. Nancy L. Rosenblum, *On the Side of Angels: An Appreciation of Parties and Partisanship* (Princeton: Princeton University Press, 2008), p. 12 (emphasis in original).
9. Rosenblum, *On the Side of Angels*.
10. Maurice Duverger, *Political Parties* (New York: Wiley, 1955).
11. Myron Weiner and Joseph Lapalombara, "The Impact of Parties on Political Development," in *Political Parties and Political Development* Joseph Lapalombera and Myron Weiner, (eds.), (Princeton: Princeton University Press, 1996), p. 403.
12. Giovanni Sartori, *Parties and Party Systems: A Framework for Analysis* (New York Cambridge University Press, 1976).
13. Scott P. Mainwaring, *Rethinking Party Systems in the Third Wave of Democratization: The Example of Brazil* (Stanford: Stanford University Press, 1999).
14. Mainwaring, *Rethinking Party Systems in the Third Wave of Democratization*.
15. Kurt Weyland, *Democracy without Equity: Failures of Reform in Brazil* (Pittsburgh, PA: University of Pittsburgh Press, 1996).
16. Philip Keefer, "Programmatic Parties: Where Do They Come From and Do They Matter?" *Paper presented at the annual meeting of the American Political Science Association, Philadelphia, PA*, Aug 31, 2006.
17. Mancur Olson, *The Logic of Collective Action: Public Goods and the Theory of Groups* (Cambridge: Harvard University Press, 1971).
18. Mark S. Bonchek, "Grassroots in Cyberspace: Using Computer Networks to Facilitate Political Participation," Paper presented at the Midwest Political Science Association, Chicago, (April 1995), p. 1.
19. Theda Skocpol, *Diminished Democracy: From Membership to Management in American Civic Life* (Norman, OK: University of Oklahoma Press, 2003).
20. Charles Tilly and Lesley J. Wood, *Social Movements, 1768–2008* (Boulder, CO: Paradigm Publishers, 2009).
21. Steve Coll, "The Internet, for Better or Worse," *New York Review of Books* (April 7, 2011), pp. 20–24.
22. Coll, "The Internet, for Better or Worse," p. 20.

23. Marc Lynch, "After Egypt: The Limits and Possibilities of Online Challenges to the Authoritarian Arab State," *Perspectives on Politics* (June, 2011), vol. 9, no. 2, pp. 301–310.
24. Robert D. Putnam with Roert Leonardi and Raffaela Y. Nanetti, *Making Democracy Work: Civic Traditions in Modern Italy* (Princeton: Princeton University Press, 1993).
25. Alan Berlow, *Dead Season: A Story of Murder and Revenge* (New York: Vintage, 1996), p. 81.
26. Quoted in Richard Gunther and Larry Diamond, "Types and Functions of Parties," in *Political Parties and Demcoracy*, Larry Diamond and Richard Gunther, (eds.), (Baltimore: Johns Hopkins Press, 2001), p. 14–15.
27. Quoted in Susan C. Stokes, "Political Clientelism," in Carles Boix and Susan C. Stokes, (eds.), *The Oxford Handbook of Comparative Politics* (New York: Oxford University Press, 2007), pp. 609–610.
28. Stokes, "Political Clientelism," p. 613.

Chapter 4

1. Haq Nawaz Khan and Tim Craig, "Separate Attacks in Pakistan Kill Dozens, Destroy a National Shrine, and Rattle Residents," *Washington Post* (June 15, 2013), http://www.washingtonpost.com/world/gunmen-seize-hospital-in-southwestern-pakistan-after-bombs-kill-at-least-13/2013/06/15/2130ea9c-d5b8–11e2-b05f-3ea3f0e7bb5a_story.html?hpid=z12
2. Polity IV Country Report 2010: Pakistan. http://systemicpeace.org/polity/Pakistan2010.pdf.
3. Hazel Rose Markus, Frontis piece to *Successful Societies: How Institutions and Culture Affect Health* Peter A. Hall and Michele Lamont, (eds.), (New York: Cambridge University Press, 2009).
4. Christian Welzel, "Political Culture," in *The SAGE Handbook of Comparative Politics*, Todd Landman and Neil Robinson, (eds.), (Thousand Oaks, CA: Sage Publications, 2009), p. 300.
5. James Bell, primary researcher, "The World's Muslims: Religion, Politics, and Society," (Washington, DC: Pew Research Center's Forum on Religion and Public Life, 2013), http://www.pewforum.org/2013/04/30/the-worlds-muslims-religion-politics-society-overview.
6. Ronald Inglehart and Christian Welzel, *Moderniztion, Cultural Change and Democracy: The Human Development Sequence* (New York: Cambridge University Press, 2005), p. 186.
7. Cited in Christian Welzel and Ronald Inglehart, "Mass Beliefs and Democratic Institutions," in *The Oxford Handbook of Comparative Politics*, Carles Boix and Susan C. Stokes, (eds.), (New York: Oxford University Press, 2009), p. 298.
8. Christian Welzel, "Political Culture," in Todd Landman and Neil Robinson, *The SAGE Handbook of Comparative Politics*, p. 302
9. Gabriel Almond and SidneyVerba, *The Civic Culture: Political Attitudes and Democracy in Five Nations* (Princeton, NJ: Princeton University Press, 1963), pp. 440, 475. The quotation is from page 440.
10. Ronald Inglehart and Christian Welzel, "Changing Mass Priorities: The Link between Modernization and Democracy," *Perspectives on Politics* 8:2 (June 2010), pp. 552–554.
11. Ronald Inglehart and Christian Welzel, *Modernization, Cultural Change, and Democracy: The Human Development Sequence*, pp. 7–26.
12. World Values Survey. http://www.wvsevsdb.com/wvs/WVSAnalizeQuestion.jsp.
13. The figure is from Ronald Inglehart and Christian Welzel, "The WVS Cultural Map of the World," http://www.worldvaluessurvey.org/wvs/articles/folder_published/article_base_54. Presenting the figure in this format was suggested by David J. Samuels, *Comparative Politics* (New York, Pearson Education, Inc., 2013), p. 194.
14. "Social Justice in the OECD: How Do the Member States Compare?" *Sustainable Governance Indicators 2011* (Bertelsmann Stiftung, 2011.), pp. 22–23, http://www.sgi-network.org/pdf/SGI11_Social_Justice_OECD.pdf.
15. Kirk Hamilton, *Where Is the Wealth of Nations? Measuring Capital for the 21st Century* (Washington, DC: The World Bank, 2006), p. xvii.
16. Christos J. Paraskevopoulos, "Social Capital: Summing Up the Debate on a Conceptual Tool of Comparative Politics and Public Policy," *Comparative Politics* 42:4 (July 2010), p. 476.
17. Malcolm Gladwell, "Small Change: Why the Revolution Will Not Be Tweeted," *The New Yorker* (October 4, 2010), www.newyorker.com.
18. Leslie T. Chang, "Egypt's Petition Revolution," *The New Yorker* (June 28, 2013), http://www.newyorker.com/online/blogs/newsdesk/2013/06/egypts-petition-rebellion.html.
19. Elizabeth C. Economy, "China: The New Virtual Political System," Council on Foreign Relations. April, 2011, http://www.cfr.org/china/china-new-virtual-political-system/p24805.
20. Bo Rothstein and Eric M. Uslaner, "All for All: Equality, Corruption, and Social Trust," *World Politics* 58:1 (October 2005), p. 45
21. Bo Rothstein and Eric M. Uslaner, "All for All," p. 42
22. Bo Rothstein, *Creating a Sustainable Solidaristic Society: A Manual*. (Goteburg, Sweden: University of Gothenburg, The Quality of Government Institute, September 2011), pp. 3, 11–15. http://www.qog.pol.gu.se/digitalAssets/1357/1357838_2011_7_rothstein.pdf

23. Rothstein and Uslaner, "All for All," pp. 44–47.
24. Bo Rothstein, "Trust, Social Dilemmas, and Collective Memories," *Journal of Theoretical Politics* 12:4 (October 2000), pp. 477–479.
25. "Society at a Glance: OECD Social Indicators 2011." OECD, p. 91, http://www.oecd.org/social/societyataglance.htm.
26. "Special Report: The Nordic Countries." *The Economist* (February 2, 2013), pp. 3–16.
27. World Economic Forum, *The Global Competitiveness Report 2012–2013*, p. 14. http://www3.weforum.org/docs/WEF_GlobalCompetitivenessReport_2012-13.pdf.
28. Francis Fukuyama, *The Origins of Political Order* (New York: Farrar, Straus, and Giroux, 2011), pp. 13–18.
29. Ashutosh Varshney, "Ethnicity and Ethnic Conflict," in *The Oxford Handbook of Comparative Politics*, Carles Boix and Susan C. Stokes, (eds.), (New York: Cambridge Oxford University Press, 2009), p. 277.
30. Max Fisher, "A Revealing Map of the World's Most and Least Ethnically Diverse Countries," *Washington Post* (May 16, 2013), http://www.washingtonpost.com/blogs/worldviews/wp/2013/05/16/a-revealing-map-of-the-worlds-most-and-least-ethnically-diverse-countries/.
31. "What Is Race?" United States Bureau of the Census, http://www.census.gov/population/race/.
32. Steve Fenton, *Ethnicity*, 2nd ed., (Malden, MA: Polity Press, 2010), p. 27–28.
33. James Habyarimana, Macartan Humphries, Daniel Posner, and Jeremy Weinstein, "Is Ethnic Conflict Inevitable? Parting Ways over Nationalism and Separatism," *Foreign Affairs* (July/August, 2008), p. 139.
34. Benedict Anderson, *Imagined Communities: Reflections on the Origins and Spread of Nationalism* (New York and London: Verso, 1991), p. 6.
35. Stephen M. Walt, "What the Olympics Can Teach Us about Nationalism," *Foreign Policy* (July 31, 2012), http://walt.foreignpolicy.com/posts/2012/07/31/olympic_fever_0?wpisrc=obinsite.
36. Liah Greenfeld and Jonathan Eastwood, "National Identity," *The Oxford Handbook of Comparative Politics*, pp. 258–261.
37. Eugen Weber, *Peasants into Frenchmen: The Modernization of Rural France, 1870–1914* (Stanford, CA: Stanford University Press, 1976), pp. 66–67, 195–220, 303–338.
38. Stephen Walt, "Nationalism Rules," *Foreign Policy* (July 15, 2011), http://walt.foreignpolicy.com/posts/2011/07/15/the_most_powerful_force_in_the_world.
39. Vali Nasr, *The Shia Revival: How Conflict within Islam Will Shape the Future* (New York: W.W. Norton & Company, 2004), p. 23.
40. For a useful presentation of these different points of view see the debate sponsored by *The Economist* magazine resolved: "This House Believes Immigration Is Endangering European Society." *The Economist*, August 9, 2011. http://www.economist.com/debate/days/view/730.
41. "The Ins and the Outs," *The Economist* (February 2, 2013). http://www.economist.com/news/special-report/21570836-immigration-and-growing-inequality-are-making-nordics-less-homogeneous-ins-and.
42. James D. Fearon and David D. Laitin, "Ethnicity, Insurgency, and Civil War," *American Political Science Review* 97 (2003), 75–90.
43. David D. Laitin, "Grievances and Civil War," The Monkey Cage Blog, June 27, 2012. http://themonkeycage.org/blog/2012/06/27/grievances-and-civil-war/#more-19372.
44. Samuel P. Huntington, *The Clash of Civilizations and the Re-Making of World Order* (New York: Touchstone, 1997), p. 130.
45. Liah Greenfeld and Jonathan Eastwood, "National Identity," in *The Oxford Handbook of Comparative Politics*, p. 257.
46. Bo Rothstein, "Creating a Sustainable Solidaristic Society," pp. 3, 11–15.
47. There are statistical tests for determining how likely the relationships shown in scatter diagrams could be due to chance. We have not included the results of such tests for the scatter diagrams because we do not believe they are needed for an introductory comparative politics text. Unless noted, the chance of the relationships shown in the scatter diagram happening by chance is 5 percent or less.
48. The updated data are from Jan Delhey, Kenneth Newton, and Christian Welzel, "How General Is Trust in 'Most People'? Solving the Radius of Trust Problem," *American Sociological Review* 76:5 (2011), pp. 786–807. The original WVS survey left who is included in "most people" unspecified. This article provides a more accurate measure of how wide the radius of trust is. The authors are grateful to Christian Welzel for providing us the raw data from the article.
49. M. Kamrul Islam, Juan Merlo, Ichiro Kawachi, Martin Lindstrom, and Ulf-G. Gerdtham, "Social Capital and Health: Does Egalitarianism Matter? A Literature Review," *International Journal for Equity in Health* 5:3 (2006). Other studies using different sets of countries have found similar results, but not all studies confirm these findings.
50. "Democracy Index 2012: Democracy at a Standstill," *Economist* Intelligence Unit, https://portoncv.gov.cv/dhub/porton.por_global.open_file?p_doc_id=1034.

Chapter 5

1. These paragraphs borrow heavily from Stephen Holmes, "What Russia Teaches us Now: How Weak States Threaten Freedom," *The American Prospect* No. 33 (July/August 1997), pp. 30–39.
2. Friedman is quoted in Robert Kuttner, *Everything for Sale: The Virtues and Limits of Markets* (New York: Knopf, 1997), p. 33.
3. Joseph E. Stiglitz, *The Roaring Nineties: A New History of the World's Most Prosperous Decade* (New York: Norton, 2003), p. xi.
4. See Eric Wolf, *Peasant Wars of the Twentieth Century* (New York: Harper & Row, 1969); and James C. Scott, *The Moral Economy of the Peasant: Rebellion and Subsistence in Southeast Asia* (New Haven: Yale University Press, 1976). For a contrary view, which contends that peasants embrace markets because they permit peasants to increase their incomes, see Samuel L. Popkin, *The Rational Peasant: The Political Economy of Rural Society in Vietnam* (Berkeley: University of California Press, 1979).
5. Richard Whitley, *Divergent Capitalisms: The Social Structuring and Change of Business Systems* (New York: Oxford University Press, 1999), p. 122.
6. On blocked exchanges, see Michael Walzer, *Spheres of Justice: A Defense of Pluralism and Equality* (New York: Basic Books, 1983). See also Judith Andre, "Blocked Exchanges: A Taxonomy," *Ethics* (October 1993), vol.103, no. 1, pp. 29–47.
7. Charles E. Lindblom, *The Market System: What It Is, How It Works, and What To Make of It* (New Haven: Yale University Press, 2001), p. 7.
8. Ibid., p. 3.
9. The metaphor applying the power of the market to invisible magnetic force fields comes from Robert L. Heilbroner, *The Logic and Nature of Capitalism* (New York: Norton, 1985), pp. 17–18.
10. Stephen Holmes and Cass R. Sunstein, *The Cost of Rights* (New York: Norton, 1999), p. 70.
11. John McMillan, *Reinventing the Bazaar* (New York: W. W. Norton, 2002), pp. 155–60.
12. John Zysman, "How Institutions Create Historically Rooted Trajectories of Growth," *Industrial and Corporate Change*, 3:1 (1994), p. 243.
13. Barzun is cited in Dani Rodrik, "Feasible Globalizations," unpublished paper (May 2002), p. 3.
14. Niall Ferguson, *The Cash Nexus: Money and Power in the Modern World, 1700–2000* (New York: Basic Books, 2001), p. 174.
15. McMillan, *Reinventing the Bazaar*, p. 222.
16. Daren Acegmolu and James Robinson, *Why Nations Fail: The Origins of Power, Prosperity and Poverty* (New York: Random House, 2012), p. 124.
17. Acegmolu and Robinson, *Why Nations Fail*, p. 77.
18. Jacob Hacker and Paul Pierson, *Winner Take All Politics: How Washington Made the Rich Richer and Turned Its Back on the Middle Class,* (New York: Simon & Schuster, 2010), p. 82.
19. Three years earlier, at a United States embassy reception in Moscow, Khrushchev challenged, "Whether you like it or not, history is on our side. We will bury you." Although Americans interpreted his boast as a military threat, Khrushchev was instead predicting that the Soviet economy would soon be bigger, wealthier, and more productive than the United States. Khrushchev is quoted in David P. Calleo, *Rethinking Europe's Future* (Princeton: Princeton University Press, 2001), pp. 119–20.
20. Thomas L. Friedman, *The Lexus and the Olive Tree* (New York: Farrar, Straus, Giroux, 1999), p. 86.
21. Robert C. Tucker, ed., *The Marx-Engels Reader*, 2nd ed. (New York: Norton, 1978), p. 477.
22. Michael Mandelbaum, "Democracy without America: The Spontaneous Spread of Freedom," *Foreign Affairs* (September/October 2007), vol. 86., no. 5, pp. 123–124.
23. Milton and Rose Freedman, *Free to Choose: A Personal Statement* (New York: Harcourt, Brace, Jovanovich, 1980).
24. Ricardo Hausmann, "Will Volatility Kill Democracy?" *Foreign Policy* (Fall 1997), no. 108, p. 55.
25. Timothy J. McKeown, "The Global Economy, Post-Fordism, and Trade Policy in Advanced Capitalist States," in *Continuity and Change in Contemporary Capitalism*, Herbert Kitschelt et al., (New York: Cambridge University Press, 1999), pp. 11–36.
26. Lindblom, *The Market System*, pp. 147–153.
27. Daniel Yergin and Joseph Stanislaw, *The Commanding Heights: The Battle between Government and the Marketplace That Is Remaking the Modern World* (New York: Simon & Schuster, 1998), p. 11.
28. Yergin and Stanislaw, *The Commanding Heights*, pp. 67–92.
29. Jonah D. Levy, ed., *The State after Statism: New State Activities in the Age of Liberalization* (Cambridge: Harvard University Press, 2006).
30. *Economist,* "The Growth of the State: Leviathan Stirs Again," (January 21, 2010).
31. Greg Linden, Kenneth L. Kramer, and Jason Dedrick, "Who Captures Value in a Global Innovation System? The Case of Apple's iPod," (Irvine, CA: Personal Computing Industry Center, 2007).
32. David Marquand, *The End of the West: The Once and Future Europe* (Princeton: Princeton University Press, 2011), p. 141.
33. The World Bank and IMF are often confused with one another, so it may be helpful to distinguish

their different missions through a metaphor. The World Bank loans money to poor store owners so they can make improvements to their businesses; the IMF loans money to poor store owners who are about to default on their mortgage.
34. Adam Przeworski, "The Neoliberal Fallacy," *Journal of Democracy* 3:3 (1992), p. 56.
35. John Williamson, "Democracy and 'Washington Consensus,'" *World Development*, 21:8 (1993), p. 1330.
36. Kevin M. Morrison, "When Public Goods Go Bad," *Comparative Politics*, (October 2011), p. 110.
37. Thomas L. Friedman, *The World Is Flat: A Brief History of the Twenty-First Century* (New York: Farrar, Straus and Giroux, 2005).
38. Austin Ramzy, "A Maker of Bikes Now Makes a Point of Riding Them," *New York Times*, August 31, 2013.
39. Jeremy Brecher and Tim Costello, *Global Village or Global Pillage: Economic Reconstruction from the Bottom Up*, 2nd ed., (Cambridge, MA: South End Press, 1998), pp. 3–33.
40. William Greider, "A New Giant Sucking Sound," *The Nation* (December 13, 2001).
41. Morrison, "When Public Goods Go Bad," p. 110.
42. Tina Rosenberg, "The Free Trade Fix," *New York Times Magazine Section* (August 18, 2002), p. 31.
43. Bruce Gilley and David Murphy, "Why China Needs a Real Central Bank," *Far Eastern Economic Review* (May 24, 2001), pp. 48–52.
44. World Bank, *2005: World Development Indicators* (Washington, DC: The World Bank, 2005), Table 5.3, "Business Environment," pp. 278–280.
45. Paul Osterman, Thomas A. Kochan, Richard Locke, and Michael J. Piore, *Working in America: A Blueprint for a New Labor Market* (Cambridge, MA: MIT Press, 2001), p. 47.
46. Chris Howell, *Trade Unions and the State: The Construction of Industrial Relations Institutions in Britain, 1890–2000* (Princeton: Princeton University Press, 2005), p. 154.
47. Morton H. Halperin, Joseph T. Siegle, and Michael M. Weinstein, *The Democracy Advantage: How Democracies Promote Prosperity and Peace* (New York: Routledge, 2005), p. 12.

Chapter 6

1. "Divisionists Beware," *The Economist* (March 4, 2010). www.economist.com.
2. Steven Levitsky and Lucan A.Way, "Why Democracy Needs a Level Playing Field," *Journal of Democracy* 21:1 (January 2010), pp. 57–58.
3. Quoted in David Held, *Models of Democracy*, 2nd ed. (Stanford: Stanford University Press, 1996), p. 71.
4. Amartya Sen, "Democracy as a Universal Value," *Journal of Democracy* 10 (July 1999), cited in Marc Plattner, "Populism, Pluralism, and Liberal Democracy," *Journal of Democracy* 21:1 (January 2010), p. 82.
5. Milan W. Svolik, *The Politics of Authoritarian Rule* (New York: Cambridge University Press, 2012), p. 22.
6. Francis Fukuyama, *The End of History and the Last Man* (New York: Simon and Schuster, 2006), p. xi.
7. Jay Ulfelder, "The 'Democratic Recession' That Isn't," May 31, 2011, http://dartthrowingchimp.wordpress.com/2011/05/31/the-democratic-recession-that-isnt.
8. Jason Brownlee, *Authoritarianism in an Age of Democratization* (New York: Cambridge University Press, 2007), p. 25; Kurt Weyland, "Why Latin America Is Becoming Less Democratic," *The Atlantic* (July 15, 2013), http://theatlantic.com/international/archives/2013/07/Why-Latin-America-Is-Becoming-Less-Democratic/277803.
9. Milan W. Svolik, *The Politics of Authoritarian Rule*, (New York: Cambridge University Press, 2012), pp. 13–14.
10. Ibid., pp. 5–8.
11. Milan W. Svolik, *The Politics of Authoritarian Rule*, p. 4.
12. The phrase "loyal and acquiescent" is from Jonathan K. Hanson, "Loyalty and Acquiescence: Authoritarian Regimes and Inequality Outcomes," Unpublished Manuscript, June 2013, Provided by the author.
13. Abel Escriba-Folch, "Repression, Political Threats, and Survival under Autocracy," (2010) unpublished manuscript, p. 7, http://papers.ssrn.com/sol3/papers.cfm?abstract_id=1705508.
14. Axel Hadenius and Jan Teorell, "Pathways from Authoritarianism," *Journal of Democracy*, 18:1 (January 2007), p. 146.
15. Michael Herb, *All in the Family: Absolutism, Revolution, and Democracy in the Middle Eastern Monarchies* (Albany, NY: State University of New York Press, 1999), pp. 7–10.
16. See Figure 2, "Autocratic regimes across time," in Barbara Geddes, Joseph Wright, and Erica Frantz, "New Data on Autocratic Regimes," (June 8, 2012), p. 8, www.personal.psu.edu/jgw12/blogs/.../GWFAutocraticRegimes1.pdf.
17. Michael Herb, *All in the Family*, pp. 1–50; Victor Menaldo, "The Middle East and North Africa's Resilient Monarchs," *Journal of Politics* 74:3 (July 2012), p. 709; Paul Brooker, *Non-Democratic Regimes*, 2nd ed. (New York: Palgrave MacMillan, 2009), p. 65.
18. Lisa Blaydes and James Lo, "One Man, One Vote, One Time," *Journal of Theoretical Politics* (2011), p. 16.
19. Marc Lynch, "Does Arab Monarchy Matter?" *Foreign Policy* (August 31, 2012), http://lynch.foreignpolicy.com/posts/2012/08/31/three_kings.
20. Michael Herb, *All in the Family*, p. 59.

21. Glen Carey and Zainab Fattah, "Saudi King Boosts Housing, Job Spending among Mideast Unrest," Bloomberg.com February 23, 2011, http://www.bloomberg.com/news/2011-02-23/king-abdullah-pours-money-into-saudi-housing-welfare-amid-regional-unrest.html.
22. William Roberts Clark, Matt Golder, Sona Nadenachek Golder, *Principles of Comparative Politics*, 2nd ed. (Thousand Oaks, CA: Congressional Quarterly Press, 2012), p. 369. Clark's data are based on Jason Brownlee, "Portents of Pluralism: How Hybrid Regimes Affect Democratic Transitions," *American Journal of Political Science* 3:3 (July 2009), pp. 515–532.
23. Barbara Geddes, Joseph Wright, and Erica Frantz, "Autocratic Regime Data," Authoritarian Regimes, Penn State College of Liberal Arts, http://dictators.la.psu.edu. The number of military regimes mentioned here does not include hybrid regimes that combine military and personal rule or military and single-party rule.
24. Personal communication from Barbara Geddes, April 29, 2010.
25. Richard Snyder, "Beyond Electoral Authoritarianism: The Spectrum of Nondemocratic Regimes," in *Electoral Authoritarianism: The Dynamics of Unfree Competition*, Andreas Schedler, (ed.), (Boulder, CO: Lynne Rienner Publishers, 2006), p. 219.
26. David Barboza, "Billions in Hidden Riches for Family of Chinese Leader," *New York Times* (October 25, 2012), http://www.nytimes.com/2012/10/26/business/global/family-of-wen-jiabao-holds-a-hidden-fortune-in-china.html?hp&_r=0&pagewanted=all.
27. Richard McGregor, *The Party: The Secret World of China's Communist Rulers* (New York: Harper Collins, 2010), p. xiv.
28. Barbara Geddes, personal correspondence, April 29, 2010.
29. Martin Kelsall and Tim Dawson, "Anti-developmental Patrimonialism in Zimbabwe," Africa Power and Politics Program, Overseas Development Institute, Working Paper 19, 2011, http://www.institutions-africa.org/filestream/20111110-appp-working-paper-19-anti-developmental-patrimonialism-in-zimbabwe-dawson-and-kelsall-nov-11; John Eligon, "Millions from Diamonds Go to Mugabe, Observers Say," *New York Times* (December 16, 2011), http://www.nytimes.com/2011/12/17/world/africa/experts-say-diamonds-help-fill-mugabe-coffers.html?_r=1&hp=&pagewanted=all.
30. Nations Development Programme, *Human Development Report 2013*, p. 12, http://www.undp.org/content/undp/en/home/librarypage/hdr/human-development-report-2013
31. Milan W. Svolik, *The Politics of Authoritarian Rule*, p. 56, and Paul Brooker, *Non-Democratic Regimes*, pp. 125–129.
32. Paul Brooker, *Non-Democratic Regimes*, pp. 125–129.
33. Barbara Geddes, Joseph Wright, and Erica Frantz, "Global Political Regimes Codebook," November 21, 2011, http://dictators.la.psu.edu/pdf/gwf-code-book-1.1.
34. Steven Levitsky and Lucan A. Way, *Competitive Authoritarianism: The Origins and Evolution of Hybrid Regimes in the Post-Cold War Era* (New York: Cambridge University Press, 2010), p. 23.
35. Levitsky and Way, p. 5.
36. Levitsky and Way, pp. 74. 374–375.
37. Levitsky and Way, pp. 5–6.
38. Levitsky and Way, p. 23. This summary omits the authors' discussion of how leverage affects the likelihood of democratization in competitive authoritarian regimes.
39. The Middle East and North Africa include Algeria, Bahrain, Djibouti, Egypt, Iran, Iraq, Israel, Jordan, Kuwait, Lebanon, Libya, Malta, Morocco, Oman, Qatar, Saudi Arabia, Syria, Tunisia, United Arab Emirates, West Bank and Gaza, and Yemen.
40. James Traub, "Last Hope: Tunisia, the One Place Where the Arab Spring Hasn't Gone to Hell," *Foreign Policy* (August 26, 2013). http://www.foreignpolicy.com/articles/2013/08/23/last_hope_tunisia_arab_spring.
41. Jason Brownlee, Tarek Masoud, and Andrew Reynolds, "Tracking the Arab Spring: Why the Modest Harvest?" *Journal of Democracy* 24:4 (October 2013), pp. 29–30.
42. World Bank. Gross National Income Per Capita, 2012, http://databank.worldbank.org/data/download/GNIPC.pdf.
43. CIA *The World Fact Book 2013*, https://www.cia.gov/library/publications/the-world-factbook/rankorder/.html. Figures based on purchasing power parity.
44. Samuel P. Huntington, *The Clash of Civilizations and the Remaking of World Order* (New York: Touchstone, 1997), p. 29.
45. Howard J. Wiarda, "Arab Fall or Arab Winter?" *American Foreign Policy Interests* 34:3 (2012), p. 136.
46. Pew Research Center, *The World's Muslims: Religion, Politics, and Society* (Washington, DC: Pew Research Center's Forum on Religion and Public Life, 2013), pp. 17, http://www.pewforum.org/Muslim/the-worlds-muslims-religion-politics-society.aspx.
47. Ibid. pp. 15, 48.
48. David Samuels, "*Comparative Politics* (New York: Pearson Education, Inc., 2013), pp. 179–180.
49. Jay Ulfelder, "How (Not) to Bring Democracy to China," Dart Throwing Chimp, (November 20, 2012), http://dartthrowingchimp.wordpress.com/2012/11.
50. Pew Research Center Global Attitudes Project, *Most Muslims Want Democracy, Personal*

Freedoms, and Islam in Political Life, (July 10, 2012), p. 1, http://www.pewglobal.org/2012/07/10/most-muslims-want-democracy-personal-freedoms-and-islam-in-political-life.

51. Marc Lynch, "A Barometer for Arab Democracy," Abu Aardvark's Middle East Blog, *Foreign Policy* (October 16, 2012), http://lynch.foreignpolicy.com/posts/2012/10/16/arabs_still_want_democracy.
52. Polity IV Project, http://systemicpeace.org/polity/polity4.htm.
53. The countries are Albania, Comoros, Indonesia, Senegal, Sierra Leone, and Turkey. The list is from Larry Diamond, "Why Are There No Arab Democracies?" *Journal of Democracy* 21:1 (January 2010), p. 94. Mali was on Diamond's list, but, a military coup d'etat overthrew the democratic government in 2012.
54. Jason Brownlee, Tarek Masoud, and Andrew Reynolds, "Tracking the Arab Spring: Why the Modest Harvest?"pp. 32–33, 37.
55. Michael Ross, "Will Oil Drown the Arab Spring?" *Foreign Affairs* (September/October 2011), http://www.foreignaffairs.com/articles/68200/michael-l-ross/will-oil-drown-the-arab-spring.
56. Jason Brownlee, Tarek Masoud, and Andrew Reynolds. "Tracking the Arab Spring," p. 33.
57. Ibid. pp. 33–35.
58. Jonathan K, Hanson, "Loyalty and Acquiescence: Authoritarian Regimes and Inequality Outcomes," Paper Prepared for Delivery at the 2010 Annual Meeting of the American Political Science Association, September 2–5, 2010, p. 1, http://faculty.maxwell.syr.edu/johanson/papers/papers.html.
59. Scholars supporting this hypothesis include Victor Menaldo, "The Middle East and North Africa's Resilient Monarchs," *Journal of Politics* 74 (July 2012), pp. 707–722; Carl Henrik Knutsen and Hanne Fjelde, "Property Rights in Dictatorships: Kings Protect Property Rights Better Than Generals or Party Bosses," *Contemporary Politics* 19:1 (2013), pp. 94–114; Nicholas Charron and Victor Lapuente, "Which Dictators Produce Quality of Government?" QoG Working Paper Series, 2010:11 (Quality of Government Institute, University of Gothenburg, 2010). http://www.qog.pol.gu.se/digitalAssets/1350/1350157_2010_11_charron_lapuente.pdf,; and William Roberts Clark, Paul Poast, Thomas Flores, and Robert R. Kaufman, "Why Some Autocracies Perform So Well," 2011, http://www.sociol.unimi.it/corsi/scienzapoliticasie_al/documenti/File/CPFKAutocracies%20Paper%20with%20figures.pdf.
60. Michael Herb, *All in the Family*, pp. 7–10; 21–35.
61. Carl Henrick Knutsen and Hanne Fjelde, "Property Rights in Dictatorships pp. 94–114.
62. The categories are from Barbara Geddes, Joseph Wright, and Erica Frantz, "New Data on Autocratic Regimes," (September 8, 2012), http://dictators.la.psu.edu. The countries used to test these hypotheses are from Barbara Geddes, Joseph Wright, and Erica Frantz, *Global Regimes Codebook*, November 21, 2011, http://dictators.la.psu.edu/data/GlobalRegimesCodebook.pdf. We have added Bahrain, Brunei, Qatar, and the United Arab Republics to the list of monarchies provided by Geddes, Wright, and Frantz.
63. James W. McGuire, *Wealth, Health, and Democracy in East Asia and Latin America* (New York: Cambridge University Press, 2010), p. 95.
64. James W. McGuire, *Wealth, Health, and Democracy in East Asia and Latin America*, pp. 18–20.
65. Author's calculations using United Nations Human Development Indicators data on infant mortality at Google Public Data Explorer, http://www.google.com/publicdata/explore?ds=kthk374hkr6tr_#!ctype=l&strail=false&bcs=d&nselm=h&met_y=indicator_57206&scale_y=lin&ind_y=false&rdim=country&ifdim=country&hl=en_US&dl=en_US&ind=false.
66. Homicide rates can be found in the Data Set for *The Good Society*, 3e.
67. World Economic Forum, *Global Gender Gap Report 2012*, http://reports.weforum.org/global-gender-gap-report-2012/#.
68. See sources in footnote 57. For an author who reaches different conclusions about monarchies, see James W. McGuire, "Political Regime and Social Performance," *Contemporary Politics* 19:1 (2013), 55–75.
69. Marc Plattner, "Populism, Pluralism, and Liberal Democracy," pp. 81–82.
70. Amartya Sen, "Democracy as a Universal Value,' p. 82.
71. Thomas Pepinsky, "The Simple Statistics of Indonesian Electoral Polling," (April 15, 2014) http://tompepinsky.com/blog
72. Andreas Schedler, "Authoritarianism's Last Line of Defense," *Journal of Democracy* 21:1 (January 2010), p. 69.
73. Reported in Bruce Gilley, "Democratic Triumph, Scholarly Pessimism," *Journal of Democracy* 21:1 (January, 2010), p. 165.
74. Marc Lynch, "Does Arab Monarchy Matter?" *Foreign Policy* (August 31, 2013), http://lynch.foreignpolicy.com/posts/2012/08/31/three_kings.
75. Jay Ulfelder, "Prospects for New Democracies in the Arab World," Monkey Cage Blog (April 26, 2011), http://themonkeycage.org/2011/04/26/prospects_for_new_democracies.

Chapter 7

1. Quoted in Niall Ferguson, *The Cash Nexus: Money and Power in*

the Modern World (New York: Basic Books, 2001), p. 353.
2. Valerie Bunce, "Comparative Democratization: Big and Bounded Generalizations," *Comparative Political Studies* (Aug.–Sept. 2000), p. 704.
3. Ira Katznelson, Mark Kesselman, and Alan Draper, *The Politics of Power: A Critical Introduction to American Government* (New York: W. W. Norton, 2011), p. 93.
4. Samuel P. Huntington, *The Third Wave: Democratization in the Late Twentieth Century* (Norman: University of Oklahoma Press, 1993).
5. Barrington Moore Jr., *The Social Origins of Dictatorship and Democracy* (Boston: Beacon Press, 1993), p. 418.
6. Quoted in Johann Hari, "The Two Churchills," *New York Times* Book Review (August 15, 2010), p. 11.
7. Seymour Martin Lipset, "Some Social Requisites of Democracy: Economic Development and Political Legitimacy," *American Political Science Review* 53 (1959), pp. 69–105.
8. Guillermo O'Donnell, *Modernization and Bureaucratic Authoritarianism: Studies in South American Politics* (Berkeley: Institute of International Studies, 1973).
9. William F. S. Miles, "The Mauritius Enigma," *Journal of Democracy* 10:2 (1999), p. 99.
10. Ibid, p. 99.
11. Larry Diamond, "Democracy's Third Wave Today," *Current History* (November 2011), p. 299.
12. Dan Slater, "Democratic Careening," *World Politics* 65:4 (October, 2013), p. 731.
13. Barbara Geddes, "What Causes Democratization," in *The Oxford Handbook of Political Science*, Robert E. Goodin, (ed.), (New York: Oxford University Press, 2009), p. 596.
14. Geddes, "What Causes Democratization."
15. Kristian Skrede Gleditsch and Michael D. Ward, "Diffusion and the Spread of Democratic Institutions," in *The Global Diffusion of Markets and Democracy*," Beth A. Simmons, Frank Dobbin, and Geoffrey Garrett, (eds.), (New York: Cambridge University Press, 2008), p. 295.
16. David Marquand, *The End of the West* (Princeton: Princeton University Press, 2011), p. 125.
17. Adam Przeworski, *Sustainable Democracy* (New York: Cambridge University Press, 1995), pp. 12–13.
18. William Bagehot, the British political journalist, wrote that, "The independence of the legislative and executive powers is the specific quality of presidential government, just as their fusion and combination is the precise principle of cabinet [parliamentary] government." Quoted in Percy Allum, *State and Society in Western Europe* (Malden, MA: Blackwell, Publishers, 1995), p. 304.
19. This particular definition is drawn from Mathew Soberg Shugart and John M. Carey, *Presidents and Assemblies: Constitutional Design and Electoral Dynamics* (New York: Cambridge University Press, 1992).
20. Michael Gallagher, Michael Laver, and Peter Mair, *Representative Government in Europe*, 3rd ed. (New York: McGraw-Hill, 2001), p. 69.
21. Juan Linz, "The Perils of Presidentialism," *Journal of Democracy* 1 (Winter 1990), pp. 51–69.
22. Alfred Stepan and Cindy Skach, "Constitutional Frameworks and Democratic Consolidation," *World Politics* 46 (October 1993), pp. 1–22.
23. Sarah Birch, "Two Round Electoral Systems and Democracy," *Comparative Political Studies* (2003), 36, pp. 2–27.
24. Steven Hill, *Europe's Promise: Why the European Way Is the Best Hope in an Insecure Age* (Berkeley: University of California Press, 2010), p. 265.
25. Andrew McLaren Carstairs, *A Short History of Electoral Systems in Western Europe* (London: George Allen & Unwin, 1980), p. 215.
26. Nolan McCarthy and Jonas Pontusson, "The Political Economy of Inequality and Redistribution," in *Oxford Handbook of Economic Inequality*, Wiemer Salverda, Brian Nolan, and Timothy M. Smeeding, (eds.), (New York: Oxford University Press, 2009), p. 677.
27. Henry Milner, "Obstacles to Electoral Reform in Canada," *American Review of Canadian Studies* 24:1 (1994), pp. 39–55.
28. Patrick Dunleavy, "Facing Up to Multi-party Politics . . .," *Parliamentary Affairs* (July 2005), vol. 59, no. 3, p. 522.
29. Quoted in Anthony Gottlieb, "Win or Lose," *The New Yorker* (July 22, 2010), p. 76.
30. Franklin Foer, "Political Pitch," *The New Republic* (June 19, 2006), pp. 15–17.
31. Amartya Sen, "Human Rights and Economic Achievements," in *The East Asian Challenge for Human Rights*, Joanne R. Bauer and Daniel A. Bell, (eds.), (New York: Cambridge University Press, 1999), p. 91.
32. Adam Przeworski and Fernando Limongi, "Political Regimes and Economic Growth," *Journal of Economic Perspectives* (Summer 1993), vol. 7, p. 65.
33. Morton H. Halperin, Joseph T. Siegle, and Michael M. Weinstein, *The Democratic Advantage: How Democracies Promote Peace and Prosperity*, (New York: Routledge, 2005), p. 34.
34. Halperin et al., *Democratic Advantage*, p. 38.

Chapter 8

1. Sharon La Franiere, "In Oil-Rich Angola, Cholera Preys upon the Poorest," *New York Times* (June 16, 2006), http://www.nytimes.com/2006/06/16/world/africa/16cholera.

1. html?pagewanted=all. This article was found in Bo Rothstein, *The Quality of Government: Corruption, Social Trust, and Inequality in International Perspective* (Chicago, IL: University of Chicago Press, 2011), p. 1.
2. Bo Rothstein, *The Quality of Government*, pp. 1–6.
3. Sharon La Franiere. "In Oil-Rich Angola, Cholera Preys upon the Poorest."
4. World Bank, "Selected Indicators: Classification of Countries by Region and Income," *World Development Report 2011*, p. 343. http://wdr2011.worldbank.org/sites/default/files/WDR2011_Indicators.pdf.
5. Bruce Cumings, *Korea's Place in the Sun: A Modern History* (New York: W. W. Norton and Company, 1997), p. 303.
6. United Nations Development Programme, "What Is Human Development?" *Human Development Report 2002*, http://hdr.undp.org/en/content/human-development-report-2002.org.
7. United Nations Human Development Programme, *Human Development Report 2013*, http://hdr.undp.org/en/media/HDR2013_EN_Statistics.pdf.
8. United Nations Development Programme, *Human Development Report, 2013*, p. 141.
9. United Nations Development Programme, *Human Development Report 2013*, p. 152.
10. United Nations Development Programme, *Human Development Report 2013*. http://hdr.undp.org/sites/default/files/reports/14/hdr2013_en_complete.pdf
11. Jean Dreze and Amartya Sen, "Putting Growth in Its Place,"(November 7, 2011), OutlookIndia.com, http://www.outlookindia.com/article.aspx?278843.
12. This question is asked by Dani Rodrik in "The Past, Present, and Future of Economic Growth," Global Citizen Foundation, Working Paper No. 1 (June, 2013), http://www.gcf.ch/?page_id=5758.
13. World Bank, "Poverty Overview," http://www.worldbank.org/en/topic/poverty/overview.
14. *Economist*, "Not Always with Us," (June 1, 2012), p. 23.
15. Shaohua Chen and Martin Ravallion, "An Update to the World Bank's Estimates of Consumption Poverty in the Developing World," World Bank, http://siteresources.worldbank.org/INTPOVCALNET/Resources/Global_Poverty_Update_2012_02-29-12.pdf. The figures are based on purchasing power parity income data.
16. Baharat Peer, "India's Broken Promise: How a Would-Be Great Power Hobbles Itself," *Foreign Affairs* (May/June 2012), http://www.foreignaffairs.com/articles/137530/basharat-peer/indias-broken-promise?page=show.
17. Geoffrey Gertz and Laurence Chandy, "Two Trends in Global Poverty," (Washington, DC: Brookings Institution (May 2011), pages 1–5, http://www.brookings.edu/~/media/Files/rc/opinions/2011/0517_global_poverty_trends_chandy/0517_trends_global_poverty.pdf.
18. Dataset for *The Good Society* 3e
19. "The Best Story in Development," *Economist* (May 19, 2012), http://www.economist.com/node/21555571#footnote1.
20. Google Public Data, "World Development Indicators, Mortality Rate under 5." http://www.google.com/publicdata/explore?ds=d5bncppjof8f9_#!ctype=l&strail=false&bcs=d&nselm=h&met_y=sh_dyn_mort&scale_y=lin&ind_y=false&rdim=region&idim=region:SSA:NAC:EAP:ECA:LAC:SAS&ifdim=region&tdim=true&hl=en_US&dl=en_US.
21. "Africa's Hopeful Economies," *The Economist* (December 3, 2011), http://www.economist.com/node/21541008.
22. "Not Always with Us," *Economist* (June 1, 2013), p. 24.
23. Peter Evans and Patrick Heller, "Human Development, State Transformation, and the Politics of the Developmental State," in Stephan Leibfried, Frank Nullmeier, Evelyne Huber, Matthew Lange, (eds.), *The Oxford Handbook of Transformations of the State* (New York: Oxford University Press, 2013), forthcoming.The authors' definition draws on the concept of infrastructural power developed by Michael Mann.
24. Lant Pritchettt and Erik Werker, "Developing the Guts of a GUT (Grand Unified Theory): Elite Commitment and Inclusive Growth," Effective States and Inclusive Development, Working Paper Series 16/12 (Cambridge, MA: Harvard Business School, December 7, 2012), p. 39, http://www.hbs.edu/faculty/Pages/item.aspx?num=44065.
25. Lant Pritchettt and Erik Werker, "Developing the Guts of a GUT," p. 39.
26. J. S. Nye, "Corruption and Political Development: A Cost–Benefit Analysis," in A. J. Heidenheimer, M. Johnston, and V. T. Levine, (eds.), *Political Corruption: A Handbook* (New Brunswick, NJ: Transaction Publishers, 1989). Cited in Paul D. Hutchcroft, "Obstructive Corruption: The Politics of Privilege in the Philippines," in Mushtaq H. Khan and Jomo K. S., (eds.), *Rents, Rent-Seeking and Economic Development: Theory and Evidence from Asia* (New York: Cambridge University Press, 2000), p. 213.
27. Carlos D. Ramirez, "Is Corruption in China 'Out of Control'? A Comparison with the United States in Historical Perspective, George Mason University Department of Economics Paper No. 12–60 (2012), http://papers.ssrn.com/sol3/papers.cfm?abstract_id=2185166.

28. Lant Pritchettt and Erik Werker, "Developing the Guts of a GUT (Grand Unified Theory), p. 51; Daron Acemoglu and James A. Robinson, *Why Nations Fail: The Origins of Power, Prosperity, and Poverty* (New York: Crown Publishers, 2012), pp. 63–68, 213–238.
29. Bo Robinson and Soren Holberg, *Correlates of Corruption* (Gothenburg, Sweden: Quality of Government Institute, University of Gothenburg, Working Paper Series 2011:12, 2012), no page numbers, http://www.qog.pol.gu.se/publications/workingpapers/2011.
30. Patrick Heller, "Degrees of Democracy: Some Comparative Lessons from India," *World Politics* 52:4 (July 2000), pp. 491–493.
31. Kenneth L. Sokoloff and Stanley L. Engermann, "History Lessons: Institutions, Factor Endowments, and Paths of Development in the New World," *Journal of Economic Perspectives* 14:3 (Summer 2000), p. 217.
32. Dani Rodrik, "The Past, Present, and Future of Economic Growth," Global Citizen Foundation, Working Paper 1 (June 2013), pp. 14–15, http://www.gcf.ch/?page_id=5758.
33. Lant Pritchett, "Divergence, Big Time," *Journal of Economic Perspectives*," 11:3 (Summer 1997), pp. 3–17.
34. Jared Diamond, *Guns, Germs, and Steel: The Fates of Human Societies* (New York: W. W. Norton and Company, 1999), p. 87.
35. Ibid., p. 78.
36. Ibid, pp. 29, 210–212.
37. Jeffrey D. Sachs, "Institutions Matter, but Not for Everything," *Finance and Development* 40:2 (June 2003), p. 39.
38. Ibid.
39. Gianfranco Poggi, *Calvinism and the Capitalist Spirit: Max Weber's Protestant Ethic* (Amherst, MA: The University of Massachusetts Press, 1983), pp. 40–47.
40. Randall Collins, *Weberian Sociological Theory* (New York: Cambridge University Press, 1987), pp. 23–37.
41. David S. Landes, "Culture Makes Almost All the Difference," in *Culture Matters: How Values Shape Human Progress*, Lawrence E Harrison and Samuel P. Huntington, (eds.), (New York: Basic Books, 2000), p. 2.
42. David S. Landes, *The Wealth and Poverty of Nations: Why Some Nations Are So Rich and Some So Poor* (New York: W. W. Norton and Company, 1998), pp. 217–218, 274–275.
43. Ibid., p. 177.
44. Ibid., p. 383.
45. Francis Fukuyama, "The Economics of Trust," *National Review* (August 14, 1995), p. 42.
46. Francis Fukuyama, "Social Capital and the Global Economy," *Foreign Affairs* 74:5 (September/October 1995), p. 90.
47. Francis Fukuyama, "Social Capital," in *Culture Matters*, Lawrence E. Harrison and Samuel P. Huntington, (eds.), p. 98.
48. Benjamin Cohen, *The Question of Imperialism: The Political Economy of Dominance and Dependence* (New York: Basic Books, 1973), p. 10.
49. Alex von Tunzelmann, "Haiti: The Land Where Children Eat Mud," *London Times* (May 17, 2009). Cited in http://chrisblattman.com, January 14, 2010.
50. For a good summary of this explanation, see John Isbister, *Promises Not Kept: The Betrayal of Social Change in the Third World*, 5th ed. (Bloomfield, CT: Kumarian Press, 2001), pages 42–49.
51. David D. Ferranti, Guillermo D. Perry, and Francisco Ferreira, *Inequality in Latin America: Breaking with History?* (Washington, D.C.: The World Bank, 2004), p. 110.
52. Patrick O'Brien, "European Economic Development: The Contribution of the Periphery," *The Economic History Review* 35:1 (February 1982), pp. 1–17.
53. Peter Evans, "The Challenges of the Institutional Turn," in *The Economic Sociology of Capitalist Institutions*, Victor Nee and Richard Swedberg, (eds.), (Princeton, NJ: Princeton University Press, 2005); and Daron Acemoglu, Simon Johnson, and James A. Robinson, "Institutions as a Fundamental Cause of Long Run Growth," in *Handbook of Economic Growth*, vol. IA, Philippe Aghion and Steven N. Durlauf, (eds.), (Maryland Heights, MO: Elsevier, 2005).
54. Daron Acemoglu and James A. Robinson, *Why Nations Fail: The Origins of Power, Prosperity, and Poverty* (New York: Crown Publishers, 2012), pp. 73–79.
55. Ibid., p. 43.
56. Ibid., pp. 79–83.
57. Daron Acemoglu and James A. Robinson, *Why Nations Fail*, pp. 80–81.
58. United Nations Development Programme, *Human Development Report 2013*, p. 12.
59. Daron Acemoglu, Simon Johnson, and James A. Robinson, "Institutions as a Fundamental Cause of Long-Run Growth," p. 446.
60. Daron Acemoglu, Simon Johnson, and James Robinson, "The Rise of Europe: Atlantic Trade, Institutional Change, and Economic Growth." *American Economic Review* 95:3 (June 2005), pp. 549–551.
61. Kenneth L. Sokoloff and Stanley L. Engerman, "Institutions, Factor Endowments, and Paths of Development in the New World," *Journal of Economic Perspectives* 14:3 (Summer 2000), pp. 220–228.
62. Daron Acemoglu and James Robinson, "Response to Fukuyama's Review," *Why Nations Fail Blog*, April 30, 2012, http://whynationsfail.com/blog/2012/4/30/response-to-fukuyamas-review.html.
63. World Bank, World Development Report 2011, p. 343.

64. Peter Evans and John D. Stephens, "Studying Development Since the Sixties: The Emergence of a New Comparative Political Economy," *Theory and Society* 17:5 (1988), p. 725.
65. CIA World Fact Book. https://www.cia.gov/library/publications/the-world-factbook.
66. The countries were chosen starting from the country reporting the lowest average per capita GDP, the Democratic Republic of the Congo in Africa, at $400 and going up the list of 226 countries, choosing every tenth country from the list. There is one difference between the countries used for Figure 1.1 and the countries used for Figure 8.1. For Figure 8.1, countries with populations of 100,000 or fewer were replaced with a country in the list with a larger population but having very similar per capita income. For example, the Cook Islands, population 10,447 and a per capita income of $9,100, were replaced with Jamaica with an income of $9,000.
67. Afghanistan is not included because literacy data are not available.
68. The Economist Economist Intelligence Unit, *Democracy Index 2012: Democracy at a Standstill*, https://portoncv.gov.cv/dhub/porton.por_global.open_file?p_doc_id=1034.

Chapter 9

1. ILO, *Global Wage Growth, 2012–2013* (Geneva: ILO, 2013), p. 11.
2. Effective tax rates were calculated on $100,000. See http://www.economist.com/blogs/dailychart/2011/09/effective-tax-rates.
3. Umut Riza Ozkan, "Comparing Formal Unemployment Compensation Systems in 15 OECD Countries," *Social Policy and Administration* 48:1(January, 2013), p. 12.
4. Alberto Alesina and Edward L. Glaeser, *Fighting Poverty in the US and Europe: A World of Difference* (New York: Oxford University Press, 2004), pp. 81–87.
5. The complete list of rich democracies includes Australia, Austria, Belgium, Canada, Denmark, Finland, France, Germany, Ireland, Italy, Japan, Netherlands, New Zealand, Norway, Portugal, Spain, Sweden, Switzerland, the United Kingdom, and the United States.
6. Eric S. Einhorn and John Logue, "Can Welfare States Be Sustained in a Global Economy? Lessons from Scandinavia," *Political Science Quarterly* (Spring 2010), vol. 125, no. 1, p. 9.
7. Gosta Esping-Andersen and John Myles, "Economic Inequality and the Welfare State," in *Oxford Handbook of Inequality*, edited by Brian Nolan, Werner Salvera, and Timothy M. Smeeding (New York, Oxford University Press, 2012), p. 655.
8. Wolf is quoted in Andrew Glyn, *Capitalism Unleashed* (New York: Oxford University Press, 2006), p. 167.
9. Perrson is quoted in Jenny Anderson, "The People's Library and the Electronic Workshop: Comparing Swedish and British Social Democracy," *Politics & Society* (September 2006), vol. 34, no. 3, p. 439.
10. Matthew Yglesias, "Why Does Sweden Have So Many Billionaires?" *Slate* (October 31, 2013).
11. See Special Report "Northern Lights" in *The Economist* (February 2, 2013), pp. 9–16.
12. Goran Therborn, "A Unique Chapter in the History of Democracy: The Social Democrats in Sweden," in *Creating Social Democracy: A Century of the Social Democratic Labor Party in Sweden*, Klaus Misgeld, Karl Molin, and Klas Amark, (eds.), (University Park, PA: Pennsylvania State University Press, 1992), pp. 1–2.
13. See Table 8.2, "Lower-Class Power," in Seymour Martin Lipset and Gary Marks, *It Didn't Happen Here: Why Socialism Failed in the United States* (New York: W. W. Norton, 2000), p. 280. Walter Korpi developed a similar, though more complex (and more dated) working-class "power resources" index in which Sweden also ranked first. See Table 3.6, "Patterns of Working Class Mobilization and Political Control in Eighteen OECD Countries, 1946–76," in Walter Korpi, *The Democratic Class Struggle* (London: Routledge & Kegan Paul, 1983), p. 40.
14. Timothy A. Tilton, "The Social Origins of Liberal Democracy: The Swedish Case," *American Political Science Review* 68 (June 1974), p. 563.
15. Arend Lijphart, *Patterns of Democracy: Government Forms and Performance in Thirty-Six Countries* (New Haven: Yale University Press, 1999), p. 2.
16. Eric S. Einhorn and John Logue, *Modern Welfare States: Scandinavian Politics and Policy in the Global Age*, 2nd ed. (Westport, CT: Praeger, 2003), p. 42.
17. Torbjorn Bergman and Niklas Bolin, "Swedish Democracy: Crumbling Political Parties, a Feeble Riskdag, and Tehcnocratic Power Holders," in *The Madisonian Turn: Political Parties and Parliamentary Democracy in Nordic Europe*, Torbjorn Bergman and Kaare Strom, eds, (Ann Arbor: University of Michigan Press, 2011) p. 273.
18. Rune Premfors, "Reshaping the Democratic State: Swedish Experiences in a Comparative Perspective," *Public Administration* (Spring 1998), vol. 76, p. 154.
19. Gosta Esping-Andersen, "The Making of A Social Democratic Welfare State," in *Creating Social Democracy: A Century of the Social Democratic Labor Party in Sweden*, Klaus Misgeld, Karl Molin, and Klas Amark, (eds.), (University Park, PA: Pennsylvania State University Press, 1992), p. 41.

20. Esping-Andersen, "The Making of a Social Democratic Welfare State."
21. Bo Sairlvik, "Recent Electoral Trends in Sweden," in *Scandinavia at the Polls: Recent Political Trends in Denmark, Norway, and Sweden*, Karl H. Cerny, (ed.), (Washington, DC: American Enterprise Institute for Public Policy Research, 1977), pp. 115–129.
22. David Arter, "Sweden: A Mild Case of 'Electoral Instability Syndrome,'" in *Changing Party Systems in Western Europe*, David Broughton and Mark Donovan, (eds.), (London: Pinter, 1999), pp. 143–163.
23. http://www.electionresources.org/se/.
24. John Logue, "The Swedish Model: Visions of Sweden in American Politics and Political Science," *The Swedish-American Historical Quarterly* (July 1999), vol. 50, no. 3, p. 167.
25. Lars Tragardh, "Sweden and the EU: Welfare State Nationalism and the Spectre of Europe," in *European Integration and National Identity: The Challenge of the Nordic States*, Lene Hansen and Ole Waever, (eds.), (New York: Routledge, 2002), pp. 130–182.
26. *The Economist*, "The Next Supermodel," (February 2, 2013), p. 9.
27. Stefan Svallfors, *Class and Attitudes in Comparative Perspective: The Moral Economy of Class: Class and Attitudes in Comparative Perspective* (Stanford: Stanford University Press, 2006), p. 59.
28. Thoams J. Anton, "Policy-Making and Political Culture in Sweden," *Scandinavian Political Studies* vol 4, no. A4 (January, 1969), p. 99.
29. Bo Rothstein, "Social Capital in the Social Democratic State," in *Democracies in Flux: The Evolution of Social Capital in Contemporary Society*, Robert Putnam, (ed.), (New York: Oxford University Press, 2002), p. 303.
30. Rothstein, "Social Capital in the Social Democratic State, p. 319.
31. Bo Rothstein and Eric M. Uslaner, "All for All: Equality, Corruption and Social Trust," *World Politics*, 58:1 (2005), pp. 41–72.
32. Maureen A. Eger, "Even in Sweden: The Effect of Immigration on Support for Welfare State Spending," *European Sociological Review*, 26:2 (2010), pp. 203–217.
33. Quoted in Eger, "Even in Sweden," p. 203.
34. Einhorn and Logue, "Can Welfare States Be Sustained in a Global Economy?" p. 12.
35. Robert Taylor, quoted in John T. S. Madeley, "'The Swedish Model is Dead! Long Live the Swedish Model,'" p. 165.
36. Gosta Esping-Andersen, *Politics against Markets: The Social Democratic Road to Power* (Princeton: Princeton University Press, 1985).
37. Einhorn and Logue, *Modern Welfare States*, p. 197.
38. Esping-Andersen, "The Making of the Social Democratic Welfare State," p. 50.
39. Richard Clayton and Jonas Pontusson, "Welfare State Retrenchment and Revisited: Entitlement Cuts, Public Sector Restructuring and Inegalitarian Trends in Advanced Capitalist Societies," *World Politics* 51:1 (1998), pp. 67–98. See also Karen M. Andersen, "The Politics of Retrenchment in a Social Democratic Welfare State," *Comparative Political Studies*, (November 2001), vol. 334, no. 9, pp. 1063–1091.
40. Anders Lindblom, "Dismantling the Social Democratic Welfare Model: Has the Swedish Welfare State Lost Its Defining Characteristics?" *Scandinavian Political Studies* 24:3 (2001), p. 17.
41. Mike Marshall, "The Changing Face of Swedish Corporatism: The Disintegration of Consensus," *Journal of Economic Issues* (September 1996), vol. 30, p. 858.
42. LO stands for Landsorganisationen i Sverige in Swedish; SAF stands for Svenska Arbetsgivareforeningen.
43. Douglas A. Hibbs Jr. and Hakan Locking, "Wage Dispersion and Productive Efficiency: Evidence from Sweden," *Journal of Labor Economics* 18:4 (2000), pp. 755–782.
44. Jonas Pontusson and Peter Swenson, "Labor Markets, Productions Strategies, and Wage Bargaining Institutions," *Comparative Political Studies* (April 1996), vol. 29, no. 2, pp. 223–250.
45. Kathleen Thelen and Ikuo Kume, "Coordination as a Political Problem in Coordinated Market Economies," *Goverance* (January 2006), vol. 19, no. 1, pp. 11–42.
46. Robert Taylor, *Sweden's New Social Democratic Model* (London: Compass, 2005).
47. Jo Blanden, Paul Gregg, and Stephen Machin, "Intergenerational Mobility in Europe and North America," *Center for Economic Performance* (London School of Economics, 2005).
48. David Brook, "How Sweden Tweaked the Washington Consensus," *Dissent* (Fall 2004), pp. 24–29.
49. Ellis Wasson, *A History of Modern Britain, 1714 to the Present* (Chichester: John Wiley & Sons, 2010), p. 210.
50. Bruce F. Norton, *Britain* (Washington, DC: Congressional Quarterly Press, 2007), p. 52.
51. Harold Clarke, et al, *Political Choice in Britain* (New York: Oxford University Press, 2004), p. 50.
52. Gabriel Almond and Sidney Verba, *The Civic Culture: Political Attitudes and Democracy in Five Nations* (Princeton, NJ: Princeton University Press, 1963).
53. Pippa Norris, ed., *Critical Citizens: Global Support for Democratic Government* (New York: Oxford University Press, 1999).
54. Rosie Campbell, "The Politics of Diversity," *Developments in British Politics 9* (New York: Palgrave, 2011) p. 214.

55. "Special Report on Britain's Turbulent Future," *The Economist* (November 9th-15th, 2013), p. 10.
56. Lane Kenworthy, *Progress for the Poor* (New York: Oxford University Press, 2011), p. 109.
57. The G7 was composed of Canada, France, Germany, Italy, Japan, the United Kingdom, and the United States.
58. Terence Casey, "'Financialization' and the Future of the Neoliberal Growth Model," Paper presented at the Political Studies Association Annual Conference (April 2011), p. 2.
59. Colin Hay, "Britain and the Global Financial Crisis: The Return of Boom and Bust," *British Politics 9* (New York: Palgrave, 2011), p. 239.
60. Quoted in Stathis N. Kalyvas, *The Rise of Christian Democracy in Europe* (Ithaca: Cornell University Press, 1996), p. 2.
61. Kalyvas, *The Rise of Christian Democracy in Europe*, pp. 222–265.
62. An early statement of Christian democratic principles is Gabriel Almond, "The Political Ideas of Christian Democracy," *Journal of Politics* (November 1948), vol. 10, pp. 734–763; for more current analyses, see David Hanley, ed., *Christian Democracy in Europe: A Comparative Perspective* (New York: St. Martin's Press, 1994); and Kees van Kersbergen, *Social Capitalism: A Study of Christian Democracy and the Welfare State* (New York: Routledge, 1995).
63. van Kersbergen, *Social Capitalism*, pp. 180–881.
64. Emmerich Talos, "Corporatism—The Austrian Model," in *Contemporary Austrian Politics*, Volmar Lauber, (ed.), (Boulder: Westview Press, 1996), p. 104.
65. Peter G. Katzenstein, *Policy and Politics in West Germany: The Growth of a Semisovereign State* (Philadelphia, PA: Temple University Press, 1987).
66. Charles Lees, *Party Politics in Germany: A Comparative Politics Approach* (New York: Palgrave, 2005), pp. 128–137.
67. Simon Green and William E. Paterson, "Introduction: Semisovereignty Challenged," in *Governance in Contemporary Germany: The Semisovereign State Revisited*, Simon Green and William E. Paterson, (eds.), (New York: Cambridge University Press, 2005), p. 3.
68. Green and Paterson, "Introduction: Semisovereignty Challenged," p. 6.
69. Hans Fuchs, newly appointed president of the North Rhine province under the Allied occupation, quoted in Konrad H. Jarausch, *After Hitler: Recivilizing Germans, 1945–1995* (New York: Oxford University Press, 2006), p. 20.
70. Jarausch, *After Hitler*, p. 45.
71. Global Competitiveness rankings can be found at: http://www3.weforum.org/docs/GCR2013-14/GCR_Rankings_2013-14.pdf.
72. Pol O'Dochartaigh, *Germany since 1945* (New York: Palgrave, 2004), p. 41.
73. Lowell Turner, *Democracy at Work: Changing World Markets and the Future of Labor Unions* (Ithaca: Cornell University Press, 1991).
74. Wolfgang Streek, *Reforming Capitalism: Institutional Change in the German Political Economy* (New York: Oxford University Press, 2009), p. 39.
75. Neil Irwin, "How Underpaid German Workers Helped Cause Europe's Debt Crisis," *New York Times* (April 12, 2014).
76. See Timothy Smeeding, "Poor People in Rich Nations," *Journal of Economic Perspectives* 20:1 (2006), pp. 69–90. See Table 2: Absolute Poverty Rates Using Official US Poverty Standards in Nine Rich Countries at the Turn of the Century.
77. OECD/HRDC, *Literacy in the Information Age: Final Report of the International Adult Literacy Survey* (Paris: Organization for Economic Cooperation and Development; and Ottawa: Human Resources Development Canada, 2000), p. x.
78. *Literacy in the Information Age*, p. xiii.
79. *OECD Skills Outlook, 2013: First Results from the Survey of Adult Skills* (Paris: OECD, 2013), p. 75.
80. UNODC Global Study on Homicide 2011 at http://www.unodc.org/unodc/en/data-and-analysis/homicide.html.
81. Economist Intelligence Unit Democracy Index, 2012

Chapter 10

1. Simon Denver, "Criminals Flourish in Indian Elections," *Washington Post* (March 5, 2012), http://www.washingtonpost.com/world/criminals-flourish-in-indian-elections/2012/03/03/gIQA1E1JsR_story.html.
2. Somini Sangupta, "Education Push Yields Little for India's Poor," *The New York Times* (January 17, 2008). http://www.nytimes.com/2008/01/17/world/asia/17india.html?pagewanted=all.
3. David De Ferranti, Guillermo E. Perry, Francisco Ferreira, and Michael Walton, *Inequality in Latin America: Breaking with History?* (Washington, D.C.: The World Bank, 2004), p. 137.
4. The Economist Intelligence Unit's Index of Democracy 2012, pp. 4–5.
5. Alexei Barrionuevo, "Violence in the Newest Olympic City Rattles Brazil," *The New York Times* October 20, 2009.
6. David De Ferranti et al., *Inequality in Latin America*, pp. 112–122, 186.
7. Atul Kohli, *State-Directed Development: Political Power and Industrialization in the Global Periphery* (New York: Cambridge University Press, 2004), p. 171.
8. Perry Anderson, "Lula's Brazil," *London Review of Books* 33:7 (March 2011), pp. 3–12, http://www.lrb.co.uk/v33/n07/perry-anderson/lulas-brazil.
9. Nicholas Lemann, "The Anointed," *The New Yorker* (December 5, 2011), p. 52; and

9. Perry Anderson, "Lula's Brazil," http://www.lrb.co.uk/v33/n07/perry-anderson/lulas-brazil.
10. Ben Ross Schneider, "The *Dessarollista* State in Brazil and Mexico," in *The Developmental State*, Meredith Woo-Cumings, (ed.), (Ithaca, NY: Cornell University Press, 1999), pp. 291–293.
11. Branko Milanovic, "Inequality and Its Discontents: Why So Many Feel Left Behind," *Foreign Affairs* August 12, 2011, http://www.foreignaffairs.com/articles/68031/branko-milanovic/inequality-and-its-discontents?page=show.
12. Charles H Blake, *Politics in Latin America: The Quest for Development, Liberty, and Governance* (Boston: Houghton Mifflin Company, 2005), p. 180.
13. Kurt Weyland, *Democracy without Equity: Failures of Reform in Brazil*. (Pittsburgh, PA: University of Pittsburgh Press, 1996), pp. 55–56.
14. Ibid., p. 4.
15. Alfred P. Montero, "A Reversal of Political Fortune: The Transitional Dynamics of Conservative Rule in Brazil," *Latin American Politics and Society* 54:1 (Spring, 2012), pp. 8–10.
16. Wendy Hunter and Natasha Borges Sugiyama, "Democracy and Social Policy in Brazil: Advancing Basic Needs, Preserving Privileged Interests," *Latin American Politics and Society* 51:2 (Summer, 2009), pp. 17–18.
17. Anderson, "Lula's Brazil."
18. Mala Htun, "From 'Racial Democracy' to Affirmative Action: Changing State Policy on Race in Brazil," *Latin American Research Review* 39:1 (February 2004), p. 61.
19. Mala Htun, "Racial Quotas for a 'Racial Democracy,'" *NACLA Report on the Americas* (January/February 2005), p. 21.
20. Ibid., p. 20.
21. Mala Htun, "From 'Racial Democracy' to Affirmative Action," p. 63.
22. Ibid., p. 64.
23. "Race in Brazil: Affirming a Divide," *The Economist* (January 28, 2012), http://www.economist.com/node/21543494.
24. "Race in Brazil: Affirming a Divide."
25. World Values Survey, http://www.wvsevsdb.com/wvs/WVSAnalizeQuestion.jsp,
26. World Values Survey, http://www.wvsevsdb.com/wvs/WVSAnalizeQuestion.jsp.
27. Ben Ross Schneider, "The *Desarrollista* State in Brazil and Mexico," p. 289.
28. World Values Survey, http://www.wvsevsdb.com/wvs/WVSAnalizeQuestion.jsp.
29. World Values Survey. http://www.wvsevsdb.com/wvs/WVSAnalizeQuestion.jsp/.
30. Ben Ross Schneider, "The *Desarrollista* State in Brazil and Mexico," pp. 280–288.
31. Nicholas Lemann, "The Anointed," p. 60
32. Nicholas Lemann, "The Anointed," p. 52.
33. Joe Leahy, "Brazil Looks to China for Industrial Policy," *Financial Times* (April 15, 2011), http://www.ft.com/cms/s/0/1f82a382-646a-11e0-a69a-00144feab49a.html#axzz2fHSUwuxy.
34. Wendy Hunter and Natasha Borges Sukiyama, "Democracy and Social Policy in Brazil: Advancing Basic Needs, Preserving Privileged Interests," *Latin American Politics and Society* 51:2 (2009), pp. 29–31.
35. Nicholas Lemann, "The Anointed," p. 61.
36. David Samuels, "Brazil Is a Stable and Growing Democracy—And We're Not Going to Take It Any More," *Monkey Cage Blog*, June 24, 2013, http://themonkeycage.org/2013/06/24/brazil-is-a-stable-and-growing-democracy-and-were-not-going-to-take-it-any-more.
37. Nicholas Barnes, "Whither Brazil: Popular Protests, Public Violence and Prospects for Change," (June 28, 2013), http://themonkeycage.org/2013/06/28/the-rio-protests-who-what-why-and-will-they-matter/.
38. Daniel N. Posner and Daniel J. Young, "The Institutionalization of Political Power in Africa," *Journal of Democracy* 18:3 (July 2007), p. 127.
39. The *Economist* Index identifies Nigeria as an authoritarian state, a few places below the cut-off point for being in the hybrid regimes category. Freedom House and Polity IV, two other respected organizations that rank countries on the degree of democracy that they display, place Nigeria in between fully democratic and fully authoritarian countries.
40. World Bank, Poverty Data, http://data.worldbank.org/indicator/SI.POV.DDAY.
41. Data Set 3e.
42. Pierre Englebert, "Pre-Colonial Institutions, Post-Colonial States, and Economic Development in Tropical Africa," *Political Research Quarterly* 53:1 (March 2000).
43. Atul Kohli, *State-Directed Development: Political Power and Industrialization in the Global Periphery* (New York: Cambridge University Press, 2004), pp. 301–306.
44. Ibid., p. 306.
45. Catherine Boone, "States and Ruling Classes in Postcolonial Africa: The Enduring Contradictions of Power," in *State Power and Social Forces: Domination and Transformation in the Third World*, Joel S. Migdal, Atul Kohli, and Vivienne Shue, (eds.), (New York: Cambridge University Press, 1994), pp. 117–118.
46. William Reno, *Warlord Politics and African States* (Boulder, CO: Lynne Rienner Publishers, 1998), p. 21.
47. Kohli, pp. 314–315.
48. Michael Roll, "Pockets of Effectiveness: Why Do Strong Public Institutions Exist in Weak States?" American Political Science Association

Annual Meeting 2013 August 29–September 1, 2013, Chicago, Illinois.
49. Wole Soyinka, *The Open Sore of a Continent* (New York: Oxford University Press, 1997), p. 15.
50. Daniel N. Posner and Daniel J. Young, "The Institutionalization of Political Power in Africa," p. 126.
51. Paul M. Lubeck, "Mapping a Sharia Restorationist Movement," in *Sharia Politics: Islamic Law and Society in the Modern World*, Robert Hefner, (ed.), (Bloomington, IN: University of Indiana Press, 2011), p. 250.
52. Lydia Polgreen, "Nigeria Turns from Harsher Side of Islamic Law," *New York Times*, December 1, 2007.
53. "A man and a morass," *Economist* (May 26, 2011), http://www.economist.com/node/18741606?story_id=18741606. "Troube in Nigeria,"*Economist* (March 1, 2014), http://www.economist.com/news/middle-east-and-africa/21597896-presidents-decision-get-rid-central-bank-governor-bad-news-now.
54. Paul M. Lubeck, "Mapping a Sharia Restorationist Movement," p. 253.
55. Brandon Kendhammer, "The Sharia Controversy in Northern Nigeria and the Politics of Islamic Law in New and Uncertain Democracies," *Comparative Politics* 45:3 (April, 2013).
56. Sudarsan Raghavan, "In Nigeria's North, Boko Haram Militia Aims to Mold the Schools through Violence," *Washington Post* (June 10, 2013), http://www.washingtonpost.com/world/africa/in-nigerias-north-boko-haram-militia-aims-to-mold-the-schools-through-violence/2013/06/09/0cc37d56-cd64-11e2-8573-3baeea6a2647_story.html
57. Kendhammer,"The Sharia Controversy in Northern Nigeria."

58. "Planned National Protest in Nigeria Could Grind Ooil-Rich Nation to Halt over End of Cheap Gas," *Washington Post* (January 7, 2012), http://www.washingtonpost.com/world/africa/planned-national-protest-in-nigeria-could-grind-oil-rich-nation-to-halt-over-end-of-cheap-gas/2012/01/07/gIQAcJh8gP_story.html.
59. AFROBAROMETER, Survey of Results Afrobarometer Round 5 Survey in Nigeria, 2012 p. 54, www.afrobarometer.org.
60. AFROBAROMETER, Survey of Results Afrobarometer Round 5 Survey in Nigeria, 2012 p. 54.
61. AFROBAROMETER, Survey of Results Afrobarometer Round 5 Survey in Nigeria, 2012 p. 12.
62. AFROBAROMETER Summary of Results, Round 4 Afrobarometer Survey in Nigeria, 2008, p. 11.–
63. Ronald Inglehart and Christian Welzel, "Changing Mass Priorities: The Link between Modernization and Democracy." *Perspectives on Politics* 8:2 (June 2010), p. 554.
64. AFROBAROMETER, Survey of Results Afrobarometer Round 5 Survey in Nigeria, 2012.
65. Paul M. Lubeck, "Mapping a Sharia Restorationist Movement," pp. 247–248.
66. David Booth and Frederick Goloola–Mutebi, "Developmental Patrimonialism: The Case of Rwanda," Africa Power and Politics Working Paper 16, Overseas Development Institute, London England (March 2011) page2. http://www.institutions-africa.org/filestream/20110321-appp-working-paper-16-developmental-patrimonialism-the-case-of-rwanda-by-david-booth-and-frederick-golooba-mutebi-march-2011", pp. 4–5.
67. Paul M. Lubeck, "Nigeria: Mapping a Shari's Restorationist Movement," p. 248.

68. Richard Joseph, "Challenges of a 'Frontier' Region," *Journal of Democracy* 19:2 (April, 2008) p. 182.
69. Paul Collier, *The Bottom Billion*: *Why the Poorest Countries Are Failing and What Can Be Done About It*(new York: Oxford University Press, 2007), p. 49.
70. World Bank, "Nigeria Economic Report" (May 2013), pp. 7–8, http://www-wds.worldbank.org/external/default/WDSContentServer/WDSP/IB/2013/05/14/000333037_20130514101211/Rendered/PDF/776840WP0Niger0Box0342041B00PUBLIC0.pdf.
71. World Bank, "Nigeria Economic Report" (May, 2013), pp. 8–9.
72. Larry Diamond," Thinking about Hybrid Regimes," *The Journal of Democracy*, 13:2 (April 2002), p. 24.
73. Political scientists operationally define electoral authoritarianism in different ways. This results in different lists of which countries have authoritarian regimes. For political scientists who list Iran as an electoral authoritarian regime, see Marc Morje Howard and Philip G. Roessler, "Liberalizing Electoral Outcomes in Competitive Authoritarian Regimes," *American Journal of Political Science* 52:2 (April 2006), p. 370; Francis Fukuyama, "Iran, Islam and the Rule of Law," *Wall Street Journal* (June 27, 2009), http://online.wsj.com/news/articles/SB10001424052970203946904574300374086282670.
74. Gunes Murat Tezcur, "Democratic Struggles and Authoritarian Responses in Iran in Comparative Perspective," in *Middle East Authoritarianisms: Governance, Constestation, and Regime Resilience in Syria and Iran*, Steven Heydemann and Renoud Leenders, (eds.), (Stanford, CA: Stanford University Press, 2012), p. 200.
75. Ray Takeyh, "Clerics Responsible for Iran's Failed Attempts at

76. Michael Axworthy, *Revolutionary Iran: A History of the Islamic Republic* (New York: Oxford University Press, 2013), pp. 137–139 and Ervand Abrahamian, "Who's in Charge?" *London Review of Books* 30:21 (November 6, 2008), http://www.lrb.co.uk/v30/n21/ervand-abrahamian/whos-in-charge.
77. Reuel Marc Gerecht, "The Koran and the Ballot Box," *The New York Times* (June 21, 2009).
78. Abrahamian, "Who's in Charge?"
79. Khamenei speech entitled "Reforms, Strategies, and Challenges," quoted in Karim Sadjadpour, *Reading Khamenei: The World View of Iran's Most Powerful Leader* (Washington, DC: Carnegie Endowment for International Peace, 2008), p. 8. http://carnegieendowment.org/2008/03/10/reading-khamenei-world-view-of-iran-s-most-powerful-leader/b1p.
80. Greg Bruno, "Iran's Revolutionary Guards," Council on Foreign Relations Backgrounder (June 22, 2009). www.cfr.org.
81. Karim Sadjadpour, "Iran Primer: The Supreme Leader," (September 2010). http://carnegieendowment.org/publications/index.cfm?fa=view&id=41753.
82. This discussion of the first three factions draws on Ray Takeyh, *Hidden Iran: Paradox and Power in the Islamic Republic* (New York: Henry Holt and Company, 2006), pp. 31–57.
83. Ray Takeyh, *Hidden Iran*, p. 48.
84. The phrase is from T. Yousef, "Employment, Development and the Social Contract in the Middle East and North Africa," Technical report, Washington, DC, 2004, cited in Dvjavad Salhehi-Isfahani, "Revolution and Redistribution in Iran: Poverty and Inequality 25 Years Later," Department of Economics, Virginia Tech University, August 2006, p. 4. http://www.filebox.vt.edu/users/salehi/Iran_poverty_trend.pdf
85. Kevan Harris, "Subsidy Payments in Iran: Too Much or Not Enough?" http://www.kevanharris.com/post/9754508505/subsidy-payments-in-iran-too-much-or-not-enough.
86. David E. Thaler, Alireza Nader, Shahram Chubin, Jerrolde D. Green, Charlotte Lynch, and Frederic Wehrey, *Mullahs, Guards, and Bonyads, An Exploration of Iranian Leadership* Dynamics (Santa Monica, CA: RAND National Defense Institute, 2010), pp. 56–58; and Kjetil Bjorvatin and Kjetil Selvik, "Destructive Competition: Factionalism and Rent-Seeking in Iran," *World Development* 36:11 (2008), p. 2317.
87. Jerry Guo, "Letter from Tehran: Iran's New Hard-Liners," *Foreign Affairs* (September 30, 2009), www.foreignaffairs.org.
88. Farideh Farhi, "The Parliament," in *The Iran Primer*, Robin Wright, (ed), (Washington, DC: United States Institute of Peace, 2010), http://iranprimer.usip.org/resource/parliament.
89. Arash Aramesh, "Iran Paralyzes Political Parties by Arresting Leaders," March 23, 2010, www.insideiran.org.
90. World Values Survey, www.worldvaluessurvey.org. The 2005 Survey is the most recent survey available.
91. Kevan Harris, "The Politics of Subsidy Reform in Iran," *Middle East Research and Information Project* 254 (Spring 2010), http://www.merip.org/mer/mer254/politics-subsidy-reform-iran
92. Ibid.
93. Kevan Harris, "The Rise of the Subcontractor State: Politics of Pseudo-Privatization in Iran," *International Journal of Middle East Studies* 45 (2013), pp. 45–47.
94. Thomas Erdbrink, "Iran Staggers As Sanctions Hit Economy," *New York Times* (September 30, 2013, http://www.nytimes.com/2013/10/01/world/middleeast/iran-staggers-as-sanctions-hit-economy.html?hp&_r=0.
95. World Bank, World Development Indicators, www.google.com/publicdata.
96. The *Economist* ranking puts Nigeria just below its hybrid regimes category and near the top of the authoritarian category We have categorized it as a semi-democracy because two other organizations widely used by political scientists, Polity IV and Freedom House, list it as a hybrid regime with a mix of authoritarian and democratic features rather than authoritarian.

Chapter 11

1. John Thornhill, "Russia's Past Is No Sign of Its Future," *Financial Times* August 25, 2011, http://www.ft.com/intl/cms/s/0/f73a9f2c-ca8c-11e0-94d0-00144feabdc0.html#axzz1W2QAduir.
2. Peter Rutland, "The Poliitical Economy of Putin 3.0," *Russian Analytical Digest* (July 18, 2013), p. 2. http://www.isn.ethz.ch/Digital-Library/Publications/Detail/?ots591=0c54e3b3-1e9c-be1e-2c24-a6a8c7060233&lng=en&id=167341.
3. Stephen F. Cohen, *Bukharin and the Bolshevik Revolution* (New York: Oxford University Press, 1980), p. 339.
4. Perry Anderson, "Two Revolutions: Rough Notes," *New Left Review* 61 (January/February 2010), p. 66.
5. Aleksandr I. Solzhenitsyn, *The Gulag Archipelago 1918–1956* (New York: Harper Collins Publishers, 1985).
6. Stephen White, "Russia," in *Politics in Europe*, 4th ed.,

M. Donald Hancock, (ed.), (Washington, DC: Congressional Quarterly Press, 2007), p. 464.

7. Vladimir Gelman, "Institutional Trap in Russian Politics: Still No Way Out?" PONARS Eurasia Policy Memo No. 151, (May 2011), p. 2.

8. Sam Green, "Putin in 2012," *The Monkey Cage Blog*, (September 25, 2011), http://themonkeycage.org/. Sept.

9. Kimberly Marten, "How Might Sanctions Affect Russia?" Monkey Cage Blog, *Washington Post* (March 4, 2014). http://www.washingtonpost.com/blogs/monkey-cage/wp/2014/03/04/how-might-sanctions-affect-russia/.

10. Brian Whitmore, "Through the Crimean Prism: Five Things We've Learned About Russia," (March 14, 2014). The Power Vertical Blog. http://www.rferl.org/archive/The_Power_Vertical/latest/884/884.html.

11. The World Bank, "Worldwide Governance Indicators," http://info.worldbank.org/governance/wgi/index.aspx#doc. The criteria used for governance effectiveness can be found by clicking on the link Government Effectiveness at this site. The quotation is from information at this link.

12. World Bank, Worldwide Governance Indicators 2012, http://info.worldbank.org/governance/wgi/index.aspx#reports.

13. Brian Whitmore, "License to Steal—A Bug or a Feature?" *The Power Vertical Blog* (December 12, 2012), http://www.rferl.org/content/license-to-steal-a-bug-or-a-feature/24795746.html.

14. Sean Guillory, "Sistema: How Power Works in Modern Russia," *Russia Direct* (September 17, 2013), http://russia-direct.org/content/sistema-how-power-works-modern-russia.

15. Gideon Lichfield, "Survey of Russia: Watch Your Back," *The Economist* (May 20, 2004), www.economist.com.

16. Julia Ioffe, "Net Impact: One Man's Cyber Crusade against Russian Corruption," *The New Yorker* (April 4, 2011), http://www.newyorker.com/reporting/2011/04/04/110404fa_fact_ioffe.

17. Transparency International, "Corruption Perceptions Index 2012," http://www.transparency.org/cpi2012/results.

18. "Russia's Economy: The S Word," *The Economist* (November 9, 2013), http://www.economist.com/news/europe/21589455-will-stagnating-economy-bring-about-much-needed-structural-reform-s-word.

19. Stephen Kotkin, "Now Comes the Tough Part in Russia," *New York Times* (March 2, 2008). http://www.nytimes.com/2008/03/02/business/worldbusiness/02shelf.html?pagewanted=print&_r=0. Accessed November 6, 2013.

20. White, pp. 489–490. Arthur S. Banks, Thomas C. Muller, and William R. Overstreet, eds., *Political Handbook of the World 2005–2006* (Washington, DC: Congressional Quarterly Press, 2006), p. 964.

21. Nikolai Petrov, Masha Lipman, and Henry Hale, "Overmanaged Democracy in Russia: Governance Implications of Hybrid Regimes," Carnegie Endowment for International Peace, Russia and Eurasia Program, No. 106, February 2010, p. 4.

22. Ibid., p. 7.

23. Thomas F. Remington, "Politics in Russia," in *Comparative Politics Today*, 9th ed., Gabriel A. Almond, G. Bingham Powell, Jr., Russell J. Dalton, and Kaare Strom, (eds.), (New York: Pearson Longman, 2008), pp. 392–393.

24. Michael McFaul and Nikolai Petrov, "What the Elections Tell Us," *Journal of Democracy* 15:3 (July 2004), p. 24.

25. Ibid.

26. Neil Buckley, "One Day in the Life of Mikhail Khodorkovsky," *Financial Times Magazine* (October 24, 2013), http://www.ft.com/intl/cms/s/2/a9adb49e-3c39-11e3-b85f-00144feab7de.html#axzz2jWGGuata.

27. "Vladimir Putin: His Many Feats of Strength," *Washington Post* (September 5, 2012), http://www.washingtonpost.com/world/vladimir-putin-his-many-feats-of-strength/2012/09/05/f7281be2-f7a7-11e1-8b93-c4f4ab1c8d13_gallery.html#photo=14.

28. Petrov, Lipman, and Hale, "Overmanaged Democracy in Russia," pp. 17–18.

29. Andrei Soldatov and Irina Borogan, "Russia's Digital Underground: How the Kremlin is Waging War on Digital Freedom," *Foreign Policy* (April 5, 2013), http://www.foreignpolicy.com/articles/2013/04/05/russia_war_on_internet_freedom?print=yes&hidecomments=yes&page=full.

30. Will Englund and Kathy Lally, "Russian Court Convicts Anti-Corruption Crusader Alexei Navalny," *Washington Post* (July 18, 2013), http://www.washingtonpost.com/world/russian-court-convicts-navalny/2013/07/18/5d058cfc-ef7c-11e2-bed3-b9b6fe264871_story.html?hpid=z3.

31. Sean Guillory, "The Party of Crooks and Thieves," *Sean's Russia Blog*, (May 3, 2013), http://seansrussiablog.org/page/8/.

32. Lilia Shevtsova, *Russia XXI: The Logic of Suicide and Rebirth* (Moscow: Carnegie Moscow Center, Carnegie Foundation for International Peace, 2013), p. 39.

33. Julia Ioffe, "#OccupyMoscow," *Foreign Policy* (December 6, 2011), http://www.foreignpolicy.com/articles/2011/12/06/occupymoscow?page=ful.

34. Michael Birbaum, "Russian Protestors Flood Moscow Demanding Reforms," *Washington Post* (December 24, 2011, http://www.washingtonpost.com/world/europe/russian-protesters-flood-moscow-demanding-

reforms/2011/12/24/gIQAIeRPFP_story.html?hpid=z4.

35. David Remnick, "The Civil Archipelago: How Far Can the Resistance to Vladimir Putin Go?" *The New Yorker* (December 19, 2011), http://www.newyorker.com/reporting/2011/12/19/111219fa_fact_remnick?currentPage=all.

36. Maria Lipman at a forum celebrating the publication of "Russia in 2020: Scenarios for the Future." Clifford Gaddy, Sam Greene, Maria Lipman, and Nikolay Petrov, "Russia in 2020: Scenarios for the Future," (Washington, DC: Carnegie Endowment for International Peace.

37. Sam Greene at a forum celebrating the publication of "Russia in 2020: Scenarios for the Future," Clifford Gaddy, Sam Greene, Maria Lipman, and Nikolay Petrov, "Russia in 2020: Scenarios for the Future."

38. World Values Survey, http://www.wvsevsdb.com/wvs/WVSAnalizeQuestion.jsp.

39. Brian Whitmore, "Russia's Silent Majority," *The Power Vertical Blog* (November 7, 2013), http://www.rferl.org/archive/The_Power_Vertical/latest/884/884.html.

40. Peter Pomerantsey, "Russia for Russians," *London Review of Books* (November 5, 2013), http://www.lrb.co.uk/blog/2013/11/05/peter-pomerantsev/russia-for-russians/.

41. Lilia Shevtsova, "Russia XXI: The Logic of Suicide and Rebirth," Carnegie Moscow Center, Carnegie Center for International Peace (2013), pp. 50–51, http://www.carnegie.ru/en.

42. Andrew Kohut, "Confidence in Democracy and Capitalism Wanes in the Former Soviet Union," Pew Global Attitudes Project (December 5, 2011), pp. 3, 21–23.

43. Amy Knight, "Putting the Watch on Putin," *New York Review of Books* 58:7 (April 14, 2011), http://www.nybooks.com/blogs/nyrblog/2011/apr/14/russia-opposition-putin-corruption/.

44. Thomas de Waal, "An Anatomy of Apathy," *The National Interest* (April 29, 2011), http://nationalinterest.org/commentary/anatomy-apathy-5239.

45. Henry E. Hale, "Trends in Russian Views on Democracy: Has There Been a Russian Democratic Awakening" *Russian Analytical Digest* 119 (September 19, 2012),p. 10. http://www.css.ethz.ch/publications/pdfs/RAD-117-9-11.pdf.," p. 10.

46. World Values Survey. www.worldvaluessurvey.org.

47. Mark Galeotti and Andrew S. Bower, "Putin's Empire of the Mind," *Foreign Policy* (April 21, 2014). http://www.foreign policy.com/profilesMark-Galeotti.

48. Joseph E. Stiglitz, *Globalization and Its Discontents* (New York: W. W. Norton 2002), p. 53.

49. Vladimir Gelman, "Russia's Crony Capitalism: The Swing of the Pendulum," *Open Democracy*, November 14, 2011, http://www.opendemocracy.net/od-russia/vladimir-gelman/russia%E2%80%99s-crony-capitalism-swing-of-pendulum.

50. Anthony Shorrocks, Jim Davies, and Rodrigo Liuberasis, Credit Suisse Research Institute, *Global Wealth Report 3=2013*, p. 28; Sean Guillory, "Russia's Widening Wealth Inequality," (October 10, 2013), http://readrussia.com/2013/10/10/russias-widening-wealth-inequality/.

51. Ruchir Sharma, "The Billionaires List," *Washington Post*, June 24, 2012, http://www.washingtonpost.com/blogs/ezra-klein/wp/2012/06/24/the-billionaires-list/?hpid=z4.

52. OECD Reviews of Labour Market and Social Policies: Russian Federation, 2011, http://www.oecd.org/els/soc/oecdreviewsoflabourmarketandsocialpoliciesrussianfederation.htm.

53. Thomas F. Remington, "Russian Regional Inequality in Comparative Perspective," Paper prepared for Benjamin F. Shambaugh Conference, "Lessons from Subnational Comparative Politics: Theory and Method in the Third Decade of Studying Russia's Regions," University of Iowa (October 6–9, 2011), pp. 13–16, http://ir.uiowa.edu/cgi/viewcontent.cgi?article=1115&context=shambaugh.

54. "Modernising Russia: Another Great Leap Forward?" *The Economist* March 11, 2010), http://www.economist.com/node/15661865.

55. "Russia's Economy: The S Word," *The Economist* (November 9, 2013), http://www.economist.com/news/europe/21589455-will-stagnating-economy-bring-about-much-needed-structural-reform-s-word.

56. Peter Rutland, "Russia's Pension System: Back to the Future," *Russian Analytical Digest* 121 (December 2012), p. 9.

57. Leon Aron, "Putin Petro State Approaching Empty," *The American* (June 5, 2013), http://www.american.com/archive/2013/june/putins-petro-state-approaching-empty.

58. Sam Greene, "Putin in 2012: Guest Commentary," September 25. 2011. http://themonkeycage.org/.

59. Andrew Nathan, *China's Transition* (New York: Columbia University Press, 1997), p. 29.

60. Yang Jisheng, "China's Great Shame," *New York Times* (November 13, 2012), http://www.nytimes.com/2012/11/14/opinion/chinas-great-shame.html?hp&_r=0.

61. Frederick C. Teiwes, "Politics at the 'Core': The Political Circumstances of Mao Zedong, Deng Xiaoping and Jiang Zemin," China Iinformation: *A Journal of Contemporary China Studies*, (date), vol. XV, No. 1, p. 27.

62. Nathan, *China's Transition*, p. 6.

63. "A Great Leap Forward," *The Economist* (October 5, 1991), pp. 19–21.
64. Minxin Pei, *China's Trapped Transition: The Limits of Developmental Autocracy* (Cambridge, MA: Harvard University Press, 2006), pp. 2–3.
65. "Entrepreneurship in China," *The Economist* (March 10, 2011), pp. 79–81.
66. "Wrangling over the New Politburo Says Much about the Prospects for Reform," *Economist* (November 12, 2012), http://www.economist.com/news/china/21566015-wrangling-over-new-politburo-says-much-about-possibility-reform-old-brooms.
67. Cheng Li, "Rule of the Princelings," *The Cairo Review of Global Affairs* (February 10, 2013), pp. 36–38, http://www.aucegypt.edu/gapp/cairoreview/Pages/articleDetails.aspx?aid=295.
68. Rodger Baker and John Minnich, "China's Inevitable Changes," *Stratfor* (November 5, 2013),http://www.stratfor.com/weekly/chinas-inevitable-changes?utm_source=freelist-.
69. Richard McGregor, *The Party: The Secret World of China's Communist Rulers* (New York: HarperCollins Publishers, 2010) p. 74.
70. Minxin Pei, *China's Trapped Transition*, p. 64.
71. Jerome Alan Cohen, "Courts with Chinese Characteristics," *Foreign Affairs* (October 11, 2012), http://www.foreignaffairs.com/articles/138178/jerome-alan-cohen/courts-with-chinese-characteristics?page=show.
72. Minxin Pei, *China's Trapped Transition*, p. 65.
73. Ibid., pp. 70–71.
74. Cheng Li, "China at the Tipping Point," *Journal of Democracy* 24:1 (January 2013), p. 45.
75. David Shambaugh, *China's Communist Party: Atrophy and Adaptation* (Washington, DC: Woodrow Wilson Center Press, 2009), p. 111.
76. Minxin Pei, *China's Trapped Transition*, pp. 89–92.
77. Shambaugh, *China's Communist Party*, p. 112.
78. Jamil Anderlini and Rahul Jacob, "Beijing City to Hike Minimum Wage 21 percent," *Financial Times* (December 28, 2010), http://www.ft.com/cms/s/0/30f7f9e0-1277-11e0-b4c8-00144feabdc0.html#axzz2lc6Utcf4.
79. Andrew Higgins, "China Trade Union Takes Up New Cause—Workers," *Washington Post* (April 28, 2011), http://www.washingtonpost.com/world/asia-pacific/chinas-trade-union-takes-up-a-new-cause--workers/2011/03/01/AFMjIN5E_story.html.
80. Qin Gao, "Redistributive Nature of the Chinese Social Benefit System: Progressive or Regressive?" *The China Quarterly* 201 (March 2010), pp. 1–19; and Wanlong Lin and Christine Wong, "Are Beijing's Policies Reaching the Poor?" *The China Journal* 67 (2012), p. 24.
81. Kevin O'Brien and Rongbin Han, "Path to Democracy? Assessing Village Elections in China," *Journal of Contemporary China* 18:60 (2009), pp. 359–378.
82. Renfu Luo, Linxiu Zhang, Jikun Huang, and Scott Rozelle, "Village Elections, Public Goods Investments and Pork Barrel Politics, Chinese-style," *The Journal of Development Studies* 46:4 (2010), pp. 662–684.
83. Cheng Li, "Rule of the Princelings," p. 45.
84. John Delury, "China's Labor's Lost," *Foreign Affairs* (November 25, 2013), http://www.foreignaffairs.com/articles/140289/john-delury/chinas-labors-lost.
85. "Top 5 Executioners in 2011," Amnesty International, http://www.amnesty.org/en/death-penalty/top-5-executioners-in-2011.
86. Cheng Li, "Rule of the Princelings, p. 46.
87. Andrew Jacobs, "Protests at Chemical Plant Forces Officials to Back Down," *The New York Times* (October 28, 2012), http://www.nytimes.com/2012/10/29/world/asia/protests-against-sinopec-plant-in-china-reach-third-day.html?hpw.
88. Elizabeth Economy, "China: The New Virtual Political System," Council on Foreign Relations (April 2011), http://www.cfr.org/china/china-new-virtual-political-system/p24805.
89. Gary King, Jennifer Pan, and Margaret Roberts, "How Censorship in China Allows Government Criticism but Silences Collective Expression," (June 18, 2012), p. 1, American Political Science Association Annual Meeting, (2012), http://papers.ssrn.com/sol3/papers.cfm?abstract_id=2104894##.
90. Peter L. Lorentzen, "Regularizing Rioting: Permitting Protests in an Authoritarian Regime," University of California, Berkeley (June 9, 2010), pp. 1–7, http://ssrn.com/abstract=995330.
91. David Shambaugh, "China's Competing Nationalisms," *International Herald Tribune* (May 5, 2008), www.brookings.edu.
92. David Shambaugh, "China's Competing Nationalisms." *International Herald Tribune*, May 5, 2008. www.brookings.edu. Accessed July 9, 2010, and Cheng Li, "Rule of the Princelings," p. 46.
93. Jie Lu, "Democratic Conceptions and Regime Support among Chinese Citizens," Asian Barometer: A Comparative Survey of Democracy, Governance, and Development: Working Paper Series Number 66 (2012), pp. 41–42, http://www.asianbarometer.org/newenglish/publications/workingpapers/no.66.pdf.
94. The 66 percent figure was provided by Professor Jie Lu from research he has done using data

from the 2011 Asian Barometer Survey of Mainland China, which had not yet been publicly released. We are grateful for his help.

95. Tianjian Shi and JieLu, "The Meanings of Democracy: The Shadow of Confucianism," *Journal of Democracy* 21:4 (2010), 123-130 and Jie Lu, "Democratic Conceptions and Regime Support among Chinese Citizens," pp. 45–47.

96. Jie Lu, "Democratic Conceptions and Regime Support among Chinese Citizens," pp. 44–47. The quoted definition of liberal democracy is from page 46.

97. Jie Lu, p. 51; and Tianjian Shi and Jie Lu, "The Battle of Ideas and Discourses before Democratic Transition: Different Conceptions of Democracy in Authoritarian China," *International Political Science Review* (forthcoming).

98. We are grateful to Professor Jie Lu for providing survey data and help in explaining this puzzle.

99. Robert J. Samuelson, "China at a Crossroads," *Washington Post* (November 24, 2013), http://www.washingtonpost.com/opinions/robert-samuelson-china-at-a-crossroads/2013/11/24/15ccd2e8-53c5-11e3-9e2c-e1d01116fd98_story.html?hpid=z3.

100. David Barboza, "Billions in Hidden Riches for Family of Chinese Leader," *New York Times* (October 25, 2012), http://www.nytimes.com/2012/10/26/business/global/family-of-wen-jiabao-holds-a-hidden-fortune-in-china.html?hp&_r=0&pagewanted=all.

101. Didi Tang, "Plague of office-buying wears at China's Image." Yahoo News. (October 31, 2012) http://news.yahoo.com/plague-office-buying-wears-chinas-image-080904130.html.

102. Credit Suisse, "Global Wealth Report 2013," pp. 27–28.

103. David S. Goodman, "Why China's Middle Class Supports the Communist Party," *The Christian Science Monitor* (October 22, 2013), http://www.csmonitor.com/Commentary/Global-Viewpoint/2013/1022/Why-China-s-middle-class-supports-the-Communist-Party.

104. An Chen, "The New Inequality," *Journal of Democracy* 14:1 (January 2003), p. 54.

105. Dorothy Solinger, "Path Dependence Re-examined: Chinese Welfare Policy in the Transition to Unemployment," *Comparative Politics* 38:1 (October 2005), p. 93.

106. Ibid., p. 96.

107. World Bank, World Development Indicators, http://data.worldbank.org/indicator/SI.POV.GINI. Dickson, "Updating the China Model," *The Washington Quarterly* 34:4 (2011). p. 46.

108. Thomas F. Remington, "Russian Regional Inequality in Comparative Perspective," Paper prepared for Benjamin F. Shambaugh Conference, "Lessons from Subnational Comparative Politics: Theory and Method in the Third Decade of Studying Russia's Regions," University of Iowa (October 6–9, 2011).

109. William Wan, "In China, Parents Bribe to Get Students into Top Schools, Despite Campaign against Corruption," *Washington Post* (October 7, 2013), http://www.washingtonpost.com/world/in-china-parents-bribe-to-get-students-into-top-schools-despite-campaign-against-corruption/2013/10/07/fa8d9d32-2a61-11e3-8ade-a1f23cda135e_story.html?hpid=z5.

110. Jamil Anderllini, "China's Rural-Urban Balancing Act," *Washington Post* (February 7, 2013), http://www.nytimes.com/2013/02/17/business/in-china-families-bet-it-all-on-a-child-in-college.html?hp&_r=0&pagewanted=all.

111. "Invisible and Heavy Shackles," *The Economist* (May 6, 2010), www.economist.com.

112. *Economist*, August 10, 2013.

113. Keith Bradsher, "China's Leaders Confront Economic Fissures, *New York Times* (November 5, 2013), http://www.nytimes.com/2013/11/06/business/international/chinas-leaders-confront-economic-fissures.html?src=rechp.

114. "Xi Jinping and the Chinese Dream," *The Economist* (May 4, 2013), p. 11.

115. Steve Barnett and Nigel Chalk, "Building a Social Safety Net," *Finance and Development* 47:3 (September, 2010), pp. 34–35, http://www.imf.org/external/pubs/ft/fandd/2010/09/Barnett.htm.

116. Cheng Li and Ryan McElveen, "Pessimism about China's Third Plenum is Unwarranted," Brookings Institution (November 4, 2013), http://www.brookings.edu/research/opinions/2013/11/04-china-third-plenum-pessimism-li-mcelveen.

117. Minxin Pei, "Beijing Fakes the Good Fight against Its Own Corruption," *The National* (November 2, 2012), http://www.thenational.ae/thenationalconversation/comment/beijing-fakes-the-good-fight-against-its-own-corruption.

118. Minxin Pei, "Beijing Fights the Good Fight against Its Own Corruption," *The National* (November 2, 2012), http://www.thenational.ae/thenationalconversation/comment/beijing-fakes-the-good-fight-against-its-own-corruption.

119. Minxin Pei, "The Politics of a Slowing China," Project Syndicate (July 6, 2013), http://www.project-syndicate.org/commentary/the-impact-of-slow-gdp-growth-on-chinese-politics-by-minxin-pei.

120. Jay Ulfelder, "Why the Communist Party of China Is Right to Worry about Popular Protests," *Dart Throwing Chimp Blog* (August 9, 2012), http://dartthrowingchimp.wordpress.com/.
121. CIA World Fact Book, https://www.cia.gov/library/publications/the-world-factbook/, accessed December 2, 2013.
122. Martin King Whyte and Zhongzin Sun, "The Impact of Market Reforms on the Health Care of Chinese Citizens: Examining Two Puzzles," *China: An International Journal* 8:1 (March 2010), pp. 2–11.
123. "Health Care Reform," *The Economist* (July 21, 2012), http://www.economist.com/node/21559379.
124. The World Bank, *China 2030: Building a Modern, Harmonious, and Prosperous China* (Washington, DC: The World Bank, 2013), p. 297, http://www.worldbank.org/content/dam/Worldbank/document/China-2030-complete.pdf.
125. Daniel Kaufmann, Aart Kraay, and Massimo Mastruzzi, *Governance Matters IV: Governance Indicators for 1996–2004* (Washington, DC: The World Bank, 2005), http://info.worldbank.org/etools/docs/library/206973/GovMatters_IV_main.pdf.